The China Reader

The China Reader

RISING POWER

David Shambaugh

EDITOR

Sixth Edition

OXFORD

UNIVERSITY PRESS

Oxford University Press is a department of the University of Oxford. It furthers
the University's objective of excellence in research, scholarship, and education
by publishing worldwide. Oxford is a registered trade mark of Oxford University
Press in the UK and certain other countries.

Published in the United States of America by Oxford University Press
198 Madison Avenue, New York, NY 10016, United States of America.

Library of Congress Cataloging-in-Publication Data
Names: Shambaugh, David L., editor of compilation.
Title: The China reader : rising power / David Shambaugh.
Description: New York, NY : Oxford University Press, 2015. | Includes
bibliographical references and index.
Identifiers: LCCN 2015025438| ISBN 978–0–19–939707–5 (hardcover : alk. paper) |
ISBN 978–0–19–939708–2 (pbk. : alk. paper)
Subjects: LCSH: China—Politics and government—2002- | China—Economic
conditions—2000- | China—Social conditions—2000- | China—Foreign
relations—21st century. | China—Foreign economic relations—21st century.
Classification: LCC DS779.4 .C464 2015 | DDC 951.06/1—dc23 LC record available at
http://lccn.loc.gov/2015025438

1 3 5 7 9 8 6 4 2
Printed by Sheridan, USA

Dedicated to Orville Schell

CONTENTS

LAW, RIGHTS, AND CIVIL SOCIETY

THE MILITARY AND SECURITY

FOREIGN RELATIONS

"GREATER" CHINA

CHINA FACES THE FUTURE

I. *Muddle Through, Adaptation, or the End of Dynasty?*   475

PREFACE

This new edition of *the China Reader* is the sixth in a series that has chronicled China's turbulent and dramatic evolution since the eighteenth century. The first three volumes were co-edited by Franz Schurmann and Orville Schell and were published together as a set in 1967, covering China's tumultuous modern history up to that point in time: *Imperial China: The Decline of the Last Dynasty and the Origins of Modern China, the 18th and 19th Centuries; Republican China: Nationalism, War, and the Rise of Communism 1911–1949; Communist China: Revolutionary Reconstruction and International Confrontation, 1949 to the Present.*[1] The third volume covered the first fifteen years of "Communist China" (as it was then known), but it came out in 1967 just after the momentous Great Proletarian Cultural Revolution erupted the previous year. The fourth volume was published in 1974 and covered the first phase (1966–1972) of the Cultural Revolution period (which, according to official Chinese communist historiography, lasted until 1976). Volume 4 was co-edited by Franz Schurmann, David Milton, and Nancy Milton and was entitled *People's China: Social Experimentation, Politics, Entry on to the World Scene, 1966–1972.*[2] These four volumes were all staples for those entering Chinese Studies in the 1970s, and they were very popular with the public—providing important insights into the closed world of the People's Republic of China at that time.

A full twenty-five years passed before Orville Schell kindly approached me about co-editing a fifth volume in the series, covering the late-Mao and post-Mao period. It was a real pleasure to collaborate with Orville on that volume, *The China Reader: The Reform Era*, which was published in 1999.[3] It was during this period that China embarked on Deng Xiaoping's path of "reform and opening" (改革与开放), and thus Volume 5 chronicled the many twists-and-turns of the period, from the twilight of the Maoist era in the mid-1970s through the early reform years of the 1980s, the traumatic political events in Tiananmen Square in 1989, and into the late-Deng era before his passing in 1997.

This collaboration cemented a long personal and professional friendship between us. Orville's perceptive insights and beautiful prose as a writer on modern China have benefitted unknown numbers of readers of his many publications over the years. Orville is that rare combination of scholar, journalist, essayist, public intellectual, educator, policy analyst, and advocate—in each of these roles he has constantly challenged conventional wisdom, entertained and educated others through his writings, contributed to on-the-ground work of non-governmental organizations in China, and participated in high-level foreign policy deliberations in the United States and other nations. His perspectives and activities have not always made him popular with the government authorities in Beijing or Washington, but his moral and scholarly integrity has always driven him to "speak truth to power." Given these many contributions to the field of China Studies, his instrumental pioneering role in *The China Reader* series, and all he has taught me about China, I admiringly and gratefully dedicate this volume to Orville Schell.

This sixth volume (6.0) in the series picks up chronologically where the fifth left off—in 1997—and brings the China story forward through 2014. It is during this nearly two-decade period that China has truly emerged as a *Rising Power* in the world (hence the subtitle to this edition). The following Introduction provides an overview of some of the impressive aspects of this historic process, to help guide readers through the subsequent selections in the book (which are ordered according to subject categories).

Through all six editions to date, *The China Reader* series has thus sought to chronicle China's convoluted evolution over a long period of time; when read in sequence and together, readers are provided with the flow of events that have shaped modern and contemporary Chinese history. Such a temporal perspective is also an interesting window into the *zeitgeist* of the time. That is, foreign analyses of China (just like those in China) are colored by certain paradigms or perspectives that are prevalent at a given time. These interpretive prisms may change over time, and therefore *The China Reader* series offers historical insights into the evolution of Western Sinology since the 1960s. Another distinguishing feature has been that the editors have consistently sought to mix together sources *from* China (primary sources) with sources published *about* China (secondary sources) written by Western scholars. This mixture has provided readers two perspectives. First, it offers a sense of China's own official and unofficial narratives: party propaganda, official documents, dissident manifestos, and literature. Even if propagandistic, it is important to know the *lingua franca* of Chinese official ideology (意识形态), terminology (提法), and slogans (口号). Secondly, it offers readers some of the best in Sinology—analyses written by scholars, journalists, and think tank analysts in the West.

As editor, in this volume (as in all previous ones in the series) I have tried to cast a wide net in the selections to be included. Not only did they need to span the seventeen years (1997–2014) since Volume 5, but they also needed to take full account of the broad spectrum of important issues concerning China internally and externally. In making these selections I have done my best to be as representative and comprehensive as possible—yet, inevitably, editorial decisions had to be made and many illustrative documents could not be included for reasons of space. In most cases, the selections appear as they did in the original—although in some cases they have been excerpted or edited down for style or length.

The following pages plunge into depth and details about China's development in many facets. To be certain, China's rise is far from over and there will be many dimensions of this incredible story to be told in future editions of *The China Reader*.

David Shambaugh

NOTES

1. Franz Schurmann and Orville Schell (eds.), *The China Reader: Imperial China* (New York: Random House, 1967); Franz Schurmann and Orville Schell (eds.), *The China Reader: Republican China* (New York: Random House, 1967); Franz Schurmann and Orville Schell (eds.), *The China Reader: Communist China* (New York: Random House, 1967).
2. Franz Schurmann, David Milton, Nancy Milton (eds.), *The China Reader: People's China* (New York: Random House, 1974).
3. Orville Schell and David Shambaugh (eds.), *The China Reader: The Reform Era* (New York: Vintage Books/Random House, 1999).

The China Reader

INTRODUCTION

The Complexities of a Rising China

David Shambaugh

"China is a sleeping giant. Let her sleep, for when she wakes she will move the world." It has been two centuries since Napoléan Bonaparte made his prophetic prediction, but it is now being realized. World history has never witnessed a nation modernize as comprehensively or rise to world power status as rapidly as has China since the 1970s. Even China's three previous "rises" (Qin-Han, Sui-Tang, Ming-Qing) were nowhere near as time-compressed or as thoroughgoing as this most recent phase.[1] This edition of *The China Reader* is about that transformation.

China's mega-economy has skyrocketed to being the second largest in the world, with a total gross domestic product (GDP) of $9.24 trillion and accounting for 15 percent of global growth in 2014. It is now the world's largest trading nation, is the largest consumer of energy, holds the world's largest foreign exchange reserves ($3.7 trillion), has had the world's highest annual growth rate for three decades (8.4 percent), and now has the world's second largest military budget and largest internal security budget. China is the world's largest producer of many goods,

earning it the moniker as the "world's workshop" and producing a plethora of goods for consumers worldwide. The physical transformation of the country has been extraordinary to witness, with infrastructure development unparalleled in human history: by the end of 2012 China had a rail network of 97,000 kilometers (including 16,000 kilometers of high-speed rail) and a national highway network of 90,000 kilometers (the longest in the world). Modern cities featuring futuristic architecture have literally risen across the country. I have personally witnessed this transformation, visiting or living in China every year since 1979.

In the process of China's dramatic growth over the past three-plus decades, more than 200 million citizens have emerged from absolute poverty, with only 6.1 percent of the population still living below the poverty line. China's per capita income has now reached approximately $6,800 in nominal terms, but nearly $11,850 in PPP (purchasing-power-parity) equivalent dollars (2014).[2] As the society has become generally more wealthy, some have become extremely well off—China now boasts the world's largest number of millionaires and second largest group of billionaires in the world.

Many other indicators illustrate China's ascent. It has an impressive space program that intends to put people on the moon by the 2020s, the world's largest museums (the Palace Museum and National Museum in Beijing), the world's largest hydroelectric dam (the Three Gorges), the world's largest military, the world's largest population, the world's largest number of gold medal winners in the Beijing and London Olympic Games, and many other global "firsts."

In 2014 the Chinese navy put its first aircraft carrier to sea (more are being planned), while a 2015 military White Paper officially stated China's goal of "building itself into a maritime power," boldly proclaiming that "the traditional mentality that land outweighs sea must be abandoned."[3] Part of the rationale for building a global naval presence has to do with the fact that China's commerce has gone global, establishing a presence all around the planet. China's outbound investment now ranks third worldwide and is growing rapidly, as its companies are establishing factories from Brazil to Bulgaria and from Kenya to Kentucky. Chinese entrepreneurs and workers have also scattered out across the world, occasionally requiring rescue (as in 2013 when 35,000 Chinese nationals were evacuated out of Libya and 2015 when 1,000 were rescued from Yemen). China's global merchandise trade and dependence on imported energy and raw materials is another reason that it believes a global naval capability is required. No less than 120 nations (out of 194) count China as their largest trading partner.

China's diplomacy has also developed as China has risen. Over the past forty years China has traveled a path from a nation isolated from the international community to one thoroughly integrated into it. Today the People's Republic enjoys diplomatic relations with 175 countries, is a member of more than 150 international organizations, and is party to more than 300 multilateral treaties. It receives a large number of visiting foreign dignitaries every year, and its own leaders travel the world regularly. It enjoys the trappings of being a major world power—being a permanent member of the UN Security Council and participant in all major international summits—although its diplomatic behavior often remains reticent and its diplomatic influence limited.

But China's rise has been about more than impressive statistics, diplomatic presence, and hard-power projection. It is important not only to conceive of China's rise in "vertical" terms—its upward trajectory—but also in what might be described as "horizontal" terms. That is, the modernization process has had numerous collateral side-effects on different aspects of Chinese society, its Asian neighbors, and the world more broadly. As in previous editions of *The China Reader*, this volume casts a broad net and intentionally covers these horizontal manifestations of China's rise—in politics, governance, social welfare, culture, intellectual life, media, social inequality, gender, demography, religion, national identity, rural and urban life, ethnicity, law and human rights, civil society, military and security, and China's roles in the world. During the seventeen-year period covered in this edition, China has passed through three distinct leadership periods—Jiang Zemin (1997–2002), Hu Jintao (2002–2012), and Xi Jinping (2012–). Each sub-period has had its own distinct characteristics and complexities. In each subsequent section, readers are exposed to these diverse elements that lurk beneath the surface of China's impressive rise. The horizontal side-effects are as significant as the impressive vertical aspects of China's rise.

Part of China's rise has also been a psychological state, whereby average Chinese citizens have been able to have ambitions and realize personal dreams that were unimaginable during the stultifying first thirty years that the Communist Party ruled the People's Republic of China.[4] China's current leader, Xi Jinping, has taken the concept of personal dreams to a national level by proclaiming the "Chinese Dream" (of national rejuvenation). Of course, the ambition to strengthen and rebuild China into a great power is not new—this has been the *leitmotif* of every Chinese leader since the Self-Strengthening Movement of the late-Qing Dynasty.[5] But today, with all of China's impressive achievements, Chinese citizens are rightfully more proud and nationalistic than ever—although this nationalism is sometimes expressed in xenophobic and hubristic outbursts against those imperialist powers that injured China during its "century of shame and humiliation" (百年国耻).

Thus, measured in many ways, China's rise to global power has been *the* most important development in world affairs in the early twenty-first century. This *zeitgeist* has produced a plethora of "China rise" books being published during the intervening years since the last edition of *The China Reader*.[6] Some observers are notably, even effusively, optimistic that China, in the words of one writer, will "rule the world."[7] Others, myself included, are much more cautious and circumspect; these observers see multiple weaknesses and fault lines in both China's domestic and international capacities.[8]

The future reality of China's rise probably lies somewhere in between these two diverse paradigms: China will be both strong and weak at the same time. How can this be? While it may not be cognitively comfortable for many analysts, it is likely to be the reality. Some dimensions of China—such as its growing military power and its sheer economic heft—auger well for its continued rise as a world power. China will continue to upgrade its intellectual capital and technological base, although it remains an open question as to whether both are capable of making the full transition to a globally cutting-edge innovative society and economy. China also has much untapped "soft power," if the government and Communist Party permits its citizens to create more freely.[9] Its growing global footprint is only going to increase. Beijing is also expected to play an ever-increasing diplomatic role in global governance.

Yet, at the same time, China remains a mass of tangled contradictions, uncertainty, and potential instability. Its Leninist political system remains repressive and anachronistic. Its demographic transition to an aging society is already underway, with significant implications for economic productivity. Various distortions caused by state intervention, debt, and corrupt practices plague the economy. China's toxic environment taxes human health and compromises sustainable development. Massive internal migration strains governments and urban institutions. Incidents of mass social unrest now total about 200,000 per year, while its peripheral regions of Xinjiang, Tibet, and Hong Kong remain restive. Taiwan also remains outside the grip of Beijing, despite the significant linkages established in recent years. Externally, as China has risen, its ties with other countries have become both deeper and more fraught simultaneously.

Managing its external relations, particularly with its neighbors in Asia and with the United States, will be an ongoing challenge for Beijing in the years ahead. The increasingly competitive dynamics of US-China relations have led many pundits to opine about the so-called Thucydides' Trap. According to research by Professor Graham Allison of Harvard, in the vast majority of "power transitions" throughout modern history (in eleven of fifteen cases since 1500), predominant powers have not been able to peacefully accommodate rising powers and rising powers have not been able to coexist in the order dominated by the existing hegemonic power—with war frequently resulting (preemptively launched either by the challenging or by the dominant power).[10] Many American scholars are skeptical and pessimistic that the Thucydides' Trap can be successful managed, and they thus anticipate an increasingly acute "security dilemma" and zero-sum contest for primacy between China and the United States—centered in East Asia but possibly becoming global—which they argue will very likely result in war between the two powers.[11] Others are more sanguine that the inevitable strategic tensions can be successfully managed, if certain reciprocal steps are taken by each side.[12] This will be the great geostrategic challenge of the twenty-first century.

Thus, the destabilizing collateral effects of China's continued rise are considerable. Yet, in many areas China will continue to impress the world with its successes. In other areas, it will likely "muddle through" and effectively manage its challenges—as flexible adaptability and incremental experimentalism have been the secrets of China's accomplishments to date. Yet, in other domains, China may stumble as it experiences the inevitable stresses of transitioning from a developing country with 1.4 billion people to a more modern nation or encounters difficulties in its foreign relations. These three pathways—continued growth, muddling through, or unstable regression—are all possibilities for China in the years ahead (and they are not mutually exclusive!)[13] We will have to await the next edition of *The China Reader* in ten or fifteen years' time to see how it all plays out. Only one thing is certain: China will continue to be one of the most intriguing stories of our era and in human history.

NOTES

1. See Wang Gungwu, "The Fourth Rise of China: Cultural Implications," *China: An International Journal*, vol. 2, no. 2 (Sept. 2004), pp. 311–322.

2. The World Bank, "GDP Per Capita in 2014," available at: http://data.worldbank.org/indicator/NY.GDP.PCAP.CD.

3. Information Office of the State Council, *China's Military Strategy* (May 2015).

4. This is so well captured in Evan Osnos, *Age of Ambition: Chasing Fortune, Truth, and Faith in the New China* (New York: Farrar, Straus, & Giroux, 2014).

5. This is best captured in Orville Schell and John Delury, *Wealth and Power: China's Long March to the Twenty-First Century* (New York: Random House, 2014).

6. See, for example, Henry Kissinger, *On China* (New York: Penguin, 2012); James Kynge, *China Shakes the World: The Rise of a Hungry Nation* (London: Weidenfield & Nicolson, 2006); Michael E. Brown et al. (eds.), *The Rise of China* (Cambridge, MA: MIT Press, 2000); Charles Horner, *Rising China and Its Postmodern Fate* (Athens: University of Georgia Press, 2009); C. Fred Bergsten et al., *China's Rise: Challenges and Opportunities* (Washington, DC: Peterson Institute for International Economics and Center for Strategic and International Studies, 2008); Robert S. Ross and Zhu Feng (eds.), *China's Ascent: Power, Security, and the Future of International Politics* (Ithaca, NY: Cornell University Press, 2008); David Kang, *China Rising: Peace, Power, and Order in East Asia* (New York: Columbia University Press, 2007).

7. Martin Jacques, *When China Rules the World: The End of the Western World and the Birth of a New Global Order* (London: Penguin, 2012). In a similar vein see Arvind Subramanian, *Eclipse: Living in the Shadow of China's Economic Dominance* (Washington, DC: Peterson Institute of International Economics, 2011); Michael Pillsbury, *The Hundred-Year Marathon: China's Secret Strategy to Replace America as the Global Superpower* (New York: Henry Holt & Co., 2015).

8. See David Shambaugh, *China Goes Global: The Partial Power* (New York and Oxford: Oxford University Press, 2013); Jonathan Fenby, *Will China Dominate the 21st Century?* (Cambridge: Polity Press, 2014); Mel Gurtov, *Will This Be China's Century? A Skeptic's View* (Boulder, CO: Lynne Reinner, 2013); Regina M. Abrami, William C. Kirby, and F. Warren McFarlan, *Can China Lead? Reaching the Limits of Power and Growth* (Boston: Harvard Business School Press, 2014); Thomas J. Christensen, *The China Challenge: Shaping the Choices of a Rising Power* (New York: W.W. Norton, 2015); Joseph S. Nye, Jr., *The Future of Power* (New York: Public Affairs, 2011); Josef Joffe, *The Myth of America's Decline* (New York: W.W. Norton, 2014); Ho-fung Hung, *The China Boom: Why China Will Not Rule the World* (New York: Columbia University Press, 2016).

9. See David Shambaugh, "China's Soft-Power Push: The Search for Respect," *Foreign Affairs* (July–August 2015).

10. Graham Allison, "Avoiding Thucydides' Trap," *Financial Times*, August 22, 2012.

11. See John J. Mearsheimer, *The Tragedy of Great Power Politics* (New York: W.W. Norton, 2001); Aaron L. Friedberg, *A Contest for Supremacy: China, America, and the Struggle for Mastery in Asia* (New York: W.W. Norton, 2011).

12. See Thomas J. Christensen, *The China Challenge: Shaping the Choices of a Rising Power* (New York: W.W. Norton, 2015); Hugh White, *The China Choice: Why We Should Share Power* (New York: Oxford University Press, 2013), James Steinberg and Michael E. O'Hanlon, *Strategic Reassurance and Resolve: U.S.-China Relations in the 21st Century* (Princeton: Princeton University Press, 2014), Geoff A. Dyer, *The Contest of the Century: The New Era of Competition with China—and How America Can Win* (New York: Vintage, 2014), David Shambaugh (ed.), *Tangled Titans: The United States and China* (Lanham, MD: Rowman & Littlefield, 2013); Henry M. Paulson, *Dealing with China: An Insider Unmasks the New Economic Superpower* (New York: Hachette Book Group, 2015).

13. I explore these possible future trajectories in *China's Future* (Cambridge: Polity Press, 2016).

Rising China

Editorial Introduction

Conceptualizing the rise of China brings to mind the ancient Indian fable of the three blind men feeling an elephant: each touched a different part of the beast and thus derived vastly different impressions of what it was. Such is the case among scholars and analysts today when they try to comprehend the rise of China and predict its future impact on the world. Vastly different perspectives are offered, and they compete with each other in the public sphere. While distinctly different (some even diametrically opposed), they all offer important insights and most hold elements of truth. China and its rise are such complicated phenomena that observers need to entertain multiple perspectives—even if all of their arguments are not persuasive.

Such is the case with the four selections in this section. They have been selected not only because they have been written by influential writers and observers of China, but also because of the stark differences in perspectives and argumentation.

Martin Jacques is a well-known public intellectual and writer in England. His book *When China Rules the World: The End of the Western World and Birth of a New Global Order* has drawn widespread acclaim around the world (and has been translated into multiple languages). As the title and subtitle suggest, Jacques offers the controversial argument that the Western-dominated world of the past two centuries is drawing to a close and a new global era is dawning with China (and other non-Western states) at the center.

This selection, which is drawn from the second edition of his book, summarizes eight features that distinguish China as a rising power and will likely characterize the new global order that Jacques envisions. A key aspect of Jacques' argument is that there are multiple pathways to development, modernity, and global order—and that China's modernization and its vision for the international system are distinctive and need to be understood and appreciated on their own terms (rather than imposing Western standards and measures of evaluation). His eight elements are valuable perspectives and correctives as they evaluate China on its own terms. Chinese are not always as persuasive in interpreting their country and its aspirations, whereas Jacques has dug deeply into the Chinese psyche and puts aside Western metrics of measurement. Yet he comes to his own conclusions about the trajectories and paths that China is likely to follow. Jacques sees deep cultural continuities connecting China's ancient past and its future. How do Chinese view the role of the state in its relations with society? He describes China as a "civilization-state" but also sees other distinguishing features of the Chinese state—such as meritocracy and adaptability. One of Jacques' more interesting insights concerns the roles of race and ethnicity in determining China's identities (plural). Geography and demography are also determining features for how China operates internally and externally. In terms of China's relations with its neighbors and the world, Jacques' envisions a return to a "tribute system" of sorts. The return of China as a great power in Asia and on the world stage will be transformational, Jacques argues—not only because of the size of China, but because of its different traditions and discomfort with the way the West has structured international relations. He, in fact, sees China's rise and future global impact as extremely disruptive. On this point, Jacques is at variance with Chinese commentators (although most of his analysis is shared by the Chinese government and commentariat). He doesn't quite predict a "clash of civilizations," as did Samuel Huntington several years ago, but Jacques does envision major fault lines emerging between Chinese and Western preferences for global order.

The second selection in this section is written by a leading Chinese intellectual-official (although it was written for a Western audience and published in the pages of the prestigious journal *Foreign Affairs*). Zheng Bijian has been a senior official and advisor to the leadership of the Chinese Communist Party (CCP) for several decades. Most of his career was spent working as a Marxist theoretician and official in the CCP propaganda system. Now retired, beginning around 2000 Zheng became very interested in how China's rise was being interpreted outside of China. Like almost all Chinese he felt that China was being misinterpreted in the West and in Asia as a threatening and disruptive force in world affairs. Zheng (and other Chinese) wonder: why won't others believe us when we say that China's rise will be benign? So he set out to try and correct these perceived misunderstandings. The result was Zheng's "theory" of China's "peaceful rise" (和平崛起). Zheng coined this concept in a speech in late 2003, and he intended it as a direct rebuttal to what Chinese commentators identified as the "China threat theory" (中国威胁论) that was prevalent in the West and parts of Asia. Zheng based his idea on a reading of history—the history of other rising powers. He found that most rising powers had not, in fact, risen peacefully—but, he argued, China was different.

Zheng's views are extrapolated in this selection. First, Zheng argues that China is weighed down by a huge population and relative poverty. While still relatively poor, Zheng nevertheless notes the dramatic progress of China's development over the past quarter-century. But Zheng argues that China's developmental path has a very long road ahead and its modernization is far from accomplished. He notes that it will not be until 2050 when China can be accurately described as a "modernized, medium-level developed country." He also describes a series of particular challenges that China will need to overcome if it is to reach this level of development. Externally, Zheng argues that China is nothing but an opportunity for the world. It is, he argues, certainly not a threat to the world. Zheng states categorically: "China does not seek hegemony or predominance in world affairs."

The third selection in this section takes direct aim at this claim by Zheng (it is also a longstanding claim by the Chinese government dating to the 1970s). In it, University of Chicago professor of political science John J. Mearsheimer stakes out the opposite position. Titled "China's Unpeaceful Rise," the author examines the issue of China as a rising power from the perspective of history and international relations theory.

Elaborated at great length in his influential book *The Tragedy of Great Power Politics*, Mearsheimer does not treat China as a unique case. Why, he assumes, should China not behave as have all other rising powers or great powers? Note that his view is the polar opposite of Martin Jacques' as well as Zheng Bijian's. In Mearsheimer's analysis there are "iron laws" (or at least repetitive patterns) of history and international relations: "My theory of international politics says that the mightiest states attempt to establish hegemony in their region of the world while making sure that no rival great power dominates another region." His view is, of course, deeply rooted in the international relations theory of "Realism," which holds that all states live in an anarchical world and thus pursue policies and take actions intended to ensure survival. This survivalist instinct leads them to compete with each other and, in his words, "The ultimate goal of every great power is to maximize its share of world power and eventually dominate the system." Why should China be any different from this age-old pattern of great powers? Why would China not follow this pattern and seek hegemony (regional first, global second)? What are the implications for China's neighbors in Asia and for the current global hegemon (the United States)? Based on his theory and analysis, not surprisingly, Mearsheimer sees major trouble on the horizon: an inevitable clash (war) between the United States and China—*unless* the United States undertakes preemptive action to restrain China's rise. For him, this is not a choice that Washington faces—it is an *imperative* that it must undertake in order to maintain American primacy and hegemony. It is also not a choice for the United States because it is *inevitable*—that is what great powers have always done: brook no tolerance of a "peer competitor." Mearsheimer thus sees calamity on the horizon, an eventuality that he terms the "tragedy of great power politics."

The fourth and final selection in this section takes yet another and different perspective on China's rise. Written by this observer, it questions some of the assumptions upon which all three of the previous analyses are based. I do not question the fact that China is rising as a world power—this is empirically indisputable. But I do question the *degree* to which China can be considered a global great power today. Over time China may well acquire most or all the attributes of the United States (the world's only true global power today) and hence, when that day arrives, we can say that China has "arrived" as a global great power. But I argue in this selection, as well as in my book *China Goes Global: The Partial Power*, that this day is a very long way away—and that when examined carefully, many dimensions of China's presumed international strength are in fact not very strong. China, in my view, continues to be characterized by far more weaknesses than strengths—which is why I term it a "partial power." Some elements of China's power profile are weak while others are simply incomplete. Over time, *if* China continues to develop anywhere near the pace it has shown since the 1980s, many of its present weaknesses will be overcome. But this is a "Big If." The world (and China itself) has grown accustomed to the dramatic growth and development of the past three decades; thus it should not *ipso facto* be assumed that such a trajectory will continue indefinitely. At the time of this book's publication (2016), China's growth rate had slowed to less than 7 percent with many economists predicting it would slow further until it levels off near 3 percent around 2020. In addition to slowing growth, China is beset by countless internal (and growing external) problems of significant magnitude. The remainder of this volume explores these in considerable detail.

Thus this selection cautions against overestimating China's current capabilities and potential as a world power. It not only questions China's capabilities, but importantly examines its power as defined by *influence*. Decades of social scientists have argued that real power is not the mere possession of instruments of power (financial, cultural, political, military, etc.), but it is rather the conversion of those assets and use of those instruments to influence other actors or situations. Here, at present, I find China to be a "partial power" at best. In the selection that follows, I inventory a variety of indices of Chinese capabilities and assess just how strong they really are on a global basis. As is explained, I conclude that China is certainly a rising power and probably the world's second leading power on aggregate after the United States—but I also argue that, depending on the category, China's power and influence on the world stage is actually closer to that of other "middle powers"—Russia, Japan, the United Kingdom, Germany, or even India. Overall it must be quickly said that China's *aggregate* power exceeds any one of these middle powers, but in individual categories (soft power, innovation, military technologies, telecommunications, and many other categories) China lags behind these other countries, which are setting global standards in various spheres.

Taken together, the four selections in this section offer readers a real diversity of views about China's status as a rising power. None deny that China is a rising power. But all disagree about the residual strengths of China's existing power, its potential development, and its intentions on how to exercise its power in the world. In these regards, assessing China is not dissimilar from the three blind Indians feeling the elephant.

I. VIEWING CHINA'S RISE: ALTERNATIVE PERSPECTIVES

The Eight Differences That Define China*

Martin Jacques

Broadly speaking, there have been two kinds of Western responses to the rise of China. The first sees China more or less solely in economic terms. We might call this the "economic wow factor." People are incredulous about the growth figures. They are in awe of what those growth figures might mean for China's position in the world. Any undue concern about their implications, moreover, is calmed by the belief that China is steadily becoming more like us, possessed of the accoutrements—from markets and stock exchanges to cars and private homes—of a modern Western society. This response is guilty of underestimating what the rise of China represents. It is a victim of tunnel vision and represents a failure of imagination. Economic change, fundamental

as it may be, can only be part of the picture. This view, blind as it is to the importance of politics and culture, rests on an underlying assumption that China, by virtue of its economic transformation, will, in effect, become Western. Consciously or unconsciously, it chimes with Fukuyama's "end of history" view: that since 1989 the world has been converging on Western liberal democracy. The other response, in contrast, is persistently skeptical about the rise of China, always expecting it to end in crisis and failure. In the light of Maoism, the collapse of the Soviet Union and the suppression of the demonstrators in Tiananmen Square, the argument runs, it is impossible for China to sustain its transformation without fundamental political change: unless it adopts the Western model, it will fail. The first view holds that China will automatically become Western, the second does not: but both share the belief that for China to succeed, it must, in effect, become Western.

---

* This selection is drawn from Martin Jacques, *When China Rules the World: The End of the Western World and the Birth of a New Global Order* (London: Penguin Books, revised second edition, 2012), 561–583.

My view is predicated on a very different approach. It does not accept that the "Western way" is the only viable model. In arguing this, it should be borne in mind that the West has seen off every major challenge it has faced, culminating in the defeat after 1989 of its greatest adversary, Soviet Communism. It has a formidable track record of growth and innovation, which is why it has proved such a dynamic force over such a long period of time. Unlike stark either/or alternatives of the great ideological era between 1917 and 1989, however, the choices are now more nuanced. The East Asian examples of modernization have all drawn from the Western experience, including China's post-1978 transformation. But to suggest that this is the key to East Asia's success or even amounts to the main story is wrong. The reason for China's transformation (like those of the other East Asian countries, commencing with Japan) has been the way it has succeeded in combining what it has learnt from the West, and also its East Asian neighbors, with its own history and culture, thereby tapping and releasing its native sources of dynamism. We have moved from the era of either/or to one characterized by hybridity.

Central is the contention that, far from there being a single modernity, there will in fact be many. Until around 1970 modernity was, with the exception of Japan, an exclusively Western phenomenon. But over the last half-century we have witnessed the emergence of quite new modernities, drawing on those of the West but ultimately dependent for their success on their ability to mobilize, build upon and transform the indigenous. These new modernities are no less original for their hybridity; indeed, their originality lies partly in their possession of this characteristic. Nor will hybridity remain an exclusively Asian or non-Western condition: in the face of the growing success of East Asian societies, the West will be obliged to learn from and incorporate some of their insights and features. In a limited way this is already the case, with the West, for example, employing some of the innovations developed by the Japanese system of manufacturing—although, given that these are very much rooted in Japanese culture, often with somewhat less success. A central question concerns which elements of the Western model are indispensable and which

are optional. Clearly, all successful examples of economic transformation currently on offer are based upon a capitalist model of development, although their economic institutions and policies, not to mention their politics and culture, display very wide variations. However, the proposition that the inheritance must, as a precondition for success, include Enlightenment principles such as Western-style rule of law, an independent judiciary, and a certain kind of representative government is by no means proven. Japan, which is at least as advanced as its counterparts in the West, is not based on the principles of the Enlightenment, nor does it embrace Western-style democracy, even though, since the early 1950s, largely for reasons of political convenience, it has routinely been seen as doing so by the West. And even if China moves in the direction of more representative government and a more independent judiciary, as it probably will in the long term, it will surely do so in very much its own way, based on its own history and traditions, which will owe little or nothing to any Western inheritance.

The desire to measure China primarily, sometimes even exclusively, in terms of Western yardsticks, while understandable, is flawed. At best it expresses a relatively innocent narrow-mindedness; at worst it reflects an overweening Western hubris, a belief that the Western experience is universal in all matters of importance. This can easily become an excuse for not bothering to understand or respect the wisdom and specificities of other cultures, histories and traditions. The problem, as Paul A. Cohen has pointed out, is that the Western mentality—nurtured and shaped by its long-term ascendancy—far from being imbued with a cosmopolitan outlook as one might expect, is in fact highly parochial, believing in its own univeralism; or, to put it another way, its own rectitude and eternal relevance.[1] If we already have the answers, and these are universally applicable, then there is little or nothing to learn from anyone else. While the West remained relatively unchallenged, as it has been for the best part of two centuries, the price of such arrogance has overwhelmingly been paid by others, as they were obliged to take heed of Western demands; but when the West comes under serious challenge, as it increasingly will from China and others, then such a parochial mentality will only serve to increase its vulnerability, weakening its ability to learn from others and to change accordingly.

The problem with interpreting and evaluating China solely or mainly in terms of the Western lexicon of experience is that, by definition, it excludes all that is specific to China: in short, what makes China what it is. The only things that are seen to matter are those that China shares with the West. China's history and culture are dismissed as a blind alley or merely a preparation for becoming Western, the hors d'oeuvres before the Western feast. Such an approach is not only demeaning to China and other non-Western cultures; it also largely misses the point. By seeing China in terms of the West, it refuses to recognize or acknowledge China's own originality and, furthermore, how China's difference might change the nature of the world in which we live. Since the eighties and nineties, the heyday of the "globalization as Westernization" era, when the Asian tigers, including China, were widely interpreted in these terms, there has been a dawning realization that such a huge country embodying such a rich history and civilization cannot be so summarily dismissed. We should not exaggerate—the Western consensus still sees history as a one-way ticket to Westernization—but one can detect the beginnings of a new Western consciousness, albeit still weak and fragile, which is more humble and realistic. As China grows increasingly powerful—while remaining determinedly different—the West will be forced, however reluctantly, to confront the nature and meaning of that difference. Understanding China will be one of the great challenges of the twenty-first century.

What then will be the key characteristics of Chinese modernity? They are eight in all, which for the deeply superstitious Chinese happens to be a lucky number. In exploring these characteristics, we must consider both the internal features of China's modernity and, given China's global importance, how these might impact upon and structure its global outlook and relations.

First, China is not really a nation-state in the traditional sense of the term but a civilization-state. True, it describes itself as a nation-state, but China's acquiescence in the status of nation-state was a consequence of its growing weakness in the face of the Western powers from the late nineteenth century.

The Chinese reluctantly acknowledged that China had to adapt to the world rather than insisting, in an increasingly utopian and hopeless mission, that the rest of the world should adapt to it. That cannot hide the underlying reality, however, that China is not a conventional nation-state. A century might seem a long time, but not for a society that consciously thinks of itself as several millennia old. Most of what China is today—its social relations and customs, its ways of being, its sense of superiority, its belief in the state, its commitment to unity—are products of Chinese civilization rather than its recent incarnation as a nation-state. On the surface it may seem like a nation-state, but its geological formation is that of a civilization-state.

It might be objected that China has changed so much during the period of its accommodation to the status of nation-state that these lines of continuity have been broken and largely erased. There was the inability of the imperial state (and, indeed, Confucianism) to modernize, culminating in its demise in the 1911 Revolution; the failure of the Nationalist government to modernize China, unify the country, or defeat the occupying powers (notably Japan), leading to its overthrow in the 1949 Revolution; the Maoist period, which sought to sweep away much of imperial China, from Confucius and traditional dress to the old patterns of land tenure and the established social hierarchies; followed by the reform period, the rapid decline of agriculture, the rise of industry, and the growing assertion of capitalist social relations. Each of these periods represents a major disjuncture in Chinese history. Yet much of what previously characterized China remains strikingly true and evident today. The country still has almost the same borders that it acquired at the maximum extent of the Qing empire in the late eighteenth century. The state remains as pivotal in society and as sacrosanct as it was in imperial times. Confucius, its great architect, is in the process of experiencing a revival and his precepts still, in important measure, inform the way China thinks and behaves. Although there are important differences between the Confucian and Communist eras, there are also strong similarities. This is not to deny that China has changed in fundamental ways, but rather to stress that China is also marked by powerful lines of continuity—that, to use a scientific analogy, its

DNA remains intact. This is a country, moreover, which lives in and with its past to a greater extent than any other: that past casts a huge shadow over its present such that, tormented by its failure to either modernize or unify, the Chinese for long lived in a state of perpetual regret and anguish. But as China now finally circumnavigates its way beyond the "century of humiliation" and successfully concludes its 150-year project of modernization, it will increasingly search for inspiration, nourishment, and parallels in that past. As it once again becomes the center of the world, it will luxuriate in its history and feel that justice has finally been done, that it is restoring its rightful position and status in the world.[2]

When China was down, it was obliged to live according to the terms set by others. It had no alternative. That is why it reconciled itself to being a nation-state, even if it never really believed this to be the case. It was a compromise borne of expediency and necessity. But as China arrives at modernity and emerges as the most powerful country in the world, it will no longer be bound by such constraints and will increasingly be in a position to set its own terms and conditions. It will feel free to be what it thinks it is and act according to its history and instincts, which are those of a civilization-state.

Second, China, in its relationship with East Asia, is increasingly likely to be influenced by the legacy of the tributary-state, rather than nation-state, system. The tributary-state system lasted for thousands of years and only finally came to an end at the conclusion of the nineteenth century. Even then, it was not entirely extinguished but continued—as a matter of habit and custom, the product of an enduring history—in a submerged form beneath the newly dominant Westphalian system. Up to a point, then, it never completely disappeared, even when China was a far less important actor in East Asia than it had been prior to the mid nineteenth century. The fact that the tributary-state system prevailed for so long means that it is deeply ingrained in the way that both China and East Asian states think about their relationship. As a consequence, any fundamental change in the position of China in the region, and therefore the nature of relations between China and its neighboring states, could well see a reversion to elements of a more tributary-type relationship,

albeit in a new and modernized form. The tributary system was undermined by the emergence of the European powers, together with Japan, as the dominant presence in the region, and by the remorseless decline of China. The European powers have long since exited the region; their successor power, the United States, is now a declining force; and Japan is rapidly being overshadowed by China. Meanwhile, China is swiftly resuming its position as the fulcrum of the East Asian economy. In other words, the conditions that gave rise to the dominance of the nation-state system in East Asia are crumbling, while at the same time we are witnessing the restoration of a defining feature of the tributary-state system.

The tributary-state system was characterized by the enormous inequality that existed between China on the one hand and its neighboring states on the other, together with a mutual belief in the superiority of Chinese culture. John K. Fairbank suggests in *The Chinese World Order* that: "If its belief in Chinese superiority persists, it seems likely that the country will seek its future role by looking closely at its own history."[3] Given that the idea of Chinese superiority remains firmly in place, China's growing economic strength, combined with its enormous population, could return the region to a state of affairs which carries echoes of the past. China is in the process of becoming once more the most important market for virtually every single East Asian country. Nor is the huge and growing imbalance in power between China and all the other states, which historically is entirely familiar, necessarily one that other states in the region will balk at or seek to resist, with the possible exception of Japan; indeed, all bar Japan have largely sought to move closer to China during the course of its rise rather than hedge with the United States against it. This is partly based on the habit and experience of history and partly on an accommodation with what these countries view as an inevitable and irresistible process. The rise of China and a return to something bearing some of the features of the tributary-state system will not necessarily be distinguished by instability; on the contrary, the tributary-state system was highly stable, rooted as it was in China's dominance and a mainly unchallenged hierarchical pattern of relationships. It would be quite wrong, however, to see any return to a tributary-style relationship as a simple rerun of the past—with, for example, the presidents and prime ministers of neighboring states making ritualized trips to Beijing bearing gifts in recognition of the greatness of the Chinese president and the superiority of the latter-day Celestial Kingdom, Rather it is likely to be defined by an acceptance that East Asia is essentially a Chinese-centric order; that it embodies an implicit hierarchy in which China's position of ascendancy is duly acknowledged; and that there is an implicit recognition and acceptance of Chinese superiority.

To what extent will such tributary influences be confined to East Asia? Could it conceivably find echoes in other parts of the world? There is, of course, no tradition of a tributary-state system elsewhere: it was only present in East Asia. That, however, was when the Middle Kingdom regarded the world as more or less coterminous with East Asia. If China should approach other parts of the world with a not too dissimilar mindset, and its power is sufficiently overwhelming, could the same kind of hierarchical system be repeated elsewhere? Could there even be something akin to a global tributary system? The most obvious objection is that the tributary system in the majority of cases embraced countries like Korea, Vietnam, and Japan with which China had a strong cultural affinity. This is not true of any other part of the world. The sphere to which even an extremely diluted version of the tribute system is least likely to extend is the West, by which, in this context, I mean the United States and Europe. The only possible long-term candidates, in this context, might be the weaker countries of southern and eastern Europe. But in the great majority of countries, both Europe and North America enjoy too much power. It should not be forgotten, moreover, that it was Europe which forced China, against its wishes, to forsake the tributary system in favor of the Westphalian system in the first place. It is not inconceivable, however, that in the long run Australia and New Zealand might enter into some elements of a tributary relationship with China given their relative proximity to it and their growing dependence on the Chinese economy. A tributary dimension might also re-emerge in China's relations with Central Asia. It would not be difficult to imagine echoes of the tributary system being found in China's relationship with Africa, given the enormous imbalance of power between them; perhaps, though less likely, in Latin America also, and South Asia, though not India. In each case, the key features would be China's overweening power, the dependency of countries in a multitude of ways on China, especially trade and finance, and an implicit acceptance of the virtues, if not the actual superiority, of Chinese civilization. But geographical distance in the case of Africa and Latin America, for example, will be a big barrier, while cultural and ethnic difference in all these instances will prove a major obstacle and a source of considerable resentment.

Third, there is the distinctively Chinese attitude towards race and ethnicity. The Han Chinese believe themselves to be a single race, even though this is clearly not the case. What has shaped this view is the extraordinarily long history of Chinese civilization, which has enabled a lengthy process of melding and fusing of countless different races. The sacrosanct and inviolable nature of Chinese unity is underpinned by the idea that the Han Chinese are all of one race, with even the non-Han Chinese being described in terms of separate nationalities rather than races. There is, furthermore, a powerful body of opinion in China that believes in polygenism and holds that the origins of the Chinese are discrete and unconnected with that of other branches of humankind. In other words, the notion of China and Chinese civilization is bolstered by a widespread belief that the difference between the Chinese and other peoples is not simply cultural or historical but also biological. The non-negotiable nature of the Chinese state's attitude towards race is eloquently illustrated by its approach towards the "lost territories" and the belief that Hong Kong and Taiwan are inseparable from China because their populations are Chinese: any idea that there might be a distinct Taiwanese identity is summarily dismissed. The Chinese attitude towards race and what constitutes being Chinese is diametrically opposed to that of other highly populous nations such as India, Indonesia, Brazil, and the United States, which explicitly recognize their multiracial and multiethnic character and, in varying degrees, celebrate that fact.

It would be wrong to describe the Chinese attitude towards race as an ideological position, because it is simply too old and too deeply rooted in Chinese history for that to be the case. Certainly it went through a profound change in the late nineteenth and early twentieth centuries, but its antecedents lie deep in the long history of Chinese civilization. Nor is the attitude towards race and identity reducible to the Chinese state or government: rather, it is ingrained in the Chinese psyche. To give one contemporary illustration: support for the return of Taiwan amongst the Chinese people is, if anything, even stronger than it is at a governmental level. Given this, any democratically elected government—admittedly, a most unlikely occurrence in the next twenty years—will almost certainly be more nativist and essentialist in its attitude towards Chinese identity than the present Communist government, which, by virtue of its lack of electoral accountability, enjoys a greater independence from popular prejudices. Nor should we anticipate any significant change in Chinese attitudes on race and ethnicity. It is true that they may have been accentuated by centuries of relative isolation from the rest of the world and China's growing integration may, as a consequence, help to weaken prejudices based on the ignorance of isolation, but the fundamental roots of Chinese attitudes will remain untouched. In fact, rather than being confined to a particular period of history, China's isolation is fundamental to understanding what I have described as the Middle Kingdom mentality. China saw itself as above, beyond, separate from, and superior to the rest of the world. "Isolation," in this sense, was integral to the Chinese world-view, even during the periods, like the Song dynasty or early Ming, when China was not isolationist in policy and outlook. It helps to explain why, for example, China has had such a different attitude from the major European states towards those who settled in other lands. Europeans viewed their settlers and colonizers as an integral part of the national civilizing mission and as still belonging to the homeland; the imperial dynasty, on the other hand, viewed those who departed the Middle Kingdom with relative and continuing indifference, as if leaving China was a step down and outside civilization. This point provides us with a way of understanding the terms on which China's growing integration with the rest of the world in the twenty-first century will take place. China is fast joining the world but, true to its history, it will also remain somewhat aloof, ensconced in a hierarchical view of humanity, its sense of superiority resting on a combination of cultural and racial hubris.

Fourth, China operates, and will continue to operate, on a quite different continental-sized canvas to other nation-states. There are four other states that might be described as continental in scale. The United States has a surface area only marginally smaller than that of China, but with a population only a quarter of the size. Australia is a continent in its own right, with a surface area around 80 percent of China's, yet its population is a meager 21 million, less than that of Malaysia or Taiwan, with the vast majority living around its coastal perimeter. Brazil has a surface area of around 90 percent of China's, but a much smaller population of 185 million. Perhaps the nearest parallel to China is India, with a population of equivalent size, but a surface area only a third of that of China's. Thus, although China shares certain similarities with each of these countries, its particular combination of population size and surface area is unique; Chinese modernity will come continental-sized, in terms of *both* population and physical size. This has fundamental implications not only for the way in which China has worked in the past but also for how it will work in the future. A continental-sized country is an utterly different kind of proposition to a conventional nation-state unless its population is tiny like Australia's, or it started off life as a settler-colony—as in the case of United States and Australia, which were essentially European transplants—with the homogeneity this implies. When a country is as huge as China in both physical scale and population, it is characterized by great diversity and, in certain respects, can be thought of as, in effect, a combination of several, even many, different countries. This is not to detract from the point made throughout this book about the centripetal forces that hold China together, but rather serves to make this unity an even more extraordinary phenomenon. We are dealing with a state that is at one and the same time a country and a continent—in other words, which is both national and multinational—and which therefore must be governed, at one and the same time, according to the imperatives of both a country and a multiplicity of countries.

For these reasons, among others, the Chinese state operates in an atypical way in comparison with conventional nation-states. The feedback loops, for example, are different. What might seem a logical consequence of a government action in an ordinary nation-state may not follow at all in China. In a country of such huge scale, furthermore, the government can conduct an experiment in one city or province without it being introduced elsewhere, which is what happened with Deng Xiaoping's reforms, even though they could hardly have been more fundamental or far-reaching in their effect. It is possible, in this context, to imagine democratic reforms being introduced in one relatively advanced province or municipality—Zhejiang or Shanghai, for example—but not others. The civilization-state embraces the concept of "one civilization, many systems," which was introduced to the wider world in 1997 with the handover of Hong Kong to China under the formula "one country, two systems"; but the idea of systemic differences within China's borders, in fact, has a very long history. It is conventional wisdom in the West that China should become "democratic" in the West's own image. The democratic systems that we associate with the West, however, have never taken root on anything like such a vast scale as China, with the single exception of India; indeed, apart from India, the only vaguely comparable example is that of a multinational institution like the European Union, and this has remained determinedly undemocratic in its constitution and modus operandi. One day China may well move, in its own fashion, towards what might be described as a Chinese-style democracy, but Western calls that it should adopt a Western-style democracy, more or less forthwith, glibly ignore the huge differences that exist between a vast continental-sized civilization-state like China and the far smaller Western nation-states (not to mention the obvious truth that China is far less developed). The fact that China's true European counterpart, the European Union, is similarly without democracy only serves to reinforce the point.

Fifth, the nature of the Chinese polity is highly specific. Unlike the Western experience, in particular that of Europe, the imperial dynasty was neither obliged, nor required, nor indeed desired to share power with other competing institutions or interest groups, such as the Church or the merchant class. China has not had organized religion in the manner of the West during the last millennium, while its merchants, for their part, instead of seeking to promote their interests by means of a collective voice, have sought favor through individual supplication. The state did not, either in its imperial or Communist form, share power with anyone else: it presided over society, supreme and unchallenged. The Confucian ethos that informed and shaped it for some two millennia did not require the state to be accountable to the people, but instead insisted on its loyalty to the moral precepts of Confucianism. The imperial bureaucracy, admission to which represented the highest possible achievement for anyone outside the dynastic circle, was schooled in Confucian morality and ethics. The efficacy of this system was evident for all to see: for many centuries Chinese statecraft had no peers in terms of efficiency, competence or its ability to undertake enormous public projects. There was just one exception to the absence of any form of popular accountability: in the event of severe popular unrest and disillusionment it was deemed that the mandate of Heaven had been withdrawn and legitimacy lay on the side of the people rather than the incumbent emperor. Apart from this *in extremis* scenario, the people have never enjoyed sovereignty: even after the fall of the imperial system, the dynastic state was replaced not by Western-style popular sovereignty but by state sovereignty.

Little has changed with Communist rule since 1949. Popular accountability in a recognizable Western form has remained absent. During the Maoist period, the legitimacy of the state was expressed in terms of a new class system in which the workers and peasants were pronounced as the new rulers; during the reform period this has partly been superseded by a de facto results-based compact between the state and the people, in which the state is required to deliver economic growth and rising living standards. As testament to the historical continuity of the Chinese state, the same key elements continue to define the nature of the Chinese polity. There is the continuing absence of any form of popular accountability, with no sign or evidence that this is likely to change—apart from the election of Hong Kong's Chief Executive, which may be introduced in 2017, and the present election of half its Legislative Council. Notwithstanding the convulsive changes over the last century, following the fall of the imperial state, with Nationalist government, war-lordism, partial colonization, the Maoist state and the present reform period, the state remains venerated, above society, possessed of great prestige, regarded as the embodiment of what China is, and the guarantor of the country's stability and unity. It is the quintessence of China in a way that is not true of any Western society, or arguably any other society in the world. Given its remarkable historical endurance—at least two millennia, arguably much longer—this characteristic must be seen as part of China's genetic structure. The legitimacy of the Chinese state, profound and deeply rooted, does not depend on an electoral mandate; indeed, even if universal suffrage was to be introduced, the taproots of the state's legitimacy would still lie in the country's millennial foundations. And herein lies the nub of the matter: the legitimacy of the Chinese state rests on the fact that it is seen by the people as the representative and embodiment of Chinese civilization and the civilization-state. It is this which explains the exceptional legitimacy enjoyed by the state in the eyes of the Chinese.

The Chinese state remains a highly competent institution, probably superior to any other state-tradition in the world and likely to exercise a powerful influence on the rest of the world in the future. It has shown itself to be capable not only of extraordinary continuity but also remarkable reinvention. The period since 1949 has seen this happen twice, initially in the form of the Maoist state, with the Communist Party providing the embryo of the new state while acting to restore China's unity, followed by the renewal and revitalization of the state during the reform era, leading to the economic transformation of the country. In the absence of any formal mechanism of popular accountability, it is reasonable to surmise that something like the Mandate of Heaven still operates: should the present experiment go seriously wrong—culminating, for example, in escalating social unrest as a result of widening inequalities, or a serious threat to the country's unity—then the hand of history might come to rest on the Communist Party's shoulder and its time be called.

Sixth, Chinese modernity, like other East Asian modernities, is distinguished by the speed of the country's transformation. It combines, in a way quite different from the Western experience of modernity, the past and the future at one and the same time in the present. I describe the Asian tigers as time-compression societies. Habituated to rapid change, they are instinctively more at ease with the new and the future than is the case in the West, especially Europe. They embrace the new in the same way that a child approaches a computer or a Nintendo games console, with confidence and expectancy—in contrast to European societies, which are more wary, even fearful, of the new, in the manner of an adult presented with an unfamiliar technological gadget. The reason is that East Asian societies have not been obliged to pass through all the various sequential stages of development—and their accompanying technological phases—that have been typical of Europe and North America, so the collective mind is less filled and formatted by older ways of doing things. China's version of modernity, however, by virtue of the country's size, must also be seen as distinct from those of other East Asian societies. While countries like Taiwan and South Korea took around thirty years to move from being largely rural to becoming overwhelmingly urban, around half of China's population still live in the countryside over three decades after 1978, and the figure will still be around one-third in 2025. This makes China's passage to modernity not only more protracted than that of its neighbors but also more complex, with various stages of development continuing to coexist over many decades as a result of the persistence of a large rural sector. This is reflected in the often sharp divergence in living standards between different provinces. This juxtaposition of different levels of economic development serves to accentuate the importance and impact of the past, the countryside providing a continuous feedback loop from history. It makes China, a country already deeply engaged with its own past, even more aware of its history.

Seventh, since 1949 China has been ruled by a Communist regime. Paradoxically, perhaps the two most significant dates of the last half-century embody what are seemingly entirely contradictory events: 1989, marking the collapse of European Communism and the demise of the Soviet bloc; and 1978, signalling not only the beginning of the most remarkable economic transformation in history but also one presided over by a Communist Party. The first represents the end of a momentous era, the second the beginning of what will probably prove to be an even more remarkable one.

Given the opprobrium attaching to Communism in the West, especially after 1989, it is not surprising that this has greatly colored Western attitudes towards the Chinese Communist Party, especially as the Tiananmen Square suppression occurred in the same year as the fall of the Berlin Wall. Indeed, following the events of 1989, the Western consensus held, quite mistakenly, that the Chinese Communist Party was also doomed to fail. Western attitudes towards China continue to be highly influenced by the fact that it is ruled by a Communist Party; the stain seems likely to persist for a long time to come, if not indefinitely. In the light of recent Chinese experience, however, Communism must be viewed in a more pluralistic manner than was previously the case: the fact is that the Chinese Communist Party is very different from its Soviet counterpart. Prior to the 1917 October Revolution, support for the Soviet Communist Party was always overwhelmingly concentrated in the cities where only a tiny minority of the population lived: in contrast, it enjoyed little backing in the countryside where the vast majority lived. As a result, the Soviet Communist Party never had widespread popular backing, which is why it became so dependent on authoritarian and coercive forms of rule after 1917. The case of the Chinese Communist Party was almost exactly the opposite. Support for it was overwhelmingly concentrated in the countryside, where the great majority lived, while it enjoyed little backing in the cities, especially compared with the Nationalists. Consequently, the Chinese Communist Party enjoyed considerable popular support, unlike the Soviet Party. This was why, when Communist rule reached its nadir after the Cultural Revolution and the death of Mao, the Party had the self-confidence and intellectual resources to undertake a fundamental change of direction and pursue an entirely different strategy. It displayed a flexibility and pragmatism which was alien to the Soviet Communist Party. Only an organization that has deep popular roots can think and act in this kind of way. In contrast, when the Soviet Party under Gorbachev finally opted for a different strategy, it was already too late and, moreover, the approach chosen was to result in the disintegration and implosion of the country.

The longer-term future of the Chinese Communist Party remains unclear: conceivably

it might metamorphose into something different (which to some extent it already has), to the point of even changing its name. Whatever the longer term may hold, the Chinese Communist Party, in presiding over the transformation of the country, will leave a profound imprint on Chinese modernity and also on the wider world. It has created and re-created the modern Chinese state; it reunited China after a century of disunity; it played a critical role in the defeat of Japanese colonialism; and it invented and managed the strategy that has finally given China the promise, after a century or more of decline, of restoring its status and power in the world to something resembling the days of the Middle Kingdom. In so doing, it has also succeeded in reconnecting China to its history, to Confucianism and its dynastic heyday. Arguably all great historical transformations involve such a reconnection with the past if they are to be successful. The affinities between the Communist conception of the state and the Confucian, as outlined earlier, are particularly striking in this respect. Given that Confucian principles had reigned for two millennia, the Chinese Communist Party, in order to prevail, needed, amongst other things, to find a way, at least in part, of reinventing and re-creating those principles.

Eighth, China will, for several decades to come, combine the characteristics of both a developed and a developing country. This will be a unique condition for one of the major global powers and stems from the fact that China's modernization will be a protracted process because of the country's size: in conventional terms, China's transformation is that of a continent, with continental-style disparities, rather than that of a country. The result is a modernity tempered by and interacting with relative rural backwardness, and such a state of bifurcation will have numerous economic, political, and cultural consequences. Chinese modernity cannot, and will not be able to, ignore the fact that a large segment of the country will continue to live in what is, in effect, a different historical period. We have already mentioned how this will bring China face-to-face with its own past for several decades to come. But it also has implications for how China will see its own interests and its relationship with other countries. Of necessity, it will regard itself as both a developing and a developed country, with the interests of both. This will find expression in many areas, including the debate over China's responsibilities concerning climate change. Over time, of course, the weight of the developing section of the economy, and the number of people that are employed in or dependent upon it, will decline, and China will increasingly behave as a developed country rather than a combination of the two. But for the next 25 years, perhaps even half a century, it will continue to display the interests and characteristics of both, an outlook which is likely to be reinforced by the sense of grievance that China feels about its "century of humiliation" at the hands of Japan and the Western powers, especially its experience of colonization. China, in fact, will be the first great power that comes from the "wrong" side of the great divide in the world during the nineteenth and first half of the twentieth century, a creature of the colonized rather than the colonizers, the losers rather than the winners. This experience, and the outlook it has engendered, will be an integral part of the Chinese mentality in the era of modernity, and will strongly influence its behavior as a global power.

A broader point can be made in this context. If the twentieth century world was shaped by the developed countries, then that of the twenty-first century is likely to be molded by the developing countries, especially the largest ones. This has significant historical implications. There have been many suggestions as to what constituted the most important event of the twentieth century: three of the most oft-cited candidates are the 1917 October Revolution, 1989 and the fall of the Berlin Wall, and 1945 and the defeat of fascism. Such choices are always influenced by contemporary circumstances; in the last decade of the last century, 1989 seemed an obvious choice, just as 1917 did in the first half of the century. Now we have come to the end of the first decade of the new century, another, rarely mentioned, candidate presents itself in the strongest possible terms. The rise of the developing world was only made possible by the end of colonialism. For the non-industrial world, the colonial era overwhelmingly served to block the possibility of their industrialization. The imperial powers had no interest in allowing competition for their own industries from their colonies. That does not mean that the effects of colonialism were entirely negative, though in some cases, notably that of Africa, they surely were. In East Asia, Japanese colonialism in the case of Korea and Taiwan, and Western colonialism in the instance of Hong Kong and the treaty ports, did at least demonstrate the possibilities offered by industrialization, and thereby helped to plant some of the seeds of their subsequent transformation. The end of colonialism, however, was a precondition for what we are now witnessing, the growth of multiple modernities and a world in which the new modernities are likely to prove at some point decisive. With hindsight, the defeat of colonialism between 1945 and the mid-1960s, the significance of which has been greatly underestimated in the West for obvious reasons, must rate as one of the great landmarks of the last century, perhaps the greatest.

In the light of these eight characteristics, it is clear that Chinese modernity will be very different from Western modernity, and that China will transform the world far more fundamentally than any other new global power in the last two centuries. This prospect, however, has been consistently downplayed. The Chinese, for their part, have wisely chosen to play a very long game, constantly seeking to reassure the rest of the world that China's rise will change relatively little. The West, on the other hand, having been in the global driving seat for so long, finds it impossible to imagine or comprehend a world in which this is no longer the case. Moreover, it is in the nature of vested interests—which is what the West is, the United States especially—not to admit, even to themselves, that the world stands on the edge of a global upheaval, the consequence of which will be to greatly reduce their position and influence in the world. China is the elephant in the room that no one is quite willing to recognize. As a result, an extraordinary shift in the balance of global power is taking place sotto voce, almost by stealth, except one would be hard-pressed to argue that any kind of deceit was involved either on the part of China or the United States. The contrast with previous comparable changes, for example the rise of Germany prior to 1914, the emergence of Japan in the interwar period, and the challenge of the Soviet Union, especially after 1945, is stark. Even though none carried anything like the ultimate significance of China's emergence, the threat that each offered at the time was exaggerated and magnified, rather than downplayed, as in the case of China. The nearest parallel to China's ascent, in terms of material significance, was that of the United States, and this was marked by a similar sense of stealth, though this was mainly because it was the fortunate beneficiary of two world wars, which in both cases it joined rather late, that had the effect of greatly accelerating its rise in relation to an impoverished and indebted Western Europe. Even the rise of the US, however, must be regarded as a relatively mild phenomenon compared to that of China.

So far, China has appeared an outsider patiently and loyally seeking to become an insider. As a rising power, it has been obliged to converge with and adapt to the existing international norms, and in particular to defer to and mollify the present superpower, the United States, since the latter's cooperation and tacit support have been preconditions for China's wider acceptance. China has struggled long and hard since 1978 to become an accepted member of the international community with the privileges and advantages that this confers. In devoting its energies to economic growth, it came to the conclusion that it could not afford for its attention and resources to be diverted towards what, at its present stage of development, it rightly deemed to be non-essential ends. In exercising such restraint and self-discipline, the Deng and post-Deng leaderships have demonstrated remarkable perspicacity, never losing sight of the long-term objective, never allowing themselves to be distracted by short-term considerations. The economic and technological demands of globalization, meanwhile, like the political imperatives just described, have similarly obliged China to replicate and converge in order to meet established international standards and adapt to existing norms. China's passage to modernity, in other words, has also set in motion powerful convergent forces as the country has sought to learn from more advanced countries, compete successfully in global markets, attract foreign capital, assimilate the disciplines of stock exchanges and capital markets, and acquire the latest technology. The fact that an increasing number of issues, most notably climate change, require global solutions with participation from all nations, especially the very largest, is acting as a further force for convergence.

Convergence, however, is only one side of the picture. Increasingly the rise of China will be characterized by the opposite: powerful countervailing pressures that push towards divergence from the established norms. In a multitude of ways, China does not conform to the present conventions of the developed world and the global polity. As a civilization-state masquerading in the guise of a nation-state, its underlying nature and identity will increasingly assert itself. The present Westphalian system of international relations in East Asia is likely to be steadily superseded by something that carries echoes of the tributary system. A nation that comprises one-fifth of the world's population is already in the process of transforming the workings of the global economy and its structure of power. A country that regards itself, for historical, cultural and racial reasons, as the greatest civilization on earth will, as a leading global power, clearly in time require and expect a major reordering of global relationships. A people that suffered at the expense of European and Japanese imperialism will never see the world in the same way as those peoples that were its exponents and beneficiaries. A state that has never shared power with any other class, group, or institution, which has never been subject to popular sovereignty, which operates on a continental scale and which, to this day, is suffused with a Confucian outlook, albeit in a distinctive and modernized Communist form, stands in sharp contrast to the credo that informs Western states and which has hitherto dominated the global community. While the West has been shaped by the Declaration of [American] Independence in 1776, the French Revolution in 1789, the British Industrial Revolution, the two world wars, the Russian Revolution in 1917 and the collapse of Communism in 1989, for China the great historical monuments are mostly very different: 221 BC and the beginnings of modern China; dynasties such as the Tang, Song, Ming, and Qing; the Opium Wars; the 1911 Revolution; Japanese colonization between 1931 and 1945; the 1949 Revolution; and the 1978 reforms. The different historical furniture betrays a different history. China, then, if convergent, is also manifestly divergent. While the rise of China since 1978 has been characterized by the predominance of convergent tendencies, well exemplified by China's current desire to reassure the world that it is a "responsible power," the divergent tendencies will in due course come to predominate as China grows more wealthy, self-confident, and powerful. But all this lies in the future; for the next twenty years or so, as China continues its modernization, it will probably remain for the most part a status-quo power.

There are two powerful forces that will serve to promote the steady reconfiguration of the world on China's terms. The fact that China is so huge means that it exercises a gravitational pull on every other nation. The nearest parallel is the United States, but the latter is on a much smaller scale. Size will enable China to set the terms of its relationships with other countries: hitherto that has been limited by China's level of development, but its gravitational power will grow exponentially in the future. China's mass will oblige the rest of the world largely to acquiesce in China's way of doing things. Moreover China's size, combined with its remorseless transformation, means that time is constantly on its side. It can afford to wait in the knowledge that the passage of time is steadily reconfiguring the world in its favor. Take its relationship with Japan: on the assumption that China's rapid growth continues, Japan will ultimately be obliged to accept China's leadership of East Asia. The same can be said, albeit less starkly, of China's relationship with the United States and Europe. With the rise of China, indeed, time itself takes on a new and different meaning: time-scales, in one sense at least, are elongated. We have become used to thinking in terms of the converse: the ever-shortening sense of time. The template for this is provided by the United States, a country with a brief history, a short memory, and a constant predilection for remaking itself. China is the opposite. It is possessed of a 5,000-year history and an extremely long memory; unsurprisingly it conceives of the future in terms of protracted time-scales. As a result, it is blessed with the virtue of patience, confident in the belief that history is on its side. If that has been the Chinese mentality since time immemorial, in the twenty-first century that belief will surely come to fruition.

So how will China act as a great power, once it is no longer confined to the straitjacket of modernization? It would be wrong to assume that it will behave like the West; that cannot be discounted, but history suggests something different. While Europe, and subsequently the United States, have been aggressive and expansionist, their tentacles reaching all over the world, China's expansion has been limited to its continent and although, in the era of globalization, that is changing and will continue to change, there is little reason to presume that it will be a West 2.0. China will become a great global hegemon, but it is likely to exercise that power in new and distinctive ways that are congruent with its history and culture. Many in the West are concerned about the absence of Western-style democracy in China, but over the last thirty years the country has become significantly more transparent and its leadership more accountable. This process is likely to continue and at some point result in a much bigger political transformation, though any democratic evolution is likely to take a markedly different form from that of the West. For the foreseeable future, however, given the success of the period since 1978, there is unlikely to be any great change. The greatest concern about China as a global power lies elsewhere, namely its deeply rooted superiority complex. How that will structure and influence Chinese behavior and its attitudes towards the rest of the world remains to be seen, but it is clear that something so entrenched will not dissolve or disappear. If the calling card of the West has often been aggression and conquest, China's will be its overweening sense of superiority and the hierarchical mentality this has engendered.

The arrival of China as a major power marks the end of Western universalism. Western norms, values, and institutions will increasingly find themselves competing with those of China. The decline of Western universalism, however, is not solely a product of China's rise, because the latter is part of a much wider phenomenon—an increasingly multipolar economic world and the proliferation of diverse modernities. The rise of competing modernities heralds a quite new world in which, perhaps, no hemisphere or country will have quite the same kind of prestige, legitimacy or overwhelming force that the West has enjoyed over the last two centuries; instead, different countries and cultures will compete for legitimacy and influence. The Western world is coming to an end; the new world, at least for the foreseeable future, will not be Chinese in the way that the previous one was Western. China, however, will enjoy a growing global hegemony and in time is likely to become, by far, the most dominant country in the world.

NOTES

1. Paul A. Cohen, *Discovering History in China: American Historical Writing on the Recent Chinese Past* (New York: Columbia University Press, 1984), p. 95.
2. Yan Xuetong, "The Rise of China in Chinese Eyes," *Journal of Contemporary China*, 10:26 (2001), pp. 33–34.

3. John King Fairbank, ed., *The Chinese World Order: Traditional China's Foreign Relations* (Cambridge, Mass.: Harvard University Press, 1968), p. 62.

CHINA'S "PEACEFUL RISE" TO GREAT-POWER STATUS[*]

Zheng Bijian

China's rapid development has attracted worldwide attention in recent years. The implications of various aspects of China's rise, from its expanding influence and military muscle to its growing demand for energy supplies, are being heatedly debated in the international community as well as within China. Correctly understanding China's achievements and its path toward greater development is thus crucial.

Getting the Facts Straight

Since starting to open up and reform its economy in 1978, China has averaged 9.4 percent annual GDP growth, one of the highest growth rates in the world. In 1978, it accounted for less than one percent of the world economy, and its total foreign trade was worth $20.6 billion. Today, it accounts for four percent of the world economy and has foreign trade worth $851 billion—the third-largest national total in the world. China has also attracted hundreds of billions of dollars of foreign investment and more than a trillion dollars of domestic nonpublic investment. A dozen years ago, China barely had mobile telecommunications services. Now it claims more than 300 million mobile-phone subscribers, more than any other nation. As of June 2004, nearly 100 million people there had access to the Internet.

Indeed, China has achieved the goal it set for itself in 1978: it has significantly improved the well-being of its people, although its development has often been narrow and uneven. The last 27 years of reform and growth have also shown the world the magnitude of China's labor force, creativity, and purchasing power; its commitment to development; and its degree of national cohesion. Once all of its potential is mobilized, its contribution to the world as an engine of growth will be unprecedented.

One should not, however, lose sight of the other side of the coin. Economic growth alone does not provide a full picture of a country's development. China has a population of 1.3 billion. Any small difficulty in its economic or social development, spread over this vast group, could become a huge problem. And China's population has not yet peaked; it is not projected to decline until it reaches 1.5 billion in 2030. Moreover, China's economy is still just one-seventh the size of the United States' and one-third the size of Japan's. In per capita terms, China remains a low-income developing country, ranked roughly 100th in the world. Its impact on the world economy is still limited.

The formidable development challenges still facing China stem from the constraints it faces in pulling its population out of poverty. The scarcity of natural resources available to support such a huge population—especially energy, raw materials, and water—is increasingly an obstacle, especially when the efficiency of use and the rate of recycling of those materials are low. China's per capita water resources are one-fourth of the amount of the world average, and its per capita area of cultivatable farmland is 40 percent of the

---

[*] This article first appeared in *Foreign Affairs*, Vol. 84, No. 5 (2005). Copyright by the Council on Foreign Relations, Inc. All rights reserved.

world average. China's oil, natural gas, copper, and aluminum resources in per capita terms amount to 8.3 percent, 4.1 percent, 25.5 percent, and 9.7 percent of the respective world averages.

Setting the Priorities

For the next few decades, the Chinese nation will be preoccupied with securing a more comfortable and decent life for its people. Since the Third Plenary Session of the Eleventh Central Committee of the Chinese Communist Party, held in 1978, the Chinese leadership has concentrated on economic development. Through its achievements so far, China has blazed a new strategic path that suits its national conditions while conforming to the tides of history. This path toward modernization can be called "the development path to a peaceful rise." Some emerging powers in modern history have plundered other countries' resources through invasion, colonization, expansion, or even large-scale wars of aggression. China's emergence thus far has been driven by capital, technology, and resources acquired through peaceful means.

The most significant strategic choice the Chinese have made was to embrace economic globalization rather than detach themselves from it. In the late 1970s, when the new technological revolution and a new wave of economic globalization were unfolding with great momentum, Beijing grasped the trend and reversed the erroneous practices of the Cultural Revolution. On the basis of the judgment that China's development would depend on its place in an open world, Deng Xiaoping and other Chinese leaders decided to seize the historic opportunity and shift the focus of their work to economic development. They carried out reforms meant to open up and foster domestic markets and tap into international ones. They implemented the household contracting system in rural areas and opened up 14 coastal cities, thus ushering in a period of economic takeoff.

In the 1990s, China once again confronted a strategic choice, due to the Asian financial crisis and the subsequent struggle between the forces for and against globalization. China's decision to participate in economic globalization was facing a serious challenge. But by carefully weighing the advantages and disadvantages of economic openness and drawing lessons from recent history, Beijing decided to open up China even more by joining the World Trade Organization and deepening economic reform at home.

China has based its modernization process mainly on its domestic resources. It has relied on ideological and institutional innovations and on industrial restructuring. By exploring the growing domestic market and transferring the huge personal savings of its citizens into investment, China has infused its economy with new momentum. Its citizens' capacities are being upgraded and its technological progress expedited. Even while attempting to learn from and absorb useful products from other societies, including those of the advanced capitalist countries, China has maintained its independence and self-reliance.

In pursuing the goal of rising in peace, the Chinese leadership has strived for improving China's relations with all the nations of the world. Despite the ups and downs in US-Chinese relations over the years, as well as other dramatic changes in international politics, such as the collapse of the Soviet Union, Beijing has stuck to the belief that there are more opportunities than challenges for China in today's international environment.

The Road Ahead

According to China's strategic plans, it will take another 45 years—until 2050—before it can be called a modernized, medium-level developed country. China will face three big challenges before it gets there. As described above, China's shortage of resources poses the first problem. The second is environmental: pollution, waste, and a low rate of recycling together present a major obstacle to sustainable development. The third is a lack of coordination between economic and social development.

This last challenge is reflected in a series of tensions Beijing must confront: between high GDP growth and social progress, between upgrading technology and increasing job opportunities, between keeping development momentum in the coastal areas and speeding up development in the interior, between fostering urbanization and nurturing agricultural areas, between narrowing the gap between the rich and the poor and maintaining economic vitality and efficiency, between attracting more foreign investment and enhancing the competitiveness of indigenous enterprises, between deepening reform and preserving social stability, between opening domestic markets and solidifying independence, between promoting market-oriented competition and taking care of disadvantaged people. To cope with these dilemmas successfully, a number of well-coordinated policies are needed to foster development that is both faster and more balanced.

The policies the Chinese government has been carrying out, and will continue to carry out, in the face of these three great challenges can be summarized as three grand strategies—or "three transcendences."

The first strategy is to transcend the old model of industrialization and to advance a new one. The old industrialization was characterized by rivalry for resources in bloody wars and by high investment, high consumption of energy, and high pollution. Were China to follow this path, it would harm both others and itself. China is instead determined to forge a new path of industrialization based on technology, economic efficiency, low consumption of natural resources relative to the size of its population, low environmental pollution, and the optimal allocation of human resources. The Chinese government is trying to find new ways to reduce the percentage of the country's imported energy sources and to rely more on China's own. The objective is to build a "society of thrift."

The second strategy is to transcend the traditional ways for great powers to emerge, as well as the Cold War mentality that defined international relations along ideological lines. China will not follow the path of Germany leading up to World War I or those of Germany and Japan leading up to World War II, when these countries violently plundered resources and pursued hegemony. Neither will China follow the path of the great powers vying for global domination during the Cold War. Instead, China will transcend ideological differences to strive for peace, development, and cooperation with all countries of the world.

The third strategy is to transcend outdated modes of social control and to construct a harmonious socialist society. The functions of the Chinese government have been gradually transformed, with self-governance supplementing state administration. China is strengthening its democratic institutions and the rule of law and trying to build a stable society based on a spiritual civilization. A great number of ideological and moral-education programs have been launched.

Several dynamic forces are noticeable in the carrying out of the three strategies. For example, there are numerous clusters of vigorously developing cities in the coastal areas of eastern and southern China, and similar clusters are emerging in the central and western regions. They constitute the main engines of growth, are the major manufacturing and trading centers, and absorb surplus rural labor. They also have high productivity, advanced culture, and accumulated international experience that the rest of China can emulate and learn from. The expansion of China's middle-income strata and the growing need for international markets come mainly from these regions.

China's surplus of rural workers, who have strong aspirations to escape poverty, is another force that is pushing Chinese society into industrial civilization. About ten million rural Chinese migrate to urban areas each year in an orderly and protected way. They both provide Chinese cities with new productivity and new markets and help end the backwardness of rural areas. Innovations in science and technology and culture are also driving China toward modernization and prosperity in the twenty-first century.

The Chinese government has set up targets for development for the next fifty years. This period is divided into three stages. In the first stage—2000 to 2010—total GDP is to be doubled. In the second stage, ending in 2020, total GDP is to be doubled again, at which point China's per capita GDP is expected to reach $3,000. In the third, from 2020 to 2050, China will continue to advance until it becomes a prosperous, democratic, and civilized socialist country. By that time, China will have shaken off underdevelopment and will be on a par with the middle rung of advanced nations. It can then claim to have succeeded in achieving a "peaceful rise."

Impact on the World

China's peaceful rise will further open its economy so that its population can serve as a growing market for the rest of the world, thus providing increased opportunities for—rather than posing a threat to—the international community. A few figures illustrate China's current contribution to global trade: in 2004, China's imports from members of the Association of Southeast Asian Nations increased by 33.1 percent, from Japan by 27.3 percent, from India by 80 percent, from the European Union by 28 percent, and from the United States by 31.9 percent. China is not the only power that seeks a peaceful rise. China's economic integration into East Asia has contributed to the shaping of an East Asian community that may rise in peace as a whole. And it would not be in China's interest to exclude the United States from the process. In fact, Beijing wants Washington to play a positive

role in the region's security as well as economic affairs. The beginning of the twenty-first century is seeing a number of countries rising through different means, while following different models, and at different paces. At the same time, the developed countries are further developing themselves. This is a trend to be welcomed.

China does not seek hegemony or predominance in world affairs. It advocates a new international political and economic order, one that can be achieved through incremental reforms and the democratization of international relations. China's development depends on world peace—a peace that its development will in turn reinforce.

CHINA'S UNPEACEFUL RISE[*]

John J. Mearsheimer

Can China rise peacefully? My answer is no. If China continues its impressive economic growth over the next few decades, the United States and China are likely to engage in an intense security competition with considerable potential for war. Most of China's neighbors—including India, Japan, Singapore, South Korea, Russia, and Vietnam—will join with the United States to contain China's power.

To predict the future in Asia, one needs a theory of international politics that explains how rising great powers are likely to act and how other states in the system will react to them. That theory must be logically sound and it must account for the past behavior of rising great powers.

My theory of international politics says that the mightiest states attempt to establish hegemony in their region of the world while making sure that no rival great power dominates another region. This theory, which helps explain US foreign policy since the country's founding, also has implications for future relations between China and the United States.

The Contest for Power

According to my understanding of international politics, survival is a state's most important goal, because a state cannot pursue any other goals if it does not survive. The basic structure of the international system forces states concerned about their security to compete with each other for power. The ultimate goal of every great power is to maximize its share of world power and eventually dominate the system.

The international system has three defining characteristics. First, the main actors are states that operate in anarchy, which simply means that there is no higher authority above them. Second, all great powers have some offensive military capability, which means that they have the wherewithal to hurt each other. Third, no state can know the intentions of other states with certainty, especially their future intentions. It is simply impossible, for example, to know what Germany's or Japan's intentions will be toward their neighbors in 2025.

In a world where other states might have malign intentions as well as significant offensive capabilities, states tend to fear each other. That fear is compounded by the fact that in an anarchic system there is no night watchman for states to call if

[*] This article was originally published in *Current History*, Vol. 105, No. 690 (April 2006).

trouble comes knocking at their door. Therefore, states recognize that the best way to survive in such a system is to be as powerful as possible relative to potential rivals. The mightier a state is, the less likely it is that another state will attack it. No Americans, for example, worry that Canada or Mexico will attack the United States, because neither of those countries is powerful enough to contemplate a fight with Washington. But great powers do not merely strive to be the strongest great power, although that is a welcome outcome. Their ultimate aim is to be the hegemon—that is, the only great power in the system.

What exactly does it mean to be a hegemon in the modern world? It is almost impossible for any state to achieve global hegemony, because it is too hard to project and sustain power around the globe and onto the territory of distant great powers. The best outcome that a state can hope for is to be a regional hegemon, and thus dominate one's own geographical area. The United States has been a regional hegemon in the Western Hemisphere since the late 1800s. Although the United States is clearly the most powerful state on the planet today, it is not a global hegemon.

States that gain regional hegemony have a further aim: they seek to prevent great powers in other regions from duplicating their feat. Regional hegemons do not want peers. Instead, they want to keep other regions divided among several great powers, so that these states will compete with each other and be unable to focus on them. In sum, my theory says that the ideal situation for any great power is to be the only regional hegemon in the world.

The American Hegemon

A brief look at the history of American foreign policy illustrates the explanatory power of this theory. When the United States won its independence from Britain in 1783, it was a small and weak country comprised of thirteen states strung along the Atlantic seaboard. The new country was surrounded by the British and Spanish empires and much of the territory between the Appalachian Mountains and the Mississippi River was controlled by hostile Native American tribes. It was a dangerous, threat-filled environment.

Over the course of the next 115 years American policymakers of all stripes worked assiduously to turn the United States into a regional hegemon. They expanded America's boundaries from the Atlantic to the Pacific oceans as part of a policy commonly referred to as "Manifest Destiny." The United States fought wars against Mexico and various Native American tribes and took huge chunks of land from them. The nation became an expansionist power of the first order. As Senator Henry Cabot Lodge put it, the United States had a "record of conquest, colonization, and territorial expansion unequalled by any people in the nineteenth century."

American policy makers in that century were not just concerned with turning the United States into a powerful territorial state. They were also determined to push the European great powers out of the Western Hemisphere and make it clear to them that they were not welcome back. This policy, known as the Monroe Doctrine, was laid out for the first time in 1823 by President James Monroe in his annual message to Congress. By 1898, the last European empire in the Americas had collapsed and the United States had become the first regional hegemon in modern history.

However, a great power's work is not done once it achieves regional hegemony. It then must make sure that no other great power follows suit and dominates its area of the world. During the twentieth century, there were four great powers that had the capability to make a run at regional hegemony: Imperial Germany (1900–1918), Imperial Japan (1931–1945), Nazi Germany (1933–1945), and the Soviet Union during the Cold War (1945–1989). Not surprisingly, each tried to match what the United States had achieved in the Western Hemisphere in the nineteenth century.

How did the United States react? In each case, it played a key role in defeating and dismantling those aspiring hegemons. The United States entered World War I in April 1917 when Imperial Germany looked like it would win the war and rule Europe. American troops played a critical role in tipping the balance against the Kaiserreich, which collapsed in November 1918. In the early 1940s, President Franklin Delano Roosevelt went to great lengths to maneuver the United States into World War II to thwart Japan's ambitions in Asia and especially Germany's ambitions in Europe. During the war the United States helped destroy both Axis powers. And after 1945, American policy makers made certain that Germany and Japan remained militarily weak. Finally, during the Cold War, the United States steadfastly worked to prevent the Soviet Union from dominating Eurasia, and in the late 1980s helped relegate its empire to the scrap heap of history.

Shortly after the Cold War ended, the first Bush administration's "Defense Guidance" of 1992, which was leaked to the press, boldly stated that the United States was now the most powerful state in the world by far and it planned to remain in that exalted position. In other words, the United States would not tolerate a peer competitor.

That same message was repeated in the famous "National Security Strategy" issued by the second Bush administration in October 2002. There was much criticism of this document, especially its claims about "preemptive war." But hardly a word of protest was raised about the assertion that the United States should check rising powers and maintain its commanding position in the global balance of power.

The bottom line is that the United States—for sound strategic reasons—worked hard for more than a century to gain hegemony in the Western Hemisphere. After achieving regional dominance, it has gone to great lengths to prevent other great powers from controlling either Asia or Europe.

What are the implications of America's past behavior for the rise of China? In short, how is China likely to behave as it grows more powerful? And how are the United States and the other states in Asia likely to react to a mighty China?

Predicting China's Future

China is likely to try to dominate Asia the way the United States dominates the Western Hemisphere. Specifically, China will seek to maximize the power gap between itself and its neighbors, especially Japan and Russia. China will want to make sure that it is so powerful that no state in Asia has the wherewithal to threaten it. It is unlikely that China will pursue military superiority so that it can go on a rampage and conquer other Asian countries, although that is always possible. Instead, it is more likely that China will want to dictate the boundaries of acceptable behavior to neighboring countries, much the way the United States makes it clear to other states in the Americas that it is the boss. Gaining regional hegemony, I might add, is probably the only way that China will get Taiwan back.

An increasingly powerful China is also likely to try to push the United States out of Asia, much the way the United States pushed the European great powers out of the Western Hemisphere. We should expect China to come up with its own version of the Monroe Doctrine, as Japan did in the 1930s.

These policy goals make good strategic sense for China. Beijing should want a militarily weak Japan and Russia as its neighbors, just as the United States prefers a militarily weak Canada and Mexico on its borders. What state in its right mind would want other powerful states located in its region? Most Chinese surely remember what happened in the past century when Japan was powerful and China was weak. In the anarchic world of international politics, it is better to be Godzilla than Bambi.

Furthermore, why would a powerful China accept US military forces operating in its backyard? American policy makers, after all, become apoplectic when other great powers send military forces into the Western Hemisphere. Those foreign forces are invariably seen as a potential threat to American security. The same logic should apply to China. Why would China feel safe with US forces deployed on its doorstep? Following the logic of the Monroe Doctrine, would not China's security be better served by pushing the American military out of Asia?

Why should we expect China to act any differently from how the United States did? Is Beijing more principled than Washington? More ethical? Less nationalistic? Less concerned about survival? China is none of these things, of course, which is why it is likely to imitate the United States and attempt to become a regional hegemon.

Trouble Ahead

It is clear from the historical record how American policy makers will react if China attempts to dominate Asia. The United States does not tolerate peer competitors. As it demonstrated in the twentieth century, it is determined to remain the world's only regional hegemon. Therefore, the United States can be expected to go to great lengths to contain China and ultimately weaken it to the point where it is no longer capable of ruling the roost in Asia. In essence, America is likely to behave toward China much the way it behaved toward the Soviet Union during the Cold War.

China's neighbors are certain to fear its rise as well, and they too will do whatever they can to prevent the Chinese from achieving regional hegemony. Indeed, there is already substantial evidence that countries like India, Japan, and Russia, as well as smaller powers like Singapore, South Korea, and Vietnam, are worried about China's ascendancy and are looking for ways to contain it. In the end, they will join an American-led balancing coalition to check China's rise, much the way Britain, France, Germany, Italy, Japan, and even

China joined forces with the United States to contain the Soviet Union during the Cold War.

Finally, given Taiwan's strategic importance for controlling the sea lanes in East Asia, it is hard to imagine the United States, as well as Japan, allowing China to control that large island. In fact, Taiwan is likely to be an important player in the anti-China balancing coalition, which is certain to infuriate China and fuel the security competition between Beijing and Washington.

The picture I have painted of what is likely to happen if China continues its rise is not a pretty one. I actually find it categorically depressing and wish that I could tell a more optimistic story about the future. But the fact is that international politics is a nasty and dangerous business, and no amount of goodwill can ameliorate the intense security competition that sets in when an aspiring hegemon appears in Eurasia. That is the tragedy of great power politics.

THE ILLUSION OF CHINESE POWER[*]

David Shambaugh

Conventional wisdom has it that the China juggernaut is unstoppable and that the world must adjust to the reality of the Asian giant as a—perhaps *the*—major global power. A mini-industry of "China rise" prognosticators has emerged over the past decade, all painting a picture of a twenty-first-century world in which China is a dominant actor. This belief is understandable and widespread—but wrong.

Recall that not so long ago, in the 1980s, similar forecasts were made about Japan being "No. 1" and joining the elite club of great powers—before it sank into a three-decade stagnation and was shown to be a single-dimensional power (economic) that did not have a broader foundation of national attributes to fall back on. Before that it was the Soviet Union that was said to be a global superpower (an assumption over which the Cold War was waged for a half century), only for

it to collapse almost overnight in 1991. The postmortem on the USSR similarly revealed that it had been a largely single-dimensional power (military) that had atrophied from within for decades. In the wake of the Cold War, some pundits posited that the expanded and strengthened European Union would emerge as a new global power and pole in the international system based on its geographical heft, history, and cultural soft power—only for the EU reveal its internal divisions and to prove itself impotent and incompetent as a global actor. Europe too was exposed as a single-dimensional power (economic). So, when it comes to China today, a little sobriety and skepticism are justified.

Certainly China is the world's most important rising power—far exceeding the capacities of India, Brazil and South Africa—and in some categories it has already surpassed the capabilities of other "middle powers" like Russia, Japan, Britain, Germany, and France. By many measures and in the eyes of many observers, China is now the world's undisputed second leading power after the United

---

[*] This article was originally published in *The National Interest*, No. 132 (July–August 2014).

States, and in some categories it has already over-taken America. China certainly possesses many of the trappings of a global power: the world's largest population, a large continental land mass, the world's second-largest economy, the world's largest foreign-exchange reserves, the world's second-largest military budget and largest standing armed forces, a manned space program, an aircraft carrier, the world's largest museum, the world's largest hydroelectric dam, the world's largest national expressway network, and the world's best high-speed rail system. China is the world's leading trading nation, the world's largest consumer of energy, the world's largest greenhouse-gas emitter, the world's second-largest recipient and third-largest originator of foreign direct investment, and the world's largest producer of many goods.

Capabilities, however, are but one measure of national and international power—and not the most important one. Generations of social scientists have determined that a more significant indicator of power is *influence*—the ability to shape events and the actions of others. As the late political scientist Robert Dahl famously observed: "A has power over B to the extent that he can get B to do something that B would not otherwise do." Capabilities that are not converted into actions toward achieving certain ends are not worth much. Their existence may have an impressive or deterrent effect, but it is the ability to influence the actions of another or the outcome of an event that matters. There are, of course, various means by which nations use their capabilities to influence the actions of others and the course of events: attraction, persuasion, co-optation, coercion, remuneration, inducement, or the threat or use of force. Power and its exercise are therefore intrinsically relational: the use of these and other instruments toward others in order to influence a situation to one's own benefit.

When we look at China's presence and behavior on the world stage today, we need to look beyond its superficially impressive capabilities and ask: Is China actually *influencing* the actions of others and the trajectory of international affairs in various domains? The short answer is: not very much, if at all. In very few domains can it be concluded that China is truly influencing others, setting global standards or shaping global trends. Nor is it actively trying to solve global problems.

China is a self-preoccupied and passive power, whose reflex is to shy away from challenges and hide when international crises erupt. The ongoing crises in Ukraine and Syria are only the most recent examples of Beijing's passivity.

Moreover, when China's capabilities are carefully examined, they are not so strong. Many indicators are quantitatively impressive, but they are not qualitatively so. It is the lack of qualitative power that translates into China's lack of real influence. The Chinese have the proverb *wai ying, nei ruan*: strong on the outside, soft on the inside. This is an apt characterization of China today. Scratch beneath the surface of the many impressive statistics about China and one discovers pervasive weaknesses, important impediments, and a soft foundation on which to become a global power. China may be a twenty-first-century paper tiger.

This can be seen in five broad areas: China's international diplomacy, military capabilities, cultural presence, economic power, and the domestic elements that underpin China's global posture. Let's examine each in turn.

In formal respects, China's diplomacy has truly gone global. Over the past forty years China has traveled a path from a nation isolated from the international community to one integrated into it. Today, Beijing enjoys diplomatic relations with 175 countries, is a member of more than 150 international organizations, and is party to more than three hundred multilateral treaties. It receives far more visiting foreign dignitaries every year than any other nation, and its own leaders travel the world regularly.

Despite this integration into the international community and Beijing's active diplomacy, the diplomatic sphere is a realm where China's position as a "partial power" is apparent. On the one hand, it enjoys the symbols of being a major world power. It's a permanent member of the United Nations Security Council, a member of the G–20 and other key global bodies, and a participant in all major international summits. On the other hand, Chinese officials still remain remarkably reactive and passive in these venues and on many global challenges. China does not lead. It does not shape international diplomacy, drive other nations' policies, forge global consensus, put together coalitions, or solve problems. Beijing is not actively involved in trying to solve *any* major global problem; rather, it is a passive and often-reluctant participant in multilateral efforts organized by others (usually the United States).

Being a global power requires getting in the middle of disputes, bringing parties together, forging coalitions and consensus, and—yes—using pressure when necessary. Beijing prefers to sit on the sidelines and simply call for nations to solve their problems through "peaceful means" and to find "win-win solutions." Such hollow invocations are hardly conducive to problem solving. Beijing also has a complete allergy to coercive measures and only goes along with UN Security Council sanctions when it is clear that not doing so would leave Beijing isolated and negatively impact China's international image. This is not the behavior of a global leader.

Instead, Beijing's high-level diplomacy is really a kind of theatrical show, more symbolism than substance. It is intended primarily to enhance the Chinese Communist Party's (CCP) legitimacy among domestic audiences by showing Chinese leaders hobnobbing with the world's elite, while signaling to the international community that the country has returned to great-power status after several centuries of impotence. As such, the Chinese government goes to extraordinary lengths to meticulously stage-manage its leaders' interactions with their foreign counterparts. Substantively, though, Chinese diplomacy remains remarkably risk-averse and guided by narrow national interests. Beijing usually takes a lowest-common-denominator approach, adopting the safest and least controversial position and waiting to see the positions of other governments before revealing its own.

The notable exception to this general passivity concerns China's own neuralgic and narrowly defined interests: Taiwan, Tibet, Xinjiang, human rights, and its contested territorial claims. On these issues Beijing is hypervigilant and diplomatically forceful, but its attempts to defend these interests are often clumsy and wind up being counterproductive to its image and its goals. Other than protecting these narrow national interests, though, Chinese diplomacy remains extremely passive for a state of its size and importance.

When it comes to global governance, which entails contributing to the common good proportionate to a nation's aggregate capabilities, Beijing's behavior generally parallels the passivity and narrow-mindedness of the rest of its diplomacy. China does contribute to—and should be given credit for—some contributions to global governance: UN peacekeeping operations, anti-piracy operations in the Gulf of Aden, counterterrorism measures in Central Asia, overseas development assistance in Africa, nonproliferation of nuclear materials, stemming public health pandemics, disaster relief, and combating international crime. In these areas Beijing deserves credit. However, China could and should do much more; it still "punches well below its weight" by not contributing proportionately to its aggregate size, wealth, or potential influence. The world should expect and demand more from China.

Why is China's global-governance diplomacy so constrained? There are three main reasons. First, there exists deep skepticism inside of China about the liberal premises and basic concept of global governance, seeing it as the latest "trap" laid by the West (primarily the United States) to "bleed" China by getting it involved in crises and places where it does not have a direct national interest—thus diverting its resources and restraining its rise. Second, Chinese citizens would criticize their government for allocating resources abroad when poverty and other pressing challenges still exist at home. Third, China has a kind of "transactional" approach to expending effort, especially when it involves money. This grows out of Chinese commercial culture but extends into many other realms of Chinese behavior. The Chinese want to know exactly what they will get back from a certain investment and when. Thus, the whole premise of philanthropy and contributing selflessly to common public goods is alien to the thinking of many Chinese.

As a result, in the realm of diplomacy—bilateral, multilateral, and global governance—Beijing still demonstrates a distinct passivity and reluctance to get involved. It is far from being the "responsible stakeholder" that Robert Zoellick called for in 2005. Chinese diplomacy remains narrowly self-interested, and Beijing's involvement in global governance is minimalist and tactical, not normative or strategic. The real business of Chinese diplomacy is, in fact, business. Examine the composition of the Chinese president's or premier's delegations abroad and one finds large numbers of corporate CEOs—in search of energy supplies, natural resources, trade and investment opportunities. Such mercantilist diplomacy does not earn Beijing international respect—and is, in fact, beginning to generate increasing criticisms and blowback around the world (most notably in Africa and Latin America).

China's military capabilities are another area where it is a partial power—increasingly a regional power, but by no means a global power. China is not able to project power outside of its Asian neighborhood (other than through its intercontinental ballistic missiles, space program, and cyberwarfare capacities), and even within Asia its power-projection capacities remain limited (although growing). It is not at all certain that China could project military power on its periphery out to five hundred nautical miles (such as in its East or South China Sea disputes) and *sustain* it long enough to prevail in a conflict. Its military forces are not battle-tested, having not fought a war since 1979.

To be sure, China's military modernization has been advancing steadily for twenty-five years. It now has the world's second-largest military budget ($131.6 billion in the 2014 official budget), largest standing armed forces, scores of new advanced weapons, a navy that is sailing further and further out into the western Pacific Ocean and occasionally into the Indian Ocean, and a modest retrofitted aircraft carrier. So China's military is no pushover. It is certainly capable of defending its homeland, and could likely now wage a successful conflict over Taiwan (absent a fast and full American intervention). China is also perceived to be a regional military power in Asia and thus is altering the balance of power in the region, but Chinese military forces still possess no conventional global power-projection capabilities. China has no bases abroad, no long-range logistics or communications lines, and rudimentary global satellite coverage. The navy is still primarily a coastal littoral force, the air force has no long-range strike ability or proven stealth capacity, and the ground forces are not configured for rapid deployment.

Moreover, strategically, China can be described as a "lonely power"—lacking close friends and possessing no allies or functional alliances. Even in China's closest relationship today (with Russia),

elements of distrust and historical suspicions percolate beneath the surface of seemingly harmonious state-to-state relations. Not a single other nation looks to Beijing for its security and protection—thus demonstrating a distinct lack of strategic influence as a major power. Quite to the contrary, other countries in Asia are seeking to bolster their defense ties with the United States and improve their coordination with each other—precisely because of the uncertainty and possible threat they perceive from China.

Turning from hard power to soft power, how does China stack up as a global cultural power? Not well. No other societies are taking their cultural cues from China, no other countries are seeking to copy the Chinese political system, and—while admirable—its economic system is not replicable elsewhere. Despite the enormous efforts and resources the Chinese government has poured into trying to build its soft power and improve its international image since 2008, China continues to have a mixed-to-negative global reputation. Surveys of public opinion reveal that everywhere in the world perceptions of China are mixed, declining and increasingly fraught with problems.

China is not a magnet for others to emulate—culturally, socially, economically, or politically. The problem for China in all four realms is that it is *sui generis*. China lacks universal appeal beyond its borders or ethnic Chinese communities. Largely because of China's cultural, economic, social and political uniqueness, its global soft-power appeal remains weak to nonexistent.

China's cultural products—art, film, literature, music, education—are still relatively unknown outside of China and do not set global cultural trends. As admirable as China's economic development is, it is the product of a unique combination of features (competitive economies of scale, Soviet-style state planning, individual entrepreneurship, a large and disciplined workforce, a large research-and-development establishment, and massive foreign investment). Even if a "China model" exists (which is debatable), it is not exportable, as this combination of growth factors exists nowhere else. China's political system is similarly an eclectic amalgam of Leninist Communism, Asian authoritarianism, Confucian traditionalism, and a strong internal-security state. Its distinctiveness cannot be replicated—there are no other states trying to do so, nor does one find foreigners seeking political asylum or citizenship in the PRC.

What about China's economic power? This is the one area where one would expect China to be a global power and trendsetter—yet China's impact is much more shallow than anticipated. As in other areas, it is quantitatively impressive but qualitatively weak. China is the world's largest trading nation, but its exports are generally low-end consumer goods; its products have poor international brand recognition; only a handful of its multinational corporations are operating successfully abroad; the total stock of its overseas direct investment (ODI) ranks only seventeenth internationally; and China's overseas aid programs are a fraction of the size of those of the United States, European Union, Japan, or the World Bank.

When evaluated qualitatively instead of quantitatively, China's global economic profile is not very impressive. It remains a processing-and-assembly economy—not a creative and inventive one. Most of the goods that are assembled or produced in China for export are intellectually created elsewhere. China's rampant theft of intellectual property and its government programs to spur "indigenous innovation" (which pour billions into domestic research and development every year) are clear admissions of its failure to create. This may, and likely will, change over time—but to date China is not setting global standards in hardly any technology or product line (or in the natural sciences, medical sciences, social sciences or humanities). Similarly, China only has two universities in the top hundred worldwide, according to the *Times Higher Education* World University Rankings for 2013–2014.

If China is to spur innovation, it will, of course, have to invest more in research-and-development funding. According to the National Science Foundation, in 2009 China spent only 1.7 percent of its GDP on research and development, compared with 2.9 percent in the United States, 2.8 percent in Germany and over 3.3 percent in Japan. The "research intensity" of China's research-and-development spending does not even rank it in the top twenty nations globally, as an estimated 80 percent is spent on product development, and only 5 percent on basic research. China's lack of Nobel Prizes is also a telling indication. Between 1949 and 2010, 584 Nobel Prizes were awarded. Ethnic Chinese won ten of these (eight in the sciences), but eight of the ten worked outside of China. The two exceptions were the Dalai Lama's 2010 Nobel Peace Prize and Mo Yan's 2011 prize for literature. Citations in professional journals are another indicator. In the world's most cited articles (across all academic disciplines), Chinese scholars account for only 4 percent—whereas Americans account for 49 percent.

As a result of China's chronic "innovation deficit," the nation is now mired in the infamous "middle-income trap." The only way out of the trap is through innovation—as Japan, South Korea, Singapore, and Taiwan previously proved. And this requires much more than government investment in research and development—it requires an educational system premised on critical thinking and freedom of exploration. This, in turn, requires a political system that is relatively open and democratic and does not permit censorship or "no-go zones" in research. Students and intellectuals must be rewarded—not persecuted or penalized—for challenging conventional wisdom and making mistakes. Until this occurs, China will be forever caught in the middle-income trap—assembling and producing but not creating and inventing.

Seen in this light, China's trade juggernaut is much weaker than it appears on the surface. Similar weaknesses are evident in China's ODI. Despite the high government priority for Chinese firms to "go out" into the world, so far China's foreign investment remains quite small. As noted above, its total stock of ODI barely places China in the top twenty globally, although its annual outflows are growing rapidly and now rank third in the world ($88.2 billion in 2012). Yet this remains only one-fourth of American ODI in the same year.

More significantly, as in other areas of China's global profile, one needs to delve beyond the quantitative statistics to ask qualitative questions: Where does it go, and is it real investment? The overseas destinations and composition of Chinese ODI have been shifting rapidly since 2011, but a large percentage remains portfolio funds flowing into locales like the British Virgin Islands and Grand Cayman Islands (which ranked as the second and third leading recipient destinations in 2011). Thus, some of this is not foreign investment per se—it is really money being parked abroad in safe havens. This is not only true for China's government and companies, but also for individual assets. The 2014 annual *Blue Book on Chinese International Migration*, compiled by the Center for China & Globalization, recently reported that since 1990 a total of 9.3 million Chinese had emigrated abroad, taking 2.8 trillion renminbi ($46 billion in US dollars) with them. This is not a new development, but has been a growing trend over the past decade. When a nation's economic elites leave in such large numbers and are so anxious to secure their personal financial savings abroad, it speaks volumes about their (lack of) confidence in their own domestic political and economic systems.

Recently, though, China's ODI profile and geographic footprint have been changing. China is ramping-up its investments and purchases across Asia, Africa, Latin America, Europe, and the United States. Chinese buyers are snatching up all kinds of assets—residential and commercial properties, factories, industrial parks, research-and-development facilities, farms, forests, mines, oil and gas fields, and various other resources. Chinese corporations are aggressively merging with or acquiring foreign companies. Individual Chinese have also been buying large amounts of valuable art on the international auction market. Thus, the profile of Chinese outbound investment is rapidly changing, but its impact remains uncertain.

What about Chinese multinational corporations? How competitive are they abroad? As in other categories, there is much more weakness than strength. On the surface, judging from the Fortune Global 500 rankings, Chinese companies now rank second only to American multinationals. But these rankings are calculated on the basis of total revenue and profit—not *where* a company makes its money. When examining the Chinese companies on the 2013 list, it is quickly apparent that relatively few even operate abroad and only a handful earn more than half their revenues overseas. So these are not truly *multinational* corporations, but rather domestic corporate actors.

Many firms may aspire to go global, but thus far those that have tried have not fared particularly well. There have been more failures than

success stories among aspiring Chinese multinationals. Chinese mergers and acquisitions often have stumbled because China's corporate leaders did not do their due diligence beforehand or because of the clash of corporate cultures. By all accounts, the major weakness of Chinese multinationals is human resources—particularly management. There are precious few multilingual and multicultural managers, and Chinese companies do not generally hire foreigners with such skills for upper-level management (Huawei and Haier are exceptions to the rule). Chinese companies and their management have frequently displayed an inability to escape their own national corporate culture and business practices. Because of their preference for hierarchy and clearly defined workplace roles, Chinese tend not to adapt well to "flatter" management structures that prize decentralization and individual initiative. These proclivities have resulted in repeated culture clashes in Chinese mergers with Western companies. Chinese companies have also demonstrated difficulties adapting to foreign legal, regulatory, tax, and political environments. Transparency and corporate governance are not attributes normally associated with Chinese companies—whose decision-making processes are usually opaque, business practices are frequently corrupt, and accounting procedures are often fraudulent. Many Chinese companies have been found to have filed fraudulent information with securities regulators in the United States prior to their IPOs.

The lack of Chinese corporate competitiveness is also evident when it comes to international brands. Only a handful of Chinese companies have been able to establish a brand presence abroad: Tsingtao beer, Haier white goods, Huawei telecoms, Air China, Geely automobiles, and a handful of others. But not a single Chinese company ranks among the *Business Week/Interbrand* Top 100 global brands.

Other measures of China's domestic capacities also do not indicate very high or positive global rankings. In 2014, Freedom House ranked China as tied for 183rd out of 197 countries for freedom of the press. Since 2002, the World Bank's composite Worldwide Governance Indicators have consistently ranked China in the thirtieth percentile for political stability and control of corruption, fiftieth percentile for government effectiveness, fortieth percentile for regulatory quality and rule of law, and below the tenth percentile for accountability. The World Economic Forum ranked China only twenty-ninth globally on its composite Global Competitiveness Index in 2013, along with sixty-eighth for corruption and fifty-fourth for business ethics. Transparency International ranked China even lower (eightieth) in its 2013 international corruption index. In virtually all these estimates and categories, China has *deteriorated* over the past decade. By these and other measures, it is clear that China's global presence and reputation is mixed at best. In many categories China finds itself clustered together with the least well-performing and least respected countries in the world.

The 2013 United Nations Human Development Report further illustrates that despite the considerable and admirable socioeconomic progress China has made since the 1980s, the nation remains very much a developing country. The PRC ranks 101st in the overall index, out of 187 countries surveyed. The average per capita income is now nearly $8,000 in purchasing-power-parity (PPP) terms, yet 13.1 percent of the population still lives on under $1.25 per day. In life expectancy, infant mortality, healthcare provision, educational quality, and inequality, China still lags well behind industrialized nations. Its environmental contamination and pollution are the worst in the world and are contributing to rapidly rising cancer rates. Despite recent government efforts to expand primary and catastrophic healthcare delivery and insurance, most Chinese still face great uncertainties when illness strikes. Its Gini coefficient (which measures income inequality, with 0 representing perfect equality and 1 representing perfect inequality) is now nearly 0.5, among the highest in the world. China's primary and secondary schools are producing world-class test results, but the university system still lags well behind global leaders.

These observations are not meant to belittle China's miraculous developmental accomplishments over the past three decades—they are simply further reminders that China is nowhere near the top of the global tables in many categories of development.

This is a snapshot of China today. Ten or twenty years from now China's global position may well improve in all of these categories and it may be operating on a global basis similar to the United States', but for now China is a partial global power at best. Yet one should not simply assume that China's growth trajectory will continue unabated. It could, but there are also two other possibilities—stagnation and retrogression.

Many China watchers are coming to the conclusion that the country is reaching a tipping point on multiple fronts. Aggregate growth is leveling off (owing to rising costs of production and declining comparative advantages) and the government is struggling to maintain the 7 percent annual growth rates deemed necessary to maintain reasonably full employment, absorb new entrants into the workforce and sustain social stability. Try as it may, the government has been unable to accomplish its announced shift from an export-and investment-driven economy to one based on increased domestic consumption and an innovative "knowledge economy." Production is not appreciably moving up the value chain and technological ladder, and the grip of the middle-income trap is setting in (and could become an indefinite condition). Local debt is soaring and many subnational governmental authorities teeter on the brink of insolvency. Social inequalities are getting increasingly acute, corruption is rampant in both state and society, frustrations abound in every social sector, the rich are fleeing the country in increasing numbers, the middle class is stagnating, and the political system remains ossified and repressive. Meanwhile, the country is not undertaking the political and legal reforms needed to spur the next phase of growth because they would directly impinge on the monopoly power of the CCP.

Several Sinologists now argue that the CCP itself is the principal impediment to future growth and development in China. The Party is an increasingly insecure, sclerotic, and fragile institution that has become paralyzed since 2008. Part of the reason for the paralysis was the leadership transition in 2012 and the factional struggle leading up to it (including the Bo Xilai affair), but it also had to do with the growing unrest around the country (particularly in Tibet and Xinjiang). There have been other contributing factors to the party's retrenchment and repression over the past five years, including fears generated by the Arab Spring, but we have not seen forward movement in political reform since the leadership transition and Xi Jinping's consolidation of power. To the contrary, the political crackdown has intensified since Xi took office. Even the vaunted Third Plenum of November 2013, which was heralded as a reformist breakthrough, has so far proved to be more hype than reality.

This is the potentially toxic cocktail that many China watchers see gripping the country today. It is a sobering and daunting set of challenges for the people and government of China to tackle. Thus, observers should not blindly assume that China's future will exhibit the dynamism of the past thirty years, or that its path to global-power status will necessarily continue.

POLITICS

Editorial Introduction

During the time that China has been rising on the world stage over the past two decades its politics and political system have also continued to evolve. It is true that they have not evolved or changed anywhere near as much as the other sectors considered in this volume. Indeed, some would argue that they have not changed *at all*—after all, China remains an authoritarian state with power concentrated in the single ruling party (CCP) that has little tolerance for dissent and attempts to control most aspects of political and civic life. But during the period of time covered in this edition of *The China Reader*, Chinese politics and the political system have continued to evolve and change.

Generally speaking, this evolution passed through two broad phases. The first (1998–2008) was throughout the remaining rule of Jiang Zemin (Jiang entered office in 1989 and stepped down at the 16th CCP Congress in November 2002) and into the first seven years of his successor Hu Jintao's reign until 2009. The second phase includes the last three years of Hu Jintao's rule (he stepped down at the 18th CCP Congress in 2012) and into Xi Jinping's period in office (2012–).

Jiang Zemin's early years as China's leader were characterized by the harsh post-Tiananmen political repression and economic retrenchment. But beginning in the mid-1990s the Jiang leadership began to embark on a series of reforms. On the economic front these were led by Premier Zhu Rongji; in the political domain they were led by Jiang's senior advisor Wang Huning and Politburo Standing Committee member Zeng Qinghong. They launched a considerable number of political reforms, albeit within the one-party system.

These reforms were aimed at strengthening the Party through reforming it. The reforms were phased in over the next decade; almost all of them derived from the CCP's careful study of the causes of collapse of the Soviet Union and other former communist states. The importance of this post-mortem analysis undertaken by the CCP cannot be overstated—as China's leaders believed that if they did not learn the correct lessons of the collapse of communist parties elsewhere, they could be next.[1]

There were multiple lessons learned, but one of the key ones was that the Party had to be proactive in reforming itself. Stasis was seen as a sure recipe for demise. In the Chinese view, the Communist Party of the Soviet Union (CPSU) had become rigid, ossified, old, overly bureaucratic, ideologically dogmatic, and isolated in the world. Among the many other "lessons learned" from the Soviet and East European collapses, were included the need to:

- Place priority on economic, material, and social development;
- Make Marxist-Leninist ideology flexible and adaptable to national conditions;
- Combat corruption and strengthen Party discipline;
- Rotate, retire, and change leading personnel in the Party, government, and military at all levels;
- Promote "inner-party democracy" and "extra-party consultation";
- Reform and reinvigorate local Party branches;
- Improve cadre competence, recruitment, and training;
- Guard against Western subversion and "peaceful evolution";
- Pay attention to a range of social development problems;
- Treat ethnic minorities and intellectuals well;
- Pursue a foreign policy of openness and integration into the international community.

Many of these conclusions and reforms were reflected in the *Decision on the Enhancement of the Party's Governing Capacity* adopted at the Fourth Plenary Session of the Sixteenth Party Congress in September 2004.

While Zeng Qinghong (who had risen to the Politburo Standing Committee) was the main mastermind behind these political reforms, President and CCP General Secretary Jiang Zemin must also be recognized as a political reformer for backing these initiatives. In retrospect, when compared with his successors Hu Jintao and Xi Jinping, Jiang appears to be a very reformist leader (something that was not anticipated when he came to power and did not really begin to manifest itself until after Deng Xiaoping died in 1997). Jiang also personally put forward the "Important Thought of the Three Represents" (三个代表重要思想)—the concept that the CCP should represent (1) "advanced social productive forces"; (2) "China's advanced culture"; (3) "the fundamental interests of the overwhelming majority of the people." While seemingly obscure ideological orthodoxy, Jiang's first "represent" opened the door to recruiting members of China's growing private sector entrepreneurial (capitalist) class into the Party. The second "represent" began a new emphasis on cultural development and soft power, while the third "represent" signaled a broadening of the mass base of the Party.

When Hu Jintao succeeded Jiang Zemin as Party and state leader in 2002, he inherited this reformist agenda. He also inherited Zeng Qinghong and many other Jiang loyalists in the leadership. Jiang had successfully managed to "stack the Politburo" with his acolytes at the Sixteenth Party Congress that year, and even continued to hold the position of Chairman of the Central Military Commission for another two years until 2004. As a result of this inheritance, Hu Jintao and Premier Wen Jiabao (both of whom were not tied to Jiang Zemin) were very constrained in what they could do. Besides, neither Hu nor Wen had the gravitas of their predecessors. So they smartly continued to implement the Jiang political agenda and the Zhu Rongji economic agenda. The former was confirmed, as noted above, at the Fourth Plenum in September 2004, and they continued through 2008. Hu did add some new initiatives of his own—most notably the "Socialist Harmonious Society" program (社会主义和谐社会) and the "Scientific Development Concept" (科学发展观).

The former was meant to address the widening income gap and rising social inequalities in Chinese society (which had become far more acute as a result of Jiang Zemin's emphasis on coastal development), while the latter was a catch-all term for the more efficient use of resources.

These political policies all continued through Hu Jintao's first term. Although Hu was viewed by many in China and abroad as a cautious *apparatchik* with a bland persona (in contrast to Jiang Zemin's flamboyant style), he nonetheless continued China on this politically reformist course begun under Jiang (Jiang was also alive and watchful behind the scenes). But at the Seventeenth CCP Congress in 2008 Zeng Qinghong retired, and beginning the very next year the CCP began a deep political retrenchment, halting most of the political reforms, and reverted to old-style harsh and repressive rule. The reasons for the retrenchment had to do with far more than Zeng's retirement. The "Arab Spring" and "Jasmine Revolution" had erupted across the Middle East, overthrowing autocratic ruling parties and promising development of democracy—and the CCP was fearful of a contagion effect. Inside of China, major ethnic uprisings in Tibet in March 2008 and in Xinjiang during the summer of 2009 further rattled the Chinese leadership. On October 1, 2009, the sixtieth anniversary of the People's Republic was to be celebrated with an impressively orchestrated military parade in central Beijing, but the leadership feared its disruption by "terrorist" elements.

As a result, for all these reasons, the CCP leadership hunkered down, dramatically strengthened their domestic controls, and unleashed a wave of repression on civil society, Tibet and Xinjiang, and the media. The internal security and propaganda apparatuses were beneficiaries of the crackdown (in 2013 it was revealed at the National People's Congress that the internal security budget actually *exceeded* that of the military's budget!). This repression was the worst witnessed in China since the early 1990s in the aftermath of the June 4, 1989, Incident. The clampdown continued through the end of Hu Jintao's term in 2012 (at the Eighteenth CCP Congress) and into the Xi Jinping era. In fact, it *intensified* under Xi's new rule—reflecting a deep *insecurity* on the part of the CCP leadership.

From 2009 to the present (2015) virtually all of the aforementioned political reforms have either been halted or diluted—with the exception of two. The first is the continuation of cadre training programs throughout the Party and state apparatus—all cadres (of which there are 45 million in China) are required to spend the equivalent of three months every three years in a Party School (of which there are nearly 1,900 nationwide) or Administration Academy learning new skills of "governance" (执政). This is a very good requirement and program that other countries would do well to emulate. The second initiative that has continued, indeed intensified significantly under Xi Jinping, are efforts to combat corruption. Since Xi came to power he has unleashed an unprecedented purge of corrupt officials in the Party, state, and military. So, these reforms continue and are real. Others continue but are really a sham—such as the "extra-party consultation" between the CCP and the eight so-called democratic parties in China. Essentially, however, political reform in China stalled badly after 2009, and it is unclear if it will resume.

Thus the period examined in this section reflects a pattern that has been noticeable in Chinese politics throughout the post-Mao era: a repetitive loosening-tightening dynamic, known as the "*fang-shou* cycle" (放-收周期). The length of each phase of political loosening (*fang*) and tightening (*shou*) has varied since the late-1970s. During this period we see a fairly prolonged period of relaxation (roughly 1998–2008) followed by a tightening of political life in China (2009–).

The following selections were chosen to illustrate these broad political trends. They are divided into four sub-sections: Elite Politics; Dissent; Ideology; and The Future of the CCP.

The first selection is written by Boston University political scientist Joseph Fewsmith, a leading expert on Chinese politics at the "elite" (i.e., leadership) level as well as intellectual trends in China. Fewsmith's contribution focuses on the changes in elite politics. He begins with the important observation that elite politics have become much more stable, predictable, and regularized in the post-Mao era—which, particularly during the Cultural Revolution decade, were anything but stable and predictable. Factionalism has permeated elite politics throughout its history, and it has remained even in the post-Mao and post-Deng eras. Fewsmith provides a careful tracing of the evolution of elite politics since Mao, but particularly in the post-Tiananmen (1989) period. He illustrates how recruitment into the elite, operation of the elite, and retirement from the elite is now far better institutionalized and regularized. Procedures have been implemented that now mandate everything from promotion criteria to Politburo operating procedures. Despite these advancements, Fewsmith describes this as a "quasi-formalized system," due to the continuing informality and unpredictability that still characterizes elite politics. Fewsmith concludes that this as a "reasonably stable situation that can exist for a prolonged period of time."

The next sub-section of entries focuses on political dissent in China. Readers must recognize that political and other forms of organized dissent in China are severely restricted and is ruthlessly repressed. The key word here is *organized*. There is scope for individual acts of dissent or protest—usually on microblogs or in face-to-face personal conversations—but even individual acts *in public* will land the person in detention. China's jails are filled with political prisoners. The two selections in this section are examples of attempts to *organize* groups in protest.

The first is the text of *Charter '08*. The document was so named to parallel *Charter '77* (written that year by a group of Czech dissidents). It was intentionally published on December 10, 2008, on the sixtieth anniversary of the United Nations Universal Declaration of Human Rights. Initially, it had about 300 individuals who endorsed it, but subsequently once it was put online more than 10,000 people inside and outside of China associated their names with the Charter. One of the principal drafters of the document was veteran dissident Liu Xiaobo, who was sentenced to an eleven-year prison sentence in Liaoning Province for "subversion of state power." Liu was subsequently awarded the 2010 Nobel Peace Prize—an act that outraged the Chinese government. *Charter '08* is a broad-gauged and inspiring manifesto that calls for nineteen specific changes in China—including separation of powers, an independent judiciary, legislative democracy, freedom of association and expression, freedom of religion, establishment of a federal republic, direct election of public officials, and other elements associated with Western democratic systems.

The second document is the closing statement of Xu Zhiyong at the end of his trial in the No. 1 Intermediate People's Court on January 22, 2014. In fact, Xu was only permitted to read a few minutes of his statement before the presiding judge intervened and ordered him removed from the courtroom. Xu was sentenced to four years in prison for "gathering a crowd to disturb public order," a charge stemming from his involvement in the New Citizens Movement (a grassroots movement to advocate for basic rights and citizen involvement in civic affairs). Xu was a practicing lawyer with a law degree from prestigious Peking University. Only 41 years old at the time of his sentencing, Xu was twice elected as an independent delegate to the district People's Congress in western Beijing (Haidian). He worked tirelessly as an advocate and lawyer for the dispossessed, most notably migrant families (his statement speaks eloquently on this issue) and official corruption. The sad irony of Xu being a defendant's attorney but being prosecuted by China's legal authorities speaks volumes about the rule *by* law rather than rule *of* law in China. Xu himself ruefully reflected on this as he was taken from the courtroom by guards: "The court today has completely destroyed what remained of respect for rule of law in China." Xu's sentencing and imprisonment were denounced by governments and human rights groups around the world.

The third sub-section segues to the role of ideology in China today. These selections are included represent three different interpretations of this issue.

The first is an excerpt from outgoing Chinese Communist Party General Secretary Hu Jintao at the Eighteenth CCP Congress in 2012. It provides a boilerplate explanation of what the CCP describes as its most central feature: "socialism with Chinese characteristics." It is an excellent example of the jargon-laden prose that populates discourse inside the CCP, and it reveals clearly how the Party seeks to justify itself in terms of Marxism-Leninism.

The second selection is drawn from *The Economist* magazine, written by its team of excellent China-based correspondents. It is interesting because it concerns the regime's recent promotion of Confucius and Confucian thought in society. This is ironic as the communist regime spent much of its existence attacking and trying to eradicate Confucius (551–479 B.C.) and his legacy. Finding that it was not so easy to destroy something so deeply embedded in China's DNA, the regime has turned 180 degrees and now venerates the ancient sage and his teachings. One reason to do so, China watchers argue, is that the regime's own ideology (as seen in the previous selection) is so vapid and hollow that it fails to resonate or inspire society (even in the Party itself). It is also the case that many of the teachings of Confucius dovetail with the current preferences of the CCP for order, obedience, authority, hierarchy, and benevolence. Thus—like many dynasties before it—the Communist Party today reaches back more than 2000 years to re-legitimize itself by cloaking its message in Confucian garb.

The third selection is very revealing of the Chinese Communist Party's assessment of the ideological weaknesses it is experiencing inside the Party and in society, and it further illustrates the paranoia the CCP has towards all forms of Western political influence. It is a high-level secret document issued by the CCP Central Committee (中发) and circulated throughout the Party system nationwide (but leaked outside of China) in 2013. Known as [Central] Document No. 9, it catalogs numerous threats to the Party's ideological dominance and steps to be taken to strengthen it. The document paints a picture of a ruling party under assault from within and without—an extremely insecure, paranoid, and unconfident party acting defensively to fend off perceived threats to its continued rule and existence. This document stands in stark contrast to the upbeat but turgid prose of Hu Jintao's speech, but it is far more revealing about the actual way that the CCP sees its rule and potential threats to it.

The final section in the Politics section looks to the future of the CCP. It contains four selections—two by Chinese leaders and two by leading American experts.

The first is another excerpt from Hu Jintao's speech to the Eighteenth Party Congress. This one focuses on what the CCP describes as "Party building" (党建). Again, it is couched in "Party-speak"—which is, in itself, an illustration of the kinds of narrative theater and dissembling that occurs in inner-Party communications. Marxists have their own lexicon—much of it propagandistic (宣传). But Hu's speech is also interesting for other reasons. On the one hand, it contains interesting admissions concerning the challenges the Party thinks it faces, that is, "[T]he whole Party is confronted with increasingly grave dangers of lacking in drive, incompetence, being out of touch with the people, corruption and other misconduct." This candor is really a remarkable admission by the Party's leader. Hu then goes on to elaborate a series of eight principles to guide "Party building" into the future. Unlike the defensive edicts of Document No. 9, Hu's speech is more of an offensive rallying cry to Party members to tighten up their work styles and combat unhealthy conduct within the rank-and-file. But the fact that Hu even mentioned these behavioral shortcomings is, in itself, an admission of the seriousness of the problems that permeate the CCP.

Hu Jintao retired and was replaced as China's paramount leader by Xi Jinping in 2012 (right after giving this speech). The next selection is one of the many speeches Xi gave in his early years in power. It was selected because it provides readers with a sense of how the CCP believes that it practices democracy. One of the principal methods the CCP argues that it is democratic is through the functioning of the so-called Chinese People's Political Consultative Congress (CPPCC) and its "consultative" relationship with the CCP. In addition to the CCP, China has eight other so-called democratic parties that participate in the CPPCC. This selection contains excerpts from Xi's speech to commemorate the 65th anniversary of the CPPCC in 2014. In it Xi elaborates the CCP's theory and practice of "socialist consultative democracy." Although few outside of China would characterize its political system as democratic, the CCP maintains just the opposite. Xi's speech offers a window into this narrative.

The next selection by American scholar Minxin Pei directly addresses the question of the longevity of the Chinese Communist Party. Pei is pessimistic about the long-term survivability of the Chinese communist regime. But he allows that the regime can survive—and *has survived*—for some time, because it has successfully employed a combination of authoritarian tactics. Pei notes three in particular: refined repression, economic statism, and political cooptation (he offers several examples in each category). While these tactics have been successful in perpetuating regime rule—what some scholars have labeled "authoritarian resilience"—Pei argues that there is an illusory quality to the seeming strength and adaptability of the CCP party-state. Beneath the surface veneer of a "resilient" regime, Pei sees deep insecurities in the leadership and deep instabilities in society. Moreover, he points to a number of systemic features of "authoritarian decay" that China shares in common with other authoritarian parties. This comparative context is important when considering the future longevity of the Chinese political system.

The next and last selection in this section also views Chinese politics through a comparative lens: that of the "Arab Spring" and "Jasmine revolution" in Tunisia and Egypt in 2011. Bruce Dickson, a leading scholar of Chinese politics, evaluates the potential for the Middle Eastern and North African uprisings to spread to China. He begins by noting the real fear in China's leadership of such a contagion—which intensified the already harsh repression and internal security measures in 2012. Dickson argues that China's leaders need not feel so insecure, as their rule is perceived as legitimate by the vast majority of Chinese citizens. Despite this cause for confidence, Dickson argues that China's leaders are right to see their society as highly volatile and potentially unstable. This is where the Arab Spring analogy comes in, Dickson aptly observes: "The lessons of the Arab Spring are that small, isolated events can explode into nationwide protests if not handled quickly and firmly, and that splits within a leadership—especially between the civilian leaders and the military—can doom the regime."

Taken together, the ten selections in this section offer a variety of insights into the state of the Chinese political system early in the second decade of the 21st century.

They collectively reveal a system and ruling party that is stressed and attempting to cope with multiple challenges to its rule. But they also show that the CCP is not sitting idly by, waiting for its inevitable demise. To the contrary, the readings in this section reveal a number of methods that the Party is employing to maintain its control and stay in power indefinitely.

NOTES

1. For a careful analysis of these lessons learned by the CCP from the collapse of the Soviet Union and other former communist party-states, see David Shambaugh, *China's* *Communist Party: Atrophy and Adaptation* (Berkeley and Washington, DC: University of California Press and the Woodrow Wilson Center Press, 2008), especially chapter 4.

I. ELITE POLITICS

Elite Politics: The Struggle for Normality[*]

Joseph Fewsmith

Today, the "Rise of China" is on everybody's lips, and books on the subject are published with regularity.[1] By the end of 2009, China was the third-largest economy in the world and set to become the second largest, and it had amassed over $2 trillion in foreign exchange reserves. The modernization of its military has provoked both analysis and concern, and China's two-decade-old pursuit of "comprehensive national power" seems well on its way to being realized.

When one looks back three decades, this sudden rise seems unlikely and indeed, improbable. In 1978, at the time of the watershed Third Plenary Session of the Eleventh Central Committee, which inaugurated the policies of economic reform and opening to the outside world, China's national income was only 310 billion yuan (about $150 billion at the then prevailing exchange rate), its foreign trade stood at a very modest $20.6 billion, the per capita income of its urban residents was 316 yuan, while the per capita income of its rural residents was only 134 yuan, making China one of the poorest countries in the world.

Over one-quarter of China's rural population had an annual income of less than 50 yuan.[2] Chen Yun, the senior economic specialist in the Party, famously warned that if the livelihood of the peasants did not improve, Party secretaries would lead them into the cities to demand food.[3]

The rise of China is, of course, an economic story, one that has been told very well by Barry Naughton and other economists,[4] but it is just as much a political story. Having recovered in the early 1950s from years of foreign and civil war, China's economic growth then stagnated between the launch of the Great Leap Forward in 1958 and the end of the Cultural Revolution in 1976 as China was repeatedly torn apart by political and ideological conflicts. As much as the poverty China faced in 1978, this legacy of political struggle, which had percolated through China's twentieth-century history, suggested that China would have a difficult time achieving the political stability and policy prescience that would allow the economy to take off.

Explaining the change from a legacy of political instability to one of at least relative stability is by no means easy. Political science is not generally well equipped as a discipline to explain political change and the changing dynamics of power in

[*] This selection first appeared in Joseph Fewsmith (ed.) *China Today, China Tomorrow: Domestic Politics, Economy, and Society* (Lanham, MD: Rowman & Littlefield, 2010).

non-democratic systems. One place to start is the relationship between formal and informal power, an issue raised pointedly by William Riker many years ago:

> Every time I convince myself that I have found an instance in which constitutional forms do make a difference for liberty, my discovery comes apart in my hand. It is, of course, all a matter of the direction of causality. Professor Ostrom believes that at least part of the reason we are a free people is that we have certain constitutional forms; but it may just as easily be the case that the reason we have these constitutional forms is that we are a free people. The question is: Does constitutional structure cause a political condition and a state of public opinion or does the political condition and state of public opinion cause the constitutional structure?[5]

Although William Riker was speaking in terms of democratic institutions, his comments can just as easily, perhaps more easily, be applied to non-democratic settings. If we understand the Cultural Revolution, in part, as a radical breakdown in the relation between formal institutions—the state constitution, the Party charter, and the various written prescriptions on the fora in which political decisions were to be made—and the informal rules of the game, in which internalized understandings of power played an important role, then it is difficult to explain why, in the years after 1978, the formal rules of the game came, gradually and uncertainly, to play a greater role in the Chinese political system. Had the formal rules gained greater credence with the passing of Mao and the end of the Cultural Revolution? If so, why, and to what extent? Had informal understandings of the rules of the game changed? These questions are important not only for the understanding of the emergence of reform, but also for comprehending the peaceful transfer of political power from one leader to another, something non-democratic systems are not generally noted for, and for our best guesses of how the exercise of political power is likely to evolve in future decades.

Part of the answer lies in the organizational response of the Party following the chaos of the Cultural Revolution. As Frederick Teiwes has argued, norms did develop within the Chinese Communist Party, even if those norms were increasingly violated by Mao's high-handed leadership style, particularly in the years following the 1959 Lushan Plenum.[6] Much as the Communist Party of the Soviet Union following the death of Stalin took organizational measures to ensure that no leader would again dominate the Party the way Stalin had, the CCP began taking steps to restore "normal" inner-party life.[7] Those measures began with the "Guiding Principles for Political Life within the Party," were followed by the 1982 Constitution, and increasingly became meaningful as the Party began to implement rules governing retirement.[8] The convocation of the Twelfth Party Congress in 1982, five years after the Eleventh Party Congress, was the first time that the Party had followed the rules in the Party charter to convene Party congresses every five years—and the CCP has managed to adhere to that schedule, regardless of whatever political conflicts and upheavals it has undergone, from that time to the present.

There was much reason to be optimistic about the progress made in the 1980s. The state began withdrawing from society. For the first time since the founding of the PRC a process of depoliticization set in; private life was restored and citizens engaged once again in leisure activities.[9] With the implementation of the Household Responsibility System, agricultural production not only revived but accelerated to the point that grain overflowed storage capacity. Industrial reform started more slowly, but gained rapidly from mid-decade. And China's new attitude toward opening to the outside world drove the growth of foreign trade and foreign investment in China. At least as important, China's relations with foreign countries, frozen by the radicalism of the Cultural Revolution, eased and then warmed as China pursued a policy of "peace and development," which might be understood as development through peace. Intellectual life revived. Ideology faded (but did not disappear).

Nevertheless, China's reforms set off tensions that ultimately could not be contained by the political system. Although reformers talked about "crossing the river by feeling the stones," conservatives were wedded by ideology, interest, and the structure of the PRC system to their understanding of "socialism." Conservatives were indeed distraught by Maoist radicalism, but they nevertheless believed that the planned economy, Marxist ideology, and Party organization could pave the way for a viable socialist system. Introduction of market forces, opening to Western ideas, and generational change challenged their ideas and unbalanced their plans; economic decentralization eroded the power of the center. Inflation, corruption, and new interpretations of Marxism fed into increasingly contentious debates over whether reform was "enlivening" the society and the economy or threatening socialism and the unity of China.[10]

The details of the spring 1989 demonstrations and subsequent crackdown have been explored in many books and articles. What is important for our purposes was the apparent reversion to politics as a game of "win all, lose all."[11] In his speech to the Fourth Plenary Session of the Thirteenth Central Committee, which took place in June following the suppression of the student movement and which fixed blame for the movement on General Secretary Zhao Ziyang, Premier Li Peng talked about the demands of the student movement as being irreconcilable with the continuation of Party rule. As he put it:

> All participants maintained that if they admit that there are "mistakes" in the *Renmin Ribao* editorial [of April 26, 1989, which accused the students of "opposing socialism"], and recognize the student movement as a patriotic democratic movement, they will necessarily force the party and government to accept their erroneous and even reactionary political programs, and to recognize all illegal student organizations as legal ones. They will make further efforts to set up other illegal organizations, including opposition factions, and opposition parties. They will try to establish a multiparty government, force the Communist Party to step down, and subvert the socialist People's Republic. This is their objective, and they will not stop until they reach this objective.[12]

The political implication of this was that Zhao Ziyang, who had suggested compromising with the student movement in order to resolve the situation peacefully, had to step down. Although not at the same level as Mao Zedong's purge of Liu Shaoqi in the Cultural Revolution, this clash was clearly a battle over succession. Deng Xiaoping and Chen Yun were getting old; the question was whether "conservatives" or "reformers" would inherit the leadership mantle. And it was a contest in which neither side was willing to compromise.

The dynamic of the 1980s and the tensions that built up—and exploded—in the CCP comport very well with Kenneth Jowitt's understanding of Leninist regimes. Leninist regimes begin as "exclusionary" systems that are bent on remaking society in their own image. As revolutionary fervor fades and economic difficulties mount, Leninist systems embark on reforms that make them more "inclusionary." But the process of inclusion—recognizing the legitimacy of societal forces—conflicts with the Leninist organization of the Party, generating tension and eventually collapse.[13] Jowitt's analysis works well in explaining the collapse of the Soviet Union and other socialist regimes, and it provides a useful framework for understanding China in the 1980s. The problem, of course, is the CCP did not collapse. Indeed, two decades after Tiananmen, the CCP is perhaps more securely in power than at any time since 1949. The economy has been doing extremely well, China's diplomatic position has never been stronger, and decentralization of state revenues, a major problem in the 1980s, has been reversed. Although many social problems remain—and burst out in frequent mass incidents—the vast majority of the people seem to accept the legitimacy of the CCP despite, or perhaps because of, its policies of cooptation.[14] In short, since 1989 the CCP has remade the political system in ways that have, to date at least, contained political conflict and appear to have paved the way for the CCP to remain in power for many years to come. How did this come about?

Putting the System Back Together

The immediate post-Tiananmen situation did not appear to bode well for the long-term future of the PRC: the political tensions within the CCP remained high, the economy stagnated under the anti-inflationary measures adopted by Li Peng, inter-enterprise debt escalated as efforts were made to strengthen the planned economy, intellectuals were cowed and dispirited, and the newly named general secretary, Jiang Zemin, did not appear to have the political heft to remain in power. Western newspapers regularly compared him to Hua Guofeng, the ineffectual leader who took over after Mao's death only to yield power to Deng Xiaoping. And Jiang's caution did not help. Yielding to the conservative leaders who dominated the post-Tiananmen political scene, Jiang eventually managed to frustrate Deng to the point that Deng seriously considered removing him.

Angered that his vision of reform was being put aside and that he himself was being ignored or worse (Deng allegedly fumed that the "*People's Daily* wants to comprehensively criticize Deng Xiaoping"[15]), Deng went to the Shenzhen Special Economic Zone in the south of China and launched a broadside of criticism against conservative leaders.[16] Convinced that Jiang would, at last, loyally uphold reform and opening (and that the political cost of removing Jiang was prohibitively high), Deng engineered a change in the political atmosphere that culminated in the Fourteenth Party Congress in the fall of 1992. Conservative leaders—most notably Yao Yilin, Song Ping, and Li Ximing—fell from power and the Congress's political report called for the creation of a "socialist market economy," employing that previously taboo word "market" for the first time in an authoritative Party document. Just as important, immediately following the close of the Congress, Deng engineered the ouster of Yang Baibing as vice chairman of the Central Military Commission (CMC) and set off a major purge of followers of Yang and his half brother, Yang Shangkun. The Yang brothers had not shown any deference to Jiang, who had been named chairman of the Central Military Commission in September 1989, thus setting up the possibility that following Deng's demise the People's Liberation Army (PLA) would not accept the leadership of Jiang.

Fearing the sort of conflict Mao had bequeathed to the Party fifteen years earlier, Deng oversaw a shakeup of the military that would ensure Jiang's ability to continue to lead China in the years ahead.[17] Contributing to Deng's efforts to pave the way for a smooth transition following his death were the actuarial tables that caught up with the most senior conservative leaders before Deng's own passing: Vice President Li Xiannian, one of Jiang's strongest supporters, died in June 1992, ideologue Hu Qiaomu followed in September 1992, and senior economic specialist Chen Yun passed in April 1995 (Deng died in February 1997).

So the first answer to the question of how the CCP put its political system back together is that Deng Xiaoping lived long enough to remove the political obstacles for Jiang Zemin to take over, and those who might have dominated the political scene in the absence of Deng died before they had a chance to. Design and luck both helped. There is an irony in this: if we think of post-Tiananmen politics as a period in which stronger institutions were created, then one of the keys to this institution building was the efforts of Deng Xiaoping, who operated largely outside the bounds of institutions. Of course, it is also important to bear in mind that part of what Deng was doing was not building institutions [...] but rather balancing political forces in a way that would support his agenda and provide political stability—which gets one back to Riker's question about the relationship between institution building and the informal distribution of power.

As actuarial realities thinned the ranks of senior leaders, major generational change was taking place. This generational change was not simply the passing of power from one generation to another, but more importantly, the passing of the revolutionary generation to a decidedly postrevolutionary generation. The revolutionary generation (and Deng Xiaoping was clearly one of the revolutionary generation despite his reference to himself as the core of the "second" generation) was one that had risen through the violence and chaos of China's civil and foreign wars and had survived the internecine conflict that engulfed that generation after the founding of the PRC. There was nothing modest about this generation. They were fighters and organizers, propagandists and mobilizers. Typically this generation had worked in many of the systems (*xitong*) of the Chinese Communist Party and thus had understandings of a wide variety of different functions and friends (and, no doubt, enemies) throughout the system. These were people who in their youth set off to "overturn heaven and earth," and they dominated Chinese politics for nearly half a century. As revolutionaries, they did not have the incremental visions of bureaucrats and more modest reformers. Mao Zedong unleashed the Great Leap Forward and the Cultural Revolution without fear that he could not rein in the forces that he had unleashed. And Deng Xiaoping embarked on market-oriented reforms without worrying that he could not control the consequences.

The postrevolutionary generation of Jiang Zemin, Li Peng, and others had fundamentally different career paths than their revolutionary elders. Most of the leaders that came to the fore in this generation were trained as engineers. Engineers tended to have fewer political problems coming out of the Cultural Revolution than those trained in the humanities and the social sciences, and thus it was easier for elders to agree on their promotion in the 1980s as China was seeking younger leadership following the Cultural Revolution. Engineers by training tend to be problem solvers rather than visionaries. Moreover, the career tracks of this generation tended to be in a single field. This generation climbed the bureaucratic ladder step by step, suggesting just how much their personalities, vision, and experience differed from those of their revolutionary elders. In addition, having stayed in narrower career tracks suggested that their ability to forge personal links across systems (*xitong*) would be limited; they would have to depend more on institutional linkages than their elders had. Perhaps more important, it was less clear what they would do with such extensive personal networks if they did have them. Securing power was one thing, and they certainly used personal relationships to achieve that goal, but they and their generation did not have the overarching political agendas of Mao Zedong with his anti-bureaucratic passion for permanent revolution or Deng Xiaoping with his desire to normalize political life and embark on market-oriented reform. The times had changed along with the generations, and there was little choice but to pursue an agenda of economic growth, political stability, and a peaceful international environment.

Generational transition also inevitably raised questions about procedure. Whereas those of the revolutionary generation could legitimize their positions by pointing to their contribution to the revolution, successors (and successors to successors) would have a more difficult time doing that. Questions would increasingly be raised (implicitly or explicitly) about why one person rather than another was promoted. And such questions led to a desire to enunciate such criteria as age, education, and experience, which the Party has increasingly done. Thus, we see positions in the Central Committee being allocated to those holding specific government, military, or Party jobs rather than simply to loyal individuals. Such procedures do not eliminate favoritism or factionalism—patrons can and do plan years in advance to promote the career of their protégés—but it does constrain the way competition can be pursued.

At the Fifteenth Party Congress in September 1997, Jiang Zemin called for "holding high the banner of Deng Xiaoping Theory," lauding the thinking of the recently deceased "architect" of reform and opening. But even as Jiang was praising Deng Xiaoping's thinking, it was evident that a new, or at least modified, approach to ideology was coming into being. Whereas the 1980s had been dominated by debates between reformers and conservatives, the trauma of Tiananmen and the collapse of the Soviet Union had revealed both the impossibility of returning to orthodox Marxism and the political unacceptability of radical reform. What emerged in the 1990s as Jiang began to consolidate his position would be a "neoconservative" approach that was, on the one hand, not intellectually satisfying—it did not articulate any political or social ideal to which people could aspire—but was, on the other hand, both pragmatic and conservative. It was conservative in the sense that it upheld the absolute primacy of the party-state against any real or perceived challenge (such as the founding of the China Democracy Party in 1998[18]), and it was pragmatic in that it accepted the absolute need for economic growth. In contrast to the immediate post-Tiananmen efforts, both ideological and practical, to shore up the old planned economy, the neoconservative approach accepted both the continued growth of the private economy and the rapid expansion of foreign trade even as it sought to revive a leaner, meaner state sector. Neoconservatism was reflected in both the new statism of the Jiang period (the tax reform of 1994 would usher in a period that continues to the present, in which the growth of central revenues outpace the growth of GDP) and the shedding of some two hundred thousand state-owned enterprises and perhaps as many as 50 million workers from state rolls.

Neoconservatism was never articulated as a formal ideology because it was primarily a pragmatic response to the exigencies of the day, but its emergence as the dominant approach to governance serves as a marker of the ideological distance that China had traveled in the two decades since Mao died. Deng Liqun, the conservative ideologue who in the 1980s became the *bête noire* of liberal reformers, tells of preparing himself for the post-Mao era by reading and rereading the Marxist classics, including the works of Mao Zedong.[19] Although Deng Liqun would be far more ideological than the pragmatic Deng Xiaoping who led the reform movement, his mastery of Marxist ideology reflects the importance of ideology and ideational manipulation in the reform movement and in moving away from Maoist ideology. A decade later, no one would think of preparing for high office by painstakingly studying the Marxist classics (indeed, no one has thought of Ding Guan'gen or Li Changchun, who have been responsible for ideological issues from the 1990s to the present, as particularly knowledgeable Marxists). Neoconservatism was not inspirational but it served as a marker of the de-ideologicalization of the Chinese political system.

The passing of the revolutionary generation, the rise of a technocratic leadership, the increasing emphasis on procedure, the decline in the importance of ideological issues in favor of practical solutions, and the adoption of neoconservative approaches to governance all point to the gradual, incomplete, but nevertheless important emergence of formal institutions as constraints on political competition, something that had been absent in China at least since the fall of the Qing dynasty. But to see post-Tiananmen China as the incremental emergence of institutionalized politics misses important dimensions of the period. First, the decline of ideology, while beneficial for the growth of the private economy, for bringing more intellectuals into the Party and for the pragmatic adoption of public policies, was not good for the organizational integrity of the Party or for public values. Public intellectuals on both the left and right lamented the loss of an idealism that could bind a large and diverse nation like China

together.[20] And membership and promotion in the Party seemed to be even more a matter of opportunism, corruption, and personal loyalty than ever. The outright sale of offices became a major problem.[21] Such issues made the building of governance difficult and the provision of public goods anemic, and those issues would, in turn, become bases for social protest and criticisms of reform—but now we are getting ahead of ourselves.

It was too much to expect that the nascent institutions being forged in the 1980s and 1990s would be strong enough to provide a solid basis for exercising political power; personal relationships remained too much a part of Chinese public life for that to happen quickly. Certainly Jiang Zemin, even as he called for the "rule of law" and for "regularization, standardization, and proceduralization" (制度化, 规范化, 程序花),[22] built his political power and indeed a good bit of his development strategy on the promotion of close associates from Shanghai, who were inevitably dubbed the "Shanghai Gang." Similarly, as the Yang brothers were being purged from the PLA, new leadership was sought from the thinning ranks of the former Third Field Army, the army that had been based in East China and to which Jiang Zemin's martyred uncle had belonged. The PLA was itself becoming more professional in this period, but personal relations between the head of the Party and top PLA generals nevertheless remained important.[23] In other words, even as there were signs that political life was indeed being institutionalized and regularized, there was the simultaneous existence and arguably growth of personalism and perhaps even factionalism. Factionalism has existed throughout the history of the PRC, but the political system has never been a factional system. Indeed, the Party has had strong injunctions against factionalism, and that has been a factor both in the centralization of power in the CCP and in the sometimes harsh conflict between leaders.[24] Factions may be more important in contemporary China than they were in the Dengist period or before, but they have not (at least not yet) come to define the political system. Rather, like the institutionalization that has emerged and the cooptation of societal interest, they stand in tension with the still Leninist structure of the party.

Hu Jintao and the Call
for a "Harmonious Society"

The pattern of a gradual leadership transition that Jiang Zemin etched, being named as general secretary in 1989 and consolidating power (if one can ever define a point in time) only at the Fourth Plenary Session of the Fourteenth Central Committee in September 1995, was followed when Hu Jintao succeeded Jiang at the Sixteenth Party Congress in November 2002. This leadership transition was not as smooth as frequently depicted, and it raised important questions about institutionalization, but it was, nevertheless, successful. Deng Xiaoping, like the Daoist strategist Zhuge Liang in the classic novel *Romance of the Three Kingdoms*, influenced events even after his death by engineering Hu Jintao's eventual succession to power even as he helped Jiang consolidate his power (it was Deng who had appointed Hu to the Politburo Standing Committee in 1992, putting him in position for succession). Unwilling to let go of the reins of power quickly or easily, Jiang expanded the size of the Politburo Standing Committee (from seven to nine) in 2002 and arranged for several of his close colleagues to sit on it, apparently to maintain watch over Hu.[25] Jiang himself held onto the critical position of head of the Central Military Commission for an additional two years, just as Deng Xiaoping had held onto that position after retiring from the Politburo at the Thirteenth Party Congress in 1987.

The personnel arrangements reflected both the limitations on the degree of institutionalization that had occurred over the previous decade and more as well as the uneasiness in relations between Jiang's followers and those of Hu Jintao. Jiang, as mentioned above, drew his closest followers from his political base in Shanghai, while Hu, who had spent much of his career in China's poor interior, drew his followers from the interior and from the Communist Youth League (CYL), which he had once headed. Jiang's coastal orientation would be—and continues to be—in tension with Hu's greater emphasis on the interior and the need for balanced development.[26] The tensions evident in this transition were by no means debilitating, but they did reflect the continuing need to carefully balance institutional rules and norms with the informal balance of power.

To an even greater degree than Jiang before him, Hu emphasized the importance of institutions and following the rules. Hu's first public appearance after being named general secretary was to deliver a speech on the twentieth anniversary of the promulgation of China's 1982 Constitution. Hu declared that "no organization or individual can be permitted the special privilege of going outside the constitution and the law."[27] Hu also emphasized such procedures as having the Politburo formally report to the Central Committee during plenary sessions, conducting collective study sessions of the Politburo in an effort to reach common understandings and policy consensus, and developing "inner-Party democracy" in an effort to regularize Party processes. Although such measures point in the direction of further institution building, it must be emphasized that they remain very preliminary as yet.

In addition, Hu began to shift China's official rhetoric in a more populist direction, emphasizing the need to build a "people-centered" society, implement his "scientific development concept," and create a "harmonious society." These ideological tropes, which began to eclipse Jiang Zemin's preferred theory of the Three Represents as Hu began to consolidate power, reflected Hu's different policy emphases. Whereas Jiang had stressed China's rapid economic development, Hu and Premier Wen Jiabao began to emphasize social justice issues—the problems left unaddressed as China, or more precisely the urban east coast of China, barreled headlong forward in pursuit of higher GDP.[28]

This change in official rhetoric is politically interesting for two reasons. First, the populist rhetoric of the Hu-Wen administration was joined by a rising tide of "New Left" criticism, directed against the policies of reform and opening up initiated by Deng and furthered by Jiang, and the Hu-Wen rhetoric, intentionally or unintentionally, seems to have encouraged further criticism. This populist upswell became quite heated, particularly over the issues of management buyouts (MBOs) and the protection of property rights, and the debates between "mainstream" (that is, market-oriented) economists and "nonmainstream" (leftist critics) became so heated that both Hu Jintao and Wen Jiabao were compelled to give strong statements reaffirming their commitment to reform and opening up in the spring of 2006.[29] The issues of how to reform, who should (or could) benefit from reform, the provision of public goods, and the direction of reform were all sensitive and foci of heated discussions among intellectuals. Public voices were playing a greater role in politics, and the issue of how the political system would or could respond to them became important. Democratization was not on the table, but issues of responsiveness were.

Second, the raising of different issues and the implicit criticism of the previous administration for neglecting these issues raised the question of how the Chinese political system could process political disputes. Those close to Jiang felt that unless Hu's populist rhetoric could be reined in, it could destabilize the political system and severely harm reform and opening. The way this issue was handled was to change the rules governing Party congresses once again to allow greater "inner-Party democracy." Whether through the expression of genuine feelings or through the mobilization of personal ties, this process resulted in the selection of Xi Jinping as heir apparent (though no official announcement has yet been made), leaving Hu Jintao's favorite, Li Keqiang, as the probable next premier. Moreover, although the congress accepted Hu's scientific development viewpoint, it relegated Hu's theme of harmonious society to a secondary position. In short, the congress reached compromise but only by constraining Hu Jintao.[30] In this instance, informal politics were at least as important as any institutional rules governing leadership selection.

As the working through of these issues suggests, Chinese politics in the contemporary period is composed of a complex interplay between the more populist forces that support Hu Jintao and his "people-centered" approach to governance and the elitist developmental approach associated with former general secretary Jiang Zemin. The difference between the two approaches should not be exaggerated. Despite some of the harsh language posted on the web by New Left intellectuals, it is difficult to imagine Hu Jintao, who is anything if not cautious, adopting the more radical, highly nationalistic policies urged by some in the New Left. Rather Hu Jintao's policies tend to address the concerns of the New Left, emphasizing the need to deliver better health care to the

rural areas, working to build social security for the poor, and reflecting economic nationalism in keeping foreign investment out of some sectors, but without adopting the populism being urged upon him. Indeed, there is little in Hu Jintao's program that would increase popular involvement in the political process, especially with regard to national policies.

Similarly, those who emphasize the need for economic growth acknowledge the need to address social justice issues. Where they differ from the New Left is first in their basic acceptance of economic theory as it is understood in the West. While China's economists have never accepted market fundamentalism, they have appreciated the value of markets and competition in the allocation of resources, decreasing the ability to engage in arbitrage, and stimulating growth. In their view, there is no need to articulate a unique Beijing consensus in contradistinction to an alleged Washington consensus. Mainstream economists also differ from their New Left critics in believing that social justice issues can only be addressed over a long period of time. Given the size of China's population and the enormity of its social needs, the ability to provide public goods can only be built over time as the overall economy grows. China, in other words, has no choice but to outgrow its problems over time. Diverting scarce resources in an effort to address social needs in the short term can only disrupt China's long-term growth.[31]

Politically these different views and emphases coexist and reach compromise because of the way in which the Chinese elite turns over. In contrast to democratic systems in which one administration ends and another, with a separate agenda and different personnel, takes over, China has a revolving elite. It now seems that the model for the transfer of power is that the senior, outgoing leader, will stay around, both by holding onto a senior portfolio (it has been the critical position of head of the CMC so far) and by surrounding the incoming Party head with close associates who both constrain the new Party head and perhaps provide policy bridges with the former leader. At the same time, the membership of the Central Committee turns over gradually. On average, about half of the membership of the Central Committee retires at each Party congress.[32] Of the newly appointed members, about two-thirds are promoted from the ranks of alternate members of the previous Central Committee, and about one-third are newly appointed. This suggests a conscious effort to mix people who have worked their way up the system with newcomers who "helicopter" onto the Central Committee—but not into top-ranked positions. In short, the newly appointed Party head has the opportunity, but only over time, of weeding out his predecessor's associates and building a Party leadership contingent more in line with his own preferences, but only in time for his own retirement—at which time he can hover over *his* successor.

This is a process which, all other things being equal, is biased toward the old leadership, not the new leadership. For instance, the critical decisions on the makeup of the Politburo that emerged from the Seventeenth Party Congress in 2007 were actually made at a Central Committee meeting on June 25, 2007. That is, the decisions on China's new leadership were not made by the incoming Seventeenth Central Committee (as the Party charter appears to prescribe) but rather by the outgoing Central Committee—on which the supporters of Jiang Zemin would have been more numerous.

What Type of System Is This?

After three decades of reform and opening, elite politics have been transformed in important ways. Rules governing retirement, qualification for higher position, and selection of new leaders have become fairly well institutionalized. There has been a remarkable transition to civilian control over the military, and the military itself seems to participate less and less in nonmilitary political issues (though 20 percent of the seats in the Central Committee are still occupied by the PLA). However, there is still a substantial amount of room in the political system for informal politics to play themselves out. Every five years the rules governing retirement or leadership selection change somewhat, and there are periodic arrests of political opponents on corruption charges that might be better understood as crimes of *lèse majesté*. That the rules governing leadership selection are not changed more radically than they are suggests that the institutional framework does constrain the pursuit of power to an important

degree; that they are nevertheless changed in important ways suggests that the informal balance of power remains important to the operation of the political system. That the rules are never committed to paper and publicized suggests that the leaders understand the continuing importance of informal politics and do not want to (or believe they can) further restrain political behavior through the use of institutions.

I have taken to calling such a situation "quasi-formalized." Such a concept is not useful if it suggests either intellectual surrender (it is a "mixed system") or a temporal oddity (it is in transition to something more identifiable), but it might be a useful concept if by it we can understand a particular interplay between formal and informal rules, such that each is seen as complementary to the other—that is to say, if we view elite politics in China as not institutionalized in important ways but also accept that the informal politics do not so overwhelm the formal rules as to render the latter meaningless. Quasi-formalization could thus be seen as describing a situation in which formal rules had indeed gained institutional traction, circumscribing the scope of informal rules, but that informal rules filled out the empty spaces not defined by the formal rules and indeed pushed against the formal institutions and importantly against the further formalization of the rules. Importantly, quasi-formalization implies that there is no third-party enforcement, including recourse either to an independent judiciary or the opinion of voters. Most important, if a concept of quasi-formalization is to make any sense, is the idea that it is not "halfway" between informal and formal, transiting in one direction or the other, but rather that it is a reasonably stable situation that can exist for a prolonged period of time. It is a deliberate blurring of the lines between formal and informal in a way that prevents formal institutions from emerging full blown and yet prevents informal political balances from overwhelming institutionalized rules.

Implications for the Future

If the concept of quasi-formalization is an adequate description of the present state of elite politics in China, then we must ask what the implications for the future are. As with all things in the future, caveats are in order. First, we see that while there are many reasons to believe that the current order seems likely to continue, there clearly will be challenges. For years, the greatest challenge to the political order has appeared to be a prolonged setback to continued economic growth. Now, with the world financial crisis, that possibility seems real, even if the Chinese economy has responded remarkably well to this challenge. We know that there have been continual challenges to the status quo in the form of "mass incidents," which grew from 8,700 in 1993 to 87,000 in 2005. If quasi-formalization works well enough as a framework in which political conflict can be mediated at the elite level, there are other arenas that simply do not accept such a framework. It is possible, if prolonged economic stagnation would result from the current global economic crisis (which does not seem likely) or from other causes, that local protests could escalate to the point that they either bring about systemic change or they bring down the whole system. Bringing down the current system seems unlikely—the government has many resources to prevent such an outcome—but the challenges presented by such protests could lead, over time, to systemic changes, such as real elections or the establishment of an independent judiciary, that would jolt China out of the current quasi-formalized setting into the realm of political contestation through formal institutional arrangements. Alternatively, the continuation of protests could exacerbate policy differences within the elite in ways that cannot be contained by quasi-formalization. Such an outcome would reflect a breakdown in the balance between the formal rules of the game and the informal balance of power, possibly triggering the sort of "game to win all" from which China has suffered so much over the past century.

Such outcomes do not seem likely to me. On the contrary, the pliability of the current system, which allows institutional rules to be stretched but not broken and thus accommodates conflict while upholding a fundamentally hierarchical order, seems sustainable over a prolonged period of time. Though this chapter has explored the development of quasi-formal arrangements at the elite level, I believe that patterns of governance at the local level are also evolving in this direction: New interests are being accommodated by a variety of quasi-formal linkages to the local state

without recognition of their separate legitimacy. New developments in law could challenge these arrangements, but quasi-formalization seems to possess durability.

If the current political arrangements do continue into the future, they augur not only for continuity in policy but also for only incremental change. The political status quo mixes different economic, political, and geographic interests and is designed to maintain a balance among diverse elements, turning political power over only incrementally and incompletely. The upside of such a political arrangement is that it is basically conservative and predictable. The downside is that it may not be able to respond quickly to crises, and crises are a normal feature of political life—as the SARS epidemic, the Asian financial crisis, the Sichuan earthquake, the bombing of the Chinese embassy in Belgrade, and the EP-3 incident all suggest. So far, China has contained the political fallout from each of these crises, but that does not mean it will continue to be able to do so. China has not yet earned high marks for crisis management, yet such skills are likely to become more important in the future.

The other problem with a political arrangement that permits only incremental change is that it can allow problems to mount. As the rising number of mass incidents suggest, China has not yet mounted an effective political response.

China has certainly talked about and experimented with political reforms at the local level, but to date these have been limited. They have been limited because more extensive political reforms would challenge the hierarchical, authoritarian nature of the political system, and that would set off political changes that would be as far-reaching as they would be unpredictable.

The pliability of China's quasi-formal arrangements could be challenged, however, by slower economic growth [...], by increased competition within the political system, or by a continued diversification of developmental goals to include environmental protection, health care, social security, and so forth, as is already happening. Such changes, singly or in combination, would put strains on China's political economy in ways that might bring very discontinuous change. Some such scenarios are pursued in the conclusion to this volume.

NOTES

1. William Overholt's 1993 book, *The Rise of China: How Economic Reform Is Creating a New Superpower* (New York: W. W. Norton) was ahead of its time, especially given the uncertainties prevailing in the post-Tiananmen period. More recently there have been many notable books on the subject, including C. Fred Bergsten, Charles Freeman, Nicholas Lardy, and Derek J. Mitchell, *The Rise of China: Challenges and Opportunities* (Washington, DC: Peter G. Peterson Institute for International Economics and the Center for Strategic and International Studies, 2008); James Kynge, *China Shakes the World: A Titan's Rise and Troubled Future* (New York: Houghton Mifflin Co., 2006); Thomas G. Rawski and William W. Keller, eds., *China's Rise and the Balance of Power in Asia* (Pittsburgh: University of Pittsburgh Press, 2007); and Robert S. Ross and Zhu Feng, *China's Ascent: Power, Security, and the Future of International Politics* (Ithaca, NY: Cornell University Press, 2008).

2. Wu Xiang, "Yang guan dao yu du mu qiao" [The broad road and the single plank bridge], *Renmin ribao*, November 5, 1980.

3. Chen Yun. "Jianchi an bili yuanze tiaozheng guomin jingji" [Readjust the national economy in accordance with the principle of proportionality], in *Chen Yun wenxuan (1956–1985)* [The selected works of Chen Yun, 1956–1985] (Beijing: Renmin chubanshe, 1986), 226–31.

4. Barry Naughton, *The Chinese Economy: Transitions and Growth* (Cambridge, MA: Massachusetts Institute of Technology Press, 2007).

5. William H. Riker, "Comments on Vincent Ostrom's Paper," *Public Choice* 27 (1976): 13–15, quoted in Douglass North, *Institutions, Institutional Change and Economic Performance* (Cambridge: Cambridge University Press, 1990), 60.

6. Frederick Teiwes, *Leadership, Legitimacy, and Conflict in China* (Armonk, NY: M.E. Sharpe, 1984).

7. George W. Breslauer, *Khrushchev and Brezhnev as Leaders: Building Authority in Soviet Politics* (London and Boston: Allen & Unwin, 1982).

8. "Guanyu dangnei zhengzhi shenghuo de ruogan zhunze" [Some guiding principles for political life within the party], in Zhonggong zhongyang wen-xian yanjiushi, ed., *Shiyijie sanzhong quanhui yilai zhongyao wenxian xuandu* [Selected readings in important documents since the Third Plenary Session of the Eleventh Central Committee], 2 vols. (Beijing: Renmin chubanshe, 1987), 1:163–84; Melanie Manion, *Retirement of Revolutionaries in China: Public Policies, Social Norms, Private Interests* (Princeton: Princeton University Press, 1993).

9. Shaoguang Wang, "The Politics of Private Time: Changing Leisure Patterns in Urban China," in Deborah S. Davis et al., eds., *Urban Spaces in Contemporary China* (New York: Cambridge University Press, 1995), 149–72.

10. Joseph Fewsmith, *Dilemmas of Reform in China: Political Conflict and Economic Debate* (Armonk, NY: M.E. Sharpe, 1994).

11. The notion of elite politics as a game to win all or lose all was central to the thinking of Tang Tsou. See, for instance, his *The Cultural Revolution and Post-Mao Reforms: A Historical Perspective* (Chicago: University of Chicago Press, 1986).

12. Li Peng, "Full Text" of Top-Secret Fourth Plenary Session Document: "Li Peng's Life-Taking Report Lays Blame on Zhao Ziyang," in Mei Qiren, ed., "Three Interviews with Zhao Ziyang," *Chinese Law and Government* 38, no. 3 (May–June 2005): 69–84.

13. Kenneth Jowitt, *The New World Disorder: The Leninist Extinction* (Berkeley and Los Angeles: University of California Press, 1992).

14. See, for instance, Bruce Dickson, *Red Capitalists in China: The Party, Entrepreneurs and Prospects for Political Change* (New York: Cambridge University Press, 2003).

15. Gao Xin and He Pin, *Zhu Rongji Zhuan* [Biography of Zhu Rongji] (Taipei: Xinxinwen, 1993), 231–32.

16. On Deng's "southern journey," as this trip is often called, see Richard Baum, *Burying Mao: Chinese Politics in the Age of Deng Xiaoping* (Princeton: Princeton University Press, 1996), 341–68.

17. On these political developments, see Joseph Fewsmith, *China Since Tiananmen*, 2nd ed. (Cambridge: Cambridge University Press, 2008), 62–77.

18. Erik Eckholm, "Beijing Sends Potential Dissidents a Message: Don't," *New York Times*, December 25, 1998.

19. Deng Liqun, *Deng Liqun zixu: Shi'erge chunqiu (1975–1987)* [Deng Liqun's narrative: Twelve years (1975–1987)] (n.d., n.p.), 11.

20. On the left, see Luo yi ning ge'er [pseudo. Wang Shan], *Disanzhi yanjing kan Zhongguo* [Looking at China through a third eye] (Taiyuan: Shanxi renmin chuban- she, 1997); on the right, see Wang Xiaoming, ed., *Renwen jingshen xunsilu* [Pondering the humanistic spirit] (Shanghai: Wenhui chubanshe, 1996).

21. John Burns, "Strengthening the Central CCP Control of Leadership Selection: The 1990 Nomenklatura," *China Quarterly*, no. 138 (June 1994): 458–91.

22. "Rule of Law" was a major theme of the Fifteenth Party Congress in 1997, and the call for standardization.

23. Gao Xin, *Jiang Zemin de quanli zhi lu* [Jiang Zemin's road to power] (Hong Kong: Jing Ming chubanshe, 1997), 58–80.

24. Tang Tsou, "Prolegomenon to the Study of Informal Groups in CCP politics," in Tsou, *The Cultural Revolution and Post-Mao Reforms*, 95–111.

25. Joseph Fewsmith, "The Sixteenth National Party Congress: The Succession That Didn't Happen," *China Quarterly*, no. 173 (March 2003): 1–16.

26. Cheng Li, "The New Bipartisanship within the Chinese Communist Party," *Orbis* 49, no. 3 (Summer 2005): 387–400.

27. "Hu Jintao zai xianfa shixing ershi zhounian dahui sang de jianghua," 2002.

28. Fewsmith, *China Since Tiananmen*, chap. 8.

29. On these debates, see Fewsmith, *China Since Tiananmen*, 262–69.

30. Joseph Fewsmith, "China in 2007," *Asian Survey* 48, no. 1 (February 2008): 82–96.

31. Wang Xing, Liu Yingting, and Lin Qi, "Shichanghua gaige zai chufa" [Relaunching market-oriented reform], *21 Shijijingji Daobao*, April 3, 2005.

32. At the Seventeenth Party Congress in 2007, 51 percent of full members of the Central Committee retired. In 2002, at the Sixteenth Party Congress, 56 percent of full members retired, and at the Fifteenth Party Congress in 1997, 57 percent retired.

II. Dissent

Charter '08*

Anonymous

I. Foreword

A hundred years have passed since the writing of China's first constitution. 2008 also marks the sixtieth anniversary of the promulgation of the *Universal Declaration of Human Rights*, the thirtieth anniversary of the appearance of the Democracy Wall in Beijing, and the tenth of China's signing of the International Covenant on Civil and Political Rights. We are approaching the twentieth anniversary of the 1989 Tiananmen massacre of pro-democracy student protesters. The Chinese people, who have endured human rights disasters and uncountable struggles across these same years, now include many who see clearly that freedom, equality, and human rights are universal values of humankind and that democracy and constitutional government is the fundamental framework for protecting these values.

By departing from these values, the Chinese government's approach to "modernization" has proven disastrous. It has stripped people of their rights, destroyed their dignity, and corrupted normal human intercourse. So we ask: Where is China headed in the twenty-first century? Will it continue with "modernization" under authoritarian rule, or will it embrace universal human values, join the mainstream of civilized nations, and build a democratic system? There can be no avoiding these questions.

_____

* An Open Petition signed by more than 2000 Chinese citizens in 2008. This document circulated for several months in China during 2008, collecting signatures, before it was banned and the principal authors were arrested and imprisoned. It was subsequently translated and republished on The Asia Society website *China File* in January 2009 (http://www.chinafile.com/chinas-charter-08).

The shock of the Western impact upon China in the nineteenth century laid bare a decadent authoritarian system and marked the beginning of what is often called "the greatest changes in thousands of years" for China. A "self-strengthening movement" followed, but this aimed simply at appropriating the technology to build gunboats and other Western material objects. China's humiliating naval defeat at the hands of Japan in 1895 only confirmed the obsolescence of China's system of government. The first attempts at modern political change came with the ill-fated summer of reforms in 1898, but these were cruelly crushed by ultraconservatives at China's imperial court. With the revolution of 1911, which inaugurated Asia's first republic, the authoritarian imperial system that had lasted for centuries was finally supposed to have been laid to rest. But social conflict inside our country and external pressures were to prevent it; China fell into a patchwork of warlord fiefdoms and the new republic became a fleeting dream.

The failure of both "self-strengthening" and political renovation caused many of our forebears to reflect deeply on whether a "cultural illness" was afflicting our country. This mood gave rise, during the May Fourth Movement of the late 1910s, to the championing of "science and democracy." Yet that effort, too, foundered as warlord chaos persisted and the Japanese invasion (beginning in Manchuria in 1931) brought national crisis.

Victory over Japan in 1945 offered one more chance for China to move toward modern government, but the Communist defeat of the Nationalists in the civil war thrust the nation into the abyss of totalitarianism. The "new China" that emerged in 1949 proclaimed that "the people are sovereign" but in fact set up a system in which "the Party is all-powerful." The Communist Party of China seized control of all organs of the state and all political, economic, and social resources, and, using these, has produced a long trail of human rights disasters, including, among many others, the Anti-Rightist Campaign (1957), the Great Leap Forward (1958–1960), the Cultural Revolution (1966–1969), the June Fourth [Tiananmen Square] Massacre (1989), and the current repression of all unauthorized religions and the suppression of the *weiquan* rights movement [a movement that aims to defend citizens' rights promulgated in the Chinese Constitution and to fight for human rights recognized by international conventions that the Chinese government has signed]. During all this, the Chinese people have paid a gargantuan price. Tens of millions have lost their lives, and several generations have seen their freedom, their happiness, and their human dignity cruelly trampled.

During the last two decades of the twentieth century the government policy of "Reform and Opening" gave the Chinese people relief from the pervasive poverty and totalitarianism of the Mao Zedong era, and brought substantial increases in the wealth and living standards of many Chinese as well as a partial restoration of economic freedom and economic rights. Civil society began to grow, and popular calls for more rights and more political freedom have grown apace. As the ruling elite itself moved toward private ownership and the market economy, it began to shift from an outright rejection of "rights" to a partial acknowledgment of them.

In 1998 the Chinese government signed two important international human rights conventions; in 2004 it amended its constitution to include the phrase "respect and protect human rights"; and this year, 2008, it has promised to promote a "national human rights action plan." Unfortunately most of this political progress has extended no further than the paper on which it is written. The political reality, which is plain for anyone to see, is that China has many laws but no rule of law; it has a constitution but no constitutional government. The ruling elite continues to cling to its authoritarian power and fights off any move toward political change.

The stultifying results are endemic official corruption, an undermining of the rule of law, weak human rights, decay in public ethics, crony capitalism, growing inequality between the wealthy and the poor, pillage of the natural environment as well as of the human and historical environments, and the exacerbation of a long list of social conflicts, especially, in recent times, a sharpening animosity between officials and ordinary people.

As these conflicts and crises grow ever more intense, and as the ruling elite continues with impunity to crush and to strip away the rights of citizens to freedom, to property, and to the pursuit of happiness, we see the powerless in our society—the vulnerable groups, the people who have been suppressed and monitored, who have suffered cruelty and even torture, and who have had no adequate avenues for their protests, no courts to hear their pleas—becoming more militant and raising the possibility of a violent conflict of disastrous proportions. The decline of the current system has reached the point where change is no longer optional.

II. Our Fundamental Principles

This is a historic moment for China, and our future hangs in the balance. In reviewing the political modernization process of the past hundred years or more, we reiterate and endorse basic universal values as follows:

Freedom Freedom is at the core of universal human values. Freedom of speech, freedom of the press, freedom of assembly, freedom of association, freedom in where to live, and the freedoms to strike, to demonstrate, and to protest, among others, are the forms that freedom takes. Without freedom, China will always remain far from civilized ideals.

Human Rights Human rights are not bestowed by a state. Every person is born with inherent rights to dignity and freedom. The government exists for the protection of the human rights of its citizens. The exercise of state power must be authorized by the people. The succession of political disasters in China's recent history is a direct consequence of the ruling regime's disregard for human rights.

Equality The integrity, dignity, and freedom of every person—regardless of social station, occupation, sex, economic condition, ethnicity, skin color, religion, or political belief—are the same as those of any other. Principles of equality before the law and equality of social, economic, cultural, civil, and political rights must be upheld.

Republicanism Republicanism, which holds that power should be balanced among different branches of government and competing interests should be served, resembles the traditional Chinese political ideal of "fairness in all under heaven." It allows different interest groups and social assemblies, and people with a variety of cultures and beliefs, to exercise democratic self-government and to deliberate in order to reach peaceful resolution of public questions on a basis of equal access to government and free and fair competition.

Democracy The most fundamental principles of democracy are that the people are sovereign and the people select their government. Democracy has these characteristics:

1. Political power begins with the people and the legitimacy of a regime derives from the people.
2. Political power is exercised through choices that the people make.
3. The holders of major official posts in government at all levels are determined through periodic competitive elections.
4. While honoring the will of the majority, the fundamental dignity, freedom, and human rights of minorities are protected. In short, democracy is a modern means for achieving government truly "of the people, by the people, and for the people."

Constitutional Rule Constitutional rule is rule through a legal system and legal regulations to implement principles that are spelled out in a constitution. It means protecting the freedom and the rights of citizens, limiting and defining the scope of legitimate government power, and providing the administrative apparatus necessary to serve these ends.

III. What We Advocate

Authoritarianism is in general decline throughout the world; in China, too, the era of emperors and overlords is on the way out. The time is arriving everywhere for citizens to be masters of states. For China the path that leads out of our current predicament is to divest ourselves of the authoritarian notion of reliance on an "enlightened overlord" or an "honest official" and to turn instead toward a system of liberties, democracy, and the rule of law, and toward fostering the consciousness of modern citizens who see rights as fundamental and participation as a duty. Accordingly, and in a spirit of this duty as responsible and constructive citizens, we offer the following recommendations on national governance, citizens' rights, and social development:

1. *A New Constitution.* We should recast our present constitution, rescinding its provisions that contradict the principle that sovereignty resides with the people and turning it into a document that genuinely guarantees human rights, authorizes the exercise of public power, and serves as the legal underpinning of China's democratization. The constitution must be the highest law in the land, beyond violation by any individual, group, or political party.
2. *Separation of Powers.* We should construct a modern government in which the separation of legislative, judicial, and executive power is guaranteed. We need an Administrative Law that defines the scope of government responsibility and prevents abuse of administrative power. Government should be responsible to taxpayers. Division of power between provincial governments and the central government should adhere to the principle that central powers are only those specifically granted by the constitution and all other powers belong to the local governments.
3. *Legislative Democracy.* Members of legislative bodies at all levels should be chosen by direct election, and legislative democracy should observe just and impartial principles.
4. *An Independent Judiciary.* The rule of law must be above the interests of any particular political party and judges must be independent. We need to establish a constitutional supreme court and institute procedures for constitutional review. As soon as possible, we should abolish all of the Committees on Political and Legal Affairs that now allow Communist Party officials at every level to decide politically

sensitive cases in advance and out of court. We should strictly forbid the use of public offices for private purposes.

5. *Public Control of Public Servants.* The military should be made answerable to the national government, not to a political party, and should be made more professional. Military personnel should swear allegiance to the constitution and remain nonpartisan. Political party organizations must be prohibited in the military. All public officials including police should serve as nonpartisans, and the current practice of favoring one political party in the hiring of public servants must end.

6. *Guarantee of Human Rights.* There must be strict guarantees of human rights and respect for human dignity. There should be a Human Rights Committee, responsible to the highest legislative body that will prevent the government from abusing public power in violation of human rights. A democratic and constitutional China especially must guarantee the personal freedom of citizens. No one should suffer illegal arrest, detention, arraignment, interrogation, or punishment. The system of "Reeducation through Labor" must be abolished.

7. *Election of Public Officials.* There should be a comprehensive system of democratic elections based on "one person, one vote." The direct election of administrative heads at the levels of county, city, province, and nation should be systematically implemented. The rights to hold periodic free elections and to participate in them as a citizen are inalienable.

8. *Rural–Urban Equality.* The two-tier household registry system must be abolished. This system favors urban residents and harms rural residents. We should establish instead a system that gives every citizen the same constitutional rights and the same freedom to choose where to live.

9. *Freedom to Form Groups.* The right of citizens to form groups must be guaranteed. The current system for registering nongovernment groups, which requires a group to be "approved," should be replaced by a system in which a group simply registers itself. The formation of political parties should be governed by the constitution and the laws, which means that we must abolish the special privilege of one party to monopolize power

and must guarantee principles of free and fair competition among political parties.

10. *Freedom to Assemble.* The constitution provides that peaceful assembly, demonstration, protest, and freedom of expression are fundamental rights of a citizen. The ruling party and the government must not be permitted to subject these to illegal interference or unconstitutional obstruction.

11. *Freedom of Expression.* We should make freedom of speech, freedom of the press, and academic freedom universal, thereby guaranteeing that citizens can be informed and can exercise their right of political supervision. These freedoms should be upheld by a Press Law that abolishes political restrictions on the press. The provision in the current Criminal Law that refers to "the crime of incitement to subvert state power" must be abolished. We should end the practice of viewing words as crimes.

12. *Freedom of Religion.* We must guarantee freedom of religion and belief, and institute a separation of religion and state. There must be no governmental interference in peaceful religious activities. We should abolish any laws, regulations, or local rules that limit or suppress the religious freedom of citizens. We should abolish the current system that requires religious groups (and their places of worship) to get official approval in advance and substitute for it a system in which registry is optional and, for those who choose to register, automatic.

13. *Civic Education.* In our schools we should abolish political curriculums and examinations that are designed to indoctrinate students in state ideology and to instill support for the rule of one party. We should replace them with civic education that advances universal values and citizens' rights, fosters civic consciousness, and promotes civic virtues that serve society.

14. *Protection of Private Property.* We should establish and protect the right to private property and promote an economic system of free and fair markets. We should do away with government monopolies in commerce and industry and guarantee the freedom to start new enterprises. We should establish a Committee on State-Owned Property, reporting to the national legislature, that will monitor the

transfer of state-owned enterprises to private ownership in a fair, competitive, and orderly manner. We should institute a land reform that promotes private ownership of land, guarantees the right to buy and sell land, and allows the true value of private property to be adequately reflected in the market.

15. *Financial and Tax Reform.* We should establish a democratically regulated and accountable system of public finance that ensures the protection of taxpayer rights and that operates through legal procedures. We need a system by which public revenues that belong to a certain level of government—central, provincial, county or local—are controlled at that level. We need major tax reform that will abolish any unfair taxes, simplify the tax system, and spread the tax burden fairly. Government officials should not be able to raise taxes, or institute new ones, without public deliberation and the approval of a democratic assembly. We should reform the ownership system in order to encourage competition among a wider variety of market participants.

16. *Social Security.* We should establish a fair and adequate social security system that covers all citizens and ensures basic access to education, health care, retirement security, and employment.

17. *Protection of the Environment.* We need to protect the natural environment and to promote development in a way that is sustainable and responsible to our descendants and to the rest of humanity. This means insisting that the state and its officials at all levels not only do what they must do to achieve these goals, but also accept the supervision and participation of nongovernmental organizations.

18. *A Federated Republic.* A democratic China should seek to act as a responsible major power contributing toward peace and development in the Asian Pacific region by approaching others in a spirit of equality and fairness. In Hong Kong and Macao, we should support the freedoms that already exist. With respect to Taiwan, we should declare our commitment to the principles of freedom and democracy and then, negotiating as equals and ready to compromise, seek a formula for peaceful unification. We should approach disputes in the national-minority areas of China with an open mind, seeking ways to find a workable framework within which all ethnic and religious groups can flourish. We should aim ultimately at a federation of democratic communities of China.

19. *Truth in Reconciliation.* We should restore the reputations of all people, including their family members, who suffered political stigma in the political campaigns of the past or who have been labeled as criminals because of their thought, speech, or faith. The state should pay reparations to these people. All political prisoners and prisoners of conscience must be released. There should be a Truth Investigation Commission charged with finding the facts about past injustices and atrocities, determining responsibility for them, upholding justice, and, on these bases, seeking social reconciliation.

China, as a major nation of the world, as one of five permanent members of the United Nations Security Council, and as a member of the UN Council on Human Rights, should be contributing to peace for humankind and progress toward human rights.

Unfortunately, we stand today as the only country among the major nations that remains mired in authoritarian politics. Our political system continues to produce human rights disasters and social crises, thereby not only constricting China's own development but also limiting the progress of all of human civilization. This must change, truly it must. The democratization of Chinese politics can be put off no longer.

Accordingly, we dare to put civic spirit into practice by announcing Charter '08. We hope that our fellow citizens who feel a similar sense of crisis, responsibility, and mission, whether they are inside the government or not, and regardless of their social status, will set aside small differences to embrace the broad goals of this citizens' movement. Together we can work for major changes in Chinese society and for the rapid establishment of a free, democratic, and constitutional country. We can bring to reality the goals and ideals that our people have incessantly been seeking for more than a hundred years, and can bring a brilliant new chapter to Chinese civilization.

FOR FREEDOM, JUSTICE, AND LOVE:
MY CLOSING STATEMENT TO THE COURT

Xu Zhiyong

You have accused me of disrupting public order for my efforts to push for rights to equal access to education, to allow children of migrant workers to sit for university entrance examinations where they reside, and for my calls that officials publicly declare their assets.*

While on the face of it, this appears to be an issue of the boundary between a citizen's right to free speech and public order, what this is, in fact, is the issue of whether or not you recognize a citizen's constitutional rights. On a still deeper level, this is actually an issue of fears you all carry within: fear of a public trial, fear of a citizen's freedom to observe a trial, fear of my name appearing online, and fear of the free society nearly upon us.

By trying to suppress the New Citizens Movement, you are obstructing China on its path to becoming a constitutional democracy through peaceful change. And while you have not mentioned the New Citizens Movement throughout this trial, many of the documents presented here relate to it, and in my view there is no need to avoid the issue; to be able to speak openly of this is pertinent to the betterment of Chinese society. What the New Citizens Movement advocates is for each and every Chinese national to act and behave as a citizen, to accept our roles as citizens and masters of our country—and not to act as feudal subjects, remain complacent, accept mob rule or a position as an underclass. To take seriously the rights which come with citizenship, those written into the *Universal Declaration of Human Rights* and China's Constitution: to treat these sacred rights—to vote, to freedom of speech and religion—as more than an everlasting IOU. And

also to take seriously the responsibilities that come with citizenship, starting with the knowledge that China belongs to each and everyone one of us, and to accept that it is up to us to defend and define the boundaries of conscience and justice.

What the New Citizens Movement calls for is civic spirit that consists of freedom, justice, and love: individual freedom, freedom without constraint that brings true happiness, will always be the goal of both state and society; justice, that which defines the limit of individual freedom, is also what ensures fairness and preserves moral conscience; and love, be it in the form of kindness, tolerance, compassion or dedication, is our most precious emotion and the source of our happiness.

Freedom, justice, and love, these are our core values and what guides us in action. The New Citizens Movement advocates a citizenship that begins with the individual and the personal, through small acts making concrete changes to public policy and the encompassing system; through remaining reasonable and constructive, pushing the country along the path to democratic rule of law; by uniting the Chinese people through their common civic identity, pursuing democratic rule of law and justice; forming a community of citizens committed to freedom and democracy; growing into a civil society strengthened by healthy rationalism.

Common to all those who identify themselves as citizens are the shared notions of constitutional democracy, of freedom, of equality and justice, of love, and faith. Because taken as a whole, civic groups are not the same as an organization as defined in the authoritarian sense, having neither leader nor hierarchy, orders or obedience, discipline or punishment, and in contrast are based fully on the voluntarily coming together of free citizens.

It is through acts of pushing for system reforms that geographically dispersed groups of citizens are able to grow spontaneously into their own, and by acting to hold authorities accountable and

---

* This is Xu Zhiyong's closing statement on January 22, 2014, at the end of his trial. According to his lawyer he had only been able to read "about 10 minutes of it before the presiding judge stopped him, saying it was irrelevant to the case." This translation of Xu's statement is available on *China File* (http://www.chinafile.com/freedom-justice-and-love).

pushing for political reforms, establishment of democratic rule of law, and advances in society, that civil groups are able to grow in a healthy way. Pushing for equal access to education, the right for children of migrant workers to sit for university entrance exams where they live, and calling on officials to disclose their assets, these are civic acts carried out in precisely this sense.

The push for equal access to education rights particularly for children of migrant workers was a three-year-long action we initiated in late 2009. Prior to that, we had received a series of requests for help from parents; it was then we realized the severity of this social issue. More than 200 million people across China had relocated to urban areas to live and work but found themselves unable to enjoy equality where they lived despite being taxpayers. Far more serious was learning that their children were unable to study or take university entrance examinations in their new places of residence, leaving no choice but to send them thousands of miles away back to their permanent registered addresses in order to receive an education, resulting in millions of Chinese children being left behind. While many feel concern for the fate of left-behind children, rarely do they realize the best help they can offer is to tear down the wall of household registration-based segregation, allowing the children to return to their parents.

Our action consisted of three phases. The first took place over the first half of 2010, with petitions to education authorities in Haidian district and across Beijing, through deliberations to allow non-local students to continue their studies in Beijing as they entered high school. The second phase, which lasted from July 2010 to August 2012, consisted of petitions to the Ministry of Education to change policies to allow non-local children of migrant workers to take university entrance examinations locally. The third phase took place between September 2012 until the end of this year. It focused on pressing the Beijing Education Commission to implement new policies issued by the Ministry of Education. To that end, we gathered signatures and expanded our volunteer team of parents, and on the last Thursday of each month, we approached the Education authorities to petition. We submitted our recommendations and we consulted experts to research actionable changes to policies regarding educational paths for non-local children of migrant workers. We wrote thousands of letters to National People's Congress delegates, making calls and arranging meetings, urging them to submit proposals during the two annual parliamentary sessions. During the "two meetings" [referring to the annual sessions of the NPC and CPPCC] in 2011, the Minister of Education said in one interview that policy changes for non-local children were then being drafted. During the two meetings in 2012, the Education minister promised publicly at a press conference that changes to university entrance examinations for non-local migrant children would be released sometime in the first half of the year, and provincial education authorities would be required to draft implementation plans over the second half of 2012. By June 28, 2012, a scheduled day for parent volunteers to continue petition work, the Ministry of Education had yet to issue any formal response. Parents decided then and there that they would return the following Thursday if by the end of the month the Ministry of Education failed to issue the new policy as it had promised. This led to the July 5th petitioning. In August, the Ministry of Education finally released a new policy regarding university entrance examination eligibility for children of non-local migrant workers, along with an order for local education authorities to draft implementation strategies. By the end of 2012, 29 provinces and cities across China released plans to implement the policy except for Beijing. One parent joked bitterly that after a three-year struggle they had managed to liberate all of China, just not themselves.

I could see the tears behind the joke, because it meant that their own children would have to leave and take up studies in a strange place, in a possibly life-changing move. As idealists, we were able to win a policy allowing children of migrant workers to continue their studies and remain with their parents, and yet the main impetus behind this change, the parents who lived and worked in Beijing without Beijing *hukou*, had not been able to secure for their own children the chance of an equal education. I felt I let all of them down, and many of them grew disheartened. I was compelled to go out and, standing at subway station entrances, hand out fliers calling for one last petitioning effort on February 28, 2013.

In the two petitioning events, one on July 5, 2012 and the other on February 28, 2013, we the citizens went to the education authority, or a government office, not a public place in a legal sense, to make an appeal. China's *Criminal Law* is very clear on the definition of public spaces, and government buildings, locations of organizations and public roads are not among them. Therefore our activities do not constitute disruption of order in a public place.

Over the past three years, our activities have remained consistently moderate and reasonable. Certain parents did get emotional or agitated during the July 5th petition, and the reason was that the Ministry of Education failed to live up to its own publicly-issued promise, nor did it provide any explanation. Yet despite this, their so-called agitation was merely the shouting of a few slogans, demanding a dialog with the Minister of Education, rather understandable considering they had gathered 100,000 signatures, behind which stand the interests of 200 million new urban immigrants.

And the response they got? Take a look at the photos of the scene. One parent who goes by the online alias "Dancing" was taken away by police pulling her hair. Was there no other way to escort her away? Was she exhibiting extreme behavior? Had she ever done anything provocative in the past three years? No, never! It hurts whenever I think of the event. We had pursued a very simple goal for three years, our approaches had been so reasonable, but we were assaulted with such viciousness. There were police officers who, with a prepared list of names in hand, sought them out and beat them.

In spite of what happened, I told them, over and over again, that they must stay calm and that we can't stoop to their level. This society needs a renewed sense of hope, and we can't behave like them. The right to an equal education, the right to take a university examination where you live, these are concepts that the New Citizens Movement encompasses. [We must start] with changes to specific public policies and concrete system changes, in this case, for the freedom of movement, for justice, for love.

When China established the household registration system, or *hukou*, in 1958, it created two separate worlds: one rural, one urban. In 1961,

China established the system of custody and repatriation. From then on, anyone born in a rural area who wanted to find work and try a new life in the city could be arrested and forcibly returned home at any time. In Beijing in 2002 alone, 220,000 were detained and repatriated. In 2003, the custody and repatriation system was abolished, but it remained a long road for new urban arrivals to integrate with the city. In 2006, we discovered through our research in Beijing that there still existed as many as 19 discriminatory policies against non-local permanent residents, the most inhumane of them being the very policy that prevented children from living with their parents and receiving an education.

We worked tirelessly for three years to win children the right to take the university entrance examination locally while living with their migrated parents. During the three years, I witnessed equal education campaign volunteers brave bitter winters and scorching summers at subway entrances, on roadsides and in shopping malls to collect more than 100,000 signatures with contact information included. I witnessed several hundred parents standing in the courtyard outside the Letters and Petition Office of the Ministry of Education and reciting their *Declaration of Equal Access to Education*. I witnessed several hundred parents and children planting trees in Qinglong Lake Park on the Clear and Bright Day (清明节) in 2012. Everyone wore caps bearing the same slogan: "Live in Beijing, love Beijing."

I also witnessed the taping of a program on Phoenix TV where a little girl sobbed because she could not bear to leave her mother and father in Beijing where she grew up to go back to a strange place where her *hukou* is to go to school. In a *hutong* in Di'anmen, I witnessed Zhang Xudong, a top eighth grader at Guozijian Secondary School, who was forced to go to a completely strange county high school in Zhangjiakou after graduating from middle school to continue his education just because he did not have Beijing *hukou*. A year later, ill-adjusted in language, environment and textbooks, he dropped out. He became withdrawn, not the happy boy he once was anymore. His parents have worked for nearly thirty years in Beijing but they are forever outsiders and second-class citizens in this city.

When I think of the hundreds of millions of children whose fates were permanently decided by the *hukou* segregation, of generation after generation of Chinese people who have been hurt by this evil system, of the countless Chinese who died in the custody and repatriation system, today I stand here as a defendant, filled with no grudges but pride for having worked to eliminate the segregation system with Chinese characteristics and for having fought for millions of children to be able to live with their parents and go to school.

The calls on officials to publicly declare their assets, these are our efforts to push the country to establish an anti-corruption mechanism. More than 137 countries and territories around the world currently have systems in place for officials to declare assets, so why can't China? What exactly is it these "public servants" fear so much? Excessive greed and undeserved wealth do not just bring luxuries, but also a deep-seated fear and insecurity, as well as public anger and enmity.

When we go online to collect signatures and distribute promotional materials, or unfurl banners on the street, all to call on officials to publicly declare their assets, we are at the same time exercising our civic rights to free speech provided for in the Constitution. Our actions did not violate the rights of any other person, nor did they bring harm to society. While the speech delivered in Xidan has a few strong words, as a speech about public policy, they did not exceed the limits of free speech provided for by the Constitution and the law.

It is a normal occurrence in a modern, civilized society for citizens to express their political views by displaying banners, giving speeches and taking other actions in public venues. Law enforcement agencies can be present to monitor and take precautionary measures, but they should not abuse their power or interfere. In fact, when banners were displayed at the west gate of Tsinghua University, Zhongguancun Square and other places where no police officers were present, they caused no disorder, nor did they hinder any other people's rights. They left after displaying banners. This conforms to our idea of a "flash action." It had taken consideration of China's reality and Chinese society's tolerance capacity. We took quick actions in small groups, instead of larger gatherings, to make these public expressions.

Of course we hope that the sacred rights enshrined in the Constitution will be realized, but reform requires stability and social progress requires gradual advancement. As responsible citizens, we must adopt a gradualist approach when exercising our constitutionally guaranteed rights and when advancing the process towards democracy and rule of law. Over the last ten years, we consistently pushed for progress through peaceful means, and we tried to effect change in specific policies through involvement in public incidents. We did so for the sake of freedom, justice, love, and for the sake of our long-held dreams.

In 2003 the custody and repatriation system was abolished, but not without Sun Zhigang paying the price of his life for it. We, as legal professionals, made every effort in the process and we recommended, in our role as citizens, constitutional review on the custody and repatriation system.

For the past decade we have continued to strive to win equal rights for new migrants in cities, resulting in the introduction in 2012 of a new policy allowing migrant children to take university entrance exams where they have relocated with their parents.

We provided legal assistance to victims of grave injustices, such as the victims of melamine-tainted milk powder and the high-speed rail accident. In 2008 when the Sanlu milk powder scandal broke, we brought together a team of lawyers and calculated the number of victims based on media reports. We proposed fair compensation schemes in accordance with the law, while working with the victims to successfully push the issuance of a government-led settlement plan. However, the government compensation package was far from adequate for the damages suffered by many children. For instance, the cost of an operation for one child was nearly 100,000 yuan, and the compensation he received was only 30,000 yuan. So we continued to seek redress for the more than 400 children we had represented, bringing lawsuits all the way to the Supreme People's Court, to more than a hundred courts across China, and to a court in Hong Kong. In July, 2009, when I was thrown in jail for the so-called Gong Meng tax evasion and when people from all walks of life made donations to help pay the fine imposed on Gong Meng, our volunteers in the south were sending a settlement of one million yuan to the home of a baby victim. I am forever proud of that moment, and we will not give up our promise to the disempowered even when we ourselves are in trouble.

We have spent many winters out on the street delivering coats, blankets and steamed buns to the poor and homeless petitioners so that they would not die of hunger or cold silently in this bustling city.

Petitioning is rights defense with Chinese characteristics. In a society like ours comprised of relationships that belie privilege, corruption, and injustice, to step forward in defense of one's rights and dignity is something only the most stubborn of us dare do. But this small minority, when gathered in the nation's capital, number in the tens of thousands. They get driven out of Beijing, or illegally detained, or beaten. In Beijing alone, there are more than forty "black jails"—and we've verified the numbers—that have been used to illegally detain people. When we visited these black jails and reported the crime taking place, showing the specific laws it violated, we were humiliated and beaten by those guarding them. Time and time again, I feel proud for sharing a little bit of their suffering.

Having chosen to stand alongside the powerless, we have witnessed far too much injustice, suffering, and misfortune over the past decade. However, we still embrace the light in our hearts and push for the country's progress in rational and constructive ways.

After proposing review on the unconstitutionality of the custody and repatriation system, we researched and drafted new measures to better manage beggars and the homeless. We pushed the educational equality campaign. We drafted a proposal for migrant workers' children to take college entrance exams locally and our draft was adopted by most provinces and cities. For our call for disclosure of officials' assets, we even drafted a "Sunlight Bill" in March 2013. Raising an issue is not enough; solutions must be found. To oppose is to construct, for we are citizens of a new era, we are citizens responsible to our country, and we love China.

Unfortunately, you [the Court] regard the existence and growth of these citizens as heresy and something to fear. You say we harbored

political purposes. Well we do, and our political purpose is very clear—it is a China with democracy, rule of law, freedom, justice, and love. What we want is not to fight to gain power, or barbaric politics by any means; but good politics, a good cause for public welfare, a cause for all citizens to govern the country together. Our mission is not to gain power but to restrict power. We aim to establish a modern and civilized system of democracy and rule of law and lay a foundation for a noble tradition of politics so that later generations can enjoy fairness, justice, freedom, and happiness.

Good politics is a result of true democracy and rule of law. On every level, the government and the legislature must be elected by the people. The power to govern should not come from the barrel of a gun but through votes. Under true democracy and rule of law, politics should be carried out within the the rule of law. Political parties should compete fairly and only those that win in free and fair elections are qualified to govern. Under true democracy and rule of law, state powers are scientifically separated and mutually subject to checks and balances; the judiciary is independent and judges abide by the law and conscience. Under true democracy and rule of law, the military and the police are state organs and should not become the private property of any political party or vested interest group. Under true democracy and rule of law, the media is a social organ and should not be monopolized to be the mouthpiece of any political party or vested interested group. Under true democracy and rule of law, the constitution stipulates and actualizes sacred civil rights, including the right to vote, freedom of speech, and freedom of belief. The promise of people's power should not be a lie.

These modern democratic values and measurements are rooted in common humanity. They should not be Eastern or Western, socialist or capitalist, but universal to all human societies.

Democracy is the knowledge to solve human problems. Our ancestors did not discover this knowledge. We should thus be humble and learn from others. Over the past thirty years, China introduced the system of market economy with free competition which brought economic prosperity. Similarly, China needs to introduce a democratic and constitutional system to solve the injustices of our current society.

Social injustice is intensifying in China. The greatest social injustice concerns political rights, which lie at the heart of other forms of injustice. The root of many serious social problems can be traced to the monopoly of all political powers and economic lifelines by a privileged interest group, and China's fundamental problem is the problem of democratic constitutionalism.

Anti-corruption campaigns are waged year after year, but corruption has become more and more rampant over the course of the last sixty some years. Without democratic elections, press freedom, and judicial independence, a clean government is not possible under a regime of absolute power. People's livelihood is emphasized year after year, yet hundreds of million of people still live below the internationally defined poverty line. In remote and mountainous areas, corrupt officials even embezzle the subsistence allowances of only 100 yuan a month for the extremely poor. The wealth gap between the elites and the general public is ever-widening.

Hostility towards government officials and the wealthy is, in essence, hostility towards power monopoly that perches high above. Tens of thousands of families toil and worry about their children's basic education, looking for connections to pay bribes just for kindergarten enrollment. How has the society become so rotten?

Humans are political animals, in need of more than a full stomach and warm clothes. Humans also need freedom, justice, and participation in governance of their own country. You say the National People's Congress is China's highest body of power, then again you say this highest body of power answers to the Party.

If the country's basic political system is such an open lie, how is it possible to build a society that values trust? You say the judiciary is just and that courts hold open trials, then you arrange for unrelated people to come occupy seats reserved for observers in the courtroom. If even the courts resort to such unscrupulousness, where can people expect to find justice? It should surprise no one that people wear frozen masks in their dealings with one another, and that whether to help a fallen elderly person can become a lasting

debate. There is toxic baby formula, kilns using child slaves, and every sort of social ill imaginable, yet the perpetrators haven't had the slightest bit of guilt or shame, and they think this is just how society is.

China's biggest problem is falsehood, and the biggest falsehood is the country's political system and its political ideology. Are you able to even explain clearly what socialism entails? Is or is not the National People's Congress the highest authority?

Political lies know no bounds in this country, and 1.3 billion people suffer deeply from it as a result. Suspicion, disappointment, confusion, anger, helplessness, and resentment are norms of life. Truly, politics affects each and every one of us intimately. We cannot escape politics, we can only work to change it. Power must be caged by the system, and the authoritarian top-down politics must change. I sincerely hope that those in power will find a way to integrate with the trends of human civilization, and take an active role in pushing for political reforms and adopt the civilized politics of a constitutional democracy, therein realizing the hundred-year-old Chinese dream of empowering the people through peaceful reforms.

More than a century ago, China missed an opportunity to turn into a constitutional democracy through peaceful transition, sending the Chinese nation into a protracted struggle marked by revolution, turmoil, and suffering. The Republic of China, with its hopes for a market economy and democratic system, didn't last long before totalitarian politics were revived and reached extremes during the Cultural Revolution. Following the Cultural Revolution, China's economic reforms led to a model of incremental reforms in which social controls were relaxed but the old system and its interests remained untouched, although new spaces created by the market slowly eroded the old system as reforms were laid out.

Political reforms in China could rely on a similar model, one in which the old system and its interests stay in place as social controls are relaxed and democratic spaces outside the system are permitted to grow in a healthy direction. A model such as this would actually prove a valuable path for China to follow.

We have built a community of citizens and rationally, remaining responsible to the country, taken the first small step. You need not fear the New Citizens' Movement; we are a new era of citizens, completely free of the earmarks of authoritarian ideology such as courting enemies, scheming for power, or harboring thoughts to overthrow or strike down. Our faith is in freedom, justice, and love, of pushing to advance society through peaceful reforms and healthy growth in the light of day—not acts of conspiracy, violence or other barbaric models.

The mission of civil groups is not to exist as an opposition party, although the creation of a constitutional democracy is inevitable for a future China built on civilized politics. Our mission is shared by all progressives in China, to work together to see China through the transition to civilized politics.

The New Citizens' Movement is a movement of political transformation leading to democratic rule of law, as well as a cultural movement for the renewal of political and cultural traditions. A constitutional democracy needs a fertile bed of civilized politics in order to function, and it's our collective anticipation and faith which serves as such a soil bed. At the same time, our country's citizens seek faith in healthy politics, unscrupulous and barbaric politics must also be forever cast out from the deep recesses of each and every soul. This calls for a group of upstanding citizens to bravely take on such a responsibility, sacrificing ego to become model citizens. Each and every Chinese person shares this responsibility.

This is my responsibility. Having been born on this land, I need no reason to love this country; it is because I love China that I want her to be better. I choose to be a peaceful reformer, carrying on with the century-old but unfinished mission of our forebears, advocating an unwavering commitment to non-violence just as I advocate freedom, justice, and love, and advocate peaceful reform as the path toward constitutional democracy. Although I possess the means to live a superior life within this system, I feel ashamed of privilege in any form. I choose to stand with the weak and those deprived of their rights, sharing with them the bitter cold of a Beijing winter the way it feels from the street or an underground tunnel,

shouldering together the barbaric violence of the black jail.

God created both the poor and the wealthy, but keeps them apart not so we can reject or despise one another, but in order for mutual love to exist, and it was my honor to have the chance to walk alongside petitioners on their long road to justice.

My decision comes at a time when my child has just been born, when my family needs me most, and when I yearn to be there by their side. After years now of witnessing the bitter struggles of the innocent and downtrodden, I remain unable to control my own sorrow—or, try as I might, to remain silent. I now finally accept judgment and purgatory as my fate, because for freedom, justice, and love, the happiness of people everywhere, for the glory of the Lord, all this pain, I am willing.

This is our responsibility as a citizen group. In a servile society prone widely to submission, there will always need to be someone to be the first to stand up, to face the risks and pay the price for social progress. We are those Chinese people ready now to stand, with utmost concern for the future and destiny of the motherland, for democratic rule of law, justice, and for the dignity and well-being of the weak and marginalized.

We are kind and pure of heart, loathe to conspire and deceive, and we yearn for freedom and a simpler, happier life. We strive to serve society, and help those most in need, pushing for better society. Bravely, we assume this responsibility, ready to forgo our privilege and secular interests—even at the cost of our freedom—to stay true to our ideals. Ready to put aside our egos with no thought of personal gain or loss, we respect the rights and boundaries of others, facing all beings with humility.

Such is the responsibility now upon you judges and prosecutors. Your responsibility is fidelity to the law and your conscience, to uphold the baseline of social justice, to neither be reduced to a lowly cog in this bureaucratic system nor debase the sanctity of rule of law. Do not say you're constrained by the bigger picture, because the bigger picture in China is not an order from above, but the letter of the law. Do not say you merely follow the logic of laws as you sentence me, and do not forget those sacred rights afforded all by law.

Do not say this is just your job, or that you're innocent, because each and every one of us is ultimately responsible for our own actions and we must at all times remain faithful to our own conscience. As a society with a history of rule by man that stretches back centuries, the law in China serves a very distinct purpose. Regardless of acting as a defendant, a juror, or a legal scholar, I have always remained true to the idea of justice and I behoove you to do the same.

It has always been my hope China's legal community will undergo an awakening of conscience, that you judges can gain the same amount of respect afforded your counterparts overseas, and it is my hope an awakening of conscience will begin with you. Those of you watching this trial from behind the scenes, or those awaiting orders, this is also your responsibility. Don't take pains to preserve the old system simply because you have vested interests in it; no one is safe under an unjust system. When you see politics as endless shadows and reflections of daggers and swords, as blood falling like rain with its smell in the wind, you have too much fear in your hearts.

So I have to tell you the times have changed, that a new era of politics is afoot in which the greatest strength in society is not violence but love. Fear not democracy or loss of privilege, and fear not open competition nor the free society now taking shape. You may find my ideas too far-out, too unrealistic, but I believe in the power of faith, and in the power of the truth, compassion, and beauty that exists in the depths of the human soul, just as I believe human civilization is advancing mightily like a tide.

This is the shared responsibility of us 1.3 billion Chinese. Dynasties, likes political parties, all pass with time, but China will always be China just as we are all Chinese. It's our responsibility to build a bright future for the country. Our China is destined to become the greatest country in the world, possessing the most advanced technology, the most prosperous economy, the greatest ability to defend equality and justice throughout the world, and the most magnificent culture to spearhead human civilization. But that is a China that cannot exist under authoritarian rule.

Ours is a China that will only exist once constitutional democracy is realized, a China that is democratic, free, and governed through rule of law. Allow us to think together what we can do for for our country, because only then can we create a bright future. This country lacks freedom, but freedom requires each of us to fight for it; this society lacks justice, which requires each of us to defend it; this society lacks love, and it is up to each and every one of us to light that fire with our truth. Allow us to take our citizenship seriously, to take our civil rights seriously, to take our responsibilities as citizens seriously, and to take our dreams of a civil society seriously; let us together defend the baseline of justice and our conscience, and refuse without exception all orders to do evil from above, and refuse to shove the person in front of you just because you were shoved from behind.

The baseline lies beneath your feet just as it lies beneath all our feet. Together, let's use love to rewaken our dormant conscience, break down those barriers between our hearts, and with our love establish a tradition for the Chinese people of noble and civilized politics.

Here in absurd post-totalitarian China I stand trial, charged with three crimes: promoting equal education rights for children of migrant workers, calling on officials to publicly disclose their assets, and advocating that all people behave as citizens with pride and conscience. If the country's rulers have any intention to take citizens' constitutional rights seriously, then of course we are innocent. We had no intention to disrupt public order; our intention was to promote democracy and rule of law in China. We did nothing to disrupt public order, we were merely exercising our freedom of expression as provided for by the constitution. Public order was not disrupted as a result of our actions, which infringed on the legitimate rights of no one. I understand clearly that some people have to make sacrifices, and I for one am willing to pay any and all price for my belief in freedom, justice, love, and for a better future of China. If you insist on persecuting the conscience of a people, I openly accept that destiny and the glory that accompanies it. But do not for a second think you can terminate the New Citizens' Movement by throwing me in jail. Ours is an era in which modern civilization prevails, and in which growing numbers of Chinese inevitably take their citizenship and civic responsibilities seriously.

The day will come when the 1.3 billion Chinese will stand up from their submissive state and grow to be proud and responsible citizens. China will become a country that enjoys a civilized political system and a happy society in which freedom, justice, and love prevail. The disempowered will be redeemed, as will you, you who sit high above with fear and shadows in your hearts.

China today still upholds the banner of reform, something I sincerely wish will be carried out smoothly allowing the beautiful dream of China to come true. But reform must have a clearly defined direction, and it is irresponsible to continue "feeling the stones to cross the river," just as it's irresponsible to treat the symptoms but not the roots of social ills, and irresponsible to sidestep the fundamental political system in designing the country.

One hundred years on, where China wants to go is still the most crucial question the Chinese nation faces. As interest groups consolidate, the economy slows down, and accumulated social injustice leads to concentrated outbursts, China has once again arrived at an historical crossroad. Reforms will succeed if the goal remains to realize democracy and constitutionalism as in line with the course of history, and without question will fail if the aim is to maintain one-party rule in contravention of history. Absent a clear direction toward democracy and constitutionalism, even if reforms deepen as promised the most likely result will be to repeat the mistakes made during the late Qing Dynasty, picking and choosing Western practices but not fixing the system. To a large extent, what we see happening around us today is re-enactment of the tragedy of the late Qing reforms, and for that reason I am deeply concerned about the future of the Chinese nation. When hopes of reform are dashed, people will rise up and seek revolution. The privileged and powerful have long transferred their children and wealth overseas; they couldn't care less of the misfortune and suffering of the disempowered, nor do they care about China's future. But we do. Someone has to care. Peaceful transition to democracy and constitutionalism is the only path

the Chinese nation has to a beautiful future. We lost this opportunity a hundred years ago, and we can't afford to miss it again today. We, the Chinese people, must decide the future direction for China.

My fellow compatriots, at any time and regardless of what happens in China, I urge everyone to maintain their faith in freedom, justice, and love. Uphold freedom of religion, stay rooted in reality, and pursue those universal rights and freedoms which were pursued and fought for and paid for in blood this past century by those also with lofty ideals. Remain steadfast in your faith in justice, always stay true to your heart, never compromise your principles in the pursuit of your goals. Pursue a rounded and just democratic society governed through rule of law, where all fulfill their duties and are provided for, where the strong are constrained and the weak are protected, a society built on the cornerstone of moral conscience. Adhere to faith in love, because this nation has too many dark, bitter, and poisoned souls in need of redemption, because there exists too much vigilance, fear, and hostility between people. These evil spirits, buried in the depths of the soul, must be cast out. It is not through hatred that we rid ourselves of them, but through salvation. We are the Redeemer.

Freedom, justice, and love, these are the spirit of our New Citizens Movement, and must become a core value for the Chinese people—for which it is up to our generation to fight, sacrifice and assume responsibility. Our faith in the idea of building a better China, one of democracy, rule of law, freedom, justice, and love, is unwavering. As long as we continue to believe in love and the power of hope for a better future, in the desire for goodness deep inside every human soul, we will be able to make that in which we have faith a reality.

Citizens, let us begin now. It does not matter where you are, what jobs you have, whether you are poor or rich; let us say in our hearts, in our everyday lives, on the Internet, on every inch of Chinese land, say with conviction and pride that what already belongs to us: I am a citizen, we are citizens.

Citizen Xu Zhiyong
January 22, 2014

III. Ideology

Achieving New Victory for Socialism with Chinese Characteristics
Report to the 18th National Congress of the Communist Party of China [Excerpts]*

Hu Jintao

Looking back at China's eventful modern history and looking to the promising future of the Chinese nation, we have drawn this definite conclusion: We must unswervingly follow the path of socialism with Chinese characteristics in order to complete the building of a moderately prosperous society in all respects, accelerate socialist modernization, and achieve the great renewal of the Chinese nation.

The issue of what path we take is of vital importance for the survival of the Party, the future of China, the destiny of the Chinese nation, and the well-being of the people. Exploring a path to national renewal in China that was economically and culturally backward is an extremely arduous task. Over the past ninety-plus years, relying firmly on the people and adapting the basic tenets of Marxism to China's conditions and the underlying trend of the times, our Party has pursued its own course independently. It has, enduring untold hardships and sufferings and paying various costs, achieved great success in revolution, development and reform, and created and developed socialism with Chinese characteristics, thus fundamentally changing the future and destiny of the Chinese people and nation.

The Party's first generation of central collective leadership with Comrade Mao Zedong at the core led the whole Party and the people of all ethnic groups in China in completing the new-democratic revolution, carrying out socialist transformation and establishing the basic system of socialism, thereby accomplishing the most profound and the greatest social transformation in China's history. This created the fundamental political prerequisite and systemic foundation for development and progress in contemporary China. In the course of socialist development, the Party developed distinctively creative theories and made tremendous successes despite serious setbacks it went through, thus providing invaluable experience as well as the theoretical and material basis for launching the great initiative of building socialism with Chinese characteristics in the new historical period.

The Party's second generation of central collective leadership with Comrade Deng Xiaoping at the core led the whole Party and the people of all ethnic groups in China in conducting a thorough review of China's experiences in building socialism, both positive and negative. On this basis and drawing on the experience of world socialism, they made the historic decision to shift the focus of the Party and country's work to economic development and to pursue the policy of reform and opening up. They gained a keen appreciation of the underlying goal of socialism and established the Party's basic line for the primary stage of socialism. They called for taking our own road and building socialism with Chinese characteristics and provided scientific answers to basic questions in this regard. On this basis, the great initiative of building socialism with Chinese characteristics was successfully launched.

The Party's third generation of central collective leadership with Comrade Jiang Zemin at the core led the whole Party and the people of all ethnic groups in China in adhering to the Party's basic theory and line. Standing the severe tests posed by complex domestic and international developments and major setbacks in world socialism, they upheld socialism with Chinese characteristics. Based on China's new realities, they reaffirmed the Party's basic program and its basic experience, set the goal of reform and developed a basic framework for achieving this goal, namely, developing a socialist market economy. They reaffirmed the basic economic system and the system

---

* This speech was published by the Communist Party of China on November 8, 2012 (http://www.china.org.cn/china/18th_cpc_congress/2012-11/16/content_27137540.htm).

of income distribution in the primary stage of socialism, ushered in a new phase in carrying out all-around reform and opening up, and pressed ahead with the great new undertaking of Party building, thus advancing socialism with Chinese characteristics into the 21st century.

In the new stage in the new century, the Party Central Committee has seized this important period of strategic opportunities and promoted innovation in practice, theory, and institutional building in the course of building a moderately prosperous society in all respects. We have emphasized the need to put people first and to pursue comprehensive, balanced, and sustainable development; we have called for building a harmonious socialist society and speeding up ecological progress, and we have adopted overall implementing steps for advancing the cause of socialism with Chinese characteristics. We have strived to ensure and improve the people's well-being, promoted social fairness and justice, worked to build a harmonious world, and strengthened the Party's governance capacity and advanced nature. We have thus upheld and developed socialism with Chinese characteristics from a new historical starting point.

Throughout the past thirty-plus years of continuous exploration for reform and opening up, we have held high the great banner of socialism with Chinese characteristics and rejected both the old and rigid closed-door policy and any attempt to abandon socialism and take an erroneous path. The path of socialism with Chinese characteristics, the system of theories of socialism with Chinese characteristics and the socialist system with Chinese characteristics are the fundamental accomplishments made by the Party and people in the course of arduous struggle over the past 90-plus years. We must cherish these accomplishments, uphold them all the time and continue to enrich them.

Taking the path of socialism with Chinese characteristics means we must, under the leadership of the Communist Party of China and basing ourselves on China's realities, take economic development as the central task and adhere to the Four Cardinal Principles and the policy of reform and opening up. It means we must release and develop the productive forces, develop the socialist market economy, socialist democracy, an advanced socialist culture and a harmonious socialist society, and promote socialist ecological progress. It also means

we must promote well-rounded development of the person, achieve prosperity for all over time, and make China a modern socialist country that is prosperous, strong, democratic, culturally advanced, and harmonious. The system of theories of socialism with Chinese characteristics is a system of scientific theories that includes Deng Xiaoping Theory, the important thought of Three Represents and the Scientific Outlook on Development, and this system represents the Party's adherence to and development of Marxism-Leninism and Mao Zedong Thought. The socialist system with Chinese characteristics includes the following: the fundamental political system—the system of people's congresses; the basic political systems—the system of multiparty cooperation and political consultation under the leadership of the Communist Party of China, the system of regional ethnic autonomy, and the system of community-level self-governance; the socialist system of laws with Chinese characteristics; the basic economic system in which public ownership is the mainstay and economic entities of diverse ownership develop together; and the specific economic, political, cultural, and social institutions based on these systems. The path of socialism with Chinese characteristics is the way to reach the goal, the system of theories of socialism with Chinese characteristics offers a guide to action, and the socialist system with Chinese characteristics provides the fundamental guarantee. The three function as an integral whole in the great practice of building socialism with Chinese characteristics, and this is the salient feature of the long-term endeavors of the Communist Party of China leading the people in building socialism.

In building socialism with Chinese characteristics, we base ourselves on the basic reality that China is in the primary stage of socialism. Our overall approach is to promote economic, political, cultural, social, and ecological progress, and our general task is to achieve socialist modernization and the great renewal of the Chinese nation. Socialism with Chinese characteristics both upholds the basic principles of scientific socialism and has distinctive Chinese features that reflect contemporary conditions. It offers from new perspectives a deeper understanding of the laws of governance by the Communist Party, laws of building socialism, and laws of the development of human society. By integrating theory with practice, it has systematically addressed the fundamental questions of what kind of socialism we should build and how we should build it in China, a big country in the East with a huge population and a weak economy to start with. Socialism with Chinese characteristics has brought about fast development and rising living standards in China. This fully shows that socialism with Chinese characteristics is what we must pursue if we are to achieve development and make progress in contemporary China and that only socialism with Chinese characteristics can enable China to develop itself.

Developing socialism with Chinese characteristics is a long-term arduous task of historic importance, and we must be prepared to carry out a great struggle with many new historical features. We must unswervingly adhere to socialism with Chinese characteristics, develop it as required by the times, constantly enrich it in both practice and theory and enhance its distinctive national features in keeping up with the times.

To achieve new victory for socialism with Chinese characteristics under new historical conditions, we must have a firm grasp of the following basic requirements and make them shared convictions of the whole Party and the people of all ethnic groups in China:

– We must maintain the people's principal position in the country. Socialism with Chinese characteristics is a cause for the people in their hundreds of millions. We should ensure that the people are the masters of the country and we should uphold the rule of law as a fundamental principle by which the Party leads the people in running the country. We should mobilize and organize as many people as possible to manage state and social affairs as well as the economy and cultural programs in accordance with the law and to devote themselves to socialist modernization, and we should better protect the people's rights and interests and ensure that the people determine their own destiny.
– We must continue to release and develop the productive forces. This is the fundamental task of socialism with Chinese characteristics. We should take economic development as the central task and pursuing development in a scientific way as the underlying guideline, advance in an all-around way economic, political, cultural, social, and ecological progress, and achieve in a scientific way development that puts people first and is comprehensive, balanced and sustainable.
– We must persevere in reform and opening up. Reform and opening up are crucial to adhering to and developing socialism with Chinese characteristics. We should always apply the spirit of reform and innovation to all aspects of governance, keep improving the socialist market economy, adhere to the basic state policy of opening to the outside world, continue to make innovations in theory, in institutions, in science and technology, in culture and in other fields, and continuously promote the self-improvement and self-development of China's socialist system.
– We must safeguard social fairness and justice. Fairness and justice are inherent requirements of socialism with Chinese characteristics. We must, relying on the concerted efforts of all the Chinese people and based on economic and social development, step up efforts to develop institutions that are vital to ensuring social fairness and justice; establish in due course a system for guaranteeing fairness in society featuring, among other things, equal rights, equal opportunities, and fair rules for all; and foster a fair social environment and ensure people's equal right to participation in governance and to development.
– We must strive for common prosperity. This is the fundamental principle of socialism with Chinese characteristics. We should adhere to the basic socialist economic system and the socialist income distribution system. We should adjust the pattern of national income distribution, tighten its regulation by secondary distribution, and work hard to narrow income gaps so that all the people can share in more fruits of development in a fair way and move steadily toward common prosperity.
– We must promote social harmony. Social harmony is an inherent attribute of socialism with Chinese characteristics. We should give higher priority to ensuring and improving the people's well-being, strengthen and conduct social management in an innovative way, strike a balance between reform, development, and stability, rally all the forces that can be rallied, maximize factors conducive to harmony, and increase the creative vitality of society. We should ensure that the people live and work in contentment, society is stable and orderly, and the country enjoys enduring peace and stability.

— We must pursue peaceful development. Peaceful development is the sure choice of socialism with Chinese characteristics. We should pursue development through opening up and cooperation to benefit all. We should develop ourselves by securing a peaceful international environment and uphold and promote world peace through our own development. We should expand common interests with all others and work to build a harmonious world of enduring peace and common prosperity.

— We must uphold the leadership of the Party. The Communist Party of China is the leadership core of the cause of socialism with Chinese characteristics. We should uphold the principle that the Party was founded for the public good and that it exercises state power for the people, enhance and improve the Party's leadership, and ensure that the Party plays its role as the leadership core in exercising overall leadership and coordinating the efforts of all. We should maintain the Party's advanced nature and purity, strengthen its creativity, cohesiveness, and capability and enhance its capacity to govern in a scientific and democratic way and in accordance with the law.

We must be soberly aware that China is still in the primary stage of socialism and will long remain so. This basic condition of China has not changed; nor has the principal problem in our society, that is,

how we can meet the ever-growing material and cultural needs of the people with backward social production; nor has China's international position as the largest developing country in the world. We must bear in mind under any circumstances the paramount reality that China remains in the primary stage of socialism and will long remain so and base ourselves on this reality in pursuing all of our endeavors of reform and development. The Party's basic line is the lifeblood of the Party and country. We must adhere to the central task— economic development—and the two basic points. The Four Cardinal Principles and the policy of reform and opening up is our great endeavor to develop socialism with Chinese characteristics. We should neither look down upon ourselves nor be arrogant. We must take solid steps to achieve new victory for socialism with Chinese characteristics.

As long as we remain true to our ideals, are firm in our conviction, never vacillate in or relax our efforts or act recklessly, and forge ahead with tenacity and resolve, we will surely complete the building of a moderately prosperous society in all respects when the Communist Party of China celebrates its centenary and turn China into a modern socialist country that is prosperous, strong, democratic, culturally advanced, and harmonious when the People's Republic of China marks its centennial. The whole Party should have every confidence in our path, in our theories and in our system.

IDEOLOGY IN CHINA: CONFUCIUS MAKES A COMEBACK—YOU CAN'T KEEP A GOOD SAGE DOWN

The Economist

"Study the past," Confucius said, "if you would define the future." Now he himself has become the object of that study.[*]

Confucius was revered—indeed worshipped— in China for more than 2,000 years. But neither the Communist Party, nor the 20th century itself, has been kind to the sage. Modern China saw the end of the imperial civil-service examinations

_____
[*] This article appeared in *The Economist*, May 17, 2007.

he inspired, the end of the imperial regime itself and the repudiation of the classical Chinese in which he wrote. Harsher still, during the Cultural Revolution Confucius and his followers were derided and humiliated by Mao Zedong in his zeal to build a "new China."

Now, Professor Kang Xiaoguang, an outspoken scholar at Beijing's Renmin University, argues that Confucianism should become China's state religion. Such proposals bring Confucius's rehabilitation into the open. It is another sign of the struggle within China for an alternative ideological underpinning to Communist Party rule in a country where enthusiasm for communism waned long ago and where, officials and social critics fret, anything goes if money is to be made.

Confucius's rehabilitation has been slow. Explicit attacks on him ended as long ago as 1976, when Mao died, but it is only now that his popularity has really started rising. On topics ranging from political philosophy to personal ethics, old Confucian ideas are gaining new currency.

With a recent book and television series on the *Analects*, the best-known collection of the sage's musings, Yu Dan has tried to make the teachings accessible to ordinary Chinese. Scholars have accused her of oversimplifying, but her treatment has clearly struck a chord: her book has sold nearly four million copies, an enormous number even in China.

Further interest is evinced by the Confucian study programs springing up all over the Chinese education system. These include kindergarten classes in which children recite the classics, Confucian programs in philosophy departments at universities, and even Confucian-themed executive-education programs offering sage guidance for business people.

But perhaps the most intriguing—albeit ambivalent—adopter of Confucianism is the Communist Party itself. Since becoming China's top leader in 2002, President Hu Jintao has promoted a succession of official slogans, including "Harmonious Society" and *"Xiaokang Shehui"* ("a moderately well-off society"), which have Confucian undertones. On the other hand, says one scholar at the party's top think-tank, the Central Party School, official approval is tempered by suspicions about religion and by lingering concern over the mixture of Buddhism and other religious elements in Confucian thinking.

The relevance of Confucian ideas to modern China is obvious. Confucianism emphasizes order, balance and harmony. It teaches respect for authority and concern for others.

For ordinary Chinese, such ideas must seem like an antidote to the downside of growth, such as widening regional disparities, wealth differentials, corruption and rising social tension. For the government, too, Confucianism seems like a blessing. The party is struggling to maintain its authority without much ideological underpinning (Deng Xiaoping questioned the utility of ideology itself when he said that it doesn't matter if a cat is black or white so long as it catches mice). Confucianism seems to provide a ready-made ideology that teaches people to accept their place and does not challenge party rule.

As an additional advantage, Confucianism is home-grown, unlike communism. It even provides the party with a tool for advancing soft power abroad. By calling China's overseas cultural and linguistic study centers "Confucius Institutes," the party can present itself as something more than just an ideologically bankrupt administrator of the world's workshop.

Yet despite this, Confucianism is not an easy fit for the party. It says those at the top must prove their worthiness to rule. This means Confucianism does not really address one of the government's main worries, that while all will be well so long as China continues to prosper, the party has little to fall back upon if growth falters.

Writing last year, Professor Kang argued that a marriage of Confucianism and communism could nevertheless be made to work. He argued that the party has in reality allied itself with China's urban elite. "It is," he wrote, "an alliance whereby the elites collude to pillage the masses," leading to "political corruption, social inequality, financial risks, rampant evil forces, and moral degeneration." The solution, he argued, was to "Confucianize the Chinese Communist Party at the top and society at the lower level."

But Stephen Angle, a Fulbright scholar at Peking University and a philosophy professor at Wesleyan University in America, argues that Confucianism may not be as useful to the party as it thinks. For a start it has little to say about one of the party's biggest worries, the tension in urban-rural relations. More important, a gap in Confucian political theory should alarm a government seeking to hold on to power in a fast-changing environment. "One big problem with Confucianism," says Mr. Angle, "is that it offers no good model for political transition, except revolution."

COMMUNIQUÉ ON THE CURRENT STATE OF THE IDEOLOGICAL SPHERE*

General Office of the Central Committee of the Communist Party of China

A Notice from the Central Committee of the Communist Party of China's General Office to Provinces, autonomous regions, municipalities directly under the Party committee, Central ministries and state organs, Party ministries, People's Liberation Army headquarters, major Party committees, and Party leadership groups of civilian organizations: This notice "A Communiqué on the Current State of the Ideological Sphere" has been approved by the central leadership, and is herewith distributed to you. Please thoroughly implement its suggestions.

April 22, 2013

(This document has been sent to local divisional levels)

Introduction

Since the Party's Eighteenth National Congress, under General Secretary Xi Jinping's strong central leadership, the nation triumphantly convened the National People's Congress and the Chinese People's Political Consultative Conference, the Party's and nation's various undertakings have made a good start, and the general mood of the Party and Government has been constantly improving. Cohesion among our nation's people has become stronger and our confidence in our path, our theory, and our system has become more resolute. Mainstream ideology is becoming healthier and more vigorous. The spirit of the Party's Eighteenth National Congress and General Secretary Xi Jinping's series of important speeches have unified the thought of the entire Party, the entire country, and the entire people enormously.

The ideological foundation of our united struggle is unceasingly solidifying.

The new session of the central leadership group has put forth a series of new principles for conduct in political administration, furnished an interpretation of the Chinese dream of the great rejuvenation of the Chinese nation, improved our work style, maintained close ties with the masses, rigorously enforced diligence and thrift, opposed extravagance and waste, increased vigor in the fight against corruption, and won the widespread endorsement of cadres and the masses. We persist in upholding scientific development as the main theme, accelerating economic transformation as the main thread, and increasing the quality and efficiency of the economy as the core. The outlook for our nation's economic development continues to be favorable, and the people's faith in China's economic prospects has risen. In an effort to improve the people's livelihood, we are putting forth new measures to benefit the people so they may look forward to a better future: disseminating thought on the cultural front as the most important political task; studying, implementing, and advancing the spirit of the Eighteenth Party Congress; rapidly arousing mass fervor, proclaiming that socialism with Chinese characteristics and the Chinese dream are the main themes of our age; expanding and strengthening positive propaganda; strengthening guidance on deep-seated problems; strengthening the management of ideological fronts; promoting unification of thought; concentrating our strength and implementing the development of a positive atmosphere and providing spiritual strength to the party and nation.

Noteworthy Problems Related to the Current State of the Ideological Sphere

While fully approving of the ideological mainstream, we must also clearly see the ideological situation as a complicated, intense struggle. Currently, the following false ideological trends, positions, and activities all deserve note:

---

* This CPC Central Committee document (中发) was translated and published on The Asia Society website *China File* on November 8, 2013 (http://www.chinafile.com/document-9-chinafile-translation) together with this explanation: "*Mingjing Magazine*, a US-based Chinese-language magazine, obtained and published the full text of the document in September 2013 in print. We are confident it is authentic and translate and re-publish it here with *Mingjing's* permission."

1. Promoting Western Constitutional Democracy: An attempt to undermine the current leadership and the socialism with Chinese characteristics system of governance. Western Constitutional Democracy has distinct political properties and aims. Among these are the separation of powers, the multi-party system, general elections, independent judiciaries, nationalized armies, and other characteristics. These are the capitalist class's concepts of a nation, political model, and system design. The concept of constitutional democracy originated a long time ago, and recently the idea has been hyped ever more frequently.

This is mainly expressed the following ways: In commemorating the thirtieth anniversary of the enactment of the [Chinese] Constitution, [some people] hold up the banners of "defending the constitution" and "rule of law." They attack the Party's leaders for placing themselves above the constitution, saying China "has a constitution but no constitutional government." Some people still use the phrase "constitutional dream" to distort the Chinese dream of the great rejuvenation of the Chinese nation, saying things like "constitutional democracy is the only way out" and "China should catch up with the rest of the world's trend toward constitutional governance." The point of publicly proclaiming Western constitutional democracy's key points is to oppose the Party's leadership and implementation of its constitution and laws. Their goal is to use Western constitutional democracy to undermine the Party's leadership, abolish the People's Democracy, negate our country's constitution as well as our established system and principles, and bring about a change of allegiance by bringing Western political systems to China.

2. Promoting "universal values" in an attempt to weaken the theoretical foundations of the Party's leadership. The goal of espousing "universal values" is to claim that the West's value system defies time and space, transcends nation and class, and applies to all humanity.

This is mainly expressed in the following ways: believe Western freedom, democracy, and human rights are universal and eternal. This is evident in their distortion of the Party's own promotion of democracy, freedom, equality, justice, rule of law, and other such values; their claim that the CCP's acceptance of universal values is a victory for "universal values," that "the West's values are the prevailing norm for all human civilization," that "only when China accepts Western values will it have a future," and that "Reform and Opening is just a process of gradually accepting universal rights."

Given Western nations' long-term dominance in the realms of economics, military affairs, science, and technology, these arguments can be confusing and deceptive. The goal [of such slogans] is to obscure the essential differences between the West's value system and the value system we advocate, ultimately using the West's value systems to supplant the core values of Socialism.

3. Promoting civil society in an attempt to dismantle the ruling party's social foundation. Civil society is a socio-political theory that originated in the West. It holds that in the social sphere, individual rights are paramount and ought to be immune to obstruction by the state. For the past few years, the idea of civil society has been adopted by Western anti-China forces and used as a political tool. Additionally, some people with ulterior motives within China have begun to promote these ideas.

This is mainly expressed in the following ways:

— Promoting civil society and Western-style theories of governance, they claim that building a civil society in China is a precondition for the protection of individual rights and forms the basis for the realization of constitutional democracy. Viewing civil society as a magic bullet for advancing social management at the local level, they have launched all kinds of so-called citizen's movements.
— Advocates of civil society want to squeeze the Party out of leadership of the masses at the local level, even setting the Party against the masses, to the point that their advocacy is becoming a serious form of political opposition.

4. Promoting Neoliberalism, attempting to change China's Basic Economic System. Neoliberalism advocates unrestrained economic liberalization, complete privatization, and total marketization and it opposes any kind of interference or regulation by the state. Western countries, led by the United States, carry out their Neoliberal agendas under the guise of "globalization," visiting catastrophic consequences upon Latin America, the Soviet Union, and Eastern Europe, and have also dragged themselves into the international financial crisis from they have yet to recover.

This is mainly expressed in the following ways:

– [Neoliberalism's advocates] actively promote the "market omnipotence theory." They claim our country's macroeconomic control is strangling the market's efficiency and vitality and they oppose public ownership, arguing that China's state-owned enterprises are "national monopolies," inefficient, and disruptive of the market economy, and should undergo "comprehensive privatization." These arguments aim to change our country's basic economic infrastructure and weaken the government's control of the national economy.

5. Promoting the West's idea of journalism, challenging China's principle that the media and publishing system should be subject to Party discipline. Some people, under the pretext of espousing "freedom of the press," promote the West's idea of journalism and undermine our country's principle that the media should be infused with the spirit of the Party.

This is mainly expressed in the following ways:

– Defining the media as "society's public instrument" and as the "Fourth Estate;" attacking the Marxist view of news and promoting the "free flow of information on the Internet"; slandering our country's efforts to improve Internet management by calling them a crackdown on the Internet; claiming that the media is not governed by the rule of law but by the arbitrary will of the leadership; and calling for China to promulgate a Media Law based on Western principles. [Some people] also claim that China restricts freedom of the press and bang on about abolishing propaganda departments. The ultimate goal of advocating the West's view of the media is to hawk the principle of abstract and absolute freedom of press, oppose the Party's leadership in the media, and gouge an opening through which to infiltrate our ideology.

6. Promoting historical nihilism, trying to undermine the history of the CCP and of New China. The goal of historical nihilism, in the guise of "reassessing history," is to distort Party history and the history of New China.

This is mainly expressed in the following ways:

– Rejecting the revolution; claiming that the revolution led by the Chinese Communist Party resulted only in destruction; denying the historical inevitability in China's choice of the socialist road, calling it the wrong path, and the Party's and New China's history a "continuous series of mistakes"; rejecting the accepted conclusions on historical events and figures, disparaging our Revolutionary precursors, and vilifying the Party's leaders. Recently, some people took advantage of Comrade Mao Zedong's 120th birthday in order to deny the scientific and guiding value of Mao Zedong thought. Some people try to cleave apart the period that preceded Reform and Opening from the period that followed, or even to set these two periods in opposition to one another. By rejecting CCP history and the history of New China, historical nihilism seeks to fundamentally undermine the CCP's historical purpose, which is tantamount to denying the legitimacy of the CCP's long-term political dominance.

7. Questioning Reform and Opening and the socialist nature of socialism with Chinese characteristics. For the past several years, the discussion of reform has been unceasing, with all kinds of voices joining one after another. Some views clearly deviate from socialism with Chinese characteristics.

This is mainly expressed in the following ways:

Some blame the contradictions and problems of development on Reform and Opening. They say "Reform and opening up has gone too far" and that "we have deviated from our socialist orientation." They question whether or not what China is doing now still truly is Socialism, or they just call it "Capitalist Socialism," "State Capitalism," or "New Bureaucratic Capitalism." Others say "reform is still distant and hasn't be realized" or that "reform of the political system lags behind and obstructs reform of the economy." They bang on about how we should use Western standards to achieve so-called thorough reform. Essentially, they oppose the general and specific policies emanating from the road taken at the Third Plenum of the Eleventh Party Congress and they oppose socialism with Chinese characteristics.

— These mistaken views and ideas exist in great numbers in overseas media and reactionary publications. They penetrate China through the Internet and underground channels and they are disseminated on domestic Internet forums, blogs, and microblogs. They also appear in public lectures, seminars, university classrooms, class discussion forums, civilian study groups, and individual publications. If we allow any of these ideas to spread, they will disturb people's existing consensus on important issues like which flag to raise, which road to take, which goals to pursue, etc., and this will disrupt our nation's stable progress on reform and development.

— Western anti-China forces and internal "dissidents" are still actively trying to infiltrate China's ideological sphere and challenge our mainstream ideology. Some of their latest major efforts include: Some people have disseminated open letters and declarations and have organized petition-signings to vocalize requests for political reforms, improvement of human rights, release of "political prisoners," "reversing the verdict on '6/4' [the counter-revolutionary rebellion]," and other such political demands; they have made a fuss over asset disclosure by officials, fighting corruption with the Internet, media supervision of government, and other sensitive hot-button issues, all of which stoke dissatisfaction with the Party and government. Western embassies, consulates, media operations, and NGOs operating inside China under various covers are spreading Western ideas and values and are cultivating so-called anti-government forces. [They are] cooking up anti-government publications overseas. Within China's borders, some private organizations are creating reactionary underground publications, and still others are filming documentaries on sensitive subject matter, disseminating political rumors, and defaming the Party and the national leadership. Those manipulating and hyping the Tibetan self-immolations, manufacturing the violent terrorist attacks in Xinjiang, and using the ethnic and religious issues to divide and break up [the nation]. [They are] accelerating infiltration of the Internet and illegal gatherings within our borders. "Dissidents" and people identified with "rights protection" are active. Some of them are working together with Western anti-China forces, echoing each other and relying on each

other's support. This clearly indicates that the contest between infiltration and anti-infiltration efforts in the ideological sphere is as severe as ever, and so long as we persist in CCP leadership and socialism with Chinese characteristics, the position of Western anti-China forces to pressure for urgent reform won't change, and they'll continue to point the spearhead of Westernizing, splitting, and "Color Revolutions" at China. In the face of these threats, we must not let down our guard or decrease our vigilance.

Pay Close Attention to Work in the Ideological Sphere

Historical experience has proven that failures in the economic sphere can result in major disorder, and failure in the ideological sphere can result in major disorders as well. Confronting the very real threat of Western anti-China forces and their attempt at carrying out Westernization, splitting, and "Color Revolutions," and facing the severe challenge of today's ideological sphere, all levels of Party and government, especially key leaders, must pay close attention to their work in the ideological sphere and firmly seize their leadership authority and dominance.

1. Strengthen leadership in the ideological sphere. Party members and governments of all levels must become fully aware that struggles in the ideological sphere are perpetual, complex, and excruciating; you must strengthen awareness of the current political situation, big picture, responsibility, and risks. Leaders at all levels of government, you must strengthen your sense of responsibility—make work in the ideological sphere a high priority in your daily agenda, routinely analyze and study new developments in the ideological sphere, react swiftly and effectively, and preemptively resolve all problems in the ideological sphere.

2. Guide our Party members and leaders to distinguish between true and false theories. Forcefully resist influential and harmful false tides of thoughts, help people distinguish between truth and falsehood, and solidify their understanding. Party members, especially high-level leaders, must become adept at tackling problems from political, big-picture, strategic, and theoretical perspective. They must clearly recognize the essence of false ideas and viewpoints, both their theoretical falsehood and the practical political harm they can cause. We must have a firm approach and clear-cut stance toward major political principles, issues of right and wrong, what to support and what to oppose. We must uphold strict and clear discipline, maintaining a high-level unity with the Party Central Committee under the leadership of General Secretary Xi Jinping in thought, political stance, and action. We must not permit the dissemination of opinions that oppose the Party's theory or political line, the publication of views contrary to decisions that represent the central leadership's views, or the spread of political rumors that defame the image of the Party or the nation.

3. Unwavering adherence to the principle of the Party's control of media. The [principle of the Party's control of media] stems from our political system and the nature of our media. We must maintain the correct political direction. We must firmly hold fast to the principle of the media's Party spirit and social responsibility, and that in political matters it must be of one heart and mind with the Party. We must persist in correct guidance of public opinion, insisting that the correct political orientation suffuse every domain and process in political engagement, form, substance, and technology. We must give high priority to building both the leadership and rank and file in the sphere of media work. We need to strengthen education on the Marxist perspective of media to ensure that the media leadership is always firmly controlled by someone who maintains an identical ideology with the Party's Central Committee, under General Secretary Xi Jinping's leadership.

4. Conscientiously strengthen management of the ideological battlefield. When facing sensitive events and complex puzzles in the ideological sphere, we should implement the principle that the people in charge assume responsibility and use territorial management.

We must reinforce our management of all types and levels of propaganda on the cultural front, perfect and carry out related administrative systems, and allow absolutely no opportunity or outlets for incorrect thinking or viewpoints to spread. Conscientiously implement the "Decision of the Standing Committee of the National People's Congress on Strengthening Information Protection on Networks," strengthen guidance of public opinion on the Internet, purify the environment of public opinion on the Internet. Improve and innovate our management strategies and methods to achieve our goals in a legal, scientific, and effective way.

IV. THE FUTURE OF THE CCP

Making Party Building More Scientific in All Respects

Report to the 18th National Congress of the Communist Party of China [Excerpts]*

Hu Jintao

Rallying and leading the people in completing the building of a moderately prosperous society in all respects, in advancing socialist modernization and in achieving the great renewal of the Chinese nation is an important mission for our Party. When the Party maintains its strength and close ties with the people, China enjoys prosperity and stability and the Chinese people live in peace and happiness. Facing the new developments, the progress in our cause and the expectation the people have of us, we should comprehensively carry out the great new undertaking of Party building in an

---

* This speech was published by the Communist Party of China on November 8, 2012 (http://www.china.org.cn/china/18th_cpc_congress/2012-11/16/content_27137540.htm).

innovative reform-driven manner and make Party building more scientific in all respects.

The whole Party must bear in mind that only by taking root among the people and delivering benefits to them can the Party remain invincible, and that only by being on guard against adversity in times of peace and forging boldly ahead can the Party remain in the forefront of the times. Under new conditions, the Party faces complicated and severe long-term tests in exercising governance, carrying out reform and opening up and developing the market economy, as well as tests from the external environment. And the whole Party is confronted with increasingly grave dangers of lacking in drive, incompetence, being out of touch with the people, corruption, and other misconduct. We should steadily improve the Party's art of leadership and governance; and increase its ability to resist corruption, prevent degeneration, and ward off risks—this is a major issue the Party must solve in order to consolidate its position as the governing party and carry out its mission of governance. All Party members must heighten their sense of urgency and sense of responsibility and focus on strengthening the Party's governance capacity, advanced nature and purity. We should continue to free up our minds and carry out reform and innovation, and uphold the principle that the Party should supervise its own conduct and run itself with strict discipline. We should make all-around efforts to strengthen the Party theoretically and organizationally and improve its conduct. We should become better able to fight corruption, uphold Party integrity, and improve Party rules and regulations. We should enhance our capacity for self-purity, self-improvement, self-development, and self-innovation and build the Party into an innovative, service-oriented and learning Marxist governing party. By taking these steps, we can ensure that the Party is always the firm leadership core guiding the cause of socialism with Chinese characteristics.

1. Be firm in our ideal and conviction and remain true to the faith of Communists. Communists' faith in Marxism, socialism, and communism is their political soul and sustains them in all tests. We should give high priority to developing the Party's theory, which is essential for Party building. We should study Marxism-Leninism, Mao

Zedong Thought and the system of theories of socialism with Chinese characteristics and intensively study and apply the Scientific Outlook on Development. We should build learning Party organizations, educate Party members and officials in our shared ideal of socialism with Chinese characteristics, and encourage them to unremittingly pursue this ideal. We should intensify education in the Party spirit, which is at the core of Party building, study Party history, and gain a full understanding of the experience and lessons reviewed in the Party's two resolutions on certain questions in its history. We should carry forward the Party's fine traditions and conduct and make its members and officials develop a firm and correct worldview and a firm and correct attitude toward power and career, take a committed political stand, and become better able to tell right from wrong on major issues of principle. We should raise the moral standards of Party members, which are the foundation of Party building, encourage Party members and officials to become role models in practicing socialist views on honor and disgrace, and urge them to observe the Party spirit and ethical standards and set good examples for the public. We should encourage Party members and officials to become paragons of socialist ethics, lead in fostering a social trend of honesty and integrity, uphold fairness and justice, and thus demonstrate with concrete actions the moral integrity of Communists.

2. Put people first, exercise governance for the people, and always maintain close ties with them. Serving the people is the fundamental purpose of the Party, and putting people first and exercising governance for the people is the ultimate yardstick for judging all the Party's performance in this regard. At all times we must put the people's interests above everything else, be of one mind with the people, share a common destiny with them, and rely on them to propel history forward. To maintain the Party's advanced nature and purity, we should carry out intensive activities throughout the Party to study and practice its mass line, with the focus on the need to serve the people and to be down-to-earth, honest, and upright in conduct. We should solve pressing problems of keen concern to the people, and raise our ability to do people-related work well under new conditions. We should improve the system for Party members and officials to maintain direct contact with the people. We should consult the people on governance, learn about their needs, seek their advice, and draw wisdom and strength from their great practices. We should endeavor to bring prosperity to the people and promote national renewal, be eager to blaze new trails and live up to our responsibility, and deliver more concrete services to the satisfaction of the people. We should always work hard and practice economy. We should make determined efforts to improve the style of writing and the conduct of meetings, and reject undesirable practices such as mediocrity, laziness, laxity, and extravagance, the practice of just going through formalities, and bureaucratism. We should use the Party's fine conduct to enhance Party cohesiveness, win popular support, and improve the conduct of the government and the general public. We should support people's organizations such as trade unions, the Chinese Communist Youth League, and women's federations in fully playing their roles as bridges linking the Party and government with the people, voicing public concern, and protecting people's legitimate rights and interests.

3. Vigorously promote intra-Party democracy and enhance the Party's creative vitality. Intra-Party democracy is the life of the Party. We should adhere to democratic centralism, improve institutions for intra-Party democracy, and promote people's democracy with intra-Party democracy. We should uphold the principal position of Party members, better protect their democratic rights, and conduct criticism and self-criticism. We should foster comradely relations based on equality and democratic principles, a political atmosphere that encourages democratic discussion, and an institutional environment for democratic oversight. We should ensure that Party members have the right to stay informed of, participate in, and oversee Party affairs, as well as the right to vote. We should improve the system of Party congresses, raise the proportion of delegates from among workers and farmers to them, implement and improve the tenure system for delegates to Party congresses, experiment with a system of annual sessions of the Party congresses at the town and township level, proceed with trials of the system of Party congresses with a fixed term in selected counties and

county-level cities and districts, and introduce the system for delegates to Party congresses to submit proposals. We should improve the system of intra-Party election, and standards governing multi-candidate nomination and election, and create procedures and a climate that fully embody the will of voters. We should strengthen the decision-making and oversight role of plenary sessions of Party committees and improve procedural rules and decision-making procedures of their standing committees. We should also improve the system for local Party committees to make decisions on major issues and appoint key officials by ballot. We should expand intra-Party democracy at the community level, improve the system for Party members to assess the performance of leading bodies of community-level Party organizations on a regular basis, make arrangements for Party members to sit in on meetings of community-level Party committees, and for delegates to Party congresses to attend relevant meetings of Party committees at the same levels, both in non-voting capacity, and thus conduct intra-Party activities in strict accordance with these principles and make them more transparent.

4. Deepen reform of the system for the management of officials and personnel and build a contingent of competent key officials for governance. To uphold and build socialism with Chinese characteristics, it is imperative to build a contingent of key officials for governance who are firm in political conviction, competent and energetic, and have fine conduct. We should adhere to the principle of the Party supervising the performance of officials. We should appoint officials on their merits without regard to their origins, select officials on the basis of both their moral integrity and their professional competence with priority given to the former, and promote officials who are outstanding in performance and enjoy popular support. We should deepen reform of the system for the management of officials and personnel so that officials with outstanding performance in all fields will come to the fore in large numbers, and we should tap their potential to the full and put their talent to best use. We should fully and strictly implement the principle of selecting officials in a democratic, open, competitive, and merits-based way, make the management of them more democratic, enhance democracy, improve the way of selecting officials through competition, increase public trust in the selection and appointment of officials, and ensure that honest people are not disadvantaged and schemers do not have their way. We should improve the system for assessing the performance of officials and require leading officials to view their performance for what it is. We should improve the system for the management of officials, conduct strict supervision over them, strengthen training and selection of officials as heads of Party and government bodies or for other key positions, and improve the public servant system. We should improve the composition of leading bodies and the mix of the ranks of officials, give high priority to training and selecting officials from among those working on the frontline or in local communities, and widen the channel for outstanding individuals from society at large to become Party and government officials. We should reform the personnel management system in state-owned enterprises and public institutions. We should strengthen and improve education and training of officials to enhance their competence. We should make greater efforts to train and select outstanding young officials, attach importance to training and selecting officials from among women and ethnic minorities, and encourage young officials to work and gain experience in local communities and in hardship areas. We should provide full services for retired officials.

5. Adhere to the principle of the Party exercising leadership over personnel management and attract outstanding individuals from all over for the cause of the Party and country. Widening channels to attract talent is important for advancing the cause of the Party and people. We should respect work, knowledge, talent, and creation, pursue at a faster pace the strategy of training competent personnel as a priority to build a large contingent of such personnel, and turn China from a country with large human resources into one with a large pool of competent professionals. We should coordinate the training of all types of personnel, implement major projects for training and attracting high-caliber personnel, give more support to the training of innovative and entrepreneurial personnel, prioritize the training of people with practical skills, and encourage the flow of talents to the frontlines of research and production. We should

fully develop and utilize human resources both at home and abroad, and actively attract high-caliber personnel from overseas, and turn them to good use. We should accelerate reform of institutions and mechanisms for talent development, adopt innovative policies for this purpose, and establish a national system of honors. We should form an internationally competitive personnel system that is capable of firing the creativity and talent of people, and thus foster a dynamic environment in which everyone can fully tap their potential and put their talent to best use.

6. Promote community-level Party building in an innovative way and consolidate the organizational foundation for the exercise of governance by the Party. Community-level Party organizations play a key role in rallying and leading the people in implementing the Party's theories, line, principles, and policies and in carrying out its tasks. We should implement the system of responsibility for Party building, strengthen Party organizations in both rural and urban communities, step up efforts to establish and strengthen Party organizations in non-public economic entities and social organizations, and carry out community-level Party building in all areas. We should expand the coverage of Party organizations and Party work, fully leverage the role of community-level Party organizations in enhancing development, serving the people, rallying public support, and promoting harmony, and ensure that efforts to strengthen community-level Party organizations also spur the development of all other community-level organizations. We should improve the network of community-level Party organizations, enhance the competence of their leaders, further integrate Party building resources in urban and rural areas, and ensure sufficient funding for community-level Party organizations. We should make community-level Party organizations more service-oriented, with serving the people and engaging in people-related work being their main tasks. We should strengthen and improve education and management of Party members, with a focus on enhancing their Party spirit and raising their overall quality, improve the permanent mechanism for encouraging them to excel in their work, and encourage them to be vanguards and role models. We should ensure that Party members participate in Party activities regularly, and improve regular review of Party members' Party spirit and democratic evaluation of their performance. We should improve education and management of Party members among the floating population and provide better services for them. We should recruit better-qualified people into the Party, and give high priority to recruiting new members from among young workers, farmers, and intellectuals. We should perfect the mechanism for recruiting and disqualifying Party members so as to improve the composition of Party membership.

7. Unswervingly combat corruption and preserve Communists' political character of integrity. Combating corruption and promoting political integrity, which is a major political issue of great concern to the people, is a clear-cut and long-term political commitment of the Party. If we fail to handle this issue well, it could prove fatal to the Party, and even cause the collapse of the Party and the fall of the state. We must thus make unremitting efforts to combat corruption, promote integrity, and stay vigilant against degeneration. We should keep to the Chinese-style path of combating corruption and promoting integrity. We should persist in combating corruption in an integrated way, addressing both its symptoms and root causes, and combining punishment and prevention, with emphasis on the latter. We should advance in an all-around way the establishment of a system of combating corruption through both punishment and prevention and see to it that officials are honest, the government is clean, and political integrity is upheld. We should strengthen education about combating corruption and promoting clean government and improve the culture of clean government. Leading officials at all levels, especially high-ranking officials, must readily observe the code of conduct on clean governance and report all important facts concerned. They should both exercise strict self-discipline and strengthen education and supervision over their family and staff; and they should never seek any privilege. We should ensure that strict procedures are followed in the exercise of power, and tighten oversight over the exercise of power by leading officials, especially principal leading officials. We should deepen reform of key areas and crucial links, improve the system of anti-corruption laws, prevent and manage risks to clean government, avoid conflict of interests, prevent and fight corruption more effectively and in a more

scientific way, and increase international anti-corruption cooperation. We should rigorously implement the system of accountability for improving Party conduct and upholding integrity. We should improve the system of discipline supervision and inspection, improve the unified management of representative offices of Party commissions for discipline inspection, and enable discipline inspectors to better play their role of supervision. We must maintain a tough position in cracking down on corruption at all times, conduct thorough investigations into major corruption cases, and work hard to resolve problems of corruption that directly affect the people. All those who violate Party discipline and state laws, whoever they are and whatever power or official positions they have, must be brought to justice without mercy.

8. Strictly enforce Party discipline and willingly uphold centralized leadership of the Party. Centralized leadership of the Party is the source of its strength and a fundamental guarantee for China's economic and social development, ethnic unity and progress, and enduring peace and stability. The more complexities the Party faces and the more arduous the tasks it undertakes, the more imperative it is for the Party to strengthen its discipline and uphold centralized leadership. Party organizations at all levels and all Party members and officials, especially principal leading officials, must willingly abide by the Party Constitution as well as its organizational principles and guiding principles for its political activities; and no one is allowed to place oneself above the Party organization. All Party organizations and members must resolutely uphold the authority of the Central Committee and maintain a high degree of unity with it theoretically, politically and in action. We must faithfully implement the Party's theories, line, principles, and policies and ensure that the decisions of the Central Committee are carried out effectively; and we will never allow anyone to take countermeasures against them or disregard them. We will strengthen oversight and inspection, strictly enforce Party discipline, political discipline in particular, and take stern actions against violations of Party discipline. We must ensure that all are equal before discipline, that nobody has the privilege of not observing it, and that no exception should be made in its enforcement. This will enable the whole Party from leadership to the ranks to advance in unison as a great force.

SPEECH ON THE 65TH ANNIVERSARY OF THE FOUNDING OF THE CHINESE PEOPLE'S POLITICAL CONSULTATIVE CONGRESS [EXCERPTS]*

Xi Jinping

Fellow Comrades and Friends:

Today we gather here ceremoniously to celebrate the 65th founding anniversary of the Chinese People's Political Consultative Conference [CPPCC]. In the past 65 years, under the CPC leadership, the CPPCC has been actively devoted to the great practice of establishing and building New China, exploring the path of reform, and realizing the Chinese dream; it has traversed a glorious course and performed historic exploits!

First, on behalf of the CPC Central Committee, I would like to extend my warm greetings to the CPPCC on its 65th founding anniversary! My lofty respects to all democratic parties and groups, All-China Federation of Industry and Commerce, non-party personages, all civic organizations, and the people of all nationalities in all circles who have jointly devoted themselves to the socialist cause with Chinese characteristics and who have made outstanding contributions to the CPPCC cause! My sincere regards to the compatriots of Hong Kong Special Administrative Region, Macau Special Administrative Region, and Taiwan as well as the overseas Chinese!

This very moment reminds us more deeply about Comrade Mao Zedong, Comrade Zhou Enlai, Comrade Deng Xiaoping, Comrade Deng Yingchao, Comrade Li Xiannian, and other leaders of the CPPCC cause of the older generation. We will forever remember the people who have contributed to the CPPCC cause and we will continue to push forward the CPPCC cause under the new conditions of our times.

---

* Excerpts from the text of Xi Jinping's speech at the meeting celebrating the 65th anniversary of the founding of the Chinese People's Political Consultative Conference on September 21, 2014, in Beijing; reprinted by Xinhua News Agency.

Fellow Comrades and Friends:

In reviewing the CPPCC's 65-year development course, we have come to more profoundly realize that the CPPCC was rooted in the Chinese history and culture; was conceived in the great struggle of the Chinese people's revolution after the modern times; has developed in the glorious practice of socialism with Chinese characteristics; possesses distinctive Chinese characteristics; and is an important force for building a prosperous and strong country, rejuvenating the nation, and bringing happiness to the people. We are fully justified to believe that the CPPCC has created a glorious history and will certainly create a more glorious future!

Fellow Comrades and Friends:

The valuable experiences accumulated in the CPPCC's 65 years of abundant practice have established important principles for us in doing well the CPPCC work. To do well the CPPCC work, we must uphold the CPC leadership. The CPC leadership is the common choice of the entire Chinese people, including all democratic parties and groups, all organizations, all nationalities, and the people of all strata and circles; it is the most essential trait of socialism with Chinese characteristics, as well as the fundamental guarantee for the development and progress of the CPPCC cause. For the CPPCC cause to develop in the correct direction, it is imperative to uphold the CPC leadership without wavering.

To do well the CPPCC work, we must characterize the CPPCC's nature. The CPPCC is a united front organization as well as a multi-party cooperation and political consultation organization; it is an important form for realizing the people's democracy, and embodies the distinctive features of the socialist system with Chinese characteristics. The CPPCC should vigorously and constantly advance its work and undertakings in all fields based on its accurate characterization by the Constitution, the laws, and the CPPCC constitution.

To do well the CPPCC work, we must uphold the grand unity and grand alliance, which are essentially required of the united front, and are important traits of the CPPCC organization. On the political foundation of ardently loving the PRC, supporting the CPC leadership, supporting the socialist cause, and jointly working to realize the Chinese nation's great rejuvenation, the CPPCC should maximally mobilize all positive factors, unite all people who can be united, and rally a powerful force for jointly performing great exploits.

To do well the CPPCC work, we must uphold and develop socialist democracy. The people's democracy is the life of socialism. The CPPCC is an important format of the people's democracy. The CPPCC should adapt to the need of modernizing the state's governing system and abilities; uphold the reform and innovative spirit; innovate the CPPCC in theory, institution, and work; enrich the forms of democracy; unclog the channels of democracy; effectively organize all parties and groups, all organizations, all nationalities, and the people of all strata and circles to jointly deliberate state affairs; and realize a widespread and effective people's democracy.

Fellow Comrades and Friends:

The CPPCC should consistently uphold and develop socialism with Chinese characteristics as the main axis for consolidating the common ideological and political foundation. We should uphold the dynamic unity of the CPC leadership, the people as masters of their own affairs, and the running of the country by law; consciously implement the CPC's policy decisions and plans when doing the CPPCC work; get an accurate grasp of the CPPCC's nature, position, functions, and roles; and steadfastly take the road of development for socialist politics with Chinese characteristics like a rock in a storm without wavering.

Second, get a tight grip of reform and development while offering suggestions and putting in the efforts. China is still in the initial stage of socialism and is still the world's largest developing

nation; development is still the crux to solving all of China's problems. The central task we face is to tightly seize and effectively use the period of important strategic opportunities, comprehensively deepen the reforms, constantly liberate and develop social productivity, advance all undertakings in an all-round way, and more effectively improve and protect the people's livelihood.

The CPPCC should fully develop its advantages of being highly representative, having broad-based contacts, and being highly inclusive; focus on the important issues of promoting scientific development and comprehensively deepening the reforms as well as the problems that the masses are most concerned about; conduct in-depth fact-finding; and strive to present practical solutions and good suggestions for reform and development. It should actively propagandize the major principles and policies on reform and development, guide the masses whom they are responsible for liaison with to support and participate in reform and development, correctly handle the readjustments in the interest layout resulting from reform and development under the new situation, and add new booster and increase the cohesive power for reform and development. It should boldly speak its mind, offer sincere advice, promptly reflect the real situation, dare to voice suggestions and criticisms, help to identify the inadequacies, resolve problems, and make sure all reform and development measures are solidly implemented.

Third, persist in letting the CPPCC play an important role in developing consultative democracy. The CPPCC is grounded on the Constitution, the CPPCC constitution, and the relevant policies; and is guaranteed by the multi-party cooperation and political consultation system under the CPC leadership; it combines consultation, supervision, participation, and cooperation into one, and is an important channel for socialist consultative democracy.

The CPPCC should develop its role as a specialized consultative organization; carry out consultative democracy throughout the process of performing its functions; develop the system of political consultation, democratic supervision, as well as participatory and deliberative politics; continue to make the CPPCC's consultative democracy a more institutionalized and regulated procedure; more effectively coordinate the relations; rally the forces; offer suggestions and plans; and serve the overall interests. It should enhance the substance of consultation; introduce richer forms of consultation; establish and perfect the mechanism for presenting the topics of consultations, organizing activities, as well as adopting, implementing, and providing feedback on the results of consultation; more flexibly and more frequently conduct special-topic consultations, paired-up consultations, sector-specific consultations, and consultations for handling motions; explore the new formats such as online deliberation of state affairs and remote consultation; increase the practical results of consultation; and create a good atmosphere for consultation where everyone can speak their minds and freely air their views in a reasonable and measured way according to the laws and regulations.

Fourth, persist in widely rallying the positive energy for realizing the Chinese nation's great rejuvenation. The CPPCC is the broadest patriotic united front organization. The united front is an important magic weapon of the CPC for winning victories in revolution, construction, and reform, as well as an important magic weapon for realizing the Chinese nation's great rejuvenation.

We should uphold and perfect the multi-party cooperation and political consultation system under the CPC leadership, perfect the working mechanism, build more platforms, and create the conditions for democratic parties and groups as well as non-party personages to more effectively play their roles in the CPPCC. We should comprehensively implement the party's policies toward ethnic and religious affairs; actively guide the masses of all nationalities to strengthen their identification with the great motherland, the Chinese nation, the Chinese culture, and the socialist path with Chinese characteristics; fully develop the positive role of religious figures and the believers in promoting economic and social development; and promote ethnic unity and religious harmony. We should unswervingly implement the principles of "one country, two systems," "the rule of Hong Kong by Hong Kong people," "the rule of Macau by Macau people," and high degree of autonomy; comprehensively and accurately implement the Basic Law; promote the hinterland's exchange and cooperation with Hong Kong and Macau; and safeguard long-term prosperity and stability of Hong Kong and Macau. We should uphold the idea that the "people across the strait belong to one family"; enhance the contact and communication with all related parties, groups, and bodies, all social organizations, and the people in all walks of life on Taiwan island; and promote peaceful development of cross-strait relations. We should strengthen connection with overseas Chinese, returned overseas Chinese, and their dependents; safeguard their legal rights and interests; support them in actively participating in and backing the motherland (homeland) modernization drive and the great cause of peaceful reunification; and promote China's cultural exchange with all nations of the world. We should hold high the banners of peace, development, cooperation, and win-win outcome; follow the state's general plans for working with foreign countries; strengthen friendly interactions with the peoples, political organizations, media, and think tanks of all nations; and actively contribute to promoting the lofty cause of mankind's peace and development.

Fifth, persist in building up the ability to perform functions. As an important component part of the state's governing system, the CPPCC should adapt to the requirement for comprehensive deepening of reforms; use the reform thinking, innovative ideas, and practical measures to vigorously build up the ability to perform its functions; and play a greater role in modernizing the state's governing system and ability.

Fellow Comrades and Friends:

Socialist consultative democracy is a specific format and unique advantage of China's socialist democratic politics, and is an important embodiment of the CPC's mass line in the political arena. The 18th CPC National Congress said that in the course of developing China's socialist democratic politics, we should perfect the system and working mechanism for consultative democracy, and develop consultative democracy as a broad and multi-tiered institution. The Third Plenary Session of the 18th CPC Central Committee emphasized that we should conduct broad consultations throughout the society under the party's leadership, focusing the contents on the important issues related to economic and social development as well as the practical issues involving in the masses' vital interests, and making sure that consultations are conducted before making policy decisions or during the implementation of policy decisions. These important expositions and plans have charted the direction for developing China's socialist consultative democracy.

We should fully understand the important assessment that socialist consultative democracy is a specific format and unique advantage of China's socialist democratic politics. By leading the people to practice the people's democracy, the CPC is guaranteeing and supporting the people to be the masters of their own affairs. Guaranteeing and supporting the people to be the masters of their own affairs is not a slogan or an empty phrase; it must be implemented in the state's political and social activities, making sure that the people can effectively exercise, according to the law, the power to manage state affairs, manage economic and cultural services, and manage social affairs.

Democracy can be realized in many diverse forms, and is not confined to a rigid model, let alone saying only one criterion is set for judging all things throughout the world. Whether the people enjoy democratic rights will depend on whether the people have the right to vote during election time, but also on whether the people have the right to persistently participate in the day-to-day political activities; it depends on whether the people have the right to hold democratic election and also on whether the people have the right to democratic policy making, democratic management, and democratic supervision. Socialist democracy not only requires a complete institution and procedures, but also requires a complete practice of participation. The people as masters of their own affairs should be specifically and realistically embodied in the CPC ruling of the country and the state's governance; specifically and realistically embodied in all aspects and all levels of work of the CPC and the state organs; and specifically and realistically embodied in the people's realization and development of their own interests.

After summing up the practice of the people's democracy in New China, we clearly stated that in a socialist country as populous and vast as ours, conducting widespread consultation under the CPC leadership on important issues vital to national economy and the people's livelihood embodies the unity of democracy and centralism;

China's socialist democracy is demonstrated in two important forms: first, the people exercise their power through election and voting; second, the people fully conduct consultations before making important policy decisions in all matters among themselves, so as to arrive at a unanimous opinion as much as possible on generic issues. In China, these two forms of democracy do not replace or negate each other, but complement and bring out the best in each other, and they jointly constitute the institutional traits and advantages of China's socialist democratic politics.

Consultative democracy is a specific, unique, and novel form of democracy in China's socialist democratic politics; it originated from the Chinese nation's excellent political culture, which has developed over many years, such as the notion that the world is for all, that we should be fully inclusive and equitable, and that we should seek common ground while accepting the existing differences; originated from the realistic process of China's political development since the modern times; originated from the longstanding practice of revolution, construction, and reform conducted by the people under the CPC leadership; originated from the great creation jointly achieved by all parties and groups, all organizations, all nationalities, and the people of all strata and circles after New China's founding; and originated from the constant innovation, since reform and opening up, of China's political structure, giving consultative democracy a profound foundation in culture, theory, practice, and institution.

We should deeply grasp the basic characterization that socialist consultative democracy is an important embodiment of the CPC's mass line in the political arena. The CPC comes from the people and serves the people; this dictates that the PRC founded by the people under the CPC leadership must closely rely on the people to run the country, conduct administration, and manage the society. The CPC has implemented the mass line in its own work, persisted in doing everything for the masses and relying on the masses in everything; it comes from the masses and goes to the masses, and turns its own correct propositions into the masses' conscious actions. The PRC Constitution stipulates that all powers of the state belong to the people, and that all state organs and state functionaries must rely on the people's support, always maintain close connection with the people, listen to the people's opinions and suggestions, accept the people's supervision, and strive to serve the people. Whether it is the CPC that rules the country or the state organs that conduct administration, they must persist in implementing the mass line and closely rely on the people.

The future and destiny of a political party and a regime will eventually be decided by popular sentiments. We have learned from the entire development course of the CPC and the PRC that success in the cause of the CPC and the PRC is attributed to their consistent efforts to maintain flesh-and-blood relations with the masses, and to represent the fundamental interests of the broadest number of people. Divorce from the masses as well as losing the people's endorsement and support will eventually lead to failure. We should put the people's interests first, and under no circumstances should we change the position of breathing the same breath and sharing the same fate with the masses, forget the purpose of wholeheartedly serving the people, or discard the historical materialistic viewpoint that firmly believes in the masses as the true heroes.

Socialist consultative democracy should be rock solid and should not be for show; it should be all-encompassing and not confined to one aspect; it should be conducted throughout the nation from the top down, and should not be confined to one level. Therefore, we must construct a system of socialist consultative democracy that has a reasonable procedure and well-developed components, and make sure that consultative democracy has an institution to depend on, rules and regulations to obey, and an order to follow.

Consultation should be genuine, and genuine consultation requires that consultation be conducted before and during the decision-making process, that we decide and readjust our policy decision and work based on the opinions and suggestions from all aspects, and that we institutionally guarantee the implementation of the consultation results, so that our policy decisions and work are more in accord with popular sentiments and the actual conditions. We should widely conduct consultations on the major issues of reform, development, and stability by using all approaches, channels, and forms, especially problems that concern the masses' vital interests; respect the majority's wishes while taking care of the minority's

reasonable demands; fully accept the collective opinions; pool the collective wisdom; build consensus; and increase cohesiveness. We should broaden the consultation channels among the CPC, NPC, the people's government, the CPPCC, democratic parties and groups, civic organizations, grassroots organizations, enterprises and public institutions, social organizations, and all types of think tanks; deeply conduct political, legislative, administrative, democratic, social, grassroots, and all kinds of consultations; establish and improve various forms of consultations for making proposals, holding meetings, discussion, validation, hearings, public announcement, assessment, counseling, and networking; and constantly improve the scientific and practical results of consultative democracy.

The people constitute the emphasis of socialist consultative democracy. Massive policy decisions and work that involve the masses' interests primarily occur at the grassroots. We should follow the requirement of holding consultations with the people and for the people, vigorously develop grassroots consultative democracy, and put the emphasis on holding consultations among the grassroots masses. In making policy decisions that involve the masses' vital interests, we should fully solicit the masses' opinions, and consult with the masses in all manners, at all levels, and in all aspects. We should perfect the system for grassroots organizations to connect with the masses, strengthen deliberative consultations, make sure that the higher ups' intents are transmitted to the lower levels, and that the lower level's situation is transmitted to the higher up; and guarantee that the people will effectively manage their own affairs according to the law. We should promote transparency and regulatory control in the exercise of power; perfect the system of disclosure of party affairs, administrative affairs, and judicial affairs, as well as disclosure in handling business in all fields; and give the people the power of supervision, so that power shall be exercised under the sun.

Fellow Comrades and Friends:

Today sixty-five years ago, Comrade Mao Zedong delivered an opening address at the CPPCC First Plenary Session, saying: "We are all convinced that our work will go down in the history of mankind, demonstrating that the Chinese people, comprising one quarter of humanity, have now stood up." Today the Chinese nation, which has long stood up, is writing a more glorious chapter of our times with its diligent work and hard struggle.

The CPPCC's sixty-five year glorious course has been written into history, and the Chinese nation's wonderful future requires the concerted efforts of all the Chinese people to create. Let us get united more closely, hold high the great banner of socialism with Chinese characteristics, forge ahead in unity, make innovation with a pioneering spirit, and continue to write new chapters for the CPPCC cause!

IS CCP RULE FRAGILE OR RESILIENT?[*]

Minxin Pei

The continuing survival of authoritarian regimes around the world and the apparent resilience of such regimes in several major countries, particularly China and Russia, have attracted enormous scholarly interest in recent years. Analysts have put forward various theories to explain the success and durability of these regimes.[1] Some theories focus on authoritarians' capacity to learn from mistakes (their own as well as those made by other authoritarians) and adapt accordingly. Others center around an observed correlation between high natural-resource rents and regime survival. Still others identify the repressive capacity of authoritarian regimes as the key to their durability, while a final group of explanations pays special attention to the capacity of authoritarian regimes to institutionalize their rule.

These theories may provide tantalizing explanations for the endurance of authoritarian regimes, but they suffer from one common weakness: they are ad hoc and inductive. Moreover, they have a selection-bias problem resulting from small sample sizes (limited by the number of surviving autocracies). As a result, when supposedly invulnerable autocracies crumble in the face of mass protest and popular uprising, the explanations of authoritarian resilience largely break down. The series of popular revolts in 2011 that toppled autocracies in Tunisia and Egypt, triggered a civil war in Libya, and sparked prolonged and bloody anti-regime protests in Syria and Yemen provide a humbling lesson for those who had viewed those regimes as "robust" and "resilient."

In terms of authoritarian resilience, the People's Republic of China (PRC) stands out as exemplary. Not only did the ruling Chinese Communist Party (CCP) survive the turbulent spring of 1989, when millions of protesters nationwide nearly toppled its rule and it put down demonstrations in Beijing's Tiananmen Square with dramatic violence, but it has since thrived. The ruling elites coalesced around a new strategy that joined the promotion of rapid (mostly export-led) economic growth to the preservation of one-party rule through selective political repression. The rapid growth of the Chinese economy in the post-Tiananmen era has lent the CCP popular legitimacy and the resources to defend its political monopoly. The Party has demonstrated remarkable tactical sophistication, a knack for adaptation, and a capacity for asserting control. It has succeeded in maintaining unity within the elite cadres, resisted the global tide of democratization, and prevented the revolution in communications technologies from undermining its grip on the flow of information. It has also manipulated nationalism to bolster its support among the young and better educated, eliminated any form of organized opposition, and contained social unrest through a combination of carrots and sticks.

The CCP's ability to consolidate authoritarian rule even as a wave of democratic openings swept much the world after 1989 raises several important questions. Does the Chinese case validate any of the theories of authoritarian resilience advanced by scholars who specialize in the study of other regions? What are the explanations for authoritarian resilience in China, and what evidence supports them? Are these explanations theoretically

[*] This article was published in *The Journal of Democracy*, Vol. 23, No. 1 (January 2012).

robust? Is authoritarian resilience in China a passing phenomenon, or is it something more durable?

Explaining Authoritarian Resilience

Theories of authoritarian survival all share a common feature: They turn theories of democratic transition upside down. Specifically, they attempt either to identify the *absence* of factors normally favorable to democratic transition or to pinpoint the *presence* of unfavorable factors associated with the prevention of democratic transition. Among all these explanations, three stand out.

The first focuses on matters of political economy. Generally speaking, authoritarian regimes that are dependent on natural-resource rents tend to be more durable. Such regimes are able to buy off the population with high welfare spending and low taxation. Resource-based rents also allow autocratic regimes to escape political accountability and maintain a strong repressive apparatus. Authoritarian regimes with significant control over economic resources, such as state-owned enterprises, have greater survival capabilities because such control allows rulers to keep their key supporters loyal through patronage and to reassert their influence over the economy.

The capacity to adapt to new social and political challenges is a second variable associated with authoritarian resilience. For example, a number of authoritarian regimes have managed to stay in power by manipulating elections. The long-ruling one-party regimes in Malaysia and Singapore stand out for the sophistication of their political institutions. During its 71-year reign, Mexico's Institutional Revolutionary Party (PRI) was said to have maintained a "perfect dictatorship" featuring highly developed political institutions that managed leadership succession and generated popular support.[2] Resilient authoritarian regimes adapt by learning to differentiate between the types of public goods that they provide. More sophisticated autocracies typically supply welfare-enhancing public goods such as economic growth but limit "coordination goods" such as the freedom of information and association, in order to reduce the opposition's ability to organize.[3]

The third explanation concerns the balance of power between the regime and opposition.

Despite its obvious importance, the role of repression in the survival of autocracies has received surprisingly little attention. Yet a simple and persuasive explanation for authoritarians' longevity is that they are ready, willing, and able to use the coercive power necessary to suppress any societal challenge. More than anything else, it is effective repression that has sustained the Middle East's autocracies.[4] As long as this balance of power favors autocratic regimes, their survival is guaranteed by the application of repression. Of course, if the military refuses support, as happened in Tunisia and Egypt in early 2011, the balance of power shifts decisively and the regime is doomed.

In the Chinese context, the discussion about authoritarian resilience has centered around three themes—regime institutionalization, organizational learning and adaptation, and organizational and administrative capacity. Regime institutionalization—the process through which important norms and rules of the game are formulated and enforced—is thought by some to be the key to the CCP regime's durability. Since 1989, the CCP supposedly has greatly improved the procedures governing political succession, defined functional responsibilities, and promoted elites on the basis of merit. These and other measures, according to Andrew Nathan, have greatly increased the degree of institutionalization within the CCP, enabling it to survive and succeed.[5] In Steve Tsang's view, the post-Tiananmen regime has evolved into a distinct and more resilient form of Leninist rule by adopting a mixture of survival strategies that focus on governance reforms (to preempt public demands for democratization), greater capacity for responding to public opinion, pragmatic economic management (considerations of socialist ideology take a back seat to the need for growth), and appeals to nationalism. Tsang calls this "consultative Leninism."[6]

Those who stress the second theme—organizational learning and adaptation—note that authoritarian elites are motivated by an urge to survive and can draw useful lessons from the demise or collapse of their counterparts in other parts of the world. As a result, a regime may adopt new policies that contribute to its longevity and power. David Shambaugh argues that the collapse of the USSR taught the CCP valuable lessons, leading it to implement effective policy responses to post–Cold War challenges both at home and abroad.[7] The third theme stresses that, compared to other developing-world autocracies, China's organizational and administrative capacity is exceptional. Since 1989, the CCP has undertaken further measures to strengthen the capacity of the Chinese state in revenue collection and regulatory enforcement. By building state capacity, the CCP has made itself more resilient.[8] These explanations of the Chinese regime's durability leave several important questions unanswered. For example, is regime survival the same thing as regime resilience? Scholars studying the persistence of authoritarian rule in China rarely make a conceptual distinction between the two. Yet the mere fact of regime survival does not necessarily indicate regime resilience; survival is an empirical measurement, whereas resilience is a subjective concept. Thus authoritarian regimes that survive are not necessarily resilient.

If it lacks strong opposition or employs brutal repression, even a decrepit autocracy—that is, one without a high degree of institutionalization or performance-based legitimacy—may hang on for a long time. It would, for example, be a definitional stretch to label the personalistic dictatorship of Zimbabwe's elderly Robert Mugabe a "resilient autocracy." What, after all, constitutes the resilience of a regime? Longevity is perhaps the most-used criterion, and by that standard, the regimes of Burma, Cuba, and North Korea would be considered resilient. But because the word "resilience" implies inherent strengths and the capacity to endure and overcome adversity, regime survival reflects only one aspect of resilience, not others. In fact, these regimes appear to live under perpetual siege and in a permanent state of crisis and insecurity, making it hard to call them resilient. Even for the more successful authoritarian regimes— China and, to a lesser extent, Russia—their degree of resilience is debatable. In the case of China, for example, the CCP faces daily instances of defiance and disturbances, ranging from hundreds of local protests to accidents and disasters caused by corruption and incompetence. It is forced to devote massive resources to maintaining domestic order.

Authoritarian resilience, however defined, may result from tried-and-true survival tactics rather than the adoption of innovative political strategies. Although many studies have focused on autocrats'

use of semi-competitive elections to legitimize their power and on authoritarian regimes' successful management of succession and promotion of regime elites,[9] the more critical variables are economic patronage, political cooptation, and ruthlessly effective repression. For all their current success and perceived strengths, authoritarian regimes have not been able to address effectively the systemic and well-known weaknesses that imperil their long-term survival and limit their policy choices in responding to public demands. Such weaknesses include political illegitimacy; endemic corruption caused by lack of political accountability and misalignment of interests between the regime and its agents; political exclusion of the middle class; and predatory state policies that victimize and alienate disadvantaged social groups. As long as such systemic weaknesses persist under authoritarian rule, autocracy is unlikely to remain resilient.

To be sure, some authoritarian regimes have helped their survival chances by improving internal rules governing succession and promotion, learning useful lessons from the success or failures of other authoritarian regimes, strengthening the administrative capacity of the state, and managing to restrict the provision of coordination goods. Such autocracies are undeniably more sophisticated in institutional and tactical terms than garden-variety dictatorships in developing countries. But an explanation of the survival of "resilient" authoritarian regimes must take into account the additional factors that enable them to maintain power and the underlying forces that threaten their long-term survival. Such a comprehensive analytical approach is likely to yield more useful insights into the political dynamics of regime survival and demise in contemporary autocracies.

In particular, we should consider simpler and more straightforward explanations for the survival of authoritarian regimes—economic performance, for example. Everything else being equal, empirical research shows that authoritarian regimes that manage to perform well economically tend to survive longer.[10] Obviously, autocracies gain political legitimacy if the standard of living rises as a result of sustained economic growth. Autocratic regimes can use the resulting rents to coopt the middle class and redistribute the benefits from growth among the ruling elites, thus avoiding internecine struggles over a more or less fixed set of spoils. Sustained economic growth in an authoritarian regime also allows ruling elites to finance and maintain an extensive repressive apparatus to suppress political opposition.

Another straightforward explanation is that the greater the range of a regime's survival strategies—the more diversified its "portfolio" of methods for staying in power—the more likely it is to endure. Force alone may sustain some authoritarian regimes, but heavy use of repression can be costly. Moreover, large military and internal-security forces will consume resources that might otherwise be spent on non-repressive survival strategies such as cooptation and patronage. Highly repressive regimes are also unlikely to instill confidence in private entrepreneurs or to create business opportunities for them. Robert Barro has found that heavy repression depresses economic growth, while moderate repression may have a positive impact.[11] In autocracies that rely solely on repression, economic performance tends to be abysmal, sowing the seeds of social discontent and sapping regime legitimacy.

Even if a regime's economic performance has been satisfactory and its survival strategies and tactics sophisticated, it must still contend with autocracy's inherent flaws—the absence of procedural legitimacy, a narrow base of social support, gross misalignment of interests between the regime and its agents, and systemic and pervasive corruption—all of which threaten its long-term durability. Thus, perceived authoritarian resilience is, in all likelihood, a temporary phenomenon that conceals fatal weaknesses.

The Keys to CCP Survival

The three keys to the CCP's survival are refined repression, economic statism, and political cooptation. Proponents of the authoritarian-resilience theory have downplayed or overlooked their role. Although autocracies may use other, sometimes more sophisticated, means of keeping power, the most important is the use of violence against political opposition. No autocracy has survived without in some way resorting to repression. The difference between more successful autocracies and less successful ones lies mainly in how they use

repression. The more successful autocracies do so more selectively, efficiently, and effectively while the less successful ones typically repress opposition in cruder, more wasteful, and less productive ways.

Since the early 1990s, China has shifted toward "smart repression." The CCP has narrowed the scope and shifted the focus of its repressive actions. While the CCP continues to restrict people's political freedoms and civil rights, it has almost completely withdrawn from their private lives and stopped meddling in lifestyle issues. At the same time, the regime has drawn a clear line against organized political opposition, which is not tolerated in any form.

Selective repression, such as brutally suppressing the quasi-spiritual group the Falun Gong or targeting leading dissidents, avoids antagonizing the majority of the population while achieving the objectives of political decapitation and preventing organized opposition from emerging. This approach also conserves the regime's repressive resources and utilizes them more efficiently. The CCP regime has become more selective in its application of harsh crackdowns both because it learned lessons from the 1989 experience and because of the party-state's institutional decentralization. China's multiple levels of authority allow the regime to avoid either using excessive repression or making needless concessions in dealing with popular resistance.[12]

The regime's repressive tactics have also grown more sophisticated, even as the Party remains ruthless in defending its political monopoly. It now favors a less brutal approach, forcing top dissidents into exile abroad, for example, rather than sentencing them to long prison terms. Routine harassment of human rights activists and political dissidents has taken on softer forms: inviting them to have tea with the police is a favorite tactic. The regime's methods for dealing with rising social unrest have likewise become more sophisticated. Confronted with hundreds of collective protests and riots each day, the party-state has shown a considerable capacity to deploy highly effective measures such as quickly arresting and jailing protest leaders to decapitate local unrest, disperse crowds, and pacify the masses.[13]

The regime's efforts at manipulating public opinion have also become more complex—a mix of harsh censorship and campaigning for popular support. Rather than simply relying on old-fashioned ideological indoctrination, the CCP's propaganda department has, in recent years, learned to influence the social agenda by showcasing the Party's success in addressing social issues such as rising housing prices and declining access to healthcare. Although this approach has not been entirely successful, it is a telling example of the CCP's growing tactical sophistication.

Through its massive investment in manpower, technology, and training, the CCP has greatly improved the operational capabilities of its already well-funded, well-equipped, and well-trained security forces. The CCP has dealt with the emergence of new threats, such as information and communication technologies, with relatively effective countermeasures that include both regulatory restrictions and technological fixes. In this manner, the regime has contained the political impact of the information revolution, although it has had to adopt new tactics in order to do so. Instead of losing its grip on the flow of information, the CCP's propaganda operations have grown more sophisticated, helping to guard the CCP's political hegemony.

The Party's operational capabilities with regard to emergency management have also improved during the last decade. In 2003, with the SARS outbreak, China faced its first major public-health crisis since the end of the Cultural Revolution. The government's initial response was incompetent and ineffective. After replacing key leaders, however, the regime quickly turned the situation around. Natural disasters, major accidents, protests, and the like are frequent in China. Because of better emergency response, however, such periodic shocks have not inflicted serious damage on CCP control.

The CCP fully understands the inseparable link between political survival and control over the country's economic resources. Without its ability to hand out economic rents, the Party would surely lose the loyalty of its supporters and its ability to retain power. Thus the CCP keeps extensive and tight control over China's state-owned enterprises so that it can dole out political patronage.[14] This means that the Party is inherently incapable of implementing market-oriented reforms beyond a certain point, since they will ultimately undermine its political base. China's stalled economic reform in recent years has vindicated this view. Indeed, the Party has not only

publicly announced its intention of retaining state control of key economic sectors such as finance, energy, telecom services, and transportation, but has also successfully defended these monopolies or oligopolies from domestic and international competition. State-owned firms dominate these industries, while private firms and foreign competitors are kept out. Such policies have slowed the pace of privatization but enabled the state to remain the country's most powerful economic actor.

Even after three decades of economic reform, firms owned or controlled by the party-state account for close to 40 percent of China's GDP. The regime's domination of the economy rose to a new level after the government used aggressive fiscal and monetary policies to maintain high rates of growth following the 2008 global economic crisis. With a fiscal-stimulus package of nearly US $700 billion and $2 trillion in new bank loans, the Chinese state further strengthened state-owned enterprises at the expense of the private sector.[15]

While the economic-efficiency losses caused by the state's continuing and deep involvement in the economy are huge, the political benefits of this strategy are clear. The Party retains the power to appoint top officials in state-owned firms and the capacity to distribute lucrative economic rents to its key constituents (bureaucrats and businessmen with ties to the ruling elites). For members of these groups, the Communist Party's patronage pays. One study shows that politically connected firms often have higher offering prices when their stocks are listed on China's equity markets.[16] Economic patronage thus serves a dual function: It is both a critical instrument for influencing economic activities and a source of incentives to secure and maintain the backing of the regime's key political supporters.

In addition to keeping a strong hand on the levers of the economy, authoritarian regimes can help to extend their lives by expanding their social bases. Since the early 1990s, the CCP has been working successfully to do just that, building an elite alliance through cooptation. Elevating the political status of the intelligentsia and the professional class and improving their material benefits—while simultaneously using regulations and sanctions to penalize and deter intellectuals who dare to challenge the regime—are the most important elements of this strategy.

The Party has systematically campaigned to recruit the intelligentsia and professionals into its fold and to award them important technocratic appointments. This effort has succeeded both in raising the CCP's technocratic capacity and in extending its base into the intelligentsia, an elite social group that was at odds with the Party in the 1980s over the issue of political reform.[17] The much publicized effort to recruit private entrepreneurs into the Party has done less to expand its social base, since the majority of private owners of nonagricultural firms were already Party members who had used their power to convert state-owned assets into private property. Nevertheless, numerous studies have concluded that the CCP has been relatively successful in coopting private entrepreneurs. Some scholars have even called Chinese private entrepreneurs "allies of the state."[18] One case study finds that local officials who are supportive of the private sector have proven to be more effective in incorporating private businesspeople into local power structures.[19]

The CCP's strategy of political cooptation has been unexpectedly successful, leading some observers to argue that China's emerging middle class mainly favors the status quo. In addition to pacifying the middle class, the CCP has managed to transform its own membership base. During the Mao era, it was predominantly a party of peasants and workers; now it is a party of elites. According to official figures released in 2010, roughly 10 percent of the Party's 78 million members at the end of 2009 were workers and 20 percent were farmers. The remaining 70 percent were bureaucrats, managers, retired officials, professionals, college students, and intellectuals. Particularly noteworthy is the high proportion of well-educated individuals in the CCP—36 percent were either college graduates or had received some college education, and 15 percent were management, technical, and professional personnel and college students.[20] By comparison, less than 8 percent of China's total population is college-educated. In short, political cooptation has turned the Party into an elite-based alliance. The incorporation of key social elites into an authoritarian regime generates significant political benefits for the rulers. Among other things, it denies potential opposition groups access to social elites and makes it much harder for lower-status groups to organize and become effective political forces.

Behind the Facade of Authoritarian Strength

There is a sharp and intriguing discrepancy between how strong autocracies seem to outsiders and how insecure the rulers themselves feel. Autocrats are constantly on guard against forces that pose even the slightest threat to their rule, expending tremendous resources and taking excessively harsh and repressive measures in the process. But if authoritarian regimes really were so strong, then such costly measures motivated by insecurity would be self-defeating and counterproductive: they would be unnecessary and, by wasting a regime's scarce resources, would undermine its long-term survival. So why is there this discrepancy? The answer is quite simple: The authoritarian strength that outsiders perceive is merely an illusion. Insiders—the authoritarians themselves—possess information about the regime's weaknesses that outsiders know little about. These weaknesses make authoritarians feel insecure and prompt them to act accordingly.

The resilience of China's authoritarian regime may be a temporary phenomenon, fated to succumb eventually to autocracy's institutional and systemic defects. These defects are inherent features of autocratic systems and therefore uncorrectable. Thus the measures that the CCP has taken since the early 1990s to strengthen its rule (regardless of how effective they may have been) merely serve to offset somewhat the deleterious effects that these flaws have on regime survival. In the long run, China's authoritarian regime is likely to lose its resilience.

Ironically, an authoritarian regime's short-term success can imperil its long-term survival and effectiveness. Success, defined in terms of suppressing political opposition and defending a political monopoly, makes it more likely that authoritarians, unrestrained by political opposition, free media, and the rule of law, will engage in looting and theft, inevitably weakening the regime's capacity for survival.

Authoritarian regimes tend to breed corruption for a variety of reasons. A principal cause is the relatively short time horizon of autocrats, whose hold on power is tenuous, uncertain, and insecure. Even where the rules of succession and promotion have improved, as they have in China, such improvement is only relative to the previous state of affairs. Succession at the top remains opaque and unpredictable in China. Although the top leadership has managed to reach compromises through bargaining, thereby avoiding destabilizing power struggles, succession politics continues to be mired in intrigue and factionalism. In the case of promotion, the only objective rule appears to be an age requirement; all the other factors that are supposedly merit-based can be gamed. The fact that many officials resort to bribery to gain promotions indicates that personal favoritism continues to play an important role in internal Party promotions.[21]

All this renders uncertain the political future of members of the CCP hierarchy and thus encourages predatory behavior. There is evidence that corruption has worsened in China in recent years despite periodic anticorruption campaigns launched by the CCP.[22] More important, because of the deep and extensive involvement of the Chinese party-state in the economy, the combination of motives (driven by uncertainty) and opportunity (access to economic rents) can create an ideal environment for regime insiders to engage in collusion, looting, and theft.

Corruption endangers the long-term survival of authoritarian regimes in several ways. It can hinder economic growth, thus reducing the regime's political legitimacy and capacity to underwrite a costly patronage system and maintain its repressive apparatus. Corruption also contributes to rising inequality by benefiting a small number of well-connected elites at the expense of public welfare, thus further fueling anti-regime sentiments and social tensions. Corruption creates a high-risk environment, making it difficult to enforce regulations governing the workplace, food and drugs, traffic, and environmental safety, thereby increasing the risks of accidents and disasters and the likelihood of mismanaged government responses to them.[23]

The Limits of Political Cooptation

By nature, autocracies are exclusionary political coalitions. Although the incorporation of social elites can generate short-term benefits for rulers, it is a costly and ultimately unsustainable strategy because the modernization process produces social elites at a faster rate than authoritarian rulers can coopt them. Eventually, the regime will be unable to afford to coopt so many social elites, thus creating a potential pool of opposition leaders.

A key test of the CCP's capacity for coopting new social elites is the employment of college graduates. Since the late 1990s, college and university enrollment in China has shot upward. In 1997, Chinese tertiary educational institutions admitted a million new students; in 2009, they admitted 6.4 million. The number of college graduates soared in the same period. In 1997, students graduating from college numbered 829,000; in 2009, that figure was 5.3million.[24]

For all its focus on coopting social elites, however, the CCP has been able to recruit into its own ranks only a small percentage of China's college graduates. In 2009, the CCP recruited 919,000 new members with a college degree (roughly 30 percent of the Party's annual new recruits).[25] In other words, so far the CCP has been able to absorb each year only about a fifth of the net increase in the college-educated population. This implies that the CCP leaves out the vast majority of newly minted college graduates. Because Party membership confers enormous material benefits, college graduates who are rejected by the CCP are bound to be frustrated politically and socially.[26] Because of the difficulty that graduates of second- and third-tier colleges have experienced in finding employment in recent years, the prospect that this group will form an anti-regime force has become ever more likely.[27]

The long-term effectiveness of political cooptation is also limited by the questionable loyalty of those social elites being targeted for recruitment into the Party and its patronage system. To the extent that these individuals join the Party or support its policies chiefly out of pecuniary interests, the CCP may not be able to count on their loyalty if its ability to satisfy their material interests declines, due to poor economic performance or constraints on the state's fiscal capacity. In a crisis, when these opportunistic supporters might be called on to risk their lives or property to defend the Party, it is doubtful that a majority would stick with a regime in danger of collapse.

For the most part, however, authoritarian regimes adapt and make adjustments in times of crisis. The CCP adopted many of its regime-strengthening measures in response to the challenges posed by the Tiananmen crisis in 1989 and the collapse of European communism that followed soon thereafter. These measures have largely been effective in addressing the challenges stemming from these twin crises: reviving the country's stagnant economy through greater liberalization and opening to the outside world; ending international isolation; placating the intelligentsia; and boosting the confidence of the business community. But the measures that helped to keep the regime in power during the tumults of the late twentieth century are not necessarily working as well in the post-crisis era.

Activist Opposition

Today, after two decades of rapid economic growth, China's political landscape and socioeconomic environment have radically changed. New threats to the CCP's hold on power have emerged, while the dangers of the early 1990s—the threats that the Party's current adaptive survival strategies were designed to meet—have disappeared or dissipated. The Chinese government no longer faces international isolation or a mass anti-regime movement led by the intelligentsia.

Instead, the CCP regime now faces an entirely new set of challenges. Rapid economic growth has greatly expanded China's middle class. Although most members of that middle class have remained politically acquiescent, some have become more active in civic affairs, such as environmental protection and charity work. While regime repression has effectively destroyed the political-dissident community, opposition to the regime has taken more innovative forms. Activists today challenge the CCP on issues that can connect them with ordinary people—labor rights, forced evictions, land disputes, environmental protection, and public health. The CCP's single-minded focus on GDP growth has led to a systemic degradation of the Chinese state's capacity for providing such essential public goods as health care, education, and environmental protection. Rising official corruption and an unbalanced economic development strategy that has depressed the growth of household income and consumption have also fueled a rapid increase in income inequality.

Most of the countermeasures that the Party has taken since Tiananmen are ill-suited to dealing with these issues. If the CCP is to address these challenges effectively, it will have to abandon many key components of its post-Tiananmen strategy. Economically, it needs to find a different development model that is less investment-intensive and socially costly. Politically, it may have to replace repression and cooptation with some form of political liberalization to gain a broader base of social support. But the leadership of the Hu Jintao administration has shown no sign that the Party is ready or willing to embrace such fundamental policy shifts. This means that the CCP is now at risk of falling into the trap of "adaptive ossification"—applying an outdated adaptive strategy that no longer works. The result can be, ironically, an accumulation of tensions and risks during the period of perceived authoritarian resilience. Just when the party-state has come to be viewed as resourceful and supremely skilled at hanging on, it may in fact have entered a time of stagnation and dwindling dynamism.

Is the PRC's authoritarianism resilient or decaying? The answer to this question will depend on whether the CCP's post-Tiananmen strategy of relying on economic growth and political repression continues to prove effective despite social and economic conditions that have changed drastically during the past two decades. Proponents of the resilience school are expecting the CCP's adaptive capacity to be equal to the challenges that lie ahead. Skeptics, meanwhile, are pointing to the institutional flaws inherent in any autocracy and expressing doubt that the CCP will manage to frame and implement a substantially different survival strategy that can help it to maintain its political monopoly and gain new sources of legitimacy.

I side with the skeptics in rejecting the argument that the post-1989 regime has made itself resilient through fundamental institutional and policy innovations. Instead, the principal reasons for the CCP's survival since Tiananmen have been robust economic performance and consistent political repression. Although it is true that the

CCP may have improved its political tactics, its survival for the last two decades would have been unthinkable without these two critical factors—economic performance and political repression.

In the future, economic performance and political repression may remain important factors for the CCP's survival, but their contribution is likely to decline for several reasons. First, the deleterious effects of authoritarian decay will offset the positive impact of economic growth. Second, political repression is likely to be less effective in defending the regime's political monopoly, as opposition groups and figures equipped with novel methods and technologies will acquire greater capabilities to challenge and delegitimize CCP rule. Finally, the probability of splits in Party ranks will rise as the CCP's fortunes fall and the choices confronting it become harder. Ironically, those at the top of the Party's hierarchy may prove the least firmly bound to it, whether by ideological commitment or political loyalty. As regime decay sets in and "crises of order" begin to increase in frequency and severity, top players within the party-state itself will be tempted to exploit the opportunities thereby presented for boosting their own power and advantages. Open factionalism will not be far behind. Splits within the rulers' highest inner councils, we should recall, are typically a prime condition for democratic transition.

NOTES

1. For representative works on the theme of resilient authoritarianism, see Olga Kryshtanovskaya and Stephen White, "The Sovietization of Russian Politics," *Post-Soviet Affairs* 25 (October 2009): 283–309; Andrew Nathan, "China's Changing of the Guard: Authoritarian Resilience," *Journal of Democracy* 14 (January 2003): 6–17; Marsha Pripstein Posusney, "Enduring Authoritarianism: Middle East Lessons for Contemporary Theory," *Comparative Politics* 36 (January 2004): 127–38; Eva Bellin, "The Robustness of Authoritarianism in the Middle East: Exceptionalism in Comparative Perspective," *Comparative Politics* 36 (January 2004): 139–57; Jason Brownlee, "Low Tide after the Third Wave: Exploring Politics under Authoritarianism," *Comparative Politics* 34 (July 2002): 177–98; Bruce Bueno de Mesquita and Alastair Smith, "Political Survival and Endogenous Institutional Change," *Comparative Political Studies* 42 (February 2009): 167–97.

2. Chappell Lawson, "Mexico's Unfinished Transition: Democratization and Authoritarian Enclaves in Mexico," *Mexican Studies* 16 (Summer 2000): 267–87.

3. Bruce Bueno de Mesquita and George W. Downs, "Development and Democracy," *Foreign Affairs* 84 (September–October 2005): 77–86.

4. See Bellin, "Robustness of Authoritarianism in the Middle East"; and Louay Abdul-baki, "Democracy and the Re-Consolidation of Authoritarian Rule in Egypt," *Contemporary Arab Affairs* 1 (July 2008): 445–63.

5. Nathan, "Authoritarian Resilience."

6. Steve Tsang, "Consultative Leninism: China's New Political Framework," *Journal of Contemporary China* 18 (November 2009): 865–80.

7. David Shambaugh, *China's Communist Party: Atrophy and Adaptation* (Berkeley: University of California Press, 2008).

8. Dali Yang, *Remaking the Chinese Leviathan: Market Transition and the Politics of Governance in China* (Stanford: Stanford University Press, 2004).

9. See Steven Levitsky and Lucan A. Way, "Elections Without Democracy: The Rise of Competitive Authoritarianism," *Journal of Democracy* 13 (April 2002): 51–65.

10. Adam Przeworski et al., *Democracy and Development: Political Institutions and Well-Being in the World, 1950–1990* (New York: Cambridge University Press, 2000).

11. Robert J. Barro, "Democracy and Growth," *Journal of Economic Growth* 1 (March 1996): 1–27.

12. Yongshun Cai, "Power Structure and Regime Resilience: Contentious Politics in China," *British Journal of Political Science* 38 (May 2008): 411–32.

13. See Murray Scot Tanner, "Chinese Government Responses to Rising Social Unrest," Testimony presented to the US-China Economic and Security Review Commission, 14 April 2005.

14. See Richard McGregor, *The Party: The Secret World of China's Communist Rulers* (New York: Harper, 2010).

15. Barry Naughton, "China's Economic Policy Today: The New State Activism," *Eurasian Geography and Economics* 52 (May–June 2011): 313–29.

16. Bill Francis, Iftekhar Hasan, and Xian Sun, "Political Connections and the Process of Going Public: Evidence from China," *Journal of International Money and Finance* 28 (June 2009): 696–719.

17. Cheng Li, "The Chinese Communist Party: Recruiting and Controlling the New Elites," *Journal of Current Chinese Affairs*, Vol. 38, No. 3 (2009): 13–33.

18. Jie Chen and Bruce J. Dickson, *Allies of the State: China's Private Entrepreneurs and Democratic Change* (Cambridge, MA: Harvard University Press, 2010).

19. Bjorn Alpermann, "'Wrapped up in Cotton Wool': Political Integration of Private Entrepreneurs in Rural China," *China Journal*, No. 56 (July 2006): 33–61.

20. Xinhua News Agency, June 28, 2010.

21. The practice of paying bribes for appointments and promotions is widespread in China. See Yan Sun, "Cadre Recruitment and Corruption: What Goes Wrong?" *Crime, Law and Social Change* 49 (January 2008): 61–79; Jiangnan Zhu, "Why Are Offices for Sale in China? A Case Study of the Office-Selling Chain in Heilongjiang Province," *Asian Survey* 48 (July–August 2008): 558–79.

22. Andrew Wedeman, "Anti-Corruption Campaigns and the Intensification of Corruption in China," *Journal of Contemporary China* 14 (February 2005): 93–116.

23. For a survey of the consequences of corruption in China, see Yan Sun, *Corruption and Market in Contemporary China* (Ithaca: Cornell University Press, 2004).

24. *Statistical Yearbook of China* (Beijing: Zhongguo tongji nianjian chubanshe, 2010), 756–57.

25. Xinhua News Agency, June 28, 2010.

26. For a study of the privileges enjoyed by CCP members, see Bruce J. Dickson and Maria Rost Rublee, "Membership Has Its Privileges: The Socioeconomic Characteristics of Communist Party Members in Urban China," *Comparative Political Studies* 33 (February 2000): 87–112.

27. A 2009 online survey of 21,057 new college graduates found that only half had found jobs. In 2007 and 2008, the percentage was 56 and 52 percent respectively; see http://edu.QQ.com, July 30, 2009.

No "Jasmine" for China[*]

Bruce J. Dickson

China's leaders seem nervous. Despite presiding over a rapidly growing economy and an ever-increasing presence in international affairs, they remain wary of the potential of a popular upsurge that would threaten their hold on power. For this reason, they crack down hard on real or perceived efforts to promote popular protests. While their actions can seem heavy-handed and exaggerated to outside observers, the consistency of their responses to signs of protest indicates that they remain insecure about the stability of the regime.

Most recently, they responded to the "Jasmine Revolution" in Tunisia and the uprising in Egypt earlier this year by blocking news of the unfolding events and temporarily censoring Internet searches—including for the word jasmine, even though jasmine is a popular variety of tea in China and the topic of a well-known traditional song.

At one point, Internet censors reportedly blocked emails with the word "tomorrow" on Saturdays and "today" on Sundays so that netizens could not find information about planned protests. While this may have complicated plans to organize demonstrations, it also wreaked havoc on delivery services and other activities that use these very common words. (These restrictions were eventually lifted as weeks passed without incident.) Meanwhile, though the political atmosphere in China has been tight for several years, in the aftermath of the Arab Spring the Chinese Communist Party (CCP) expanded the reach of repression to a wider assortment of activists, bloggers, lawyers, and even artists.

Several explanations have been offered for this year's crackdowns. First, the regime fears a "color revolution" in China. After seeing the ouster of authoritarian leaders in Georgia's Rose Revolution, Ukraine's Orange Revolution, and now the revolutions in Tunisia and Egypt, China's leaders recognize their vulnerability to mass protest. Although the possibility that the Jasmine Revolution will snowball from Northern Africa and the Middle East seems farfetched, they are extremely risk-averse when it comes to the survival of their regime. This is why they are so often hypersensitive to real or potential regime threats, and to international

[*] This article was first published in *Current History*, Vol. 110, No. 737 (September 2011).

criticism of what they deem to be internal affairs.

A second explanation concerns timing: China's leaders are tightening up their country's political space in anticipation of a planned leadership succession in 2012. They wish to preempt demands for more wide-ranging political change when they are pre-occupied with internal bargaining over which leaders will be promoted to which positions. However, the political tightening did not begin in the spring of 2011, but several years earlier. Political pressure was ratcheted up in anticipation of the 2008 Olympics and after an uprising in Tibet in March 2008, the online publication of the pro-democracy Charter '08 in December 2008, and protests in Xinjiang in July 2009. The more recent repression is a continuation of those earlier episodes.

Some observers claim the political closing began even earlier. Despite hopes that President Hu Jintao would initiate ambitious political reforms, the Party has actually pulled back from both economic and political liberalization since he became CCP general secretary in 2002. Leadership succession alone, then, is not a sufficient explanation for the party-state's response to the Jasmine Revolution.

A third explanation concerns bureaucratic politics. The response to the Arab Spring was not a consensus decision by a unified elite but an effort by security forces to strengthen their political clout. If they can claim they have prevented an existential threat to the regime, they can justify the growth of their budgets in recent years and seek additional resources. (According to China's finance ministry, the budget for internal security increased by 15.6 percent in 2010 and 13.8 percent in 2011. The officially announced budget for internal security now exceeds that for national defense.) This explanation was prevalent within China: The crackdown was not the action of a monolithic Party but a cynical attempt by one part of the regime to increase its influence.

These are not mutually exclusive explanations. The CCP clearly wants to avoid wide-scale protests that would destabilize the country and threaten its hold on power, and may feel particularly vulnerable with the upcoming succession. Security forces can point to the potential of a color revolution as a justification for their actions. For their part, CCP leaders may be unwilling to rein in the security forces, recognizing they are an important constituency within the political system and that their loyalty will be particularly necessary during the leadership transition. Each of these explanations captures an important aspect of the current political context in China.

But why were CCP leaders so concerned that the Jasmine Revolution might snowball from Northern Africa and the Middle East, or why were security services able to frame their actions as a response to those foreign events? After all, the underlying conditions are remarkably different. The economies of Tunisia and Egypt have been stagnant for years; most wealth in those countries is concentrated in the hands of the ruling families and their cronies, and much of the rest of the population has seen few opportunities.

In contrast, China's economic growth has averaged 10 percent per year for over a decade, and most Chinese feel the benefits of that growth. The vast majority of Chinese say that their incomes have been rising, and that they are even more optimistic about their future prosperity. That combination—recent progress and future optimism—is not normally a context for social revolution.

The leadership dynamics are also quite different. Tunisia's Zine el-Abidine Ben Ali had been president for 23 years before fleeing his country in January 2011. Egypt's Hosni Mubarak had been in power for almost 30 years and was about to be reelected president in elections scheduled for the fall of 2011 before he was forced to resign in February. In contrast, China's leaders now face term limits and mandatory retirement ages. They are about to undergo a long-planned and wide-ranging change of party and government leaders in 2012–2013.

In fact, the upcoming succession will be a key test of whether China's term and age limits are norms that can be relaxed when they are not convenient, or institutionalized rules of elite politics that prevent individual leaders from remaining in office indefinitely. This routinized process for replacing ruling elites is a remarkably rare practice among authoritarian regimes, and sharply distinguishes China from Egypt and Tunisia.

Sources of Legitimacy

Although China's leaders do not face election or reelection by the public at large, and are therefore not legitimized by the consent of the governed, that does not mean that they do not enjoy popular support. Every public opinion poll has found high levels of support for the status quo, especially for the central party and government institutions.

There are often strong complaints about specific policy issues and local leaders, but most Chinese recognize how extensive economic reforms and more limited political reforms have provided them with tangible material benefits. Because most people benefit from the regime's policies, and because there is no guarantee that they would maintain those benefits under an alternative regime, they tend to support the continuation of the status quo, at least for the near term. As Teresa Wright has written, most Chinese accept authoritarianism because it is in their material interests to do so.

Regime legitimacy in China is not based on the consent of the governed, nor on the Weberian ideal types of traditional, charismatic, or legal-rational authority. Instead, to the extent that the Chinese public regards the current regime as legitimate, it is primarily on the basis of performance legitimacy—specifically with regard to modernization, nationalism, and political stability.

Without question, economic growth is the primary—but by no means the only—source of popular support for the regime in China. Sustained double-digit rates of growth not only have brought rising living standards to China; they also have made its economy the second largest in the world, having surpassed Japan in 2010. Even though economic wealth is not as impressive in per capita terms—China ranked 94th in per capita GDP in 2010, according to the International Monetary Fund—the aggregate size of the economy has fostered self-respect at home and both envy and concern among many countries in the world.

This remarkable record of growth has also produced tremendous national pride in the country's accomplishments. Chinese nationalism is a curious mix of patriotic pride in the recent past and bitter memories of more distant interactions with the international community. China's history in the decades after the Opium Wars of the 19th century is often described as the "century of humiliation," a period when the Chinese government was too weak to defend the country against economic and military pressures. China's newfound role in global affairs, best symbolized by the hosting of the 2008 Summer Olympics, is seen by many as a vindication of the CCP's policies of economic reform and opening and the return of China to its rightful place in the world.

Another element in the CCP's popular support is the need to preserve political stability, seen as a necessary precondition for continued economic growth. Fear of chaos and instability is a distinctive aspect of traditional Chinese political culture, and remains a cause of concern today. In 2010, there were an estimated 180,000 popular protests, up from 87,000 in 2005. The greater frequency in protests led to the sharp increases in spending on internal security in recent years.

These protests are often a direct consequence of the economic growth policies of local governments: land seizures for industrial and commercial redevelopment without adequate compensation, unregulated pollution, corrupt deals between officials and businessmen, and not-in-my-backyard disputes over the placement of new construction and transportation projects. But the protests are primarily about material issues and isolated to specific locales. They have not engendered sustained social movements, multi-regional mobilization, calls for fundamental political change, or—with rare exceptions—demands for the replacement of incumbent officials. In each of these ways, political protests in China are a far cry from those that created the Arab Spring.

In T. H. Rigby's classic formulation, the CCP has become part of the "normal order of things" for most Chinese. Although complaints are raised about specific policy issues, the regime and its accomplishments enjoy general support.

Critics and Democrats

This is not to say that government critics or supporters of democratization do not exist in China. They certainly do, and they often pay a high price for their activism. In recent years, the repressive hand of the state has been used more often and more severely against those who challenge the regime or sympathize with those who do.

But the regime's repression is selective: It targets the CCP's critics but does not envelop the public at large. The regime had a typically over-the-top reaction to the awarding of the Nobel Peace Prize to the political activist Liu Xiaobo in 2010, but many in China were unaware of him, and many who did know of him did not share his democratic goals. One of the challenges confronting activists in China today is that they face both state repression and societal indifference.

Exceptions to the selective use of repression concern the dissemination of ideas and the maintenance of national unity. On the Internet, state censorship can frustrate even the most patriotic of citizens. The CCP cannot completely shut the country off from the worldwide web, even though it occasionally indicates it would like to. The nation's economy is so integrated with the international market and so dependent on access to buyers and suppliers that gaps must exist in the "great firewall of China." But Chinese netizens, activists and gamers alike, are plagued by slow connections, the scrutiny of messages, and the removal of even tongue-in-cheek comments that tweak but do not oppose the regime.

In minority regions, the state also relies on broad-gauged repression when violent protests arise. A fatal traffic accident in Inner Mongolia in May 2011, for example, led to a crackdown that followed the pattern set by uprisings in Tibet in 2008 and Xinjiang in 2009: Internet access was cut off, Mongolian websites were shut down, and a wide range of adults were taken into custody even though they had not participated in protests.

Even those who do favor political reform are often patient about the timing of such change. In casual conversations, one often hears an implicit endorsement of modernization theory. Many Chinese say that they hope for democracy in the future, but that the country is too poor (in per capita terms), too traditional, and above all too rural for democracy at present. The willingness to wait indefinitely for these conditions to change is yet another factor in public support for the status quo, and another reason to question the regime's worried response to the Jasmine Revolution abroad.

The greater irony is that many in China feel their country is already democratic, though with different definitions of democracy. Many Chinese define democracy not in terms of political rights, institutions, and procedures, but as a government that works on behalf of the people and offers freedom and equality. Although China remains in many ways a closed political system, significant liberalization has occurred during the more than 30 years of economic opening and reform.

Those who remember the Maoist era in particular recognize how different the political system is today. The Chinese people still lack a say in who their leaders are, and cannot adequately defend themselves against an occasionally oppressive state. But they also experience less state intrusions now into their daily lives. And opportunities for social mobility, access to information, travel, and other daily activities are much broader than before, even if they fall short of what is taken for granted by those who live under democratic governments.

These trends in China are in sharp contrast to the conventional wisdom that the middle class is the natural source of support for democratization. This truism is the basis for numerous scholarly studies on the growth of the middle class in China and its potential political impact. So far, there is little evidence that the political values of the middle class are significantly different from those of the rest of society, or in particular that it favors Western-style liberal democracy.

In fact, the CCP has been actively promoting the expansion of the middle class by dramatically increasing college enrollments, occupational mobility, and the level of domestic consumption. To the extent that middle class Chinese are able to enjoy the perks of prosperity, they credit the CCP's reform and opening policies.

In the future, a growing middle class may develop rising expectations and seek greater representation. That is why scholars and journalists watch the middle class with great interest, but there is little evidence of this sort at present. The CCP is promoting the interests of Chinese in the middle class in order to maintain their support for, or at least acceptance of, the status quo. So far, the strategy is working.

Local Legitimacy Deficit

If public opinion surveys reveal remarkably high levels of popular support for the status quo, they also indicate a local legitimacy deficit. Most Chinese express high levels of support and even trust in central-level institutions and leaders, but are much less supportive of their local governments. While high-level officials give lofty statements about policy goals—fighting corruption, cleaning up the environment, narrowing the gap between rich and poor, providing much needed public goods such as affordable housing and health care, and so forth—ordinary Chinese often do not see the achievement of these goals where they live.

Scholars have debated the reasons for this gap between rhetoric and reality. One explanation is that the center is committed to better governance and public goods provision, but its intentions are undermined and blocked by local officials. An alternative explanation is that the center provides the rhetoric but not the resources necessary to achieve success; local officials are left with unfunded mandates that they cannot meet, and therefore take the blame.

Regardless of which explanation is correct, the result is the same: Public support for the center remains high, and the public is more critical of local officials. For example, according to a nationwide survey of almost 3,900 urban Chinese that I conducted in the fall of 2010, the public's trust in individual officials declines steadily as they move down the political ladder: 75.5 percent say they trust central-level officials, 66.4 percent trust

provincial officials, 58.7 percent trust city and county officials, and only 47.7 percent trust civil servants. The more familiar they are with different types of officials, the less they trust them.

Since 2004, the CCP has made improvements in the quality of governance and the provision of public goods a top priority. The intention is to enhance local stability as a precondition for economic growth and to preempt demands for more expansive political reforms. The results to date have been decidedly mixed. Survey respondents were asked about key policy areas such as housing, transportation, job creation, poverty alleviation, medical care, care for the elderly, and other issues. Across the board, respondents said there had been no demonstrable change in any of these policy areas, and evaluated the policy performance of local governments as mediocre.

Corruption has accompanied rapid economic development, and many believe it is now endemic to the political system. In the same nationwide survey, respondents were roughly equally divided on whether corruption in recent years had gotten better (35.5 percent), gotten worse (32.2 percent), or stayed the same (32.3 percent). In addition, they viewed corruption as primarily a local issue: 77.2 percent said corruption was at least somewhat common among local officials, but only 49.4 percent said the same for central-level officials.

This is a consequence of the government's treatment of corruption. The state-run media give extensive coverage to cases of corruption, but most target local officials, at the county level and below. Higher-level officials, especially Politburo members and their families are shielded from scrutiny. State Council ministers are occasionally charged with corruption (as was the minister of railways in February 2011), but these cases are rare.

As portrayed by the media and perceived by many Chinese, corruption is a plague that afflicts local officials far more commonly that central leaders. The more people believe corruption is a severe problem, the less likely they are to support their local governments; however, perceptions of corruption do not have a significant influence on support for the center.

Meanwhile, the CCP is trying to be more consultative and responsive in the policy making process. Chinese citizens have been encouraged to offer opinions on new policy initiatives, such as a Labor Law in 2006 and a new national health care system in 2008. At the local level, some governments consult extensively with their communities on policy and budget priorities. These are often successful tactics, and allow the state to respond to public opinion before policies are implemented.

Other attempts at state-society interaction have been less successful. For many years, the state has encouraged citizens to use formal legal channels to address their grievances and appeal decisions by local officials. At the same time, the center has instructed local officials to restrict appeals—by force if necessary, sending police to Beijing and provincial capitals to seize petitioners and take them home.

As scholars such as Mary Gallagher, Lianjiang Li, and Yu Jianrong have shown, people who use official channels only to have their complaints ignored become disillusioned and cynical about the regime. By publicly encouraging people to use these channels, but simultaneously instructing localities to restrict access to them, the center is pursuing a shortsighted and counterproductive course of action.

The Surprise of Change

We are much better at explaining political change after it happens than predicting where and when it will occur. A stable situation can turn unstable very quickly, often for unexpected and idiosyncratic reasons. The Jasmine Revolution began after a Tunisian street vendor was slapped by a female police officer. After failing to get redress from the local government, he set himself on fire and died several weeks later. He was an unlikely martyr, but became the symbol of a movement that toppled the government in his country and spread throughout the region.

Similarly, few people expected political protests to erupt in China in the spring of 1989. Yet the death of Hu Yaobang, a former general secretary of the CCP who lost the support of Chinese leader Deng Xiaoping and consequently his political post in 1987, triggered a nationwide movement that lasted for weeks and nearly brought down the CCP.

Regimes can survive even when change seems imminent. After the protests in 1989, the former US ambassador to China Winston Lord predicted that the survival of the CCP would be measured in days or weeks, not months or years. In fact, it has survived for more than two decades after his prediction. Many others have also predicted the collapse of the CCP, and yet it remains the ruling party in China. These inaccurate assertions reflect the inherent difficulty in making predictions, but also a tendency among China watchers to underestimate the CCP's ability to adapt itself to the changing social and political environment in China, an environment its policies have created.

With this in mind, CCP leaders may not be wrong to be nervous about the stability of Chinese society, and therefore the security of their hold on power. Popular protests have been on the rise for years, and although they are generally focused on specific issues in specific localities, they could crystallize into a broader movement that deals not just with policy failures but with the propriety of the policies themselves and the legitimacy of the leaders who decide them.

The lessons of the Arab Spring are that small, isolated events can explode into nationwide protests if not handled quickly and firmly, and that splits within a leadership—especially between the civilian leaders and the military—can doom the regime; these lessons are certainly not lost on CCP leaders. The support of the People's Liberation Army was essential for the survival of the CCP in 1989; the loss of support of the Egyptian military was the tipping point in Mubarak's fall from power.

At the same time, Chinese society may not be wrong for not being inspired by the Jasmine Revolution. The underlying conditions are quite different in China, with growing prosperity for most people and great optimism about the future, in stark contrast to the stagnation and desperation that fueled the Arab Spring. The turmoil that has engulfed some Arab countries and the uncertainty that followed the fall of governments in Tunisia and Egypt offer a cautionary tale (a theme self-servingly promoted in China's official media). Among other things, they are a reminder that the alternative to an authoritarian regime is not necessarily a stable democracy, at least not immediately. The hopes and dreams of people who fill the streets are not always honored by the political elites who emerge after the revolution.

Growing prosperity, optimism, patience for political change—this is not a recipe for revolution. On the contrary, public attitudes may provide a cushion for China's next generation of leaders who will be selected in the fall of 2012. Although these new leaders will face a host of challenging domestic and international issues that need immediate attention, they likely will not face a mobilized society demanding political change. For every activist who wants democracy now, there are many others who are willing to wait and see.

ECONOMIC DEVELOPMENT

Editorial Introduction

There is no aspect of China's rise that has been more spectacular than its economic growth. Never before in world history has any nation developed as quickly or as greatly as has China since the late 1970s when the Chinese government initiated its "reform and opening" (改革与开放) policies. From 1978 through 2012 China's GDP increased more than tenfold to $13.4 trillion, which accounted for 15.4 percent of global GDP in 2013 (in purchasing power parity, PPP, terms). Its growth rate during this period averaged an astounding 8.4 percent, nearly three times the global average. The Chinese economy ranks as the second largest in the world on aggregate—and various estimates indicate that China will surpass the United States sometime between 2020 and 2030 to be the largest aggregate economy in the world. In purchasing power parity (PPP) terms, the International Monetary Fund indicated that China already surpassed the United States in 2014. Foreign direct investment into China, which has been a key element of China's manufacturing revolution, has averaged around $100 billion per year during the same period. Meanwhile, China's foreign exchange reserves (including gold) ballooned to $3.8 trillion by the end of 2013—the largest in the world by a considerable margin (Japan ranks second with $1.2 trillion). Trade has been another driving source of China's dramatic growth—giving the country the moniker "workshop of the world." China's $2.21 trillion in exports (2013) ranks it first worldwide.

There are many other quantitative indicators that demonstrate China's economic prowess and importance to the global economy. These indicators are captured well in the first selection in this section—an overview of key statistics provided in the US Government's Central Intelligence Agency's annual *The World Factbook* (2014 edition).

The second selection is authored by one of the world's leading specialists on the Chinese economy, Professor Barry Naughton of the University of California–San Diego. Writing in 2010, the year after the global financial crisis, Naughton's analysis was prescient. He saw the need for China's economy to transition from what he describes as a "high growth to high quality" model. That is, China needed to move up the value chain and shift from basically a low-end manufacturing economy to a higher-end technology and knowledge economy. This requires a recalibration of domestic investment away from hard infrastructure to soft innovation. Consumer consumption also needs to be increased. The Chinese government itself recognizes these (and many other) needed transitions and codified them in the 18th Central Committee Third Plenary Session (2013) *Decision on Deepening of Reforms.* Naughton's analysis builds off of these goals and assesses the opportunities and constraints on China achieving this macroeconomic reorientation.

The next selection, another excerpt from former CCP General Secretary Hu Jintao's speech to the 18th Party Congress in 2012, illustrates how the Chinese government itself views its economic challenges. It speaks specifically about building an innovative society and economy, a modern service industry, boosting domestic demand and consumption, training a higher-quality workforce, developing capital markets and the financial services sector, investing in strategic industries, and further opening the economy to the outside world. Hu also speaks of the need for various structural reforms in the economic system so as to lessen the role of the state while increasing the role of the market. All in all, Hu lays out an ambitious "wish list" for qualitatively adjusting the Chinese economy.

The next selection concerns the provision of "public goods" to Chinese society. Written in 2002 by leading China scholar Minxin Pei, this article identifies a "governance crisis" that would come to characterize China over the following decade. Pei's piece speaks to the growing inequalities that emerged in Chinese society after the go-go 1990s economic boom. But he sees the problems as affecting more than society at large—Pei argues that they are symptomatic of corrosive elements in the party state system. Perhaps presciently, he argues that the endgame of the Chinese communist regime may be underway. More than a decade later, the regime had not collapsed—but many of the factors Pei identified had become even more pronounced.

By contrast, the next selection is much more optimistic and upbeat about China's economic future. Written by Justin Yifu Lin, this selection was a speech that he gave to the US Federal Reserve Bank of San Francisco in 2009. Lin, a Taiwan-born scholar who escaped and defected from Taiwan to the Chinese mainland and then was trained as an economist at the University of Chicago before returning to China and the Peking University faculty, had become Chief Economist at the World Bank (the first Chinese to be appointed to this prestigious position). Lin's contribution particularly focuses on China's role in the global economy. While Lin sees many fragilities and uncertainties in the global economy, he identifies few in China's economy. While acknowledging some "structural imbalances," he is very optimistic about China's future growth potential and therefore its contribution to global growth.

The final selection in this section by David Shambaugh (this volume's editor) examines a recent and newer feature of China's economic development—its rapidly expanding international investment (Outbound Direct Investment or ODI), which reached $120 billion in 2014, and the growing presence of China's multinational corporations on the global corporate landscape. By 2014, 89 Chinese corporations made the *Global Fortune 500* rankings. This impressive number is second only to American corporations (with 128). While this article was originally written in 2012 and is based on 2010 data, it still offers a good glimpse into China's companies. And what does one find? In brief, Chinese companies exhibit a number of weaknesses. They do not really operate globally—only a handful of the companies in the *Fortune* rankings earn the majority of their revenue outside of China. They are really primarily domestic corporations. And they are largely state-owned enterprises (SOEs).

They lack competitiveness in the global marketplace because of a number of inherent weaknesses: human resources, politicization, rigid management practices, an insular corporate culture, lack of transparency and accountability, corruption, and other characteristics. They do not understand well foreign legal and investment regulations, and have very poor brand presence abroad. Many of their mergers and acquisitions (M&As) have been failures. Thus, while China's corporations have been instructed by the government to "go out" (走出去) into the world, most have struggled in doing so to date. This will likely change over time, but thus far Chinese multinationals have not fared very well in the hyper-competitive globalized marketplace.

Taken together, the selections in this section offer a variety of important insights into the state of the Chinese economy and its role in the world.

I. BUILDING AN ECONOMIC SUPERPOWER

China: Economy—Overview[*]

Central Intelligence Agency

Since the late 1970s China has moved from a closed, centrally planned system to a more market-oriented one that plays a major global role—in 2010 China became the world's largest exporter. Reforms began with the phasing out of collectivized agriculture, and expanded to include the gradual liberalization of prices, fiscal decentralization, increased autonomy for state enterprises, growth of the private sector, development of stock markets and a modern banking system, and opening to foreign trade and investment. China has implemented reforms in a gradualist fashion. In recent years, China has renewed its support for state-owned enterprises in sectors considered important to "economic security," explicitly looking to foster globally competitive industries. After keeping its currency tightly linked to the US dollar for years, in July 2005 China moved to an exchange rate system that references a basket of currencies. From mid-2005 to late 2008 cumulative appreciation of the *renminbi* against the US dollar was more than 20%, but the exchange rate remained virtually pegged to the dollar from the onset of the global financial crisis until June 2010, when Beijing allowed resumption of a gradual appreciation and expanded the daily trading band within which the RMB is permitted to fluctuate.

The restructuring of the economy and resulting efficiency gains have contributed to a more than tenfold increase in GDP since 1978. Measured on a purchasing power parity (PPP) basis that adjusts for price differences, China in 2013 stood as the second-largest economy in the world after the US, having surpassed Japan in 2010. The dollar values of China's agricultural and industrial output each exceed those of the US; China is second to the US in the value of services it produces. Still, per capita income is below the world average. The Chinese government faces numerous economic challenges, including: (a) reducing its high domestic savings rate and correspondingly low domestic consumption; (b) facilitating higher-wage job opportunities for the aspiring middle class, including rural migrants and increasing numbers of college graduates; (c) reducing corruption and other economic crimes; and (d) containing environmental damage and social strife related to the economy's rapid transformation.

Economic development has progressed further in coastal provinces than in the interior, and by 2011 more than 250 million migrant workers

[*] This assessment and data appeared in the Central Intelligence Agency, *The World Factbook* (2014), https://www.cia.gov/library/publications/the-world-factbook.

and their dependents had relocated to urban areas to find work. One consequence of population control policy is that China is now one of the most rapidly aging countries in the world. Deterioration in the environment—notably air pollution, soil erosion, and the steady fall of the water table, especially in the North—is another long-term problem. China continues to lose arable land because of erosion and economic development. The Chinese government is seeking to add energy production capacity from sources other than coal and oil, focusing on nuclear and alternative energy development.

Several factors are converging to slow China's growth, including debt overhang from its credit-fueled stimulus program, industrial overcapacity, inefficient allocation of capital by state-owned banks, and the slow recovery of China's trading partners. The government's 12th Five-Year Plan, adopted in March 2011 and reiterated at the Communist Party's "Third Plenum" meeting in November 2013, emphasizes continued economic reforms and the need to increase domestic consumption in order to make the economy less dependent in the future on fixed investments, exports, and heavy industry. However, China has made only marginal progress toward these rebalancing goals. The new government of President Xi Jinping has signaled a greater willingness to undertake reforms that focus on China's long-term economic health, including giving the market a more decisive role in allocating resources.

Economic Indicators

- GDP (purchasing power parity): $13.39 trillion (2013 est.); $12.43 trillion (2012 est.); $11.54 trillion (2011 est.).
- GDP (official exchange rate): $9.33 trillion [Note: because China's exchange rate is determined by fiat, rather than by market forces, the official exchange rate measure of GDP is not an accurate measure of China's output; GDP at the official exchange rate substantially understates the actual level of China's output vis-à-vis the rest of the world; in China's situation, GDP at purchasing power parity provides the best measure for comparing output across countries (2013 est.)].

- GDP—real growth rate: 7.7% (2013 est.); 7.7% (2012 est.); 9.3% (2011 est.).
- GDP—per capita (PPP): $9,800 (2013 est.); $9,100 (2012 est.); $8,300 (2011 est.).
- Gross national saving: 50% of GDP (2013 est.); 51.2% of GDP (2012 est.); 50.1% of GDP (2011 est.).
- GDP—composition, by end use: household consumption: 36.3%; government consumption: 13.7%; investment in fixed capital: 46%; investment in inventories: 1.2%; exports of goods and services: 25.1%; imports of goods and services: 22.2% (2013 est.).
- GDP—composition, by sector of origin: agriculture: 10%; industry: 43.9%; services: 46.1% (2013 est.).
- Agriculture—products: world leader in gross value of agricultural output; rice, wheat, potatoes, corn, peanuts, tea, millet, barley, apples, cotton, oilseed, pork; fish.
- Industries: world leader in gross value of industrial output; mining and ore processing, iron, steel, aluminum, and other metals, coal; machine building; armaments; textiles and apparel; petroleum; cement; chemicals; fertilizers; consumer products (including footwear, toys, and electronics); food processing; transportation equipment, including automobiles, rail cars and locomotives, ships, aircraft; telecommunications equipment, commercial space launch vehicles, satellites.
- Industrial production growth rate: 7.6% (2013 est.).
- Labor force: 797.6 million [Note: by the end of 2012, China's population at working age (15–64 years) was 1.0040 billion (2013 est.)].
- Labor force—by occupation: agriculture: 33.6%; industry: 30.3%; services: 36.1% (2012 est.).
- Unemployment rate: 4.1% (2013 est.); 4.1% (2012 est.) [Note: data are for registered urban unemployment, which excludes private enterprises and migrants].
- Population below poverty line: 6.1% (2013) [Note: in 2011, China set a new poverty line at RMB 2300 (approximately US $3,630)].
- Household income or consumption by percentage share: lowest 10%: 1.7%; highest 10%: 30% [Note: data are for urban households only (2009)].
- Distribution of family income—Gini index: .473 (2013); .474 (2012).
- Budget: revenues: $2.118 trillion; expenditures: $2.292 trillion (2013 est.).

- Taxes and other revenues: 19.4% of GDP (2013 est.).
- Budget surplus (+) or deficit (−): −2.1% of GDP (2013 est.).
- Public debt: 22.4% of GDP (2013 est.); 26.1% of GDP (2012) [Note: Official data; data cover both central government debt and local government debt, which China's National Audit Office estimated at RMB 10.72 trillion (approximately US$1.66 trillion) in 2011; data exclude policy bank bonds, Ministry of Railway debt, China Asset Management Company debt, and non-performing loans].
- Fiscal year: calendar year.
- Inflation rate (consumer prices): 2.6% (2013 est.); 2.6% (2012 est.).
- Central bank discount rate: 2.25% (December 31, 2013 est.); 2.25% (December 31, 2012 est.).
- Commercial bank prime lending rate: 5.73% (December 31, 2013 est.); 6% (December 31, 2012 est.).
- Stock of narrow money: $5.532 trillion (December 31, 2013 est.); $4.911 trillion (31 December 2012 est.).
- Stock of broad money: $18.15 trillion (31 December 2013 est.); $15.5 trillion (December 31, 2012 est.).
- Stock of domestic credit: $11.79 trillion (December 31, 2013 est.); $10.02 trillion (December 31, 2012 est.).
- Market value of publicly traded shares: $6.499 trillion (December 31, 2013 est.); $5.753 trillion (December 31, 2012); $3.389 trillion (December 31, 2011 est.).

- Current account balance: $182.8 billion (2013 est.); $215.4 billion (2012 est.).
- Exports: $2.21 trillion (2013 est.); $2.049 trillion (2012 est.). Exports—commodities: electrical and other machinery, including data processing equipment, apparel, radio telephone handsets, textiles, integrated circuits. Exports—partners: Hong Kong 17.4%, US 16.7%, Japan 6.8%, South Korea 4.1% (2013 est.).
- Imports: $1.95 trillion (2013 est.); $1.818 trillion (2012 est.). Imports—commodities: electrical and other machinery, oil and mineral fuels; nuclear reactor, boiler, and machinery components; optical and medical equipment, metal ores, motor vehicles; soybeans. Imports—partners: South Korea 9.4%, Japan 8.3%, Taiwan 8%, United States 7.8%, Australia 5%, Germany 4.8% (2013 est.).
- Reserves of foreign exchange and gold: $3.821 trillion (December 31, 2013 est.); $3.388 trillion (December 31, 2012 est.).
- Debt—external: $863.2 billion (December 31, 2013 est.); $737 billion (December 31, 2012 est.).
- Stock of direct foreign investment—at home: $1.344 trillion (December 31, 2012 est.); $1.232 trillion (December 31, 2011 est.). Stock of direct foreign investment—abroad: $541 billion (December 31, 2013 est.); $531.9 billion (December 31, 2012 est.).
- Exchange rates: *Renminbi yuan* (RMB) per US dollar—6.2 (2013 est.); 6.3123 (2012 est.); 6.7703 (2010 est.); 6.8314 (2009); 6.9385 (2008).

ECONOMIC GROWTH FROM HIGH-SPEED TO HIGH-QUALITY

Barry J. Naughton

China has grown faster and longer than any other economy in history.[*] China is thus unique, yet in its broad outlines, the Chinese growth experience also resembles other successful developing

countries and, in particular, recapitulates earlier East Asian growth miracles. Developing countries can grow very rapidly for twenty or more years, but eventually growth must slow. Growth slows down, in the first place, for structural reasons: the transformation from a traditional rural economy to a mostly modern urban economy is completed when the vast majority of agricultural

---

[*] This selection first appeared in Joseph Fewsmith (ed.) *China Today, China Tomorrow: Domestic Politics, Economy, and Society* (Lanham, MD: Rowman & Littlefield, 2010).

workers have transitioned into nonagricultural work. After this turning point, growth must slow and growth strategy must adapt to new conditions. In fact, there is no precise turning point, because in most countries growth strategy is already being adapted before this structural turning point. Policy starts to be driven by new imperatives, such as upgrading of labor skills and improvement of the natural and built environment. Moreover, policymaking around the time of the turning point usually takes place with a sharp increase in public participation, and sometimes even coincides with full-blown democratization. Third, and finally, these changes take place amidst rapidly changing external conditions that are often perceived as crises. Growth and policy both adapt to these sharp changes in external conditions. It is hard to disentangle all these effects: the transition from high-speed growth to moderate growth is hardly ever smooth.

China today seems to be hurdling into just such a turning point. Growth has been consistently fast for thirty years, but then accelerated to "superfast" growth rates above 10 percent per year between mid-2003 and mid-2008. This five-year growth surge moved China toward the structural turning point much more quickly than most observers anticipated. Even Chinese policymakers were far from confident that growth at such a pace could be healthy or sustained. Since nearly the beginning of the five-year growth surge, Chinese policymakers have been talking about pursuing more "balanced" growth that is "higher quality" and more "friendly to the environment." However, this high-level talk has had little impact on the actual pattern of growth. By most measures, Chinese growth became *more* unbalanced throughout the five-year growth surge. Then, in the second half of 2008, the Chinese economy ran into a perfect storm: the US financial crisis caused a dramatic slowing of external demand just at the time when the domestic economic cycle was turning down. Faced with this challenge, Chinese policymakers moved decisively to reinstate the investment-driven growth that their system is particularly well suited to deliver (and which they understand so well). By the end of 2009, this policy had succeeded in stabilizing growth, and China was one of the first economies recovering from the global crisis.

As it emerges from the global financial crisis, China faces many immediate questions. Will China settle into a new growth trajectory with slower speeds and different characteristics? Will China's recovery be smooth, or must an additional crisis be overcome before the economy reaches a sustainable long-run growth path? While these questions are still open, China's long-run economic challenge is recognizably the same as what it was before the crisis. Having successfully powered through the developmental and systemic transitions at warp speed, China must now adapt to a new phase of growth. When the dust settles, we will see China making a shift from "quantity" (speed) to "quality," that is, to slower growth but with more than proportionate improvements in the quality of life.

How will China adapt to this potentially wrenching set of changes? In the following I address this question by first looking back on the experience of growth thus far. The first section examines the way that policymakers have subordinated nearly every consideration to the quest for economic growth, a quest that has been remarkably successful. The second section then looks at some of the most important concomitants of the "unbalanced" growth pattern that was followed. Quite obviously, rapid growth has had costs as well as benefits. I do not attempt a full analysis of the growth process, but confine myself to sketching some of the most important outcomes. The third section looks at the attempt of Chinese policymakers to move to a more balanced growth strategy, an attempt that today appears to have been too feeble to make much difference. I argue that the attempt at a radical recasting of Chinese growth strategy was probably doomed from the start, given China's institutional and economic environment. The fourth section looks at the impact of the economic crisis on China, while a fifth section looks to the future, and speculates about the coming transition to higher-quality economic growth.

Economic Growth Before Everything Else

For thirty years, the Chinese leadership has subordinated every other consideration to the quest for economic growth. The beginnings of economic reform were inseparable from the burgeoning disillusionment with Maoism's failure to bring adequate economic development. Subsequently, at a key crossroads of the economic reform process, in late 1991, Deng Xiaoping declared, "Development is the only hard truth," and brought two years of vacillation and backsliding in the reform process to an end. When competing objectives confront Chinese policymakers, they have almost invariably chosen to give priority to economic growth over whatever the other objective has been. This can be seen in virtually any policy arena examined, and most crucially in those core policy realms where choices are made that shape the overall development process. For example, China's foreign policy has been shaped by the desire to avoid overt confrontations with the dominant powers—in practice, the United States—and to maintain a positive environment for China's economic growth. Again, a dictum from Deng Xiaoping is crucial here: "Keep a low profile; never take the lead." Therefore, when we say that no nation has grown as fast as long as China, we should quickly add that no nation has more single-mindedly pursued policies designed to power an economy through the structural transformation required to reach "modernization." In order to make economic growth a reality, Chinese leaders subordinated nearly everything to the mobilization of resources for the growth process.

The relative priority given to growth is so consistent that it is often seen as simply reflecting Chinese "pragmatism," as if there were no implicit trade-offs involved. But in fact it is not so much that Chinese policymakers are pragmatic, as that it is virtually impossible to find a "revealed value" that competes with growth itself. A simple example that exemplifies the argument is China's overwhelming dependence on coal for energy (almost 70 percent of consumption, far higher than any other country). At first glance, this seems to be simply another case of Chinese pragmatism, since coal is abundant, cheap, and relatively widespread. But in fact China has never been able to mobilize sufficient technology and capital resources to allow state enterprises to produce enough coal, so in order to take advantage of coal's abundance, China has allowed entry into this sector by small-scale township and village enterprises and private firms. In 2005, for example, over 10 percent of output by value came from private firms, and over a third from other small-scale firms. This has been

a consistent part of China's development approach for the past thirty years.

Yet this simple outcome is possible only because Chinese policymakers are willing to override at least three potentially competing principles. First, China's mineral resources are owned by the national government, and we might expect the government to closely guard these valuable resources, just as it closely guards other strategic monopolies. But in fact, China has consistently allowed new entrants to appropriate natural resource rents that theoretically belong to the state. Second, China's mines produce an enormous output of extremely low-quality coal, heavy to transport and laced with impurities that are pumped into the air and water. While Chinese policymakers have repeatedly recognized the enormous environmental costs, they have never significantly restricted the use of low-quality coal. Third, small mines operate with appalling disregard for safety and work conditions. As a result, coal mines are deadly, killing over 6,000 miners annually until the early 2000s (SAWS Annual)—this compares to 22 deaths in coal mines in the United States in 2005. In fact, a recent study sponsored by Greenpeace and carried out by reputable Chinese economists concluded that coal use imposed an annual cost on China equal to 7 percent of gross domestic product (GDP). Each ton of coal—which sells for 300–400 yuan—causes an additional 150 yuan of costs in terms of environmental and health damage. These unpriced negative externalities are not accounted for in any decision-making (Mao, Sheng, and Yang 2008). We would normally expect to see the Chinese government carry out regulatory, natural resource, and pricing policies that internalize the cost of some of these externalities, or prevent their emergence in the first place. This would balance to some extent the trade-offs between highly desirable economic growth and other goods, such as safety and environmental quality. Yet until the recent shift in declared development objectives—discussed later—we see little effort and no successful efforts in this direction.

Broadening the discussion, we can ask in which strategic policy arenas do policymakers decide the most important developmental outcomes? That is, what are the broad policy areas in which policymakers must balance growth with other social and political objectives? In the Chinese context, we can identify three strategic policy arenas that are most crucial for shaping economic growth, while also inevitably shaping other aspect of society's evolution. I call these three transition strategy, industrial development strategy, and the repurposing of the Communist Party hierarchy. In all three of these we see the privileging of rapid economic growth above other considerations.

Transition Strategy

Given the prominence of rapid economic growth among policymakers' objectives, rapid "big bang" scenarios of transition were rejected. It was never conceivable that China would willingly sacrifice a year or two of growth in order to complete a rapid and thorough transition to a market economy, as reformers in Poland, for example, envisaged. Instead, Chinese policymakers adopted measures that would increase growth in the short run, by lowering entry barriers, encouraging the growth of markets alongside the plan, strengthening incentives for increased output, and so on. This has already been well covered in the transition literature. Not only have specific measures of economic reform repeatedly been judged on the basis of their contribution to growth (Heilmann 2008), the entire strategy of reform can be seen as subordinate to the quest for growth.

Industrial Development Strategy

China's development strategy has been an aggregation of multiple industrial policies. In the cases of Japan and Korea we can describe clearly the focus of industrial policies in certain eras, and reasonably trace the impact those policies had on developmental outcomes. Thus, industrial policy in the late 1970s accelerated Korea's transition to heavy and chemical industries. Efforts in Taiwan in the 1980s to promote the semiconductor and related industries are plausibly related to Taiwan's emergence as a high-tech hub in the 1990s. It is virtually impossible to make similar judgments about China. There are many cases where government industrial promotion policies are associated with successful subsequent development, but just as many cases where industrial promotion was an abject failure (Marukawa 2000; 2001). More crucially, it

is not clear that industrial policies targeted at specific sectors do not simply cancel each other out, as preferences and priorities given for one type of investment cancel out those given to another. Chinese industrial policy reflects fragmented policy formulation and multiple, inconsistent interests at play, and ends up being hit and miss.

However, all of the various industrial policies tend to promote investment. Tax breaks, subsidized land development, and public utilities all serve to subsidize investment. While the sectoral impact of industrial policy may be ambiguous, the net impact in tilting priorities toward industrial and infrastructure investment is quite strong. The diversity of industrial policies may be the natural outcome of an enormous and diverse economy like China; diverse and competing national and regional policies might even be an efficient solution, as long as competition washes out the least effective policies. The point is that a congeries of inconsistent industrial policies adds up to a consistent policy priority to industrial and infrastructure investment, at the expense of other objectives.

Repurposing the Communist Party Hierarchy

The most fundamental thing that a communist party does is manage personnel. A communist party is a human resources department that, in an economy with a large state presence, manages the allocation and reward of personnel throughout the economy. Since China entered the reform era, it has not left this personnel system unchanged. Rather, the entire personnel system has been regularized, given much stronger incentives, and focused on the objective of economic growth. Since the early 1980s, national "cadre responsibility systems" have provided for systematic evaluation of government officials at all levels through a system of success indicators (*kaohe zhibiao* 考核指标) and their reward with year-end bonuses. Cadres are annually assigned points for performance in several different policy arenas, and the total score determines the cadre's annual bonus. A large bonus can easily double a cadre's annual income. Crucially, for general government officials, indicators directly related to economic growth—GDP growth, tax collections, and industrial output—typically accounted for 60–65 points out of the 100 total possible (Edin 2000, 125–40; Whiting 2001; Whiting 2004; Zhuang Guobo 2007). As a result, government officials at all levels are strongly "incentivized" to support specific pro-growth policies.

Combining transition strategy, development strategy, and the manner in which incentives are built into the political system, it is clear that pro-investment and pro-growth policies are built into the Chinese system in an extremely profound way. Indeed, a pro-growth bias is integral to the functioning of the system as a whole. To be sure, China may be uniquely well positioned to generate rapid growth and, as mentioned above, China is in the midst of the highest-growth phase of the development process. But on top of these structural factors, the policy and systemic features of China over the past thirty years have been clearly focused on promoting precisely the outcome of maximum speed growth.

There is nothing irrational or misconceived about China's ranking of economic growth above other objectives. No country as poor as China was in the 1980s could hope for international respect or ever attain objectives that were in competition with other, more powerful nations. Nor could a rich and satisfying life for its people be attained without

economic development. Elevating economic growth to the top of a poor country's objectives is entirely reasonable. But emphasizing the implicit choices behind the growth strategy reminds us that no strategy is inevitable or immutable. Moreover, any choice, no matter how reasonable, involves costs as well as benefits. A choice that seemed overwhelmingly obvious at one time may gradually become less compelling, and over time, the balance among different objectives will gradually shift. That is particularly true as countries move from one set of developmental conditions to another.

The Concomitants of China's Growth Strategy

The commitment to rapid growth has in practice meant an enormous mobilization of resources for investment. China's investment rate—fixed investment as a share of GDP—is higher than any other country has achieved on a sustained basis. China's investment rate was already as high as any other country in the ten-year period from 1993 to 2002, and it then rose over 40 percent during the five-year growth surge from 2003–2008 (figure 1). Moreover, as discussed later, the investment rate

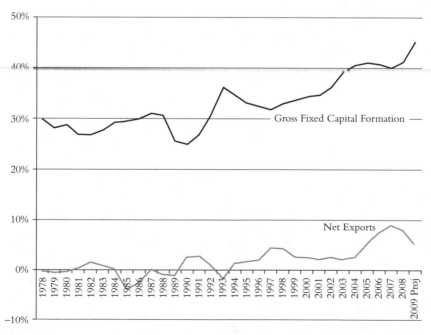

Figure 1 Investment and Net Exports (Share of GDP)

jumped even higher in 2009 in the wake of the global financial crisis. In addition, figure 1 shows that China has run a consistent large trade surplus since 2004 (peaking at 8.9 percent of GDP in 2007) that stands in marked contrast to the modest surpluses and occasional deficits that China generated before 2004. These numbers show that China's growth pattern is certainly "unbalanced," in the sense that it has been accompanied by extremely high levels of investment, and extraordinarily large international imbalances as well.

Investment and Net Exports (Share of GDP) The huge effort expended on investment and exporting inevitably implies that consumption—and particularly household consumption—is a correspondingly small part of the Chinese economy. As figure 2 shows, the consumption share of GDP declined dramatically after 2003, corresponding to the surge in investment and net exports in that period. It is worth tracing the roots of this dramatic decline by reading figure 2 from left to right. As Chinese households began to emerge from the planned economy in 1978, they consumed less than 50 percent of GDP. However, successful rural and urban reforms put more money into the

hands of households, and rapid growth of household income pushed consumption expenditures significantly above 50 percent of expenditure-side GDP by the mid-1980s. But after 1989, China's economic structure began to swing back to earlier patterns. The mid-1990s brought a surge of investment, such that household consumption dropped to around 45 percent of GDP and then stabilized. During the new millennium, though, household consumption as a share of GDP dropped again, to just above 35 percent of GDP in 2008, much lower than it had been during the Maoist period. Again, this is internationally unprecedented. US household consumption was about 62 percent of GDP from the 1950s through the early 1980s (Parker 1999). US household consumption rose to exceed 70 percent of GDP after 2001, but this reflected the unsustainable housing and financial bubbles in the United States in those years. In any case, the consumption-dominated economy of the United States is something of an outlier, and the more relevant comparison may be with Japan in the early 1970s. Between 1970 and 1973, Japan devoted 49 percent of its GDP to household consumption, and 37 percent to fixed capital formation. Net exports were only 2 percent of GDP,

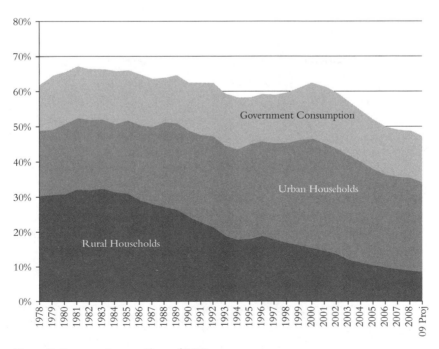

Figure 2 Consumption as a Share of GDP

and government consumption was 11 percent of GDP, compared to China's 13–16 percent (World Bank). Generally speaking, these macro-structural figures tell us that China in the 1980s and 1990s was quite similar to Japan in the early 1970s, as both economies pumped a comparatively high level of resources into investment and enjoyed rapid growth. However, China's experience in the 2000s has diverged from Japan's earlier experience. In Japan, the early 1970s were the final years of the high growth era, and subsequently investment declined, while growth dropped off markedly. In China, however, investment, net exports, and economic growth all reached more extreme values, and surpassed all historical precedent.

The huge volume of resources devoted to new investment created a very powerful process of transformation that included exceptionally rapid structural change. During the period of maximum structural change, the benefits to a high investment policy are also arguably at a peak. Each worker who leaves agriculture for a nonagricultural job creates a demand for new fixed capital for productive machinery, housing, and urban infrastructure. At the same time, the productivity of that new investment is high because it enables a previously under-employed agricultural worker to perform much more productive tasks. Figure 3 shows that rapid structural change in employment has followed on high investment. There are numerous problems

with the official labor data, but the pattern they portray is so strong that it would survive any plausible data revision. During three periods, agricultural workers have left the farms in large numbers. From 1983 through 1988, following the success of rural reforms and the growth of township and village enterprises; from 1991 through 1996, as the economy surged back from the post-Tiananmen recession; and again from 2002 through 2007. During this last five-year growth surge, the agricultural labor force declined from 369 million to 314 million, a net decrease of 55 million people. Since the natural increase in the agricultural labor force over this period would have been at least 4 million per year, a total of 75 million people—about 10 percent of the total labor force—left the farm sector in the past five years. As these people move from low productivity farm jobs to higher productivity urban jobs—even at the margins of the urban economy—they provide a huge impetus to the growth process.

Consumption as a Share of GDP Given China's size, and the fact that few farmers leave the land after age thirty-five, mass rural-urban migration will probably slow down before the agricultural labor force sinks below 30 percent of the labor force, with the remainder of the transformation taking place more slowly as the labor force ages. In any case, the process of transformation today

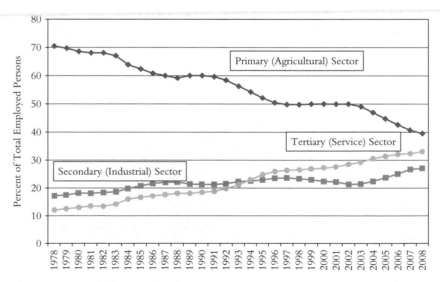

Figure 3 Structural Change in Employment

is certainly not exhausted, but the bulk of it has passed astonishingly rapidly. In the Yangtze Delta, with a total population approaching 150 million, less than 20 percent of the labor force is left in agriculture; in Guangdong—with 94.9 million people in 2007, China's most populous province (!)—only 29 percent of the labor force is in agriculture. These nation-sized entities have transformed into middle-income economies, like Korea and Taiwan in the 1980s. However, figure 3 tells an additional story as well. After each surge of structural change, the economy has suffered a setback that temporarily brought structural change to a halt, and even threw it into reverse for a period. Another of these temporary phases of recoil took place in 2008–2009, but appears to have lasted for only one year.

China's high investment rate relies on a financial system that mobilizes resources into investment. The banking and fiscal systems play a large role in this outcome, and they have been extensively studied. State-run banks channel household saving into new investment. The crucial role of the fiscal system was temporarily occluded by the crisis of state capacity that appeared immediately after the Tiananmen debacle, but has come back strongly in fifteen years since fiscal reforms were enacted at the end of 1993. The additional piece of the system that needs to be emphasized is the importance of retained profits, particularly within the industrial system. Pro-producer policies have succeeded

in stabilizing the state-run industrial sector and in boosting the profits of industrial enterprises, whether state-owned or not. As figure 4 shows, the turnaround has been particularly striking since 2002. The surge in profitability of the industrial sector was the proximate source of the increase in the investment share after 2003. Flush with cash, industrial enterprises channeled funds into expansion, feeding the great Chinese boom of 2003–2008. Only after midyear 2008 did the growth of profits stall with the onset of the global crisis.

Structural Change in Employment For China as a society, these patterns lead directly to the disproportionate power of the corporate and government sectors as compared to the household sector. Resources are concentrated in large organizations, often state-owned and staffed by the Communist Party. Access to a position in the large-scale sector is an important determinant of wealth as well as status. Access can come through entrepreneurship and cultivation of personal networks, as well as through political power and influence. The system is thus dramatically different from the old Maoist system, under which only political power provided meaningful access to resources. But it is still a system in which access is selective and control over resources is highly concentrated. These disproportions support corruption and breed resentment among the general population. Society, especially rural society, is low-powered.

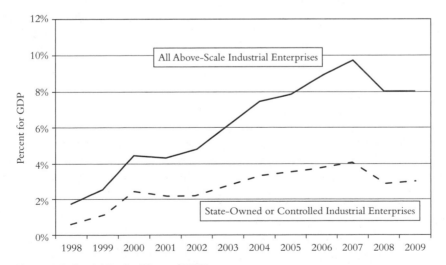

Figure 4 Industrial Profits (Share of GDP)

More indirectly, the high growth system contributes to high levels of income inequality across the board in society. Despite high levels of rural to urban migration, the income gap between urban and rural households has hardly shrunk, and may even have widened. High rates of investment equip the new urban immigrant with fixed capital, but also increase the capital that existing urbanites dispose of, and raise their income directly and indirectly. Urban economies—especially coastal cities—continue to surge ahead of rural areas. China's income inequality, as measured by the Gini coefficient, has increased from its low point below .3 in the early 1980s (after successful rural reforms) to .45 in 2002, according to Ravallion and Chen (2007). These household survey-based calculations do not capture the extremes of power and income inequality referred to in the previous paragraph. Both kinds of inequality breed resentment and, under certain circumstances, can lead to lower returns to investment in human capital among those at the lower end of the income scale (Chauduri and Ravallion 2006; Li et al. 2005).

Industrial Profits (Share of GDP) China's growth strategy also has huge environmental costs. In part this is simply because in any given decision process, environmental factors will almost always play a secondary role compared to the overriding goal of economic growth. The utilization of coal, as discussed above, is the most obvious case of repeated subordination of environmental considerations to the growth imperative. The environmental costs of China's development are also high simply because the high investment strategy inevitably implies that demand for energy-intensive and often polluting heavy industrial products is large. China's limited progress in continuing to improve energy efficiency over the past five years has been largely due to the remarkable growth of energy-using heavy industry (Rosen and Houser 2007). Finally, the concentration of the governmental incentive system on the pursuit of economic growth—so useful in adapting the Communist hierarchy to the needs of a market economy—stands in the way of increasing the weight of environmental considerations in decision making. Even if the center declares its support for a given environmental outcome, the officials on the ground charged with implementing that

decision still find their incentives shaped by a system that prioritizes growth above anything else. In other words, this is a system that has been tuned up; it is optimized for supporting growth policies. As a result, policies designed to achieve other objectives typically get short shrift, and are weakly implemented by a system that is not really set up to deliver those goods.

The Shift from Growth to a "Harmonious Society"

Chinese policymakers are acutely aware of the problems sketched out in the previous paragraphs. Since the Hu Jintao–Wen Jiabao administration assumed power at the end of 2002, policy has shifted in numerous areas. Government policymakers have adopted a broad array of policies designed to improve social security, protect the disadvantaged, improve living conditions in rural areas, and improve the overall environment (Naughton 2008b). Ambitious goals have been laid out in general programmatic documents, including the Eleventh Five Year Plan (Naughton 2005). Concrete policy measures have been successively implemented. The most dramatic set of policies, and the most successful, have been those policies by which the central government has assumed budgetary responsibility for core social programs in rural areas. Central government budget transfers have begun to fund primary education in most of rural China, and have made significant contributions to the new rural health insurance program. These have been combined with the abolition of the agricultural tax and the institution of direct subsidies to grain growers to significantly increase the profitability of farming.

In fact, it is fair to ask a very general question: which of the social problems spawned by China's rapid economic growth have been addressed by new policies in China in the last five years? The answer is clear, but may be surprising: all of them. The sheer range of issue areas in which new policy initiatives have emerged over the past five years is staggering: in rural areas, along with the income-related policies mentioned above, new land policies seek to strengthen farmers' rights to control, buy and sell, and lease their land. Policies toward rural-to-urban migrants have shifted mark-edly, with government increasingly recognizing the huge contribution such migrants make to development. Local areas now often provide premigration training classes to prepare departing young people for the challenges of urban life. The State Council has issued a series of documents designed to establish the rights of migrants: migrants have a right to live and work in cities; cities have a responsibility to educate migrant children; and migrants should not be subjected to exorbitant fees or police harassment.

In the urban workplace, enormous effort is now going into the support of worker rights. The number of members of the government-run union, the All China Federation of Trade Unions (ACFTU) has gone from 87 million in 1999 (the recent low), to 193 million in 2007 (NBS 2008a, 875). The new Labor Law that came into effect on January 1, 2008, gives workers the right to a labor contract, and the right to a clearly specified severance pay, calculated according to a simple formula (one month of pay per year of seniority). A major effort to improve workplace safety has been put into effect, with a special focus on coal mines. The coal mine death toll has been brought down by more than half, falling below three thousand in 2009 (SAWS Annual).

In the area of environment, enormous steps have been taken in principle, steps that are only beginning to have an effect. The Eleventh Five Year Plan was followed by an ambitious programmatic document drafted at the Chinese Academy of Sciences, declaring that China had to side-step further deterioration of the environment as implied by an environmental Kuznets curve. Again, looking to coal for evidence of implementation, we find that several thousand small coal mines have been shut down in the last two years, as a process of inspection and licensing finally begins to come into effect (SAWS 2007). The government has finally acknowledged that pure automobilization on the American model is not feasible in the Chinese context, and State Council [2005] Article 46 decreed that cities must quickly give priority to public transport in allocation of street space, and urged cities to proceed with the construction of mass transport systems for the medium to long run. There is no area of Chinese policymaking that has not been affected by the new thinking, and the push for a more harmonious and scientific growth path.

And yet, seen from thirty thousand feet, the Chinese growth path reveals absolutely no impact from this apparent change of course. It is relatively easy to see why not: while the government has made important new allocations of resources around the margins of the existing system, and while institutions have been tinkered with to address new needs, all of the core elements of the existing growth engine are still in place. The resource allocation decisions involving really large sums of money are still made on the same basis; the incentive structure rewards the same types of behavior and decision making; and the opportunities for rapid development are still enticing. Given that the basics of the high investment growth pattern were still in place, the early and modest efforts toward a more "balanced" and higher quality society were simply swamped by a cyclical intensification of the old pattern.

By 2004, Chinese economists and planners had begun to seriously worry about an over-heated economy. But continued productivity improvements kept a lid on costs and macroeconomic policy adjustments prevented the imbalances from erupting into sustained open inflation. Instead, China pulled into a sustained boom, led by investment and a steadily growing trade surplus. Although China let the value of its currency drift upward slowly after mid-2005, the currency remained distinctly undervalued. Only at the end of 2007, as new inflationary pressures emerged, did China allow the currency to appreciate significantly. In the meantime, sustained productivity growth drove a steady increase in exports, and China's homegrown heavy industries increasingly substituted for imports of heavy and machinery industry products. Demand for investment goods fueled additional new investment, which fed into a virtuous growth cycle. But in the process, all of the core imbalances of the economy became more pronounced (Lardy 2008). Moreover, China became, willy-nilly, more dependent on external demand than it had ever been before. It was in this context—as Chinese policymakers struggled with their own ambivalence and with their limited success in taming their overheated and unbalanced economy—that the global financial crisis arrived in China with unexpected force.

The Crisis and China's Response

China's growth turned down sharply after August 2008. Chinese policymakers hesitated only a few months as they digested the magnitude of the internal and external economic challenges they faced. Then, in early November 2008, policymakers launched an economic stimulus program of enormous scale. Planners laid out a two-year program of government infrastructure investment with a total value of about 4 percent of GDP. Crucially, the leadership then used the hierarchical political system to send a message to local leaders: initiate work immediately on your most urgent local investment projects; submit lists of "shovel-ready" projects to the central government; get started as soon as possible. Policymakers then opened the spigots of the state-owned banking system. Beginning in January 2009 a massive flood of credit flowed to support investment by local governments and (primarily) state-owned enterprises. The flood of liquidity into the system was more than enough to offset the decline in profits in the industrial system in 2008–2009 (shown in figure 4). Bank credit grew an average of 9.2 percent during the first half of the years 2002 through 2008. By that standard, "normal" credit growth in 2009 would have been about 2.8 trillion RMB. Instead, credit surged more than twice that much, jumping to 7.4 trillion RMB. That part of 2009 credit growth that was *above normal*—4.6 trillion RMB—was equal to 14 percent of annual GDP, giving an indication of the huge stimulus provided the economy in this way. Finally, the government rolled out measures to stimulate consumption as well, providing tax breaks and rebates to a range of goods from small autos to electronics products in the countryside (Naughton 2009).

This vigorous program had the desired effect. China's response was one of the most "Keynesian" of all the national responses to the global crisis, in that it combined size and speed, with increased activity in the real economy evident within ninety days of the policy's birth (by February 2009). In addition, the government infrastructure investment program was fairly well targeted, with a focus on transportation and rural infrastructure. Of course, the flood of funding from bank credits far exceeded the needs of the initial infrastructure

investment program, and could not possibly have been so precisely targeted. By the second quarter of 2009, economic growth had stabilized and began to increase. Virtually all the impetus to growth in the first half of 2009 came from the expansion of government investment. While consumption grew as well, it was barely enough to offset the decline in net exports. China rode a surge of government investment out of the global financial crisis.

Figures 1 and 2 include a projection of 2009 data based on data through the first three quarters of the year. While preliminary, the figures show a striking fact. In response to the crisis, the Chinese economy has become even more unbalanced than it ever was before. By conservative estimate, the Chinese investment rate will soar to 45 percent of GDP in 2009 (as figure 1 shows). Household consumption, despite turning in a solid growth performance, will continue to erode as a share of GDP, dropping below 35 percent of GDP for the first time (figure 2). Net exports (the trade surplus) do show a trend toward "rebalancing," as the surplus will decline to just over 5 percent of GDP. This is still a large surplus, but down significantly from its peak two years earlier. Even more than in the past—and more than any economy in history—China is dependent on domestic investment to drive growth.

In brief, China has responded to the crisis by reinstating its existing growth model. Ironically, the unprecedented economic crisis has caused a reversion to old habits. But in the successful response to the crisis, we have also seen China's existing growth model display its most characteristic features. The concentration of power allowed decision makers to be extremely decisive in changing policy in November 2008. The growth-compatible incentives in place throughout the hierarchical system facilitated an extraordinarily rapid implementation of the policy turn. Direct government influence over the banking system elicited a flood of credit, quickly. Most important, the ever-present demand for new investment and new growth-supporting measures implied that decision makers at all levels jumped at the opportunity to roll out new projects, and thus supported the recovery of final demand. Not surprisingly, Chinese leaders during 2009 began to display a degree of pride about their success in dealing with the crisis, the achievements of their economic and political system, and their newly prominent place among the leading nations of the world as well.

The Future

China appears to have successfully sidestepped the worst of the global financial crisis. In this, we see a recapitulation of one of the most striking aspects of China's growth experience over the past thirty years. One of the most surprising things about China's economic growth since 1978 has been the virtual absence of crisis. The political crisis around Tiananmen in 1989 shook the political system to the core, it is true, but the political recovery was quick and fairly predictable—circle the wagons and hang together—and the economic recovery was even swifter. But ever since Tiananmen, people have been predicting crisis for China. All these predictions have proved wrong, whether they came from China pessimists or from China optimists. Given this background, it would be foolhardy to predict a crisis for the Chinese economy in the immediate future, and this assessment does not make any such prediction. However, we cannot neglect the fact that a newly complex mix of economic challenges currently faces China.

While China has been able to reinstate growth and its old growth model, it is unlikely that this will lead to a smooth return to pre-crisis growth levels. China's dramatic expansion of exports is likely to slow permanently, given the long-term reductions in the purchasing power of American consumers, who lay behind so much of the global boom of 2003–2008. Government investment simply cannot keep expanding at the rates it grew during 2009. Overall, then, China probably has no choice but to adjust to a somewhat slower overall pace of economic growth, reliant to a larger extent on domestic consumption growth. The problem here is that consumption is such a small share of China's GDP that even large increases in consumption will not be enough to restore very rapid growth. The transition to moderately fast growth in the 8 percent range (down from the 10–12 percent range in the five-year growth surge) is probably unavoidable.

Beyond this stabilization of growth, China will soon be facing the shift to a different kind of growth strategy as discussed at the beginning of this chapter. The shift has been temporarily deferred by the expansionary policies of 2009, but cannot be put off indefinitely. With structural change ongoing in 2009, the abundant labor surplus in the rural areas is already beginning to face exhaustion. Labor force growth is beginning to slow down, and will reach zero growth by around 2015. To be sure, China has taken many steps that may position it well to make the transition to a "higher quality" growth path. Education standards have risen dramatically in the past five years. New industries have been created that may play a role in future environmental cleanup. Consumer living standards have increased and an urban middle class is growing. There is nothing in economic theory that tells us that such a transition cannot be smoothly made (Holz 2008).

However, past experience of rapidly growing East Asian economies tells us that such transitions are rarely entirely smooth. Japan grew at 10.4 percent per year between 1950 and 1973, raising its investment effort to a peak in the last three years of the period. But after the first global energy shock, Japan's growth rate dropped sharply, and after 1974 Japan never grew more than 6 percent in a single year. Korea, Thailand, and Malaysia made their largest investment efforts in the early 1990s and enjoyed very rapid growth. But after the East Asian financial crisis in 1997–1998, investment and growth dropped sharply and has never fully recovered to pre-crisis levels. The transition in Taiwan was less dramatic, perhaps because of the opportunity to transplant export networks to the China mainland, but eventually led to a similar growth slowdown. Looking backward, it is obvious that crisis punctuates—and punctures—long-run trends, marking turning points or sudden shifts from one apparently stable long-run path to another. These crises often appear inevitable in retrospect, yet hardly anybody predicted them beforehand, and even fewer were those who adapted their behavior beforehand to the brewing storm. As the crisis recedes—having been dealt with effectively or not—many find that their behavior has adapted to something new, that things don't ever return to the way they were, and that the crisis has marked the beginning of a new era. There are crises; they don't disappear; they are very difficult to predict; and then they end up changing everything.

We can predict with a fairly high degree of confidence that by around 2015—that is, within five years of this writing—China will be undergoing a transition to a slower but higher quality growth path. We are on the threshold of a new era, and the extraordinary growth bonus that China reaped in the early part of this century is either over or will soon be over. The one certainty is that the China that develops from this different growth model will be quite different from the China we know today: it will be more sophisticated, more prosperous, with an older population, and a much more desirable living environment. How the transition to that new era happens is hard to predict, even more so in the wake of the uncertainties caused by the global financial crisis. Perhaps China will indeed experience an acute short-run crisis, if stimulus measures ultimately fail to revive high-speed growth and a "W-shaped" recovery emerges in 2010–2011. It is also possible that China will be forced into a painful and protracted shift of economic growth model, struggling to find a new set of economic relationships that work. Yet it is also possible that China will move aggressively, in the immediate future, to increase consumption, democratize its economy, and spread the benefits of growth more widely. In that case, slower growth might be smoothly achieved, along with rapid increases in well-being. In that case, China will have surprised us again with its ability to avoid crisis.

REFERENCES

Chaudhuri, Shubham, and Martin Ravallion. 2006. "Partially Awakened Giants: Uneven Growth in China and India." Policy Research Working Paper 4069. Washington, DC: World Bank, November.

Edin, Maria. 2000. *Market Forces and Communist Power: Local Political Institutions and Economic Development in China.* Uppsala: Uppsala University Printers.

Heilmann, Sebastian. 2008. "Policy Experimentation in China's Economic Rise." *Studies in Comparative International Development* 43, no. 1 (March): 1–26.

Holz, Carsten. 2008. "China's Economic Growth 1978–2025: What We Know Today About China's Economic Growth Tomorrow." *World Development* 36, no. 10: 1665–91.

Lardy, Nicholas R. 2008. "Sustaining Economic Growth in China." In C. Fred Bergsten, Charles Freeman, Nicholas R. Lardy, and Derek J. Mitchell, *China's Rise: Challenges and Opportunities*, chap 6. Washington, DC: Peterson Institute for International Economics.

Li Rongrong. 2009. *Fully Implement the Perspective of Scientific Development to Raise the Quality of State Enterprise Growth*, December 24, 2009, www.sasac.gov.cn/n1180/n1566/n259730/n264153/6870745.html (accessed December 30, 2009).

Li Shi, Bai Nansheng, et al. 2005. *China Human Development Report*. Beijing: UNDP and China Development Research Foundation.

Marukawa, Tomoo, ed. 2000. *Iko-ki Chugoku no Sangyo Seisaku* [China's industrial policy in transition]. Chiba: Institute of Developing Economies.

———. 2001. "WTO, Industrial Policy and China's Industrial Development." In Ippei Yamazawa and Ken-ichi Imai, eds., *China Enters WTO; Pursuing Symbiosis with the Global Economy*. Chiba: Institute of Developing Economies.

Mao Yushi, Sheng Hong, and Yang Fuqiang, 2008. *The True Costs of Coal*. Greenpeace. www.greenpeace.org/international/en/publications/reports/cost-of-coal/.

National Bureau of Statistics (NBS). 2008a. *China Statistical Yearbook*. Beijing: Zhong-guo Tongji.

———. 2008b. *Zhongguo Fazhan Baogao* [China development report]. Beijing: Zhongguo Tongji.

———. 2009. "Industrial Profit Shot Up from January to November." December 29. www.stats.gov.cn/enGliSH/newsandcomingevents/t20091229_402610800.htm (accessed December 30, 2009).

Naughton, Barry. 2005. "The New Common Economic Program: China's Eleventh Five Year Plan and What It Means." *China Leadership Monitor*, no. 16 (Fall), www.hoover.org/publications/clm/issues/2898936.html.

———. 2008a. "Market Economy, Hierarchy and Single Party Rule." In Janos Kornai and Yingyi Qian, eds., *Market and Socialism Reconsidered (with Particular Reference to China and Vietnam)*, 135–61. London: Macmillan, for the International Economic Association.

———. 2008b. "China's Left Tilt: Pendulum Swing or Mid-course Correction?" In Cheng Li, ed., *China's Changing Political Landscape: Prospects for Democracy*, 142–58. Washington, DC: Brookings Institution Press.

———. 2009. "Understanding the Chinese Stimulus Package." *China Leadership Monitor*, no. 28 (Spring), www.hoover.org/publications/clm/issues/44613157.html.

Parker, Jonathan. 1999. "Spendthrift in America? On Two Decades of Decline in the U.S. Saving Rate." *NBER Macroeconomics Annual* 14: 317–70.

Ravallion, Martin, and Chen Shaohua. 2007. "China's (Uneven) Progress Against Poverty" *Journal of Development Economics* 82, no. 1: 1–42.

Rosen, Daniel, and Trevor Houser. 2007. "China Energy: A Guide for the Perplexed." The China Balance Sheet: A Joint Project by the Center for Strategic and International Studies and the Peterson Institute for International Economics. Washington, DC: Peterson Institute for International Economics.

SASAC. 2006. "Guanyu tuijin guoyou ziban tiaozheng he guoyou qiye zhongzu de zhidao yijian" [Guiding opinions on advancing the readjustment of state capital and the reorganization of state-owned enterprises]. www.sasac.gov.cn/2006rdzt/2006rdzt_0021/gzw/03/200702050217.htm.

———. 2009. "General Operating Conditions of Central Enterprises in 2008." September 18, 2009. www.sasac.gov.cn/nll80/nl566/n258203/n258329/6649463.html (accessed December 30, 2009).

State Administration of Work Safety (SAWS). Annual. "Annual Statistical Analysis Page." www.chinasafety.gov.cn/newpage/aqfx/aqfe_ndtjfe.htm (accessed December 19, 2009). [Contains safety reports for most years since 2000.]

———. 2007. "State Administration of Work Safety Announcement No. 15 on Closure of Unsafe Coal Mines in 2007." www.chinasafety.gov.cn/2007-09/19/content_260837.htm (accessed December 19, 2009).

Whiting, Susan H. 2001. *Power and Wealth in Rural China: The Political Economy of Institutional Change.* New York: Cambridge University Press.

———. 2004. "The Cadre Evaluation System at the Grass Roots: The Paradox of Party Rule." In Barry Naughton and Dali Yang, eds., *Holding China Together: Diversity and National Integration in the Post-Deng Era*, 101–19. New York: Cambridge University Press.

World Bank. Annual. World Development Indicators (WDI). web.worldbank.org/WBSITE/EXTERNAL/DATASTATISTICS/0,,menuPK:232599~pagePK:64133170~piPK:64133498~theSitePK:239419,00.html.

Xinhua. 2006. "Guoziwei: Guoyou jingji ying baochi qige hangye de juedui kongzhili" [SASAC: The state-owned economy ought to maintain absolute control over seven sectors]. December 18, 2006. www.gov.cn/jrzg/2006-12/18/content_472256.htm (accessed December 19, 2009).

Zhuang Guobo. 2007. *Lingdao ganbu zhengji pingjia de lilun yu shijian* [Theory and practice of evaluation of political performance by leadership cadres]. Beijing: Zhongguo jingji.

ACCELERATING THE IMPROVEMENT OF THE SOCIALIST MARKET ECONOMY AND THE CHANGE OF THE GROWTH MODEL

Report to the 18th National Congress of the Communist Party of China [Excerpts]*

Hu Jintao

Taking economic development as the central task is vital to national renewal, and development still holds the key to addressing all the problems we have in China. Only by promoting sustained and sound economic development can we lay a solid material foundation for enhancing the country's prosperity and strength, improving the people's well-being, and ensuring social harmony and stability. We must unwaveringly adhere to the strategic thinking that only development counts.

In contemporary China, pursuing development in a scientific way best embodies the thinking that only development counts. Taking the pursuit of development in a scientific way as the underlying guideline and accelerating the change of the growth model as a major task is a strategic choice we have made for promoting China's overall development. In response to changes in both domestic and international economic developments, we should speed up the creation of a new growth model and ensure that development is based on improved quality and performance. We should fire all types of market participants with new vigor for development, increase motivation for pursuing innovation-driven development, establish a new system for developing modern industries, and create new favorable conditions for developing the open economy. This will make economic development

---

* This speech was published by the Communist Party of China on November 8, 2012 (http://www.china.org.cn/china/18th_cpc_congress/2012-11/16/content_27137540.htm).

driven more by domestic demand, especially consumer demand, by a modern service industry and strategic emerging industries, by scientific and technological progress, by a workforce of higher quality and innovation in management, by resource conservation and a circular economy, and by coordinated and mutually reinforcing urban-rural development and development between regions. Taking these steps will enable us to sustain long-term development.

We should keep to the Chinese-style path of carrying out industrialization in a new way and advancing IT application, urbanization, and agricultural modernization. We should promote integration of IT application and industrialization, interaction between industrialization and urbanization, and coordination between urbanization and agricultural modernization, thus promoting harmonized development of industrialization, IT application, urbanization, and agricultural modernization.

Deepen Economic Structural Reform Across the Board

Deepening reform is crucial for accelerating the change of the growth model. The underlying issue we face in economic structural reform is how to strike a balance between the role of the government and that of the market, and we should follow more closely the rules of the market and better play the role of the government. We should unwaveringly consolidate and develop the public sector of the economy; allow public ownership to take diverse forms; deepen reform of state-owned enterprises; improve the mechanisms for managing all types of state assets; and invest more of state capital in major industries and key fields that comprise the lifeline of the economy and are vital to national security. We should thus steadily enhance the vitality of the state-owned sector of the economy and its capacity to leverage and influence the economy. At the same time, we must unswervingly encourage, support, and guide the development of the non-public sector, and ensure that economic entities under all forms of ownership have equal access to factors of production in accordance with the law, compete on a level playing field, and are protected by the law as equals.

We should improve the modern market system and strengthen institutional procedures for setting macro-regulation targets and employing policy tools. We should accelerate the reform of the fiscal and taxation systems and ensure that the central and local governments have sufficient financial resources to exercise their respective powers and fulfill their respective responsibilities. We should improve the public finance system to ensure equal access to basic public services and promote the building of functional zones. We should also institute local tax systems and improve the structure of the taxation system to promote social fairness. We should establish a mechanism for equitable sharing of proceeds from public resource transfers. We should deepen reform of the financial system and improve the modern financial system so that it will better contribute to macroeconomic stability and support development of the real economy. We should accelerate development of a multilevel capital market, take steady steps to make interest rates and the RMB exchange rate more market-based, and promote the RMB's convertibility under capital accounts in due course. We should speed up the development of private financial institutions. We should improve financial supervision and oversight, promote financial innovations, improve the competitiveness of banking, securities, insurance and other sectors, and ensure financial stability.

Implement the Strategy of Innovation-Driven Development

Scientific and technological innovation provides strategic support for raising the productive forces and boosting the overall national strength, and we must give it top priority in overall national development. We should follow a path of making innovation with Chinese features and take steps to promote innovation to catch up with global advances. We should increase our capacity for making original innovation and integrated innovation and for making further innovation on the basis of absorbing advances in overseas science and technology, and place greater emphasis on making innovation through collaboration. We should deepen reform of the system for managing science and technology, promote close integration of science and technology with economic development, and speed up the development of the national innovation system. We should establish a system of technological innovation in which enterprises play the leading role, the market points the way, and enterprises, universities, and research institutes work together. We should improve the knowledge-based innovation system, and strengthen basic research, research in frontier technologies, and public benefit-oriented research and development; and we should improve research and our capacity for applying research results to production to ensure that we can obtain the leading strategic position in research and development. We should launch important national science and technology projects to remove major technological bottlenecks. We should speed up the research, development, and application of new technologies, products, and production processes, strengthen innovation in integration of technologies, and develop new business models. We should improve standards for evaluating scientific and technological innovations and mechanisms for rewarding such innovations and applying them to production. We should implement the strategy concerning intellectual property rights and strengthen their protection. We should efficiently allocate and fully integrate innovation resources, and ensure that the wisdom and strength of the whole society are directed toward promoting innovation-driven development.

Carry Out Strategic Adjustment of the Economic Structure

This is the major goal of accelerating the change of the growth model. We must strive to remove major structural barriers to sustained and sound economic development, with a focus on improving the demand mix and the industrial structure, promoting balanced development between regions, and advancing urbanization. We should firmly maintain the strategic focus of boosting domestic demand, speed up the establishment of a long-term mechanism for increasing consumer demand, unleash the potential of individual consumption, increase investment at a proper pace, and expand the domestic market. We should focus on developing the real economy as a firm foundation of the economy. We

should adopt policies and measures to better facilitate the development of the real economy. We should make the economy more demand-driven, promote the sound growth of strategic emerging industries and advanced manufacturing industries, speed up the transformation and upgrading of traditional industries, develop and expand the service sector, especially modern service industries, and make the geographical and structural layout of the development of infrastructure and basic industries more balanced. We should develop next-generation information infrastructure and modern IT industry, better ensure information security, and promote the application of information network technologies. We should enhance the core competitiveness of large- and medium-sized enterprises and support development of small and micro businesses, especially small and micro science and technology companies. We should continue to implement the master strategy for regional development and fully leverage the comparative advantages of different regions. We should give high priority to large-scale development of the western region, fully revitalize old industrial bases in northeast China, work vigorously to promote the rise of the central region, and support the eastern region in taking the lead in development. We should increase support for old revolutionary base areas, ethnic minority areas, border areas, and poor areas through pairing assistance and other means. We should make scientific plans for the scale and layout of urban agglomerations; and we should make small and medium-sized cities and small towns better able to develop industries, provide public services, create jobs, and attract population. We should accelerate reform of the household registration system, conduct registration of rural migrant workers as permanent urban residents in an orderly way, and endeavor to ensure that all permanent urban residents have access to basic urban public services.

Integrate Urban and Rural Development

Resolving issues relating to agriculture, rural areas, and farmers is the number one priority in the Party's work, and integrating urban and rural development provides the fundamental solution to these issues. We should better balance urban and rural development, boost rural development, work to narrow the gap between urban and rural areas, and promote their common prosperity. We should continue to encourage industry to support agriculture in return for agriculture's earlier contribution to its development and encourage cities to support rural areas. We should give more to farmers, take less from them, and lift restrictions over their economic activities. We should increase policy support to boost agriculture, benefit farmers, and increase rural prosperity, and encourage the rural population to participate in modernization on an equal footing and share in its fruits. We should speed up the development of modern agriculture, raise the overall production capacity of agriculture, and ensure food security and effective supply of major agricultural products in China. We should give high priority to rural areas in developing infrastructure and social programs in the country. We should work harder to build new rural areas, carry out programs of poverty alleviation through development and fully improve rural working and living conditions. We should ensure sustained and fast growth of rural income. We should uphold and improve the basic system for rural operations and protect in accordance with the law farmers' rights to farm the land they have contracted, to use the land on which their houses sit, and to share in the proceeds from rural collective operations. We should strengthen the collective economy, develop specialized cooperatives and joint stock partnerships for farmers, foster new types of agricultural business entities, and develop large-scale agricultural operations in diverse forms. We should establish a new type of system for intensive agricultural operations that are specialized, well organized, and commercialized. We should reform the land expropriation system and increase the share of gain in land value to farmers. We should speed up improvements to institutions and mechanisms for promoting integrated urban and rural development, with a focus on integrating urban and rural planning, infrastructure, and public services. We should ensure equal exchange of factors of production between urban and rural areas and balance allocation of public resources between them. What we aim to achieve is a new type of relations between industry and agriculture and between urban and rural areas in which industry promotes agriculture, urban areas support rural development, agriculture and industry benefit each other, and there is integrated urban and rural development.

Promote All-Around Improvements to China's Open Economy

In response to new developments in economic globalization, we must implement a more proactive opening-up strategy and improve the open economy so that it promotes mutual benefit and is diversified, balanced, secure, and efficient. We should move faster to change the way the external-oriented economy grows, and make China's open economy become better structured, expand in scope, and yield greater returns. We should make innovations in the mode of opening up; encourage coastal, inland, and border areas to draw on each other's strengths in opening up; develop open areas that take the lead in global economic cooperation and competition; and form leading areas of opening up that drive regional development. We should continue to attach equal importance to export and import, better coordinate trade and industrial policies, and make China's exports more competitive in terms of technology, brand, quality, and service. We should transform and upgrade processing trade, develop service trade, and promote balanced development of foreign trade. We should make full use of our overall advantageous position in utilizing foreign capital and make better use of such investment. We should step up efforts to attract investment, technology, and high-caliber professionals from overseas. Chinese companies should expand overseas presence at a faster pace, enhance their operation in an international environment, and develop a number of world-class multinational corporations. We should make overall planning for bilateral, multilateral, regional, and subregional opening up and cooperation, accelerate implementation of the strategy of building free trade areas, and promote infrastructure connectivity with our neighboring countries. We should become better able to defuse international economic risks.

We must have firm confidence in winning the tough battle of deepening reform of the economic structure across the board and of accelerating the change of the growth model so as to increase the vitality and competitiveness of China's economy.

II. State Capacity and Governance

China's Governance Crisis[*]

Minxin Pei

More Than Musical Chairs

Predicting the outcome of China's upcoming leadership succession has become a popular parlor game in certain Washington circles. The curiosity aroused by the transition is understandable, given the huge stakes involved for the world's largest country. If all goes well, the Chinese Communist Party (CCP) is scheduled to select a new and younger leadership at its Sixteenth Party Congress this fall. The incumbent CCP general secretary, 76-year-old Jiang Zemin, may step down and be replaced by China's Vice President Hu Jintao, who is 59. The all-powerful Politburo Standing Committee will see most of its members retire, as will the important Central Committee. In addition, Chinese Premier Zhu Rongji is to step down in March, and Li Peng, the leader of the National People's Congress (the country's legislature), may be heading for the exit as well.

In a country ruled largely by man, not law, succession creates rare opportunities for political intrigue and policy change. Thus, speculation is rife about the composition, internal rivalries, and policy implications of a post-Jiang leadership. The backgrounds of those expected to ascend to the top unfortunately reveal little. By and large, the majority of new faces are technocrats. Some have stellar resumes but thin records; other front-runners boast solid experience as provincial party bosses but carry little national clout.

In any case, conjectures about the immediate policy impact of the pending leadership change are an exercise in futility, because Jiang will likely wield considerable influence even after his semi-retirement. A truly dominant new leader may not emerge in Beijing for another three to five years. And regardless of the drama that the succession process might provide, a single-minded focus on power plays in Beijing misses the real story: China is facing a hidden crisis of governance. This fact ought to preoccupy those who believe that much more is at stake in Beijing than a game of musical chairs.

The idea of an impending governance crisis in Beijing may sound unduly alarmist. To the outside world, China is a picture of dynamism and promise. Its potential market size, consistently high growth rates, and recent accession to the World Trade Organization have made the Middle Kingdom a top destination of foreign direct investment ($46 billion in 2001), and multinational corporations salivate at the thought of its future growth. But beneath this giddy image of progress and prosperity lies a different reality—one that is concealed by the glitzy skylines of Shanghai, Beijing, and other coastal cities. The future of China, and the West's interests there, depends critically on how Beijing's new leaders deal with this somber reality.

Dot Communism and Its Discontents

China's current crisis results from fundamental contradictions in the reforms that it has pursued over the past two decades—a period that has seen the amazing transformation of the communist

---

[*] This article appeared in *Foreign Affairs*, Vol. 81, No. 5 (Sept./Oct. 2002): 96–109. Copyright by the Council on Foreign Relations, Inc. All rights reserved.

regime from one that was infatuated with class struggle to one obsessed by growth rates. This "dot communism," characterized by the marriage of a Leninist party to bureaucratic capitalism with a globalist gloss, has merely disguised, rather than eliminated, these contradictions. But they are growing ever harder to ignore. The previously hidden costs of transition have begun to surface: Further change implies not simply a deepening of market liberalization but also the implementation of political reforms that could endanger the CCP's monopoly on power.

These emerging contradictions are embedded in the very nature of the Chinese regime. For example, the government's market-oriented economic policies, pursued in a context of autocratic and predatory politics, make the CCP look like a self-serving, capitalistic ruling elite, and not a "proletarian party" championing the interests of working people. The Party's professed determination to maintain political supremacy also runs counter to its declared goals of developing a "socialist market economy" and "ruling the country according to law," because the minimum requirements of a market economy and the rule of law are institutionalized curbs on political power. The CCP's ambition to modernize Chinese society leaves unanswered the question of how increasing social autonomy will be protected from government caprice. And the Party's perennial fear of independently organized interest groups does not prepare it for the inevitable emergence of such groups in an industrialized economy. These unresolved contradictions, inherent in the country's transition away from communism, are the source of rising tensions in China's polity, economy, and society.

During the go-go 1990s, the irreconcilable nature of these contradictions was obscured by rising prosperity and relative political tranquility. Economically, accelerating liberalization and deepening integration with the world marketplace produced unprecedented prosperity, even though some tough reforms (especially those affecting the financial sector and state-owned enterprises, or SOEs) lagged behind. Politically, the ruling elite drew its own lesson from the collapse of Soviet communism ("It's the economy, stupid") and closed ranks behind a strategy that prioritized economic growth and left the political system untouched.

This strategy worked for a decade. Within the regime, conservatives who opposed market reforms

were marginalized. China's pro-democracy movement, which peaked with the Tiananmen Square protest in 1989, also waned after its leadership was decapitated through exile or imprisonment. The resulting tranquility ended the polarized debate between liberals and conservatives of the 1980s. But ironically, this shift also silenced those at both ends of the ideological spectrum who would have cried that the emperor had no clothes. Thus, the regime escaped pressure to adopt deeper political reforms to relieve the tensions produced by the contradictions of dot communism. With rising wealth and loose talk of a "China century," even some skeptics thought the CCP had managed to square the circle.

The incompatibilities between China's current political system, however, and the essential requirements of the rule of law, a market economy, and an open society have not been washed away by waves of foreign investment. Pragmatists might view these contradictions as inconsequential cognitive nuisances. Unfortunately, their effects are real: they foreclose reform options that otherwise could be adopted for the regime's own long-term good. To be sure, China's pragmatic leaders have made a series of tactical adjustments to weather many new socioeconomic challenges, such as the CCP's recent outreach to entrepreneurs. But these moves are no substitute for genuine institutional reforms that would reinvigorate and relegitimize the ruling party.

The Bubble Bursts

In retrospect, the 1990s ought to be viewed as a decade of missed opportunities. The CCP leadership could have taken advantage of a booming economy to renew itself through a program of gradual political reform built on the rudimentary steps of the 1980s. But it did not, and now the cumulative costs of a decade of foot-dragging are becoming more visible. In many crucial respects, China's hybrid neo-authoritarian order eerily exhibits the pathologies of both the political stagnation of Leonid Brezhnev's Soviet Union and the crony capitalism of Suharto's Indonesia.

These pathologies—such as pervasive corruption, a collusive local officialdom, elite cynicism, and mass disenchantment—are the classic symptoms of degenerating governing capacity. In most political systems, a regime's capacity to govern is measured by how it performs three key tasks: mobilizing political support, providing public goods, and managing internal tensions. These three functions of governance—legitimation, performance, and conflict resolution—are, in reality, intertwined. A regime capable of providing adequate public goods (education, public health, law and order) is more likely to gain popular support and keep internal tensions low. In a Leninist party-state however, effective governance critically hinges on the health of the ruling party. Strong organizational discipline, accountability, and a set of core values with broad appeal are essential to governing effectively. Deterioration of the ruling party's strength, on the other hand, sets in motion a downward cycle that can severely impair the party-state's capacity to govern.

Numerous signs within China indicate that precisely such a process is producing huge governance deficits. The resulting strains are making the political and economic choices of China's rulers increasingly untenable. They may soon be forced to undertake risky reforms to stop the rot. If they do not, dot communism could be no more durable than the dot coms.

The Party's Over

The decline of the CCP began during the rule of Mao Zedong, as the late leader's political radicalism, culminating in the madness of the Cultural Revolution (1966–76), deeply damaged the ruling party. The ascent of Deng Xiaoping and his progressive reforms slowed this process, as economic gains, the end of mass repression, and the expansion of personal freedoms partially repaired the CCP's tarnished image.

But Deng's pro-market reforms produced a different set of dynamics that began to corrode the CCP's support. As economic reform deepened, large segments of Chinese society became poorer (such as grain-producing farmers and workers in SOEs). The revenue-starved state was unable to compensate these losers from reform. Consequently, the CCP had little means to secure the political support of these disaffected groups beyond exhorting self-sacrifice and making empty promises of better times ahead.

Some members of the ruling elite also converted their political power into economic gains, building and profiting from patronage machines. In one survey, about two-thirds of the officials being trained at a municipal party school said their promotion depended solely on the favors of their superiors; only 5 percent thought their own efforts could advance their careers. A ruling party fractured from within by such personalized patronage systems is hardly capable of building broad-based support within society.

It is worth noting that mass political campaigns, a previous hallmark of the CCP's prowess, have virtually vanished from the Chinese political scene. An obvious explanation is that such campaigns tend to be disruptive and lead to political excesses, as they did during the Mao years. A more likely cause, however, is that the CCP no longer possesses the political appeal or the organizational capacity required to launch such campaigns even when it desires them (as was the case during Beijing's efforts to contain prodemocracy dissidents in the late 1980s and the Falun Gong spiritual movement in the late 1990s). Increasingly, when faced with direct challenges to its authority, the CCP can rely only on repression rather than public mobilization to counter its opponents.

Immobilized

The extent of the CCP's decline can be measured in three areas: the shrinkage of its organizational penetration, the erosion of its authority and appeal among the masses, and the breakdown of its internal discipline. The organizational decline of the CCP is, in retrospect, almost predetermined. Historically, Leninist parties have thrived only in economies dominated by the state. Such an economy provides the economic institutions (SOEs and collective farms) that form the organizational basis for the ruling party. By pursuing market reforms that have eliminated rural communes and most SOEs, the CCP has fallen victim to its own success. The new economic infrastructure, based on household farming, private business, and individual labor mobility, is inhospitable to a large party apparatus. For instance, an internal CCP report characterized half of the party's rural cells as "weak" or "paralyzed" in recent years. In urban areas, the CCP has been unable to penetrate the emerging private sector, while its old organizational base has collapsed along with the SOEs. In 2000, the CCP did not have a single member in 86 percent of the country's 1.5 million private firms and could establish cells in only 1 percent of private companies.

The CCP's organizational decay is paralleled by the decline of its authority and image among the public. A survey of 818 migrant laborers in Beijing in 1997–98 revealed that the prevailing image of the ruling party was that of a self-serving elite. Only 5 percent of the interviewees thought their local party cadres "work for the interests of the villagers," and 60 percent said their local officials "use their power only for private gains." Other surveys have revealed similar negative public perceptions of the CCP. A 1998 study of 12,000 urban and rural residents across 10 provinces conducted by the CCP's anti-graft agency found that only 43 percent of respondents agreed that "the majority of party and government officials are clean," and that fully one-third said "only a minority of party and government officials are clean."

At the same time as public officials are losing respect, the party's ideological appeal has all but evaporated. Polls conducted by the official national trade union in 1996 showed that only 15 percent of the workers surveyed regarded communism as "their highest ideal," while 70 percent said that their top priority was to pursue individual happiness. Even members of the ruling elite are beginning, albeit reluctantly, to admit this reality. A poll conducted in 1998 among 673 CCP officials in the northeastern province of Jilin found that 35 percent thought the status and authority of government officials had declined.

At the heart of the CCP's organizational and reputational decline is the breakdown of its members' ideological beliefs and internal discipline. Cynicism and corruption abound. The sale of government offices by local CCP bosses was unheard of in the 1980s but became widespread in the 1990s. A 1998 survey of 2,000 provincial officials, conducted by the official anti-graft agency, found that 45 percent of respondents thought such practices were continuing unabated.

Even more worrying, the CCP appears unable to enforce internal discipline despite the mortal threat posed by corruption, which has surpassed unemployment as the most serious cause of social instability. Recent official actions, especially the prosecution and execution of several senior officials, create the impression that the CCP leadership is committed to combating corruption. But a comprehensive look at the data tells a different story. Most corrupt officials caught in the government's dragnet seem to have gotten off with no more than a slap on the wrist. For example, of the 670,000 party members disciplined for wrongdoing from 1992 to 1997, only 37,500, or 6 percent, were punished by criminal prosecution. Indeed, self-policing may be impossible for a ruling party accountable to no one. According to a top CCP official, the Party has in recent years expelled only about 1 percent of its members.

Perhaps the greatest contributing factor to the CCP's political decline is, ironically, the absence of competition. Competition would have forced the party to redefine its mission and recruit members with genuine public appeal. But like monopoly firms, the CCP has devoted its energies to preventing the emergence of competition. Without external pressures, monopolies such as the CCP inevitably develop a full range of pathologies such as patronage systems, organizational dystrophy, and unresponsiveness. Moreover, one-party regimes can rarely take on the new competitors that emerge when the political environment changes suddenly. The fall of the Soviet bloc regimes and the defeat of similar monopolistic parties in the developing world (such as Mexico's Institutional Revolutionary Party) show that an eroding capacity for political mobilization poses a long-term threat to the CCP.

Failing State?

In a party-state, the ruling party's weakness unavoidably saps the state's power. Such "state incapacitation," which in its extreme form results in failed states, is exemplified by the government's increasing inability to provide essential services, such as public safety, education, basic health care, environmental protection, and law enforcement. In China, these indices have been slipping over the past two decades. This decline is especially alarming since it has occurred while the Chinese economy has been booming.

Most of the evidence of the government's deteriorating performance is mundane but telling. Take, for example, the number of traffic fatalities (a key measure of a state's capacity to regulate a routine, but vital, social activity: transportation). Chinese roads are almost twice as deadly today as they were in 1985; there were about 58 road fatalities per 10,000 vehicles in 2000, compared to 34 in 1985. An international comparison using 1995 data shows that traffic fatality risks were much higher in China than in India or Indonesia. Indeed, China fared better only than Tonga, Bangladesh, Myanmar, and Mongolia in the Asia-Pacific region.

Although China has made tremendous progress in improving education, its recent performance lags behind that of many developing countries. China's education spending in 1998 was a mere 2.6 percent of GDP, below the average of 3.4 percent for low-income countries. In fact, China spends almost a third less on education than does India. As a result, access to primary and intermediate education is as low as 40 percent among school-age children in the country's poor western regions.

China's public health-care system has decayed considerably in recent years and compares poorly with those of its neighbors. According to the World Health Organization, China's health system ranked 144th worldwide, placing it among the bottom quartile of WHO members, behind India, Indonesia, and Bangladesh. China's agricultural population has been hit especially hard, as government neglect has led to a near-total collapse of the rural public-health infrastructure. According to the 1998 survey conducted by the Ministry of Health, 37 percent of ill farmers did not seek medical treatment because they could not afford it, and 65 percent of sick peasants needing hospitalization were not admitted because they could not pay. Both figures were higher than in 1993, when a similar survey was carried out. Poor health has become the chief cause of poverty in rural China; 40–50 percent of those who fell below the poverty line in 2000 in some provinces did so only after becoming seriously ill. Even more troubling, the crumbling public-health infrastructure is a principal cause of the rapid spread of HIV and AIDS in China. The United Nations warned in a recent study that "China is on the verge of a catastrophe that could result in unimaginable human suffering, economic loss, and social devastation."

State incapacitation also manifests itself in worsening environmental degradation. This problem poses perhaps the deadliest threat to China's continued economic development. About a third of the country suffers from severe soil erosion, 80 percent of wastewater is discharged untreated, 75 percent of the country's lakes and about half its rivers have been polluted, and nine of the ten cities with the worst air pollution in the world in 1999 were located in China.

China suffers huge direct economic losses from this environmental damage. The World Bank estimated in the mid-1990s that major forms of pollution cost the country 7.7 percent of its GDP. Beyond this measurable cost, environmental degradation, together with the collapse of much of the agricultural infrastructure built before the 1980s, may have exacerbated the effects of natural disasters. Grain losses resulting from natural disasters have more than doubled in the last 50 years, with most of the increase recorded in the 1990s.

Busting the Budget

The central cause of the declining effectiveness of the Chinese state is a dysfunctional fiscal system that has severely undercut the government's ability to fund public services while creating ample opportunities for corruption. Government data misleadingly suggest that the state experienced a massive loss of revenue over the last two decades, as its tax receipts fell from 31 percent of GDP in 1978 to 14 percent in 1999. The truth, however, is quite different. Aggregate government revenue over the past 20 years has held steady at about 30 percent of GDP. What has changed is the massive diversion of revenue from the government budget; increasingly, income collected by the government is not listed in the official budget. At their peak in the mid-1990s, such off-budget earnings exceeded budgeted tax revenue by two to one.

Provincial and municipal governments are the primary beneficiaries of this system because it allows them to raise revenue outside the normal tax streams. Because local officials are more likely to get promoted for delivering short-term growth or other such tangible results, off-budget revenue tends to be spent on building local industries and other projects that do little to improve education, health, or the environment. Moreover, since normal budget rules do not apply to such revenue, officials enjoy near-total discretion over its spending. Consequently, corruption is widespread. Large portions of this off-budget money have been found stashed away in secret slush funds controlled by government officials. In 1999, the National Auditing Agency claimed to have uncovered slush funds and illegal expenditures that amounted to 10 percent of 1998's tax revenue.

An important consequence of this dysfunctional fiscal system is the near collapse of local public finance in many counties and townships, particularly in the populous rural interior provinces (such as Henan, Anhui, and Hunan). Although counties and townships provide most government services, they rely on a slim tax base, collecting only 20 percent of total government revenue. In 1999, counties generated revenue barely equal to two-thirds of their spending, and about 40 percent of counties can pay for only half their expenditures.

The fiscal conditions for township governments are even more precarious because townships have practically no tax base and must extract their revenue from farmers, mostly through inefficient and coercive collection. The responsibilities of providing public services while supporting a bloated bureaucracy have forced many township governments deeply into debt. For instance, a survey in Hunan in 2000 found that township debts equaled half the province's total revenue.

In most countries, the state's declining fiscal health portends more serious maladies. The problems of the rural provinces should serve as an urgent warning to Beijing because these are historically the most unstable regions in the country, having previously generated large-scale peasant rebellions. Indeed, it is no coincidence that these agrarian provinces (where per capita income in 2000 was about half the national average) have in recent years seen the largest increase in peasant riots and tax revolts. Left to their own devices, local governments will not be able to provide effective remedies. A workable solution will require reforming the flawed fiscal system at the top and restructuring local governments at the bottom to make them more efficient and responsive.

Anger Management

The institutional decline of the ruling party and the weakness of the state have caused rising tensions between the state and society. The number of protests, riots, and other forms of resistance against state authorities has risen sharply. For instance, the number of collective protests grew fourfold in the 1990s, increasing from 8,700 in 1993 to a frightening 32,000 in 1999. The size and violence of such incidents have grown as well. There were 125 incidents involving more than 1,000 protesters in 1999, and the government itself admits that protests with more than 10,000 participants have become quite common. For example, in March 2002, more than 20,000 laid-off workers participated in a week-long protest in the northern city of Liaoyang. In rural areas, many towns have reported mob attacks by peasants on government buildings and even on officials themselves.

To be sure, rising social frustration results partly from the hardships produced by China's economic transition. In recent years, falling income in rural areas and growing unemployment in the cities have contributed to the rising discontent among tens of millions of peasants and workers. But the increasing frequency, scale, and intensity of collective defiance and individual resistance also reveal deep flaws in Chinese political institutions that have exacerbated the strains of transition. Social frustration is translated into political protest not merely because of economic deprivation, but because of a growing sense of political injustice. Government officials who abuse their power and perpetrate acts of petty despotism create resentment among ordinary citizens every day. These private grievances are more likely to find violent expression when the institutional mechanisms for resolving them (such as the courts, the press, and government bureaucracies) are inaccessible, unresponsive, and inadequate.

In rural China, where institutional rot is much more advanced, the tensions between the state and the peasantry have reached dangerous levels. In a startling internal report, the Ministry of Public Security admitted that "in some [rural] areas, enforcement of family-planning policy and collection of taxes would be impossible without the use of police force." In some villages, peasant resistance has grown so fierce that local officials dare not show their faces; these areas have effectively become lawless.

The most important source of this anger is the onerous tax burden levied on China's most impoverished citizens. The effective tax rate in 1996 for the agrarian sector (excluding village enterprises) was estimated at 50 percent. In fact, collecting taxes and fees has become practically the only task performed by public officials in rural areas, consuming 60–70 percent of their time. In some areas, local officials have even recruited thugs in their collection efforts; such practices have resulted in the illegal imprisonment, torture, and even deaths of peasants who are unable to pay. What has irked the peasantry even more is that their high taxes appear to have brought few government services in return. The combination of high payment, heavy-handed collection, and inadequate services has thus turned a large portion of the rural population against the state. Recent polls conducted in rural areas found that peasants consistently identify excessive taxes and fees as the most important cause of instability.

Significantly, relations between the state and society are growing more tense at a time of rising income inequality. To be sure, the reasons behind this process are extremely complex. Although the most important causes of overall inequality are the growing rural-urban income gap and regional disparities, the level of income inequality within regions and cities has been rising at an alarming pace as well. Recent surveys have found that inequality has become one of the top three concerns for the public. In the context of rampant official corruption, this rising inequality is likely to fuel public ire against the government because most people believe that only the corrupt and privileged can accumulate wealth. Such a perception is not off the mark: one academic study estimated that illegal income contributed to a 30 percent increase in inequality during the 1980s.

The absence of pressure valves within the Chinese political system will hamper the regime's ability to reduce and manage state-society tensions. Recent reforms, such as instituting village elections and improving the legal system, have proved inadequate. The CCP's failure to open up the political system and expand institutional channels for conflict resolution creates an environment in which aggrieved groups turn to collective protest to express frustrations and seek redress.

The accumulation of state-society tensions will eventually destabilize China, especially because the dynamics that generate such tensions trap the CCP in a hopeless dilemma. Rising tensions increase the risks that any reforms, even implemented as remedies, could trigger a revolution. Alexis de Tocqueville first observed this paradox: repressive regimes are most likely to be overthrown when they try to reform themselves. This sobering prospect could deter even the most progressive elements within the CCP from pursuing change.

Think Again

Remedying China's mounting governance deficits should be the top priority of the country's new leaders. At present, these problems, brought on by the contradictions of dot communism, are serious but not life-threatening. If the new leadership addresses the institutional sources of poor governance, the CCP may be able to manage its problems without risking a political upheaval. The unfolding succession drama, however, will get in the way of meaningful change in the short term. Proposing even a moderate reform program could jeopardize a leader's political prospects. Moreover, undertaking risky reforms would require a high level of party unity—unlikely from a leadership jockeying for power.

Thus, China's governance deficits are likely to continue to grow and threaten the sustainability of its economic development. The slow-brewing crisis of governance may not cause an imminent collapse of the regime, but the accumulation of severe strains on the political system will eventually weigh down China's economic modernization as poor governance makes trade and investment more costly and more risky. The current economic dynamism may soon fade as long-term stagnation sets in.

Such a prospect raises questions about some prevailing assumptions about China. Many in the Bush administration view China's rise as both inevitable and threatening, and such thinking has motivated policy changes designed to counter this potential "strategic competitor." On the other hand, the international business community, in its enthusiasm for the Chinese market, has greatly discounted the risks embedded in the country's political system. Few appear to have seriously considered whether their basic premises about China's rise could be wrong. These assumptions should be revisited through a more realistic assessment of whether China, without restructuring its political system, can ever gain the institutional competence required to generate power and prosperity on a sustainable basis. As Beijing changes its leadership, the world needs to reexamine its long-cherished views about China, for they may be rooted in little more than wishful thinking.

III. GOING GLOBAL

China and the Global Economy*

Justin Yifu Lin

It is a great pleasure to be here with you today to discuss the role of Asia in the post-crisis global economy—that is, to the extent that the global economy is truly "post-crisis." My focus will be on my home country—China is obviously the biggest story out of Asia in terms of economic growth in recent decades, and the growth in China has been a driving force for the recovery from the global crisis since 2009. As a Chinese economist and specialist on economic development, I have had the good fortune to witness and participate in the policy debate over this remarkable period since returning to China with a PhD in economics in 1987.

I will organize my remarks around the following four themes: (1) China's achievements since the initiation of economic reforms in 1979; (2) prospects for China's growth in the coming decades; (3) challenges for China's future growth; and (4) the role of China in the multipolar growth world.

China's Achievements Since the Reform and Opening in 1979

China started its reform and opening in 1979 and achieved an annual growth rate of 9 percent between 1979 and 1990. At the end of that period and even up to early 2000s, many scholars still believed that China could not continue that growth rate much

longer due to the lack of fundamental reforms.[1] However, China's annual growth rate during the period 1990–2010 increased to 10.4 percent. On the global economic scene, China's growth since the reform and opening started has been unprecedented. This was a dramatic contrast with the depressing performance of other transitional economies in Eastern Europe and the former Soviet Union.

As a result of the extraordinary performance, there has been a dramatic change in China's status in the global economy. When China embarked on its economic reform program in 1979, the world's most populous country barely registered on the global economic scale, commanding a mere 1.8 percent of global gross domestic product (GDP) (measured in current US dollars). Today, it is the world's second-largest economy and produces 9.3 percent of global GDP (Figure 1).

China's exports grew by 16 percent per year from 1979 to 2009. At the start of that period,

* Speech at the Federal Reserve Bank of San Francisco, November 29, 2011 (http://www.frbsf.org/economic-research/events/2011/november/asia-role-post-crisis-global-economy-cpbs/ConferenceVolume.pdf).

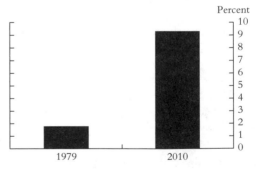

Figure 1 China's Share of World GDP (share measured in current USD)

(a) China's Share of World Exports of Goods and
Nonfactor Services (share measured incurrent USD)

(b) Merchandise Exports, 2009
(in trillions of USD)

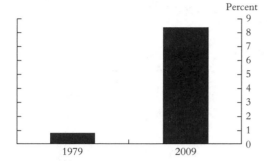

China	1.20
Germany	1.13
United States	1.06
Japan	0.58

Figure 2 China's Place in the World as an Exporter

China's exports represented a mere 0.8 percent of global exports of goods and nonfactor services. Now China is the largest exporter of goods in the world, with 9.6 percent of the global share and an 8.4 percent share of goods and nonfactor services (Figure 2).

In 1980, China was still a low-income country; in fact, its income per capita (measured in purchasing power parity or PPP) was only 30 percent of the level of the average sub-Saharan African country.[2] Today, its income per capita of $7,500 (in terms of PPP; $4,400 in current dollars) is over three times the level of sub-Saharan Africa, and China is well established as a middle-income country (Figure 3).

Behind this growth, there has been a dramatic structural transformation—in particular, rapid urbanization and industrialization. At the start of economic reforms in the 1980s, China was primarily an agrarian economy. Even in 1990, 73.6 percent of its population still lived in rural areas, and primary products composed 27.1 percent of GDP. These shares declined to 27.1 percent for the rural population and 11.3 percent for primary products composition of GDP in 2009. A similar change occurred in the composition of China's exports. In 1984, primary products and chemicals composed an important share of merchandise exports (about 55 percent). Now, almost all of China's exports are manufactures (Figure 4).

Accompanying the change in the composition of China's exports is the accumulation of foreign reserves. In 1990, China's foreign reserves were $11.1 billion USD, barely enough

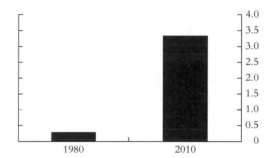

Figure 3 Ratio of China's GDP per Capita Relative to Sub-Saharan Africa (ratio measured in current PPP-adjusted dollars)

to cover 2.5 months of imports, and its reserves today exceed $3 trillion USD—the largest in the world.

Globally, China's economic performance was outstanding during the East Asian financial crisis (1998) and the current global crisis (2008) (Figure 5). China withstood the shocks and maintained dynamic growth in both crises. China's decision to maintain the *renminbi*'s stability helped other East Asian economies avoid a competitive devaluation, which contributed tremendously to the quick recovery of the crisis-affected countries. China's dynamic growth in the current global crisis has been a driving force for the global recovery.

The reasons for China experiencing such remarkable growth over the past 30 years were:

1. China adopted a dual-track approach and was able to achieve stability and dynamic transformation simultaneously.

(a) 1984 Structure of Chinese Exports

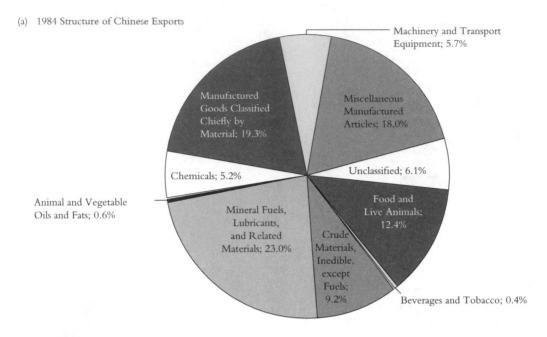

(b) 2009 Structure of Chinese Exports

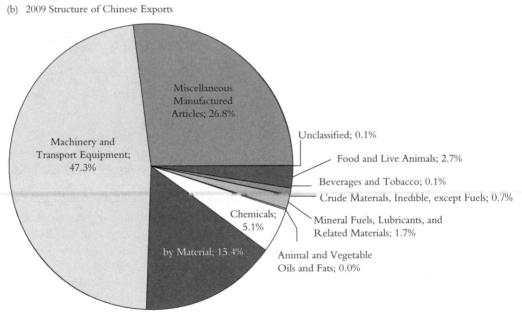

Figure 4 The Structural Transformation of China's Exports

2. China was a latecomer, developed according to its comparative advantage, and tapped into the potential advantage of backwardness.[3]

Many authors, myself included, have written extensively about the Chinese government's pragmatic approach to reforms. The result was to achieve "transition without tears." This was no accident: It was based on the government's recognition that big-bang reforms could be self-defeating. It was necessary to let private enterprises prosper wherever feasible, but to continue to support important state-owned enterprises while reforming them gradually.

The second point is the latecomer advantage. As I wrote in my article "China's Miracle Demystified,"[4]

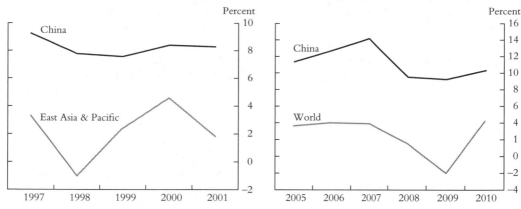

(a)   GDP Growth during the Asian Crisis

(b)   GDP Growth during the Global Crisis

Figure 5 China Glides Past Regional and Global Financial Crises

A developing country such as China, which started its modernization drive in 1949, potentially has the advantage of backwardness in its pursuit of technological innovation and structural transformation (Gerschenkron 1962). In advanced high-income countries technological innovation and industrial upgrading require costly and risky investments in research and development, because their vanguard technologies and industries are located on the global frontier. Moreover, the institutional innovation required to accommodate the potential of new technology and industry often proceeds in a costly trial-and-error, path-dependent, evolutionary process (Fei and Ranis 1997). By contrast, a latecomer country aspiring to be at the global technological and industrial frontiers can borrow technology, industry, and institutions from the advanced countries at low risk and costs. So if a developing country knows how to tap into the advantage of backwardness in technology, industry, and social and economic institutions, it can grow at an annual rate several times that of high-income countries for decades before closing its income gap with those countries.

Prospects for China's Growth in the Coming 20 Years

Looking forward, China can still rely on the advantage of backwardness, and it has the potential to maintain dynamic growth for another 20 years or more because of the following reasons:

1. In 2008, China's per capita income was 21 percent of US per capita income measured in PPP.[5] The income gap between China and the United States indicates that there is still a large technological gap between China and industrialized countries. China can continue to enjoy the advantage of backwardness before closing up the gap.

2. Maddison's (2010) estimation shows that China's current relative status to the United States is similar to that of Japan's in 1951, Korea's in 1977, and Taiwan's in 1975. The annual growth rate of GDP grew 9.2 percent in Japan between 1951 and 1971, 7.6 percent in Korea between 1977 and 1997, and 8.3 percent in Taiwan between 1975 and 1995. China's development strategy after the reform in 1979 is similar to that of Japan, Korea, and Taiwan. China has the potential to achieve another 20 years of 8 percent growth. By that time, China's per capita income measured in PPP may reach about 50 percent of US per capita income. (Note that Japan's per capita measured in PPP was 65.6 percent of that of the United States in 1971, Korea's was 50.2 percent in 1997, and Taiwan's was 54.2 percent in 1995.) Measured by PPP, China's economic size may then be twice as large as that of the United States; and measured by market exchange rates, China may be at least the same size as the United States.

That said, now China is becoming an innovator in its own right. As a middle-income country, in many sectors that China has comparative advantage;

other higher income countries have graduated, or are close to graduating, from those sectors—for example, household electronics and the high-speed train. If China wants to maintain leadership in those sectors, it will need to develop the technology/product innovation when it reaches the frontier. China can then become a global technological/industrial leader in those sectors. There are also some new sectors, such as green technology, which are important for China's sustainable growth. China has the potential to be a leader due to its large domestic market.

Challenges of China's Growth in the Twelfth Five-Year Plan—The Global Crises and the "New Normal"

Over the last three years, the global economy has witnessed its most tumultuous times since the Great Depression. The impressive coordinated policy response of the G-20 nations has helped the world avoid the worst possible scenario. Economic activity started to recover around the world in 2009. Global GDP performance improved from a contraction of 2 percent in 2009 to a growth of 4.2 percent in 2010, and a projected growth of 2.7 percent in 2011.[6]

However, we are observing a two-speed recovery. On the one hand, high-income countries' growth rates in 2010 and 2011 are estimated 3.1 percent and only 1.6 percent, respectively—far below the historical average following other crises. On the other hand, developing countries have been growing at 7.6 percent in 2010 and are likely to be at 6.0 percent in 2011, much faster than advanced countries and returning to their pre-crisis rates (Figure 6). Developing countries, especially China

and India, but others too, have increasingly become engines of the world economy growth.

However, there are tremendous risks underneath this global outlook. First and most importantly, the high-income countries are still beset with high unemployment rates and large excess capacities in housing and manufacturing sectors, which repress private consumption and investment and dampen growth. The combination of low returns and high risks on financial investment in these countries, caused by low growth and high unemployment rates, has been referred to as the "new normal" (Clarida 2010).

Second, the sovereign debts in a number of European countries and the government debts in some states in the United States may require restructuring, and they present a threat to the stability of global financial markets.

Third, the large short-term capital inflows to a number of middle-income countries create appreciation pressures, and may damage their external competitiveness and stymie their growth prospects. The capital influx may also lead to the emergence of unsustainable bubbles in their equity and real estate markets.

Fourth, the resurgence in food, commodity, and fuel prices has hurt the poor and threatened social stability, as demonstrated by events in North Africa.

These risks to a sustained recovery are directly or indirectly related to the simultaneous existence of large excess capacity in the high-income countries. In spite of the recovery, industrial production in these countries is estimated to be more than 10 percent below its peak in 2008 (World Bank 2011, p. 36). The high unemployment rate is a reflection of their high underutilization of capacity. The need to increase social spending and provide stimulus to counter these conditions at the same time that public revenue is under stress presents a dilemma. Fiscal deterioration is a looming concern and has led to state and sovereign debt problems in the United States and several European countries. The adoption of low-interest rates in high-income countries as a countercyclical measure at the same time that investment opportunities are constrained by the underutilization of capacity encourages investors to seek high yields, resulting in large short-term capital outflows to emerging markets and contributing to the spikes of food, fuel, and commodity prices.

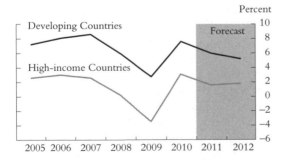

Figure 6 The Two-Speed Economic Recovery GDP Growth

The Challenge of Triple Imbalances

Given the inevitable slowdown in exports to high-income countries in the coming years and the need to reduce trade surplus, it is prudent and pragmatic to consider ways to rebalance the Chinese economy towards domestic demand. Much is said about stimulating consumption, but the process should be balanced between consumption and continuing strong growth in investment. The latter is critical for industrial upgrading and sustainable increases of per capita income, as well as developing green economy sectors and investing in environmental protection. This shift towards domestic demand represents the first rebalancing.

A second form of rebalancing is a structural transformation to reduce income disparities. In spite of the general improvement of living standards, China has shifted from a relatively egalitarian society at the beginning of reforms in 1979 to a country with alarming income inequality. The Gini index reached 41.5 in 2005, approaching the level of Latin American countries (World Bank 2011, p. 94). The widening disparity may threaten social stability and hinder economic growth.

There is a third form of rebalancing that is overlooked by macroeconomists. China's extraordinary growth has come with almost inevitable environmental costs. China needs to rebalance short-term growth and long-term environmental sustainability. This poses a challenge for the future in terms of shifting the structure of production towards cleaner technologies. The question then becomes: How can China engineer this triple rebalancing?

Rebalancing toward Domestic Demand and Reducing Income Disparities

The first two rebalancing themes are closely related in the case of China, since in the end improving the distribution of income is the key to rebalancing towards domestic demand (see Lin, Dinh, and Im 2010). Specifically, I am referring to the distribution of income between aggregate households on aggregate and the corporate sector (essentially the functional distribution of income) and the distribution of income across households (or the size distribution of income). We know from the national accounts and from industry data that a large share of Chinese national income accrues to large corporations, and we also know that an increasing share of income accrues to rich people. Both groups have higher propensities to save than the middle-income and low-income households. Figure 7 displays the increasing share of corporate savings as a share of GDP and the rising Gini coefficient that summarizes the increasing concentration of household income. This pattern of income distribution increases investment and the accumulation of productive capacity while repressing domestic consumption, leading to a large current account surplus. Shifting more

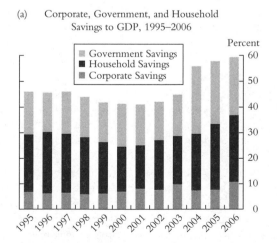

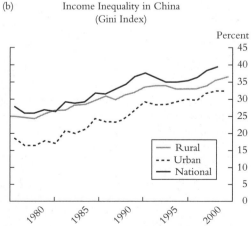

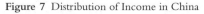

Figure 7 Distribution of Income in China

income towards workers can rebalance income between rich and poor and between the corporate sector and households. This redistribution would also reduce external imbalances.

After the economic reforms in 1979, China's economic development changed from a capital-intensive industry-oriented strategy, which went against China's comparative advantage, to a strategy that follows China's comparative advantage. In theory, as noted in my Marshall Lectures, following comparative advantage to develop industries should lead to improvements in the distribution of income. More specifically, I have noted, when an economy's development is in its early stage—with relatively abundant labor and scarce capital—enterprises will initially enter labor-intensive industries and adopt more labor-intensive technologies. This will create as many employment opportunities as possible and transfer labor from traditional sectors to modern manufacturing and service sectors. Accompanied with the upgrading in the endowment structure, labor abundance will be replaced gradually with labor scarcity and capital scarcity will gradually become capital abundance. Accordingly, the cost of labor will increase and the cost of capital will decrease. Because capital income is the major source of income for the rich, while labor is the major source of income for the poor, such changes in relative prices will make it possible to achieve economic growth and equity simultaneously (Lin 2009, p. 47).

In practice, however, the concentration of income in the corporate sector and among rich people is a consequence of the dual-track reform process, which retains certain distortions as a way to provide continuous support to nonviable firms in the priority industries. Those distortions favor large corporations and rich people. Major remaining distortions include the concentration of financial services in the four large state-owned banks, the almost zero royalty on natural resources, and the monopoly of major service industries, including telecommunications, power, and banking.

Those distortions contribute to the stability in China's transition process. They also contribute to the rising income disparity and other imbalances in the economy. This is because only big companies and rich people have access to credit services provided by the big banks, and the interest rates are artificially repressed. As a result, big companies and rich people are receiving subsidies from the depositors who have no access to bank credit services and are relatively poor. The concentration of profits and wealth in large companies and the widening of income disparities are unavoidable. Low royalty levies on natural resources and monopoly in the service sector have similar effects.

Therefore, it is imperative for China to address structural imbalances by removing the remaining distortions in the finance, natural resources, and service sectors so as to complete the transition to a well-functioning market economy. The necessary reforms include (1) removing financial repression and allowing the development of small local financing institutions including local banks to increase financial services, especially access to credit, to household farms as well as small- and medium-size enterprises in manufacturing and service sectors; (2) reforming the pension system, removing the old retired worker's pension burden from the state-owned mining companies and levying appropriate royalty taxes on natural resources; and (3) encouraging entry and competition in telecommunications, power, and financial sectors.

In recent debates about the rebalancing toward domestic demand in China, much is made of the need for social safety nets to stimulate domestic demand. I would argue that a social safety net is needed for social harmony rather than for increasing the ratio of consumption in China. This is because, while households may increase the propensity for consumption with improved social safety nets, the government needs to increase savings in order to accumulate the provision funds for covering pension and other social program costs. As a result, the total aggregate savings of private households and the government may not change much.[7] The reforms in social safety nets are desirable mainly for protecting the vulnerable and for providing transitory support to relieve temporary shocks to jobs and health and to maintain social harmony. The reforms can be based on lessons from international experience from both developed and developing countries. Note that there have been mixed results from pension privatization reforms, despite the need for a fiscally sustainable old-age security system. The question of full funding can be addressed separately from the question of who manages the savings, and a multipolar design is generally recommended.[8] In other social programs, the lessons from the experience of conditional cash transfers are quite positive, and this is something that China could explore.[9]

The Environment: Rebalancing Short-Term Growth and Long-Term Sustainability

Pollution and global warming are real challenges for long-term sustainability. China is a continental economy, and as a result, environmental externalities from economic activity are internalized within China's borders. This implies that there are direct impacts of pollution on the health of the population. Another challenge is that China is still in the high-carbon phase of development. These challenges for sustainable growth create the opportunity for China to become a technological leader in green growth. Theory and experience has shown that innovation in this area can have important positive spillover effects for technological upgrading more broadly in the economy as well.

I should note that the reforms I have discussed are the main items in the Twelfth Five-Year Plan, which covers 2011–15.

China and the Multipolar Growth World

It is important to place this moment in history in a broader historical context. After the Industrial Revolution, the world was polarized. Growth in industrialized countries accelerated. Later in the 20th century, a few developing economies in East Asia were able to accelerate growth, and they caught up with the industrialized countries. Most other developing countries failed to have sustained and accelerated growth. As a result, there is a great divergence between the developed and developing countries, as Figure 8 shows.

Given this history, the global economy was dominated by the G-7 economies consistently throughout the latter half of the 20th century. At market exchange rates, the G-7 represented about two-thirds of the global economy. Even accounting for purchasing power parity, half of global income was concentrated in the G-7, as displayed in Figure 9.

With the rapid growth in the past 20 years, China has become a major driving force for the emergence of a multipolar growth world. As shown in Figure 10, in the 1980s and the 1990s, except for China, the other top five contributors to the growth of global GDP were all members of the G-7 industrialized countries, and China's contributions were respectively 13.4 percent and 26.7 percent of the contributions of the United States in those two decades. However, in the decade beginning in 2000, China became the top contributor to the growth of global GDP. Among the G-7 countries only the United States and Japan remained in the top-five list, and China's contribution exceeded that of the United States

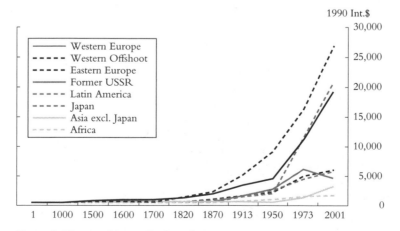

Figure 8 History of Economic Growth

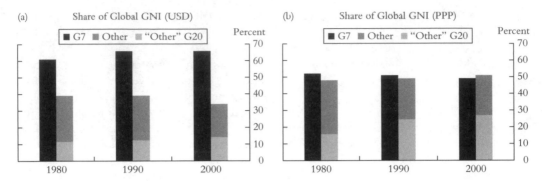

Figure 9 Global Shares of Gross National Income

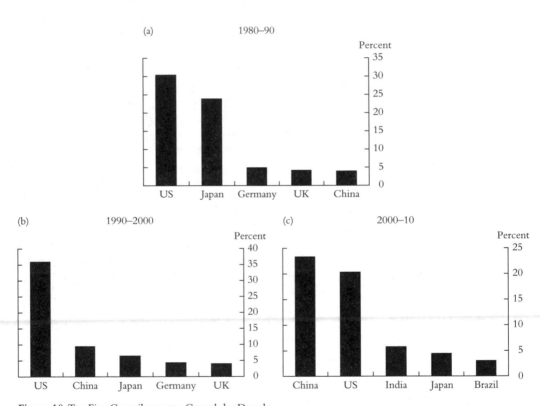

Figure 10 Top Five Contributors to Growth by Decade

by 4 percentage points. A multipolar growth world emerged in the 21st century, with many of the new growth poles in emerging market economies.

Leading up to the global crisis, a burst of convergence occurred, as developing countries grew substantially faster than the high-income countries. As we can see in Figure 11, this superior growth was widespread in developing countries across regions. This tendency is likely

to continue as growth prospects in developing countries remain favorable and prospects for high-income countries remain subdued. This is not to say that the latter will not affect the former, but there is sufficient momentum in developing countries' own demand—combined with increasing south-to-south economic linkages—that should sustain a gap in growth rates between the developing and the high-income countries. Fortunately this convergence has also been fairly broad-based across regions of the developing world.

As a result of this superior growth in the developing world, we have witnessed a shift toward a more multipolar growth world. Figure 12 shows this shift in economic weight from the G-7 economies to the developing economies—both the larger members of the G-20 and other countries beyond the G-20.

As discussed [previously] China has the potential of maintaining an 8 percent annual growth rate for another two decades. If China can maintain this growth rate in the coming years, it may contribute to the multipolar growth world in many other ways in addition to GDP growth and trade.

There will be benefits shared and opportunities created by China's growth—for both high-income and developing countries. For high-income countries, China's growth will expand the markets for capital goods and intermediate goods exports.

Many developing countries are still major producers of agricultural and natural resource commodities. Chinese consumption and production growth will continue to support adequate prices for commodities and thus help these exporters.

In addition, the Chinese government and Chinese firms will also provide funds for natural resource and infrastructure investment in emerging markets and low-income countries. This is already happening, and it is likely to continue

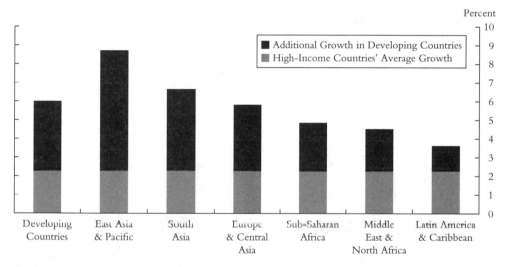

Figure 11 Growth Acceleration in Developing Countries (average for 2000–08)

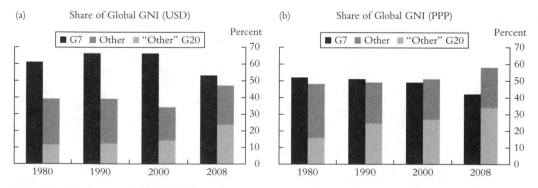

Figure 12 Rebalancing of the Global Economic Landscape

into the future. In particular, there is a growing role for Chinese finance in the African region—the developing region with the most constrained access to finance (Wang 2009).

The continued structural transformation of the Chinese economy will create other opportunities. As China undergoes industrial upgrading to more sophisticated product markets, it will leave the market space for other developing countries to enter the more labor-intensive industries. Chinese enterprises are expected to relocate their existing production to other lower-wage countries as they upgrade to higher value-added industries, like Japan and East Asian economies did a few decades ago. The difference is that, because of its size, China may become a "leading dragon" for other developing countries instead of a "lead goose" in the traditional flying geese pattern of the international diffusion of industrial development.[10]

China also has an important and expanding role in the new global economic architecture. As the economic landscape changes to a multipolar

growth world, the international architecture will reorganize, as evidenced by the shift from the old G-7 to the broader G-20. China has become a key member in regional and international forums, such as APEC and the G-20. Over time, there is also the possibility of the gradual emergence of the Chinese *renminbi* as a global reserve currency. This is something that would require many fundamental reforms in the Chinese economy; however, it is almost inevitable given the growing relative strength of China in the multipolar world.

Whether we are on the verge of an Asian century or not, one thing is clear: There has already been a dramatic shift in the geographic center of the global economy. China is very much at the center of this transformation, and its role as a leading dragon can be beneficial for growth prospects for the overall economy. The world is desperately in need of engines of growth right now, and fortunately—with continued strong and pragmatic economic policymaking—China can provide that impetus for economic growth.

NOTES

1. Chang (2001) was one representation of such views.
2. PPP data do not go back to 1979 in the World Development Indicator database.
3. For further discussion of these two points, see Lin (2012).
4. Lin (forthcoming).
5. The national data used in this and next paragraphs are taken from Maddison (2010).
6. Historical data from World Development Indicators. The forecast for 2011 is from a preliminary World Bank projection.

7. An example of this phenomenon is Singapore, which has one of the best social safety nets in the world, but its savings as a percentage of GDP have been as high as 40 percent.
8. See Holzmann and Hinz (2005).
9. Conditional cash transfers form one of the most carefully analyzed public policy programs in developing countries, with numerous impact evaluations completed. For a survey, see Fiszbein and Schady (2009).
10. For the flying geese pattern of industrial diffusion, see Akamatsu (1962).

REFERENCES

Akamatsu, Kaname. 1962. "A Historical Pattern of Economic Growth in Developing Countries." *The Development Economies* 1 (Issue supplement 1), pp. 3–25.

Chang, Gordon G. 2001. *The Coming Collapse of China.* New York: Random House.

Clarida, Richard. 2010. "The Mean of the New Normal Is an Observation Rarely Realized: Focus Also on the Tails." *Global Perspectives*, PIMCO, July.

Fei, John, and Gustav Ranis. 1997. *Growth and Development from an Evolutionary Perspective.* Oxford: Blackwell Publishing.

Fiszbein, Ariel, and Norbert Schady. 2009. *Conditional Cash Transfers: Reducing Present and Future Poverty.* Washington, DC: World Bank.

Gerschenkron, Alexander. 1962. *Economic Backwardness in Historical Perspective: A Book of Essays.* Cambridge, MA: Belknap Press of Harvard University Press.

Holzmann, Robert, and Richard Hinz. 2005. *Old-Age Income Support in the 21st Century: An International Perspective on Pension Systems and Reform.* Washington, DC: World Bank.

Lin, Justin Yifu. 2009. *Economic Development and Transition: Thought, Strategy, and Viability.* Cambridge: Cambridge University Press, p. 47.

Lin, Justin Yifu. 2012. *Demystifying the Chinese Economy*. New York: Cambridge University Press.

Lin, Justin Yifu. Forthcoming. "China Miracle Demystified." Proceedings of Econometric Society Congress in Shanghai, 2011.

Lin, Justin Yifu, Hinh T. Dinh, and Fernando Im. 2010. "United States-China External Imbalance and the Global Financial Crisis." Paper prepared for the Edward Chen Distinguished Lecture, Hong Kong University.

Maddison, Angus. 2010. *Historical Statistics of the World Economy: 1–2008 AD*. Figure 8 data set, available at www.ggdc.net/maddison/Historical_Statistics/horizontal-file_02-2010.xls.

Ravallion, Martin, and Shaohua Chen. 2007. "China's (Uneven) Progress Against Poverty." *Journal of Development Economics* 82(1), pp. 1–42.

Wang, Yan. 2009. "Development Partnership for Growth and Poverty Reduction: A synthesis of the first event organized by the China-DAC Study Group," held October 28–29, Beijing.

World Bank. 2011. *World Development Indicators 2010*.

ARE CHINA'S MULTINATIONAL CORPORATIONS REALLY MULTINATIONAL?[*]

David Shambaugh

Following the Chinese government's mandate that companies should "go out" (走出去) or "go global" (走向世界), many observers anticipate that Chinese multinational corporations (MNCs) will secure a growing share of the international consumer market around the world. This may eventually occur, but for the time being China's multinational corporations remain a very long way from playing in the premier leagues of international commerce.

How many Chinese corporations can you name? Most likely fewer than ten, or even five. We are all familiar with Tsingtao Beer, Air China, Bank of China, and Lenovo computers —and some may know names like Huawei Technologies, Haier appliances, or China Mobile. But not a single one of these firms made the 2011 "Top 100 Global Brands" list compiled annually by *BusinessWeek* and Interbrand. The global brand presence of China's best-known multinationals is nowhere near the likes of Coca-Cola, GE, Intel, McDonald's, Google, Disney, Honda, Sony, Volkswagen, and similar global giants.

Yet when measured in terms of total revenue, it is clear that Chinese companies have steadily climbed up the global rankings. Twelve Chinese companies were included in *Fortune's* Global 500 list in 2001. And only a decade later, in 2011, that number rose to 61 (including four with headquarters in Hong Kong). China now ranks third on the global list, only slightly behind Japan but well behind American firms. In 2010 these 61 Chinese enterprises had a combined annual revenue of US $2.89 trillion and an estimated overall profit of US $176.1 billion. Of the 57 mainland companies, 49 are state-owned enterprises (SOEs).

While ranking on the *Fortune* Global 500 list indicates the growing clout of Chinese corporations, it does not mean that a company is internationally active or even that it is a real multinational. When these companies are ranked by foreign assets and sales, it becomes clear that, with few exceptions, they all operate predominantly within China. In other words, despite the government's directives and financial incentives to "go global," many leading Chinese corporations have yet to do so.

So why have Chinese multinational corporations encountered such difficulties in going global? Ten possible factors may explain it.

First, very few Chinese firms can operate truly globally. Haier, Huawei, and the national oil companies Sinopec, CNOOC, and CNPC are often the only ones that have capital, operations and sales on a global scale. Many of China's other multinationals (banks, auto companies, natural resource companies or IT) really only invest in and operate on some continents;

---

[*] This article appeared in the *East Asia Forum Quarterly* (April–June 2012).

most are far from possessing global production, marketing, distribution, logistics, supply, research and development, and human resource networks.

Second, the Achilles heel of Chinese multinationals is human resources—particularly management. Multilingual and multicultural managers are few and far between, and all assessments of Chinese corporations note this to be a fundamental weakness. A 2005 study by the global multinational consulting firm McKinsey & Company estimated that Chinese multinationals will require 75,000 global managers by 2020. As a result, Chinese students are flooding into foreign MBA programs as well as business schools in China. Distance-learning MBAs tailored to the Chinese market are also taking off.

But classroom training alone will not suffice because there is no substitute for extensive international experience. Some Chinese companies have taken advantage of the global financial downturn by hiring (preferably young) laid-off staff in New York, London, Hong Kong, and elsewhere. In 2010, for example, the *China Daily* reported that Chinese companies operating overseas had hired a total of 800,000 foreign employees.

Third, and related, Chinese companies and their management have displayed an inability to escape their own national corporate culture and business practices. Chinese business culture values interpersonal over institutional relationships and business decisions are often oriented towards short-term profit. There is also a lack of transparency and oversight, which has been linked to a high degree of corruption.

Moreover, Chinese companies are politicized: that is, many have Communist Party cells and members embedded within the firm. Most of China's state-owned "national champion" firms have CEOs appointed by the Organization Department of the Chinese Communist Party, and this is also true of multinationals. Unlike their Chinese competitors, though, most Western multinationals are apolitical. And this is not where the differences end. Western business culture emphasizes teamwork and cooperation between management and staff, detailed long-term planning, transparency and oversight, multiculturalism,

prosecution of corruption, and the institutionalization of relationships.

Fourth, as noted above, Chinese companies have a very poor global brand presence. Establishing this type of presence requires investing large and sustained resources into advertising and cultivating clientele. Having distinctive, non-Chinese names will also help in this endeavor.

Fifth, mergers and acquisitions have become the preferred modality for Chinese corporations to go global because they are a quick means of acquiring advanced technology, sales networks, established brand names, and other strategic assets overseas. Precisely because Chinese corporations have very few multilingual staff who have experience working in cross-cultural environments, and many who are inexperienced in local business practices, it is much easier for Chinese multinationals to simply buy a share of an established foreign firm in order to gain these elements and offset their deficits in one stroke. Even though in recent years China's mergers and acquisitions have spiked in number and sometimes in value, they have not been very successful so far.

One report estimates that 90 percent of China's 300 overseas mergers and acquisitions conducted between 2008 and 2010 were unsuccessful, with Chinese companies losing 40–50 percent of their value after the acquisition. This has particularly been the case in the technology, communications and natural resource sectors.

Sixth, while some Chinese firms develop business plans and strategies to globalize, the majority do not. Instead, efforts to "go global" tend to be driven by pent-up cash in search of a place to invest outside China's saturated domestic market; a strong mandate by the government to "go out," with incentives to do so and penalties for not doing so; naïveté about the complexities of foreign countries; a desire to maximize profits as quickly as possible, rather than produce steady revenue streams; and a fickle management tendency to frequently change decisions and directions.

Seventh, while Chinese firms do tend to have clear performance indicators and incentive programs and do provide job security, they do not score as well in other aspects of management. Big Chinese firms—and the Chinese government is no exception—are extremely hierarchical. Chinese organizational culture stresses discipline and conformity, which creates a climate of risk aversion and discourages initiative. Being entrepreneurial (which Chinese companies certainly are) is different from being innovative and creative. Moreover, the Chinese notion of teamwork is geared towards following leaders' instructions, rather than the more egalitarian and collegial model prevalent in Western organizations.

This preference for clearly defined workplace roles and hierarchies often means that Chinese do not adapt well to management structures that prize decentralization and individual initiative—and this has resulted in repeated culture clashes in Chinese mergers with Western companies.

The practice of mid-career (re)training is similarly alien to Chinese multinationals, while it is intrinsic to most Western corporations. Chinese firms tend to train a worker for a precise skill and job, which they are expected to do indefinitely—whereas many Western firms adopt much more flexible personnel policies that emphasize self-improvement, retraining and job mobility within the firm, and generalization over specialization.

Often this is done within the firm through training aimed at developing new job skills, but also via mid-career management training outside the firm—so-called executive education. A one-month stint in an "Executive Ed" program at the Wharton School, Kennedy School, INSEAD, London Business School or similar institutions offers an "escalator effect" for corporate management. Chinese business schools—such as Shanghai's China-Europe International Business School, Hong Kong University of Science and Technology's Business School, or Peking University's Guanghua School of Management—are all seen to be improving, but are yet to enter the premier league internationally. Though mid-career training has become *de rigueur* in the Chinese Communist Party and government, this organizational culture is yet to become prevalent in the corporate world.

Eighth, Chinese companies have demonstrated difficulties in adapting to foreign legal, regulatory, tax, and political environments. Transparency and corporate governance are not exactly attributes associated with Chinese companies, which have a reputation for opaque decision-making processes, frequently corrupt business practices, and often-fraudulent accounting procedures. Few Chinese firms have in-house legal counsel who are knowledgeable about foreign legal and regulatory environments. This impatience with the regulatory environment of host countries has had a negative impact on business operations abroad, particularly when Chinese companies have tried to list on foreign stock markets: many Chinese companies have filed fraudulent information with securities regulators in the United States before their initial public offerings. They also often run afoul of foreign politicians who are suspicious of Chinese investments on national security grounds.

Ninth, Chinese firms rarely apply due diligence when dealing with their competitors abroad, which often means they overlook both the strengths and weaknesses of their potential partners and competitors. As a result, they find it harder to exploit comparative advantages.

Finally, in looking for foreign partners, many Chinese multinationals run up against the "reciprocity problem." Many foreign multinationals with which Chinese corporations seek to partner have either been operating in China for many years or are seeking to enter the Chinese market. The former have most likely experienced years of Chinese red tape, investment obstacles, and have had very frustrating and costly experiences (even if they have become profitable), while the latter want an entrée. In both cases they look to the Chinese firm to make life easier for them inside China; for them, there is an informal quid pro quo: you help us in China, we help you abroad. The problem is that many Chinese multinationals have a bifurcated corporate structure, which means that domestic and international divisions often have a bureaucratic firewall between them and do not communicate well with each other. Moreover, the Chinese partner firm is not necessarily responsible for improving a foreign company's situation or solving its problems in China—this is often the domain of domestic government authorities. These competing motivations often lead to a mismatch of expectations between Chinese and foreign multinationals.

For all these reasons, Chinese corporations face a number of impediments in going global. They have a steep learning curve ahead. Over time, they will no doubt learn and adapt—as Chinese in all professional pursuits seem so capable of doing—but these obstacles are not insignificant. China's multinationals are still taking baby steps in global business.

RESOURCES AND ENVIRONMENT

Editorial Introduction

China's reforms have brought many miraculous and positive changes for the nation and people of China. But the frantic pace of development has also brought many unintended and negative consequences. China's environment is probably the most noticeable and pronounced such manifestation. This includes diminishing (and polluted) water resources, life-threatening and cancer-causing air pollution, desertification, deforestation, climate change, inefficient energy usage, and so on. It directly and negatively affects human health, economic growth, the planet's global warming. It is also potentially a volatile political issue. The first selection in this section by Beina Xu of the Council on Foreign Relations details the realities of China's polluted landscape, air, and water—and she elaborates many of the sources, costs and consequences for the country, China's neighbors, and the world. Some of the statistics are chilling. Environmental degradation rightfully has the status of being the number one public concern.

Consequently, the government is placing high priority on trying to mitigate and reverse the harmful damage to public health and the environment. The second selection includes a series of excerpts from China's official *White Paper* on climate change. It lists a wide variety of governmental directives and initiatives—from restructuring the industrial economy, to investing huge amounts in green technologies, to establishing strict caps and penalties on pollution, to controlling greenhouse gas emissions, to changing China's energy usage and mix. Time will tell if these initiatives are too little, too late—or if they are able to ameliorate the immediate horrific consequences while putting in place more sustainable policies for the future. As with many dimensions of government policy in China, the problem is not that the state does not have adequate regulations, provisions, and laws in place—it is that they are not implemented or are ignored at local levels.

The third selection, by China analyst Damien Ma, explicitly examines China's energy consumption. He notes how China has become the world's largest energy user and energy importer (60 percent of oil and 30 percent of natural gas). Yet China also remains heavily dependent on coal for basic heating and other usage, while fossil fuel use is skyrocketing along with the middle class's voracious appetite for private auto-mobiles (China has the world's fastest growing auto market). Perhaps China's greatest energy challenge is not overall consumption but its inefficient usage. Ma not only describes the need for China to fashion a more sensible energy policy, but he also reveals the economic impediments. He argues that more rational pricing of energy, with a much greater role for market rather than state-determined prices will be a key to a more sustainable long-term strategy.

I. ENVIRONMENT AND CLIMATE CHANGE

China's Environmental Crisis[*]

Beina Xu

China's environmental crisis is one of the most pressing challenges to emerge from the country's rapid industrialization. Its economic rise, which has averaged around 10 percent annual GDP growth for the past decade, has come at the expense of its environment and public health. As the world's largest source of carbon emissions, China is responsible for a third of the planet's greenhouse gas output and has sixteen of the world's twenty most polluted cities. Life expectancy in the north has decreased by 5.5 years due to air pollution, and severe water contamination and scarcity have compounded land deterioration problems. Environmental degradation cost the country roughly 9 percent of its gross national income in 2008, according to the World Bank, threatening to undermine the country's growth and exhausting public patience with the government's pace of reform. It has also bruised China's international standing as the country expands its global influence, and endangered its stability as the ruling party faces increasing media scrutiny and public discontent.

A History of Pollution

While China's economic boom has greatly accelerated the devastation of its land and resources, the roots of its environmental problem stretch back centuries. Dynastic leaders consolidating territory and developing China's economy exploited the country's natural resources in ways that contributed to famines and natural disasters, writes the Council on Foreign Relations' Elizabeth Economy in *The River Runs Black: The Environmental Challenge to China's Future.* Moreover, China's Confucian roots helped spur policies that often promoted man's use of nature, hindering the development of a conservation ethos. "China's current environmental situation is the result not only of policy choices made today but also of attitudes, approaches, and institutions that evolved over centuries," Economy writes.

It wasn't until the 1972 United Nations Conference on the Human Environment that China began to develop its environmental institutions. It dispatched a delegation to the conference in Stockholm, but by then the country's environment was already in dire straits that were further exacerbated by economic reforms of the late 1970s. Spearheaded by Deng Xiaoping in 1978, these reforms boosted China's industrial output at an average annual rate of more than 11.4 percent.

The legacy of decentralization characterized by Deng's reforms remains at the heart of China's environmental struggles today. The reforms diffused authority to the provinces, creating a proliferation of township and village enterprises (TVEs) to encourage development in rural industries. In

1997, TVEs generated almost a third of the national GDP. But local governments were difficult to monitor and therefore seldom upheld environmental standards. Today, environmental policies remain difficult to enforce at a local level, where officials often retain economic incentives to ignore them.

China's modernization has lifted hundreds of millions out of poverty and created a booming middle class. In some ways, the country's trajectory of industrialization is not unlike those of other modernizing nations, such as Great Britain in the early nineteenth century. But experts point to the nation's staggering size and pace of its growth, noting that its environmental effect on the world is *far greater* than that of any other single country. "It's on a scale and speed the world has never known," says Jennifer Turner, director of the China Environment Forum at the Woodrow Wilson Center.

How Bad Is It?

China's energy consumption has ballooned, spiking 130 percent from 2000 to 2010. In January 2013, Beijing experienced a prolonged bout of smog so severe that citizens dubbed it "airpocalypse"; the concentration of hazardous particles was forty times the level deemed safe by the World Health Organization (WHO). Later that year, pollution in the northern city of Harbin shrank visibility to less than 50 meters. *China Daily* reported that December was the worst month in 2013 for air quality, with more than 80 percent of the seventy-four cities with air-monitoring devices failing to meet national standards for at least half the month. Based on a 2012 Asian Development Bank report, less than 1 percent of China's 500 largest cities meet the WHO's air quality standards.

China Coal Plant Emissions by Health Impact

Coal has been the main culprit in the degradation of air quality. China is the world's largest coal producer and accounts for almost half of global consumption. Coal is also the source of as much as 90 percent of the country's sulfur dioxide emissions and half of its particulate emissions. Mostly burned in the north, it provides around 70 percent of China's energy needs. However, emissions levels from coal plants alone in 2011 potentially contributed to a quarter of a million premature deaths that year, according to a Greenpeace analysis. Another troubling trend compounding air problems has been the country's staggering pace of urbanization, with the government planning to move 70 to 75 percent of China's population to cities between 2000 and 2030. China is the world's largest emitter of greenhouse gases, having overtaken the United States in 2007.

Yet experts cite water depletion and pollution as the country's biggest environmental hazards. Overuse, contamination, and waste have produced severe shortages; approximately two-thirds of China's roughly 660 cities don't have enough water despite the fact that China controls the river water supply of thirteen neighboring countries and has dammed every major river on the Tibetan plateau. The impact is particularly felt in rural areas, where some 300 to 500 million people lack access to piped water. Industry along China's major water sources has also polluted the supply heavily; in 2005, a plant explosion leaked around one hundred tons of toxic chemicals into the Songhua River.

The pace of contamination has garnered increased media attention: in March 2013, Shanghai came under scrutiny when roughly 16,000 dead pigs were discovered floating through the Huangpu River. Lack of waste removal and proper processing has exacerbated the problem; almost 90 percent of underground water in cities and 70 percent of China's rivers and lakes are now polluted. Combined with negligent farming practices, the water crisis has turned China's arable land into desert, which today claims around 27.5 percent of China's total land mass. Some 400 million Chinese lives are affected by desertification, according to the government, and the World Bank estimates that the overall cost of water scarcity associated with pollution is around 147 billion RMB, or roughly 1 percent of GDP.

The Cost of Environmental Damage

Environmental depredations pose a serious threat to China's economic growth, costing the country roughly 9 percent of its gross national income, according to most recent figures from the World Bank. China's Ministry of Environmental Protection calculates its own "green GDP" number, estimating the cost of pollution at around 1.5 trillion RMB, or roughly 3.5 percent of GDP, according to its 2010 figures. Due to the sensitivity of the topic, the ministry has only been releasing such figures since 2006, and intermittently since then.

Data on the public health toll of China's pollution paint a devastating picture. According to a Global Burden of Disease study, air pollution contributed to 1.2 million premature deaths in China in 2010. In late 2013, an eight-year-old girl in Jiangsu province became China's youngest lung cancer patient; doctors attribute her illness to air pollution. Epidemiological studies conducted since the 1980s in northern China suggest that urban air in China causes significant health complications, including respiratory, cardiovascular, and cerebrovascular diseases. The pollution has also been linked to the proliferation of acute and chronic diseases; estimates suggest that around 11 percent of digestive system cancers in China may stem from unsafe drinking water. Human cases of the Avian Flu (H7N9 virus), which broke out in China in March 2013 and has claimed more than forty lives, were caused by exposure to infected poultry and contaminated environments.

China's neighbors, including Japan and South Korea, have also expressed concern over acid rain and smog affecting their native populations. In May 2013, government officials of the three countries added air pollution and climate change to a list of diplomatic issues for the region to solve. Moreover, a recent study reported that emissions from China's export industries are worsening air pollution as far away as the western United States.

The damage has also affected China's economic prospects as it continues to pursue resources and pump investment into other countries. Its close economic partners, particularly in the developing world, face costly environmental burdens attached with doing business with China.

Citizen Outrage

Environmental damage has cost China dearly, but the greatest collateral damage for the ruling Communist Party has likely been growing social unrest. Demonstrations have proliferated as citizens gain awareness of the health threats and means of organized protest (often the Internet). In October 2012, demonstrations against an $8.9 billion petrochemical plant expansion in the eastern city of Ningbo suspended the project. Several months later, anger boiled over in Shanxi Province, where a factory spilled thirty-nine tons of toxic chemicals into local water sources. In May 2013, thousands of demonstrators gathered in the southwest city of Kunming to protest the building of a nearby chemical plant, which would produce half a million tons of a carcinogenic chemicals annually.

Elizabeth Economy points out that one of the most important changes in China's environmental protest movement has been a shift, beginning in the late 2000s, from rural-based protests to urban movements. The issue has worried the top leadership, which views the unrest as a threat to the party's legitimacy and authority. A February 2013 poll by *People's Daily* named the environment as one of the top issues citizens wanted addressed by the central government. By early 2013, public protests had succeeded in consistently gaining concessions from local governments, and in March 2013, Li Keqiang, China's new premier, pledged that his government would show "even greater resolve" in tackling China's pollution crisis. Such remarks from the central government reflect "a changing understanding within China about the relationship between economic development and societal well-being," Economy and Levi write. But experts say the jury is still out on the current government, which has shown more resolve in cracking down on public dissent. "It seems to me that environmental protests could well fall within the sphere of concern over threats to China's domestic security," says Economy.

What's Being Done?

The government has mapped out ambitious environmental initiatives in recent five-year plans, although experts say few have been realized. In December 2013, China's National Development and Reform Commission, the country's top economic planning agency, issued its first nationwide blueprint for climate change, outlining an extensive list of objectives to achieve by 2020. Since January 2014, the central government has required 15,000 factories, including large state-owned enterprises, to publicly report real-time figures on their air emissions and water discharges. And the government has pledged to spend $275 billion over the next five years to clean up the air. More recently, China's legislature amended the country's environmental protection law to allow for stricter punishments against companies or individuals caught polluting the environment.

China is also one of the biggest investors in renewables; its spending could total 1.8 trillion RMB ($300 billion) in the five years through 2015 as part of its pledge to cut its carbon intensity. According to its National Energy Administration, renewable energy sources comprised 57 percent of newly installed electricity-generating capacity in the first ten months of 2013. "China is also reaching out and partnering with international companies to jointly create technologies," says the Wilson Center's Jennifer Turner.

The Internet has facilitated greater information transparency. Since 2008, the US embassy in Beijing has issued pollution readings via a Twitter feed, a service that also spread to consulates in other major Chinese cities. In 2012, Beijing publicly demanded—to no avail—that Washington cease the practice. Later that year, it began publishing its own hourly data in seventy-four cities.

While policy implementation has been inconsistent, a thriving environmental NGO community has grown to push the government to stay on track. Tens of thousands of these groups—often working with US and foreign counterparts—push for transparency, investigate corruption, and head grassroots campaigns. Friends of Nature is one of its oldest; Global Village and Green Home are among other well-known NGOs. Despite state support, these organizations inevitably face constraints from government fear that their activities could catalyze democratic social change. Beijing, for instance, has advanced an amendment to China's environmental protection law that would bar such groups from suing polluters. The central government has structured its efforts in much of the same way it has pursued economic growth, Elizabeth Economy writes, "by granting local authorities and factory owners wide decision-making power and by actively courting the international community and Chinese NGOs for their expertise while carefully monitoring their activities."

Yet some are sanguine about China's prospects. Despite the political reforms that will be needed to catalyze any real change in the environmental sphere, the public response to China's crisis has sprung some optimism about the future. "If there's any country in the world that can turn it around, it's China," says Jennifer Turner. "The Chinese people believe they have a right to a clean environment. How can you not be optimistic about that?"

China's Policies and Actions for Addressing Climate Change[*]

(2013 White Paper) [Excerpts]

Information Office of the State Council

Mitigating Climate Change

The Chinese government has reached its goal of reducing the energy consumption and CO_2 emissions per unit of GDP and has achieved positive results since 2012 by controlling greenhouse gas emissions by adjusting the industrial structure, improving the energy structure, making energy use more efficient, and increasing carbon sinks.

Adjusting the Industrial Structure

Transforming and upgrading traditional industries. The National Development and Reform Commission (NDRC), the Ministry of Environment Protection, and the Ministry of Land and Resources have raised the entry threshold for

---

[*] This White Paper was published by the State Council Information Office in November 2013.

industries by enhancing the evaluation and examination for energy saving, and improving the assessment of environmental impact and the pre-examination of land resources for construction, to strictly control the launch of the industries with high energy consumption, high emissions or excess capacity, and exports of the products from high energy consumption or high emission industries. In February 2013, the NDRC cooperated with relevant administrations to amend the 2011 edition of the *Guideline Catalogue for Industrial Restructuring*, highlighting the strategic principle of energy saving and emission reduction by improving and upgrading the industrial structure. In March 2013, the National Development and Reform Commission issued the *Restructuring Plan on the Old National Industrial Bases (2013–2022)*, in which it pointed out that China needs to restructure and upgrade its traditionally advantageous industries, enhance its competitiveness, and improve its industrial structures by adopting new technologies. In the 12th Five-Year Plan period, the NDRC initiated the National Low Carbon Tech Innovation and Model Industries Projects, among which 34 model projects have been launched in the coal, electric power, construction, and building materials industries in 2012.

Supporting the development of strategic and newly emerging industries. In July 2012, the State Council issued the *Development Plan for National Strategic Emerging Industries* during the 12th Five-Year Plan. It charts the road map for seven strategic emerging industries—energy conservation and environmental protection, new-generation information technology, biology, high-end equipment manufacturing, new energy, new materials, and new-energy vehicles. It has mapped out a sequence of specific plans for the seven strategic and newly emerging industries and over 20 areas of science and technology, such as modern biological manufacturing. It has also issued several policies and measures, such as the *Catalogue of Key Products and Services in Strategic Emerging Industries*, the *2012 Strategic Emerging Industries Categories,* and *Several Opinions on the Work of Enhancing the Intellectual Property Rights of the Strategic Emerging Industries*. Twenty-six provinces and cities, such as Beijing and Shanghai, have issued plans or guidelines on the development of the strategic

emerging industries. So far, 138 venture capital funds have been set up, managing 38 billion yuan. Among these funds, 38, with a total of 11 billion yuan, are designed to stimulate the development of the energy-saving, environmental protection and new energy sectors.

Vigorously developing the service industry. China has continuously implemented the State Council *Opinions on Accelerating the Development of the Service Industry*, the *Opinions of the State Council General Office on Implementing the Policy Measures for Accelerating the Development of the Service Industry*, and other relevant documents. In December 2012, the State Council issued the *12th Five-Year Plan on the Development of the Service Industry*, stipulating that the *12th Five-Year Plan* marks an important period in stimulating the development of the service industry. China needs to strive to achieve the goals, which include increasing the ratio of the tertiary industry, raising the quality of the industry, pushing forward the reform, and opening up of the industry and increasing the industry's capability to create jobs. The pattern of the development of the tertiary sector will eventually take shape as the industry has improved structure, heightened standards, and adopted open and win–win cooperation and complementary models.

In May 2012, the NDRC drew up the *Guidelines for Speeding up and Cultivating International Cooperation and Improved Competitiveness* in cooperation with relevant administrations, putting forward the mission of developing service industry trade, establishing a service trade system, and raising the quality of international services trade. The ratio of the tertiary industry in 2012 increased by 1.5 percentage points compared with 2010.

Speeding up the elimination of backward production capacity. The State Council issued the *Instructive Opinions on Solving the Problem of Overcapacity* in October 2013, which proposed the general principle of respecting the law, tailoring policies to industries, multiple-measure approach and addressing both symptom and root cause, and also put forward the opinions on how to implement policies according to the characteristics of industries of steel, cement, electorlytic aluminum, glass, and shipbuilding and set eight main tasks to solve the current overcapacity issue. The State Council further implemented the *Notice on Issuing the Evaluation Measures on the Work of Eliminating*

Backward Production Capacity, improved the phasing-out system of the backward production capacity, encouraged local governments to set strict standards on energy consumption and emission standards, and sped up the process of eliminating the backward production capacity. In June 2012, the Ministry of Industry and Information Technology set a goal of eliminating nineteen industries with backward production capacity and subsequently announced a name list of the enterprises concerned. It required local governments to break down the tasks and assign them to cities, towns, and enterprises. After the evaluation in 2012, China eliminated obsolete production capacity in the following industries: iron smelting, 10.78 million tons; steel production, 9.37 million tons; coke, 24.93 million tons; cement (clinker and mill), 258.29 million tons; plate glass, 59.56 million cases; paper, 10.57 million tons; printing and dyeing, 3.26 billion meters; lead battery, 29.71 million kVah.

Optimizing Energy Structure

Promoting the clean utilization of fossil fuel. In October 2012, NDRC issued the Natural Gas Development Plan During the 12th Five-Year Plan Period, [estimating] the supply capacity of natural gas will reach 176 billion cubic meters in 2015, among which conventional natural gas will reach 138.5 billion cubic meters, synthetic natural gas 15–18 billion cubic meters, and mining and production of coal bed gas about 16 billion cubic meters. About 18 percent of residents from cities and towns will use natural gas. In 2012, NDRC and the National Energy Administration announced the *Development Plan for Shale Gas (2011–2015)*; the Ministry of Finance and the National Energy Administration issued the *Notice on Issuing the Subsidy Policies of Exploring and Utilizing Shale Gas*, and arranged special funds to support shale gas projects. In September 2013, the State Council issued the *Airborne Pollution Prevention and Control Action Plan*, which stipulates the goals and requirements for controlling the consumption cap of coke and increasing the utilization of clean energy. The plan also requires increasing control over fossil fuel consumption and advancing the development of clean energy. By the end of 2012, the rate of thermal power units above 300,000 KWH was

75.6 percent, a year-on-year growth of 1.2 percent; a total of 54 supercritical coal-fired units were in operation, the highest figure in the world; the demonstration power station Tianjin Huaneng IGCC, designed, constructed, and operated by China, was put into operation in December 2012. The power station marked a major breakthrough in China's clean coal generator technology.

Developing non-fossil fuel. In July 2012, the State Council issued *Several Opinions on the Sound Development of the Photovoltaic Industry*, articulating the policies and measures on developing the market for the adoption of photovoltaics, speeding up the adjustment of the industrial structure, regulating industrial development, and improving the management and service of grid connections. The National Energy Administration issued the *Development Plan for Solar Energy Generation during the 12th Five-Year Plan Period*, the *Development Plan for Biomass Energy during the 12th Five-Year Period,* and *the Guidelines on Promoting the Exploration and Use of Geothermal Energy*, stipulating the guidelines, principles, goals, planning, and key parts of the development of solar, biomass, and geothermal energies and mapping out measures and institutions to guarantee and implement the development. China will continue to increase investments on renewable energy. It invested 127.7 billion yuan in hydropower stations, 77.8 billion yuan in nuclear power plants, and 61.5 billion yuan in wind power in 2012. To encourage the purchase and grid integration of renewable energy power, the Ministry of Finance, the NDRC and the National Energy Administration issued the *Interim Measures on the Management of the Additional Subsidy Funds for Prices of Electricity from Renewable Energies*, in order to subsidize renewable energies. In August 2013, the NDRC issued the *Interim Measures on the Management for Distributed Electricity Generation*, setting out different supporting policies for distributed generation of wind, solar, biomass, ocean, and geothermal energies. By the end of 2012, power generation capacity had reached 1.147 billion kw, up by 7.9 percent. Within this, the capacity of hydropower, which ranked first globally, reached 249 million kw, registering a year-on-year growth of 7.1 percent; nuclear power plants, 12.57 million kw, were equal to last year and the largest in the world; on-grid wind power capacity, which was the largest in the world, amounted to 61.42 million kw, increasing 32.9 percent year on year; on-grid solar power reached 3.41 million kw, growing 60.6 percent from a year earlier. The generation sets of non-fossil fuel, including, hydro, nuclear, wind, and solar energies, took up 28.5 percent of the whole, 4.2 percentage points higher than the 2005 figure. The electricity generated from non-fossil fuel accounted for 21.4 percent of the total of on-grid electricity.

After efforts from all over the country, by the end of 2012, the one-time energy consumption of standard coal equivalent was 3.62 billion tons, among which, the coal accounted for 67.1 percent, dropping 1.3 percentage points compared with 2011; oil and natural gas was 18.9 percent and 5.5 percent, up 0.3 percentage points and 0.5 percentage points from the previous year; and non-fossil fuel made 9.1 percent, up 1.1 percentage points compared with 2011.

Conserving Energy and Improving Energy Efficiency

Enhancing the evaluation of energy saving accountabilities. The State Council has issued the plans on energy saving, emissions reduction, and the development of energy-saving and environmental-protection industries, further stipulating the missions and goals for local governments, and specifying the policies and measures. In line with the plans, China releases quarterly reports on the completion of energy conservation targets in each region. China has improved the evaluation system, adjusted evaluation content and created a comprehensive process for evaluation. In 2013, the NDRC cooperated with relevant ministries and administrations to evaluate the energy saving accountabilities of the provincial-level governments, and the results will be an important reference to the evaluation system of local governments and officials. China also awarded 530 model units and 467 people in energy saving during the 11th Five-Year Plan Period.

Implementing key energy conservative projects. Since 2012, China has invested 4.896 billion yuan within the central government's budget and 2.61 billion yuan worth of the central fiscal bonus in supporting 2,411 projects regarding high-efficiency,

energy-saving technologies, model products and industries, contracted energy management, developing energy-saving monitoring institutions, energy-saving buildings, and green lighting. Among the projects, around 1,215 monitoring institutions received 1.066 billion yuan from the budget of the central government, and 17 restructuring projects were financed with 130 million yuan from the central government's fiscal funds. Support for the 495 contracted energy management projects was enhanced with 302 million yuan coming from the central fiscal bonus. Energy-saving projects have saved energy equivalent to more than 19.79 million tons of standard coal.

Improving energy efficiency standard and labeling scheme. [The] NDRC and the Standardization Administration collaborated to implement the *One Hundred Energy Efficiency Standard Promotion Projects*, issuing over sixty energy-saving standards since 2012, including limiting unit product energy consumption for high-consumption industries, and energy capacity and efficiency of terminal-use products, and fundamental standards for energy saving. The Ministry of Housing and Urban Rural Development approved and issued ten industrial standards, including the *Standards of the Labels on the Energy Capacity and Efficiency of Buildings and Regulation on Energy Saving Technology in Heating Systems in Towns.* The Ministry of Industry and Information Technology and other ministries issued over sixty standards concerning new energy vehicles and the Ministry of Transport announced twenty-one batches of qualifying vehicles in line with limits set on fuel consumption in operational vehicles by the end of 2012, in a bid to improve energy-saving projects and the standardized systems of new energy vehicles. By the end of May 2013, the energy-efficiency labeling scheme has covered 28 kinds of terminal-use products, after the implementation of the project.

Expanding energy conservative technologies and products. The NDRC issued the fifth batch of the *Catalogue on the Promotion of National Key Energy Saving Technologies*, listing forty-nine technologies from twelve industries. The five batches of the catalogue have recommended 186 key energy-saving low carbon technologies to the public. The Ministry of Industry and Information Technology, the Ministry of Science and Technology and the Ministry of Finance collaborated to issue the *Notice of the Selection, Evaluation and Promotion on Advanced and Appropriate Technologies to Enhance*

Industrial Energy Saving and Emission Reduction and selected the first batch of 600 technologies from eleven key industries, including steel, chemicals, and building materials. They jointly issued the *Recommended Catalogue (3rd Batch) of Energy-Saving Mechanical and Electrical Equipment (Products)*, and the *Catalogue (2nd Batch) of Obsolete Mechanical and Electrical Equipment (Products) Eliminated due to High Energy Consumption*, and completed the construction of the platform of the industrial information concerning energy conservation and emission reduction. The ministries jointly issued the *Implementation Plan on the Special Action of Industrial Energy Conservation and Green Development*, the *Notice on the Plan to Raise the Energy Efficiency of Electrical Machines (2013–2015)*, and the *Opinions on the Energy Conservation and Emission Reduction of Internal Combustion Engines*, which pushed for restructuring and energy conservation of electrical machines in key industries, improved the emission-reducing technologies of internal combustion engines, and the promotion of new products. The Ministry of Finance and NDRC have promoted the government procurement of the energy-saving products by issuing two batches of procurement lists. China will continue to expand the benefits of energy-saving projects to its citizens. The government has set aside more than 30 billion yuan of fiscal grant for the projects, saving energy equal to 12 million tons of standard coal. The projects distributed over 90 million energy-saving electric home appliances, over 3.5 million energy-saving vehicles, over 14 million kw of energy-efficient electrical machines, and 160 million energy-saving green lighting products.

Promoting energy conservation in construction industry. The General Office of the State Council circulated the *Action Plan for Green Buildings*, which was jointly drafted by the NDRC and the Ministry of Housing and Urban-Rural Development. The Ministry also issued the *Special Blueprint of Conserving Energy in the Construction Sector during the 12th Five-Year Plan Period*. By the end of 2012, the country had completed heat metering and energy-efficiency renovations on 590 million square meters of existing residential buildings in northern China, saving energy equivalent to 4 million tons of standard coal and reducing about 10 million tons of CO_2 emissions. All new buildings in cities and towns, or a total of 6.9 billion square meters of floor space, have reached the new energy-saving standard, saving energy equivalent to 65 million tons of standard coal, or 150 million tons of CO_2 emissions.

Driving energy conservation in transportation industry. The Ministry of Transport has continued to improve energy saving, emission reduction, as well as climate change in key areas of the transportation industry. It gave a boost to supporting policies, and continued to undertake the special action on low-carbon transport for 1,000 companies dedicated to vehicles, ships, roads, and ports. The ministry issued the *Guidelines for Pedestrian and Bicycle Transport*, in order to encourage local governments to promote the construction of city pedestrian and bicycle transport system by showcasing model pedestrian and bicycle transport systems. The Ministry of Science and Technology has rolled out a pilot green car project, billed as "10 cities, 1000 green cars," in 25 cities across the nation. It is estimated that the energy-saving capacity in transport industry is equivalent to 4.2 million tons of standard coal or 9.17 million tons of CO_2 emissions.

Increasing Forest Carbon Sinks

The State Council approved the second stage of the plan to curb the source of sandstorms in Beijing and Tianjin. The plan has been expanded to six provinces (autonomous regions, municipalities) and 138 towns. The State Forestry Administration issued the *Plan on the Division of Work on Enhancing the Forest's Role in Tackling Climate Change to Implement the Durban Climate Change Conference Agreement*, began to draft the fifth stage of the plan on the shelterbelt construction in northeast, northwest, and northern China, announced the third stage plan on the shelterbelt construction along the Yangtze River, the Pearl River, as well as the greenery work on plains and Taihang Mountain. China will continue to improve forest management. Forestry subsidies from central fiscal revenue have been expanded from pilot regions to the whole country. China initiated a mid- and long-term plan to manage national forests, decided to build fifteen model forests management bases, and issued measures on how to examine and evaluate the cultivation of forests as well as the regulations for their management. It launched a pilot program for sustainable management in 200 towns (forestry farms), taking lumbering as the center of the management. It also issued the *Notice on Further Protection and Management of Forest Resources* to proactively protect forest resources. The construction of the national monitoring system on forest sinks has made steady progress, as the program expanded from 17 pilot provinces (autonomous regions and municipalities) to the whole country from 2012 to 2013, and a national data base and parameter model base for forestry sink calculation has been built at the initial stage. From 2012 to the first half of 2013, a total area of 10.25 million hectares was greened in afforestation drives, and 4.96 billion trees were planted in volunteer tree-planting drives and 10.68 million hectares of forests were cultivated, further strengthening forest sink capabilities.

Controlling Emissions in Other Areas

Controlling greenhouse emission from agriculture. In 2012, the central government allocated 700 million yuan in special fund to support 2,463 fertilizer projects. The Ministry of Agriculture initiated and carried out a project categorizing formulas for fertilizers for different types of soil in thousands of villages. The central government earmarked 30 million yuan for special agrarian project funds and 300 million yuan for protective agrarian projects, promoting protective agrarian technologies in 204 towns (cities). The area of protective agrarian land increased to 1.64 million hectares. The central government invested 3 billion yuan to continue standardizing farming areas for pigs and cows. It also put emphasis on the renovation of livestock and poultry farms. The projects will set up several waste treatment facilities, including manure pits and sewage treatment sites. Biological resources and new energies, such as manure, solar, and wind, will be used for biomass generation, biomass energy projects, methane projects, and the replacement of fossil fuels with solid bio-fuels and biomass in heating.

Tightening control over CO_2 greenhouse gas. The State Council issued the *12th Five-Year Construction Plan on the Facilities for the Treatment and Reuse of Sewage* and the *12th Five-Year Construction Plan on the Treatment of Domestic Garbage in Cities and Towns*, actively controlling the methane emissions during garbage treatment. By the end of 2012, the garbage treatment rate had reached 76 percent, signaling that the majority of dumping grounds had collected, tunneled, and treated emissions when burying garbage underground. China planned under the guideline of the Montreal Protocol to speed up the elimination of HCFCs. By June 2012, it had approved six plans for consumer industries and one plan for contracted capacity amid the first phase of the elimination of HCFCs. Emissions of HCFCs are expected to reach zero in 2013, saving energy equivalent to 200 million tons of CO_2. China has launched research projects on current controlling technologies over non-CO_2 greenhouse gas emissions from coal and charcoal manufacturing, garbage treatment, chemical manufacturing, refrigeration, electric power, electronics, metallurgy, and foundries, both across the country and abroad, and has proposed technologies and policies to control non-CO_2 greenhouse gas emissions.

II. ENERGY CHALLENGES

China's Search for a New Energy Strategy[*]

Damien Ma

Much like the United States, China has an "all of the above" energy strategy: it plans to continue

[*] This article was published in *Foreign Affairs* (June 2013). All rights reserved, Council on Foreign Relations.

to rely on traditional sources of energy even as it makes the transition to cleaner fuels. And this is only natural. Both countries are continent-sized economies with diverse energy needs and geographically dispersed resources.

But China's energy situation differs from that of the United States in several notable ways. For starters, the Chinese state's role in energy looms large, and its hand is seen and deeply felt when it comes to prices. Even more important, China's per capita resource availability is below the world average—and even below that of some other developing countries—yet its total energy consumption could potentially be the largest in history. It is little wonder that China's energy strategy has been guided by the need to supply enough fuel to power an economy that grew from under $1 trillion in 1997 to more than $8 trillion in 2012.

Over that same fifteen-year span, China has become staggeringly dependent on imported energy: today, nearly 60 percent of its oil and almost 30 percent of its natural gas is imported. These developments have all but supplanted Beijing's traditional concept of equating energy security with energy self-sufficiency. But China has little alternative, as just about the only resource it possesses in abundance is coal. (China now devours about four billion tons per year, or nearly half the world's annual coal output. The bulk of those needs are met by domestic production.)

China's rampant consumption of coal and fossil fuels has imposed an exorbitant cost on the country's economic development, including severe environmental despoliation and thousands of deaths in coal mines. These environmental and pollution hazards have been regularly chronicled, and they are eroding the already limited resource base on which future growth depends. Resource scarcity, unfortunately, is a daily reality that China cannot evade.

Such constraints on future economic development are reflections of the growth model according to which the Chinese economy was built. While this model has come in for criticism from many angles, few have appreciated one of its most important features: cheap and highly regulated energy prices. But it is these suppressed prices that drive China's uncontrolled energy consumption and its negative side effects.

Much Ado About Industrialization

Ever since the late 1990s, China has been in a phase of development that requires affordable and abundant energy, which feeds the country's hyper-industrialization. Its development strategy has focused on heavy industry such as steel, aluminum, and cement—the inputs needed to accommodate an astronomical expansion of infrastructure and housing. This sprawling network of low-efficiency heavy industry has been by far the largest consumer of energy, making up about three-quarters of total consumption. (In comparison, industry in the United States is responsible for about one-third of total energy consumption.) Today, China churns out about half the world's steel. Its steel sector is so big, in fact, that Chinese demand has largely determined world iron ore prices over the last decade.

Supporting the vast expansion of industry in a relatively poor country, however, meant that the government needed to keep inflation in check, a difficult task given that China's huge appetite for foreign commodities risked importing inflation along with them. China has to buy iron ore at global market prices from Australia and Brazil, for example, because it does not have adequate domestic reserves. So, to keep Chinese industry humming—often with razor-thin margins—the Chinese government decided on a policy that both managed inflation and offered an important industry-wide subsidy: artificially suppressing energy prices.

Although the prices of many commodities and consumer goods were liberalized during China's economic reforms of the 1980s and 1990s, energy prices have been a holdout because the state has had to ensure that industry could continue to support urbanization and export growth. In other words, China's economic model has determined its energy strategy.

Much like a devalued currency can function as a market-wide subsidy for exports, the energy price subsidy worked spectacularly well for China's production-oriented economy. Up until 2011, energy demand from industry and the hundreds of millions of new urban dwellers seemed so great that the government's main preoccupation was to ensure that supplies were abundant enough to keep prices low. And if that was not enough, the state regularly intervened to prevent prices from rising.

Consequently, over the past decade, the energy required to generate one unit of Chinese GDP, or energy intensity, rose rather than declined as it did in the 1990s, suggesting that overall efficiency was probably decreasing as well. The government's emphasis on industrialization encouraged local governments to approve hundreds of thousands of energy-intensive infrastructure projects that boosted local growth and supported employment. In turn, industry received all sorts of subsidies, and efficiency and environmental considerations became afterthoughts. What is more, in the absence of clear market prices set by energy supply and demand, industry and consumers had to depend on the government to raise or cut prices.

Inflation Bites

The government's control of prices has hurt Chinese energy security, broadly defined. Throughout the last decade, China experienced major power shortages virtually every year, often forcing the state to raise energy prices on industry to manage demand. Some have blamed coal shortages for the blackouts, but a more compelling explanation is that they have been brought on by government policy and represent a symptom of China's illiberal pricing system.

Although the market determines domestic coal prices, the government continues to set the price at which power generators sell electricity to the state's transmission and distribution monopoly. But markets usually move much faster than the government does, so even when coal prices are rising, the state often refuses to raise power prices, causing power utilities to bleed profits. In response, the power companies often take the only action they know to be effective in getting a price hike: idling or fully cutting power generation. Over the past decade, rolling blackouts have become a regular occurrence in China, with one of the most severe episodes in 2004.

The government's continued grip on energy prices is rooted in its fear of spiraling inflation. Reform of energy prices makes the government nervous, because once the market takes over, prices could get out of control, undermining the economic stability that Beijing has diligently maintained. Even a marginal rise could seriously pinch the still relatively poor Chinese people, whose meager incomes are disproportionately spent on necessities such as food and electricity.

Those concerns have made energy price reforms a torturously slow affair. And even when attempted, efforts have been botched. Take, for example, recent actions to make Chinese gasoline prices more aligned with global crude-oil prices. In 2009, the government announced what was supposed to be an important step toward liberalizing energy prices. It decided on a fairly complex formula that would allow Beijing to change retail gasoline prices according to whether global crude prices moved up or down by 4 percent over a 22-day period. The policy turned out to be both exceedingly confusing and highly unpopular with major interest groups. Chinese car owners felt that the government used the mechanism as a ploy to make gasoline more expensive and serve the interests of the big oil companies. The oil companies, meanwhile, remained dissatisfied over the long lag between market movements and the time when the government would raise prices.

The policy eventually devolved into a charade when, immediately before the 22-day period expired, there were reports of runs on diesel and gasoline products at gas stations across China in anticipation of a price hike. As a result, the government essentially abandoned the policy de facto, deciding to change prices when the public was least expecting it. But rumors of imminent price hikes inevitably got around, and it became a game of cat and mouse.

Where the Economy Goes, Energy Follows

Energy price reforms were lackluster and disappointing because Beijing never made them a priority. The economic logic that underpinned the Chinese growth model was simply not conducive to energy price liberalization. But left in the wake of the reforms' failure are serious problems of unchecked energy consumption, poor energy efficiency, and an industry beset by severe overcapacity. The steel industry, for instance, has about 35 percent more capacity than necessary to meet domestic needs, even as global demand has shrunk after the financial crisis and China itself has imposed austerity measures on the property sector.

But these dynamics appear poised to change, as the country undertakes the transition to a more sustainable economic model. Central to this effort is beginning the process of reaching a better equilibrium between production and consumption, what many observers call "rebalancing."

To its credit, the Chinese government has, over the last several years, clamped down on heavy industry and forced the most environmentally harmful producers to shut down. But liberalizing energy prices will send a significant nationwide signal that the era of energy subsidies is coming to an end, forcing companies to either improve production efficiency quickly or exit the market because they can no longer survive in an unsubsidized environment. Its effect would be similar to moving to a more flexible exchange rate system, which would signal to exporters that their days are numbered if they conduct business as usual.

Pricing energy right will also play an important role in shifting to cleaner sources of energy. This is particularly true in the near term as China intends to boost natural gas consumption. The official goal is to double gas's share in total primary energy consumption from roughly 4 percent today to around 8 percent in 2015, but various estimates suggest the increase could be even higher. In recent years, domestic consumption of gas has been growing at a rate roughly double that of domestic production, again forcing China to tap the international market to make up the difference.

But unlike China's oil reserves, which are limited, the country's natural gas reserves are potentially immense. Preliminary estimates put China's shale gas reserve on par with that of the United States. Consequently, China is intent on developing its domestic energy resources such as coal-bed methane and shale. But doing so will require deregulating domestic gas prices, which continue to be below global prices, to incentivize domestic production.

Getting the Price Right

As China begins to transition from an investment- and export-driven economy to a consumption-driven one, its energy policy must shift from a focus on supply-side security to demand-side management. Although the perennial concern about inflation is unlikely to abate anytime soon, market-based energy prices offer a powerful tool to help shape consumer behavior on energy consumption. And with a rising cohort of relatively prosperous urban dwellers, the Chinese government should reassess its long-held belief that the Chinese public has a low tolerance for inflation.

Perhaps in recognition of these changing dynamics and China's future demands, Beijing has already begun testing the ground for a more liberalized energy price regime. In Guangdong and Guangxi provinces, pilot programs on reforming natural gas prices have been under way for more than a year. Even the gasoline mechanism that turned out to be a farce has been revived under a purportedly more flexible formula. In the current low-inflation environment, conditions appear conducive for the government to engage in bolder pricing experiments that could put China on a path to more rational energy pricing.

Most important, instead of paying lip service, the new government appears to have seriously prioritized pricing reform as an important component of China's economic transition. If recent reports are any indication, the government intends to make resource prices a key part in a comprehensive reform package expected to be unveiled at the Third Plenum this fall. Beijing is unlikely to liberalize all prices at once and will likely proceed in stages. It is possible that one of the changes will allow utilities and industry to negotiate power prices without government involvement.

Of course, energy price reforms alone would not be a panacea for China's diverse economic challenges. Deindustrialization will take time and require a strong commitment to shifting economic growth toward domestic consumption and expanding less-energy-intensive sectors such as services. But liberalizing prices would, at the very least, send a strong signal that Beijing is committed to putting China on a path toward more sustainable economic development. And just as important, it would send an unambiguous message that one of the most stubborn legacies of the planned economy is finally being written off.

SOCIETY

Editorial Introduction

Those scholars and analysts who study the rise of China tend to focus their main attention on China's foreign relations, its military modernization and impact on Asian and international security, and the nation's growing global economic clout. Their focus is primarily *external* rather than *internal*. Yet, many of the very forces that have catalyzed China's dramatic development and rise in the world have simultaneously impacted Chinese society. The rise of China is also very much a *domestic* story. No nation in world history has developed as rapidly and dramatically as has China, and with a fifth of the world's population! Many of the social consequences of development have been extremely positive—universal education, universal literacy, universal primary health care delivery, reduced infant mortality, eradication of many infectious diseases, prolonged longevity, improved housing and standard of living, and many other notable accomplishments. In many ways, China has been an exemplar model of social development.

Yet, such dramatic social changes have also spawned a wide range of unanticipated and negative consequences. This section examines a number of these developments.

The first selection, by leading China sociologist Martin King Whyte of Harvard University, examines the issue of inequality. With ever-widening gaps between rich and poor, China has become one of the world's most unequal societies. Its Gini coefficient of 0.47 (2012), the main index of inequality, ranks China in the top 10 percent worldwide. On one end of the scale, China now has the largest number of millionaires in the world (1.09 million in 2013 with net worth of at least $1.6 million) and the second largest number of billionaires (152 plus 45 in Hong Kong in 2014) after the United States (492 in 2014), according to *Forbes* annual surveys. On the other end of the scale China still has 82 million people who live on less than $1 per day, but if international standards of the "absolute poor" poverty line were applied the number would rise to 200 million (2014). As Professor Whyte points out, this is a dramatic departure from China's emphasis on egalitarianism under Mao. Deng Xiaoping famously proclaimed that some could "get rich first," but this has occurred on an unexpected and unprecedented scale. Whyte's article traces the historical evolution and economic sources of how inequality has developed during the reform era in China, and he concludes with some astute observations about its implications for the future.

The second selection by demographer Wang Feng considers the "looming crisis" in China's population. Actually, Professor Wang notes multiple pending problems with China's population—but, among them, he notes that the rapid aging of the population may be the most serious. At present, China's population over the age of sixty is 200 million (2015) and will grow to over 300 million by 2030. This mass retirement of China's "baby boomer" generation will put extraordinary stress on individual families as well as the central and local governments to support this huge cohort of the population. The combination of China's declining fertility rate combined with the rapid aging of the population will create a negative "scissors effect" on the economy by shrinking the student population and entrants into the labor force.

The third selection includes excerpts from a Chinese government White Paper on "Gender Equality and Women's Development in China." It offers a variety of statistics concerning women in the workforce, in society, in education, and in politics.

The next selection addresses the complex issue of nationalism in China. Leading French Sinologist Jean-Pierre Cabestan explores the complexities of how modern-day Chinese nationalism has been shaped and its impact on Chinese identity, politics, and approach to the world. These complexities include the role of ethnicity and race (Han and non-Han), the searing impact of the "century of shame and humiliation," recurrent xenophobia, the impact of China's brutish encounter with Japan, the attraction of the West before 1989, and the subsequent rejection of Western values. All of these (and other) forces have contributed to the complex and rather confused nature of contemporary Chinese nationalism—leaving China with a fairly deep "identity crisis." Cabestan also demonstrates the importance of nationalism for the Communist Party's legitimacy, and how the regime has manipulated popular sentiments for its own purposes. Finally, he links nationalism to contemporary Chinese foreign policy and the externalities it creates in Beijing's relations with its neighbors and the United States.

The fifth selection examines the subject of religion in China today. Richard Madsen, a leading sociologist at the University of California–San Diego, shows how—despite unremitting official hostility by the communist regime towards religion for many years—it has nonetheless germinated and sunk deep roots in Chinese society (both urban and rural). Madsen observes that: "Religion is growing rapidly, and has overwhelmed the CCP regime's systems of surveillance and control. Clumsy methods of suppressing unwanted forms of religion have backfired, raising rather than lowering the temperature of conflicts involving religion and the state." There are five legally recognized religions in China: Taoism, Buddhism, Islam, Catholicism, and Protestantism—but many more religious groups and sects exist underground in China. This includes movements such as Falun Gong (which is officially outlawed). Nor has the state been successful in channeling various offshoots of these five official religions into official "patriotic associations." Underground "house churches" thrive across the country. Marx declared religion to be the "opiate of the masses"—and the Chinese Communist regime is finding it ever more difficult to contain and control the rapid spread of religion across China. Religion is also closely tied to the politics of "national sovereignty" concerning Tibetans and Uighurs—large ethnic groups who chafe under Han and communist rule. On the other hand, as Madsen shows, the government has invested large sums of money in restoring churches, temples, monasteries, and other places of worship around the nation (including in Tibet and Xinjiang). Compared with the first few decades of the People's Republic, when religion was brutally repressed (particularly during the Cultural Revolution), today's government exhibits far greater tolerance and support. But there will always be limits to the permissible and an underlying tension between practitioners and the state.

The next entry concerns China's "angry youth." Authored by Evan Osnos, *The New Yorker* correspondent in China and a prize-winning book author (*The Age of Ambition*), the article takes the reader inside the world of a subset of Chinese youth. Not all Chinese youth are over-achieving, hardworking, education-obsessed, professional wannabies—Osnos takes us inside the substrata of society populated by nonconforming individualists. Many live in cyberspace. While some are on the fringes of conventional society, others are enrolled in universities. They seem equally angry with their own society and with the West—a profile in youthful alienation. They are hypernationalists who decry and defame the United States.

The next two selections juxtapose rural and urban China. Lianjiang Li, a professor at the Chinese University of Hong Kong and a noted expert on politics in the Chinese countryside, writes about social unrest in rural China. Writing in 2006, he describes the 87,000 mass protests ("collective incidents") that swept China the previous year. Li chronicles the various and multiple grievances that give rise to this collective action: expropriated land; polluted farmland and water; illegal mining; the state's one-child birth control policy; the controls of the *hukou* system; predatory rent-seeking behavior of local cadres; and rigged local elections. He observes that protest is a last resort for many desperately seeking redress: "With few exceptions, Chinese villagers resort to disruptive protests only after they have exhausted all lawful procedures." He describes the various legal avenues open to rural inhabitants, but also the many factors that limit the effectiveness of these formal channels. Li also documents the harsh repression of protests and protesters. Fully one-quarter of a sample of 1,314 protesters he surveyed in 28 provinces had been beaten by local security authorities. Since Li's article was first published in 2006, the government has taken several steps to try and alleviate the causes of rural discontent and protest—by raising grain procurement prices (and hence incomes), abolishing rural taxes, making rural education free, increasing funding for a revitalized rural health care system, and cracking down on corrupt and predatory cadres. To some extent, these measures have helped—yet rural protests continued to grow to approximately 200,000 nationwide in 2011.

The next selection is an extended assessment of China's cities by the British magazine *The Economist*. It is filled with statistics and stories describing China's urban landscape today and the extraordinary plans the government has for its "urbanization" initiatives. This is a high priority of the current government and particularly Premier Li Keqiang. The government's goal is to have 60 percent of the population living in urban areas by 2020—requiring the relocation of 260 million rural inhabitants, creating 110 million new jobs, permanently absorbing 160 million migrants already living in metropolitan areas, and providing them with legitimate rights for dwelling, education, health care, and other basic social services. By 2030, *The Economist* notes, China's cities will be home to close to 1 billion people, or about 70 percent of the population, compared with 54 percent today (2014). The magnitude of the undertaking is nothing short of staggering—essentially relocating the entire American population from rural to urban areas by 2020! Much of this "relocation" will be accomplished, though, through redistricting and expanding outward urban jurisdictions into suburban and rural areas—rather than a zero-sum displacement of population. Nonetheless, the visionary plan is remarkable. And it will have all kinds of side effects. The middle class is expected to balloon, with increased incomes and consumer spending. The service sector will expand. Infrastructure will need to be built to accommodate the vastly increased urban populace. But the burden on municipal governments to provide a wide range of public services will be intense. As the article explains, the urbanization plans will require the likely abolition of the antiquated *hukou* household registration system, thus abolishing the apartheid and legitimating the current underclass of illegal migrants. The article also discusses the impact on inter-city connectivity and the creation of a continental transport grid. It also examines the environmental implications of such rapid and extensive urbanization, as well as the government's plans to build "Eco-Cities." Finally, *The Economist* article looks at the possible political repercussions of a predominantly urban China—the "revolution of rising expectations" and the electronic connectivity of modern society will certainly pose new challenges to China's authoritarian state.

The final selection in this section examines China's ethnic conflicts and particularly the situation of Tibetans and Uighurs. Yan Sun, a political science professor at Queens College in New York, explores the roots of discontent and unrest in these border regions: religious, economic, racial, cultural, linguistic, historical, and political. The disenfranchisement, apartheid, and brutal repression experienced by Tibetans and Uighurs (but also Mongols and other practitioners of Islam) have driven these groups to acts of desperation (such as self-immolation) and terrorism.

Taken together, the nine selections in this section offer readers a kaleidoscope through which to view and understand the complexities of Chinese society today. No nation in history has experienced as comprehensive or rapid social change as has China over the past 35 years—and it is remarkable that it has done so with so little upheaval. But it is hard to imagine the dramatic changes that will occur over the next quarter century given the demographics and urbanization China will experience.

I. Rich and Poor

China's Post-Socialist Inequality[*]

Martin King Whyte

Since the death of Mao Zedong in 1976 and the launch of market reforms under Deng Xiaoping's leadership in 1978, China has undergone dramatic changes that have affected the lives of Chinese citizens in multiple ways. With the step-by-step dismantling of China's system of centrally planned socialism and other reforms, growth rates have accelerated, producing rising living standards, reduced poverty, and rapid increases in the skyscrapers, highways, and other symbols of a modern society.

Inequality on the Rise

However, in many analyses there is also concern about one consequence of these reforms. Whatever the problems of the Mao era, in this view, social equality was a primary goal, and China in the 1970s boasted an unusually egalitarian social order, one that was popular at home and admired by many around the world. Since 1978, in pursuing economic growth at all costs, so this argument goes, the goal of social equality has been abandoned, and China has become an increasingly unequal and unfair society. Many suggest that the

[*] The article was published in *Current History* (September 2012).

widening gaps between rich and poor in China, and the contrasts of such gaps with the egalitarianism of Mao's day, are creating anger and resentment among the citizens, fueling mass protests that increasingly threaten China's political stability.

Certainly there is much about this view that is accurate. One can imagine Mao turning over in his crystal sarcophagus in Beijing at the news of foreign capitalists once again exploiting Chinese workers and of Chinese millionaires residing in palatial mansions while many of their fellow citizens lose jobs, housing, and health insurance, with some destitute Chinese even forced to sell their blood to buy food. However, this picture of a nation transformed from egalitarianism under Mao into rampaging inequality over the past three decades is at best oversimplified, and in some respects dead wrong. China at the end of the Mao era was, in reality, a highly unequal and unfair society, and while the country today is much more unequal in many respects, most Chinese view the current social order as fairer.

The Socialist Legacy

The social revolution carried out by the Chinese Communist Party (CCP) after 1949 under the leadership of Mao (with Deng as one of his leading lieutenants) was aimed at transforming China from a very unequal, petty capitalist society into a centrally planned socialist economy modeled after the Soviet Union. That transition was completed by 1956. Until Mao's death two decades later, familiar institutions of a state socialist system shaped the contours of inequality in China.

In the countryside, the Chinese-style collective farms created in 1955–56 were consolidated into larger variants, people's communes, in 1958. In the 1960s and 1970s, following Soviet precedent, peasant families retained small private plots and could raise food and a few animals there for their own consumption, or for sale in nearby markets (but not in the cities). However, most of their labor time and energy were spent in collective field work directed by production team cadres, with the efforts of family members recorded in work points whose value would not be known until after the harvest. After 1960, strict enforcement of the CCP's household registration (*hukou*) system

prohibited villagers from leaving farming or their villages to seek better opportunities in the cities.

As a result, while inequalities among families in a production team were relatively modest, income differences across teams, brigades, communes, and rural regions were larger. Moreover, income and other gaps between villagers and favored urbanites became much wider than they had been before the revolution, when no restrictions prevented geographical and social mobility. Ironically, the result of China's rural revolution was a system of de facto socialist serfdom for the peasantry, who constituted over 80 percent of the population.

In the urban economy, socialist transformation meant that all private ownership of businesses and other productive assets disappeared after 1956, and all production and employment were organized into state-owned or state-controlled firms subject to bureaucratic rather than market regulation. Upon completing school, urban youths were bureaucratically assigned to jobs, and with each job came a bureaucratically designated ladder of wage grades, a package of benefits, and often assignment to subsidized housing, with access as well to dining, child care, recreational, and other facilities. Such facilities frequently were organized within work unit compounds, many demarcated by walls with gatekeepers.

The Iron Rice Bowl

The security of this employment package in state-owned enterprises (SOEs), often referred to as the "iron rice bowl," contrasted sharply with the insecurity of jobs, incomes, and much else before the revolution. However, individuals were expected to accept their assignments and continue their labors unless bureaucratically transferred, and they had very little ability to choose their first jobs, seek other work, move elsewhere, or refuse to accept a transfer. In some periods authorities mobilized educated youths by the millions to leave cities and settle down in the countryside, rather than assigning them urban jobs.

As in the Soviet Union, within any urban work organization there were relatively modest differences in wages, the size and quality of housing assigned, and other benefits, although those with the highest ranks were often entitled to special privileges, such as access to a chauffeured limousine and special medical clinics and vacation resorts. The paucity of supplies in state stores in combination with strict rationing of grain, cooking oil, cotton cloth, and much else also tended to keep urban consumption differences within modest ranges.

However, as in the countryside, socialism did not equalize or redistribute across urban organizations and locales. Those working in high-priority organizations located in China's largest cities operated under higher wage scales and enjoyed access to more generous benefits and scarce commodities that were not available to those at the lower end of the bureaucratic hierarchy. As in other state socialist systems, inequality was organized more in terms of local variations in organizational affiliation and rank, rather than via differential incomes and property that translated into class differences in purchases and lifestyles. (From 1962 onward Mao convulsed society with class struggle campaigns, even though China lacked social classes in any meaningful sense after the socialist transformation was completed in 1956.)

The Cultural Revolution launched by Mao in 1966 added new radical elements to China's Soviet-inspired organizational template. All material incentives, production bonuses, and prizes were eliminated, and any remaining displays of status differences in clothing or adornment (even signs of rank on military uniforms) became taboo, leading to the fairly uniform (and unisex) style of dress that struck visitors to China during the 1970s. Also, intellectuals, political elites, and professionals were required to spend extended periods away from their offices, cleansing themselves of their elitist attitudes through manual labor and other menial tasks (for example, surgeons emptying hospital bedpans).

University entrance exams were abolished, and youths finishing secondary school had to work for several years in a commune, factory, or military unit before they could even be considered for college, with selection based on recommendations from workmates and supervisors, rather than on academic records or test scores. These Cultural Revolution reforms all pursued greater social equality by "leveling down" to the "masses," rather than through any affirmative action assistance to the disadvantaged.

To sum up, the increased equality at the end of the Mao era was of a very unusual and selective sort. Primarily it entailed reduced gaps in incomes, consumption, and lifestyles within each local unit, but across organizations and locales, and across the rural-urban divide, if anything inequalities increased. Furthermore, the remaining inequalities were not ones that Chinese citizens were likely to view as fair, since they were based on where you were born (for villagers) or where you had been bureaucratically assigned (for urbanites), rather than on your own talents and efforts. Within organizations Chinese were likely to see such patterns as inequitable because they violated the socialist formula of "rewards according to contributions." Mao condemned any desires for rewards or advancement as "bourgeois" sentiments.

The Reform Model

After Mao's death, Deng emerged as China's reform leader. The Cultural Revolution's "leveling down" policies were repudiated. Nationwide university entrance examinations were revived in 1977. In 1978 authorities launched a more fundamental departure from planned socialism and toward market reforms, though in a step-by-step fashion rather than via "big bang" rapid privatization. Starting in the 1950s Japan and other East Asian societies had implemented a development strategy that combined rapid economic growth with improved popular living standards. With some oversimplification, we can characterize Deng's strategy as abandoning Soviet-style central planning and adopting instead a version of the Japanese development model.

At the core of this new model was a commitment to implement whatever policies and institutional changes were necessary to stimulate productivity and economic growth in a labor-intensive, export-promoting, market-driven development process, even if by doing so inequalities increased. But the abandonment of Mao-style egalitarianism was more direct than this statement implies. Deng rejected Mao's egalitarianism as "everyone eating from the same big pot," an approach he saw as destroying incentives. Instead, he argued, "it is good to allow some people to get rich first," as this would stimulate others to try to do so as well. Much of the reform effort focused on fostering competition and providing rewards (to organizations and localities as well as individuals) to stimulate productivity and economic growth.

The specific institutional changes adopted after 1978 are well known and too complex to summarize here, but a few deserve emphasis. Market reforms began first in the countryside, with de-collectivization of agriculture and the dismantling of communes allowed and then required. This resulted in a return to family farming, though without rural families enjoying full private property rights to their fields. Prior restrictions on rural marketing and family businesses were eliminated, and very rapidly village families redirected their energies to growing produce and making handicrafts for sale in the cities, and to establishing factories that made goods for sale elsewhere and even overseas. Migration restrictions were relaxed, and soon millions of rural migrants began leaving their villages to seek better opportunities, particularly in the cities.

By the mid-1980s the rapid improvements in agricultural production and rural incomes stimulated by these changes reduced the gap between average urban and rural incomes, while rapid increases in food production and marketing enabled rationing in the cities to be phased out, a development that in turn facilitated more rural to urban migration. However, China's migrants, who numbered well over 100 million by the mid-1990s and over 200 million by 2010, in virtually all cases still retained their agricultural household registrations and were thus not entitled to full urban citizenship rights and the benefits enjoyed by urbanites.

Two trends early in the reform period were potentially harmful to rural interests in spite of the increased opportunities generated by de-collectivization and non-farm employment. The altered fiscal terrain that accompanied these reforms led to a collapse of most Mao-era village medical insurance plans, producing anxiety about how to pay for medical bills out of pocket. (Even so, rising incomes and improved diets enabled rural health and life expectancy to improve, despite the decline in medical insurance coverage.) In addition, the rising opportunity costs of extended schooling and the weakened financial base of rural schools led to sharp drops in rural secondary school enrollments in the 1980s.

Both of these trends were eventually addressed through new state policies—by a government effort after 1986 to make enrollment at least through nine years of schooling compulsory, and by an effort launched in 2003 to develop new but very basic medical insurance plans in all Chinese villages. As a result, by 2010 about 90 percent of rural residents were once again covered by medical insurance, and almost all rural children were completing lower middle schooling.

Inequality Redux

In the cities, market reforms began in the 1980s with a strategy that the economist Barry Naughton has termed "growing out of the plan." This involved allowing private and foreign enterprises to operate in China for the first time since 1955, while initially not privatizing state firms. However, the latter were required to become more efficient in order to compete with the new entrants, rather than being able to rely on bureaucratically guaranteed funding and distribution of their products. After 1979 China established special economic zones (SEZs) along the coast where tax relief and other incentives attracted foreign companies to set up factories.

Foreign direct investment began to pour in, soon making China the largest FDI recipient among developing countries. Within a few years sleepy rural towns designated as SEZs, such as Shenzhen, were transformed into major cities, swelled by waves of migrant laborers attracted to the new jobs offered via foreign investment. Migrants have become vital to the economies even of long-established cities. They do much of the construction and hauling work as well as laboring in domestic and hotel services, sales, and manufacturing—though they continue to suffer systematic discrimination in wages, benefits, and everything else (including having their children excluded from urban public schools, at least until quite recently).

As a result of these and other market-oriented reforms, China's coastal cities and SEZs began to develop very rapidly, and after the mid-1980s the gap in average incomes between the coast and the interior, and between urban areas in general and the countryside, began to widen once again. On the latter point, available evidence indicates that the ratio of the average household income of urbanites (not including migrants) to rural households was something on the order of 3:1 before the reforms. It closed slightly to approximately

2.5:1 in the mid-1980s, but then rose to more than 3:1 again by the early 1990s, and by 2007 had widened further to about 4:1. (Even if urban migrants and their lower incomes are included in the calculation, China's urban-rural income ratio is currently around 3:1, among the most extreme on earth, comparable to nations such as Zimbabwe and South Africa.)

No Guarantees

During the 1990s two major institutional reforms further altered the structures of inequality affecting Chinese cities. First, China's leaders abandoned their previous strategy of "growing out of the plan" by tackling the reform of remaining SOEs. The new effort aimed to preserve, reform, and provide enhanced funding for the largest and most important state-owned enterprises, while requiring smaller and less profitable SOEs to either merge, privatize, or go out of business.

Within remaining SOEs, the aim was to "smash the iron rice bowl" of lifetime jobs and guaranteed wages and benefits by mandating that managers reward and promote their most essential employees, while laying off large numbers of others deemed expendable. From the mid-1990s into the early years of the new millennium, millions of SOE workers were laid off, and SOE employment totals plummeted (from 113 million in 1995 to 41 million in 2002). Although efforts were made to soften the blow through basic subsistence payments and by ramping up re-employment service agencies, for a decade Chinese cities had millions of former SOE employees who had thought their livelihoods were secure but now found themselves scrambling to find new ways to earn a living.

However, the downsizing of SOEs had another, more positive side. From the 1990s onward, growing private and foreign businesses provided employment alternatives to SOEs, and increasing numbers quit their state jobs to join such firms or to start their own companies. So two modes of exit from state employment developed that had quite different implications—*xiagang* (layoffs) and *xiahai* ("going down into the sea")—for private business. For youths finishing their schooling in urban areas after the early 1990s, these reforms meant competing for jobs in a revived labor market, rather than accepting a bureaucratic assignment.

Joining or starting a private business held out the possibility of becoming very rich, though also the peril of failing and becoming destitute, as in other market economies. In 1990 stock markets were opened in Shanghai and then Shenzhen, so that both state and private firms could by being listed gain access to equity funding, a development that enabled urbanites fortunate enough to have extra funds to try to get rich by playing the stock market.

The other major urban reform of the 1990s was the mass privatization of housing. Most urbanites until then had lived in cramped apartments rented from their work organizations or city housing bureaus. A government-launched initiative to privatize housing at first mainly involved providing families with subsidized financing to enable them to buy the apartments that they already lived in. By 2005 more than 80 percent of all urbanites had become homeowners in this fashion.

But that was not the end of the process. Once they owned their own apartments, many urbanites began to play the housing market, buying up additional housing, renting out their own apartment while moving elsewhere, or even starting up housing development companies to take advantage of the pressing demand for new and better housing fueled by both Chinese and foreigners in rapidly expanding cities. (By 2011 China had reached the milestone of having 50 percent of its population living in cities, up from about 20 percent at the time the economic reforms were launched.)

Conspicuous Consumption

These trends had several important implications for social inequality. First, it became less common for an organization's managers, workers, and janitors to live together in work unit housing compounds. Those who could afford it could now rent out or sell their current apartments and buy a flat in one of the new apartment complexes that were springing up, or even purchase a mansion in one of the gated and guarded compounds built to cater to the truly wealthy. At the same time many urban families living in older neighborhoods found their homes condemned and destroyed to make way for construction of such new housing complexes, and thereby were forced to move to more distant apartments provided as compensation.

By 2010, work unit housing complexes no longer dominated China's urban housing patterns. Instead cities increasingly displayed the full range of housing from run-down and crowded working-class neighborhoods to glittering new apartment towers and fancy detached homes with all the amenities. Income rather than bureaucratic affiliation increasingly became the sorting device for urban housing, as it had been in China before 1955.

An additional implication of these changes is that a portion of urban residents ceased to rely mainly on wage or pension income, but instead derived a growing share of their incomes from property they owned—from housing, from businesses, and from investments. At the top of the income pyramid created by the reforms arose large numbers of millionaires and even billionaires, many of them deriving their wealth from housing development firms or other private business empires, their newfound riches often made possible by the close ties they cultivated with political elites. China now has more than one million US-dollar millionaires according to media estimates, and perhaps 200 to 600 billionaires.

Today this new wealth makes possible conspicuous consumption that would have been unimaginable, not to mention politically suicidal, under Mao. In addition to lavish mansions, China's newly rich display a growing demand for private jets, for very expensive foreign cars (Ferraris, Lamborghinis, or Maseratis, with a Porsche or Mercedes for those with more modest tastes), for foreign travel and foreign schooling for their children, and for the luxury clothing, nightlife, and private clubs that the very rich enjoy in other countries.

Below this layer of the super-rich is a growing Chinese middle class, mostly urban and increasingly well-educated holders of white-collar jobs. The growth of the middle class has been fueled not only by China's hectic growth, but also by a massive expansion of higher education in recent years.

At the time of Mao's death, China had barely half a million college students nationwide, a number much smaller than at the end of the 1950s. But in the reform era college enrollments expanded steadily, to 1.5 million in 1985, over 2 million in 1990, and close to 3 million in 1996. In 1998 China's leaders made a decision to expand college enrollments at a breakneck pace, exceeding 20 million by 2008.

This extraordinary expansion has several implications for social inequality. Most of the added college spaces have gone to urban youths, with children of villager and migrant families facing much greater obstacles in completing upper middle school and passing college entrance exams. Overall, about 75 percent of those who take the college exams now gain admission, so the university dreams of urban parents (almost all with only one child) are now more in reach than is the case in much richer societies.

However, the unprecedented expansion of higher education has created new problems, including a growing number of college graduates who cannot find white-collar work, ending up instead in what is called the "ant tribe" (yizu), those who remain unemployed or compete with rural migrants for menial jobs. The standards for being considered middle class are also rising, with a well-educated man in some large cities increasingly expected to own his own apartment and car before he can hope to find a young woman willing to marry him. So conspicuous consumption and status competition reverberate up and down the stratification hierarchy.

Unequal but Mobile

China's reforms and impressive economic growth since 1978 have transformed inequality patterns. Social stratification in China today is a complex hybrid. It retains some features of the socialist era—for example, the CCP's political monopoly, state supported and controlled large firms dominating many lines of business, and paths to upward mobility involving political vetting and promotion in the party-state bureaucracy, not to mention the hukou system that aggravates China's largest and most inequitable cleavage, between city and countryside. At the same time, contemporary social stratification also features a re-emerging class hierarchy based on education, income, and personal assets obtained through competition in China's revived markets.

Overall it is clear that China is a much more unequal place than it was in 1976 when Mao died, at least in terms of income and personal wealth. At that time nobody possessed substantial personal wealth, the maximum monthly income was only about 800 yuan, and China's national Gini coefficient of income distribution (a statistic that can range from 0 = total equality to 1 = total inequality) was below 0.30, a very moderate figure compared to other societies. Today things are very different, with millionaires and even billionaires in growing numbers, and with China's Gini coefficient now estimated at close to 0.50, among the highest in the world (though still below the levels of nations like South Africa and Brazil).

The country's sharp increase in income inequality is not the result of the rich getting richer while the poor become poorer. China's extraordinary economic growth has raised the living standards of most of the population dramatically, and the World Bank estimates that more than 500 million Chinese have been raised above internationally recognized poverty lines. Thus many fewer Chinese are desperately poor today (less than 10 percent, rather than over 60 percent at the start of the reforms), but the income of the rich has been increasing faster than the income of the poor. The tide of economic development is lifting almost all Chinese boats, but at unequal speeds.

Despite increased inequality, China today is also not a society in which most individuals are locked in place by where they were born or assigned, thereby forced to accept the work, compensation, and benefits decided for them by socialist bureaucrats. Instead, individuals can and do change jobs, move to other locales, start businesses, and plan strategies to try to get ahead without worrying that they will be criticized for having bourgeois attitudes. Bureaucratic officials still wield considerable power in China's hybrid stratification hierarchy, but they don't have the nearly total control over those they supervise that they did in the Mao era.

Socialist serfdom has also ended, with hundreds of millions of villagers leaving farming for local nonagricultural jobs or for work in the cities. Even though the rural-urban income gap is still huge and growing, and migrants face systematic discrimination and denial of basic citizenship rights in the cities, most migrants regard their opportunities as far preferable to staying in the countryside, as Mao forced them to do. In some ways China has returned to a familiar social order, as stark inequalities combined with much upward and downward social mobility were the rule in China in past centuries.

Surveys that colleagues and I have been conducting in China in recent years (in Beijing in 2000, and then nationally in 2004 and 2009) indicate that, despite the dramatic increases in income gaps unleashed by reforms, most citizens feel optimistic about their own chances to get ahead. A majority also believe that talent, hard work, and schooling are the primary routes to mobility, rather than viewing most of the benefits of the reforms as a monopoly enjoyed by the already rich and powerful.

Given these survey findings, the mass protest incidents that have become ever more common in recent years are mainly a response to abuses of power and other procedural justice issues, rather than being fueled by feelings of distributive injustice and anger at the rich. However, whether China's leaders can continue to generate economic growth rapid enough to sustain popular acceptance of current inequalities, while also keeping suspicions of system unfairness at bay, remains to be seen.

II. Demography and Gender

China's Population Destiny: The Looming Crisis*

Wang Feng

Observers of China's rise, when assessing the implications for global peace and prosperity, have largely focused their attention on the country's

economy, on its energy and resource needs, on the environmental consequences of its rapid expansion, and on the nation's military buildup and strategic ambitions. Yet, underlying all these dazzling changes and monumental concerns is a

---

* This article was published in *Current History* (September 2010).

driving force that has been seriously underappreciated: China's changing demography.

With 1.33 billion people, China today remains the world's most populous country. In a little more than a decade, however, it will for the first time in its long history give up this title, to India. But, even more important, China's demographic landscape has in recent decades been thoroughly redrawn by unprecedented population changes. These changes will in the future drive the country's economic and social dynamics, and will redefine its position in the global economy and the society of nations. Taken together, the changes portend a gathering crisis.

One number best characterizes China's demographics today: 160 million. First, the country has more than 160 million internal migrants who, in the process of seeking better lives, have supplied abundant labor for the nation's booming economy. Second, more than 160 million Chinese are 60 years old or older. Third, more than 160 million Chinese families have only one child, a product in part of the country's three-decade-old policy limiting couples to one child each. (The total populations of countries like Japan and Russia do not reach 160 million; Bangladesh's population is roughly equal to that number.)

But the relative size of these three Chinese population groups of 160 million will soon change. As a result of the country's low fertility rates since the early 1990s, China has already begun experiencing what will become a sustained decline in new entrants into its labor force and in the number of young migrants. The era of uninterrupted supplies of young, cheap Chinese labor is over. The size of the country's population aged 60 and above, on the other hand, will increase dramatically, growing by 100 million in just 15 years (from 200 million in 2015 to over 300 million by 2030). The number of families with only one child, which is also on a continued rise, only underscores the challenge of supporting the growing numbers of elderly Chinese.

Why should one care about these demographic changes, and why should the overused label "crisis" be attached to such slow-moving developments? The aging of China's population represents a crisis because its arrival is imminent and inevitable, because its ramifications are huge and long-lasting, and because its effects will be hard to reverse.

Political legitimacy in China over the past three decades has been built around fast economic growth, which in turn has relied on a cheap and willing young labor force. An aging labor force will compel changes in this economic model and may make political rule more difficult. An aging population will force national reallocations of resources and priorities, as more funds flow to health care and pensions.

Indeed, increased spending obligations created by the aging of the population will not only shift resources away from investment and production; they will also test the government's ability to meet rising demands for benefits and services. In combination, a declining labor supply and increased public and private spending obligations will result in an economic growth model and a society that have not been seen in China before. Japan's economic stagnation, closely related to the aging of its population, serves as a ready reference.

China's demographic changes will also have far-reaching implications for the world economy, which has relied on China as a global factory for the past two decades and more. The changes may also affect international peace and security. An aging population is likely to lead to a more peaceful society. But at the same time, the projected 20 to 30 million Chinese men who will not be able to find wives, due to the country's decades-long imbalanced sex ratio at birth, may constitute a large group of unhappy, dissatisfied people. Claims that these future bachelors will harbor criminal intentions and a propensity to form invading forces against China's neighbors are unsubstantiated and overblown. Still, the fact that such a large number of Chinese men will not be able to marry is clearly a serious social concern, and the issue should not be neglected.

The ripple effects of fertility decline have begun to emerge everywhere in China these days. What also makes China's demographic future a looming crisis is that, so far, the changes have largely taken place under-the-radar. This is so in part because China still has the world's largest population and its population is still growing. It is also due in part to a continued tendency in China and elsewhere to believe that overpopulation is the root cause of all problems. Hence, China's hesitation, even reluctance, to phase out its one-child policy—an important cause of the country's demographic challenges.

Something little understood by the outside world, and indeed to the Chinese government and public, is that today's demographic changes mark only the beginning of a crisis that will be increasingly difficult to mitigate if action is not taken soon.

A New Era

China has entered a new demographic era. Its mortality rate has dropped to a level not very different from that of the developed countries. Its fertility has dropped to a level lower than that of many developed countries, including the United States, Britain, and France—indeed, it is among the lowest in the world. And China has witnessed the largest flow of internal migrants in world history, resulting in an urbanization process that is of comparable historical proportions. These forces combined have created a population that is rapidly aging and rapidly urbanizing.

China's mortality over the past three decades has been on a path of continuous decline. Despite concerns over the collapse of the rural collective public health care system in the 1980s and increasing incidents and reports of air pollution, food poisoning, and public health crises (such as the SARS epidemic in 2003), the Chinese population's overall health has continued to improve with the spread of affluence. The latest numbers based on nationally representative surveys put life expectancy at birth at 74.5 years for females and 70.7 for males, levels that approach those of the world's more developed countries. Longer life expectancy means more old people in the population and an increasing demand for services and expenditures related to health care.

But more important than increased life expectancy in defining China's new demographic era—and determining China's demographic future—is declining fertility. For nearly two decades, the average number of children a couple is expected to produce has been less than 2, recently falling as low as approximately 1.5. Such a number is below the replacement level (the level required for a population to maintain its size in the long run).

China's low fertility, however, is a fact that has been established as real only relatively recently, in part because of problems associated with deterioration in the country's birth registration and statistical data collection system, and in part because of the government's reluctance to acknowledge declining fertility. The current period of fertility decline began quietly and remained unnoticed for almost a decade. When the first signs that fertility had dropped below the replacement level were reported in the early 1990s, they were quickly dismissed in the context of what was believed to be widespread underreporting of births.

By the turn of the twenty-first century, China's demographic transition could no longer be doubted. Today the national fertility level is around 1.5 and possibly lower. In the country's more developed regions, fertility has been even lower for more than a decade—barely above one child per couple, a level that rivals the lowest fertility rates in the world.

The ripple effects of fertility decline have begun to emerge everywhere in China these days. In 1995, primary schools nationwide enrolled 25.3 million new students. By 2008, that number had shrunk by one-third, to only 16.7 million. In 1990, China had over 750,000 primary schools. By 2008, due to the combined effects of fertility decline and educational reforms, the number of primary schools nationwide had fallen to about 300,000. In a country where getting into a university has always been a matter of intense competition and anxiety, the number of applicants to universities has begun to decline in the past couple of years.

The challenges posed by these demographic changes will be more daunting in China than in other countries that have experienced mortality and fertility declines. The reason for this does not lie in the size of China's population, but in the speed with which the People's Republic has completed its transition from high to low birth and death rates. China has achieved in 50 years—increasing life expectancy from the 40s to over 70—what it took many European countries a century to accomplish. In 2000, when the ratio of income levels in the United States and China was still about 10 to 1, female life expectancy in China was only about five years below that of the United States (75 versus 80). China, in other words, completed its mortality-decline transition while per capita income was still at a very low level.

Major fertility reduction in China took even less time. In just one decade, from 1970 to 1980, the total fertility rate (TFR) was more than halved, from 5.8 to 2.3, a record unmatched elsewhere (TFR extrapolates an average woman's fertility over her lifetime from a society's fertility rate in a given year). In contrast to Western European countries, where it took 75 years or longer to reduce TFR from around 5 to the replacement level, in China a similar decline took less than two decades. As a result, in 2008, China's rate of population growth was only 5 per thousand, down from over 14 per thousand in 1990 and 25 per thousand in 1970.

Such a compressed process of demographic transition means that, compared with other countries in the world, China will have far less time to prepare its social and economic infrastructure to deal with the effects of a rapidly aging population. And for the People's Republic the challenge is all the more difficult because the country is undergoing an economic upheaval at the same time that its population is rapidly changing. While China continues to transform itself from an agrarian to an industrial and post-industrial society, and from a planned to a market-based economy, it not only will need, for example, to provide health care and pensions for a rapidly growing elderly population that has been covered under government-sponsored programs. It also will need to figure out how to expand the scope of coverage to those who were not covered under the old system.

Reversal of Fortunes

China's astonishing economic expansion over the past two decades took place within a highly, almost uniquely favorable, demographic context. But the country is at the end of reaping economic gains from a favorable population age structure.

Economic growth relies on a number of basic factors. Aside from institutional arrangements, these include capital, technology, markets, and labor. In China's case, foreign direct investment, especially from overseas Chinese, brought not only capital but also technology and management know-how. Foreign consumer demand, especially in the United States (fueled first by the dot-com boom and then by the housing and stock market boom), supplied a ready market for China's export industries. But capital, technology, and overseas markets alone would not have made China a global factory in the last two decades of the twentieth century. The country's economic boom relied on another crucial factor: a young and productive labor force.

Such a labor force, a non-repeatable historical phenomenon resulting from a rapid demographic transition, was fortuitously present as the Chinese economy was about to take off. The large birth cohorts of the 1960s and 1970s were at their peak productive ages when the boom began. This good fortune, measured as a demographic dividend, is estimated to have accounted for 15 to 25 percent of China's economic growth between 1980 and 2000.

The term "demographic dividend" refers to gains (or losses) in per capita income brought about by changes in a population's age structure. It is expressed as the ratio of the growth rate of effective producers to the growth rate of effective consumers. It resembles but is not the same as the commonly used "dependency ratio," which is the ratio of the dependent-age population (such as 0–14 years old and 60 and above) to the productive-age population (such as 15–59 or 20–59). The demographic dividend, unlike the dependency ratio, takes into account people in the productive age cohort who are not contributing to income generation (for example, because they are unemployed) as well as those within the dependent age range who generate income (such as from after-retirement earnings).

For the most part, China has exhausted its demographic fortune as measured by the demographic dividend—that is, by the changing support ratio between effective producers and effective consumers. Between 1982 and 2000, China enjoyed an average annual rate of growth in the support ratio of 1.28 percent. Using the World Bank's figure of per capita annual income growth during this same period, 8.4 percent, we find that the demographic dividend accounted for 15 percent of China's economic growth. Today, the net gain due to favorable demographic conditions has been reduced to only one-fifth of the average level maintained from 1982 to 2000.

By 2013 China's demographic dividend growth rate will turn negative: That is, the growth rate of net consumers will exceed the growth rate of net producers. Starting in 2013, such a negative growth rate will reduce the country's economic growth rate by at least half a percentage point per year. Between 2013 and 2050, China will not fare demographically much better than Japan or Taiwan, and will fare much worse than the United States and France.

As a result of China's very low fertility over the past two decades, the abundance of young, inexpensive labor is soon to be history. The number of workers aged 20 to 29 will stay about the same for the next few years, but a precipitous drop will begin in the middle of the coming decade. Over a 10-year period, between 2016 and 2026, the size of the population in this age range will be reduced by about one-quarter, to 150 million from 200 million. For Chinese aged 20 to 24, that decline will come sooner and will be more drastic: Over the next decade, their number will be reduced by nearly 50 percent, to 68 million from 125 million.

Gender Equality and Women's Development in China[*]

Information Office of the State Council

The following are some facts and figures published in the White Paper:

— In 1990, the state's spending on women and children's healthcare and epidemic prevention and treatment stood at 305 million yuan and 1.203 billion yuan, respectively, which rose to 1.046 billion yuan and 3.388 billion yuan in 1999, and further to 1.579 billion yuan and 9.054 billion yuan in 2003.

— During the period from 1998 to 2003, women's federations nationwide endeavored to get small-sum credit loans to directly aid a total of 2.5 million women to get re-employed.

— By the end of 2004, the number of both urban and rural women workers reached 337 million nationwide, accounting for 44.8 percent of the total employed; and the number of women workers in urban work units stood at 42.27 million, accounting for 38.1 percent of the national total.

— At present, women owners of small- and medium-sized enterprises account for about 20 percent of the national total number of entrepreneurs, and 60 percent of them have emerged in the past decade.

— By the end of 2004, women accounted for 43.6 percent of the total number of professionals and technicians in state-owned enterprises and institutions nationwide, up 6.3 percentage points over the 37.3 percent of 1995, among whom, the number of senior- and intermediate-level women professionals and technicians rose from 20.1 percent and 33.4 percent to 30.5 percent and 42 percent, respectively.

— By the end of 2004, the practice of overall social planning had been introduced in 28 provinces, autonomous regions and municipalities directly under the central government, with 43.84 million employees, or 60 percent of the total number of urban employees covered.

— China is basically an agricultural country, and women account for more than 60 percent of the rural labor force and are a major force in farming activities. The *Law of the People's Republic of China on Rural Land Contracting*, which came into effect in 2003, states that women and men enjoy equal rights in contracting land in rural areas, and no organization or individual shall deprive women of the right to contract and operate land or infringe upon their right to do so.

— With the implementation of large-scale and effective special poverty-reduction development programs, the government has succeeded in reducing the poverty-stricken rural population, the majority of whom are women, by 53.9 million—from 80 million in 1994 to 26.1 million in 2004.

---

[*] This news report was published by Xinhua News Agency on August 24, 2005.

– During the period from 2001 to 2004, a total of 13.52 billion yuan in small-sum credit loans for rural households were granted from the state poverty-reduction discount loans, and more than half of the money went to women. Since 2001, the Chinese government has taken poverty-reduction projects in the form of participation of the poor as the main way to "enhance the whole village," and such projects now cover 148,000 poverty-stricken villages nationwide.

– The project of "Love of the Earth, Water Cellars for Mothers," initiated by the China Women's Development Foundation, has raised funds for building more than 90,000 rain-water collecting cellars and 1,100 small water supply projects in water-deficient northwest part of China, benefiting nearly 1 million poverty-stricken people.

– In the past decade, women have displayed great enthusiasm in participating in electing deputies to the people's congresses at all levels and exercising their democratic rights. Some 73.4 percent of women turned out to elect deputies to local people's congresses. Of all the deputies to the various National People's Congresses, more than 20 percent have been women.

– At present, three of the vice-chairpersons of the National People's Congress Standing Committee are women. Four of the vice-chairpersons of the National Committee of the Chinese People's Political Consultative Conference are women.

– In 2004, female membership in the Communist Party of China was 12.956 million, accounting for 18.6 percent of all CPC members, an increase of 3 percentage points over 1995.

– By the end of 2004, 368 incumbent or vice mayors (commissioners and prefects) were women; and women cadres at or above the provincial (ministry) level accounted for 9.9 percent of the total at that level, an increase of 2.8 percentage points over 1995.

– At present, China has one woman Vice-Premier and one woman State Councilor on the State Council, and 25 women incumbent or vice ministers or ministerial-level directors or heads in the Supreme People's Court, the Supreme People's Procuratorate, and the ministries and commissions under the State Council.

– The proportion of women civil servants recruited in 2003 nationwide was 27.8 percent of the total; and that in the organs of the CPC Central Committee and central government was 37.7 percent.

– In 2004, the enrollment of boys and girls was 98.97 percent and 98.93 percent, respectively. The difference in access to education between boys and girls was reduced from 0.7 percentage point in 1995 to 0.04 percentage point.

– In 2004, the educational appropriation from the state treasury for compulsory education in rural areas reached 139.362 billion yuan, two times the amount in 1995.

– In 2004, the proportion of girl students in junior and senior middle schools reached 47.4 percent and 45.8 percent, respectively; the proportion of girl students in secondary vocational schools reached 51.5 percent; the number of girl students in institutions of higher learning nationwide reached 6.09 million, accounting for 45.7 percent of all students in such schools and an increase of 10.3 percentage points over 1995. The proportion of female postgraduate and doctoral students was 44.2 percent and 31.4 percent, 13.6 percentage points and 15.9 percentage points higher respectively over the figures for 1995.

– In 2004, the proportions of women teachers in junior and senior middle schools were 45.9 percent and 41.7 percent, respectively; and the proportions of full-time women teachers in secondary vocational schools and institutions of higher learning were 46.5 percent and 42.5 percent, respectively.

– In 2004, the illiteracy rate among women 15 years of age and above in urban areas was 8.2 percent, a decrease of 5.7 percentage points from that of 1995; the illiteracy rate among women 15 years of age and above in rural areas was 16.9 percent, a decrease of 10.5 percentage points from that of 1995. The illiteracy rate among young and middle-aged women across the country was 4.2 percent, a drop of 5.2 percentage points from that of 1995.

– According to the fifth national census, conducted in 2000, the average number of years of education of Chinese women was seven—one and a half years more than in 1990—and the gap between the genders had been narrowed by half a year in that decade.

- By the end of 2004, there were 2,997 healthcare institutes for women and children throughout China, with 243,000 beds for women.
- For years, the healthcare departments at all levels have considered the examination and treatment of gynecological diseases to be routine work. Every year, over one third of married women under the age of 65 across China go through examinations for gynecological diseases. In 2004, some 37.3 percent of them had this examination.
- The average life expectancy for women was 74 years in 2003.
- In the 2000–2001 period, the state invested 200 million yuan in a project intended to "lower the mortality rate of women in pregnancy and childbirth and eliminate tetanus among the newborn," which covered 378 state-level poor counties. From 2002 to 2005, the central treasury and relevant local areas allocated an additional 400 million yuan for the continuation of this project, extending it to 1,000 counties and benefiting more than 300 million people.
- In the past decade, the mortality rate of women in childbirth has declined steadily—from 61.9 per 100,000 in 1995 to 48.3 per 100,000 in 2004.
- Over the last decade, the rate of early marriage among women has dropped, the average age for first marriage has gone up, and the general childbirth rate was kept at a fairly low level—1.8 per couple in 2004.

- From 2001 to 2004, the central government earmarked 9.7 billion yuan to solve the problem of drinking water for rural residents, providing safe drinking water for an average of 6.9 million rural women a year. In 2004, as many as 53.1 percent of rural households in China had access to sanitary toilets. The sanitary disposal rate of night soil in rural areas rose quickly from 28.5 percent in 1998 to 57.5 percent in 2004. The upgrading of public toilets and sewage facilities has eased the heavy burden of many rural women to carry water, and reduced health hazards for them and their family members, thus effectively improving their living and development conditions.
- In the last decade, China has enacted and revised, in succession, the Marriage Law, the Population and Family Planning Law, the Law on Rural Land Contracting, and the Law on Protection of Rights and Interests of Women, and promulgated and implemented over 100 rules and regulations concerning the protection of women's rights and interests, such as the Regulations on Implementing the Law on Mother and Infant Healthcare.
- In recent years, local statutes outlawing domestic violence have been enacted in 22 provinces (autonomous regions and municipalities directly under the central government) by the end of 2004.

III. Nationalism and Identity

The Many Facets of Chinese Nationalism*

Jean-Pierre Cabestan

Chinese nationalism is a more ambiguous reality than it might seem. Its existence cannot be denied. It has great power and intensity, as shown over the last few years by the demonstrations against

the American bombing of the Chinese embassy in Belgrade in May 1999, the EP-3 incident in April 2001, the denunciation of the Japanese Prime Minister's visits to the Yasukuni Shrine, the virulent criticisms of Taiwanese leaders, from Lee Teng-hui to Chen Shui-bian, and, more recently, the ambition to make China not only a great economic and military power but to surpass the United States as the greatest power in the world.

* This article was published in *China Perspectives*, No. 59 (May–June 2005). Translated from the French original by Michael Black.

Nationalism seems today to be the most widely-shared value both in Chinese society and in the government, which is perfectly aware of this, and has repeatedly instrumentalized it with the aim of strengthening its hand in the face of its foreign partners and also of preventing any "peaceful evolution" of the regime towards democracy.

Yet at the same time, motivated by self-interest, many international actions by the Beijing government, and many expressions of society, have remained impervious to this feeling of nationalism. The opening up of the Chinese economy and society to the outside world, the establishment of diplomatic and trade links with those powers who had once "humiliated" China (the United States, Japan, Great Britain, Germany, France, etc.), Beijing's accession to the World Trade Organization (WTO) and the acceptance (provisional, it is true) of a form of status quo in the Taiwan Strait, are evidence of a certain "bringing under control" of nationalist emotions which can affect government circles and the intellectual elite. Similarly, within Chinese society, the pursuit of individual success, the desire—and perhaps even more the possibility—to become rich and to improve one's standard of living, the increasing power of provincialism and localism, the fascination with an America which is both powerful and prosperous, the attraction of a modernity which is often synonymous with the "American way of life," as well as a general curiosity about a long-forbidden outside world—as shown by the growth of Chinese tourism abroad—and the emigration of millions of Chinese towards the developed world, are all evidence, if not of an absence, at least of a relative weakness of nationalism. This attitude has led a number of writers to put forward the concept of "pragmatic nationalism."[1]

Moreover, 9/11 and the worldwide war against terrorism have contributed to creating solidarities between Chinese and Western governments, solidarities which have attenuated, at least up to the spring of 2005, the most spectacular and extreme manifestations of Chinese nationalism. Finally, the last ten years have brought to light a spectrum, wider than one might previously have expected, of international behavior on the part of both Chinese government and society, putting into perspective the nature and extent of Chinese nationalism and making it possible to distinguish more

clearly between ordinary times and the brief—but intense and emotional—moments of more or less spontaneous manifestations of nationalism.

While, for historical reasons, Chinese nationalism is in many ways specific, because it is based on what is perceived as past humiliation (*xiuru*), it has shown since the beginning of the modern era, which is to say since the Opium War of 1840, a profound feeling of insecurity. However, beyond this feeling of insecurity, several forms of nationalism co-exist in this country, as they do in any other.

It is, first of all, an *official nationalism*—inspired by communist ideology and the preoccupation of the Chinese Communist Party (CCP) with maintaining its monopoly of politics: this is synonymous in China with "patriotism." It is also a *revanchist nationalism* with racist tendencies, which is disseminated in society by the most xenophobic elements among the Chinese elite—in particular the "New Left"—which rely on popular ignorance of foreign countries and the traditional mistrust towards them to spread their ideas. Based more on the need to wash away past humiliations than on a rational analysis of reality, influenced by communist patriotism but going beyond it, this form of nationalism was particularly influential in the second half of the 1990s. Its manifestations more frequently took the form of anti-foreign emotions and violence than of structured discourse or coherent action. Stimulated by the elites close to government circles, it was once again instrumentalized by the latter in the spring of 2005.

One may well wonder if there is not another form of Chinese nationalism, a nationalism which derives its legitimacy both from cultural specificity and from current Chinese economic and social realities, without however rejecting foreign influence out of hand. While seeking to modernize China and to make it regain the place and influence which are its due in the international community, while preserving its culture, this nationalism seeks to be less aggressive and more peaceable, showing a desire to favor convergence, in particular political convergence, with the rest of the world. Symbolized by the concept, favored by Hu Jintao, of China's "peaceful rise," can this nationalism eventually give birth to a democratic nationalism, at once measured, open, and concerned with defending not only the interests of the Chinese nation but also those of the men and women who belong to it? Is not this nationalism the only one capable of expressing a real ideological consensus in society, far from the manipulations of political and intellectual elites driven above all by ambition and the struggle for power?

Elitist Nationalism of a Great Power Dispossessed and Humiliated

It is widely accepted that Chinese nationalism took form only as a reaction to the shock of forced contact with the West, after the Opium War of 1840. It is true that before this historic turning point, China was much more an empire than a nation state, a civilization and a culture dominated by one race (*zu*)—the Han—rather than a society brought together by a national project, and even less so by a modern citizenship. This is why several Sinologists have contrasted the old "culturalism" with the nationalism of the Chinese after 1840.[2] In fact, despite earlier contacts with the outside world, in particular with Russia, it is this emblematic event which truly transformed the Chinese empire into a modern state, and China into a nation, thus confirming the theses of Ernest Gellner and Eric Hobsbawm on the decisive role played by the state in the construction of the nation and consequently on the formation of nationalism.[3]

However, the main specificity of imperial China may lie elsewhere: many non-Western societies did not have the characteristics of the old European nations (in particular France and England), while being brought together by clear and specific racial origins, in short an ethnic or "objective" nationalism, which, in contact with the West, could only be exacerbated. On this last point, Japan and Korea come to mind—in the languages of these countries, as in Chinese, the idea of nationalism (*minzuzhuyi*) introduced in the nineteenth century includes the idea of race (*minzoshugi* in Japanese and *minjokchuyi* in Korean).[4] These nations therefore also constituted, in their own ways, "imagined communities," to use Benedict Anderson's classic formulation.[5] Moreover, also in the West, "subjective" nationalism, as a feeling and a movement, is a phenomenon scarcely older than modern Chinese nationalism,

brought about directly by the consolidation of states, the drawing of frontiers and the ideological changes of the eighteenth century.[6]

The specificity of Chinese nationalism stems from the almost permanently dominant position occupied by the Chinese Empire within the world with which it maintained relations prior to 1840. After its fall from the pedestal, the impact of the West was all the more strongly felt, the humiliation provoked all the more profound, China's resistance to outside ideas all the stronger, causing the failure of numerous reforms at the end of the Manchu era, at the very moment when Meiji Japan, having become Europe's pupil after having been China's, was modernizing on an economic level as well as in political and institutional matters. We know that Chinese nationalists, and the Communist Party in particular, continue to accuse Western imperialism of being the main instigator of these failures, in particular by imposing inequitable treaties on their country, whereas historiography as a whole has shown that the weakening of the Empire predated 1840, and was due to a number of internal causes (in particular the doubling of the population between 1700 and 1800). What is interesting to focus on here is the foundational dimension of the trauma of 1840 in the debate on Chinese nationalism. Since then the debate has been between those who favored resistance to the West and the partisans of modernization by the introduction, not only of Western sciences and techniques, but also of Western ideas, modes of organization (political institutions and law) and of management.

The second specificity we would venture to put forward is the essential role played in China by the political and intellectual elites in the formation of contemporary nationalism. As both Wilfred Pareto and Roberto Michels have shown, the role played by the elites in the conceptualization, manipulation and propagation of this ideology is universally important. Despite the relevance of the work of both Pierre Birnbaum and Ezra Suleiman on the elites in France, this influence tends to grow as a particular regime moves away from democracy and leans towards authoritarianism. The elitist character of Asian and especially Confucian societies, for example those of Japan and Korea, gives the elites a specific influence in this undertaking. As we shall see, certain nationalist movements which appeared in China after 1840—the Taiping and the Boxers—were not entirely the preserve of the "counter-elites" but of social strata who perceived foreign ascendancy (respectively the Manchu and the Westerners) to be the source of their problems. The hypothesis we seek to put forward here, however, and which seems to be borne out in the People's Republic today, is that of the virtual monopoly exercised by the elites in the formation of nationalism, and the low level of interaction between them and the rest of society, which, structured as it is around personal and family obligations, remains, except in times of major crisis (even in the case of the Sino-Japanese war) relatively impervious to this ideology, and especially to its translation into action.[7]

A reflection of the distanced relations between society and the state in China, this gap is much less obvious elsewhere, particularly in Japan or in Korea. This specificity favors a more energetic manipulation of nationalism by the elites, particularly those which have privileged interaction with government.

The Diversity of Nationalist Responses to China's Problems

The apparent binary of the choices put forward by the Chinese elites after 1840—either resisting the West or learning from it—did not lead to an inevitable monopolization of nationalism by the detractors of the West. On the contrary, what is shown by a century and a half of contemporary Chinese history is the great diversity of discourses and political and economic projects that the country produced. It is enough to briefly recall the debates among the elites at the end of the Manchu era (1644–1911) and the way in which these structured the political forces in the Republican period (1912–1949) to be convinced of this.

Constrained against its will to open up, subjected to the regime of "inequitable treaties," of zones of influence and of foreign concessions, China after 1840—and once again its elites above all—could not be other than unanimously nationalist and anti-Western. But at the same time, this nationalism was not turned against the European powers only: it was also aimed at the "foreign," which is to say non-Han, power of the Manchu dynasty, and militated for the restoration of the

Ming; as was shown by the Taiping Rebellion (1851–1864), it could both draw inspiration from Western religions, in this case Christianity, and display profound xenophobia. After the humiliating military defeat against Japan in 1895, it was fuelled by both enduring jealousy towards that country and a strong determination to learn from it. Above all, nationalist reaction to Western domination was plural from the beginning.

At one end of the spectrum, under the impact of the West and of the "break-up of China" in 1898, which is to say the race for foreign concessions, was the formation of a rural and populist "primitive nationalism" based on an "ethno-cultural awareness" of which the Boxer Rebellion in 1900 was the best-known manifestation.[8] This rebellion, molded by religions and popular millenarian beliefs, consolidated a xenophobic nationalist tradition, racist and above all anti-Western, as well as anti-Christian. Sanctified by the Communist Party, the Boxer movement experienced a certain extension during the Maoist period, particularly during the Cultural Revolution (even though the Red Guards, often offspring of the *nomenklatura*, can be considered a "counter-elite," anxious to instrumentalize, for uniquely political and personal purposes, their rejection of the outside world). Although the manifestations of nationalism which have appeared since the reopening of China in 1979 have never equaled that degree of fanaticism and xenophobia, one cannot bank on the disappearance of this tradition, particularly among the elites. Indeed, despite a certain evolution in historiography, not only does the present Chinese government continue to consider the Boxers as nationalist heroes and to propagate this idea in the country's school textbooks, but the many who have been pushed aside by economic growth—while certain sections of the elite like to manipulate them and use them in the service of their political ambitions—might well in future find in the expatriate population in China the most obvious scapegoats for their misfortunes.

Right next to this movement lies an "instrumentalist" nationalist tradition which has constantly sought to introduce into China only those "recipes" of the West which are likely to strengthen the state with the exclusive aim of enabling it better to resist both domination and ideas from outside. Personified in the nineteenth century by Zhang Zhidong, whose aim was to adopt only the sciences and techniques of Europe in order to maintain "Chinese learning for essence" (*zhongxue wei ti*), and by the statesman Li Hongzhang, this conservative tradition advocated the maintenance of an unalloyed Confucianism, opposed to any opening to the West. It contributed to the failure of the prudent reforms of the Hundred Days in 1898, launched by Kang Youwei and Liang Qichao. It also influenced a number of Chinese reformers and constitutionalists at the beginning of the twentieth century, who conceived the law and political institutions more as weapons for the consolidation and modernization of the state than as comprehensive values aimed at guaranteeing the rights of citizens in the face of the state.[9]

This tradition was long maintained by the Communist Party. In fact, the foundation of the People's Republic in 1949 allowed this kind of nationalism, officially anti-Confucian and modernizing, but in reality conservative and favorable to the maintenance of a traditional rural society, to impose itself for over thirty years. The alliance with the Soviet Union, and then the falling-out between the two countries, led Mao Zedong's China to accept Western techniques and modes of organization only extremely sparingly, establishing a de facto nationalist isolation which seemed to link up with the Empire before 1840. While this current of thought is weaker now, it would be wrong to think that it has disappeared, for it is present within the Communist Party of Deng Xiaoping, Jiang Zemin and in particular Hu Jintao, and helps to explain the Party's persistent ambiguity towards the West.[10]

A third current of thought is based on what Yves Chevrier calls "the modernizing nationalism of the reformist elite." Its first and principal promoter at the end of the nineteenth century was probably Kang Youwei, one of the architects of the Hundred Day reforms. While he favored the study not only of the techniques but also of the ideas of the West, Kang was nevertheless a supporter of a renovated Confucianism. While he hoped, in 1898, to introduce reforms in three years, particularly in the institutions, which Meiji Japan had applied over the course of thirty years, he had no intention of calling into question his country's Confucian legacy, but sought, by means of reforms decided on high, to establish a utopian

consensus, the great unanimity (*datong*). Today one is struck by the similarities between Kang's ideas and plans, and those of Deng Xiaoping, Jiang Zemin, and Hu Jintao. All three of these leaders are unquestionably modernizers and reformers. However, the official rehabilitation of Confucianism over which they presided from 1979 on, their exaltation of traditional morality and of virtue (*de*), in the same way as the "socialist rule of law" and the protection of human rights, their determination to maintain the leadership role of the Communist Party, which they see as the only guarantor of social consensus (in particular through the theory of the "three represents"), betray a nationalist resistance to the globalization of ideas and to democratization.[11] While it is less anti-Western than previous ones, this form of nationalism seeks nonetheless to contrast the path chosen by China with that followed by the West. It is therefore frequently instrumentalized in order to reinforce the unity of society around the political establishment, and to defend the international interests of the country.

Lastly, there does exist in China a form of nationalism that is broadly pro-Western. Despite his ambiguities, Yan Fu (1852–1921) is one of the first and the most representative of this trend.[12] Having introduced the most important Western political thinkers to his compatriots (including John Stuart Mill and Montesquieu), Yan held up the British parliamentary system as a model for his country. While he influenced the communists and Mao Zedong in particular, he left his mark above all on the democratic nationalist tradition embodied by Sun Yat-sen, Hu Shi, and Lu Xun. It is true that Yan Fu, and then Sun Yat-sen, felt that they had to move forward prudently and prepare the people by education, and therefore by what were once again Confucian methods, for democracy. Thus Yan Fu, towards the end of his life, gave his support to the dictatorship of Yuan Shikai (1912–1916) and Sun Yat-sen, after the failure of the revolution in 1911, conceived of the establishment of a constitutional government (*xianzheng*) in three stages—which would have to be preceded by a military government (*junzheng*), and then by political control (*xunzheng*) of the Kuomintang (KMT) over society.

Nevertheless, while it sought to build on those aspects of Chinese tradition that could favor the modernization of the country, this form of nationalism was largely inspired by the West. Sun

Yat-sen established, at the beginning of the republican period, the "three principles of the people": nationalism (*minzuzhuyi*), democracy (*minquan*), and the well-being of the people (*mins-heng*). He also proposed the establishment of democratically elected political institutions—the five Yuan or Councils—which combined the separation of the three powers of the Enlightenment (the legislative, the executive and the judiciary) with the Chinese administrative tradition (the powers of examination, stemming from the imperial competitive examinations, and of control, inspired by the censorship). While his successors, particularly Chang Kai-shek, were for a while attracted by the Soviet Union's anti-colonialism or Germany's militarism, they turned to the West above all in order to modernize their institutions, their laws, their economy, and their education system. As an active participant in the nationalist movement of the May Fourth 1919, which is to say the protests of the elites and of the students against the decision contained in the Treaty of Versailles to transfer to Japan the former German possessions in China, the Kuomintang largely contributed to the dismantling of the concessions, which became definitive in 1943, and more generally to the reintegration of the Chinese nation among the world's great powers. It was partly thanks to these efforts that in 1945, at the end of the Second World War and the Sino-Japanese conflict, China, with the support of the United States, became a permanent member of the UN Security Council.

It is clear that, giving priority to the strengthening of the central government in Nanking, which was the capital of the Republic of China from 1928, and to the subjugation of local potentates and of the communist rebellion, Chiang Kai-shek dithered over launching a hopeless counterattack against Japan's territorial violations, which allowed Mao and his partisans to appear in the eyes of many Chinese, and above all of important sections of the Chinese elite, as the only upholders of the nationalist cause. Having taken refuge in Chungking from 1938 to 1945, the Kuomintang government largely abandoned the political territory of the occupied zones to the Communist Party, which reinforced the identification of the Party with resistance to the Japanese (and allowed Mao to extend his hold over that part of the country). The Kuomintang remained nevertheless highly nationalist, having sacrificed its best officers to the defense of Nanking in 1938 and later negotiating inch by inch with the Allies, and particularly with the Americans, the return of the Chinese possessions which had been snatched by Japan, among them Taiwan (at the Cairo Conference of 1943). The Sino-Japanese war did nevertheless favor the political victory in China in 1949 of the conservative nationalism, totalitarian and with xenophobic tendencies, of the Communist Party over the liberal, constitutional, and pro-Western, if not yet democratic nationalism of the post-war Kuomintang.

This historical framework is important because these four main nationalist movements are still represented in the People's Republic. Thanks to the reforms of 1979, and then the clamp-down which followed the Tiananmen massacre in 1989, the respective influence of these various facets of Chinese nationalism has evolved. But as we shall see, this evolution is far from over. Because of the slow death of communist ideology under the successive batterings of the reforms, of the opening-up and of the collapse of the Soviet Union, the leadership of the Communist Party has been increasingly tempted since 1989 to instrumentalize the anti-Western and especially anti-Japanese dimensions of Chinese nationalism. Certain segments of the Chinese elites have used this ideological movement to strengthen either their influence over the government or their opposition to the current system. The partial withdrawal of control over intellectual debate has favored the reappearance of several competing forms of nationalism, bringing to light once again the fundamentally plural character of this phenomenon, particularly among the elites.

Nationalism in China Today

Nationalism has always formed a part of the official discourse of the Chinese Communist Party. However, for reasons which stem from its ideology and from its links with the Communist International, it preferred for a long time the idea of "patriotism" (*aiguozhuyi*) which was supposed to be more easily reconcilable than nationalism properly speaking (which had once been denounced by Mao and his comrades) with the "proletarian internationalism" which the Party claimed to embrace.[13] The collapse of the international communist movement and the dismemberment of the Soviet Union did not call the idea of patriotism directly into question. The authorities in the People's Republic still today consider as "patriotic" any Chinese person who shows allegiance to the state, renders it service and accepts the directives of the Communist Party, whether they are communist or not. Thus Peking continues to award this honorary "seal of quality" to many overseas Chinese who have chosen the mainland over Taiwan. However, since Tiananmen and the collapse of the Soviet Union, the idea of nationalism has gradually regained its place in Communist Party discourse, clearing the way for the expression among the intellectual elites of a "new nationalism," more populist and autonomous, which, since the mid-1990s, has gone beyond the bounds of the nationalism set by the Party.[14] This evolution has led leadership circles in return to adopt an ambivalent attitude to this trend, hesitating between instrumentalization and control, particularly with the aim of maintaining more margin for [maneuvering] on the international level.

The Increase in the Power of State Nationalism after Tiananmen

The increase in the power of nationalism after Tiananmen has been multidimensional from the beginning. There was first of all the irruption of a state nationalism which some dubbed "nationalism of substitution,"[15] because to a large extent it replaced a communist ideology which had shown its futility and above all its inadequacy in the face of the economic and social realities which the Communist Party was allowing to take root in China. Appearing in 1991, this form of nationalism was part of the transformation of the Communist Party into a "ruling party" (*zhizhengdang*), offering daily proof of its management abilities and presiding over the destiny of a "great country" (*daguo*), whose power is to grow irresistibly and thus eventually overtake the United States.

While this state nationalism was, for a period in the 1990s, attracted by "Asian values," today it is seeking above all to find in the Chinese Confucian and Imperial tradition the foundations of a legitimate national territory, of an authoritarian national identity and of government by virtue

or by benevolence (*renzheng*). On the foreign level, this form of nationalism favors diplomacy and a security policy entirely based on national interests (*guojia liyi*), an idea which had been absent from the discourse of the Chinese Communist Party before, and the reconquest of the Manchu Imperial area (in particular Taiwan). It is above all more often used by the authorities in Beijing, who always seek to place their partners in a position of inferiority, for example by constantly alluding to their five millennia of history and culture, or to strengthen their hand in negotiation, by throwing into the balance the supposed nationalist feelings and even anger of their compatriots.

Having targeted Western countries as a whole after Tiananmen, who were suspected of favoring China's "peaceful evolution" (*heping yanbian*) towards "bourgeois democracy," this state nationalism then concentrated its attacks on two countries which are close to China and have a particular interest in the question of Taiwan: the United States and Japan. The private visit by the Taiwanese President Lee Teng-hui to the United States in 1995 unleashed an unprecedented official offensive against Washington centered on the theme of the inevitability of the rebel island's reunification with the so-called Motherland.[16] The perspective of the return of Hong Kong (1997) and Macau (1999) was not foreign to this instrumentalization of the question of Taiwan. However, these attacks against the United States, which was accused of seeking to hamper the satisfaction of China's legitimate demands, were part of an increase in bilateral tensions, which were themselves exacerbated by a variety of frictions.[17]

During the same period, the Chinese Communist Party intensified its criticisms of Japan, stigmatizing it for a whole range of reasons: on the one hand for its desire to strengthen its security links with the United States (shown in particular by the adoption in 1997 of new Guidelines for US-Japan Defense Co-operation and in February 2005 of a declaration which identified Taiwan as a common strategic objective) and to enhance its relations with Taiwan, and, on the other hand, for its persistent refusal to present a "sincere apology" for the crimes it committed during the Second World War, to put an end to the visits to the Yasukuni Shrine where are preserved the funerary stones of the 2.5 million soldiers killed during the Second World War, among them fourteen war criminals, to exercise more control over the publishing of history textbooks with revisionist tendencies, and finally, to yield on the question of the Senkaku (Diaoyutai) archipelago. The presentation by Tokyo of a written apology to Seoul in 1998 was the occasion for an official offensive by Peking, aimed at obtaining the same commitment (when a verbal apology had already been made in 1995). However, because Jiang Zemin did not wish to promise to put an end to Chinese criticisms of the Japanese government's attitude to the events connected with the war, the latter refused to accede to his demand, provoking, after the failure of Jiang's visit to Japan in 1998, a further salvo of nationalist attacks from the Chinese Communist Party.

Fueled by certain intellectuals who chose to serve the government after Tiananmen, such as He Xin,[18] this state nationalism has also favored the eruption of a populist nationalism whose most extreme manifestations have recalled the xenophobia and anti-Western attitudes of the "primitive nationalism" at the end of the nineteenth century.

A New Populist Nationalism in China

The central place occupied by nationalism in the ideology of the Chinese Communist Party since 1989 has favored the expression, particularly among the intellectual elites, of an autonomous popular nationalism with populist tendencies, beginning in the second part of the 1990s, a period marked by the crisis in the Taiwan Strait (1995–1996), the American bombing of the Chinese embassy in Belgrade (1999), and more recently the demonstrations of April 2005 against Japan. The adjectives "popular," "autonomous," and "populist" deserve explanation. To what extent does this form of nationalism reflect the feelings of significant sections of Chinese society? Is it really autonomous from the state nationalism propagated by the Chinese Communist Party? In a country where the state tightly controls the media and organized demonstrations, is not this autonomy inevitably limited and subject to manipulation by the government, or certain sections of the government? Are the supporters of this form of nationalism tempted to seek the support

of society by criticizing what they perceive to be a series of weaknesses and compromises on the part of the government, and of the official elites, in the face of the outside world?

The 1980s were not without autonomous nationalist movements. For example, the student demonstrations against the revision of Japanese school textbooks in 1985 were already aimed at influencing government policy towards Japan (and in fact contributed to the fall of Hu Yaobang, a convinced supporter of reconciliation with Tokyo). But generally speaking, Chinese society, fascinated by the discovery of the outside world, was much more bent on learning from the West, envying its prosperity and seeking its freedom, than on rejecting it, distrusting it, or criticizing its dominant position. Moreover debates on foreign policy were still highly regulated, restricting any autonomous and public participation by society, and above all by the intellectuals, in them.

Things changed gradually after Tiananmen. It was probably the publication in 1994 of a book by Wang Shan, a former Red Guard who had become a writer and author of *Looking at China Through the Third Eye*, which heralded the re-emergence in China of a form of nationalism and of critical foreign policy discourse which were in fact autonomous and populist. Worried by the growing gaps in society brought about by the reforms and nostalgia for the Maoist period, Wang believed that only an autocratic and elitist state could allow China to remain stable, to develop successfully and to become a great power again. In parallel he developed a discourse opposed to liberalism, and in particular to the United States, which he accused of having encouraged and supported the Beijing Spring of 1989, and of seeking to overthrow the Chinese Communist Party, because, among other reasons, it possessed nuclear weapons. However, as if to reassure himself, and following the discourse of state nationalism, he was of the opinion that America was in decline and that the future belonged to the East.[19]

At the time these opinions were still in a minority among the intellectual elites and were carried by few publications, apart from a new journal, *Strategy and Management* (*Zhanlüe yu Guanli*), which, launched at the end of 1993 with the support of major leaders in the Communist Party and in the army (among them Generals Xiao

Ke and Zhang Aiping), had begun to develop, in the writings of authors such as Yan Ping and Wang Xiaodong, a prickly, aggressive and populist nationalism.

It was the crisis in the Taiwan Strait which probably contributed the most to the rise of populist nationalism in Chinese society. By 1994–1995, several opinion polls showed obvious popular support for a pro-active and aggressive policy of reunification with Taiwan and a clear increase in anti-American feelings among young Chinese. Carried out in a closed society where outside viewpoints are systematically distorted or censored, these polls produced results that are clearly questionable. They nevertheless directly inspired a number of nationalist books published after 1996, of which the best-known was *China Can Say No! (Zhongguo Keyi Shuo Bu!).* Written by young intellectuals (Qiao Bian, Zhang Zangzang, and Song Qiang) based on the model of *Japan Can Say No!* by the far-right member of parliament Shinaro Ishihara, this book was followed by many others which, often for primarily commercial reasons, sought to exploit this new "seam."

These intellectuals had managed to pick up the feelings of a fairly substantial part of public opinion and to systematize them into a discourse which, without contradicting that of the Party, went beyond it. Nevertheless these nationalist tracts, which demonized the United States, were produced by a relatively small elite. Most of the authors were young intellectuals who were brought together in what the Chinese press then called "The No Club" (*shuo bu julebu*), with about ten members. Among them at the time were Liu Kang and Li Xiguang who, in December 1996, published *Behind the Scenes of the Demonization of China (Yaomohua Zhongguo de Beihou),* a vitriolic denunciation of the American media.[20]

The outrageous statements, the idea of a Western, and particularly an American, plot aimed at preventing China from developing itself and thus becoming stronger, as well as the determination—and the certainty—displayed to raise China to the rank of most powerful nation in the world and thus to put an end to American hegemony, all these themes expressed, within the Chinese elites, both a growing awareness and a deep feeling of insecurity. An awareness, related to the 1980s, that the West could not provide all the answers to China's problems, and a feeling of insecurity in the face of foreign criticism of their country, and especially the dangers of economic failure or of social instability which their criticisms alluded to.

Fascinated by Western success during the first decade after opening up, these intellectuals were now tempted to perceive in the West, if not always the cause of their ills, at least the main obstacle to the realization of their country's destiny as a great power. This is why, worried by the implications of the globalization of the Chinese economy, they were often hostile to China's accession to the World Trade Organization (WTO), and critical of the supposed weakness of their government during the negotiations. Lastly, they developed the idea that because of the antiquity of their civilization, the greatness of their culture, and the intrinsic qualities of the "Chinese race" (*hanzu*), their country could legitimately claim the first rank in the world, which the Americans, whose culture was constantly presented as young and superficial, had usurped by taking advantage of China's temporary weakness. It was thus a question for China, by rising above the United States, of washing away the humiliation inflicted by the West (and Japan) from 1840 onwards.

One can obviously see in this discourse the direct influence of the domestic communist propaganda that can be found, for example, in school textbooks. This has always more accurately reflected the position of the Communist Party leadership than the more civilized discourse that it broadcasts on the international scene, and is molded by a deep feeling of superiority (which classically conceals an obvious feeling of inferiority). The same is true of the nationalism propagated within the armed forces, some studies of which have revealed its deeply anti-American and anti-Japanese character.[21] Nonetheless, nationalist intellectuals developed anti-American, anti-Japanese, anti-WTO, and sometimes racist ideas that manifestly went beyond even the internal discourse of the Beijing authorities. It is true that the authorities allowed these theses to be published and broadcast. In this sense, one cannot help suspecting a certain collusion or, as noted above, a temptation to instrumentalize this extremist discourse, which allows the Chinese government to appear in the eyes of the world as supporting a moderate, tolerant, or so to speak "centrist" form of nationalism. The fact remains that Wang Xiaodong, Song Qiang, and others like them developed from this period onwards an autonomous strategy and position which largely contributed to the spontaneous demonstrations in May 1999, protesting against the accidental bombing of China's embassy in Belgrade by NATO forces, and to the violent and probably less spontaneous demonstrations in April 2005 against Japan.[22]

The Demonstrations in May 1999: A Turning Point in Chinese Nationalism?

Much has been said and written about these demonstrations. With hindsight, one can first of all state that there was then a very clear convergence between the position of the government and the feelings expressed in the streets. The reasons for this encounter were, however, far from being identical. On one side the Chinese Communist Party reacted all the more strongly to the bombing because it had taken sides with the Yugoslav regime of Milosevic which it supported militarily, and had opposed the NATO airstrikes against Serbia. Consequently, it deliberately kept its citizens ignorant of the human tragedy in Kosovo. Moreover, certain sections of society that were already "wound up" against the United States saw in the bombing a deliberate desire to "humiliate" China. The outcome of this convergence was the inability of most Chinese to believe in the hypothesis of an accident, a hypothesis that their government also strongly denounced (and subsequently never accepted). Moreover, the government was late publishing the official apologies given by the Clinton administration and by NATO, which, as soon as they were received, were called into question and considered by many demonstrators to be "lacking in sincerity."

In any case, this protest movement also constituted a turning point in nationalist expression in China, and in relations between the state and society. Firstly, this movement developed independently, giving rise to violence, which having been tolerated, was partly controlled in Peking, and much less so in Chengdu, where the American Consulate was burned to the ground. For about two weeks, the many foreigners resident in China were advised to reduce as much as possible their contacts with a local population which was galvanized against the Americans, and Westerners more generally. Hu Jintao, then the regime's second-in-command, was given the task of asking the demonstrators to put an end to their movement, apparently convincing them that the best way to avoid other "humiliations" was to work hard and contribute to the development and thus to the strengthening of their country. This was not a risk-free strategy, but it was successful in calming things down.

Second, the leaders of this movement mostly came from the universities, showing once more to what extent Chinese nationalism had become a weapon that allowed the elites and the future elites (the students) to express themselves and to influence the government. Moreover this movement shed light on the deeply emotional character of Chinese nationalism. Rather than expressing itself through constant pressure on the authorities or on foreigners, it manifests itself through moments of intense mobilization, which can lead to surges of anti-Western violence. In 1999, there were no foreign casualties. But one cannot exclude such a possibility in the future, so punctuated is the history of Chinese nationalism, in its populist and primitive dimension, with aggression against foreigners. The anti-Japanese violence perpetrated over the last few years, and particularly during the demonstrations in the spring of 2005, has shown that such an evolution remains possible.

At the same time, the excesses of this movement led to important divisions among Chinese nationalists. On the one hand, these excesses brought the writers of popularizing tracts closer to the best-known nationalist intellectuals of the "New Left," as well as to conservative Communist Party leaders opposed to China's accession to the WTO. Moreover the demonstrations in May 1999 gave them an opportunity to denounce the supposed concessions made by Zhu Rongji on the question during his journey to the United States the previous month. Fang Ning and Wang Xiaodong, the two main organizers of the opinion polls in 1994–1995, wrote with Song Qiang, one of the authors of *China Can Say No!*, an equally anti-American sequel to that book entitled *China's Path in the Shadow of Globalization* (*Quanqiu Yinying Xia de Zhongguo Zhilu*). Published in November 1999, the book received the explicit support of Yu Quanyu, former Vice-President of the Chinese

Human Rights Commission, directed by the arch-conservative Zhu Muzhi. On the other hand, the increasing power of populist nationalism worried certain intellectuals who had initially perceived in it a stabilizing factor. In 1998, the journal *Strategy and Management* excluded Wang Xiaodong from its list of contributors. The events of 1999 furthered this development. For example, these events led Xiao Gonqin, an intellectual described as a neo-conservative during the 1990s, but in reality fairly liberal although a nationalist, to denounce the extremism and the emotional and destabilizing character of this new movement, in his eyes the source of the failure of numerous reforms in China (including those of Kang Youwei).[23]

Finally, the nationalist mobilization in May 1999 was a lesson for the leadership of the Chinese Communist Party, or at least for some of them. Having for ten years nourished and fed the nationalist feelings of society, the government in Beijing realized that these were getting out of control and could not only reduce its margin for maneuver in international matters, but eventually destabilize it. This is the reason why, after 1999, while not overtly suppressing "populist nationalism," the Chinese authorities sought for several years to direct it, gradually toning down, particularly from 2000–2001 onwards, a foreign policy strategy which had done more to build the perception of a Chinese menace, particularly in the United States and in Japan, than to satisfy the demands of the populist nationalists. In this respect 9/11 made the Chinese government's task easier. But the latter's attitude towards nationalism has remained deeply ambivalent, so central is this ideology to the survival of the present regime. Thus the relative prudence advocated by Jiang Zemin after the demonstrations in 1999 was clearly called into question by Hu Jintao in the spring of 2005.

The Anti-Japanese Demonstrations in the Spring of 2005

The anti-Japanese mobilization in the spring of 2005 was of a kind that set certain limits, probably temporary but nonetheless real, to the emergence of any autonomous nationalist movement in the People's Republic. The question here is not to pass judgment on the moral grounds for the Chinese movement of protest against the visits paid by the Japanese Prime Minister to Yasukuni, or against the approval by the Minister of Education of school textbooks with revisionist tendencies: both of these problems, which give rise to equally negative reactions in South Korea for example, show beyond a doubt the massive ambiguity of the Japanese Right towards the period of the war. Neither is it to disregard the general context of the rise in anti-Japanese feeling within Chinese society, nourished from a tender age by the education system and by government propaganda but also connected with China's emergence onto the world scene and marked by numerous incidents over the last few years. The physical and verbal violence that surrounded the football matches between China and Japan, held in Chengdu and in Beijing in the course of the Asian Cup during the summer of 2004, were a striking illustration.

Nevertheless, the dialectic between, on the one hand, the mobilization observed in China from March 2005, and on the other, the government's offensive against a number of Japanese initiatives is too close to believe that the latter did not instrumentalize the former, and was very likely at its origin.

Indeed, what unleashed the Chinese Communist Party's campaign against Tokyo was the joint American and Japanese declaration on February 19th, 2005, on security in [Northeast Asia], in which, among the many shared strategic objectives on display, there appeared the peaceful settlement of the question of Taiwan. Although insignificant because it added hardly any substance to previous commitments, this declaration nonetheless appeared at a difficult time, marked in particular by clearer military rivalry between China and Japan (sharpened by the intrusion of a Chinese submarine in Japanese territorial waters in November 2004), the lack of summit meetings between the two countries, because of Prime Minister Koizumi's repeated visits to Yasukuni, and dissension over the underwater gas deposits at *Chunxiao*, which lie in an area which is claimed by both countries.

In this context, the petition against Japan's candidacy for a permanent seat on the UN Security Council, which was launched at the end of February by the "Alliance to preserve the truth about the Sino-Japanese war," based in the United States, and then taken up by several Chinese websites which are tightly controlled by the Chinese government, could seem somewhat suspicious.[24] Although there is no tangible evidence that the authorities in Beijing played any part in this initiative, the role they play in manipulating the debates taking place on the Internet unavoidably casts doubts on the spontaneity of this campaign.[25] This petition was enormously successful, with 22 million electronically collected signatures within a month, and 40 million by the end of April.[26] Shortly after, in early March, two books by the liberal author Yu Jie, including *The Iron and the Plough*, which exhorted his compatriots to find out more about Japan before "hating" it, were withdrawn from the bookshops.[27]

A month later, at the beginning of April, several demonstrations broke out in various cities in China, denouncing both Japan's candidacy for the UN Security Council and its general attitude to its own past, particularly the approval by the Japanese Ministry of Education of a school textbook (which was distributed to 0.1% of pupils) which plays down the massacres committed in China during the war, and the visits to Yasukuni. China's claim over the Senkaku [Diaoyudao] islands was also brought up. First organized in Chengdu and Shenzhen on April 5th, these demonstrations reached Beijing on April 9th, and then Shanghai on April 16th. In Beijing, and especially in Shanghai, verbal and physical violence was committed against Japanese representations with the permission of the Chinese authorities, and, even in Shanghai, against shops that sold Japanese products and several Japanese people, without the police showing any clear determination to prevent these people from being beaten up.[28] The verbally and physically destructive excesses which took place in Shanghai led the Communist Party leadership to bring a halt to the demonstrations it had allowed to go ahead, revealing its power to suddenly muzzle a nationalist movement which one might have thought had acquired a certain autonomy.

Admittedly, the authorities in Beijing, while refusing to present an apology to the government in Tokyo for the damage caused to its embassy and consulates in China, decided under the pressure of international reaction—particularly Japanese—to prosecute those who had committed the violence, and to pay for repairs to the damaged buildings (at least in Shanghai). But information received after the events makes it possible to think that Public Security and the Communist Youth League, in other words the government, played a decisive role in setting off and organizing the April demonstrations. Those responsible for these demonstrations were not the spontaneous representatives of an autonomous civil society, but the cadres of those organizations. Those who participated belonged either to the student community, which is to say the future elite of the country, or to the new educated middle classes, such as those that now live around Zhongguancun, the new business district located near the capital's universities.[29] A final point is that these demonstrations brought together a fairly limited number of participants (between 10,000 and 20,000), for a country supposedly unanimously hostile to Japan. The order given on April 19 by the Minister for Foreign Affairs, Li Zhaoxing, to stop the movement, was meekly obeyed by these temporary demonstrators and the boycott against Japanese products they had launched fizzled quickly away. In a way the failure of this campaign showed how little it was "popular" and above all how unrealistic, in a country whose trade with the nation which is the target of its invective reached $168 billion in 2004, ranking it second among China's trading partners, after the United States (with $252 billion according to American statistics).

One might well consider, however, that the temptation for Hu Jintao and the present authorities in China to brandish the nationalist weapon and to manipulate society for reasons of foreign policy, in this case with the aim of preventing Japan from rising to the status of Asian Great Power, has not been without its dangers. It has revealed an unappealing and rather undemocratic facet of Chinese society, and especially of its rising elites, who did not hesitate to resort to racist slogans (comparing the Japanese to pigs, for example) and physical violence in order to advance their cause. This temptation also allowed other, more anti-authoritarian forces, to interfere in the movement, particularly in Shanghai, revealing the potential for anti-government protest that exists in China.

The loss of control of the movement probably explains the editorial published in the paper *Jiefang*

Ribao (Liberation Daily), Shanghai's official daily, which claimed to perceive a "plot" in the anti-Japanese demonstrations rather than a patriotic movement.[30] The renewed instrumentalization of nationalism decided on by Hu Jintao also caused dissension within the Communist Party leadership. The article in *Jiefang Ribao* was also a virtually transparent denunciation of Hu's strategy and of its deplorable effects on social and political stability, and on the business environment, particularly in a city where Japanese economic presence is very strong. This is why the article was not reprinted in the national press and, according to outside sources, why the leaders in Shanghai were scathingly criticized for having allowed it to be published.[31]

Hu's strategy also turned its back on several years of efforts by Chinese specialists on Japan (Ma Licheng, Shi Yinhong, Lu Zhongwei, etc.) to convince their government to improve relations with this important partner, which is also strongly nationalist, and less willing nowadays to yield to the pressures of its former victims, and whose regional ambitions, as these experts see it, will have to be taken into account in one way or another.[32]

However, this episode showed how useful nationalism is to the government, both in order to legitimize its domination over society and to further its interests on the international scene, and particularly in its regional environment, even if it means fuelling the syndrome of a Chinese menace in Japan and a negative image abroad. It also showed the limitations of the emergence of an autonomous populist nationalism whose existence no longer needs to be demonstrated but whose propensity for being manipulated by the government has also been proved.

Chinese Nationalism and the New Dialectic Between the State and Society

Since 1999 a complex interaction has appeared between government and society around the question of nationalism. Today the discussions about the theme of nationalism go far beyond international questions and tend to concern the legitimacy of the political regime and its ability to raise China to the rank of Number One World Power, however much this ambition may be a dream. Since the end of the 1990s, the growth

of electronic communications and forums has favored wider expression by society on political matters and particularly on nationalism.[33] Certain fora specialize in nationalist diatribes (such as *Qiangguo Luntan* (Strong Country Forum), or *Jianchuan Zhishi* (Knowledge of Warships). These fora are tolerated, particularly because of the support they receive from certain leadership circles, but they are also used by the authorities, since they are seen as polls on the opinions of society and particularly on the opinions of the educated population with Internet access (there were about 100 million Internet users in 2005). However, the Chinese Communist Party remains particularly vigilant over the subversive uses some might be tempted to make of nationalist sentiment.

Nationalism and Foreign Policy

Today, questions of foreign policy are debated by a much larger number of Chinese, particularly in discussion forums and in intellectual journals, such as *Strategy and Management*, which was banned during the summer of 2004 for having published an iconoclastic article on the question of North Korea's nuclear program.[34]

This episode also highlights a greater diversification of opinion on foreign policy. In other words, even among the fora and journals that have served as carriers of nationalist ideas, these are far from dominating all the debates. On the contrary, some research tends to show that the emergence of an urban middle class has contributed to the moderation of society's nationalist sentiment.[35] The internationalization of China and of its modes of consumption is doubtless not unconnected to this evolution. Having said that, the Chinese government remains strongly tempted to instrumentalize nationalism, and particularly its populist component, above all where its relations with the United States and Japan are concerned.

Where the former is concerned, Taiwan continues to occupy an important place. More generally, the strategic role played by the United States in East Asia and in the world, as well as its determination, perceived as imperial, to export its political system, its values and its mass culture, are the targets of denunciation by the Communist Party and by the nationalist sections of the intellectual elites which continue to irrigate Chinese society. It is a similar case with perception of Japan, which remains largely in thrall to trends from a past that is long gone. Thus the Chinese government persists in placing at the center of bilateral relations the problems connected with the war, with the apologies and with the Yasukuni Shrine, even going so far as to mobilize the man in the streets against the Japanese government.

Thus, China's policies towards America, Taiwan and Japan have become largely dependent on a "public opinion" which is manipulated by the most nationalist political and intellectual elites, and sometimes by the leadership of the Communist Party. The government uses it to strengthen its hand in its relations with Washington, Taipei, and Tokyo. But it also finds itself constrained to use cunning and to conceal any flexibility under an intransigent and even aggressive discourse when it decides to reach a compromise.

The attraction of the United States for many Chinese, and the importance of the economic and human exchanges with Japan can be helpful for those within the government who strive to maintain the stability of these bilateral relations, both of which are essential to China.[36] But nationalist pressure is likely to remain strong, and in conjunction with the temptation to instrumentalize it which is often present in official circles, will continue to influence China's foreign policy as a whole, including that towards neighboring countries such as Russia, India, or Vietnam, with which border problems have not been completely settled, or even towards the European Union, which still refuses to grant China the status of a market economy and sometimes raises its voice in protest against the most visible human rights violations in that country.

Nationalism and the Stability of the Regime

Chinese nationalists have often proclaimed that: "If Taiwan declares independence and the Communist Party does nothing, we will overthrow it!" This provocative statement sheds light on the link that has always existed in China between the legitimacy of a government and its ability to defend the fundamental national interests of the country. And in the eyes of the majority of mainland Chinese, or at least of the elites who have

the right to speak in their name, the question of Taiwan is part of those fundamental interests.

This relationship has led some reformers who favor the establishment of a democratic regime in China to also claim to be nationalists. This is particularly the case of Wu Guoguang, now a Professor at the University of Victoria in Canada, and of Ding Xueliang, a Professor at the Science and Technology University of Hong Kong. One can perceive behind this strategy a desire to avoid allowing nationalism to become the monopoly of conservative forces close to the Communist Party. This approach, which has been criticized by some Chinese reformers and democrats, such as Ma Licheng, a former journalist with the *People's Daily*, and Chen Yang, a journalist with Radio France International, because they see it as "killing freedom" and as being a source of tensions with the outside world, cannot be easily brushed aside.[37] This is also the reason why others theorists of an exit from authoritarianism, such as Zheng Yongnian, a scholar at the University of Nottingham and National University of Singapore, seek to construct a "democratic nationalism" in opposition to the "ethnic nationalism" of the populist movement.[38] But one can appreciate the difficulty of such an undertaking, so easily can the debates about nationalism be taken over by the country's most xenophobic and demagogic powers.

All in all, Chinese nationalism constitutes a more complex ideology than might appear at first glance. In fact, both within the Communist Party and in society, the various forms of nationalism examined here still exist, and will probably continue to cohabit in future. Associated with the Cultural Revolution, which was still very present in people's minds, populist nationalism was little in evidence in the 1980s. In contrast, from the middle of the following decade, its influence grew rapidly, concentrating its attacks on the United States and on Japan. Since it expresses a feeling of insecurity in the face of richer and more powerful countries, could this form of nationalism not decline as China sees its own power grow and its standard of living improve? Possibly. But for all that one cannot rule out the Party leaders and certain intellectuals of the New Left being tempted in the future, for political ends, to hive off into extreme nationalism the reservoir of frustration and discontent contained in Chinese society. Having said that, and despite the anti-Japanese demonstrations in April 2005, this form of nationalism is today less perceptible within Chinese society, and even among the elite as a whole, which is perhaps a sign of a positive development. Is this to say that the globalization of the economy and society in China have already contributed to marginalizing this trend of thought? Or is this decline to be attributed to the increase in "face" (*mianzi*), capable of washing away past "humiliations," that the country's economic successes have provided to society?

The game is not yet won, so loaded is the process with jolts and even social crises. Pandering to nationalism in society while marginalizing its populist and aggressive corruptions, "the path of peaceful rise" advocated by Hu Jintao in 2004 had precisely the aim of reassuring China's partners, and avoiding the trap which pre-war Germany and Japan fell into. But the anti-Japanese violence which the same Hu Jintao tolerated in April 2005 showed that the Communist Party remains in part a prisoner of its old demons. The future of Chinese nationalism will depend heavily on the Chinese elites and their ability to give society an image that is both independent and accurate, of the intentions of their country's main partners.

There is no doubt that much will also depend on the way in which these partners manage this nationalism, and, without acceding to its unreasonable demands, find ways to provide it with balanced and persuasive answers. One obviously thinks of Japan, which has not managed to come to terms completely with its past. Lastly, much will also depend on the Chinese authorities, and their ability to embark on real political reform. Only a genuine diversification of the Chinese political system will be capable of guaranteeing the reconciliation of Chinese society with its own history, independent access to information about the outside world, the marginalization of populist nationalism and thus the irruption of a tolerant and democratic nationalism into Chinese society, which—reviving Yan Fu, Sun Yat-sen, and Hu Shi—will find ways to co-exist smoothly with the other nationalisms which the world, and particularly East Asia, have produced. As such an evolution remains unlikely in the foreseeable future, we have no choice but to remain vigilant and attentive to the various manifestations of Chinese nationalism.

NOTES

1. Zhao Suisheng, *A Nation-State by Construction: Dynamics of Modern Chinese Nationalism* (Stanford: Stanford University Press, 2004), pp. 29–31. This is the idea taken up by Jia Qingguo of Beijing University in his article, "Disrespect and Distrust: The External Origins of Contemporary Chinese Nationalism," in a special issue "The Limits of Chinese Nationalism" introduced by William A. Callahan, *Journal of Contemporary China*, Vol. 14, No. 42 (February 2005), pp.11–21.
2. James Harrison, *Modern Chinese Nationalism* (Hunter College of the City of New York, Research Institute of Modern Asia, 1969), quoted by James Townsend, "Chinese Nationalism," in John Unger (ed.), *Chinese Nationalism* (Armonk, NY: M.E. Sharpe, 1996), p. 2.
3. Ernest Gellner, *Nations and Nationalism* (Ithaca: Cornell University Press, 1983); Eric Hobsbawm, *Nations and Nationalism Since 1780: Program, Myth, Reality* (Cambridge: Cambridge University Press, 1992).
4. On the links between Chinese nationalism and the Han race, see Frank Dikötter, *The Discourse of Race in Modern China* (Stanford: Stanford University Press, 1992).
5. Benedict Anderson, *Imagined Communities: Reflection on the Origins and Spread of Nationalism* (New York: Verso Books, 1991).
6. Eric Hobsbawm, *Nations and Nationalism Since 1780*, op. cit.
7. The work of Lucien Bianco illustrates this point in many ways. See, for example, *Origins of the Chinese Revolution, 1915–1949* (Stanford: Stanford University Press, 1973). One is tempted to apply E. M. Foster's personalism to Chinese society: he used to say that if he had to choose between betraying his country and betraying a friend, he hoped he would have the courage to betray his country. *Dictionnaire de la pensée politique: Hommes et idées* [A Dictionary of Political Thought. Men and Ideas] (Paris: Hatier, 1989), p. 565.
8. Yves Chevrier, *La Chine Moderne* [Modern China], "Que sais-je?" (Paris, PUF, 1983), p. 20.
9. Andrew Nathan, *Chinese Democracy* (New York: Knopf, 1985).
10. Jean-Philippe Béja, "Naissance d'un national-confucianisme?" [The Birth of National Confucianism?] *Perspectives Chinoises*, No.30 (July–August 1995), pp. 6–11. Since he succeeded Jiang, Hu Jintao has been tempted to strengthen this "Confucianist nationalism."
11. The Chinese government's recent decision to set up a sizeable network of Confucius Institutes abroad is part of this nationalist project.
12. Benjamin Schwartz, *In Search of Wealth and Power: Yen Fu and the West* (Cambridge: Cambridge University Press, 1964).

13. Cf. Chapter XVIII "Patriotism and internationalism" in *Quotations from President Mao Tse-tung* (Peking: Foreign Language Editions, 1966), pp. 193–198. Here he declares in particular: "We must beware of harboring the slightest pride inspired by great power chauvinism and of ever becoming presumptuous after our victory in the revolution and certain successes obtained in the field of construction. Whether great or small, each nation has its strong and weak points." Directly inspired by the Leninist and Marxist tradition, this advice seems to have been long forgotten.

14. Peter Hays Gries, *China's New Nationalism: Pride, Politics and Diplomacy* (Berkeley: University of California Press, 2004).

15. Chen Yan, *L'Eveil de la Chine. Les bouleversements intellectuels apres Mao, 1976–2002* [China's Awakening; Intellectual Upheavals After Mao, 1976–2002] (La Tour d'Aigues, Edition de l'Aube, 2002), pp. 151 and after.

16. Edward Friedman, "Chinese Nationalism, Taiwanese Autonomy and the Prospects of a Larger War," *Journal of Contemporary China*, Vol. 6, No. 14 (1997), pp. 5–32.

17. In particular the failure in 1993 of China's candidacy to host the 2000 Olympic Games, and the unexpected inspection by the Americans in the same year of the Chinese ship *Yinhe*, which was suspected—wrongfully—of transporting forbidden chemical products to Iran, two episodes which contributed largely to the discourse of all Chinese nationalists.

18. He Xin stated in 1992, for example: "Our country must start up the propaganda machine to denounce to the Chinese people the American determination to annihilate China, cultivate a mentality of hatred towards our enemies and form a centripetal national spirit," quoted by Chen Yan, *L'Eveil de la Chine*, op. cit., p. 158.

19. Wang Shan (pseudonym, Luo yi ning ge er), *Di sanzhi yanjing kan Zhongguo* (Taiyuan: Shanxi renmin chubanshe, 1994); cf. also Joseph Fewsmith, *China Since Tiananmen: The Politics of Transition* (Cambridge: Cambridge University Press, 2001), pp. 146–151.

20. Beijing: Zhongguo shehui kexue chubanshe, 1996.

21. Michael Pillsbury, *China Debates the Future Security Environment* (Washington, DC: National Defense University, 2000).

22. For a worthwhile analysis of the ambiguities and pluralities of this nationalist discourse, cf. Christopher R. Hughes, "Interpreting Nationalist Texts: A Post-Structuralist Approach," *Journal of Contemporary China*, Vol. 14, No. 43 (May 2005), pp. 247–267.

23. Xiao Gongqin, "The Kosovo Crisis and the Nationalism of Twenty-First Century China," in Jean-Philippe Beja and Jean-Pierre Cabestan (eds.), "The Responses of Intellectuals to the Challenges of the Twenty-First Century in China," Part II, *Contemporary Chinese Thought*, Vol. 35, No. 1 (Autumn 2003), pp. 21–48; cf. also Fewsmith, *China Since Tiananmen*, op. cit., p. 217.

24. This initiative was reported in a very positive manner by the Chinese media; cf. *China Daily*, March 23rd 2005 (Internet).

25. *Nanfang zhoumo* (Southern Weekend), May 19, 2005.

26. *New York Times*, April 1, 2005.

27. BBC, March 30, 2005.

28. According to eyewitness reports, the police impassibly watched stone-throwing and other violence against the Japanese Embassy in Beijing, and then after half an hour their leaders amiably told the demonstrators: "Comrades, you are getting tired! It's time to get back to your campuses" *(Tongzhimen, nimen xinku le! Xianzai nimen huiqu xuexiao!).* Interviews, Beijing, May 2005. Japanese TV stations repeatedly broadcast these attacks on their compatriots. Among the verbal excesses, slogans as "Death to the Japanese Pigs!" were repeatedly shouted.

29. Interviews, Beijing, May 2005; Reuters, April 9, 2005; Associated Press, April 16, 2005.

30. *Jiefang ribao*, April 25, 2005.

31. *Zhengming*, May 2005, pp. 6–8. Another explanation put forward is that the Shanghai municipality deliberately allowed these excesses to take place in order to weaken Hu Jintao in the struggle which, since the compulsory retirement of Jiang Zemin in September 2004, has pitted the new government in Peking against the "Shanghai clique" formerly supported by Jiang and still represented at the top by Wu Bangguo, Zeng Qinghong, Huang Ju and Chen Liangyu, the Shanghai Party Secretary. However, there is no evidence to confirm the use of this "worst possible strategy."

32. Their views were published prominently in the journals *Zhanlue yu Guanli* (*Strategy and Management*) and *Xiandai guoji guanxi* (*Contemporary International Relations*).

33. Joseph Fewsmith and Stanley Rosen, "The Domestic Context of Chinese Foreign Policy: does 'Public Opinion' Matter?" in David M. Lampton (ed.), *The Making of Chinese Foreign and Security Policy in the Era of Reform* (Stanford: Stanford University Press, 2001), pp. 151–187.

34. No. 4 (July–August 2004). In this article, the researcher Wang Zhongwen advised the United States to distance itself from the problem, and to let China assume its responsibilities, which is to say to influence Pyongyang itself, since its interests really lie in favoring the establishment of a de-nuclearized Korean peninsula.

35. Alastair Iain Johnston, "Chinese Middle Class Attitudes Toward International Affairs: Nascent Liberalization?" *The China Quarterly*, No. 179 (September 2004), pp. 603–628.

36. The idea of "positive nationalism," discussed by Chen Zhimin, takes these constraints into account and to some extent accords with the concept of "pragmatic nationalism," cf. Chen Zhimin, "Nationalism, Internationalism and Chinese Foreign Policy," *Journal of Contemporary China*, Vol. 14, No. 42 (February 2005), pp. 35–53. On the relations between nationalism and foreign policy cf. also William A. Callahan, "Nationalism, Civilization and Transnational Relations: The Discourse of Greater China," *Journal of Contemporary China*, Vol. 14, No. 43 (May 2005), pp. 269–289.

37. Chen Yan, *L'Eveil de la Chine*, op. cit., pp. 160 on.

38. Zheng Yongnian, *Discovering Chinese Nationalism in China: Modernization, Identity, and International Relations* (Cambridge: Cambridge University Press, 1999).

IV. RELIGION

The Upsurge of Religion in China*

Richard Madsen

Over the years, these pages have featured many essays devoted to analyzing the prospects for democracy in China. Such analyses have focused on studying the resiliency (or fragility) of the current Chinese Communist Party (CCP) regime, and on weighing the significance of various protest movements or other actual and potential sources within China of pressure for democratic change. Among the latter, attention has been devoted to workers, rural dwellers, the middle classes, and online activists. But very little note has been taken of what may turn out to be the biggest threat of all to the CCP's ability to maintain its control—namely, the extraordinary growth of religious belief and religious movements in Chinese society.

Unlike liberal democracies, which generally accord their citizens the right to complete freedom of religious belief and practice, the People's Republic of China claims that it needs to control religion in order to preserve social harmony and economic modernization. The government has a bureau that is officially in charge of religious affairs—the State Administration for Religious Affairs (SARA). The state claims the prerogative of determining what counts as "true" and "false" religion, and uses its police power to attempt the eradication of "false" religion (often termed, in the parlance of Chinese officialdom, "evil cults" or "feudal superstition"). The state also chooses the leaders of approved religions and monitors many religious activities.

The Chinese government shares an assumption that is often encountered in liberal democracies—namely, that secularity is inseparable from modernity.[1] Liberal-democratic *governments* (as distinguished from various influential schools of thought found within liberal-democratic societies) are neutral on the matter, of course, and take no position on the question of whether religion

has any future in the modern world. China's government is not neutral, but maintains instead that religion is destined to recede as modernization continues to proceed. Chinese officialdom derives its version of this "secularization thesis" from Marxism, and China's religious policy (like all government policy in that country) is set by the ruling CCP. The framework for religious policy comes from "Document 19," which the CCP's Central Committee promulgated in 1982 under the title *The Basic Viewpoint on the Religious Question During Our Country's Socialist Period.*[2]

This document parallels the liberal-democratic handling of religious belief by relegating it to the private sphere of life: The "crux of the policy of freedom of religious belief is to make the question of religious belief a private matter, one of individual free choice for citizens." (Unlike liberal democracies, however, China has a constitution that offers no guarantee of freedom of association to complement freedom of belief.)

In a sharp contrast to the neutral, liberal-democratic approach to religious claims regarding what is true, however, Document 19 goes on to declare that religion is false, and makes government the active agent of a modernizing project that is meant to eventually eliminate religion altogether: "[W]e Communists are atheists and must unremittingly propagate atheism." In contrast to the "leftist" policies put in place during the Cultural Revolution that began in 1966—policies that tried forcibly to obliterate religion from public life—Document 19 is a product of the early Reform program of Deng Xiaoping, who was CCP leader from 1978 to 1992. Its approach toward religion is based on patiently waiting for scientific education, not political coercion, to spread atheism.

As suggested above, the notion that science and modernity will put an end to religion is not confined to Communist functionaries: It is in fact an assumption that elite social scientists in liberal

* This article was published in *Journal of Democracy*, Vol. 21, No. 4 (October 2010).

democracies widely share. Until fairly recently, these social scientists would probably have overwhelmingly agreed with Document 19 that religion is a historical phenomenon whose demise will inevitably come with modernization, albeit probably not until a period of "cultural lag" has run its course: "Old thinking and habits," cautions Document 19, "cannot be thoroughly wiped out in a short period." Therefore, "Party members must have a sober-minded recognition of the protracted nature of the religious question under Socialist conditions. . . . Those who expect to rely on administrative decrees or other coercive measures to wipe out religious thinking and practices with one blow are even further from the basic viewpoint that Marxism takes toward the religious question. They are entirely wrong and will do no small harm."

The problem for the secularization thesis—and hence for the CCP—is that it appears to be wrong. Far from inexorably receding, religions all over the world are growing and seeking increasingly vigorous engagements with public affairs. Recognizing this, many Western social theorists (even confirmed agnostics such as Jürgen Habermas) are now searching for "postsecular" social theories.[3] Although there is great disagreement over the content of such theories, they all note that religions do not simply "rise and fall" according to a linear pattern. The theories also note that in modernized societies religion not only persists, but continues to evolve dynamically. Theorists now recognize that there are "multiple modernities," defined by different interactions between religious belief and practice on the one hand, and modern political and economic developments on the other.[4] It is generally conceded, moreover, that religion cannot typically be confined altogether to private life, but instead is (for better or worse) an active part of public life.[5] Finally, scholars are growing increasingly suspicious of definitions that conceive of religion in overly narrow, ethnocentric terms based on Western historical experience.[6]

There are heated arguments and unresolved issues concerning religion and its relation to public life in liberal democracies such as the United States, of course, but these are at least openly debated. In China, the secularist assumptions that underpin official religious policy are proving unworkable. The policies that Document 19 lays out are a complete failure, even in terms of their own goals of constraining the growth of religion, confining it to the private sphere, and keeping it out of politics and ethnic relations. Religion is growing rapidly, and has overwhelmed the CCP regime's systems of surveillance and control. Clumsy methods of suppressing unwanted forms of religion have backfired, raising rather than lowering the temperature of conflicts involving religion and the state. And attempts to decouple religion from the ethnic awareness of minority nationalities that might fuel opposition to the dominant Han nationality have failed as well. The policy debacle has become obvious enough that CCP leaders have begun to acknowledge it more or less openly, and some within the government are searching for a new approach to religious policy. But constraints on debate about sensitive religious matters are making it hard for the CCP and the state to move beyond the old policy, with its untenable assumptions; and when they do move, it is not in the direction of more liberal-democratic rights to religious freedom.

Official Policy and Social Reality

The problems with the official policy of containing religion, making it serve state aims, and keeping it within regime-approved channels start with the government's attempts to define religion itself. Official policy views religion in terms of private belief expressed through voluntary participation in congregations organized via institutions that have clearly delineated leaderships separated from the economy and polity. This fits the understanding of religion developed by nineteenth-century Western scholars who, consciously or not, were working from a secularized notion of Western Protestantism. Based on this definition, the Chinese government recognizes five (and only five) religions in China: Taoism, Buddhism, Islam, Catholicism, and Protestantism. At least some manifestations of all five are organized into distinctive institutions with recognized leaders, and are practiced through congregations of voluntarily associating believers.

The containment of religion is part of a policy that seeks to contain all the associations of a civil society. There is in principle no space in official Chinese policy for an independent civil society, and therefore no space for independent religious associations. The officially recognized institutions are thus placed under the supervision of "patriotic associations" that in turn are supervised by SARA, and above it the United Front Department of the CCP.

Yet SARA has no jurisdiction over any form of religion that has not received official recognition, even though such generally recognized world religions as Russian Orthodoxy, Judaism, Mormonism, and the Bahá'í Faith can all be found in China. Rural China, moreover, is home to millions of temples—many of them built in just the last decade—that serve as centers for local folk religions and their associated festivals. By no means do these temples and their liturgies represent a simple return to ancient traditions. Traditional rituals, myths, and practices are being enacted with modern technology such as video cameras and websites, and reconfigured to fit the sensibilities of villagers who are no longer farmers, but factory workers, entrepreneurs, and even professionals.[7] These folk religions are more a matter of public practice than private belief, and they are not organized into institutions clearly separate from local economic and political life. Such activities have been defined by the Chinese authorities as "feudal superstition," in contrast to real religion. But modern anthropologists would want to consider these activities, through which hundreds of millions of people in China seek fundamental meaning and celebrate community, as religious. In any case, none of these activities are under the purview of SARA, and there is confusion within the Chinese government about who should monitor them and what should be done about them. In fact, regulation of folk religion often depends on ad hoc arrangements by local officials, and different provinces follow different policies in handling its growth.

Even within the five officially recognized religions, moreover, most of the growth is taking place outside the state-supervised patriotic associations and hence not under the jurisdiction of SARA. For example, there is an extensive "underground" Catholic Church that is about three times larger than the officially recognized Chinese Patriotic Catholic Association. And even more amazing from a sociological point of view, there is an extremely wide array of rapidly growing unregistered Protestant "house churches."

When Mao Zedong and his Communists triumphed over the Nationalists and established the People's Republic in 1949, there were fewer than a million Protestants in all of China. Under Mao, who died in 1976, restrictions on religion and the religious were severe. Since 1979, however, the ranks of Chinese Protestants have grown exponentially. A conservative estimate favored by many leading scholars of religion within China puts their strength at around fifty million.[8] (Some Protestant leaders claim that there are really twice that number.) The vast bulk of this astounding growth has taken place outside the institutional bounds of the state-supervised Three-Self Patriotic Movement (TSPM). The fastest-growing sectors of all have been those dominated by evangelical and Pentecostal Christian assemblies that hew to a premillennial theology positing the imminent end of the world, the "rapture" of the faithful into heaven, and the arrival of global tribulations heralding the second coming of Christ.

Although most new Chinese Christians concern themselves with spiritual matters and have no interest in active efforts to bring on the apocalypse, some sects do see their faith as a mandate to bring about radical change in this world. The Chinese government's attitude toward unregistered Protestant "house churches" has been one of great suspicion, and it certainly does not like eschatological talk. It will also have noticed that a disproportionate number of those "rights lawyers" and other activists (including imprisoned dissident Liu Xiaobo) who have been pushing for political reforms are also Christians associated with urban house churches.[9]

The house churches have been growing so fast, however, that the government can neither stop them nor ignore them. Thus, parts of the government are trying to distinguish between those evangelical Protestants who take a relatively passive, spiritual stance toward their religious convictions and the minority with the potential for political confrontation. Since the Protestants outside the TSPM are not under the purview of SARA, however, other central-government agencies have been entering into discussions with those house-church leaders who seem to pose no danger to social stability and who want to distance themselves from the more militant religious activists. The Chinese State Council's Development Research Center held an important meeting for such leaders—its title was "Christianity and Social Harmony"—in the latter part of 2008. Meanwhile, however, agencies of repression such as the Public Security Bureau take a less conciliatory approach and have been increasingly prone to arrest house-church leaders since the first half of 2009. But since there are too many leaders in too many decentralized organizations for even China's security forces to arrest, the detentions seem arbitrary, with the great majority of house churches being unaffected.

Finally, there is the growth of new religious movements with flexible organizations that combine traditional social networks with sophisticated multimedia communications technologies. The best-known of these is the Falun Gong, which mixes Buddhist and Taoist ideas in a modernized form. Founded in 1992 as part of a wave of meditation practices for promoting spiritual harmony and physical health, the Falun Gong expanded rapidly to include perhaps ten million followers by 1999.[10] In April of that year, in response to criticisms in the national media, the Falun Gong gathered 10,000 of its practitioners for a demonstration in front of the government headquarters in Beijing. Even though the demonstration was peaceful, CCP leaders considered it an illegal provocation and feared that it could set a precedent for more independent mass action.

Since the summer of 1999, the government has carried out a massive campaign to crush the movement, arresting and sometimes allegedly torturing and killing its leaders. Followers living abroad have organized their activities and publicized their plight through a newspaper (the *Epoch Times*), a television station (Tang Dynasty TV), and elaborate websites. Along with similar religious movements that have challenged the government's authority, the Falun Gong has been put into the category of "evil cults" that the state strives to crush by mobilizing new forms of police power on a vast scale, despite Document 19's warning that harsh coercive measures are "wrong and will do no small harm." The Falun Gong has been driven deep underground within China, yet at the same time it has become a force worldwide.

Meanwhile, other "evil cults," including offshoots of Christianity, continue to spread.[11]

Back to the Future?

The first response to the breakdown of the old policies has been to tolerate different experimental, ad hoc responses to local religious developments, while officially maintaining the framework of Document 19. But in the absence of any unified theoretical approach to guide them, these responses produce an incoherent patchwork of disparate local policies. Moves to tolerate some religious activities are joined with new methods of repressing others. There does not seem to be much central coordination of these developments, and they proceed at their own respective paces according to the ambitions of the various bureaucratic units that initiate them. Recognizing the incoherence of its ad hoc policies, the Party is looking for a new understanding to guide its approach toward religion.

As with all "sensitive" issues in China, discussions about religious policy go forward not in public forums, but rather in closed-door meetings that bring together academic experts and political leaders. While spending a year at Fudan University in Shanghai not long ago, I myself was invited to give a lecture to one such group, the United Front Department of the Fudan University Communist Party Committee, which has been designated a "theoretical base" for developing policies toward religion. My sense, from that experience and other interactions I had in China, is that leading Chinese experts agree on the unworkability of Document 19. Whether top CCP leaders will openly admit this is doubtful, given the Party's need to maintain an air of infallibility. But whether it is spelled out or not, the Party's strategy seems to be evolving along the lines suggested by leading experts such as Zhuo Xinping, the director of the Institute of World Religions at the Chinese Academy of Social Sciences. Zhou's paper on "The Situation of Chinese Religion and Its Direction of Development" has been presented to the CCP Politburo. He begins with a long introduction on the place of religion in Chinese history and the relationship between religion and the state under the emperors. He discusses Marxism, but treats it as social science—subject to all the canons of empirical verification and so on—not as sacred dogma. When things are handled this way, it is the emperors and not Karl Marx who provide the touchstone for religious policy.

What is gradually emerging from all this is a somewhat more coherent policy that differs from Document 19 in being more accepting of many of the different forms of Chinese religiosity and more flexible in seeking to regulate them. But it is by no means a liberal-democratic policy. Instead, it is a back-to-the-future policy—a modern throwback to the viewpoint of the Ming (1368–1644) and Qing (1644–1912) imperial dynasties.

In Ming and then Qing China, the emperor was the "Son of Heaven." His main duty was to mediate between Heaven (considered a deity) and Earth. The legitimacy of his authority rested on this sacral role, which of course depended on a "Mandate of Heaven" that could be lost through imperial malfeasance. The emperor fulfilled his role by performing important rituals in the capital and elsewhere in order to secure Heaven's blessings for his subjects, and he had the ultimate authority to distinguish between "true teaching" (*zhengjiao*) and "deviant teaching" (*xiejiao*). He thus combined the Western roles of king and pope.

Although the elites who furnished emperors with their chief advisors were schooled in a Confucian tradition that was skeptical about most forms of popular religious practice, the emperors often tolerated and even encouraged village cults, which usually drew on some mixture of Taoist, Buddhist, and Confucian traditions. Such rituals and myths would count as "true teachings" if they solidified the proper hierarchical relations within families, helped to build strong communities rooted in local agriculture, and thus bolstered social stability under imperial rule. As for large-scale Buddhist and Taoist monasteries, the emperors kept them in line through imperial patronage, which helped such institutions to thrive while ensuring that their leaders remained imperial loyalists.

By contrast, sectarian organizations that gathered people from different communities, contravened gender distinctions by allowing men and women to worship together as equals, preached an imminent end to the present era, and sometimes became the organizational basis for rebellion might be labeled heterodox (or in the English

translation of the term *xiejiao* that is officially preferred today, "evil cults").[12] Their fate would be intense persecution.

Often the facts that might justify this distinction were ambiguous. When Jesuit missionaries such as Matteo Ricci brought Catholic Christianity to China in the sixteenth century, there was considerable debate within the imperial court about whether this "foreign teaching" should be considered orthodox or heterodox. The Jesuits eventually convinced the emperor that their teaching was compatible with the other teachings that sustained imperial rule, and the long-ruling Kangxi emperor declared in 1692 that Catholicism would count as an "orthodox teaching." But when, in what has become known as the "Chinese-rites controversy," Pope Clement XI ruled against the Jesuit missionaries' interpretation of what was acceptable for Chinese converts and thus contradicted the judgment of the emperor, Kangxi denounced Christianity as a heterodox teaching. Designations of orthodoxy and heterodoxy could change, but the infallible arbiter of such distinctions was always the emperor.[13] As Zhuo Xinping has noted, the basic imperial policy toward religion was that "the government is the master, religion is the follower" (*zhengzhu, jiaocong*).

In 2008, Xi Jinping, the CCP leader who is the presumptive successor to current general-secretary Hu Jintao, declared that the Party was now a "ruling party" rather than a "revolutionary party."[14] The CCP will now justify itself by driving China's economic development, defending its territorial integrity, and promoting its rich cultural heritage. The regime's main slogan now lauds the "harmonious society," a notion with Confucian echoes. Harmony is said to depend above all on "social stability." In religious affairs, at least, it is imperial hierarchs and not Marx and Lenin who furnish the models to be followed.

The new line suggests that the state will tolerate a wide range of religious practices under the rubric of respecting "cultural pluralism." In line with official pronouncements, scholars such as Zhuo insist that the cornerstone of religious policy is the constitutional guarantee of religious freedom. But this is not freedom as understood in the Western liberal tradition. In some ways, the Chinese policy gives *more* support to religion than is the norm in countries such as the United States, where church and state are strictly separated and the latter may provide no direct economic support to the former.[15] In China, the government pays religious functionaries their salaries and funds the building of churches—provided that the functionaries and the churches alike belong to one of the officially accepted patriotic associations.

This government patronage is in line with the imperial state's custom of doling out patronage to temples. This is not a liberal toleration, based on an unalienable right to freedom of religious association. Rather, it is a modern manifestation of the old imperial principle that the state is the master, and religion is the follower. The state reserves for itself the prerogative of determining which practices make up orthodox "true religion" and which betoken a heterodox "evil cult." In 2008, the Propaganda Department produced a video that made just this kind of distinction. The state's chief criterion is the religion's practical effect: Does it or does it not contribute to a "harmonious society" under the direction of the party-state? In order to be fully legitimate, the official thinking goes, religions must work actively to build the harmonious society. If they are not working actively toward this end, the state must guide them so that they do fulfill their obligations. If they refuse to accept guidance, the state must crush them.

In its new incarnation, the supposedly secular CCP assumes a holy aura. It now presents itself as the carrier of a sacred national destiny. It carries out spectacular public rituals such as the opening ceremonies of the 2008 Beijing Olympics—ceremonies that powerfully evoked the glorious cultural heritage of Confucianism, Buddhism, and Taoism, but gave no mention at all to Mao Zedong or even to socialism.

This can lead to new patterns of religious tolerance and repression. Village temples and festivals that were once suppressed as examples of "feudal superstition" are now permitted and even encouraged, as long as they keep villagers happy and perhaps draw in some tourism. Like the imperial government of old, the CCP is partial to polytheism—a multitude of local cults keep rural society divided and incapable of mass action. Christianity is more problematic; it is a foreign religion, not part of the Chinese cultural heritage. But as long as Christian groups thoroughly indigenize—which in practice means that they accept the principle that the government is the master, religion the follower—they can be accepted. Even local house churches may be tolerated if they preach strong families and hard work and avoid challenging the police forces of the harmonious society. The encouragement of local folk religion seems to have slowed the recent growth of evangelical Christianity in the countryside. The Christian God then becomes one in a pantheon of local gods among whom the rural population divides its loyalties.

With the collapse of a religion policy based on the presumed inevitability of secularization, the CCP is thus falling back upon the old scripts of an enchanted imperial age. This may not work, however, because the Chinese state is ironically both too strong and too weak for it.

The modern state has the power to subject society to much more complete surveillance and control than did the imperial state. In order to fulfill its sacral ambition to exercise a modern Mandate of Heaven, the Communist party-state must attempt to exert that control. In imperial China, some religious practices gave people a chance to withdraw to spaces that were beyond the state's reach, but also so marginal as to be politically harmless. Now, because of the very success of the Chinese state in extending its power, free space is so rare that even the attempt to retreat to it can seem like resistance. Moreover, events at the margins of society can now affect state power. Finally, because of the very communications technologies with which the modernizing government has crisscrossed China, marginalized groups can forge ties, exchange ideas, and influence one other. If these groups eventually end up undermining the CCP regime, that outcome will have come to pass at least in part because the regime had inadvertently laid down some of the conditions for its own destruction.

As the evolution of grassroots religion in China grows more dynamic, the government must now decide which of the churning changes in religious life are orthodox and which are not. Scholars and officials concerned with religious affairs are adopting the Chinese-American sociologist Fenggang Yang's idea that there are "red" (legitimate), "black" (illegitimate), and "grey" markets for religion.[16] The government's task is to sort the points of "grey" into clear-cut "red" and "black." Yet the "grey" market is so huge and diversified that this is very hard to do, and in any case it would require a degree of expertise that is in short supply in China.

The second problem stems from the Chinese government's inability to seal China off and completely control all its relationships with the outside world. The emperors could choose not to tolerate foreign faiths whose leaderships lay beyond imperial control. But in an age of globalization, the Chinese government cannot easily stop such faiths from influencing China.

Challenges of Religious Globalization

The Ming and Qing emperors had problems with universalist religions whose teachings transcended the boundaries of any particular empire and indeed could be invoked to call earthly rulers to account. Such religions could be tolerated only if thoroughly "indigenized"—that is, made supportive of established social order and imperial rule. Even religions that aspire to universalism can become all too easily absorbed into the immanent power structures of this world, of course. In the nineteenth century, both Catholic and Protestant Christianity came to China on the heels of Western imperialism and played a role in justifying colonialist projects that in Chinese eyes made the era a "century of shame" never to be permitted again. In the twenty-first century, by contrast, the flow of universalist religious movements into China—Christianity, Islam, and globalized forms of Buddhism—is mostly the result not of imperialist power politics but of the fluidity of networks and the porosity of borders in an age of global hypercommunication. Yet the Chinese government still worries—not without cause—that foreign governments might use the promotion of universal religions for the purpose of fomenting "color revolutions" that would undermine the party-state.[17]

As China rises to world-power status, its rulers seek to showcase its glory by exporting their country's "nonmaterial cultural heritage" around the globe. The government is establishing "Confucian institutes" to teach Chinese language and culture in Europe and the Americas. State-sponsored films, art troupes, and other efforts celebrate the Chinese past, including the legacies of Taoism, Buddhism, and Confucianism—all interpreted in ways that comport with the dominant Han Chinese culture and the state's preferred "government master, religion follower" formula. The regime appears to have few qualms about importing foreigners' "nonmaterial cultural heritage" in the form of globalized popular culture, but remains highly wary of absorbing global religious culture, especially to the degree that it may be influenced by authorities outside China.

Christianity, Islam, and Tibetan Buddhism all pose severe challenges to the CCP's neoimperial sacral hegemony. Although in many respects the Chinese Catholic Church has been indigenized, its theology still commits its leadership to be loyal to the pope. The Chinese government concedes that Catholics can accept Rome's "spiritual" authority, but it reserves the right to draw the exact line between spiritual and temporal. The pope, of course, thinks that Rome knows the proper boundary. For the state, global communications make the threat of foreign influence on the Catholic Church ever harder to eliminate. Negotiations between the Chinese government and the Vatican about normalizing diplomatic relations have been going on fitfully for more than two decades, but they are currently at an impasse. The main problem is that the Vatican seeks more religious freedom for Catholics than the government is willing to give. And the Chinese government is afraid that even if the Vatican formally agrees to its conditions, the pope has enough spiritual authority to influence Catholics in ways beyond the government's ability to control.

Protestant Christianity in China is much more decentralized, and does not pose the threat of a centralized ecclesiastical power attempting to impose its version of orthodoxy on Chinese believers. But as a global faith, it too is open to influence spread through modern media (and often carried directly by missionaries) from around the world. Thus, however indigenized Protestant Christianity becomes in China, it will remain in touch with spiritual movements from abroad. A completely secular liberal government would not have much problem with such cosmopolitan religious influence, but a government that claims a modern Mandate of Heaven cannot in principle tolerate it. The likeliest prospect is that the CCP will work on two fronts, trying to restrict Christianity's spread while also fostering indigenous folk religion as a rival. The restrictions, however, will most likely prove ineffective. Christianity will keep growing, China's ruling elite will keep arguing internally about how to respond, and the upshot will be a grab bag of seemingly arbitrary, incoherent policies toward Christianity.

From its beginnings, Buddhism transcended all boundaries of kinship and nation, but most of the Buddhism practiced by the Han Chinese in mainland China is closely identified with Han Chinese culture, and its leaders have been very willing to accept guidance from the state. The problem for the CCP is Tibetan Buddhism, which over the last fifty years has surged beyond the boundaries of Tibetan and Mongolian nationality and become a world religion, with enthusiastic devotees in the Americas, Europe, and elsewhere. Since his 1959 flight into exile, the Dalai Lama has become a global celebrity, welcomed and respected as a great spiritual leader by popes, kings, publics, and presidents. Both his office and his charisma bring him huge respect from most Tibetans, who already have plenty of nonreligious reasons to resist Han Chinese colonialism. But their allegiance to a faith whose most revered leader is beyond the control of the Chinese state makes their resistance even more threatening in the eyes of the Chinese government. According to the logic of sacral imperial rule, all lamas should accept the suzerainty of the Chinese emperor, even though in practice they might have wide leeway in their religious affairs. Following the logic of sacral emperorship, the CCP is not content merely to dispute the Dalai Lama's positions on Tibet, but seeks thoroughly to demonize the man. He is portrayed as equal in evil to Osama bin Laden, a person utterly devoid of any claim to spiritual leadership. Given the Dalai Lama's immense and far-flung popularity, such attacks are counterproductive. They merely alienate global public opinion and, if anything, increase the religious zeal of embattled Tibetans.[18]

A final challenge to the CCP's neoimperial sacral hegemony comes from Islam.[19] The Qing dynasty in the nineteenth century and the Republican government in the 1930s both faced uprisings from the Uyghur minority that inhabits China's far-western region of Xinjiang. The Uyghurs are Muslims, but the Islamic religion was not necessarily the major cause of previous rebellions among these Turkic people. Indeed, they practiced a variety of strands of Islam that divided rather than united them. But globalization has brought Uyghur Muslims into contact with worldwide Islamic movements.

There are pragmatic reasons for the Chinese government to worry about the radicalism that might come with such a religious revival, but the reaction against it seems so extreme as to be counterproductive. In the name of suppressing "separatism," some Chinese authorities have begun to attack Islamic practice itself. During Ramadan in 2008, for example, they forced Uyghur men to shave their beards, restricted access to mosques, and discouraged ritual fasting. This perhaps can only be explained in terms of the affront that a globalized Islam poses to neoimperial sacral hegemony. Such actions serve to add religious grievances to the many others that Uyghurs have against Han Chinese and could drive Uyghur movements closer to global movements of political Islam. It does not seem that such connections were made during the Uyghur uprisings of July 2009. But the Chinese government's general hostility to globalized Islam adds dangerous fuel to the fires of ethnic resentment.

With its "Great Firewall" of Internet filtering and massive surveillance resources, the Chinese party-state can inhibit the influence of universalizing religious movements, but it cannot block them completely. Moreover, even partial repression of such influences exposes China to censure from increasingly assertive global movements for religious freedom.

This will be confounding to a policy modeled on the sacral hegemony of premodern Chinese emperors. The one way to keep universalizing global religious movements from undermining that policy is for China to become so powerful that it can set the terms of its relationship with the rest of world. Then it can use its military and economic might to enforce its claim that universal standards of religious freedom do not apply to China and that universal religions can enter China only if they accept the "government master, religion follower" principle. Some political leaders think that they can accomplish this.

If they do completely succeed, they might one day come to regret it, because the accumulated pressure from frustrated religious believers could become explosive. The likelihood, however, is that China's political authorities will succeed only in part, and will experience ongoing frictions with global proponents of religious freedom. One can easily imagine grim scenarios of intensified conflict over religion's relationship to the state. In more auspicious scenarios, however, such international frictions will drive all sides to seek better ways of balancing the rights of increasingly assertive religions with the requirements of governance in a post-secular world.

NOTES

1. See Daniel Bell, "The Return of the Sacred: An Argument on the Future of Religion," in *The Winding Passage: Essays and Sociological Journeys, 1960–1980* (New York: Basic Books, 1981), 327.

2. Translated in Donald E. MacInnis, *Religion in China Today: Policy and Practice* (Maryknoll, N.Y.: Orbis, 1989), 8–26. In the nearly three decades since Document 19's promulgation, additional regulations regarding religion have supplemented it, but these have all been within the framework that Document 19 lays out.

3. See Jürgen Habermas, *Rationality and Religion: Essays on Reason, God, and Modernity* (Cambridge, Mass.: MIT Press, 2002). See also the introduction to Craig Calhoun, Mark Juergensmeyer, and Jonathan VanAntwerpen, *Rethinking Secularism* (New York: Oxford University Press, 2010).

4. Shmuel Eisenstadt, ed., *Multiple Modernities* (New York: Transaction, 2002).

5. Jose Casanova, *Public Religions in the Modern World* (Chicago: University of Chicago Press, 1994).

6. Mayfair Mei-hui Yang, ed., *Chinese Religiosities: Afflictions of Modernity and State Formation* (Berkeley: University of California Press, 2008).

7. Kenneth Dean, "Local Communal Religion in Southeast China," in Daniel L. Overmyer, ed., *Religion in China Today* (Cambridge: Cambridge University Press, 2003), 32–52.

8. Yu Jianrong (Institute of Rural Development, Chinese Academy of Social Sciences), "Religious Demography and House Churches, 2008," *Compass Direct News Service*, 3 July 2009.

9. Gerda Wielander, "Bridging the Gap? An Investigation of Beijing Intellectual House Church Activities and Their Implications for China's Democratization," *Journal of Contemporary China* 18 (November 2009): 849–64.

10. David A. Palmer, *Qigong Fever: Body, Science, and Utopia in China* (London: Hurst, 2007), 260–61.

11. The best-known "heterodox" Christian sect is the Eastern Lightening, which began in Henan Province, is quite strong in Shaanxi, and now seems to be spreading in Wenzhou. It has a female leader whose followers consider her a reincarnation of Jesus. There are at least ten other such quasi-Christian sects, with names like "The Established King," "The Lord God Sect," and "Three Ranks of Servants." See Richard Madsen, "Chinese Christianity: Indigenization and Conflict," in Elizabeth J. Perry and Mark Selden, eds., *Chinese Society: Change, Conflict, and Resistance*, 3rd ed. (London: Routledge, 2010), 246.

12. The term *xiejiao* has usually been translated in the English-language scholarly and historical literature as "heterodoxy." The phenomenon does not necessarily conform to the definition of a "cult" in a modern sociological sense. But official Chinese translations of the term into English render it as "evil cult," probably to intimate sinister connotations that would seem to justify crackdowns on such activities.

13. Richard Madsen, *China's Catholics: Tragedy and Hope in an Emerging Civil Society* (Berkeley: University of California Press, 1998). See also Richard Madsen, "Catholicism as Chinese Folk Religion," in Stephen Uhalley, Jr., and Xiaoxin Wu, eds., *China and Christianity: Burdened Past, Hopeful Future* (Armonk, N.Y.: M.E. Sharpe, 2001), 233–49.

14. He first made this statement in a speech at the Central Party School in Beijing on 1 September 2008. The speech was later reprinted in the school's official newspaper.

15. Zhuo Xinping, *Quanqiuhuade Zongjiao yu Dangdai Zhongguo* [Global religions and contemporary China] (Beijing: Shehuikexue wenxian chubanshe, 2008), 30. A major mission of the Chinese Academy of Social Sciences is to give scholarship-based advice to China's central government.

16. Fenggang Yang, "Red, Black, and Grey Markets for Religion in China," *Sociological Quarterly* 47 (February 2006): 93–122.

17. Zhuo Xinping, Quanqiuhuade, 174.

18. Melvyn C. Goldstein, *The Snow Lion and the Dragon: China, Tibet, and the Dalai Lama* (Berkeley: University of California Press, 1999).

19. Dru Gladney, *Muslim Chinese: Ethnic Nationalism in the People's Republic*, 2nd ed. (Cambridge, Mass.: Harvard East Asian Monographs, 1996).

V. YOUTH

Angry Youth*

Evan Osnos

On the morning of April 15th, a short video entitled *2008 China Stand Up!* appeared on Sina. com, a Chinese website. The video's origin was a mystery: unlike the usual YouTube-style clips, it had no host, no narrator, and no signature except the initials "CTGZ."

It was a homespun documentary, and it opened with a Technicolor portrait of Chairman Mao, sunbeams radiating from his head. Out of silence came an orchestral piece, thundering with drums, as a black screen flashed, in both Chinese and English, one of Mao's mantras: "Imperialism will never abandon its intention to destroy us." Then a cut to present-day photographs and news footage, and a fevered sprint through conspiracies and betrayals—the "farces, schemes, and disasters" confronting China today. The sinking Chinese stock market (the work of foreign speculators who "wildly manipulated" Chinese stock prices and lured rookie investors to lose their fortunes). Shoppers were beset by inflation, a butcher counter where "even pork has become a luxury." And a warning: this is the dawn of a global "Currency War," and the West intends to "make Chinese people foot the bill" for America's financial woes.

A cut, then, to another front: rioters looting stores and brawling in Lhasa, the Tibetan capital. The music crescendos as words flash across the scenes: "So-called peaceful protest!" A montage of foreign press clippings critical of China—nothing but "rumors, all speaking with one distorted voice." The screen fills with the logos of CNN, the BBC, and other news organizations, which give way to a portrait of Joseph Goebbels. The orchestra and the rhetoric climb toward a final sequence: "Obviously, there is a scheme behind the scenes to encircle China. A new Cold War!" The music turns triumphant with images of China's Olympic hurdler Liu Xiang standing

in Tiananmen Square, raising the Olympic torch, "a symbol of Peace and Friendship!" But, first, one final act of treachery: in Paris, protesters attempt to wrest the Olympic torch from its official carrier, forcing guards to fend them off—a "long march" for a new era. The film ends with the image of a Chinese flag, aglow in the sunlight, and a solemn promise: "We will stand up and hold together always as one family in harmony!"

The video, which was just over six minutes long and is now on YouTube, captured the mood of nationalism that surged through China after the Tibetan uprising, in March, sparked foreign criticism of China's hosting of the 2008 Summer Olympics. Citizens were greeting the criticism with rare fury. Thousands demonstrated in front of Chinese outlets of Carrefour, a French supermarket chain, in retaliation for what they considered France's sympathy for pro-Tibetan activists. Charles Zhang, who holds a Ph.D. from M.I.T. and is the founder and C.E.O. of Sohu, a leading Chinese web portal along the lines of Yahoo!, called online for a boycott of French products "to make the thoroughly biased French media and public feel losses and pain." When Speaker of the House Nancy Pelosi denounced China's handling of Tibet, Xinhua, China's official news service, called her "disgusting." State-run media revived language from another age: the magazine *Outlook Weekly* warned that "domestic and foreign hostile forces have made the Beijing Olympics a focus for infiltration and sabotage." In the anonymity of the Web, decorum deteriorated. "People who fart through the mouth will get shit stuffed down their throats by me!" one commentator wrote, in a forum hosted by a semi-official newspaper. "Someone give me a gun! Don't show mercy to the enemy!" wrote another. The comments were an embarrassment to many Chinese, but they were difficult to ignore among foreign journalists who had begun receiving threats. (An anonymous letter to my fax machine in Beijing

---

* This article appeared in *The New Yorker*, Vol. 84, Issue 22 (July 2008).

warned, "Clarify the facts on China . . . or you and your loved ones will wish you were dead.")

In its first week and a half, the video by CTGZ drew more than a million hits and tens of thousands of favorable comments. It rose to the site's fourth-most-popular rating. (A television blooper clip of a yawning news anchor was No. 1.) On average, the film attracted nearly two clicks per second. It became a manifesto for a self-styled vanguard in defense of China's honor, a patriotic swath of society that the Chinese call the *fen qing*, the angry youth.

Nineteen years after the crackdown on student-led protests in Tiananmen Square, China's young elite rose again this spring—not in pursuit of liberal democracy but in defense of sovereignty and prosperity. Nicholas Negroponte, the founder of M.I.T.'s Media Laboratory and one of the early ideologists of the Internet, once predicted that the global reach of the Web would transform the way we think about ourselves as countries. The state, he predicted, will evaporate "like a mothball, which goes from solid to gas directly," and "there will be no more room for nationalism than there is for smallpox." In China, things have gone differently.

A young Chinese friend of mine, who spends most of his time online, traced the screen name CTGZ to an email address. It belonged to a twenty-eight-year-old graduate student in Shanghai named Tang Jie, and it was his first video. A couple of weeks later, I met Tang Jie at the gate of Fudan University, a top Chinese school, situated on a modern campus that radiates from a pair of thirty-story steel-and-glass towers that could pass for a corporate headquarters. He wore a crisp powder-blue oxford shirt, khakis, and black dress shoes. He had bright hazel eyes and rounded features—a baby face, everyone tells him—and a dusting of goatee and mustache on his chin and upper lip. He bounded over to welcome me as I stepped out of a cab, and he tried to pay my fare.

Tang spends most of his time working on his dissertation, which is on Western philosophy. He specializes in phenomenology; specifically, in the concept of "intersubjectivity," as theorized by Edmund Husserl, the German philosopher who influenced Sartre, among others. In addition to Chinese, Tang reads English and German easily, but he speaks them infrequently, so at times he swerves, apologetically, among languages. He is working on his Latin and Ancient Greek. He is so self-effacing and soft-spoken that his voice may drop to a whisper. He laughs sparingly, as if he were conserving energy. For fun, he listens to classical Chinese music, though he also enjoys screwball comedies by the Hong Kong star Stephen Chow. He is proudly unhip. The screen name CTGZ is an adaptation of two obscure terms from classical poetry: *changting* and *gongzi*, which together translate as "the noble son of the pavilion." Unlike some elite Chinese students, Tang has never joined the Communist Party, for fear that it would impugn his objectivity as a scholar.

Tang had invited some friends to join us for lunch, at Fat Brothers Sichuan Restaurant, and afterward we all climbed the stairs to his room. He lives alone in a sixth-floor walkup, a studio of less than seventy-five square feet, which could be mistaken for a library storage room occupied by a fastidious squatter. Books cover every surface, and great mounds list from the shelves above his desk. His collections encompass, more or less, the span of human thought: Plato leans against Lao-tzu, Wittgenstein, Bacon, Fustel de Coulanges, Heidegger, the Koran. When Tang wanted to widen his bed by a few inches, he laid plywood across the frame and propped up the edges with piles of books. Eventually, volumes overflowed the room, and they now stand outside his front door in a wall of cardboard boxes.

Tang slumped into his desk chair. We talked for a while, and I asked if he had any idea that his video would be so popular. He smiled. "It appears I have expressed a common feeling, a shared view," he said.

Next to him sat Liu Chengguang, a cheerful, broad-faced Ph.D. student in political science who recently translated into Chinese a lecture on the subject of "Manliness" by the conservative Harvard professor Harvey Mansfield. Sprawled on the bed, wearing a gray sweatshirt, was Xiong Wenchi, who earned a Ph.D. in political science before taking a teaching job last year. And to Tang's left sat Zeng Kewei, a lean and stylish banker, who picked up a master's degree in Western philosophy before going into finance. Like Tang, each of his friends was in his twenties, was the first in his family to go to college, and had been drawn to the study of Western thought.

"China was backward throughout its modern history, so we were always seeking the reasons for why the West grew strong," Liu said. "We learned from the West. All of us who are educated have this dream: Grow strong by learning from the West."

Tang and his friends were so gracious, so thankful that I'd come to listen to them, that I began to wonder if China's anger of last spring should be viewed as an aberration. They implored me not to make that mistake. "We've been studying Western history for so long, we understand it well," Zeng said. "We think our love for China, our support for the government and the benefits of this country, is not a spontaneous reaction. It has developed after giving the matter much thought."

In fact, their view of China's direction, if not their vitriol, is consistent with the Chinese mainstream. Almost nine out of ten Chinese approve of the way things are going in the country—the highest share of any of the twenty-four countries surveyed this spring by the Pew Research Center. (In the United States, by comparison, just two out of ten voiced approval.) As for the more assertive strain of patriotism, scholars point to a Chinese petition against Japan's membership in the U.N. Security Council. At last count, it had attracted more than forty million signatures, roughly the population of Spain. I asked Tang to show me how he made his film. He turned to face the screen of his Lenovo desktop P.C., which has a Pentium 4 Processor and one gigabyte of memory. "Do you know Movie Maker?" he said, referring to a video editing program. I pleaded ignorance and asked if he'd learned from a book. He glanced at me pityingly. He'd learned it on the fly from the help menu. "We must thank Bill Gates," he said.

When people began rioting in Lhasa in March, Tang followed the news closely. As usual, he was receiving his information from American and European news sites, in addition to China's official media. Like others his age, he has no hesitation about tunnelling under the government firewall, a vast infrastructure of digital filters and human censors which blocks politically objectionable content from reaching computers in China. Younger Chinese friends of mine regard the firewall as they would an officious lifeguard at a swimming pool—an occasional, largely irrelevant, intrusion.

To get around it, Tang detours through a proxy server—a digital way station overseas that connects a user with a blocked Web site. He watches television exclusively online, because he doesn't have a TV in his room. Tang also receives foreign news clips from Chinese students abroad. (According to the Institute of International Education, the number of Chinese students in the United States—some sixty-seven thousand—has grown by nearly two-thirds in the past decade.) He's baffled that foreigners might imagine that people of his generation are somehow unwise to the distortions of censorship.

"Because we are in such a system, we are always asking ourselves whether we are brainwashed," he said. "We are always eager to get other information from different channels." Then he added, "But when you are in a so-called free system you never think about whether you are brainwashed."

At the time, news and opinion about Tibet was swirling on Fudan's electronic bulletin board, or B.B.S. The board was alive with criticism of foreign coverage of Tibet. Tang had seen a range of foreign press clippings deemed by Chinese Web users to be misleading or unfair. A photograph on CNN.com, for instance, had been cropped around military trucks bearing down on unarmed protesters. But an uncropped version showed a crowd of demonstrators lurking nearby, including someone with an arm cocked, hurling something at the trucks. To Tang, the cropping looked like a deliberate distortion. (CNN disputed this and said that the caption fairly describes the scene.)

"It was a joke," he said bitterly. That photograph and others crisscrossed China by e-mail, scrawled with criticism, while people added more examples from the *Times* of London, Fox News, German television, and French radio. It was a range of news organizations, and, to those inclined to see it as such, it smacked of a conspiracy. It shocked people like Tang, who put faith in the Western press, but, more important, it offended them: Tang thought that he was living in the moment of greatest prosperity and openness in his country's modern history, and yet the world still seemed to view China with suspicion. As if he needed confirmation, Jack Cafferty, a CNN commentator, called China "the same bunch of goons and thugs they've been for the last fifty years," a quote that rippled across the front pages in China and for which CNN later apologized. Like many of his peers, Tang couldn't figure out why foreigners were so agitated about Tibet—an impoverished backwater, as he saw it, that China had tried for decades to civilize. Boycotting the Beijing Games in the name of Tibet seemed as logical to him as shunning the Salt Lake City Olympics to protest America's treatment of the Cherokee.

He scoured YouTube in search of a rebuttal, a clarification of the Chinese perspective, but he found nothing in English except pro-Tibet videos. He was already busy—under contract from a publisher for a Chinese translation of Leibniz's "Discourse on Metaphysics" and other essays—but he couldn't shake the idea of speaking up on China's behalf.

"I thought, O.K., I'll make something," he said. Before Tang could start, however, he was obligated to go home for a few days. His mother had told him to be back for the harvest season. She needed his help in the fields, digging up bamboo shoots.

Tang is the youngest of four siblings from a farming family near the eastern city of Hangzhou. For breaking China's one-child policy, his parents paid fines measured in grain. Tang's birth cost them two hundred kilos of unmilled rice. ("I'm not very expensive," he says.)

Neither his mother nor his father could read or write. Until the fourth grade, Tang had no name. He went by Little Four, after his place in the family order. When that became impractical, his father began calling him Tang Jie, an abbreviated homage to his favorite comedian, Tang Jiezhong, half of a popular act in the style of Abbott and Costello.

Tang was bookish and, in a large, boisterous household, he said little. He took to science fiction. "I can tell you everything about all those movies, like 'Star Wars,'" he told me. He was a good, though not a spectacular, student, but he showed a precocious interest in ideas. "He wasn't like other kids, who spent their pocket money on food—he saved all his money to buy books," said his sister Tang Xiaoling, who is seven years older. None of his siblings had studied past the eighth grade, and they regarded him as an admirable oddity. "If he had questions that he couldn't figure out, then he couldn't sleep," his sister said. "For us, if we didn't get it we just gave up."

In high school, Tang improved his grades and had some success at science fairs as an inventor. But he was frustrated. "I discovered that science can't help your life," he said. He happened upon a Chinese translation of a fanciful Norwegian novel, *Sophie's World*, by the philosophy teacher Jostein Gaarder, in which a teen-age girl encounters the history of great thinkers. "It was then that I discovered philosophy," Tang said.

Patriotism was not a particularly strong presence in his house, but landmarks of national progress became the backdrop of his adolescence. When Tang was in junior high, the Chinese were still celebrating the country's first major freeway, completed a few years before. "It was famous. We were proud of this. At last we had a highway!" he recalled one day, with a laugh, as we whizzed down an expressway in Shanghai. "Now we have highways everywhere, even in Tibet."

Supermarkets opened in his home town, and, eventually, so did an Internet cafe. (Tang, who was eighteen at the time, was particularly fond of the websites for the White House and NASA, because they had kids' sections that used simpler English sentences.) Tang enrolled at Hangzhou Normal University. He came to credit his country and his family for opportunities that his siblings had never had. By the time he reached Fudan, in 2003, he lived in a world of ideas. "He had a pure passion for philosophy," Ma Jun, a fellow philosophy student who met him early on, said; "A kind of religious passion."

The Internet had barely taken root in China before it became a vessel for nationalism. At the Atlanta Olympics, in 1996, as the Chinese delegation marched into the stadium, the NBC announcer Bob Costas riffed on China's "problems with human rights, property right disputes, the threat posed to Taiwan." Then he mentioned "suspicions" that Chinese athletes used performance-enhancing drugs. Even though the Web in China was in its infancy (there were just five telephone lines for every hundred people), comments spread instantly among Chinese living abroad. The timing couldn't have been more opportune: after more than fifteen years of reform and Westernization, Chinese writers were pushing back against Hollywood, McDonald's, and American values. An impassioned book titled *China Can Say No!* came out that spring and sold more than a hundred thousand copies in its first month. Written by a group of young intellectuals, it decried China's "infatuation with America," which had suppressed the national imagination with a diet of visas, foreign aid, and advertising. If China didn't resist this "cultural strangulation," it would become "a slave," extending a history of humiliating foreign incursions that stretched back to China's defeat in the first Opium War and the British acquisition of Hong Kong, in 1842. The Chinese government, which is wary of fast-spreading new ideas, eventually pulled the book off the shelves, but not before a raft of knock-offs sought to exploit the same mood (*Why China Can Say No, China Still Can Say No*, and *China Always Say No*).

Xu Wu, a former journalist in China who is now a professor at Arizona State University, says in his 2007 book *Chinese Cyber Nationalism* that groups claiming to represent more than seventy thousand overseas Chinese wrote to NBC asking for an apology for the Costas remarks. They collected donations online and bought an ad in the *Washington Post*, accusing Costas and the network of "ignominious prejudice and inhospitality." NBC apologized, and Chinese online activism was born.

Each day, some 3500 Chinese citizens were going online for the first time. In 1998, Charles Zhang's Sohu launched China's first major search engine. The following spring, when a NATO aircraft, using American intelligence, mistakenly dropped three bombs on the Chinese Embassy in Belgrade, the Chinese Web found its voice. The United States apologized, blaming outdated maps and inaccurate databases, but Chinese patriotic hackers—calling themselves "honkers," to capture the sound of *hong*, which is Chinese for the color red—attacked. As Peter Hays Gries, a China scholar at the University of Oklahoma, details in *China's New Nationalism*, they plastered the home page of the US Embassy in Beijing with the slogan "Down with the Barbarians!," and they caused the White House Web site to crash under a deluge of angry e-mail. "The Internet is Western," one commentator wrote, "but . . . we Chinese can use it to tell the people of the world that China cannot be insulted!"

The government treated online patriots warily. They placed their pride in the Chinese nation, not necessarily in the Party, and leaders rightly sensed that the passion could swerve against them. After a nationalist website was shut down by censors in 2004, one commentator wrote, "Our government is as weak as sheep!" The government permitted nationalism to grow at some moments but strained to control it at others. The following spring, when Japan approved a new textbook that critics claimed glossed over wartime atrocities, patriots in Beijing drafted protest plans and broadcast them via chat rooms, bulletin boards, and text messages. As many as ten thousand demonstrators took to the streets, hurling paint and bottles at the Japanese Embassy. Despite government warnings to cease these activities, thousands more marched in Shanghai the following week—one of China's largest demonstrations in years—and vandalized the Japanese consulate. At one point, Shanghai police cut off cell-phone service in downtown Shanghai.

"Up to now, the Chinese government has been able to keep a grip on it," Xu Wu told me. "But I call it the 'virtual Tiananmen Square.' They don't need to go there. They can do the same thing online and sometimes be even more damaging."

Tang was at dinner with friends one night in 2004 when he met Wan Manlu, an elegantly reserved Ph.D. student in Chinese literature and linguistics. Her delicate features suited her name, which includes the character for the finest jade. They sat side by side, but barely spoke. Later, Tang hunted down her screen name—gracelittle—and sent her a private message on Fudan's bulletin board. They worked up to a first date: an experimental opera based on "Regret for the Past," a Chinese story.

They discovered that they shared a frustration with China's unbridled Westernization. "Chinese tradition has many good things, but we've ditched them," Wan told me. "I feel there have to be people to carry them on." She came from a middle-class home, and Tang's humble roots and old-fashioned values impressed her. "Most of my generation has a smooth, happy life, including me," she said. "I feel like our character lacks something. For example, love for the country or the perseverance you get from conquering hardships. Those virtues, I don't see them in myself and many people my age." She added, "For him, from that kind of background, with nobody educated in his family, nobody helping him with schoolwork, with great family pressure, it's not easy to get where he is today."

They were engaged this spring. In their years together, Wan watched Tang fall in with a group of students devoted to a charismatic thirty-nine-year-old Fudan philosophy professor named Ding Yun. He is a translator of Leo Strauss, the political philosopher whose admirers include Harvey Mansfield and other neoconservatives. A Strauss student, Abram Shulsky, who co-authored a 1999 essay titled "Leo Strauss and the World of Intelligence (By Which We Do Not Mean Nous)," ran the Pentagon's Office of Special Plans before the invasion of Iraq. Since then, other Strauss disciples have vigorously ridiculed suggestions of a connection between Strauss's thought and Bush-era foreign policy.

I saw Mansfield in Shanghai in May, during his first visit to China, at a dinner with a small group of conservative scholars. He was wearing a honey-colored panama and was in good spirits, though he seemed a bit puzzled by all the fuss they were making about him. His first question to the table: "Why would Chinese scholars be interested in Leo Strauss?"

Professor Ding teaches a Straussian regard for the universality of the classics and encourages his students to revive ancient Chinese thought. "During the nineteen-eighties and nineties, most intellectuals had a negative opinion of China's traditional culture," he told me recently. He has close-cropped hair and stylish rectangular glasses, and favors the conspicuously retro loose-fitting shirts of a Tang-dynasty scholar. When Ding grew up, in the early years of reform, "conservative" was a derogatory term, just like "reactionary," he said.

But Ding and others have thrived in recent years amid a new vein of conservatism which runs counter to China's drive for integration with the world. Just as America's conservative movement in the nineteen-sixties capitalized on the yearning for a post-liberal retreat to morality and nobility, China's classical revival draws on a nostalgic image of what it means to be Chinese. The biggest surprise best-seller of recent years is, arguably, Yu Dan's *Reflections on the Analects*, a collection of Confucian lectures delivered by Yu, a telegenic Beijing professor of media studies. She writes, "To assess a country's true strength and prosperity, you can't simply look at GNP growth and not look at the inner experience of each ordinary person: Does he feel safe? Is he happy?" (Skeptics argue that it's simply "Chicken Soup for the Confucian Soul.")

Professor Ding met Tang in 2003, at the entrance interview for graduate students. "I was the person in charge of the exam," Ding recalled. "I sensed that this kid is very smart and diligent." He admitted Tang to the program, and watched with satisfaction as Tang and other students pushed back against the onslaught of Westernization. Tang developed an appetite for the classics. "The fact is we are very Westernized," he said. "Now we started reading ancient Chinese books and we rediscovered the ancient China."

This renewed pride has also affected the way Tang and his peers view the economy. They took to a theory that the world profits from China but blocks its attempts to invest abroad. Tang's friend Zeng smiled disdainfully as he ticked off examples of Chinese companies that have tried to invest in America. "Huawei's bid to buy 3Com was rejected," he said. "C.N.O.O.C.'s bid to buy into Unocal and Lenovo's purchase of part of I.B.M. caused political repercussions. If it's not a market argument, it's a political argument. We think the world is a free market."

Before he could finish, Tang jumped in. "This is what you—America—taught us," he said. "We opened our market, but when we try to buy your companies we hit political obstacles. It's not fair."

Their view, which is popular in China across ideological lines, has validity: American politicians have invoked national-security concerns, with varying degrees of credibility, to oppose Chinese direct investment. But Tang's view, infused with a sense of victimhood, also obscures some evidence to the contrary: China has succeeded in other deals abroad (its sovereign-wealth fund has stakes in the Blackstone Group and in Morgan Stanley), and though China has taken steps to open its markets to foreigners, it remains equally inclined to reject an American attempt to buy an asset as sensitive as a Chinese oil company.

Tang's belief that the United States will seek to obstruct China's rise—"a new Cold War"—extends beyond economics to broader American policy. Disparate issues of relatively minor importance to Americans, such as support for Taiwan and Washington's calls to raise the value of the yuan, have metastasized in China into a feeling of strategic containment. In polls, the Chinese public has not demonstrated a significant preference for either Barack Obama or John McCain, though

Obama has attracted negative attention for saying that, were he President, he might boycott the opening ceremony of the Olympics. Tang and his friends have watched some debates online, but the young patriots tend to see the race in broader terms. "No matter who is elected, China is still China and will go the way it goes," one recent posting in a discussion about Obama said. "Who can stand in the way of the march of history?"

This spring, Tang stayed at his family's farm for five days before he could return to Shanghai and finish his movie. He scoured the Web for photographs on the subjects that bother him and his friends, everything from inflation to Taiwan's threats of independence. He selected some of the pictures because they were evocative—a man raising his arm in a sea of Chinese flags reminded him of Delacroix's *Liberty Leading the People*—and chose others because they embodied the political moment: a wheelchair-bound Chinese amputee carrying the Olympic flame in Paris, for instance, fending off a protester who was trying to snatch it away.

For a soundtrack, he typed "solemn music" into Baidu, a Chinese search engine, and scanned the results. He landed on a piece by Vangelis, a Yanni-style pop composer from Greece who is best known for his score for the movie "Chariots of Fire." Tang's favorite Vangelis track was from a Gerard Depardieu film about Christopher Columbus called "1492: Conquest of Paradise." He watched a few seconds of Depardieu standing manfully on the deck of a tall ship, coursing across the Atlantic. Perfect, Tang thought: "It was a time of globalization."

Tang added scenes of Chairman Mao and the Olympic track star Liu Xiang, both icons of their eras. The film was six minutes and sixteen seconds long. Some title screens in English were full of mistakes, because he was hurrying, but he was anxious to release it. He posted the film to Sina and sent a note to the Fudan bulletin board. As the film climbed in popularity, Professor Ding rejoiced. "We used to think they were just a post-modern, Occidentalized generation," Ding said. "Of course, I thought the students I knew were very good, but the wider generation? I was not very pleased. To see the content of Tang Jie's video, and the scale of its popularity among the youth, made me very happy. Very happy."

Not everyone was pleased. Young patriots are so polarizing in China that some people, by changing the intonation in Chinese, pronounce "angry youth" as "shit youth."

"How can our national self-respect be so fragile and shallow?" Han Han, one of China's most popular young writers, wrote on his blog, in an essay about nationalism. "Somebody says you're a mob, so you curse him, even want to beat him, and then you say, We're not a mob. This is as if someone said you were a fool, so you held up a big sign in front of his girlfriend's brother's dog, saying 'I Am Not a Fool.' The message will get to him, but he'll still think you're a fool."

If the activists thought that they were defending China's image abroad, there was little sign of success. After weeks of patriotic rhetoric emanating from China, a poll sponsored by the *Financial Times* showed that Europeans now ranked China as the greatest threat to global stability, surpassing America.

But the eruption of the angry youth has been even more disconcerting to those interested in furthering democracy. By age and education, Tang and his peers inherit a long legacy of activism that stretches from 1919, when nationalist demonstrators demanded "Mr. Democracy" and "Mr. Science," to 1989, when students flooded Tiananmen Square, challenging the government and erecting a sculpture inspired by the Statue of Liberty. Next year will mark the twentieth anniversary of that movement, but the events of this spring suggest that prosperity, computers, and Westernization have not driven China's young elite toward tolerance but, rather, persuaded more than a few of them to postpone idealism as long as life keeps improving. The students in 1989 were rebelling against corruption and abuses of power. "Nowadays, these issues haven't disappeared but have worsened," Li Datong, an outspoken newspaper editor and reform advocate, told me. "However, the current young generation turns a blind eye to it. I've never seen them respond to those major domestic issues. Rather, they take a utilitarian, opportunistic approach."

One caricature of young Chinese holds that they know virtually nothing about the crackdown at Tiananmen Square—known in Chinese as "the June 4th incident"—because the authorities have purged it from the nation's official history.

It's not that simple, however. Anyone who can click on a proxy server can discover as much about Tiananmen as he chooses to learn. And yet many Chinese have concluded that the movement was misguided and naive.

"We accept all the values of human rights, of democracy," Tang told me. "We accept that. The issue is how to realize it."

I met dozens of urbane students and young professionals this spring, and we often got to talking about Tiananmen Square. In a typical conversation, one college senior asked whether she should interpret the killing of protesters at Kent State in 1970 as a fair measure of American freedom. Liu Yang, a graduate student in environmental engineering, said, "June 4th could not and should not succeed at that time. If June 4th had succeeded, China would be worse and worse, not better."

Liu, who is twenty-six, once considered himself a liberal. As a teen-ager, he and his friends happily criticized the Communist Party. "In the nineteen-nineties, I thought that the Chinese government is not good enough. Maybe we need to set up a better government," he told me. "The problem is that we didn't know what a good government would be. So we let the Chinese Communist Party stay in place. The other problem is we didn't have the power to get them out. They have the Army!"

When Liu got out of college, he found a good job as an engineer at an oil-services company. He was earning more money in a month than his parents—retired laborers living on a pension—earned in a year. Eventually, he saved enough money that, with scholarships, he was able to enroll in a Ph.D. program at Stanford. He had little interest in the patriotic pageantry of the Olympics until he saw the fracas around the torch in Paris. "We were furious," he said, and when the torch came to San Francisco he and other Chinese students surged toward the relay route to support it. I was in San Francisco not long ago, and we arranged to meet at a Starbucks near his dorm, in Palo Alto. He arrived on his mountain bike, wearing a Nautica fleece pullover and jeans.

The date, we both knew, was June 4th, nineteen years since soldiers put down the Tiananmen uprising. The overseas Chinese students' bulletin board had been alive all afternoon with discussions of the anniversary. Liu mentioned the famous photograph of an unknown man standing in front of a tank—perhaps the most provocative image in modern Chinese history.

"We really acknowledge him. We really think he was brave," Liu told me. But, of that generation, he said, "They fought for China, to make the country better. And there were some faults of the government. But, finally, we must admit that the Chinese government had to use any way it could to put down that event."

Sitting in the cool quiet of a California night, sipping his coffee, Liu said that he is not willing to risk all that his generation enjoys at home in order to hasten the liberties he has come to know in America. "Do you live on democracy?" he asked me. "You eat bread, you drink coffee. All of these are not brought by democracy. Indian guys have democracy, and some African countries have democracy, but they can't feed their own people.

"Chinese people have begun to think, One part is the good life, another part is democracy," Liu went on. "If democracy can really give you the good life, that's good. But, without democracy, if we can still have the good life why should we choose democracy?"

When the Olympic torch returned to China, in May, for the final journey to Beijing, the Chinese seemed determined to make up for its woes abroad. Crowds overflowed along the torch's route. One afternoon, Tang and I set off to watch the torch traverse a suburb of Shanghai. At the time, the country was still in a state of shock following the May 12th earthquake in the mountains of Sichuan Province, which killed more than sixty-nine thousand people and left millions homeless. It was the worst disaster in three decades, but it also produced a rare moment of national unity. Donations poured in, revealing the positive side of the patriotism that had erupted weeks earlier.

The initial rhetoric of that nationalist outcry contained a spirit of violence that anyone old enough to remember the Red Guards—or the rise of skinheads in Europe—could not casually dismiss. And that spirit had materialized, in ugly episodes: when the Olympic torch reached South Korea, Chinese and rival protesters fought in the streets. The Korean government said it would deport Chinese agitators, though a Chinese Foreign Ministry spokeswoman stood by the demonstrators' original intent to "safeguard the dignity of the torch." Chinese students overseas emerged as some of the most vocal patriots. According to the *Times*, at the University of Southern California they marshalled statistics and photographs to challenge a visiting Tibetan monk during a lecture. Then someone threw a plastic water bottle in the monk's direction, and campus security removed the man who tossed it. At Cornell, an anthropology professor who arranged for the screening of a film on Tibet informed the crowd that, on a Web forum for Chinese students, she was "told to 'go die.'" At Duke University, Grace Wang, a Chinese freshman, tried to mediate between pro-Tibet and pro-China protesters on campus. But online she was branded a "race traitor." People ferreted out her mother's address, in the seaside city of Qingdao, and vandalized their home. Her mother, an accountant, remains in hiding. Of her mother, Grace Wang said, "I really don't know where she is, and I think it's better for me not to know."

Now in summer school at Duke, Grace Wang does not regret speaking up, but she says that she misjudged how others her age, online but frustrated in China, would resent her. "When people can't express themselves in real life, what can they do? They definitely have to express their anger toward someone. I'm far away. They don't know me, so they don't feel sorry about it. They say whatever they want." She doesn't know when she'll return home (she becomes uneasy when she is recognized in Chinese restaurants near campus), but she takes comfort in the fact that history is filled with names once vilified, later rehabilitated. "This is just like what happened in the Cultural Revolution," she said. "Think about how Deng Xiaoping was treated at that time, and then, in just ten years, things had changed completely."

In the end, nothing came of the threats to foreign journalists. No blood was shed. After the chaos around the torch in Paris, the Chinese efforts to boycott Carrefour fizzled. China's leaders, awakening to their deteriorating image abroad, ultimately reined in the students with a call for only "rational patriotism."

"We do not want any violence," Tang told me. He and his peers had merely been desperate for someone to hear them. They felt no connection to Tiananmen Square, but, in sending their voices out onto the Web, they, too, had spoken for their moment in time. Their fury, Li Datong, the newspaper editor, told me, arose from "the accumulated desire for expression—just like when a flood suddenly races into a breach." Because a flood moves in whatever direction it chooses, the young conservatives are, to China's ruling class, an unnerving new force. They "are acutely aware that their country, whose resurgence they feel and admire, has no principle to guide it," Harvey Mansfield wrote in an e-mail to me, after his visit. "Some of them see . . . that liberalism in the West has lost its belief in itself, and they turn to Leo Strauss for conservatism that is based on principle, on 'natural right.' This conservatism is distinct from a status-quo conservatism, because they are not satisfied with a country that has only a status quo and not a principle."

In the weeks after Tang's video went viral, he made a series of others, about youth, the earthquake, China's leaders. None of his follow-ups generated more than a flicker of the attention of the original. The Web had moved on—to newer nationalist films and other distractions.

As Tang and I approached the torch-relay route, he said, "Look at the people. Everyone thinks this is their own Olympics." Venders were selling T-shirts, big Chinese flags, headbands, and mini-flags. Tang told me to wait until the torch passed, because hawkers would then cut prices by up to fifty percent. He was carrying a plastic bag and fished around in it for a bright-red scarf of the kind that Chinese children wear to signal membership in the Young Pioneers, a kind of Socialist Boy Scouts. He tied it around his neck and grinned. He offered one to a passing teenager, who politely declined.

The air was stagnant and thick beneath a canopy of haze, but the mood was exuberant. Time was ticking down to the torch's arrival, and the town was coming out for a look: a man in a dark suit, sweating and smoothing his hair; a construction worker in an orange helmet and farmer's galoshes; a bellboy in a vaguely nautical getup. Some younger spectators were wearing T-shirts inspired by China's recent troubles: "Love China, Oppose Divisions, Oppose Tibetan Independence," read a popular one. All around us, people strained for a better perch. A woman hung off a lamppost. A young man in a red headband climbed a tree.

The crowd's enthusiasm seemed to brighten Tang's view of things, reminding him that China's future belongs to him and to those around him. "When I stand here, I can feel, deeply, the common emotion of Chinese youth," he said. "We are self-confident."

Police blocked the road. A frisson swept through the crowd. People surged toward the curb, straining to see over one another's heads. But Tang hung back. He is a patient man.

VI. Urban and Rural

Driven to Protest: China's Rural Unrest*

Lianjiang Li

Today the Chinese countryside has become noticeably less stable. One indicator is that the number of "collective incidents"—a euphemism for popular protests—has jumped tenfold in the past dozen years, from 8,706 in 1993 to 87,000 in 2005, with about 40 percent occurring in the countryside. The number of people involved in such incidents also grew at a similar pace, from about 700,000 in 1993 to as many as 5 million in 2005. At the same time, large protests and the crackdowns that often ensue have become much more violent. Recent bloodshed in Guangdong and Hebei over insufficient compensation for valuable farmland is only the tip of an iceberg. Although no national data on casualties are available, scholarly research suggests a grim picture. In 2004, for instance, a research team at the Chinese Academy of Social Sciences found that hundreds of farmers were injured, 3 killed, and over 160 arrested in 87 clashes that year between farmers and police over land appropriation.

Political unrest in some parts of the countryside is no longer a distant danger, though few would argue that a political crisis is imminent. Chinese authorities, who almost always downplay political challenges, publicly admit that popular protests have become a major destabilizing factor. In 2004, the minister of public security acknowledged that "collective incidents" had become a prominent problem that threatened social stability. And just last year Prime Minister Wen Jiabao sternly warned local officials to avoid "historic

blunders" when dealing with compensation for land seizures, hinting that such mistakes could drive peasants toward rebellion.

Research by the Chinese Academy of Social Sciences shows that land expropriation is now the most volatile issue in the countryside, particularly in coastal areas. Other issues near the top of the list of villager grievances are rampant cadre corruption, rigged village elections, government violence against protesting villagers, and, until recently, thanks to the gradual abolition of agricultural taxes that began in 2004, excessive local taxation and the use of violence to collect taxes and fees. A 2003–2005 survey by this author of 1,314 rural petitioners from 28 Chinese provinces confirmed the wide range of peasant discontent, also noting grievances such as pollution of farmland and drinking water, illegal mining, and vote buying by the newly rich.

A closer look at these complaints suggests an interesting pattern. Chinese villagers have numerous grievances, some of which arise out of central policies—for example, Beijing's birth control policy, a household registration system that still bars free migration to cities, and systematic discrimination against rural dwellers in education, medical care, and social welfare. Overall, however, rural protests have thus far been directed almost exclusively at local authorities, especially county and township governments. Protesters often accuse local officials of violating central policies or state laws that are designed to protect them. Moreover, they demand that the government respect their lawful rights and interests, which have been laid out in central policies or state laws.

---

* The article was published in *Current History* (September 2006).

The Villagers' Dilemma

If Chinese villagers are generally not proactively demanding new rights, why do they resort to disruptive protests and even, sometimes, violence? The authorities frequently accuse protesters of lacking "legal consciousness." Zhou Yongkang, the public security minister, argues that a main reason the number of "collective incidents" has exploded is that "people's consciousness of their lawful rights and interests has grown fast but their legal consciousness remains low." According to Zhou, because of this gap between high rights consciousness and low legal consciousness, ordinary citizens do not express their views and make their claims through lawful procedures but instead "rashly take excessively radical actions to apply pressure on the party and government in [an] attempt to achieve reasonable objectives through illegal means." Plausible as this might sound, this puts the cart before the horse. With few exceptions, Chinese villagers resort to disruptive protests only after they have exhausted all lawful procedures.

Chinese villagers have employed, usually without success, at least six lawful methods to defend their rights and interests in the past two decades. Most commonly, they petition. This typically involves visiting a government office to submit a letter of complaint against specified officials or a government. The Chinese constitution grants citizens a right to lodge complaints against officials who violate the law or neglect their duties. But this constitutional right is severely limited in practice. The State Council's Regulation Concerning Letters and Visits allows people to petition as a group, but does not allow them to send more than five representatives at once. It also allows petitioners to appeal to higher levels if they are unsatisfied with a ruling, but it requires that they petition level by level, while in effect allowing a government to take as much time as it would like to make a ruling. (In 2005 the State Council's regulation was revised to further restrict the right to petition by allowing petitioners to visit no more than three levels of government.)

Restrictions like these often place villagers in a dilemma. If they pursue their claims strictly in accordance with the law, their likelihood of winning is slim because they cannot apply sufficient pressure on their foes. If they wish to be effective, they have to work around or brush against the law by, for example, sending multiple teams of representatives, bypassing levels of government, going to Beijing en masse, or camping out in a government compound and refusing to leave until a grievance is redressed.

Other than petitioning, Chinese villagers have also tried to make their voices heard by staging mass demonstrations. Here they find themselves in a similar predicament. The constitution grants Chinese citizens freedom of assembly, of procession, and of demonstration. These freedoms, however, exist almost exclusively on paper. The 1989 Law on Assembly, Procession, and Demonstration requires that all demonstrators obtain police approval in advance. But the police rarely grant such a permit. A group of petitioners from Hunan, for instance, applied to the Beijing City Public Security Bureau in 2003 to hold a peaceful demonstration in Tiananmen Square. The application, in the words of a cosigner, was "like a clay ox entering the sea"—never to be heard from again. The petitioners went ahead with the demonstration, only to be rounded up immediately by the police as soon as they knelt down in front of the Monument to the People's Heroes.

A third lawful procedure through which China's rural residents have sought redress against abusive or negligent local officials is administrative lawsuits. The Administrative Litigation Law allows Chinese citizens to sue local governments for unlawful administrative acts. But this legal right is limited in important ways. There are a number of restrictions on whom villagers can sue. They cannot sue any party committee or secretary, for example, because the party is not subject to administrative litigation—even though the party and government are often difficult to disentangle. Local authorities sometimes try to use this overlap and the party's immunity to deflect lawsuits.

Villagers, moreover, can sue only for specific misdeeds, not "abstract" decisions. And party committees may issue internal orders forbidding courts to accept suits on sensitive matters. Even when such prohibitions do not exist, a local court will often consult the party committee and government at the same level before it accepts litigation on a hot-button issue.

When villagers have managed to get cases into court, officials may intervene directly in the legal proceedings, employ unlawful means to induce plaintiffs to drop an action, or apply pressure on the judge who presides over a case. Even when villagers emerge victorious from the courtroom, it does not mean their grievances will be redressed. Rulings for plaintiffs sometimes go unexecuted when local governments either ignore or subvert them.

In some cases where villagers prevail and the verdict is duly executed, their gains are soon lost when officials retaliate. A survey of rural petitioners who went all the way to Beijing produced a suggestive finding. Of 450 complainants from 28 provinces who had filed administrative lawsuits, 32 percent said the court rejected their cases, 63 percent said that the court did not rule according to law, and 6 percent said they won the suits but the rulings were never enforced.

Hollow Rights

A fourth legal maneuver available to Chinese peasants is the right to reject unlawful fees imposed by local governments. In 1985 the central government granted villagers the right to reject financial demands that were not authorized by township people's congresses. The right was then reaffirmed in a 1991 State Council ruling and in the Agriculture Law, which was passed by the National People's Congress in 1993. Can Chinese villagers effectively exercise this right? Often they cannot because neither the 1991 regulation nor the 1993 law says anything about the procedure through which villagers may reject illicit impositions.

The right to reject illegal fees, significant as it is, amounts only to an individual, on-the-spot right to dodge if one can. It is not a right to actively resist a tax collector when he or she knocks down your door, let alone a license to engage in proactive prevention. Put another way, by granting this right the central government only allowed villagers to flee a fire that is coming their way. But it does not condone stomping out fires, or preventing them from starting in the first place. This is why local officials often feel free to ignore this right.

Local officials may even go so far as to employ coercion and explicit violence against those who insist on their rights. According to interviews conducted by Wang Xingfu, a well-known petitioner

from Yiyang county, Henan province, over 200 villagers were badly beaten during a "strike-hard" campaign against "tax-resisters" in 2002. None of the victims owed any state tax, and they were beaten simply because they refused to pay illicit local fees. If villagers can rarely defend their rights and interests alone, can they instead organize and negotiate with local governments over issues such as taxation and fees? By law they may. In practice they seldom can. The Chinese constitution grants all citizens freedom of association. Yet such freedom does not mean much, because the State Council's Regulation Concerning Registration and Management of Civil Organizations makes it virtually impossible for peasants to legally establish an organization for the purpose of defending their rights and interests against government infringement.

The regulation requires that all organizations register at a local civil affairs bureau. To register however, an organization must find a government department as its "professional supervisory unit" (*yewu zhuguan danwei*). Of course, it is usually impossible for villagers who wish to restrain government power to find such a unit in the same level of government they wish to charge with misconduct. In the words of a villager from Anhui who established a "peasant society for rights defense" without going through the formal registration procedure: "Where can we find such a unit? Nobody will accept us. If I want to find such a government department, I will have to beg the relevant officials. They will tell me: we can be your supervisory unit if you listen to us, pay all required fees, and do not engage in any excessive activities. Even if we find a supervisory unit, the civil affairs bureau will find a reason not to register us. If we go to the civil affairs bureau, they will say, it is a good thing, but we cannot register the organization for you because there is no precedent and there is no relevant regulation in the law."

Fixed Elections

Finally, because Chinese villagers have found defending their rights and interests by themselves difficult, perhaps a better alternative is the election of their own political representatives through local elections. But here again, the door appears to be open yet in fact is barely cracked. Chinese villagers have three occasions to vote. The first allows them to elect the director and members of villagers' committees, which have a responsibility to "convey residents' opinions and demands and make suggestions to the people's government." Two other pieces of legislation allow Chinese villagers to elect deputies to township and county people's congresses, who in turn elect heads and deputy heads of township and county governments.

So in theory Chinese peasants can hold administrators at the county, township, and village levels accountable by voting malfeasant officials out of office. In fact, however, elections of township and county people's congress deputies have remained under tight control by the Communist Party and government. Consequently, election of township and county government heads by people's deputies is little more than a formality in most places.

The exception is village elections, which have become freer and fairer since reasonably specific election procedures were laid out in the 1998 revised Organic Law of Villagers' Committees. In some places village elections have indeed improved the responsiveness of the village leadership and some elected cadres have become more assertive in raising objections to illicit taxes imposed by township governments. But the power of elected villagers' committee directors is still highly constrained because appointed village party secretaries remain by law the "leadership core" in the village. In other words, although a villagers' committee director may be popularly elected by hundreds or over a thousand villagers, he or she is, according to the Organic Law, only a lieutenant to the village party secretary, who is either handpicked by the township party committee or at best elected by several dozen party members in the village.

Furthermore, township governments in many places have continued to manipulate village elections to prevent independent-minded candidates from winning or even standing for election. Township governments have illegally recalled or suspended many popularly elected village leaders. In Shandong, Sichuan, and Hunan, some village directors who actively led the opposition to illicit fees and corrupt village party secretaries have even been jailed or sentenced to labor education.

Outside the Law

Chinese peasants engage in disruptive protests or even violence not because they lack "legal consciousness," but because lawful methods to redress their grievances generally do not work. They are fully aware of the risk of protest, but are, in the words of the Anhui villager quoted earlier, driven to protest, much like peasants in imperial China who were "forced to join the Liangshan Mountain rebels."

They petition in groups because individual petitioning or sending no more than five representatives to file a collective complaint typically takes them nowhere. They bypass lower levels of government because officials often procrastinate in making a ruling and protect each other. They take to the streets and hold demonstrations without police permission because they know they will never get permission. They petition Beijing in large numbers because they have failed to find a fair arbiter below. They resort to disruptive measures such as blocking public transportation, besieging government compounds, and holding sit-ins in government offices because they have no other way to pursue their lawful claims.

Government repression also drives villagers who seek to defend their rights and interests through lawful procedures toward confrontation and opposition. Numerous peaceful petitioners, especially leaders of collective petitioning, have experienced harsh crackdowns over the past two decades. My survey conducted in 2003–2005 painted a grim portrait of government repression. Of 1,314 petitioners from 28 provinces, many said they had been fined. Others had their homes ransacked or destroyed, their properties confiscated, or their valuables taken away. Some were sent to political study classes, which were in fact detention centers.

Cadres had beaten a fourth of the surveyed petitioners. Others were detained and arrested, sentenced to labor education camps or prisons, or paraded through the streets and publicly humiliated. A large number were framed for other crimes—for example, wrongfully accused of theft, tax evasion, or violation of the birth control policy. Some had family members beaten by cadres, or experienced retaliation by thugs hired by cadres.

Altogether, over 60 percent of the petitioners suffered one or more forms of local repression.

In some places, grassroots officials have even used annual "strike-hard anti-crime campaigns" to suppress protest leaders in the name of maintaining stability and safeguarding law and order. In late 1998 and early 1999, the Hengyang county government in Hunan had hundreds of protest leaders and their family members rounded up, many of whom were beaten badly, paraded through the streets like criminals, and even put up on makeshift stages to be denounced in "mass struggle meetings."

Yet forceful repression, either by the police or hired local toughs, often backfires. Large meetings to denounce protest leaders can, for instance, generate even stronger popular support for "rightful resisters" and can inspire efforts to rescue them or mount large-scale protests on the subject of the initial grievance.

Beijing's Blindness

Anxious to head off further rural unrest, China's leaders have greatly stepped up their efforts to appease popular discontent and rein in wayward local officials. In 2004, Prime Minister Wen pledged to abolish all agricultural taxes in five years—and then followed through three years ahead of schedule. More recently, Beijing has launched a campaign to "build a new socialist countryside," the centerpiece of which is a pledge to "give more and take less."

So far, however, the leadership has been emphasizing making new promises rather than finding ways to secure better implementation of beneficial policies that are already on the books. Beijing does not seem to appreciate that, since most "collective incidents" aim to defend rights recognized by the center that are being violated locally, the only long-term solution is to narrow the gap between what the central government promises and what local officials deliver. Or perhaps the leaders do understand this, but have not yet figured out how to make local officials do their bidding. Top-down measures have so far generally proved ineffective, and Beijing remains unwilling to ally itself with mistreated villagers by introducing democratic elections at the township or county levels.

Instead of checking local misconduct through the rule of law, enlarging freedom of the press, and introducing local elections at higher levels, the current leaders have instituted one feeble campaign after another. They first launched a campaign to indoctrinate local officials with a "scientific view of development" and a "correct view of political achievement." Then they initiated a campaign to "maintain the advanced nature of the party." The most recent campaign has sought to educate people about the "eight honors and eight shames." Even high-ranking central officials do not hide their contempt for such ineffective efforts to combat serious problems. Local officials, for their part, have innumerable political jokes about the "education" they have to endure, many of which spare no one and are frankly obscene.

The Chinese leadership has failed so far to address the political cause of mounting protests in the countryside: farmers do not have the right to act as a legitimate interest group. Beijing has done little more than allow villagers to defend their "lawful rights and interests" individually. They have not responded to various proposals that aim to improve rural governance by empowering Chinese peasants—such as suggestions to open up the election of deputies to township and county people's congresses, to introduce direct election of township heads, to reestablish "peasant societies," and to merge the petitioning system with the people's congress system so that local people's congresses may acquire more power and resources to supervise local governments, courts, and procurators. This latter proposal would move offices of letters and visits (*xinfang ban*) that are currently affiliated with the government, the judiciary, the police, and similar entities to the people's congress so that elected people's deputies will be in charge of receiving petitions.

Politics by Other Means

It remains to be seen whether current leaders have the courage and wisdom to overcome the party's longstanding distrust of an organized citizenry. One thing, however, is certain. Until they secure the right to defend themselves in organized groups, Chinese villagers will continue to launch more and more "collective incidents" to uphold rights that they believe they have, but which are not being respected by local officials. Beijing may wish to keep the rural population as apolitical and passive as possible, but it must understand that this is fast becoming an impossible task.

As Chinese villagers become better educated and better informed about laws and policies, their "consciousness of their lawful rights and interests" will only continue to grow. As the income gap between rural residents and urban dwellers widens, rural residents will become increasingly aware of various kinds of discrimination they suffer. Some of them, then, will seek a political resolution of their problems. And if the villagers cannot find solutions through lawful procedures like petitioning, litigation, group negotiation, and the ballot box, they will naturally turn to politics by other means.

BUILDING THE (CHINA) DREAM[*]

The Economist

Some historians believe that Marco Polo never went to China. But even if the 13th-century Venetian merchant did not lay eyes on the coastal city of Hangzhou himself, he certainly reflected the awe it inspired in other foreign traders when he described it as "beyond dispute the finest and the noblest in the world." And, "incredible as it may seem," he wrote, Hangzhou (which he called Kinsay) was but one of more than 1,200 "great and wealthy cities" in southern China. "Everything appertaining to this city is on so vast a scale ... that it is not easy even to put it in writing."

In Marco Polo's day it was the ornate palaces, paved roads and meticulously planned layouts of Chinese cities that impressed visitors; in today's megacities it is some of the world's tallest skyscrapers and largest shopping malls, interlinked by the world's longest bullet-train network. And if all goes according to the Communist Party's plan, the coming two decades will evoke a few more gasps.

By 2020 the high-speed rail network will expand by nearly two-thirds, with the addition of another 7,000 kilometers (4,300 miles). By then almost every city with a population of half a million or more will be connected to it. Tens of millions more migrants will have poured in from the countryside. Between now and 2030, says the World Bank, the average rise in the number of city-dwellers each year is likely to be around 13 million, roughly the population of Tokyo. In 2030 China's cities will be home to close to 1 billion people, or about 70% of the population, compared with 54% today. By some estimates the urban population will peak around 2040, still just shy of the 1 billion mark but close enough. As James McGregor, an American businessman, put it in his book *One Billion Customers*, published in 2005, the notion of a billion Chinese spenders has come to symbolize "the dream of staggering profits for those who get here first, the hype and hope that has mesmerized foreign merchants and traders for centuries."

After taking over as Party chief in 2012, Xi Jinping (now also president) launched his expected decade in power with a catchphrase: "The Chinese Dream." It was a striking break from the party's tradition of ideology-laden slogans. Now endlessly invoked in official speeches and the subject of numerous books and songs, the phrase is clearly intended to appeal to upwardly mobile urban residents striving for the comforts of their rich-world counterparts.

Only 15 years ago such a middle class barely existed in China. In 2011, when the country reached 50% urbanization, it had become obvious that the party's fate rested with the stability of cities and the contentedness of their middle-class residents. The largely rural country that Deng Xiaoping (himself of peasant stock) set out to "reform and open up" in the late 1970s had become overwhelmingly urban in its economic and political focus. Thanks mainly to a tide of migration, China's urban population had grown

---

[*] This article was published in *The Economist*, April 19, 2014.

by more than 500 million since Deng launched his reforms: the equivalent of all the people in the United States plus three Britains.

Li Keqiang, who took over as premier in 2013, sees further urbanization as critical to China's economic success. He has called it a "gigantic engine" for growth. Mr. Li and other officials are fond of quoting Joseph Stiglitz, a Nobel prize–winning American economist, who said that technological innovation in America and urbanization in China would be "two keys" to mankind's development in the 21st century.

A new grand plan for China's cities, overseen by the prime minister and published last month, admits to a number of problems, such as worsening pollution, urban sprawl, and congestion, as well as growing social tensions. It also points out that China's urbanization lags behind that of other countries at similar levels of development (typically around 60%), and that there remains "quite a lot of room" for further urban growth.

Getting cities right will help China to keep growing fast for years to come. Getting them wrong would be disastrous, bringing worsening inequality (which the World Bank says has approached "Latin American levels," although Chinese officials insist it has recently been improving), the spread of slums, the acceleration of global climate change (cities consume three-quarters of China's energy, which comes mainly from coal), and increasing social unrest.

After more than a decade of spectacular growth in China, much of it in double digits, doubts are setting in both at home and abroad about the sustainability of the "China Model." Growth is slowing. Lavish spending by local governments has piled up huge debts. Increasing numbers of middle-class Chinese are looking for bolt holes abroad for themselves, their families and their assets. Scandals involving senior officials have revealed corruption on a gargantuan scale. Censors generally succeed in preventing antiparty messages from spreading widely but micro bloggers with thousands of followers still boldly relay damning critiques.

Mr. Xi describes the country's problems and his approach to solving them in colorful terms. Reforms, he says, have entered a "deep-water area." China must "venture along dangerous paths to break through barriers to reform." In tackling

corruption it will need the resolve of a man who must "cut off his own snake-bitten hand to save his life." At a plenum of the Central Committee in November the party declared that market forces must play a "decisive role," the strongest support it has ever expressed for the market. This seems all the more stirring after years of vacillation under Mr. Xi's predecessor, Hu Jintao, who retreated from reform in the face of powerful resistance by vested interests, above all local governments, huge state-owned enterprises and, ironically, the new middle class, which would rather not share the fruits of growth with rural migrants.

Why Cities Matter

All the most important reforms that Mr. Xi needs to tackle involve the movement to China's cities. He must give farmers the same property rights as urban residents so they can sell their homes (currently all but impossible) and leave the land with cash in hand. He must sort out the mess of local-government finances, which depend heavily on grabbing land from farmers and selling it to developers. He must loosen the grip of state-owned enterprises on the commanding heights of the economy and make them hand over more of their profits to the government. He must move faster to clean up the urban environment, especially its noxious air, and prevent the growth of China's cities from exacerbating climate change. And he must start giving urban residents a say in how their cities are run.

This list is both daunting and urgent. The recent growth of China's cities has created two new social forces whose concerns Mr. Xi cannot afford to ignore. One is a vast migrant population (including the urban-born children of recent migrants from the countryside) that now makes up more than one-third of the urban total of 730 million. It is far harder for a member of this group to gain official recognition as a city-dweller in his own country, with all the welfare benefits and access to public services that status confers, than to gain citizenship in America or Europe if he were to migrate there. The harsh treatment of China's internal migrants is creating huge social divisions that could erupt in serious unrest.

The other new force is the urban middle class, now thought to be roughly the same size as the migrant population, which numbers around 260 million. It has been kept reasonably content by the rapid growth of the past few years, but that may not last. China's middle classes, like those elsewhere, worry about property: how to protect it from the whims of urban planners and party officials, what is happening to prices, and what to do if the bubble bursts. Increasingly unaffordable house prices, or conversely a steep drop, might prompt different ends of the middle-class spectrum to protest. So too might the party's many sins and blunders: a food-safety scandal, perhaps, linked to official corruption.

Like his predecessors, Mr. Xi is nipping signs of unrest in the bud. Dissidents who have done little more than briefly raise protest banners in tiny groups are being thrown into jail. But there are also some positive signs. He has taken charge of a new party organ, a small group of officials with a wide range of portfolios, who are working to improve policy coordination and overcome bureaucratic resistance to change. It even has a task force dedicated to building "democracy and the legal system," although that may not get very far. Mr. Xi has also launched a fierce campaign against high-level corruption which, though unlikely to offer a lasting cure to the endemic problem of graft, could scare officials into compliance with his reform plans.

A Dwindling Labor Supply

As economic growth slows and the pool of surplus labor in the countryside shrinks, the speed of urbanization will diminish. For the past few years about 9 million people have been moving into cities every year. The number will fall to 7 million in the second half of this decade and 5 million in the 2020s, according to Jin Sanlin of the Development Research Centre, a government think-tank. By 2017, he writes, that supply of surplus labor in the countryside will have all but disappeared.

Chinese officials note that the speed of urbanization in China has been far faster than in Western countries during their industrial transformations. It took China only 30 years to climb from 20% urbanization to today's 54%. In Britain the equivalent journey took 100 years and in America 60. However, in more recent times, population growth

in urban China has been slower than in countries such as South Korea and Indonesia during their period of rapid economic development, mainly because of China's discriminatory policies against migrants and its state monopoly on rural land sales.

By any measure, the country's urbanization has been impressive. Shanghai is about to finish a 121-story American-designed skyscraper that will be the world's second tallest building (after Dubai's Burj Khalifa). Whole new urban districts, underground railways, modern airports and inter-city expressways have been built on a scale and at a pace most countries would be proud of. But China has failed to reap the full benefits of city growth. This is becoming a pressing problem in the face of diminishing returns from pouring ever more concrete.

Spreading the Wealth: A Billion Shoppers

Deng Hong's ambition, according to a Chinese newspaper, was to build a city inside a single building: a "temperature-controlled paradise." Last September his dream edifice, the New Century Global Center, formally opened in the south-western city of Chengdu. China's official media call it the world's largest building. Its centerpiece is a shopping mall of such arresting dimensions that many visitors pause on arrival to take souvenir photographs. It boasts a 300-meter indoor beach, a skating rink and an IMAX cinema. The Chinese often say that theirs is a country of too many people and too little land. The cavernous Global Center building begs to differ.

Mr. Deng did not attend the launch ceremony. He was in custody, suspected of being involved in a corruption scandal that has also ensnared a former mayor of Chengdu, who in turn may be linked to an even bigger case linked to a former member of the Politburo Standing Committee, Zhou Yongkang. Mr. Deng's troubles are an uncomfortable reminder of the perils of hubris. Massive buildings help to boost local officials' egos and brand their cities. According to the Council on Tall Buildings and Urban Habitat, an American industry association, China has about 200 skyscrapers over 250 meters tall, four times as many as America. Close to Mr. Deng's building is an office complex reminiscent of Beijing's "bird's nest" stadium that cost 1.2 billion *yuan* ($175m) to build. It was supposed to become the city government's headquarters, but after a public outcry over its extravagance its leaders decided to move to more modest buildings nearby.

The Global Center, though, is also a monument to an increasingly essential ingredient of China's economic development: consumption on a scale that helps to lessen the country's dependence on infrastructure investment as an engine of growth. China's leaders want citizens to save less and spend more. Mr. Deng's brainchild is a proud declaration by a local government far inland that it wants a consumer culture like that in megacities such as Beijing, Shanghai, Guangzhou, and Shenzhen. The capital's most iconic new structures are stadiums, office buildings and a colossal egg-shaped center for the performing arts. Chengdu's is a jaw-dropping shopping experience.

Chengdu, the capital of Sichuan province, is a "second-tier" city, a loosely defined category that includes most provincial capitals; yet it is rapidly gaining the "first-tier" status of Shanghai, 1,600 kilometers (1,000 miles) to the east. That suits China's leaders, who are trying to boost consumption in regions that have fared less well in China's almost uninterrupted boom of the past 35 years. Thanks to massive government investment since the turn of the 21st century the gap between the wealthy east and the far less developed west of China has narrowed. According to the Economist Intelligence Unit, average GDP per person in China's western provinces in the late 1990s had dropped to about one-third the figure in the nine eastern coastal provinces; but by 2012 it had recovered to more than half, the highest level since China launched its economic reforms in the late 1970s.

The Global Center seems to be reckoning on a fair number of wealthy spenders in Chengdu: it provides 15,000 parking spaces. It is also readily accessible by the city's first metro line, which opened in 2010 (there are now two lines, and plans for an underground network of more than 350 kilometers by 2020, close to the length of London's). But Chengdu's new middle classes much prefer to drive. The city has more than 3m private cars, second only to the number in Beijing. And on weekends the center already seems to be packing visitors in.

Consuming Passions, Continued

Like the rest of the country, though, Chengdu is beginning to slow down. The city estimates that its GDP last year grew by about 10%, two percentage points less than it was aiming for and the lowest rate since 1999. Nationally the picture is much the same. This year's overall growth target is for 7.5%, the same as last year's and a far cry from the double-digit advances of most of the past decade. But that does not mean household spending will falter. Andy Rothman of Matthews Asia, an investment firm, calls China "hands down the best consumption story on the planet." Retail sales last year went up by 11.5% in real terms, after 12.1% in 2012 and 11.6% in 2011. China's household spending over the past few years was holding up well, he argues. It was just that investment grew even faster.

A "rebalancing" may be under way. Except for a dip last year, the share of GDP growth contributed by households and the government has been rising. In 2011 and 2012 it exceeded that contributed by investment for the first time since the middle of the past decade. Last year China overtook Japan to become the world's second-largest consumer economy.

However, there is a lot more that China's leaders could do to achieve the goal set by the premier in March: that the country should "fully tap the enormous consumption potential of more than a billion people." The Global Center was not built for the mass market, as attested by a display inviting shoppers to invest in luxury resort property in Thailand. A large group of people living in China's cities is, in effect, "shut out of the urban consumer economy," says Tom Miller, author of *China's Urban Billion*: the one-third of urban residents who have migrated from the countryside. They make up about 40% of urban labor and the majority of China's workforce in manufacturing and services, but they spend very little.

As Mr. Miller notes, this is changing, thanks to a shift in China's demography. In 2012 China's working-age population (those between 15 and 59; most Chinese retire young) began to shrink. In response to shortages of young, unskilled labor, local governments have been raising minimum wages. This has been good for inland cities like Chengdu, which have benefited from production shifting westward in search of lower labor costs. It has also been great for migrants: their average wages doubled between 2005 and 2011, to about 2,050 *yuan* ($322) a month, and last year rose by nearly 14%. But a lot remains to be done to turn these migrants into big spenders.

A good start would be to change their official household registration, or *hukou*, to the city entitling them to the welfare benefits and access to public services enjoyed by other city dwellers and thus releasing some of their spending power. Migrants have an unusually high savings rate, far higher than that of either urbanites or rural dwellers, perhaps to compensate for the absence of welfare benefits. According to Chi Fulin of the China Institute for Reform and Development, rural migrants on average spend 2.7 times as much when they move to urban areas as they did at home. But they still need to save to make up for their lack of entitlement to housing and other benefits. If they also change their *hukou*, their expenditure more than triples.

Yet for most migrants changing *hukou* is next to impossible. They continue to be called *mingong* (peasant workers) no matter how long they have been living in the city and so do their children, even if urban-born and raised. For reasons of equity as well as economic advantage, *hukou* reform has become urgent.

The Rural-Urban Divide: Ending Apartheid

For China's reforms to work, its citizens have to be made more equal. Migrants encounter barriers of speech, habits and manners the world over, but in China these are heavily reinforced by the system of *hukou*, or household registration, which permits routine discrimination against migrants by bureaucrats as well as by urbanites (a term applied in this special report to city-dwellers who have no rural connections themselves, and nor do their parents). In a survey conducted by the Chinese Academy of Social Sciences, nearly one-third of respondents in Shanghai said they would not like to live next door to a migrant, against only one-tenth who said they would rather not live next to a poor person. In Changchun, a less outward-looking city in the north-east, nearly two-thirds said they did not want to live next to a migrant.

Chinese urbanites seem as anxious as Europeans about migration from poor to rich places, even though in China the migrants are fellow citizens.

In one crucial respect, however, they fall short of that status. A migrant may have been living in a city for many years, but his *hukou* will still identify him as rural. The document acts as an internal passport. China's first constitution in 1954 said that citizens enjoyed "freedom of residence and freedom to change their residence." Four years later Mao Zedong introduced the *hukou* system in order to prevent a flood of migrants pouring into the cities. It was eased only in the 1980s when China needed cheap labor for its factories. But the pernicious legacy of *hukou*-induced apartheid persists today.

If China's level of urbanization were calculated on the basis of *hukou*, rather than residency, it would be a mere 36%, not far ahead of India's (31%). Very few of those who have migrated to the cities over the past three decades have obtained urban *hukou*. This matters a lot because a person's *hukou*, rather than his place of residence, determines the level of welfare benefits he is entitled to. The city-born children of migrants suffer the same discrimination, often being denied access to urban state-run schools and having to clear higher hurdles to get into university.

The *hukou* divide is sharpest of all in China's "first-tier" megacities, which are among the biggest magnets for migrants. In some, including Beijing, they are not allowed to buy cars or houses unless they meet what for most would be impossibly exacting conditions. Thus, as China's middle class has expanded rapidly, a similarly large group of urban "second-class citizens" (as even the official media have sometimes called the migrants) has grown in parallel. Not that it matters in a one-party autocracy but migrants and their urban-raised offspring are not even allowed to vote in the cities.

In the decade to 2010 the migrant population living in cities grew by more than 80%, a colossal influx that pushed up the total number of urban residents by some 200 million. China has been remarkably successful in controlling the spread of urban slums: over the same period the proportion of city-dwellers living in slums fell by one-quarter to below 30%, according to a UN study. Many of these slum dwellings are relatively smart compared with their counterparts in other developing countries, thanks to tough controls on building shanty towns.

Risking an Explosion

Even so, migrants often live in grim conditions. Out of sight are pockets of wretchedness similar to slums in developing countries such as India. One such is the village of Dongxiaokou north of Beijing, just beyond the edge of the city's urban core. A village only in name, it is essentially a center for processing waste. Thousands of migrants, most of them from impoverished villages in a single prefecture of the central province of Henan, prepare sacksful of tin cans, piles of iron scrap and mountains of plastic bottles for bulk sale to recycling plants.

It is a scene of Dickensian poverty with migrants packed into tiny brick shacks off muddy, rubbish-strewn streets. Their children go to ramshackle private schools that charge around 4,500 *yuan* ($725) a year, several weeks' income for many migrants. For most of them there are no places at state schools. If migrants fall seriously ill, they have little choice but to go back to their villages; their government-subsidized rural medical insurance is often not valid in a different province (or even, until last year, in a different part of Henan). The only migrants who have urban health insurance are those with formal job contracts, but not even one in five enjoys that privilege.

The party appears to be waking up to the disruptive potential of an urban underclass. Early in 2013 Li Keqiang, the premier, began calling for a "human-centered new style of urbanization." In November last year the party decided to speed up the pace of *hukou* reform. Officials have been calling for "equal rights" for all urban residents. A new word has entered the party lexicon: *shiminhua,* which means turning a migrant into an urbanite with all the perks of a city *hukou*-holder. The declared aim of urbanization now is not just to move people into cities, but more importantly to make urbanites of them.

That will be both costly and hugely contentious. Mr. Li's plan for a new style of urbanization was published in March after many months of bickering among officials. It glossed over the crucial question of how to pay for it all, which hints at strong resistance by local governments

that do not want to foot the bill, and by urbanites who fear their privileged access to education and health care will be stripped away. Li Tie, a government researcher, in a book last year wrote that online support for *hukou*-related reforms was "not running high." Part of the problem, he said, was that policymakers, journalists, and online commentators were themselves urban *hukou*-holders and as such formed a "rigid interest group," posing a "severe" challenge to reforms.

At the same time many holders of rural *hukou,* despite the discrimination they suffer, are suspicious of moves to give them urban status. They fear that it might lose them the right (conferred by rural *hukou*) to a small patch of farmland and a residential plot in their village of registration. Mr. Li's urbanization plan failed to provide reassurance.

In July last year the agriculture ministry conducted a survey of nearly 7,000 rural *hukou* holders, mostly male and living in the countryside, which found that only about a quarter regarded getting an urban *hukou* as important. Even among those whose entire families were living in urban areas, the share was only just over half. The main reason for not wanting urban *hukou,* the survey found, was fear of losing entitlements to land. Last October a senior official on the National Health and Family Planning Commission said that as many as 70% of rural migrants wanted to stay in the cities but had no wish to give up their rural *hukou.* That chimes with the views of the waste-recycling migrants of Dongxiaokou village. One middle-aged man standing by the roadside says he would far rather have his tiny patch of land in backward Henan province than a promise of a pension in wealthy Beijing.

Losing the Plot

Given the discrimination they face, it seems odd that migrants themselves resist reform, but they will continue to do so until the government allows them to sell their land and sever their ties with the countryside for good. Mr. Li has promised this, but local governments, used to seizing land at will, are loathe to give up that privilege.

The new urbanization plan calls for 100 million migrants to be given urban *hukou* by 2020, but there will still be conditions: at a minimum, applicants will need a stable job and a legal place of residence. That would rule out most migrants, who often live in unauthorized lodgings and work without contracts.

Officials sometimes hold up the city of Zhongshan in the southern province of Guangdong as an example of how *hukou* reform could work. Since 2007 migrants into the city (who make up more than half its population) have been able to apply for city *hukou* on the basis of points scored for educational qualifications, ownership of property, payments of social-security contributions, and volunteer work (such as giving blood). Yet since the scheme was launched, only around 30,000 out of a total migrant population of 1.6 million have gained local *hukou* this way. Migrants can also use their points to apply for just some of the benefits associated with urban *hukou,* which has enabled them to secure places at state-run schools for about 25,000 of their children. But that is out of a total of 200,000 migrant children attending school in Zhongshan (and many more who are studying in their parents' villages of origin). All the same, in January Zhongshan won a prestigious award in Beijing for its points system.

In June 2012 three days of large-scale rioting erupted in Shaxi, a satellite town of Zhongshan, fed by rumors that security agents had maltreated the son of a migrant worker who was involved in a fight. Peng Ronghui of Zhongshan's department in charge of migrant management admits that the city's migrant population has created "a problem of social control." She says they "lack a sense of belonging and their morale and self-discipline is relatively poor."

Cities like Zhongshan worry that lifting *hukou* restrictions would require massive extra spending on public services such as education, health care and housing. Yet most local governments would simply not be up to the task.

Seizing Land and Running Up Debts Is No Way to Finance Local Government

Residents of Chaobei New City know what it is like to be "upstairsed"—the word for turfing farmers off their land, pushing them out of their homes and making them move into newly built clusters of blocks of flats without lifts. It is forced urbanization, to which local governments have taken with relish in their rush to acquire precious land. Chaobei New City is the reincarnation of six flattened villages: a desolate, prison-like, rubbish-strewn ghetto. On a concrete wall along one side, billboards spell out the risks of protesting. For example, depositing funeral wreaths, ashes from cremations, or corpses at government petitioning offices could be treated as crimes.

Chaobei New City's very name conveys the mindset of those who ordered it built: officials who hoped that by destroying the villages and building 56 blocks of flats in their place they could create a semblance of urbanity. The residents would still be classified as peasants for welfare purposes, but the statistics would count them as urban. To local officials, who take enormous pride in urbanization rates, such numbers matter. Xianghe County to which the "new city" belongs, is in Hebei province, about 45 kilometers (30 miles) east of Beijing. Like almost every other local government in China, Xianghe's has an urbanization target: 60% by 2017, up from around 50% today and ahead of the national target of 60% by 2020. Since the global financial crisis in 2008, governments have been hardening such objectives as a way of stimulating growth, and have been borrowing heavily to meet them. The result has been a rapidly growing pile of debt that has spooked global investors.

Seizing land is an easy way of acquiring cash or collateral for borrowing, and since the 1990s this technique has become a favorite of local governments. Some have used the pretext of building what they call "new-style rural communities," such as Chaobei New City. Such schemes have uprooted millions of farmers around the country. In one prefecture alone, Chinese media quoted a local leader in 2010 as saying he planned to flatten villages with a total population of 1 million within three to five years. The coastal province of Shandong has moved more than 12.5 million villagers into nearly 5,200 "new-style rural communities" since 2009, according to the local government. It calls this "urbanization on the spot."

Mod Cons from Hell

Central-government officials have expressed alarm and (ineffectually) reminded local governments that resettlement must be voluntary. Beijing newspapers have run several exposés of the horrors of being "upstairsed," comparing the phenomenon to Britain's enclosure movement of the 18th and 19th centuries when landlords stripped farmers of their right to use common land. Last September *Xinmin Evening News,* a Shanghai newspaper, described cracks in Chaobei New City's buildings, flooded basements, sagging ceilings and a leaky sewage system.

Angry victims of forced appropriations are legion. According to state-controlled media, seizures of rural land by local governments are the cause of 60% of mass petitionings in China and of nearly 4 million disputes every year. Lynette Ong of the University of Toronto says almost all compulsory relocations involve gangs or secret societies, often hired by local governments to push farmers out. Occasionally evictions trigger large-scale protests, but strong-arm tactics usually deter farmers from putting up much resistance. The thuggery, often brought to light by social media, is a political embarrassment to the central government. But what is behind these land grabs is of far greater concern: a financial system that has gone wrong and a system of local governance that has become dangerously dysfunctional.

Chaobei New City is symptomatic of both. The local government sold ten hectares (25 acres) of the land seized from the villagers to a local developer, Xiu Lan Real Estate Group. The company is using it to build Rivedroite Town, a cluster of lavish French-style houses separated by a wide road from the farmers' new flats. It is unclear how much Xiu Lan is investing or where the money is coming from, but the company's website suggests it has a close relationship with large state-owned trust companies. Such institutions are a widespread and openly acknowledged source of financing for property projects. Their lending is less strictly regulated than that of formal banks. A cozy relationship between both types of institution has enabled what Stephen Green of Standard Chartered calls "shadowy activity" by formal banks, which use their informal counterparts to channel lending into property and other risky projects.

Some trust companies and banks raise funds by selling fixed-term investments known as wealth-management products (WMPS). These promise better returns than bank deposits, interest rates on which are capped at extremely low or even negative real levels—a legacy of Maoist banking that has proved hard to shake-off. But this short-term finance often supports long-term projects, creating a dangerous maturity mismatch. And some institutions may be repaying maturing products with fresh funds raised from new ones. In 2012 Xiao Gang, then chairman of the state-owned Bank of China and now in charge of regulating the country's stock markets, described this as "to some extent . . . a Ponzi scheme."

In theory banks are not liable when WMPS go wrong. In practice, when defaults have occasionally loomed, ways are almost always found of keeping investors from losing much, if anything (including in the biggest potential default so far, of a $490 million trust product issued through China's biggest bank, ICBC, that was due to mature in January; a stalled mining venture related to the project suddenly got official permission to go ahead).

Local governments, which in China cannot borrow from formal banks or sell municipal bonds without central-government backing, are among the biggest borrowers through such shadow channels. They mostly use the money to finance public works (including knocking down villages in the hope that resulting "urbanization" might stimulate growth). In response to the global financial crisis of 2008 the central government loosened controls on bank lending. The volume of new loans doubled in 2009. Much of the money found its way indirectly into the hands of local governments which used it in a spending binge in an effort to maintain growth. As a result, debts soared. Along with WMPS, this has become the biggest worry to bearish observers of China's economy.

There are good reasons for concern about local-government borrowing, and about the banks and trust firms, but financial meltdown looks unlikely. An audit made public in December showed that in mid-2013 local governments directly owed 10.9 trillion *yuan* ($1.8 trillion), an increase of more than 60% on 2009. This is by no means crippling. Taken together with other debts for which local governments are, or might be, liable, such as those of local state-owned enterprises, it amounts to one-third of GDP. The central government would never allow a local government to default, so these debts are for the center to worry about. GK Dragonomics, a research firm, says total government debt may be 70–80% of GDP, still well below the levels of many rich countries with lower growth.

Local Governments Receive Half the Nation's Fiscal Revenue—But Are Responsible for 80% of Spending

Risks are certainly growing. Standard & Poor's, a credit-rating agency, points out that projects which once looked viable may cease being so as growth slows. It outlines a possible scenario: a WMP fails, investors stop buying new products, and non-bank credit dries up. Investment slows and property prices drop. Non-performing loans rise, putting pressure on banks. Credit slows further, and growth with it. In the event of such a crisis, however, the central government could take bad loans off the banks' books and order them to resume lending. It could also ramp up its own spending. It would not solve the problem, but could avert an immediate crisis.

To reduce such risks, China must introduce a range of reforms. The most pressing of these is to lift controls on bank-deposit interest, which would reduce depositors' incentives to shift money into riskier WMPS. There are signs that it is gradually moving that way, but for all the recent talk of the importance of markets, progress remains slow. Zhou Xiaochuan, the governor of China's central bank, in March held out the possibility of full liberalization of interest rates in a year or two. Banks themselves are not keen because higher rates would cut their profit margins.

Reform is also slow in two areas that are key to local governments' woes: the way in which their spending obligations, such as on public works, are funded; and the ownership of rural land. Changes in both are vital if China's new "human-centered" urbanization is to succeed and officials' rapacious instinct to grab land is to be tamed.

Local governments' lack of money to cover their spending needs is a problem of the Communist Party's own making. In 1994, worried about the central government's rapidly declining share of the country's total revenue, the party reorganized the tax system to boost the Center's takings. But it failed to reduce the burden on local governments, which have remained responsible for such coffer-draining activities as providing education and health care. The central government transfers funds to local ones (via provincial governments) to cover basic costs, but this is often far from enough. Local governments receive half of the nation's fiscal revenue but are responsible for 80% of spending.

To make up shortfalls, local officials turn to rural land. Whereas the property rights of urbanites were strengthened from the late 1990s, thanks to the privatization of urban housing and legislation to protect it from government interference, the property rights of villagers have remained vulnerable to abuse. Landesa Rural Development Institute, an American NGO, found that in 1,791 villages it surveyed, the number of land seizures had nearly tripled between 2007 and 2011. Land-related income, which in 2001 made up one-sixth of local-government revenue, had soared to three-quarters a decade later.

Counting the Cost

Giving urban benefits to migrants will cost a lot of money. Unless a new way of funding local governments can be found, they are likely to solve the problem in the time-honored manner: by seizing yet more land. The central government might help, but could it afford to? Estimates of the likely expense vary widely. A report this year by the Chinese Academy of Social Sciences put the cost of providing a migrant worker with full urban benefits at 130,000 *yuan*. A government study in 2010 came up with a figure of 80,000 *yuan*. But Kam Wing Chan of the University of Washington writes that even at about 100,000 *yuan* per migrant, the total would still be manageable.

Mr. Chan calculates that it would add up to around 23 trillion *yuan*, or more than 44% of China's GDP in 2012. That would be more than any economy could cope with, but it would not happen all at once. If it were done gradually, bringing in 20 million migrants annually, it would mean spending a far more manageable 3.8% of 2012 GDP a year. But in fact those 100,000 *yuan* of healthcare and other expenses would be stretched out over a lifetime, so the actual annual cost of converting 20 million people to full urbanite status would be 0.1% of 2013 GDP, Mr. Chan reckons: about one-fifth of what China spent on the 2008 Olympic Games.

That would leave the task of giving full property rights to farmers. Doing so would make it more difficult for local governments to seize land, which in turn would make it harder for them to find ready collateral for piling up huge debts. Most importantly, it would empower farmers, and perhaps even end the tyranny of village officials who use their control over land to fill their pockets. Last November the Party pledged to allow rural land (though not arable land) to enter the market on the same terms as any other property. This will take time: even deciding who owns what in the countryside will be tricky. And local governments are not keen to dispense with a ready source of cash.

But the Party has to press ahead. If financial and social stability are not sufficiently powerful incentives, there is another to consider: the rampant urban sprawl encouraged by local governments' ability to seize rural land at will. Such unrestrained expansion may work in parts of America where there is plenty of empty land (albeit at a cost to the environment and often to the quality of life). In China, where urbanization has forced around 40 million farmers off their land over the past three decades, usually with little or no compensation, it will not.

Urban Sprawl: People, not Paving

China's largest cities can mostly cope with population growth. The spread of concrete is a bigger problem. To grasp the size of China's largest cities, and the pace of expansion of even the remotest of them, consider the southwestern city of Kunming. Looking at a map, it would be easy to dismiss it as a backwater, tucked in a mountainous subtropical corner of China that borders on some of Southeast Asia's poorest countries: Vietnam, Laos, and Myanmar. Yunnan, the province of which Kunming is the capital, is one of China's most backward, with a nominal GDP per person roughly that of Albania. By the standards of China's provincial capitals Kunming's urban population is merely middling, yet at 3.8 million it roughly equals that of America's second-largest city, Los Angeles. By the end of this decade it is likely to have risen by 50%.

There will, however, be no mushrooming of shanty towns along the shore of Dian Lake, Yunnan's largest and the one-time pride of Kunming (ill-regulated urban growth has since turned it so toxic that its water is deemed unfit even for industrial use). Officials have what they think is a far better plan: building a new suburb called Chenggong. This will account for most of a projected 40% expansion of the built-up area of the city of Kunming. Kunming's urban-planning exhibition promises "a beautiful environment" for Chenggong.

Work on the new addition is already well underway. Thickets of residential tower blocks and office buildings are sprouting. Chenggong was connected to Kunming's new metro network last year. City-government offices and local universities have already moved there. By 2016 it will have a $525 million bullet train station with one of its 30 tracks connecting to Shanghai, 2,000 kilometers (1,200 miles) to the east. By the end of this decade the population of Chenggong is expected to reach nearly 1 million, three times its current level. Not so long ago Chenggong was derided as a ghost city in the making. Few are now so scornful.

Kunming's orgy of urban expansion sits oddly with a long-established Chinese policy of seeking to limit the population growth of large cities. An urban-planning law adopted in 1989 calls for strict control. Even after a decade of huge expansion in which the urban population of Beijing (including its satellite towns) grew by about 7 million to nearly 17 million, the party still clings to the hope that it can keep such expansion in check. When it unveiled plans for wide-ranging economic reforms last November, it called again for "strict control over the population size of extra-large cities." For all the party's recent emphasis on the role of market forces, they are still not allowed to determine people's movements.

Kunming could now argue that it is not "extra-large." The central government's new urbanization plan released in March suggests that the term applies only to cities with urban populations over 5 million. On this definition only about 15 cities qualify, and they do not include Kunming. Previously, however, "extra-large" had meant any city with more than 1 million people, of which China has more than 130. (America, by contrast, has a mere nine in this category.) A little redefinition goes a long way.

The central government wants cities to grow, but prefers the smaller ones to grow faster than the rest. Its new urbanization plan calls for *hukou* barriers to be scrapped altogether in cities with fewer than 500,000 urban residents. Those bigger than 500,000 have been asked to remove or relax *hukou* rules, but in an "orderly" or "reasonable" manner, meaning not all at once. In extra-large cities tough *hukou* restrictions are to remain in place. Yet in the past decade the populations of small cities have been shrinking, largely because bigger ones have proved to be a much more powerful draw for migrants.

Plenty of Room for More

The government's worries about population size are overblown. Chinese cities are by no means unusually crowded. Three Chinese scholars, Ming Lu and Zhao Chen of Shanghai's Fudan University, and Zheng Xu of the University of Connecticut, argue in a recent paper that apart from cities with 10 million people or more, the average big city in China has "a lot of room for growth." Even greater Beijing, which city officials think is bursting at the seams, is far less densely populated than greater Tokyo.

Rather than try to control population size, the central government would do better to have a go at curbing the spatial expansion of cities. Local bureaucrats have a predilection for vast areas of concrete. Plazas, broad boulevards, and colossal airports and railway stations have become their badges of honor. In the central city of Zhengzhou, what local officials called the largest bullet train station in Asia opened in 2012: a $2.4 billion edifice with a plaza in front which together covers around 240 hectares (about 340 football fields). The station is half-deserted.

Such extravagant use of land and money will only increase if the government continues to encourage cities to expand their populations. Built-up areas across the country have recently been growing by an average of 8% a year whereas their populations have been rising by only 5%. In western China the gap is far wider, with urban areas growing three times faster than their populations, according to Fudan University's Mr. Lu. Kunming provides evidence of extravagant habits. Luo Chun, a professor at Yunnan University, reckons his institution's new campus in Chenggong district is five times the size of its old one in the center of Kunming. The original campus remains in use.

Central officials are concerned about this, but for the wrong reasons. They fear that urban sprawl could make it more difficult for China to maintain near-self-sufficiency in staple foods. The country is already hovering close to what officials describe as a "red line" of 120 million hectares available for planting such crops. Even so, grain production has been rising. Thanks to fewer people in the countryside, farming is becoming more efficient.

A better reason to worry about sprawl is that it is making China's cities less "harmonious and livable," to use a phrase in vogue among the country's city planners. Old neighborhoods are being demolished, their inhabitants scattered into far-flung gated communities, commuting times are lengthening, car-dependence is growing and the spatial divide between rich and poor is widening. All this contributes to what officials call the country's growing "urban disease."

Greenery: Let Us Breathe

The term "Eco City" first took off with a book written in 1987 by Richard Register, a green thinker based in California. Now what may become the world's first city with the word in its name is beginning to take shape in the unlikely setting of a smog-shrouded expanse of salty mud on the northern Chinese coast. Around a lake that not so long ago was a sewage farm, energy-efficient apartment blocks are going up. Electric buses ply the still largely empty streets. Public litter bins are equipped with solar lighting so that residents can find them more easily at night. China's urban growth is warming up the planet, and the elaborately named Sino-Singapore Tianjin Eco-City is being touted as a cool solution.

Few other countries could dream of building a large city from scratch, let alone an eco one, but China has the advantage of an autocratic approach to urban planning (and to governance in general). It can decree that a piece of land will become a green city commandeer it and sell it cheaply to developers. That is how the eco-project began in 2007 when Singapore proposed a co-operative green-city venture. China's leaders agreed, having recently awoken to the environmental horrors wrought by breakneck urban expansion. Later that year the party formally declared that its goal was to build an "ecological civilization." The 30 square kilometers of inhospitable terrain near the northern port city of Tianjin became a test bed.

China has tried a couple of eco-city projects before and failed. About 60 kilometers (40 miles) farther along the coast to the east of Tianjin, in Caofeidian, work began in 2009 on an eco-city aiming for 500,000 residents by 2020. Yet most of the site remains a wilderness, too remote to attract developers. In Shanghai, plans a decade ago for a similar-sized eco-city on an alluvial island became entangled in local corruption and never got off the ground. But Tianjin's, with strong backing from central and local governments, is making progress.

To give it a flying start, officials designated it as China's first industrial park devoted to the animation industry. The $690 million state-funded zone opened in 2011 and has attracted hundreds of businesses. To lure in more residents, the government built a Victorian-style school in brown brick with lavish facilities, including a room full of stuffed animals to help children learn about nature ("all real, except the tiger and the panda," says a proud teacher). A 350-bed hospital, supposedly one of the best in China, is due to be completed next year, at a cost of $110 million.

At a control center a dozen officials watch a giant screen displaying readings from heating and water systems, as well as feeds from closed-circuit cameras at traffic intersections. "If an emergency happens, we can respond," says an official surveying the images of lifeless streets. Officials are not deterred by the "ghost city" label. The city opened two years ago and now has 10,000 residents. By 2030 it aims to have 350,000. Work is due to begin this year on subway lines that will make it easier for locals to get to Tianjin, currently about an hour's drive away, and nearby industrial zones.

The government has a powerful incentive to support the project. Within China, public resentment of its deteriorating environment, particularly the noxious haze over its cities, is growing, and abroad the country is being criticized for its contribution to global warming. In 2006 China became the world's biggest emitter of carbon from energy, overtaking America; it is now spewing out nearly double America's level. The spread of Chinese smog across the region is worrying neighbors such as South Korea and Japan.

Ho Tong Yen, the Singaporean CEO of the eco-city's development company (and a director of Mr. Register's Californian consultancy, Eco-city Builders), says he believes many of the eco-city's methods will eventually become "a key part of urbanization in China." A decade ago, he recalls, Chinese officials he met at conferences would boast about their cities' GDP growth. Now they brag about how green their cities are.

A Work in Progress

This sounds like a bit of a stretch. China's urban landscapes appear to be the antithesis of green: smog, foul-smelling streams and canals, roads jammed with exhaust-belching cars, shoddy buildings erected with little heed to building codes. But growing public discontent with the urban environment is beginning to change at least the rhetoric of officials, and in some cities their actions as well. In recent years about a third of China's 600-plus municipalities have announced plans to turn themselves into eco-cities. The central government has imposed stricter controls on emissions of carbon and smog-forming pollutants. In March the premier, Li Keqiang, declared "war" on pollution. Smog, he said, was nature's "red-light warning against the model of inefficient and blind development." It was a remarkable admission of urbanization gone wrong.

Since there is no agreed definition of an eco-city, local governments interpret the term to suit themselves. They often use it as an excuse for prettification, or worse, for seizing yet more land from farmers and using it to build luxury housing, with golf courses next to them (because grass is "green"). Even the eco-city in Tianjin, a drought-prone area, has a golf course, supposedly irrigated with recycled water. Mr. Register himself is not altogether bowled over by the project. In 2012 he wrote that its layout, with the wide streets and long blocks typical of modern Chinese cities, looked "every bit as if created to encourage driving." Its plan for 20% of its energy to come from renewable sources does not sound much bolder than the nationwide target of 15% by 2020, against 9% now.

And for all its claims to greenery, the eco-city lacks a vital ingredient: a thriving civil society that is free not only to protest about the environment but to put pressure on the government to live up to its promises. The party talks green and sometimes even acts tough, but all the while it has been machinating to prevent the growth of an environmental movement. It does not want residents to set their own agenda for the way cities are run.

Politics: China's New Middle Classes, Quiescent So Far, May Soon Become More Demanding

Cao Tian is a property dealer who dreamed of changing his city. As a poet and writer chosen by the government of Henan in central China as one of the province's ten cultural personalities of the year in 2006, he clearly did not lack imagination. When in May 2011 the mayor of Zhengzhou, Henan's capital, announced he was stepping down, Mr. Cao said that he would stand for election to replace him. Not only would he take no salary, he would put up 100 million *yuan* ($15.4 million) as a guarantee of good behavior while in office.

It was a good try, but he knew it was doomed. Chinese law says that independent candidates can stand for the post of mayor in cities. In theory all they need is the support of 20 members of a city's legislature, which in Zhengzhou is less than 4% of the total. But legislators are hand-picked by the Communist Party. Most of them are officials and party members. Mr. Cao says he spoke to half a dozen he knew and got nowhere; they were all "very obedient" to the party. "You can eat with them, you can gamble with them, but you cannot talk [about standing for election]," he says. The authorities made that clear enough. They launched a tax investigation into his company a common tactic for intimidating dissenters. Mr. Cao left town for a few months. To no one's surprise, the acting mayor, Ma Yi, was elected by Zhengzhou's legislators to fill the post.

Mr. Cao's challenge was an act of rare bravado. In China, entrepreneurs like him are usually reluctant to cross the line into political activism because business deals often depend on good ties with the party. At the time of Mr. Cao's mayoral bid China's leaders were more than usually jittery following a series of pro-democracy uprisings in the Arab world. Internet activists were anonymously calling for China to stage its own "jasmine revolution," the name given to Tunisia's revolt in late 2010. Online censors were busy trying to expunge any reference to the word "jasmine"; police were rounding up dissidents and even telling florists not to sell the flower.

It was a bad moment to provoke the authorities, especially for someone like Mr. Cao, who had form. After the pro-democracy unrest of 1989 he had been sentenced to 12 years in prison for "counter-revolutionary" behavior (he had organized a protest against the bloody crackdown in Beijing). Thanks, he believes, to foreign pressure on China he served less than three years, but recalls jail as "hell." His punishment, he says, included having to watch condemned prisoners being shot.

The rapid growth of a middle class in China increases the risk, as the party sees it, that more people like Mr. Cao will begin to find their political voice. Unusually for a man who makes his living from property, Mr. Cao says that as mayor he would have tried to control soaring prices. He thinks a property tax would help, but would be opposed by the many corrupt officials who own expensive properties.

Many argue that China's new middle class is largely in favor of the political status quo; many of its more affluent members are officials, former officials or closely in league with officialdom. But the economic make-up of middle-class China is rapidly changing. McKinsey, a consultancy, reckons that in 2012 only 14% of urban households belonged to what it calls the "upper middle class" (with an annual household income of 106,000–229,000 *yuan*, or $16,000–34,000, in 2010 real terms) and 54% to the "mass middle class" (with an income of 60,000–106,000 *yuan*). By 2022, it estimates, the upper segment will have expanded to more than half and the mass part will have shrunk to 22%. With this rise of what McKinsey calls "sophisticated and seasoned shoppers" will come demands for a bigger say in how their cities are run. "Unmet, these demands could raise social tensions," as the World Bank and China's Development Research Centre observed in a joint report in 2012. A second joint report by the two organizations, *Urban China*, published in March, called for comprehensive reforms.

Very few are challenging the party politically, but growing numbers are getting involved in campaigns to protect their neighborhoods from government projects that might affect their health and comfort or the value of their property. Such protests occasionally take on a political hue, providing cover for a wealth of grievances about the opacity of city management, the high-handedness of officials, and pervasive corruption.

The biggest middle-class protests have been mostly about factories producing paraxylene, a chemical used in the production of polyester. Since 2007 large-scale protests have erupted in five cities over plans to build such facilities, the main concern being that the factories might release poisonous fumes. The fears are probably overblown, but reflect wide-spread and profound distrust in officialdom. The demonstrators' ability to gather in public places in their tens of thousands, with the help of mobile text messages and microblogs, has highlighted the weakness of China's censorship system. PX, as the chemical is often called, has become a cover for poking at the party. Those of dissident bent gleefully count off the cities that have witnessed PX protests: Xiamen in June 2007, Dalian in August 2011, Ningbo in October 2012, Kunming in May 2013, and Maoming earlier this month.

Zhou Min, a restaurant reviewer in Kunming, is one of them. She says she used not to care about politics. But in response to the protests in her city last May the police detained dozens of activists. Officials even briefly attempted to stop the sale of medical face-masks for fear they might be donned by demonstrators. "Now I've changed my mind," says Ms. Zhou, who was herself interrogated by police, accused—falsely she says—of being an organizer. "If only we had the vote, then we could veto projects like these," she says, visibly angry. During the recent anti-PX protests in the southern city of Maoming police used tear gas and batons against demonstrators.

Most of the time urban China displays few obvious signs of discontent. Since the late 1990s the party has managed a period of rapid middle-class growth, along with huge urban expansion thanks to an upsurge of migration, with remarkably little unrest in the cities. Protests have been far more common in the countryside, mainly against the government's seizure of land from farmers.

The mostly peaceful PX protests have been a rare exception to widespread middle-class quiescence.

Looking on the Dark Side

But the mood in China's cities could be changing. Middle-class urban residents look ahead with greater anxiety: about the slowing of China's growth; about the harmful effects of air pollution and contaminated food; about rising house prices that are making middle-class dreams of property ownership ever less achievable; about the burden of looking after an ageing population that is growing ever faster; and (especially among recent graduates) about the difficulty of finding a job. Richer Chinese worry about whether they can protect the wealth they have accumulated in the past few years. Could a marginalized urban underclass turn against them? Could an anti-corruption campaign such as President Xi Jinping's current drive land them in jail? Growing numbers are voting with their feet. When in 2012 and 2013 researchers at Shanghai University surveyed nearly 2,000 people in urban areas of Shanghai and five provincial capitals across China, nearly one in five said they would emigrate if they had the chance. Those in the wealthiest cities were most eager to leave. In Shanghai one-third said they would go if they could, and in Guangzhou nearly 40%. *Hurun Report*, a company that monitors China's rich people, said in January that 64% of nearly 400 Chinese with personal wealth of at least 10 million *yuan* ($1.6 million) that it surveyed were emigrating or planning to do so, compared with 60% a year earlier.

With his talk of a "Chinese Dream," Mr. Xi has prompted debate among his countrymen about how far they feel they are from a dream state. A survey last year by the Chinese Academy of Social Sciences (CASS) on attitudes to the "Chinese Dream" found that only just over half of the 7,300 respondents believed they lived in a "good society." Equality democracy and being rich and powerful were rated most highly as the hallmarks of such a society. The party itself bandies around such terms, but Li Chunling of CASS says that what China's middle class understands by democracy is closer to Western ideas.

China's leaders clearly worry about this, as evidenced by the cottage industry that has sprung up to produce translations and analyses of Alexis de Tocqueville's work on the French revolution, *The Old Regime and the Revolution*, published in 1856. This was prompted by a recommendation of the book in 2012 by Wang Qishan, who is now a member of the Politburo's Standing Committee. Exactly what drew Mr. Wang to the book is not known, but Chinese media have focused on one of its main arguments: that revolution is more likely to occur when an authoritarian society begins to reform than during its period of maximum repression. *China Daily,* a government-controlled newspaper, notes that copies of the book have been prominently displayed in the Beijing bookshop of the Communist Party's main training school for senior officials. New versions carry blurbs such as "Recommended by Wang Qishan." One is subtitled: "Why Does Prosperity Hasten the Advent of Revolution?" The possibility of revolution still appears remote, but the risk of larger-scale social unrest in urban areas is growing. To divert attention from trouble at home, China's leaders may be tempted to flex their muscles abroad.

A New Society: Pushing the Boundaries

Few outside China have heard of Sansha, the country's biggest city. Its administrative area is 150 times larger than Beijing's, or roughly the size of Kazakhstan. Yet Sansha's population is no bigger than that of a village and consists mostly of fishermen. Its government is on an island too small even to fit in an airport; the military airstrip stretches out into the South China Sea, where most of the city's watery territory lies. It is a city only in name, setup to assert China's claims in a vast swathe of sea encompassing some of the world's busiest sea lanes. If Shanghai inspires awe, Sansha causes alarm.

The city was created (in bureaucrats' minds, though probably not the fishermen's) seven years ago and upgraded in 2012 to "prefectural level." Its tiny land area comprises about 200 islets clustered in three groups that are bitterly contested. Two of the groups, the Spratlys (*Nansha* in Chinese) and the Paracels (*Xisha*), are claimed by Vietnam. The third, known as *Zhongsha* in Chinese, includes Scarborough Shoal, which is claimed by the Philippines but has in effect been controlled by China since 2012. Some of the Paracels were controlled by South Vietnam until 1974, when it was expelled after a battle with China. It was on one of these, Woody Island, that the party installed Sansha's legislature, which duly elected a man likely to be the country's least busy mayor.

An Empty Threat

Sansha is one of China's most bizarre, and unsettling, attempts at city-building: an undertaking motivated by a desire to stake out territory and scratch the itch of nationalism. Some 2.6 million of the South China Sea's total area of 3.5 million square kilometers are said to be under the city's jurisdiction, giving access to a wealth of resources: an estimated 5 million tons of harvestable fish and huge reserves of oil and natural gas. Parts of the vast area are also claimed by five other countries. The creation of Sansha was intended to rebuff them.

China's spectacular urban-led growth in recent years has been changing the way the country behaves abroad in important ways. First, it has been fuelling a voracious demand for imports of commodities, from oil to iron ore. More than half of China's supplies of both are now bought from abroad. As a result, much more of China's diplomatic attention is being focused on cultivating relations with commodity-exporting countries, mostly in the Middle East, Africa, and Latin America (several of them no friends of the West).

Second, China is now much more worried about the security of its supplies. It feels uneasy about leaving America to patrol vital shipping lanes such as those through the South China Sea. And third, China's growth has given it much greater confidence, increased by the West's economic malaise in recent years. The country is asserting itself more visibly especially in nearby seas that have long been under America's sway.

Xi Jinping himself also happens to be a far more confident leader than his predecessor. He has not been afraid to take steps that raise tensions with American allies, notably Japan and the Philippines. This suggests to some in Asia that China has had enough of America as the region's dominant power and is beginning to do something about it. Certainly the risk has increased that a small incident might escalate into a bigger conflict. For now, however, Mr. Xi does not appear to be spoiling for a fight. China cozies up to America's rivals, most notably Russia, but it also sees its economic interests, and hence its strategic ones, as closely linked with America's.

It is developments inside China, in real cities, that should worry the outside world more. Urbanization, especially over the past decade, has handed Mr. Xi a daunting legacy. When his predecessor, Hu Jintao, came to power in 2002, urban China was far less of a challenge. The country was recovering well from the Asian financial crisis of 1997–98. Its north-east had been wracked by large-scale protests by workers laid off during the massive downsizing of the state sector from the 1990s, but Mr. Hu kept the region largely quiet by directing dollops of cash to it. The Internet was still the preserve of a small urban minority.

A Harder Place to Run

The picture today is very different. Economic growth is slowing. As this special report has explained, rapid urbanization has spawned two huge new social forces: a middle class and an underclass. Both are much bigger than they were a decade ago; both are suspicious of, and sometimes hostile towards, each other; and both often distrust the Communist Party.

Just in the past five years social media such as Sina Weibo and WeChat have connected hundreds of millions of Chinese in a conversation held in near-real time, much of it less than flattering about the party. More than 60% of urban residents now use the Internet. The shoots of civil society are beginning to grow; small, scattered groups are working on everything from helping HIV/AIDS sufferers to cleaning up the environment. The security apparatus keeps close tabs on them but rightly worries that urban China may be changing too fast for it to keep up.

Double-digit growth for much of this century has not only made many ordinary Chinese better off but bestowed breathtaking riches on the families of some members of the political elite (including some of Mr. Xi's extended family). This has proved impossible to cover up. Mr. Xi's anti-corruption efforts risk causing strife among political clans eager to protect their privileges. He may be China's strongest leader since Deng Xiaoping,

but urbanization has fuelled the growth of other, often countervailing, powers too: large state-owned enterprises that have gorged on property and commodities, local governments bloated by reckless borrowing to build ever bigger cities, and an internal security apparatus that now spends more than the army, most of it on policing cities.

Mr. Xi and his team have correctly identified the need for a better approach to urbanization: one that will help ease social tensions which have built up over the past decade, bring local governments into line, and make big SOEs contribute much more to welfare and share more of their markets with the private sector. They have been making encouraging noises about the need to reform the iniquitous *hukou* system, strengthen farmers' property rights and make cities more "livable."

But Mr. Xi needs to go much further. The party still cannot bring itself to talk of a "middle class" (too unsocialist-sounding), much less acknowledge that its aspirations are more than just material ones. In January a famous actor, Huang Bo, introduced a new song about the "Chinese dream" on state television's most popular show of the year, the Spring Festival gala. It was called "My Needs Are Modest." The middle-class fantasy it described (without naming it as such) was an advance on the usual calls for selfless devotion to the nation, but it was still politically sterile: "I can earn money, and still have time to go to Paris, New York and the Alps. I stroll through the shopping mall and go skiing in the mountains. Days like these are so carefree."

Optimists still wonder whether Mr. Xi might eventually allow a little more political experimentation. At the party's 19th Congress in 2017, five of the Politburo Standing Committee's seven members are due to step down, leaving only Mr. Xi and Mr. Li, the prime minister. Of the replacements expected to join them, at least two are thought to have liberal(ish) leanings. But few observers are holding their breath.

In 1997 China's leaders set a goal of making China "moderately well off" by 2020, just in time for the party's 100th birthday celebrations the following year. Judgment on whether this has been achieved will be passed while Mr. Xi is still in office. As long as China's GDP keeps on growing at about 7% a year (as is plausible, possibly even making China's economy bigger than America's by then), it will not be hard for him to tick off the economic targets. But the party has said that "moderately well off" also means a more democratic China, and one that respects human rights.

Ignoring those aspects risks antagonizing the constituency that has become most vital to sustaining the party's power: the urban middle class. Mr. Xi would do so at his peril.

VII. ETHNIC TENSIONS

The Roots of China's Ethnic Conflicts*

Yan Sun

A surge of ethnic violence in China in recent years has revealed growing social tensions in a country beset by developmental strains, with a political system lagging behind epic economic change. In the first half of 2014 alone, there were at least five instances of what the state defines as terrorism associated with Xinjiang, the Muslim borderland in the west. A May attack at a vegetable market in Urumqi, Xinjiang's capital, killed 43 people. In August, clashes in Xinjiang left nearly 100 dead. And the spread of violence to other provinces—notably in Beijing's Tiananmen Square last October and at the rail station in the southwestern city of Kunming this March—has brought home the reality of ethnic tensions to Chinese citizens outside sensitive minority regions.

What has caused this eruption of ethnic riots and violence? Is Beijing guilty of political, economic, cultural, and religious discrimination against minorities, as its critics claim? Or is China vulnerable to ethnic separatism, as its leaders fear? A combination of sticks and carrots in Beijing's policies—especially inappropriate carrots—deserves most of the blame for the deteriorating situation.

Peripheral Zones

Until the nineteenth century, China defined itself as a "Celestial Empire" with a three-tier topography. The imperial bureaucracy governed the central agrarian zone, where the Sinic communities were concentrated, based on bureaucratic and legal rules. Inner and outer zones of tribal and peripheral territories encompassed the other two administrative tiers. Most of these territories—whether peacefully absorbed or conquered—were managed by a "loose rein" system based on ritualistic obligations and titles. This history of center-periphery relations makes a difference in contemporary ethnic relations. The inner peripheral zone, ethnically and culturally close to the central zone, became increasingly incorporated into China's regular governance system over time. The inhabitants of the outer peripheral zone—largely nomadic as well as ethnically and culturally more remote—faced fewer obligations and were left alone as long as they did not present military threats to agrarian communities.

Ethnic tensions in today's China, which has 55 official minority groups, mainly concern the historical outer peripheries, Tibet and Xinjiang. These two regions were incorporated, respectively, by the two nomadic dynasties in Chinese history, the Mongols and the Manchus. Xinjiang became a regular province in 1884 under Manchu rule, while much of Tibet did not. After the founding of the People's Republic of China (PRC) in 1949, Beijing established a new system of governance across all ethnic regions. Known as the autonomous system, it has lately come under much criticism in China for providing either too little autonomy or excessive ethnic prerogatives.

In the autonomous system, Soviet features replaced historical practices. Following the Soviet definition of nationalities based on the practice of ethnic classification, the PRC launched a

* This article was published in *Current History* (September 2014).

classification campaign in the 1950s and has since registered an official "nationality" for every citizen. This superseded neutral approaches to ethnicity under Confucian universalism. The PRC created uniform ethno-regional units named after the principal local nationality; in this way, indirect and diverse rule gave way to direct rule and political synchronization. The PRC adopted socioeconomic strategies, including preferential policies, as a means of promoting social and other forms of equality across ethnic groups. Thus the historical practice of co-opting ethnic elites was replaced by a coalition between the party-state and the ethnic proletariat.

The Party's class-based appeal helped to legitimize and rally support for the new system, while the socialist redistributive state helped to guarantee egalitarianism and prevent economic competition among ethnic groups. At the same time, the system of regional autonomy incorporated China's three-tier topography in an unprecedented way: It required that all autonomous areas accept their institutional frameworks under the PRC's unitary political system—namely, under the centralized leadership of the party.

In the post-Mao era, reform policies have eroded the Party's solidarity with its ethnic support base, replacing class politics with identity politics. In the early 1980s, the Party rehabilitated former ethnic elites, leaving the lower classes ideologically and politically abandoned. Since the early 1990s, economic liberalization has ended guaranteed employment and encouraged competition—leaving the lower classes socioeconomically abandoned. In ethnic regions with theocratic traditions, new policies have served to reconnect ethnic masses with former religious authorities, consolidating identities weakened during the socialist era. And new developmental initiatives—along with growing concerns regarding social stability—have intensified preferential policies for sensitive ethnic regions, further increasing the role of the state in local affairs.

Meanwhile, the built-in tensions of the autonomous system persist. It has reduced actual political autonomy for the constituent regions of China's traditional dynastic empire, while the enduring Soviet influence contributes to what Terry Martin of Harvard University has called an "affirmative action empire."

Religious Revival

Religious policy is a prime example of this mix of sticks (limited autonomy) and carrots (excessive ethnic prerogatives); lately, it has been the leading cause of terrorism in Xinjiang. In the early post-Mao era, the state encouraged and even sponsored the revival of religion, especially in Tibet and Xinjiang. The extent to which this state role helped to undermine secular forces and strengthen religious influences is a matter of much debate recently in China. Critics blame state sponsorship for playing a legitimizing and enabling role; supporters continue to defend the policy, which was led by Hu Yaobang, the Party's general secretary in the early 1980s.

Notably, state sponsorship of religious revival occurred mainly in sensitive ethnic regions. Monasteries and mosques, enthusiastically destroyed by members of formerly oppressed classes during the Cultural Revolution, were restored with public funding in the 1980s. Construction of new houses of worship boomed. Former religious elites were restituted and compensated, and thousands of them received positions in local people's congresses, state agencies, and religious associations. Those associated with major monasteries received government salaries, along with fringe benefits and professional ranks. As mosques and clergymen resurged in social status and influence, private religious schools mushroomed, filling the spiritual void left by the end of the Mao era.

The revival of private madrassas in Xinjiang has posed one of the secular state's biggest problems, and has led to a cycle of restrictions and an increasingly violent backlash. The state's initial worry was education, as many Uighur students abandoned public schools for madrassas starting in the early 1980s. The Uighurs, a Turkic Muslim people, comprise over 80 percent of the population in southern Xinjiang. Rural parents want their children to learn traditional values and religious rituals and scripts—knowledge respected in the local communities. But today, due to government constraints, there are just a few officially established schools for Islamic teaching throughout Xinjiang, open only to students above 18 years of age.

This conflict between community needs for religious education and state bans on private madrassas defines the religious problem in

Xinjiang. Since the late 1980s, local restrictions have created demand for imported Islamic sects in China's black market of religions. Wahhabism, a puritanical strain of Saudi origin previously marginalized in Xinjiang's mostly Sunni communities, arrived by way of Muslims returned from pilgrimages to Mecca, visiting foreign religious groups, and newly independent Central Asian states just across Xinjiang's borders. Spreading through existing and new madrassas, Wahhabism won converts through its simplified rituals, exemption of dues, and emphasis on helping the poor.

Wahhabism distinguishes itself from Xinjiang's traditional Islamic sects by claiming the exclusive supremacy of Allah and promoting resistance against the secular state. As Wahhabism spread traditional imams began to seem old and outdated, unable to prevail over the young *talibs* trained in the underground madrassas. Local authorities initially viewed their clashes as an intrafaith matter and refused to intervene, leaving the new sect's madrassas to grow uncontrolled. Less educated youths dominated the ranks of its adherents, especially among the unemployed, the self-employed, and students.

Wahhabi groups have been responsible for the spread of violence since 1990. More than a dozen major incidents of such violence reportedly occurred in Xinjiang in the 1990s; over half were targeted assassinations of traditional Uighur imams and local Uighur officials. The killings were often carried out in the name of various "East Turkestan" parties, inspired by a movement for Uighur independence in the 1930s and '40s. Authorities traced all the attacks to Wahhabi assailants, particularly students from one madrassa in the Kashgar prefecture of Xinjiang. Its senior imam advocated a pure Islamic and moral society—a message that appealed to Uighurs thrust into China's turbulent social transition in the reform era.

The violence in the 1990s led the central and local governments to tighten religious policy. Subsidies to officially sanctioned imams increased; Uighur officials have been assigned to supervise mosques. In Uighur and Tibetan regions, children under the age of 18, public school teachers, party members, and government employees are banned from practicing religion in public and communal spaces. Symbols of religious faith are banned in public schools. The failure to distinguish between a sect and Islam in general has alienated non-Wahhabi Muslims, and strengthened Wahhabism as a form of populist resistance against the state.

The global US antiterrorism campaign after 9/11 and Washington's listing of the East Turkestan Islamic Movement as a terrorist group briefly stemmed violence from Xinjiang between the early 2000s and 2008—the year Beijing hosted the Summer Olympics. During that period, however, two international jihadist organizations entered Xinjiang: Hizb ut-Tahrir and the Hijrat movement. Hizb ut-Tahrir's stated aim is the unification of all Muslim nations in a single Islamic state or caliphate; in post-Soviet Central Asia, it has filled the ideological and socioeconomic void left by the retreat of socialism and the rise of unemployment, and has appeal among the young. Its association with violence led to crackdowns in Central Asian states and Russia. In Xinjiang, local studies indicate that Hizb ut-Tahrir may not be directly responsible for violence associated with Islamic and separatist East Turkestan groups, but some members have belonged to Hizb ut-Tahrir organizations.

The Hijrat movement advocates leaving behind one's earthly possessions and traveling to engage in jihad. Loosely organized and operating through underground madrassas, it is regarded by Xinjiang's local authorities as the main perpetrator of violence emanating from the region at present.

Uighur Alienation

By the late 2000s, the cumulative effects of economic liberalization and marginalization had frustrated Uighur society. This discontent manifested itself in massive unemployment, a surge in crime, epidemic drug problems, family breakdown, disintegration of traditional moral fabrics, spreading fundamentalism and cultural conservatism, and, not least, a growing hatred of the Han people, China's majority ethnic group. Han–Uighur relations ruptured with violent riots in Urumqi on July 5, 2009, when a Uighur student protest escalated into the worst ethnic rioting in the history of the PRC, leaving 197 people dead, most of them Han pedestrians. The riots created an opening for extremist groups to exert panethnic pressure on Uighur communities. The line between boycotting the Chinese state and traditional Uighur society is now increasingly blurred, as extremists make an emphatic distinction between what is Muslim and not Muslim, inter- as well as intra-ethnically.

Lately a so-called Arabianization of Uighur costumes and mores has become prominent. The conservative black *hijab,* which covers a woman's entire face and body, has spread more widely; traditionally, Uighur women wore colorful headpieces and dresses. More men, especially among the younger generation, now wear beards and refuse to drink or smoke. Anything issued by the state, from marriage licenses to free television sets and earthquake-proof houses, is rejected as "un-Muslim," perhaps as a form of political resistance. But in a trend that troubles many Uighur intellectuals, traditional Uighur art forms are also discouraged. Extremists in the rural south ban dance and music on celebratory occasions and crying at funerals. But local governments can be just as draconian: Bans aimed at fundamentalist practices may be brusquely implemented or make little distinction between fundamentalist and traditional Uighur customs, further alienating the Uighurs as a group. For example, head scarves are banned in public schools and workplaces, and during Ramadan in the summer of 2014, local agencies barred government employees, teachers, and students from fasting.

The state's heavy-handed policies in both promoting and restraining religious revival in Xinjiang have backfired. More autonomy might have allowed local communities to sort out their own strategies—and perhaps find a means of effectively thwarting radical forms of Islam. Uighur intellectuals had qualms from the beginning about the state's vigorous restoration of religion, fearing that this would impede secular progress.

Tibet in Flames

Whereas Uighur parents prefer some religious education for all their children, Tibetan families have a tradition of each sending one child to a Buddhist monastery. Despite the ban on religious practice by minors, the Tibetan system of full-time monasticism creates various pretexts, such as taking care of an uncle who is a monk. As long as one child is in a monastery, most Tibetan parents

encourage their other children to attend regular schools. These factors contribute to a far better equilibrium between secular and religious education than in Xinjiang.

Recently, religion has been linked to violence in a different way in Tibetan regions: the self-immolation of low-level monks. The most important cause lies in the deep tensions between the Chinese state and the Gelugpa sect of Tibetan Buddhism—historically the leading sect, headed by the Dalai Lama. State control is felt more acutely among monasteries of this sect, because when the government urges the monks to endorse its chosen Panchen Lama or to denounce the Dalai Lama, the Gelugpa monasteries have no option to dodge the issue, as the non-Gelugpa sects can. They face a chronic challenge to the heart of their sect.

Since its first occurrence in 2009, self-immolation has primarily been associated with Gelugpa monasteries—specifically, the Kirti monastery in the Ngawa region of western Sichuan. Until their conflict with Beijing over the selection of the Panchen Lama, monks and lamas there enjoyed relative freedom to travel to India and study in exile monasteries.

Based on an analysis of their last words by the Tibetan dissident writer Woeser, the self- immolators' major motives were to take an action (54 percent) and to offer themselves to the Dalai Lama as a religious sacrifice (38 percent). The exact meaning of the action was not always clear, but the immolations were often timed to coincide with commemorations of political events and thus presumably an implicit form of political protest. As in Xinjiang, Beijing's conflation of religious sentiments and separatism has led to an overly politicized religious policy in Tibet.

Anemic Economies

The massive unemployment among Uighurs—especially college graduates and youths—raises the question of why intensive economic growth in post-Mao China has not sufficiently lifted a key minority region such as Xinjiang. To be sure, there has not been a lack of carrots in this area: State subsidy has exceeded 90 percent of the total annual revenue of Tibet in recent decades, and at least 60 percent of the revenue of three of the other four autonomous regions in recent years (Inner Mongolia is the exception). There is also a myriad of other assistance and antipoverty programs for Tibet and Xinjiang.

Chinese analysts have blamed the futility of these carrots on diffusion bias in the state's developmental strategy—that is, an obsession with transplanting the practices of interior provinces to ethnic regions. In Tibet, despite unsuitable conditions for developing industries on the high plateau, the state vigorously promoted industrialization in the socialist era, generating huge deficits and chronic dependency on state subsidies. In the post-Mao era, Tibet received extra preferential treatment in the form of assistance from almost all interior provinces and major cities, as well as central ministries and large state firms. This assistance must be coerced by the central government because the aid donors have little interest in Tibet's natural resources (it is unknown whether these are significant, since the formidable elevations make the area unsuitable for exploration). The projects funded by this "partner assistance" are not always practical, since they tend to be based on economic models from the donors.

For resource-rich Xinjiang, central government jurisdiction over strategic resources and developmental patterns has left little room for local autonomy over development priorities and benefit distribution. Starting in 1997, Xinjiang became the other major recipient of partner assistance, with 19 partner provinces and cities involved, plus central agencies and large state firms. After the riots of 2009, these programs intensified with the intention of creating "leap forward" development in Xinjiang. Critics complain that aid projects have brought little direct stimulation to the local economy, as the diffusion of coastal models pays little attention to local needs. For efficiency's sake, project donors bring their own managers, workers, and construction materials, contributing little to local job creation. Citing skill gaps, they usually hire locals only for low-end jobs.

Likewise, economic zones with special incentives have been created to attract businesses, but lack of skilled labor is again an inhibiting factor. Some participating companies pay taxes through their headquarters located elsewhere in the country, depriving local governments of revenue windfalls. Low-income housing projects, which make up the bulk of partner assistance, have not always benefited those most in need. While local policy gives priority to poor households, many cannot afford the small matching fund required.

This vicious cycle of economic diffusion and dependency is vividly summed up in two phrases commonly heard in southern Xinjiang and the Tibetan regions: State subsidies and partner assistance sustain "blood transfusions," but do little to improve the regions' own capacity for "blood generation." Unconditional aid has nurtured a culture of dependency known as the "anemia complex." The more aid transfusions an ethnic region receives, the worse its anemia gets, as local officials, farmers, and pastoralists develop the habit of expecting, relying on, and asking for outside assistance.

Migrant Competition

The issue of population resettlement often frames Western perceptions of ethnic conflict in Tibet and Xinjiang. The general view is that Han settlers and migrants are overrunning these regions, in a process typically referred to as "population swamping" or "transfer." Close observers rightly suggest that this perception is essentially an urban-centric assessment of ethnic shares in the local populations, since Tibetans and Uighurs are still concentrated in rural areas. But important questions remain. What has pulled migrants to Tibet and Xinjiang in the reform era, when the state no longer sponsors population resettlement? And why has random and temporary migration in the reform era led to serious tensions, while the larger-scale and long-term migration of the Mao era did not do so to the same extent?

According to available data, during 1995–2000, the autonomous regions with the highest in-migration rates were Xinjiang, Tibet, and Ningxia. These three regions also happened to have received the highest per capita investment during that period. Analyses of demographic trends in Tibet from 1991 to 2005 suggest that significant fluctuations in the numbers of Han residents and migrants correlated with central government developmental policies. Migrant workers in Tibet and Xinjiang come mostly from poor provinces that lack economic opportunities. Sichuan, Gansu, and Henan top the list.

These migrant workers have been drawn to Tibet and Xinjiang by the spillover effects of the state's elaborate investment and aid projects, often toiling as temporary laborers on construction projects, as tenant farmers for local ethnic land-owners, or as owners and employees in small retail and catering services. Most are seasonal workers and few settle permanently. Demand for Mandarin-speaking, hard-working migrant labor is a major reason for their presence, not deliberate population transfer by the state.

Such unskilled migrants have posed direct competition to ethnic labor within the minority regions. During the 2008 Tibetan riot in Lhasa and the 2009 Uighur riot in Urumqi, participants were mostly vagrants from rural regions outside the provincial capitals. They face greater difficulties than Han and Hui (Mandarin-speaking Chinese Muslim) migrants in finding jobs in urban centers. Many are illiterate, whereas the Han migrants often have had secondary education. Rural ethnic youths also tend to be unfamiliar with life and employment opportunities in cities, or lack skills and work habits suited to urban employment.

Differences in migrant labor trends also account for greater tensions in Xinjiang than in Tibet. Han settlers are often physically unfit for long-term residence on Tibet's high plateau, whereas Xinjiang's terrain poses no such problem. Han migrants' activities in Tibet are concentrated in urban businesses and coal mining, posing little threat to the core of the Tibetan economy and society in the pastoral regions. Han migrants in Xinjiang, both recent and long established, present a more comprehensive competitive challenge for the native Uighurs—urban as well as rural, economic as well as political, cultural as well linguistic. The result has been a shrinking of survival space for Uighurs since the 1990s, leading to intense resentment of the Han.

The state-sponsored migration of the Mao era did not produce the same direct competition with the local population. In Xinjiang, most immigrants settled on state farms away from local ethnic communities. The small number of Hans assigned to state and professional sectors did not overwhelm the natives linguistically or culturally. These professionals were required to receive training in ethnic languages and urged to respect local people and customs. Members of local ethnic groups

enjoyed protected employment in the public sector, which also guaranteed equal remuneration. Children grew up together, speaking each other's languages. Han migrants of the reform era, by contrast, are voluntary and short-term oriented, and care little about the local communities.

Trouble at School

Preferential treatment in college admissions is perhaps the most polarizing carrot in China's minority policies. In interior regions, Han students complain that minorities look like them and go to the same schools but receive extra points on college entrance exams. In heavily ethnic regions, minority students may take those exams in their native language and receive a significant amount of extra points. The exams in ethnic languages are also easier in content.

Critics complain that lower academic standards, most visible in sensitive regions, have been responsible for minority students' poor employment prospects after college. State responses, however, have promoted bilingual education, on the ground that Mandarin proficiency will enhance employability. Draconian approaches to bilingual education in the lower grades, especially in Xinjiang, have in turn ignited serious tensions.

Of the two prevalent models in bilingual education, the so-called complementary model is balanced and popular. Humanities classes are taught in a minority language, while math and science classes are in Chinese. In the far more aggressive "immersion" model, Chinese is used for teaching all subjects, while one class in the ethnic language is offered; 13.7 percent of minority students were enrolled in this model in Xinjiang by 2009. Logistical difficulties would have slowed further progress, but the riots of 2009 led authorities to expand the immersion model. Some local officials, in their zeal to get fast results, adopt a top-down "political task" approach, issuing extreme commands that distort the meaning of bilingual education.

Moderate Uighur intellectuals worry about adverse effects on children's cultural values and identity. Dissidents contend that the latest promotion of bilingual education amounts to accelerated and forced assimilation by political methods. The immersion model has been tempered in

Xinjiang since 2012 due to local opposition, but underlying resentment over Mandarin hegemony persists. In regions where other options are available, bilingual education has proceeded more smoothly and successfully In Tibetan regions of Qinghai and Gansu provinces, local educational authorities and schools are allowed to pick models of instruction that they deem appropriate for local conditions. Local authorities in Qinghai have responded accommodatingly to Tibetan students' protests against the immersion model. In China's Korean and Mongol regions, balanced approaches have made their bilingual programs exemplary models.

Seeking Balance

The key to progress is improving China's understanding of the roots of its ethnic problems. A misunderstanding of Western support for minority human rights in China is perhaps the biggest source of a prevalent Chinese belief in a Western (especially American) conspiracy to destabilize the country. Sensationalist and nationalist Chinese media organs, lacking an understanding of pluralist domestic politics in Western countries, equate the support that Tibetan and Uighur exiled leaders enjoy in the West to Western governments' support for separatism—or even to indirect sympathy for "terrorist forces." Authorities have blocked more extreme statements on the Internet, such as those by the ultranationalist Dai Xu, a professor at China's National Defense University. But the idea of "behind-the-scenes forces" lingers in the popular imagination, preventing a clear-eyed assessment of counterproductive elements in China's own policy.

In an encouraging sign, at a Communist Party work symposium on Xinjiang in May 2014, after the latest attack in Urumqi, President Xi Jinping spoke of cracking down on illicit religious practices but "protecting legitimate religion." Following Tibet's example after the 2008 Lhasa riot, Xinjiang is trying a policy of guaranteeing employment to at least one adult child in each Uighur household. The policy is said to serve as a stabilizing factor for each family and to provide a good example for other young adults.

A better understanding of the flaws in China's ethnic policy would help ease the vicious cycle of ever more sticks and carrots in dealing with sensitive regions. In ongoing Chinese debates about policy failures, liberal critics have blamed a lack of regional autonomy, while integrationists criticize an excess of preferential policies. Little is noted in terms of the trade-offs between the two approaches. A more candid discussion about these trade-offs would be a good beginning to reassess and adjust a policy approach that has alienated both minority and majority groups in the name of interethnic equality and harmony.

LAW, RIGHTS, AND CIVIL SOCIETY

Editorial Introduction

China's rise has also impacted its domestic law and social order. Not only have there been increased pressures from the international community for China to adhere to the UN Charter on Social and Economic Rights (which China has ratified) and the Charter on Civil and Political Rights (which it has not ratified), but demands have also arisen within China for improved human rights, the rule of law, and activities of civil society organizations. As China has economically developed, gradually the population has grown more aware of its rights as *citizens*. As this social consciousness has developed, demands on the Chinese government to ensure rights under domestic law and international norms have increased. The government has responded both positively and negatively.

On the positive side of the ledger, a multitude of laws have been passed to govern society as well as the state. Compared with the totalitarian Maoist era, respect for human rights has expanded across the board. Ordinary Chinese now enjoy broad freedoms unimaginable forty years ago. Arbitrary arrests, detentions, and disappearances have dramatically declined since the Mao era (although all still occur). While still a "police state" in many ways, many of the more draconian features of Maoist period—such as the sprawling network of "reform through labor" (劳动改造) camps—have been abolished. The penal system has been modernized, the court system has become more professional, and nearly 200,000 lawyers are licensed to practice. Civil society organizations have sprung up in the tens of thousands (although they do not enjoy real autonomy and operate under the watchful eye of the state).

Thus, compared with the dark features of China's totalitarian past, the nation and society has made many advances in the civil-legal sphere. Nonetheless, this progress should not be overstated. China remains a harsh authoritarian system with one of the world's most repressive regimes. Since 2009, the limited openings of the previous decade have been rolled back and China's internal security state has engaged in widespread and substantial repression (the domestic security budget now exceeds the military budget). The court system remains a tool in the hands of the Communist Party (although some steps were initiated after the Fourth Plenum of 2014 to reduce interference by local party officials in court cases). Basic rights of *habeas corpus* do not exist. Disappearances and arbitrary detentions still occur with regularity—ordinary citizens are held in "black jails" while officials are subjected to the *shuanggui* (双规) system. Torture remains a common practice. Any kind of political activity is dealt with harshly—with both dissidents and "rights lawyers" being given prison terms. Many others, including the families of incarcerated dissidents, are subject to house arrest and around-the-clock surveillance. The Chinese government has instituted the world's most sophisticated network of controls on the Internet, email communications, and social media (see next section). Certain groups in society—notably Tibetans, Uighurs, and Falun Gong spiritual practitioners—are subject to severe repressive measures.

As reform and repression have both advanced, other manifestations of China's rapidly developing society have burst forth: crime and corruption. For a nation of its gargantuan size China has a remarkably low crime rate. This may have much to do with the size and strength of the internal security forces, which maintain tight surveillance and control of the population. Nonetheless, China is hardly crime-free. Robbery, homicide, human trafficking, drug smuggling, and a variety of domestic abuse crimes afflict China like every other nation. One particularly striking feature of China's criminal world, though, is the rampant white-collar corruption. But unlike most capitalist economies, corruption in China permeates more than the private sector—it is deeply embedded in government at local and central levels, inside the Communist Party itself, and throughout the military and security forces. It is systemically rooted and has reached epidemic proportions. The mixed private-state economy has bred much of the graft, as officials are susceptible to bribes for making decisions to authorize projects while, at the same time, they engage in "rent seeking" behavior in a wide variety of local transactions. At the time of this writing, China was undergoing a sweeping anti-corruption campaign launched in 2013 by strongman ruler Xi Jinping. So far the campaign is proceeding with vigor—with a number of high-ranking party, state, and military officials under investigation or having been punished. Large numbers of ministerial-level, provincial-level, and local-level officials have also been investigated: altogether in 2013 over 180,000 CCP members and government officials, as well as 4024 PLA officers (including 82 generals) were punished. In 2014 this included 68 ministerial and vice-ministerial level officials.

All in all, while China has moved forward in many ways in the civil-legal sphere during the reform (post-1978) era, it remains one of the most repressive governments in the world. The following selections elaborate the various dimensions of both the progress and the severe limits on basic human rights and freedoms in China.

The first selection, by Yale University law professor Jamie Horsley, presents an excellent overview of the state of the legal system in China during the early 2000s. The growth of the legal system has paralleled the increasing social and economic complexities of the process of modernization—Chinese courts now hear nearly 11 million cases per year. Professor Horsley begins by tracing the evolution of the system during the reform era. Despite the considerable progress, she finds that China still suffers from rule *by law* instead of rule *of law*. That is, law remains primarily an instrument in the hands of the party-state to enforce its writ and rule—rather than an impartial adjudicator among individual and institutional actors in the country. This said, Horsley argues that the laws such as the Administrative Litigation Law, State Compensation Law, State Reconsideration Law, Administrative Penalties Law, Administrative Licensing Law, and the public petition (信访) system all have given citizens unprecedented means to challenge the decisions and actions of officials. She notes that, over the past quarter century, "China has been building a body of administrative law to better regularize government behavior and the government's interaction with the public." Since coming to power in 2012, Xi Jinping has made improving the legal system a high priority; the Fourth Plenum of the 18th Central Committee in November 2014 issued a detailed blueprint for the further development of a law-based society. Despite the progress, much of it admirable, China's legal system remains underdeveloped, untransparent, underinstitutionalized, and susceptible to intervention and manipulation by the party-state. Indeed, the just-noted Fourth Plenum communiqué made explicitly clear that the Party "guides" the legal system and, by implication, remains above the law.

The second selection by Minxin Pei, a noted expert on Chinese politics at Claremont McKenna College in California, focuses on the corruption problem in China. Filled with statistics and examples of real cases, Professor Pei's analysis provides exhaustive details of the depth and breadth of the cancer that permeates China. One of the more shocking types of corruption is the prevalence of buying and selling of official jobs in the Party, government, and military—a phenomenon known as *maiguan-maiguan*. Normally controlled by the Communist Party's Organization Department, the State Council's Ministry of Personnel, and the PLA's General Political Department, Pei makes clear that this *nomenklatura* system has become beholden to corrupt cadres. Although written before the post-2013 anti-corruption drive launched by Xi Jinping and the CCP's Central Discipline Inspection Commission (中央监察委员会), Professor Pei's article provides deep insights into the widespread and large-scale corruption problem in China. As Chinese leaders Jiang Zemin, Hu Jintao, and Xi Jinping have all candidly admitted publicly: "[Controlling] corruption is a matter of life and death for our Party."

The next selection, from *The Economist* magazine, discusses crime in China—specifically homicide. China has an official annual murder rate of 1.1 per 100,000 people, ranking among the lowest in the world—while the United States, by contrast, has 5 homicides per 100,000 (much of the contrast has to do with the non-availability of guns in Chinese society). China's low homicide rate, *The Economist* points out, is paralleled more generally with other categories of crime. This is one of the "good news" stories in China, but perhaps also a by-product of China's extraordinary state investment in "stability maintenance" procedures.

This brings us to the broader issue of human rights in China. The next selection is the China section of the 2014 annual "World Report" by Human Rights Watch, a global rights-monitoring NGO. As the report pithily puts it:

Rapid socio-economic change in China has been accompanied by relaxation of some restrictions on basic rights, but the government remains an authoritarian one-party state. It places arbitrary curbs on expression, association, assembly, and religion; prohibits independent labor unions and human rights organizations; and maintains Party control over all judicial institutions. The government censors the press, the Internet, print publications, and academic research, and justifies human rights abuses as necessary to preserve "social stability." It carries out involuntary population relocation and rehousing on a massive scale, and enforces highly repressive policies in ethnic minority areas in Tibet, Xinjiang, and Inner Mongolia. Though primary school enrollment and basic literacy rates are high, China's education system discriminates against children and young people with disabilities. The government obstructs domestic and international scrutiny of its human rights record, insisting it is an attempt to destabilize the country.

The remainder of the report details the situation and violations of essential human rights in each of these categories. Since around 2009 there has been across-the-board repression in China, and it intensified after Xi Jinping took over from Hu Jintao. The repression and abuse of human rights is the worst it has been in China since the early 1990s. Whether it will continue indefinitely into the future is to be determined, but it does not reflect well on the Chinese government and speaks volumes about its insecurity.

The next section includes two entries concerning civil society in China. The first, by *The Economist*, is subtitled "Beneath the Glacier." This is a metaphor for what the article aptly describes as "social forces bubbling up from below in a stubbornly top-down state." China's non-governmental organizations (NGOs) that are registered with the state—and they are *all* mandated to register—now number over 500,000. But it is precisely the registration process that compromises their autonomy and activities. Strictly speaking, by definition, civil society organizations can not exist in any society unless they are completely autonomous of state control. From this defini-tional perspective, many would question whether, in fact, civil society actually exists in China. In other words, these are not *non*-governmental organizations—but, rather, *government organized* non-governmental organizations, or GONGOs. The Chinese government co-opts and controls them. That is when they are allowed to exist in the first place—since 2008, as part of the government's broad sweep of repression, many NGOs have been investigated, raided, and shut down. The article also notes that a large percentage of these supposed NGOs are, in fact, shell organs of Party and state institutions. But, more generally, the party-state fears NGOs as agents of (foreign-inspired) political subversion and "peaceful evolution." Nonetheless, some NGOs are finding space to operate and are addressing pressing social problems that the govern-ment often ignores, for example drug users, prostitutes with HIV/AIDS, migrants, and orphans. Even philanthropy with social conscience has begun to germinate in China. Thus, the cat-and-mouse game between the government and NGOs will con-tinue into the future.

The final selection in this section also concerns civil society, but through the prism of university students. Written by the eminent historian–political scientist Elizabeth Perry of Harvard, it shows how the government has sought to simultaneously intimidate and co-opt university students since 1989—tactics the state has used more generally vis-à-vis civil society. Chinese university students have a long history of political activism, dating to the May Fourth Movement of 1919. They were the main impetus to the May–June uprising of 1989. After detailing the complex web of controls that the state employs on college campuses, Professor Perry also interestingly shows how Chinese students today are much less interested in political activism and much more interested in personal advancement. However, she also notes that they are becoming more and more engaged in civic and social activities (community service). While preferable to political agitation, this still makes the state very nervous—as it brings idealistic youth in direct contact with workers and other sectors of society. Nonetheless, she concludes that:

> Counterintuitively, the recent increase of popular protest and associational activity in the PRC has proved more of a help than a hindrance to the perpetuation of Communist party-state rule. Rather than providing a platform for political agitation and democrati-zation, the burgeoning of civil society in mainland China has offered an outlet for public service that relieves the state of some of its own onerous welfare burden while also fulfill-ing citizens' growing desire for social engagement. The pervasive contestation that takes place outside the gates of university campuses, while sometimes sparked by grassroots NGOs, has concentrated on economic and environmental issues that do not directly challenge CCP authority. And the campuses themselves, the cradle of political ferment in twentieth-century China, have remained uncharacteristically quiet for the past 25 years.

Whether they will remain quiescent in future years is very much a question, but given the broad range of challenges facing China (and outlined in this volume) it would be surprising if Chinese students did not find their social conscience and voice again in the future.

I. Progress and Limits in the Rule of Law

The Rule of Law: Pushing the Limits of Party Rule*

Jamie Horsley

Thirty years ago at the historic Third Plenum of the Eleventh Central Committee in December 1978, the Chinese Communist Party adopted as part of its reform and opening platform the twin goals of "democratic institutionalization and legalization," launching China onto the path of establishing a modern legal system. Borrowing from a speech that had been delivered by Deng Xiaoping at the meeting, the Plenum Communiqué looked to law and democracy to defend against a resurgence of the violent and arbitrary Cultural Revolution politics of the 1960s and early 1970s:

> In order to safeguard people's democracy, it is imperative to strengthen the socialist legal system so that democracy is institutionalized and legalized, in such a way as to ensure the stability, continuity and full authority of this type of system and law; *there must be laws to follow, these laws must be observed, they must be strictly enforced and lawbreakers must be dealt with.*[1]

Since the 1978 Third Plenum, "legalization" has been intertwined with China's political, economic, and social modernization. By the Seventeenth Communist Party Congress in October 2007, "ruling the country in accordance with law" had been enshrined in China's Constitution and was espoused as essential, alongside party leadership and the position of the people as masters of their own country, to the promotion of political development under "socialism with Chinese characteristics."[2] Nonetheless, thirty years after reform and opening, and ten years after making rule of law a constitutional principle, law and legal institutions are still unable to effectively manage the complex tensions and rising conflicts caused by China's wrenching transition from a command to a market economy and the emergence of a more pluralistic society.

While China has successfully established over the past three decades a respectable body of law to follow, its leaders are having great difficulty in achieving the other three interrelated goals expressed above: broad compliance with and enforcement of the law, and holding lawbreakers accountable. The challenges to making China a truly law-based nation are complex and multifaceted, and ultimately implicate the continued dominance and extralegal status of the Chinese Communist Party, which exerts influence both legitimately through state structures but also through parallel, nontransparent mechanisms that place it outside and above the law.

China's leadership moved quickly to establish the laws necessary to accomplish Deng's modernization vision, including what would be called the "socialist market economy." Focused on the goals of using law to safeguard the nation against future chaos, promote social stability, and spur economic development, the National People's Congress (NPC), China's lawmaking body, adopted in the next few years new criminal and criminal procedure laws, a trial civil procedure law, a provisional environmental protection law, domestic contract and tax regulations, trademark and patent laws, and [a number] of laws and regulations to permit private foreign investment in China for the first time since the country's establishment in 1949.

China also revised its Cultural Revolution Constitution, adopting a new version in 1982 that replaced explicit party control of the state with party leadership and restored a system of government through state organs duly constituted through lawful procedures set forth in the Constitution. This Constitution called for the state to uphold the uniformity and dignity of the "socialist legal system," proclaimed that no organization, political party, or individual was above the Constitution and the law, articulated an impressive-sounding

---

* This article was first published in Joseph Fewsmith (ed.), *China Today, China Tomorrow: Domestic Politics, Economy, and Society* (Lanham, MD: Rowman & Littlefield, 2010).

list of rights and duties of Chinese citizens, and formally endorsed the "open-door policy" for foreign trade and investment.

China's rapid and substantial economic reforms called for new legislation to regulate and guide China's transformation. Many laws and regulations were adopted on a "provisional" basis or "for trial implementation," to permit for trial and error. China's legal reform model, paralleling its economic approach, has been notable for its experimental and incremental approach of trying new ideas on an approved local or sectoral basis before applying them to the entire country. Chinese officials began cautiously to study foreign legal experience, especially with regard to how to regulate foreign companies and foreigners who were arriving in increasing numbers and setting up shop within China's borders.

Looking back over the past thirty years, China has done a remarkable job of creating a fairly complete system of substantive law. As of March 2009, China counts 231 laws, some 600 administrative regulations, and 7,000 local rules and regulations currently in force,[3] as well as roughly 600 regulations issued by the autonomous regions of China and "numerous" departmental rules at all levels that regulate different aspects of daily life.[4] Although China's Legislation Law differentiates between "laws" that can create rights and can only be passed by the NPC and local enactments passed by local people's congresses and governments, these legally binding, official documents are, following the Chinese practice, all generally referred to herein as "legislation" or "law."

China's domestic law is supplemented by a large number of bilateral and international treaties and agreements that China has joined, including forty-eight international conventions on environmental protection,[5] twenty-two international agreements on human rights,[6] and the World Trade Organization agreements, accession to which required China to commit to many changes in China's legal system and helped to promote China's move toward a more transparent governance model. China is becoming ever more engaged in the international economic and legal "order," although it reserves the right to adopt its own interpretations of these norms.

The 1982 Constitution has been amended four times. In 1999 the NPC added the principles that China exercises the rule of law and is "building a socialist country governed according to law" and, in 2004, that the state is to "respect and preserve human rights," as well as protect private property. While constitutional principles are important in articulating general aspirational principles, constitutional rights are not directly enforceable in Chinese courts. Realization of these rights normally requires enactment by the NPC of specific laws to provide the relevant details and procedures for carrying out these principles.

Over the years, lawmaking has also moved from emphasis on regulating the socialist market economy to achieving greater social fairness and justice. China's leadership recognizes that the legitimacy of its one-party rule depends not only on delivering economic growth but also on ensuring that its people are treated fairly and on creating a "harmonious society." In its embrace of the market economy, the government recognizes that it has withdrawn perhaps too far from such fundamental areas as public health and education. Recent NPC legislative plans have included more laws on social security, welfare and social relief, health insurance, labor protection, food safety, and the environment.

China's leaders have also come to realize that law is useful not only as a tool to regulate the economy and society, but also to restrain abuse of state power by government bureaucrats. In the absence of direct elections or other effective mechanisms to hold government officials directly accountable to the public, corruption and abuse of power have led to widespread feelings of disaffection between the Chinese people and their "people's government." Reported incidents of mass unrest increased from 58,000 in 2003 to roughly 90,000 in 2006,[7] at which point the authorities stopped disclosing specific statistics on protests and other manifestations of unrest.

While local leaders continue to rely on heavy-handed tactics to put down disturbances, the central leadership realized the governance model had to change in order to better address the underlying causes of social unrest, including environmental degradation, illegal land seizures and forced relocations for urban development, unpaid wages, police malfeasance, and government and business corruption, as well as to better deal with that unrest. Recent central policies and legislation seek to provide clearer procedural restraints upon, and clearer rights in the public to protect their interests against, state power.

After a brief overview of how the legal institutions of the people's congresses, the government, the courts, and the legal profession have developed over the past thirty years, this chapter explores in more depth how the party-state is working through administrative reforms to transform the lawmaking and policymaking process, to improve administrative mechanisms to manage conflict, and to help achieve better compliance with the law by both the public and the state.[8]

Having lots of laws, even good laws, is not sufficient to ensure that the law is broadly complied with and enforced, that is, what we think of as the rule of law. In contrast with the traditional "rule of man" that characterized imperial China and the Maoist era, or the instrumentalist "rule *by* law" that arguably describes reform-era China, under which the state views and uses law as a tool to regulate the public, the concept of "rule *of* law" requires that the state itself—and the party—also be subject to law. The 1982 Constitution stipulated that in principle everyone—including the state, the military, and all political parties—must abide by the Constitution and the law and that no one is above the Constitution and the law.[9] It also provides for basic legal institutions including lawmaking congresses and governments at all political levels, and law-enforcing courts and procuracies, and articulates a list of basic rights of Chinese citizens. Even the Party's own Constitution requires its members to abide by the laws and regulations of the state.[10]

Yet, despite its notable legislative and institutional accomplishments, Chinese leaders recognize that China's rule of law enterprise is not yet complete and admit that at least in some localities and departments "laws are *not* observed, they are *not* strictly enforced, and lawbreakers are *not* dealt with" (emphasis added).[11]

They have concluded that an important reason why the rule of law remains so elusive is that the formulation of laws and regulations has been insufficiently "scientific and democratic," resulting in laws that are inadequate to address the rapid economic, social, and political changes taking place in China and the lack of public support. Accordingly, the party-state is undertaking to make the lawmaking and law-enforcement institutions more professional, rules-based, participatory, and transparent.

The Legislative and Rulemaking Institutions

Under China's Constitution, all power ostensibly belongs to the people, and state power is to be exercised by the people through the "democratically elected" National People's Congress (NPC) and local people's congresses (together with the NPC, referred to collectively herein as "PCs") at the provincial, county, and township levels. The PCs make law and local regulations, supervise government organs, and approve the government budgets. [People's Congress] elections are becoming incrementally more competitive, and PC deputies somewhat more assertive and representative, but the PC system is still heavily influenced by the party, which essentially controls the appointment and election of PC delegates and congressional and government leaders.

The NPC and local PCs now meet regularly, but only once a year. Standing committees make most of the PCs' decisions between annual meetings in close consultation with the party, which sets the annual agendas for the full PC meetings at its own party congresses. Full-time legislative affairs committees under the standing committees are responsible for drafting and submitting national and local laws for approval either by the relevant standing committee or the full PC. In recent years these legislative committees are increasingly staffed by legally trained employees, including former law professors, in an attempt to improve the quality of legislation.

The State Council, China's cabinet appointed by the NPC, is the highest executive body and the center of state power, headed by the premier. It oversees China's central government ministries and commissions and the work of local governments at each level. Legislative affairs offices (LAOs) at each level of government draft administrative rules and regulations to carry out and enforce the laws and to regulate the government bureaucracy, as well as handle administrative appeals brought by the regulated public. The party controls the appointment or "election" by the PCs of high-ranking government officials at the corresponding political level. However, lower-ranking staff are part of an increasingly competitive and merit-based civil service system, and the trend is for LAO personnel to be trained in law.

Both of these lawmaking institutions are also moving toward a more transparent and participatory legislative process involving the use of public hearings, advice from subject matter experts, and written public input, drawing on research into international practices and experimentation.[12] Public participation is encouraged, but not required, for legislation deemed to be of particular public interest under the Legislation Law and its implementing regulations.

The PCs have historically been somewhat more open than the government, utilizing discretionary mechanisms such as visiting localities to listen to the people's opinions directly and permitting the public to "audit" or observe their annual meetings. While local PCs started experimenting with legislative hearings in 1999, the NPC Standing Committee held its first public hearing in September 2005, on draft revisions to the Individual Income Tax Law. Prior to 2008, the NPC selectively released a number of draft laws since 1949, including the 1954 Constitution, for public comment. In April 2008, the NPC Standing Committee announced that, going forward, all drafts submitted to it for review and adoption will ordinarily be made public as a standard practice, observing that an open and transparent legislative process would better ensure the public's "right to know, participate, express and supervise" and provide the people with a better understanding of new laws through participation in their formulation.[13] It has also promised to continue to experiment with public hearings and the broadcasting of its deliberations.

Following initial experiments by some central ministries and local governments, the State Council LAO first released draft regulations for public comment in October 2002. Thereafter, it gradually increased the number of draft regulations that it made public each year, until it announced in 2008 that it and the central ministries should henceforth release virtually all draft rules and administrative regulations—other than those relating to state secrets or national security—for public comment. State Council Work Rules

adopted in 2008 similarly call for increased public participation in major policy decisions and draft regulations, through written input as well as hearings when appropriate, and Premier Wen Jiabao directed in his 2008 Work Report that governments at all levels should henceforth release information about and hold public hearings before making major decisions.

The Courts

China's judicial system, which applies and enforces the law, comprises some 3,631 people's courts at four levels corresponding to the political structure, with the Supreme People's Court (SPC) at the apex, and staffed by roughly 200,000 judges. It also includes the 160,000-member procuracy that prosecutes cases and the public security apparatus, China's police.[14] The procuracy and public security organs primarily handle criminal cases.

Institutionally, the courts are not an independent branch of government but rather part of the government structure, subject to oversight by the procuracy and answerable to the PCs at the same political level. The NPC Standing Committee, rather than the SPC, has the authority to interpret national law, although the SPC issues judicial interpretations on questions arising out of specific application of law. Some of these interpretations are as a practical matter tantamount to supplemental legislation, and some draft interpretations have even been released for public comment, following the practice of government agencies and PCs in recent years.

Chinese courts are supposed to exercise their adjudicatory power independently, in principle through open trials and free from interference.[15] However, judges are appointed (in accordance with party guidance) and remunerated by the PCs at the corresponding governmental level, a system that fosters local protectionism and undue political influence. In practice, government officials may apply pressure on courts in particular cases, and the party may intervene through court-based adjudication committees that supervise the work of the judges and other channels. Consequently, the courts frequently decline to accept jurisdiction over sensitive cases, such as lawsuits relating to land seizures, official corruption, or "hot" social issues like government liability for the shoddily constructed elementary schools that collapsed and killed thousands of children in the Sichuan Province earthquake of May 2008.

In addition to institutional constraints on their authority and independence, the courts have traditionally been plagued by incompetence, lack of professionalism, and corruption, which undermine the public's trust. In the early days of the People's Republic, judges were frequently drawn from the ranks of the retired military and were not required to have any legal training. Now, new judges must hold university degrees and pass a national unified judicial exam, as well as participate in ongoing legal education programs. However, the quality of judicial personnel outside the major cities is still uneven, and low salaries contribute to widespread judicial corruption.

Lack of transparency in the judicial system also contributes to potential corruption. Since China follows a continental or civil law system, court decisions do not have binding precedential value as in a common law system like the United States, and legal opinions have not normally been made public, although selected decisions are published for reference by other courts and lawyers. Moreover, trials are frequently closed off to the public and media even though, in principle, they are supposed to be open to the public. The SPC announced reforms in early 2009 to introduce greater judicial transparency, including publishing court opinions and enforcement decisions online and permitting greater public access to trials,[16] as well as to prohibit acceptance of gifts and *ex parte* communication between judges and lawyers and to otherwise curb inappropriate and corrupt judicial behavior.

The appointment in March 2008 of Wang Shengjun as president of the SPC caused some pessimism about the road to judicial independence and rule of law. Wang's background was in party politics and public security rather than in law, and his appointment raised concern that the courts were being politicized. Continued momentum on a variety of judicial reforms, including some movement toward centralized funding of all courts to help overcome local protectionism, judicial transparency, and the promotion of judicial ethics, suggests that incremental progress toward a more professional and somewhat autonomous judiciary might continue.

Nonetheless, the Party seems conflicted about the degree of judicial independence it wants to actually foster, and it is not clear, thirty years after China began to develop a modern legal system, whether the courts will be permitted to effectively carry out their potentially critical role in resolving conflict, especially with the government, and in strengthening rule of law.

Lawyers

Of little relevance in traditional China, lawyers enjoyed a tenuous status in Republican China and the early years of the People's Republic. Less than 2,000 lawyers could be identified at the beginning of Reform and Opening in 1978. By the end of 2008, however, China had more than 600 institutions of higher learning offering bachelor's degrees in law, nearly 157,000 licensed lawyers, and over 14,000 law firms.[17]

The overall number of practicing lawyers for a country the size of China is still low (slightly more than one lawyer per one thousand people), and they are subject to the often strict "supervision and guidance" of local judicial bureaus under the Ministry of Justice (MOJ), which supervises the legal profession. Nonetheless, the legal profession is increasingly recognized as an important institution to help ensure that law is understood, observed, and enforced. Like lawyers around the world, Chinese lawyers not only handle a wide range of criminal, civil, and administrative cases and counseling; many lawyers and legal scholars also undertake "public interest" lawyering and get involved in drafting and proposing legislation.

Government agencies have begun to hire law graduates as "public service lawyers," although many of these seem to be assigned to perform legal aid for government-sponsored legal aid centers rather than fill the same kind of role as government lawyers do in the United States. Indeed, most legally trained officials working within government agencies are not technically qualified to be lawyers under the current Lawyers Law.

Government-supported and private legal aid are also developing rapidly. China's legal aid system dates back to 1994 but only began to flourish in recent years. The MOJ now requires all lawyers to handle a certain number of legal aid cases each year, and Chinese law now requires that criminal defendants must have access to legal assistance if they cannot afford it. Moreover, low-income citizens can apply for legal aid when seeking state compensation, social security, welfare, pensions, alimony, maintenance, child support, and labor payments.

Chinese trade unions are beginning to offer legal aid to migrant workers and others with labor disputes, and the government-supported All-China Consumers Association announced in early 2009 that it had received authorization to bring lawsuits. Law schools and non-governmental organizations sponsor legal aid clinics that assist low-income citizens with criminal defense, employment discrimination, family disputes, juvenile justice, urban relocations, and rural land takings. Although rural areas remain significantly underserved, legal aid seems to be becoming firmly rooted in China's changing legal culture and helping to raise rights consciousness among sectors of society that have not had much access to the formal legal system in the past.

Chinese lawyers are also becoming more politically active. A lawyer was elected as a deputy to the NPC for the first time in 1988. Since then law school professors and lawyers increasingly seek posts on local PCs to promote their law reform agendas, sometimes winning appointment by the local party but sometimes running as independent candidates. As of 2008, some 519 lawyers reportedly served as deputies to the PCs at all levels, and 2,845 are members of various levels of the Chinese People's Political Consultative Conference, a political advisory body.[18]

A growing number of Chinese lawyers have begun to file "public interest" cases that highlight particularly difficult or widespread social problems. Some practitioners estimate there are only about 120 public interest lawyers throughout the country, although the establishment of a nationwide public interest lawyers network in March 2009 to share and tap into professional expertise,[19] taking advantage of the Internet in China, may expand these numbers. While these lawyers frequently lose their lawsuits, the public attention thereby drawn to the issues through litigation often leads to beneficial changes in law or policy.

In recent years, a small number of courageous lawyers—sometimes referred to as "rights defenders"—have taken on and publicized sensitive cases

involving criminal defendants, peasant activists, displaced urbanites, religious worshippers, unpaid migrant laborers, and others who find themselves in conflict with the state. Such representation frequently places these lawyers in direct conflict with the local governments that license them. Criminal defense lawyers in particular and others who speak out on politically sensitive issues face the prospect of being jailed on such grounds as falsifying evidence or revealing state secrets and may lose their jobs and their licenses to practice law. As one prominent Chinese lawyer put it, "You cannot be a rights lawyer in this country without becoming a rights case yourself."[20]

Despite the sobering limitations on the role of the courts and the legal profession in helping realize rule of law in China, statistics show that these two institutions are in fact playing an ever greater role within Chinese society. In the five-year period 2003–2007, the courts heard approximately 26 million cases,[21] and the total number of cases heard in 2008 alone increased by 11 percent to over 10.7 million.[22] During this period, lawyers handled millions of criminal and civil cases, as well as administrative proceedings against the government, and provided a wide range of advisory services to both the public and the government.[23] Today, the coercive power of the party-state generally intervenes in the normal functioning of the judicial process only when a private interest is at odds with an important government or party interest. However, it is precisely these kinds of cases, involving state or party power, that most call into question the role of law in China and are most likely to cause widespread social unhappiness and unrest.

Law as an Instrument to Restrain State Power

The idea of using law to constrain state power is a relatively recent development in China. Traditional Chinese law contained numerous administrative regulations and codes, but these were primarily designed to regulate government practices, not to establish rights in the public to contest state actions. Only with adoption of the unprecedented Administrative Litigation Law (ALL) in 1989 were ordinary Chinese citizens for the first time given the right to challenge the legality of official action through lawsuits in the people's courts. Since then, China has been building a body of administrative law to better regularize government behavior and the government's interaction with the public.

Allowing the Chinese public to sue the government was heralded as a "revolution" in legal system development. The administrative tribunals have recorded a respectable plaintiff success rate of 20–40 percent over almost two decades. However, after an initial enthusiastic response, the number of administrative lawsuits leveled off, fluctuating around 95,000 per year. This flattening was attributed to a combination of lowered expectations due to the ALL's limits on what cases the courts can adjudicate and the reluctance of courts to accept complaints in more politically sensitive cases, rather than to a decline in grievances against the government.[24]

Nonetheless, plaintiffs (and groups of plaintiffs) have won some notable successes, including in the areas of environmental protection and land takings, and the number of administrative lawsuits seems to be inching upward in recent years, exceeding 109,000 in 2008,[25] with a plaintiff success rate of about 30 percent.[26] It is not clear whether this uptick in administrative lawsuits represents a long-term trend, but revision of the ALL is on the NPC's legislative agenda and many scholars and officials are working to broaden its scope to allow more cases to be heard in the courts.

The 1994 State Compensation Law permitted citizens to sue the government for monetary compensation for injuries caused by official action. Possibly due to its low levels of mandated compensation and some of the same limitations that discourage litigation against the government generally, relatively few compensation claims have been filed and only 34 percent of those awarded compensation, leading many to refer to it as the "State Non-Compensation Law." This law is also undergoing revision by the NPC.

As an alternative to suing the government, the 1999 Administrative Reconsideration Law (ARL) permits citizens aggrieved by unlawful or inappropriate government action to request review or "reconsideration" within the government agency itself. An average of slightly over 80,000 disputes—less than those taken to the courts—have been filed under the ARL every year since it came into effect.[27] Applicants can normally appeal the final administrative decision to the courts or bypass the administrative reconsideration (AR) system altogether and sue directly in the courts.

In principle, AR should be quicker than court proceedings, broadly accessible, and free of charge, and, because it is handled by career government personnel who may better understand the relevant regulatory background, potentially more professional. In practice, AR is fundamentally constrained by the same political environment that undermines the effectiveness of administrative litigation: the lack of truly independent or neutral adjudicators. While the officials who review the case may be somewhat removed from the issues in dispute, they are still within the same chain of agency command. Both the party and government leadership support reforms to make AR more professional and neutral, so the Chinese public will trust and accept the outcome, and begin to use this "in-house" dispute resolution mechanism more frequently.

Instead, a large number of disputants remain unsatisfied with both administrative litigation and reconsideration and have preferred resorting to a traditional petitioning or "letters and visits" system called *xinfang* (信访), which is governed by State Council Regulations on Letters and Visits. The State Council has a Letters and Visits Office, whose function is replicated throughout the bureaucracy at each level of government and in individual government agencies, the courts, the procuracies, and the PCs. While the courts nationwide heard close to 11 million cases in 2008, Chinese government agencies, including the courts themselves, have been flooded in recent years with upward of 11–12 million citizen petitions seeking assistance to resolve a range of grievances, including complaints about government behavior. Many Chinese legal scholars call for the abolition of the *xinfang* system altogether on the premise that it perpetuates disputes and undermines rule of law and the role of the courts, which need to be strengthened so that they can more effectively and finally resolve disputes.

The above laws seek to restrain Chinese state action by providing some redress to aggrieved citizens *after* the fact. Others seek to impose procedural constraints on government action *in advance* and have introduced unprecedented requirements of procedural due process.

The 1996 Administrative Penalties Law gave the Chinese public clear procedural rights for the first time, by requiring government agencies not only to publicize the range and standards for potential penalties, but also to give affected persons advance notice when the government proposes to impose a penalty, such as shutting down production, revoking a license, or levying a fine. This law further affords Chinese citizens the right to provide a defense to the charges and proposed penalty and to request a public hearing at no cost. The 1998 Price Law subsequently introduced the hearing into the broader administrative decision-making process, requiring that public hearings be held when government-set or guided prices are being determined or changed.

The 2003 Administrative Licensing Law also established procedural requirements for government action. Responding to a nationwide proliferation of government approval requirements that were unduly burdening both economic and social activity and fueling official corruption, it restricts government from imposing a license or permit requirement unless it can demonstrate that individual initiative, associations, or the market are not able to regulate the activity effectively. This law, which has no counterpart anywhere in the world, limits the government entities that have authority to issue licenses and the types of activity that can be so regulated. The law also stipulates procedures, including public hearings, to ensure transparency, fairness, and impartiality in the establishment and implementation of licensing requirements and in the licensing process. The number of matters requiring approvals at all levels has been nearly halved since the law's adoption, and some plaintiffs have successfully sued to stop polluting projects based on their failure to obtain required environmental licenses under this law.

Most recently, the State Council adopted nationally applicable regulations that require governments at all levels to disclose a broad range of records on their own initiative as well as upon request, albeit subject to broadly crafted exceptions for information constituting state secrets, commercial secrets, or privacy. The Regulations on Open Government Information (OGI), which took effect May 1, 2008, are yet another part of China's evolving administrative law and are seen as an important step toward a national law on information disclosure that will further promote government transparency.

Unlike many of the administrative laws discussed above, the OGI Regulations do specifically provide that agency failure to abide by their requirements can be appealed through administrative reconsideration or directly in the courts. Within the first seven days after they took effect, Chinese media reported seven cases brought by retired workers and peasants, in addition to lawyers and law professors. Many of the initial lawsuits were rejected or not acknowledged, but a few courts did rule that government agencies had to comply with the regulations and disclose the requested information. Moreover, the publicity surrounding some information requests pressured government to respond positively. For example, a Shanghai lawyer in January 2009 filed a request for details on China's stimulus plan to counter the global economic downturn starting in 2008 and, after he threatened to sue, the National Development and Reform Commission publicly pledged to disclose the plan on its website once it was approved by the NPC.

Other legislation to round out the administrative law framework and standardize government behavior is being drafted, including a law to regulate and prevent abuse of compulsory law enforcement measures, to regulate the imposition of administrative or user fees, and to require disclosure of civil servants' assets to curb corruption.

Law-Based and Open Government

Recognizing that the remedies provided by the administrative laws described above were insufficient on their own to address the continuing failures in observance and enforcement of law as well as holding lawbreakers accountable, and that these failures were undermining the government's credibility, the party-state has begun to promote a Chinese version of "reinventing government" under the rubric of "administration in accordance with the law" ([...] 依法行政). The State Council committed itself in 2004 to a ten-year reform program,[28] extending it down to the municipal and county levels in 2008.[29] The program calls for establishing clear rules on the scope of administrative power; fair, rational, and transparent administrative procedures to regulate the exercise of government power; more open government information and "scientific and democratic decision-making" with greater public participation; doing a better job of preventing and administratively resolving social tensions; introducing better law-enforcement mechanisms; and ensuring greater accountability for government actions. Some of these systems have been "legalized" through the administrative laws discussed above or in planned amendments thereto. Others are still at the policy stage.

Party Secretary Hu Jintao promoted the complementary theme of Party "governance in accordance with the law," calling for protection of the people's rights and interests and ensuring social fairness and justice in pursuit of a "harmonious society." Hu and Premier Wen Jiabao urged all segments of government and society to experiment with "innovations" in governance to "build a just, transparent, hard-working, efficient, honest, upright and clean government that follows a well-defined code of conduct, a government with which the people are satisfied."[30]

The Party and the central government have identified reform of the way decisions are made and laws and regulations formulated as critical to improving the entire administrative process. Public participation and increased transparency in lawmaking were identified as key mechanisms to build trust in government, curb rampant corruption, and help maintain social stability. The 2008 Government Work Report to the NPC promised to improve the quality of legislation by seeking views from many sources and publishing drafts to solicit the public's opinions, as well as developing the positive role of civic organizations to expand public participation in government affairs and give voice to the concerns of the people.[31]

To be sure, the handling of various forms of public participation is still in the experimental stage. The solicitation of written public input on legislative drafts, while steadily spreading in practice, is not yet standardized. Legislative or decision-making hearings in China all too often suffer from inadequate openness, hand-picked participants who are not necessarily representative of the diversity of views on a matter, and the lack of a public record of the hearing proceedings. Both the written comment process and public hearings need to provide better feedback to the public on the impact of their input on the final decision. Chinese commentators complain that these proceedings are often just "for show" and call for more standardized and transparent procedures

that would truly serve to curb arbitrary exercise of power and safeguard citizens' rights and interests.

Another area where China is introducing greater "open government" is in making various kinds of official meetings open to the public. Peoples' congresses have permitted citizens to "audit" or observe their meetings for a number of years. Some localities have begun experimenting with holding open government meetings, a "government under the sunshine" practice that is encouraged under Hunan Province's pioneering 2008 Administrative Procedure Provisions.[32] As another sign of increasing openness, many governors and mayors now provide mailboxes for public comments and questions on their official government websites and hold online chats to discuss current issues with the public, a modern channel for interacting with the people that has even been utilized by China's top leaders, Party General Secretary and President Hu Jintao and Premier Wen Jiabao.

More recently, in a new model for better dealing with protests, high-level local officials have held hearings or informal meetings with aggrieved protesters to discuss their issues and promised to do a better job of soliciting their input to prevent future problems. A series of taxi strikes prompted by largely similar grievances concerning unlicensed competition, fuel prices, and fees unrolled in different cities throughout the country in November 2008. In one of the first, the party secretary of Chongqing Municipality held a televised and podcast open hearing with aggrieved taxi drivers following a citywide strike.[33] Quick action, promises to address the complaints, the meeting with the party secretary, and a government apology to the public for not having managed the taxi system effectively convinced most drivers to go back to work, while the responsive handling of the incident was reported to have improved the Chongqing government's credibility.[34]

In the wake of these taxi-driver strikes, and other well-publicized protests and riots in 2008, former public security minister and Politburo member Zhou Yongkang observed that "more channels should be opened to solicit public opinion and local governments should spare no effort to solve people's problems,"[35] so as to prevent these problems from intensifying and leading to social instability. Clearly, the benefits of greater transparency and interaction with the public are increasingly recognized by Chinese leaders, if not always implemented.

While public participation procedures are not yet legally mandated at the national level, their increasing use and adoption of the OGI Regulations seem to reflect a growing appreciation of how greater openness and consultation can elicit public support and compliance with law and policy, as well as a growing confidence on the part of the Chinese leadership about their ability to interact with, respond to, and manage conflict with the Chinese public.

The Next Thirty Years

Thirty years after launching the Reform and Opening program, China has achieved at least one important plank of its legal reform objectives, that of establishing a sound and fairly complete body of law and regulations for not only the people, but also the government, to abide by. Basic legal institutions, including the people's congresses, the courts, the legal profession, and government agencies themselves, are becoming more professional, transparent, and responsive to public concerns.

However, the Chinese leadership recognizes it continues to face formidable challenges in achieving the other three goals of general compliance with and strict enforcement of the law and accountability for violations of the law. The conclusion to China's 2008 White Paper on establishing the rule of law observes:

> The development of democracy and the rule of law still falls short of the needs of economic and social development; the legal framework . . . calls for further improvement; in some regions and departments, laws are not observed, or strictly enforced, violators are not brought to justice; local protectionism, departmental protectionism and difficulties in law enforcement occur from time to time; some government functionaries take bribes and bend the law, abuse their power when executing the law, abuse their authority to override the law, and substitute their words for the law, thus bringing damage to the socialist rule of law.[36]

What the White Paper does not acknowledge is that undoubtedly the largest obstacle to achieving those goals is the ambivalence of the party itself about how far it is willing to permit the country to move toward true rule of law. Despite continued lip service to the importance of rule of law and the principle that party members must also be subject to the Constitution and the law, the party remains unwilling to give judges the authority to decide cases independently and the legal profession the latitude to zealously help the public achieve justice, particularly when cases involve the party-state. Moreover, the party maintains its own parallel, secretive system of "justice," under which the Party Central Discipline Inspection Commission investigates corruption and other forms of wrongdoing by party members, subjects them to the extralegal *shuanggui* (双规) or "double treatment" system, and only at its discretion turns those cases over to the judicial system for disposition.

In part due to its reluctance to permit the courts to handle the rising number of increasingly complex social conflicts, the party is advocating "transformation" of the Chinese government. The premise is that enhanced transparency, participation, and accountability will make government more efficient and effective and thereby reduce and better resolve disputes over government actions and policies and achieve better compliance with laws and policies. With increasing confidence, the party-state is beginning to standardize the use of public participation in different forms in legislation and policymaking and has already issued executive regulations requiring government at all levels to disclose a wide range of information both on its own initiative and upon request by the public.

The party-state is experimenting with making more government decisions publicly available, holding face-to-face adjudicatory hearings, improving the use of negotiation or mediation to resolve administrative disputes, and making the in-house administrative reconsideration system more professional, effective, and credible. The goal of these reforms is to satisfactorily settle disputes with the government so the people feel they have been fairly treated and do not subsequently resort to overburdened and often unhelpful courts or the *xinfang* system.

China's legislative accomplishments, the cautious movement toward a new model of government administration that is regulated and constrained by law, the rise of the beleaguered but resilient "rights protection" lawyers movement, and the Chinese people's seeming enthusiasm for continuing to use the courts and other legal avenues even though the track record seems so dismal, all do reflect substantial progress over the past three decades. From this perspective, China can be said to be moving further along the continuum from the traditional rule of man that Deng Xiaoping denounced, beyond the instrumental concept of rule *by* law that appeared pervasive in the first years of Reform and Opening, toward a rule *of* law under which all citizens, government entities, and political parties are truly subject to law.

China had no tradition of either democracy or rule of law on which to draw when it began this journey. We have learned in the United States that democracy and law are not settled but are dynamic works in progress. Both China's leadership and the Chinese people are experimenting with new practices, adopting new perspectives, and continually refining their unique "legal system with Chinese characteristics."

Looking back to reflect on the legal reform accomplishments over the past thirty years, the Chinese have established a comprehensive, modern, and sometimes innovative body of law. They are professionalizing their legislative and enforcement institutions. They are cautiously "democratizing" the legislative and decision-making processes through greater transparency and public participation to better involve the public and obtain their compliance with the law, and they are moving to make the judicial system more transparent and accessible.

The continuation of the generally positive trends of the past thirty years is by no means inexorable. The paradox, of course, is that China's Communist Party continues to espouse a rule of law that also constrains state power while insisting on the primacy of the Party. The tension between promotion of greater rule of law and one-party rule permeates the entire legal system.

However, the official rhetoric of legality and positive development of law and the legal institutions and processes discussed above, including the rapid growth of administrative law to not only regulate but also limit state power, is fostering a new culture of legality in the public and the party-state. These developments suggest that an increasingly transparent, participatory, and accountable China may well continue to progress further along the continuum toward rule of law.

NOTES

1. The Communiqué of the Third Plenum of the Eleventh Central Committee of the Communist Party of China of December 22, 1978, *Peking Review* 21, no. 52 (December 29,1978) at 14, www.marxists.org/subject/china/peking-review/1978/PR1978-52.pdf. The Chinese of the italicized language is *youfa keyi, youfa biyi, zhifa biyan, weifa bijiu.*

2. Hu Jintao, "Hold High the Great Banner of Socialism with Chinese Characteristics and Strive for New Victories in Building a Moderately Prosperous Society in All," Report to the Seventeenth Party Congress, October 15, 2007, English translation at www.china.org.cn/english/congress/229611.htm.

3. "Highlights of NPC Standing Committee Chairman Wu Bangguo's Work Report," National People's Congress, March 9, 2009, at www.npc.gov.cn/english-npc/Special_11_2/2009-03/09/content_1487180.htm.

4. State Council Information Office, *White Paper: China's Efforts and Achievements in Promoting the Rule of Law,* February 28, 2008, www.gov.cn/english/2008-02/28/content_904901.htm [hereafter "Rule of Law White Paper"].

5. Wang Canfa, "Chinese Environmental Law Enforcement: Current Deficiencies and Suggested Reforms, *Vermont Journal of Environmental Law* 8 (2006–2007): 159, 163.

6. Rule of Law White Paper, *supra* note 4.

7. "Post-Olympic Stress Disorder," *The Economist,* September 11, 2008, www.economist.com/world/asia/displaystory.cfin?story_id=12209848.

8. Some of the themes and examples discussed in this chapter draw on the author's chapter on "Rule of Law in China: Incremental Progress," in C. Fred Bergsten, N. Lardy, B. Gill, and D. Mitchell, *The China Balance Sheet in 2007 and Beyond* (Washington, DC: Center for Strategic and International Studies and The Peterson Institute for International Economics, 2007). For a general overview of the Chinese legal system, see Jianfu Chen, *Chinese Law: Context and Transformation* (Leiden: Martinus Nijhoff Publishers, 2008). For earlier classics on the Chinese legal system, see Stanley Lubman, *Bird in a Cage: Legal Reform in China after Mao* (Stanford: Stanford University Press, 1999) and Randall P. Peerenboom, *China's Long March toward Rule of Law* (Cambridge: Cambridge University Press, 2002).

9. Article 5, Constitution of the People's Republic of China, as amended March 2004, English translation at www.npc.gov.cn/englishnpc/Constitution/node_2825.htm.

10. Article 3, Constitution of the Communist Party of China, as amended October 2007, English translation at news.xinhuanet.com/english/2007-10/25/con-tent_6944738.htm.

11. Rule of Law White Paper, *supra* note 4 (in Chinese: *youfa buyi, zhifa buyan, weifa bujtu*).

12. See, Jamie P. Horsley, "Public Participation and the Democratization of Chinese Governance," in Yang Zhong and Shipin Hua, eds., *Political Civilization and Modernization in China: The Political Context of China's Transformation* (Hackensack, NJ: World Scientific Press, 2006).

13. Zhu Zhe, "NPC to Make All Draft Laws Public," *China Daily*, April 21, 2008, www.chinadaily.com.cn/china/2008-04/21/content_6630400.htm.

14. Jerome A. Cohen, "China's Reform Era Legal Odyssey," *Far Eastern Economic Review* 34 (December 2008).

15. Constitution, *supra* note 9, Article 126; ROL White Paper, *supra* note 4.

16. Xinhua News Agency, "Courts to Allow Easier Access to Judicial Services," February 19, 2009, www.chma.org.cn/government/central_government/2009-Q2/19/con-tent_17299842.htm.

17. China Law Society, *"Zhongguo fazhi jianshe niandu baogao (2008 nian)"* [2008 report on China's rule of law construction], June 3, 2009, news.xinhuanet.com/legal/2009-06/03/content_11478996.htm [hereafter "2008 ROL Report"].

18. "Association: Lawyers Play Bigger Role in China's Politics," *People's Daily Online*, October 26, 2008, english.people.com.cn/90001/90776/90785/6521573.html.

19. "'*Gongyi Ivshi wangluo' zai Beijing qidong zhenghe gongyi susong ziyuan*" [Public interest lawyers network started in Beijing, pooling public interest litigation resources], March 15, 2009, www.bj.xinhuanet.com/bjpd_sdzx/2009-03/15/content_15959074.htm.

20. Joseph Kahn, "Lawyer Takes on China's 'Unwinnable' Cases," *New York Times*, December 12, 2005.

21. Xinhua News Agency, "Highlights of Work Report of China's Supreme People's Court," March 9, 2008, english.sina.com/china/1/2008/0309/149438.html.

22. Xinhua News Agency, "Highlights of Work Report on China's Supreme People's Court," March 10, 2009, english.people.com.cn/90001/90776/90785/6610940.html.

23. "Practicing Lawyers in China Reach 140,000," *People's Daily Online*, October 27, 2008, english.people.com.cn/90001/90776/6522103.html.

24. Joseph Kahn, "When the Chinese Sue the State, Cases Are Often Smothered," *New York Times*, December 28, 2005.

25. 2008 ROL Report, *supra* note 17.

26. *Zuigaoyuan xin gongbu xingzheng anjian sifa jieshi* [SPC issues new judicial interpretation on administrative cases], *Caijing*, January 17, 2008, www.caijing.com.cn/2008-01-17/100045594.html.

27. Xinhua News Agency, "China Gives Public More Leeway to Disagree with Government Decisions," June 8, 2007, news.xinhuanet.com/english/2007-06/08/con-tent_6217625.htm.

28. *Quanmian tuijin yifa xingzheng shishi gangyao* [Outline for promoting the comprehensive implementation of administration in accordance with the law] adopted March 22, 2004, news.xinhuanet.com/zhengfu/2004-04/21/content_1431232.htm.

29. *Guowuyuan guanyu jiaqiang shixian zhengfu yifa xingzheng de jueding* [State Council decision on strengthening administration in accordance with the law by municipal and county governments], issued May 12,2008, www.gov.cn/zwgk/2008-06/18/ content_1020629.htm.

30. Wen Jiabao, "VI. Strengthening Government Reform and Improvement Efforts," Report on the Work of the Government to the National People's Congress, March 5, 2007, news.xinhuanet.com/english/2007-03/16/content_5857166_5.htm.

31. Wen Jiabao, "Report on the Work of the Government to the National People's Congress," March 5, 2009, www.npc.gov.cn/englishnpc/news/Events/2009-03/14/con-tent_1493265.htm.

32. *Hunansheng xingzheng chengxu guiding,* effective October 1, 2008, hn.rednet.cn/c/2008/04/18/1487353.htm.

33. Christopher Bodeen, "Chinese Official Talks to Striking Taxi Drivers," November 6, 2008, Associated Press, biz.yahoo.com/ap/081106/as_china_taxi_strike.html?.v=l.

34. Bodeen, "Chinese Official Talks."

35. "Public Must Be Allowed to 'Air Grievances,'" *China Daily*, November 26, 2008, www.chinadaily.com.cn/china/2008-ll/26/content_7239377.htm.

36. Rule of Law White Paper, *supra* note 4.

II. CORRUPTION AND CRIME

Fighting Corruption: A Difficult Challenge for Chinese Leaders*

Minxin Pei

The task of fighting and preventing corruption determines the party's legitimacy and survival.
—Hu Jintao, "Political Report to the 17th Party Congress" (2007)

---

* This article was first published in Cheng Li (ed.), *China's Changing Political Landscape: Prospects for Democracy* (Washington, DC: Brookings Institution Press, 2008).

Of all the potential risks for instability that dot China's changing political landscape, none may be more lethal than corruption by government officials. The abuse of power for personal gain, the classic definition of corruption, today permeates nearly all layers and departments of the government.[1] Anticorruption investigations have ensnared officials of all ranks, from members of the powerful Politburo of the ruling Chinese Communist Party (CCP) to senior generals and commanders of the armed forces, provincial Party secretaries and governors, top executives in financial institutions and state-owned enterprises, county magistrates, and village chiefs. In September 2006, the CCP dismissed Chen Liangyu, Shanghai's Party chief and a member of the Politburo, for alleged involvement in a corruption scandal. Each year since the 1980s, the CCP's top antigraft agency, the Central Discipline Inspection Commission (CDIC), metes out various forms of disciplinary action and punishment to roughly 100,000–170,000 CCP members and officials for various forms of wrongdoing (see Table 1). And each year Chinese courts prosecute more than 30,000 cases of corruption involving "large sums of money." Yet repeated campaigns against corruption and harsh penalties for lawbreakers, including the death sentence and life in jail for the worst offenders, have failed to restrain rapacious officials and curb abuses of power.

Despite some optimistic, though questionable, observations that corruption in China has not hurt its economic growth, endemic corruption threatens China's future prospects in many ways.[2] Politically, corruption by the members of the ruling elite undermines the legitimacy of the CCP, erodes the authority of the state, impedes the effective implementation of government policies, and fuels public resentment against the government. Economically, corruption creates distortions, increases the costs of commerce, causes waste and inefficiency, and stunts growth and employment. Socially, corruption exacerbates inequality, harms public safety, victimizes the poor and the powerless, and increases social injustice.[3] Ultimately, if the Party fails to curb corruption, China will most likely witness the rise of a form of authoritarian crony-capitalism that marries unaccountable political power with ill-gotten private wealth. Such a development would pose an enormous hurdle to the democratization of China in the future because the socioeconomic inequality embedded in a society dominated by

crony-capitalists hinders democratic transition and subverts democratic processes (this often continues to be true even after a democratic transition occurs).[4] Given the corrosive effects of corruption, it would be hard to imagine how China could confront its manifold economic, social, and political challenges in the decade ahead without waging a more committed and effective campaign against official corruption.

Corruption in China: Enforcement, Magnitude, and Scope

A frustrating difficulty in understanding corruption in China is the dearth of quality time-series data that accurately capture both the magnitude and the trends of corruption. For obvious reasons, the Chinese government does not publish such data, even though it is reasonable to assume that the CDIC collects such information. Another difficulty lies in interpreting the data on the investigation and punishment of corrupt officials.

The Enforcement Record While such data can be used to gauge the magnitude and trends of corruption, they actually reflect only the intensity of anticorruption efforts. In other words, although more intense anticorruption efforts yield more investigations and prosecutions, and therefore increase the number of corruption cases exposed and prosecuted, this does not necessarily indicate a worsening of corruption per se. However, any such worsening could be masked by lax enforcement, and to judge by the three key measurements of enforcement effectiveness—the rate of investigation, the rate of prosecution, and the rate of imprisonment—China does not have a tough enforcement record against corrupt officials.

If the number of CCP members punished for corruption and misdeeds is taken as an indicator of the scope of corruption, it seems that corruption grew significantly in the 1990s, given the average number of CCP members disciplined each year was about 50 percent higher in the mid-1990s than in the early 1980s (Table 1). Then in the early years of the twenty-first century, especially after 2004, these figures dipped: the number of CCP members punished from December 2004 to November 2005 was about 55,000 fewer, or about a third less, than in 2004. In 2006 only 97,260 CCP members received disciplinary actions, about 18,000 fewer, or 16 percent less, than in 2005. Furthermore, the punishment meted out to CCP members found to have committed wrongful deeds is generally mild (Tables 1 and 2). A huge majority—two-thirds—got away with only a mild to serious warning that appeared to have no real punitive consequences. Less than 3 percent were stripped of their CCP positions, only 9 percent received expulsion on probation, and roughly 20 percent were immediately expelled from the

Party. Only 6 percent were criminally prosecuted in the 1980s and 1990s. In more recent years, with the exception of the spike in the prosecution rate in 2004, only about 3 percent of the CCP members disciplined were prosecuted as criminals.

Is such relatively light punishment for wayward CCP members justified? Further details on the exact nature of the various violations and misdeeds perpetrated by such CCP members (Table 3) indicate that 48 percent of the CCP members disciplined and punished in 2006 committed very serious, and most likely criminal

Table 1 CCP Members Punished by the Party's Disciplinary and Inspection Committees, 1982–2006

Years	Average number punished and disciplined a year[a]	Percent expelled	Percent criminally prosecuted[b]
1982–86	130,000	23.4	n.a.
1987–92	146,000	21.0	5.8
1993–June 1997	190,000	18.2	5.6
October 1997–September 2002	169,230	16.2	4.5 (37,790)
December 2002–November 2003	174,580	n.a.	5.0 (8,691)
2004	170,850	n.a.	2.9 (4,915)
2004–05	115,143	21.0	13.1 (15,177)
2006	97,260	21.7	3.6 (3,530)

Sources: Yan Sun, *Corruption and Market in Contemporary China*, p. 47; Xinhua News Agency, November 19, 2002; www.chinanews.com.cn, February 22, 2004, January 21, 2005, and February 14, 2007; and *People's Daily Online*, February 13, 2006.
a. I use the twelve-month average for this column because the CDIC provides only five-year aggregate numbers for the period 1982–2002.
b. Number of members prosecuted in parentheses.

Table 2 Types of Disciplinary Actions against CCP Members, 2004–06

Action[a]	December 2004–November 2005	2006
Warning	44,836 (38.9)	37,343 (38.4)
Serious warning	32,289 (28.0)	27,185 (28.0)
Dismissal from CCP positions	3,173 (2.8)	2,744 (2.8)
Expulsion, on probation	10,657 (9.3)	8,777 (9.0)
Expulsion	24,188 (21.0)	21,120 (21.7)
Criminal prosecution[b]	15,177 (13.1)	3,530 (3.6)
Total number disciplined	115,143 (100)	97,260 (100)

Sources: People's Daily Online, February 13, 2006; www.chinanews.com.cn, February 14, 2007.
a. Figures in parentheses are percentages.
b. The numbers in these two columns are most probably already included in the "expulsion" category since only expelled CCP members are criminally prosecuted.

Table 3 Types of Infractions Punished by the CCP Disciplinary and Inspection Committees, 2006

Infraction	Number punished	Percent
Negligence	3,196	3.3
Obstructing and harming social order[a]	31,218	32.1
Violating rules of integrity, self-discipline, and financial matters[b]	15,350	15.8
Other	47,496	48.8
All	97,260	100.0

Source: www.chinanews.com.cn, February 14, 2007.

a. The Chinese term is *fanghai shehui guanli zhixu*.

b. The Chinese term is *weifan lianjie zilu be caijing jilu*.

offenses (such as obstructing and harming social order, violating the rules of integrity and self-discipline, or engaging in corrupt financial practices). The unspecified types of wrongdoing committed by 49 percent of the disgraced CCP members in 2006 also most likely included serious criminal acts. On this evidence, the severity of administrative and criminal sanctions against corrupt CCP members is fairly low.

The near quadrupling of the prosecution rate in 2004–05 appears to be an aberration. Intriguingly, it occurred during the transition from the Jiang Zemin era to the Hu Jintao era, which suggests a connection with inner-party political rivalry. Conceivably, the new leadership might have been motivated to use corruption charges to remove officials perceived as loyalists of the retired leadership, thus prosecuting many more miscreants within the CCP and causing the prosecution rate to spike in 2005. Alternatively, the high prosecution rate in 2005 might indicate that the new leadership is far more committed to fighting corruption and has taken a tougher approach. Unfortunately, the facts do not support this hypothesis because, after the unusual rise in 2005, the rate of prosecution fell to 3.6 percent in 2006—the second lowest level recorded since 1982. At least one thing seems clear about the new leadership's record on fighting corruption: the number of CCP members punished by the CDIC since 2004 has inexplicably collapsed, despite the prosecution of several high-level CCP and government officials in the same period (see Table 1).

What does this recent decline in the number of CCP members punished signify? As depicted in Table 1, it gives the government's anticorruption campaign an inverted U-shape: the number punished was low in the 1980s, began to rise steadily and apparently peaked during the period of 1992–97 (on an average annual basis), held steady until 2004, then fell dramatically after 2004. Unfortunately, the evidence points only weakly to declining corruption and more reasonably to lax enforcement as the cause, as corroborated by the falling rate of prosecution since the late 1990s. This rate declined by almost half between the mid-1990s and 2006 (see Table 1).

Indeed, paralleling the fall in the number of CCP members punished for corruption, the number of cases received by prosecutors began a precipitous decline after the mid-1990s (Table 4).[5] From 1996 to 2005, this number fell by nearly two-thirds. Moreover, only about half of the cases received by the prosecutors led to investigation and prosecution, demonstrating further a relatively low rate of prosecution of corrupt officials.

At the same time, the government appears to have been focusing greater attention on the more egregious cases (see Table 5). An estimate of the magnitude of corruption, as measured by the percentage of so-called major cases (defined in terms of the sums of money involved) and the number of cases involving officials at and above *xian* (county) and *chu* (division) levels, is telling. Roughly half of all prosecuted corruption cases involve large sums of money, called *da'an* (literally "big cases"). Apparently this category was reclassified in 1998 (when the sum was adjusted upward to reflect inflation); this led to a dramatic fall in the share of such cases among all cases filed. Subsequently, however, the share of *da'an* began to rise rapidly,

Table 4 Cases of Corruption and Abuse of Power Prosecuted by Courts, 1996–2005

Year	Number received by prosecutors	Number filed	Number concluded	Cases filed as a share of Cases received	Major cases (da'an)[a]	Key cases (yao'an)[b]
1996	180,186	82,356	88,574	45.7	39,727	2,700
1997	153,946	70,477	62,336	45.7	42,194	2,577
1998	108,828	35,084	34,081	32.2	9,715	1,820
1999	103,356	38,382	34,806	37.1	13,059	2,200
2000	104,427	45,113	40,770	43.2	16,121	2,872
2002	86,187	43,258	40,776	50.2	18,496	2,925
2003	71,032	39,562	37,042	50.1	18,695	2,728
2004	68,813	37,786	35,138	54.9	18,611	2,960
2005	63,053	35,028	32,616	55.5	18,416	2,799

Source: *Zhongguo falu nianjian* (Law yearbooks of China) (Beijing: *Zhongguo falu chubanshe*, various years).

a. Major cases, based on the amount of money involved (filed cases only). Such cases mirror one of the following criteria applied since 1998: embezzlement or bribes involving more than ¥50,000; misuse of public funds in excess of ¥100,000; collective misappropriation of public funds, unexplained wealth, and undeclared foreign bank accounts in excess of ¥500,000.

b. Key cases based on involvement of *xian-chu* officials (filed cases only).

Table 5 Share of Major (*da'an*) and Key (*yao'an*) Cases in Total Filed by Prosecutors, 1996–2002

Year	Total number filed	Major cases		Key cases	
		Number[a]	Percent	Number[b]	Percent
1996	82,356	39,727	48.2	2,700	3.3
1997	70,477	42,194	59.9	2,577	3.7
1998	35,084	9,715	**27.7**	1,820	5.2
1999	38,382	13,059	34.0	2,200	5.7
2000	45,113	16,121	35.7	2,872	6.4
2002	43,258	18,496	42.8	2,925	6.8
2003	39,562	18,695	47.3	2,728	6.9
2004	37,786	18,611	49.3	2,960	7.8
2005	35,028	18,416	52.6	2,799	8.0

Source: *Zhongguo falu nianjian* (Law yearbooks of China) (Beijing: *Zhongguo falu chubanshe*, various years).

a. Major cases based on amount of money involved.

b. Key cases based on involvement of *xian-chu* officials.

reaching 52 percent in 2005. Note, too, that the absolute number of *da'an* fell considerably after the reclassification in 1998 but has stayed at around 18,000 a year in the past five years, which suggests that such cases are of some concern.

Similarly, the number of officials with the rank of *xian* or *chu* and above prosecuted for corruption in the so-called *yao'an* (key) cases has held remarkably steady, at about 2,700–2,900 in the past decade, despite the significant decline in 1998 and 1999. Because of the huge decline in the number of cases filed by the prosecutors in this period, however, the relative share of major cases has more than doubled (from 3.3 percent to

8 percent). Again, this signals that the government has maintained its focus on addressing corruption by key officials even though the overall anticorruption efforts appear to have grown much less intense. Also significant is the increase in the number of bribery and embezzlement cases involving more than ¥1 million: from January to November 2005 this number rose by 8 percent over the comparable period in 2004; the number of corruption cases involving officials at, or above, *ting* level also rose 8 percent.[6]

If anything, the stabilization of the number of prosecuted key cases (at about 18,000) and the number of *xian-chu* officials prosecuted (now averaging 2,800 a year) may indicate the existence of a fragile anticorruption equilibrium. The Chinese government may have, in other words, routinized its anticorruption work, prosecuting a fixed number of key cases and officials each year. This equilibrium may have several implications. First, given the CCP's limited commitment to combating corruption (and its fear of undermining its own political authority and support base), the CDIC is not likely to refer as many corrupt CCP members as possible to government prosecutors. Second, the CCP nevertheless has an interest in maintaining a minimum level of internal discipline and wants to keep corruption by its own agents within certain limits. As a result, it uses criminal prosecution to punish officials whose actions blatantly exceed the CCP's implicit levels of tolerance, thus deterring those who might be tempted to follow suit. Third, without external political pressure, such as a mass political movement or extreme agitation in public opinion, it will probably be hard to break this equilibrium.

Although the data in Tables 1 do not reveal definitively whether corruption is increasing or decreasing in China, they do confirm that corruption is a very serious problem and involves large numbers of CCP and government officials. From October 1997 to September 2002, 28,996 *xian-* or *chu*-level and 2,422 *ting-* (department) or *ju*-level (bureau) officials were prosecuted. According to official statistics, China has 170,000 *difang ganbu* (local officials). This means that almost one in five local officials were prosecuted for corruption in a five-year period (assuming the number of officials did not expand significantly during the same period).[7] Despite the epidemic proportions of

official corruption, anticorruption efforts are less intense today than before, and the number of cases filed for prosecution has been declining, as has the rate of prosecution of CCP members found to have committed wrongful acts. Indeed, for all the CCP members punished for misdeeds today, only 3 percent are eventually prosecuted. Astonishingly, the actual punishment meted out to these individuals after they are prosecuted and convicted appears to be very mild. According to an official report, of all the 33,519 individuals convicted of using their official positions to commit crimes (*zhiwu fanzui,* a term referring mostly to official corruption) during 2003–05, 52 percent received suspended sentences and did not serve jail time. In comparison, only 20 percent of convicted common criminals receive suspended sentences.[8]

Magnitude and Scope By its very nature as an illicit activity, corruption is inherently difficult to measure in magnitude and scope. In this section, I employ a variety of measures to this end, ranging from public opinion surveys to officially reported figures and scholarly estimates.

Polling data suggest that the elite and the public consider corruption a serious social problem. In surveys conducted by researchers at the CCP's Central Party School, which trains midlevel and senior officials, the officials who participated in these surveys have consistently rated corruption as one of the most serious social problems in China since 1999. From 1999 to 2004, corruption was ranked either the most or second most serious problem facing the country. Only in 2005 and 2006 did other social problems—such as income inequality, crime, and lack of access to health care—top their concerns.[9]

Recent public opinion surveys show similar concerns with corruption. In a survey of 5,000 readers conducted by the influential official publication *Banyuetan* (Fornightly Discussion Forum) in July 2006, the issue of "intensifying anticorruption measures" was the fifth top concern of the respondents (behind rising income inequality; high costs of health care, education, and housing; unemployment; and an inadequate social safety net).[10] In an August 2006 survey of 4,586 business executives (87 percent of them in non-state firms) by the State Council's Development Research Center, only 20 percent rated their local officials as "very good" or "quite good" in terms of integrity, 45 percent rated them "so-so," 23 percent said "bad," and 12 percent said "very bad." In addition, 30 percent reported that they had to pay "extra fees" on top of standard interest rates in order to secure bank loans.[11]

Second, the magnitude of corruption may also be measured by the amount of misspent or misappropriated public funds found each year by the National Audit Agency's investigations. When the agency audited 22,000 government officials from January to November 2005, for example, it found that ¥290 billion had been spent in violation of laws and regulations (*weifa weigui*). In a two-year period (2004 and 2005), government auditors uncovered ¥14.5 billion in misspent funds by the various departments and ministries of the central government.[12] From 1996 to 2005, the National Audit Agency uncovered, altogether, ¥1.29 trillion in government spending categorized as *weigu* (in violation of the rules), averaging ¥129 billion a year, or about 8 percent of the on-budget spending in 2000.[13]

Third, the economic costs of corruption may be derived from a set of certain assumptions. One notorious example of corruption is officials' misuse of government-provided automobiles. In 2006 the government spent about ¥70 billion on purchasing such automobiles (and an undisclosed but presumably very large amount for the maintenance of said vehicles). If even as little as 10 percent of the spending on such automobiles is unjustified, then the cost of automobile-related corruption alone would amount to ¥7 billion in 2006. The total government procurement budget in 2005 (which includes the purchase of official automobiles) was ¥300 billion. If at least 10 percent of the procurement budget goes to corruption, then the amount that can be misappropriated from the procurement budget is, at a minimum, ¥30 billion (or 0.25 percent of gross domestic product [GDP] that year). If the price tag of corruption includes the costs of unjustified overseas visits by government officials, it rises considerably. In 2004 alone, officials' overseas visits cost Chinese taxpayers ¥480 billion. Assuming that a quarter of these trips are junkets, the costs of corruption in this area of spending would be ¥120 billion.[14] The so-called administrative spending in the budget, about 20 percent of the total budget (¥470 billion in 2003), is easily subject to misappropriation and theft. If illegal

activities constitute 10 percent of the administrative spending budget, this would cost ¥47 billion in 2003, or 0.4 percent of GDP that year.[15]

The cost of corruption in land transactions, known to be one of the most tainted economic activities, is presumably very high. In 2005 the government claimed that it generated ¥580 billion in revenues from land leases.[16] It is common knowledge that local governments underprice land leases for well-connected developers, often by a very significant margin. If these land transactions were underpriced by 20 percent, then the loss of revenue to the government in 2005 from land leases would be ¥115 billion. The biggest black hole of corruption appears to be fixed-asset investment, mainly infrastructure projects. In 2003, for example, state-owned firms and institutions spent ¥2.1 trillion (19 percent of GDP that year) on fixed-asset investments. If 10 percent of this massive amount of government spending were siphoned off in corruption, China would lose roughly 1.9 percent of GDP.[17] Thus a conservative estimate of the direct costs of corruption in the areas of government procurement, administration, and state spending on fixed-asset investments in 2003 would be 2.5 percent of GDP, assuming that 10 percent of such spending is diverted to private benefits illegally every year. If the loss of revenue from land transactions is added, then the cost of corruption would be 3 percent of GDP. Previous estimates by various scholars put the costs of corruption at 3–17 percent of GDP.

At the high end of the estimate, Hu Angang argued that corruption cost the Chinese economy about 13.3–16.9 percent of GDP in 1998. He included both the direct and indirect costs of corruption resulting from tax evasion (7.6–9.1 percent), siphoning off government investments and public expenditures (3.4–4.5 percent), income from the underground economy (0.4–0.5 percent), and "rents" from monopoly industries (1.7–2.7 percent).[18] At the lower end, I estimated that corruption in 1998 cost the Chinese economy about 3–4 percent of GDP. The share of tax evasion was much lower in my estimate. I also excluded the costs of rents from government-run monopolies.[19]

High-Risk Sectors By and large, corruption in China springs from the same causes as in other

societies: a combination of political and economic monopolies (that is, a lack of political and
economic competition). According to official
reports, it tends to be concentrated in the sectors
where China's government exercises a monopoly
or has extensive involvement. Termed "commercial corruption" (*shangye huiru*), such illegal
practices typically consist of bribes, kickbacks,
and misappropriations.[20] Anticorruption agencies
have repeatedly identified the high-risk areas, as
reflected in their priorities. In 2006 the Supreme
People's Procuratorate listed the following six priorities in prosecuting corruption: (1) attacking
bribery and embezzlement involving CCP and
government officials; (2) battling corruption committed by government officials using their power
of personnel appointment and project approval;
(3) fighting corruption committed by officials
in the process of the restructuring, bankruptcy,
and management of state-owned enterprises;
(4) combating corruption in the judiciary and law
enforcement agencies; (5) rooting out corruption
in major infrastructural projects, the financial sector, and land management; and (6) uncovering
and punishing bribes paid to officials in order to
advance illegal private interests.[21] In April 2007,
the Supreme People's Procuratorate announced
that four economic sectors, all highly lucrative,
would receive special attention: urban infrastructural projects, land sales and leases, construction,
and real estate.[22]

Infrastructural Projects Given the huge amounts
of public investment in infrastructural projects, it
is no surprise that kickbacks are common in this
sector. Kickbacks range from about 10 percent
to 20 percent of the total costs of infrastructural
projects.[23] Proportionally, infrastructural projects
account for a large share of all corruption scandals.
Of all the commercial corruption cases investigated by government prosecutors from January to
July 2006, one-quarter were related to infrastructure projects.[24] Anecdotally, the pervasiveness of
corruption in the infrastructure sector can be seen
in the downfall of many local officials in charge
of transportation (mainly highway construction)
and urban planning (project approval) policies. In
Henan, three successive directors of the provincial
transportation department were jailed for corruption. The same pattern was observed in many

other provinces. Altogether, provincial transportation chiefs in almost half of the provinces have
been arrested and sentenced for corruption.[25]
During 2002–07, three successive directors of the
Bureau of Urban Planning of Kunming, which
approves real estate projects, were arrested for corruption. One was sentenced to life in prison and
another to thirteen years.[26] Government officials
have generally engaged in the following corrupt
practices in the infrastructure sector: demanding
bribes in exchange for project approval, colluding
with architects and designers, reporting inflated
expenses for relocation, rigging the bidding process, subcontracting to favored firms in exchange
for bribes, accepting illegal commissions from
suppliers of building materials, lowering quality
control standards, inflating the costs of finished
projects, and conducting superficial inspections
and certifications following the completion of the
projects.[27]

Land Acquisition and Leases Since only a small
proportion of all land transactions are market based, corruption here consists largely of
bribes paid by developers to the local officials
in charge of land leases. Moreover, these officials often use illegal means to acquire the land
that they later lease to developers at low prices.
Following a satellite survey of sixteen cities in
2005, the Ministry of Land Resources concluded
that half of the land used for development was
acquired illegally.[28] Zhang Xinbao, director of the
Regulatory Enforcement Bureau at the Ministry
of Land Resources, disclosed that between 1999
and 2005 the government uncovered more than
1 million cases of illegal land acquisition, affecting more than 5 million *mu* (about 825,000 acres)
of land. Provinces that are more developed appear
to have fewer violations than less developed ones.
In some cities on the coast, about 10 percent of
all land acquisitions violated government rules.
In some cities in the central region, about 60–
70 percent of land acquisitions violated government rules.[29]

Violations of government regulations and illegal acquisitions allow local officials to pocket the
lion's share of the proceeds from land deals or
divert the benefits to their family members and
friends. According to one study, 60 percent of village and township cadres who had been accused

of using their powers to commit a crime were under suspicion of embezzling revenues from land deals.[30] Corruption in the real estate sector often implicates senior leaders. A vice governor of Anhui, the chief prosecutor of Tianjin, a vice mayor of Beijing, a large number of local leaders in Fujian, and many other local Party bosses, have been arrested and sentenced for getting involved in corrupt real estate transactions.[31]

The Financial Sector Poor regulation, weak governance, and inadequate internal control have made the financial sector (banks, brokerage houses, trust companies, insurance firms, and credit cooperatives) a rich target for corrupt officials and thieving insiders. In 2004 alone, bank regulators uncovered ¥584 billion in misused funds, 244 senior executives in the industry were arrested or dismissed, and a total of 1,219 individuals were deemed to be involved in corrupt practices in one way or another. In 2005 the situation seemed worse: regulators uncovered ¥767 billion in misused funds, and 1,466 individuals were allegedly involved in their misuse.[32] That same year, the Bank of China disciplined eight provincial branch chiefs and dismissed another eleven provincial branch chiefs (totaling two-thirds of its top provincial executives) for various causes, most likely corruption and negligence.[33] Several senior executives in the four mega state-owned banks have been jailed for corruption, including Wang Xuebing (chairman of the Bank of China), Liu Jingbao (chairman of the Bank of China Hong Kong), Zhang Enzhao (chairman of the China Construction Bank), and dozens of provincial branch chiefs.

As just mentioned, bank insiders are often involved as well. In 2006 the influential investigative business publication, *Caijing*, exposed evidence of collusion between senior state-owned bank officials and real estate developers who used fraudulent means to get loans from the state-owned banks, causing billions of yuan worth of losses to the banks in the form of nonperforming loans.[34] In one particularly egregious case, according to the chief auditor of the State Audit Agency, Li Jinghua, one company took out ¥1.1 billion in fraudulent bank loans and used ¥300 million of it to bribe various officials, presumably including bank insiders.[35] Indeed, corruption and fraud are rife in the financial services sector. In a survey of 3,561 employees in banks, state-owned enterprises (SOEs), private firms, brokerage houses, and farming households in 2003, 82 percent of the respondents said that corruption was "pervasive" or "quite pervasive" in financial institutions. Because of corruption, firms and borrowers were forced to pay bribes averaging roughly 9 percent of the loan amount.[36] China's nascent insurance industry is similarly plagued by the pervasive use of kickbacks, which sometimes amount to as much as 50 percent of the premiums paid out.[37] Media reports, too, charge that corruption in the financial sector often entails collusion between outsiders and bank insiders.[38] *Caijing* published a long investigative story in 2006 that exposed a real estate developer who colluded with two branch chiefs of the Beijing City Cooperative Bank in an elaborate scheme to defraud various state- and city-owned banks of as much as ¥2 billion.[39]

State-Owned Enterprises Transactions in the restructuring, privatization, and transfer of state-owned assets, especially in SOEs, breed corruption because such activities are monopolized by insiders—usually local officials or SOE executives, or both. Because market forces play a negligible role in these transactions, insiders can more easily underprice state assets and thereby reap huge profits. In 2004 SOEs owned by the central government declared asset losses close to 10 percent of the value of their net assets. It is suspected that a large portion of these losses were siphoned off by SOE executives.[40]

The Pharmaceutical Industry Official reports indicate corrupt practices are common in the approval, sale, purchase, and prescription of pharmaceuticals. Kickbacks are prevalent and often involve doctors, who can get illegal commissions from pharmaceutical companies for prescribing their products. Even top industry regulators are routinely bribed to get them to approve drugs of dubious effectiveness. Zheng Xiaoyu, the director of the State Drug Administration, which regulates the pharmaceutical industry, was arrested in March 2007 after investigators found that he had taken ¥5 million to ¥6 million in bribes from drug companies in exchange for approving their products.[41]

Corruption Across Sectors

The extent of corruption across various sectors can be assessed from the findings of a major study conducted by the prosecutors office of Jiyuan City in Henan Province, as reported in the weekly newspaper *Lianzheng zhoukan* (Government Integrity Weekly) in 2006. In 3,067 "representative" cases of *zhiwu fanzui* (using one's official position to commit crime), about half related to infrastructural projects and land transactions, 20 percent to government procurement scandals, and 13 percent to corrupt or fraudulent loan approvals. When the ranks of the corrupt officials were examined in more detail, those at or above the *chu*-level, 1,348 altogether, accounted for almost 44 percent of all the cases in the study. Of this group, 608 (45 percent) were implicated in infrastructure and land transaction scandals, 216 (16 percent) in *maiguan-maiguan* (the buying and selling of government appointments), 120 (9 percent) in illegal loan approvals, 95 (7 percent) in questionable sales practices such as kickbacks, and 67 (5 percent) in asset-stripping during SOE restructuring.[42]

Corruption in Key Institutions China's most vital political institutions—the CCP, the judiciary, law enforcement, and local bureaucracies—have all been severely damaged by corruption. Perhaps most serious of all is its easy penetration of the legal system, which remains heavily politicized and lacking in transparency despite small efforts at modernization. In the absence of systematic data, the extent of judicial corruption is unclear, but several anecdotes provide strong hints of its depth. In 2003, for example, thirteen judges of Wuhan's Intermediate Court, including two vice presidents, were arrested and sent to jail for corruption; forty-four lawyers were also implicated in the same scandal. Surprisingly, even all of these arrests combined failed to curb corruption in this particular court: in 2006 the president of the court, Wu Zhenghan, was arrested for taking ¥3 million in bribes.[43]

In Fuyang City, one of the most corrupt regions in Anhui, a large number of senior judges of the Fuyang Intermediate Court were implicated in corruption scandals, including three successive presidents of the Fuyang Intermediate

Court who were arrested and tried for corruption. Other disgraced judges included a vice president of the court, the chief and deputy chief of the criminal tribunal, the chief and deputy chief of the enforcement division, and the chief judge of the economic chamber.[44] In Shenzhen, one vice president and four senior judges (heads of the civil tribunals) of the Intermediate Court were arrested for corruption in 2006. They all took huge bribes.[45] In addition, the chief prosecutor of Jiangsu Province, Han Jianlin, and the chief prosecutor of Tianjin were both brought down in corruption scandals in 2006.

Like the judiciary, China's other key institutions are now rife with the most insidious forms of corruption: the buying and selling of government appointments (*maiguan-maiguan*) and collusion among local ruling elites. These activities usually signify late-stage political decay.

Buying and Selling Government Appointments The practice of *maiguan-maiguan* was practically unheard of in the 1980s but has become prevalent since the 1990s, as is evident from shocking news accounts of local officials taking large bribes in exchange for appointments to desirable government positions. This is a particularly pernicious activity because it completely undermines the integrity of the state and turns government positions into nothing more than investments for rapacious individuals. In one of the most notorious cases, Ma De, the Party boss of Suihua in Heilongjiang Province, sold hundreds of government appointments in return for millions of yuan in bribes. Han Guizhi, a long-serving powerful Heilongjiang CCP organizational chief, also sold government positions for bribes. A similar scandal brought down Xu Guojian, the CCP organizational chief of Jiangsu Province in 2004. Xu sold positions to the province's deputy chief prosecutor, the provincial chief of the anticorruption bureau, and the head of the provincial transportation department, the chairman of the provincial toll-road operations board, the director of the provincial state-asset investment and trust company, and the head of the provincial state-asset management group. Altogether, these individuals oversaw state-owned assets in excess of ¥60 billion.[46]

Just a few examples can serve to illustrate how lucrative this practice can be. In a fourteen-month period during 2003–04, Wu Bao'an, a county Party boss in Shanxi Province, took in ¥5 million in bribes from individuals who paid him to secure government appointments.[47] Xu Guojian, Jiangsu's organization chief, netted ¥6.4 million (¥2 million from one deal alone).[48] Han Guizhi, the provincial CCP organization chief in Heilongjiang, pocketed ¥7 million in bribes from officials seeking promotions between 1993 and 2003. And Tian Fengshan, former governor of Heilongjiang, received ¥4.4 million in bribes from 1996 to 2003 for handing out juicy government positions to those willing to pay.[49] The national record for *maiguan-maiguan* belongs to the aforementioned Ma De, the former CCP boss in Suihua prefecture in Heilongjiang. From 1997 to 2002 he collected bribes worth ¥24 million, for an average of more than ¥10,000 (approximately US$1,250) a day.[50] The most extreme case of *maiguan-maiguan*, which occurred in Heilongjiang, involved 265 officials, including five officials at the deputy governor level.[51]

Collusion Widespread collusion among members of the ruling elite completely subverts the political hierarchy and state authority and thus is widely regarded as a symptom of almost incurable institutional decay. Previously unknown or rare in China, collusive corruption—termed *wo'an* (literally, nest cases)—has become common since the 1990s. In retrospect, its emergence was predictable. Since the Cultural Revolution, members of the ruling elite have become quite negative about mass political movements, and since Tiananmen, they have been shielded from the scrutiny of the mass media and civil society by the conservative political environment. As a result, those engaged in corrupt activities are under no serious threat other than denunciation by their colleagues. Collusion and the sharing of the spoils of corruption have therefore become the preferred strategies of cooperation among the ruling elite.

Anecdotal evidence from various localities indicates that 30–65 percent of all corruption cases can be classified as *wo'an*.[52] In the previously cited study of more than 3,067 corruption scandals, 552 (or 18 percent), were *wo'an*. Collusive corruption has brought down numerous senior officials, sometimes numbering in the hundreds. In one study it was blamed for 29 of 36 corruption cases involving officials at the vice ministerial level

and above.[53] In Suihua, where Ma De ran a racket of selling government appointments for years, 260 officials, including the chiefs of fifty government agencies and Party organizations, were involved in the scandal.[54] Collusive corruption can turn an entire city or town into a local mafia state, as in the case of Fuyang City, a major region in Anhui with a population of 9 million. The impoverished city has the distinction of producing a string of corrupt Party chiefs and mayors. Hundreds of local officials above the rank of *ke* (section) were investigated and punished for corruption. Most of the chiefs of the city's main bureaucracies, including the police and the finance bureau, have been involved in corruption.[55]

In a very large number of jurisdictions, local officials even collude with and protect mafia elements. The government reported that, as of January 2004, nearly 1,000 officials had been exposed for providing protection for organized crime. From March 2006 to March 2007, the government prosecuted fifty-four cases involving sixty-two officials who protected organized criminal groups.[56] He Qinglian, a leading social critic, has gone so far as to argue that the behavior of the state has increasingly assumed the style of organized crime (*heishehui hua*).[57]

In one of the most notorious such cases, Hou Wujie, a vice governor and third highest official in Shanxi Province, was arrested in 2004 for protecting a local mafia boss. In another highly publicized case, the deputy chief of police of Jiangxi Province, Xu Xiaogang, asked a local crime boss to pay ¥450,000 to his mistress in 2003 to set up a business. Xu had provided protection for the crime boss for years.[58]

Collusion and protection have made it much harder for the authorities to crack down on corruption, with the result that many corrupt officials have been able to engage in extended predatory activities and even get promoted through the CCP and government hierarchies. For a full fifteen years, from 1990 to 2005, Wang Zhaoyao accepted bribes totaling ¥7 million on 294 occasions while he was a vice governor of Anhui Province. He could not explain where another ¥8.1 million came from. Another official, the toll-road administration chief of Hunan Province, took in nearly ¥3 million in bribes from 1994 to 2004 (in addition to ¥2.6 million in unexplained wealth); despite his actions, he kept getting promoted during this period.[59] Collusion also appears to account for as much as 61 percent of all financial corruption and crime cases.[60]

Conclusion: Corruption and Prospects for Democracy

To be sure, the Chinese government has promulgated numerous laws and rules to combat corruption. By one account, China has more than 1,200 laws, rules, and regulations designed to curb official corruption. Clearly the problem is not a lack of legal injunctions against corruption but their weak implementation and effectiveness.[61] In recent years, Beijing has taken additional measures and begun various experiments to combat corruption.

Recent Anticorruption Measures In fighting corruption within the elite, the CCP is forced to strike a delicate balance. On the one hand, it needs to restrain greedy officials from undermining economic development and stoking public resentment. On the other hand, it is afraid of unleashing popular opinion and unwanted civic participation that could threaten its legitimacy and rule. As a result, most recent measures tend to be top-down organizational initiatives or administrative adjustments that attempt to curb corruption within the current institutional framework of the one-party state.

In one of its most notable moves, the CCP Central Committee has begun rotating provincial anticorruption chiefs (known as secretaries of the provincial CCP discipline and inspection committees) and dispatching the CDIC's own senior personnel to assume such provincial positions. By the end of 2006, ten of the newly appointed fifteen provincial discipline chiefs (*jiwei shuji*) were either from another province or from the CDIC.[62] Even though these new discipline chiefs now occupy a lower rank because the number of deputy provincial Party secretaries has been reduced (the discipline chief is now a member of the standing committee of the provincial Party committee), they are supposedly more accountable to the central government since the CCP Central Committee controls the nomination and appointment of such officials.[63] Through similar recentralization initiatives in 2004 and 2005, the CDIC

eliminated the previous system of "dual control," under which the CDIC's inspectors stationed in fifty-six critical government ministries, agencies, and SOEs used to report both to the CDIC and the bureaucracy's Party organization. As a result, the inspectors now report only to the CDIC, without the threat of interference from these bureaucracies. In another move to overcome local obstruction, Beijing established nine land supervisory bureaus to enforce land laws. In addition, five environmental inspection centers, directly reporting to Beijing, were set up in 2006 to monitor local compliance with environmental regulations.

In August 2003, the CCP had already formed roving local inspection teams to increase the monitoring of powerful provincial Party chiefs. A staff of forty-five serves five "central teams," which report to the CDIC and the Central Organization Department. Each team is headed by a ministerial official who has recently stepped down but is not yet formally retired. In a period of three years, the inspection teams visited 150 cities. However, such teams are unlikely to be effective because the heads of inspection teams lack political power, their staffs are too small, and they have restricted local access.[64] According to a former head of the Central Organization Department, when the CCP evaluates a senior provincial official, it usually solicits opinions of *ju* (bureau) and *ting* (department) officials. But local social and political networks are so complex that the CCP's evaluation team rarely obtains an accurate picture of the official being evaluated.[65]

With the aid of modern technology, the Supreme Procuratorate plans to publish the names of those who pay bribes and wants to set up a national electronic database on the individuals who have committed bribery in construction, finance, education, pharmaceuticals, and government procurement (though it has yet to implement these plans).[66] In 2004, during the height of the campaign against *maiguan-maiguan*, the Central Organization Department set up a special hotline, 12380, to allow whistle-blowers to report cases of corruption involving organizational matters, especially *maiguan-maiguan*.[67]

While these are welcome measures that should have some effect in Beijing's campaign against corruption, more drastic political reforms are needed to root it out among officials. International experience suggests that the most effective weapons against official graft are greater governmental transparency (often enforced by democratic political institutions), judicial independence (which ensures punishment of the guilty and maintains deterrence), a free media, and monitoring by nongovernmental organizations (NGOs). Indeed, some inside the CCP have recognized the need for outside pressure. In the opinion of Lu Dingyi, a veteran revolutionary who was the Party's propaganda chief before the Cultural Revolution, "self-discipline" alone cannot solve the corruption problem within the CCP, which cannot be its own "referee" in this fight. The power to adjudicate and monitor corruption within the CCP, said Lu, must reside outside the Party, in the hands of the people and the mass media. This, added Lu, was the only effective solution.[68]

Prospects for Democratic Change Ironically, worsening corruption may precipitate democratic change even as it threatens to undermine China's democratic prospects by giving birth to crony-capitalism and derailing economic development. The CCP's incremental steps to fight corruption could gradually help expand the role of the media

and civil society, thus introducing political liberalization through the back door. Indeed, China's mass media today already function as key players in exposing official wrongdoing and galvanizing public opinion against corruption. If it is serious about combating corruption, China must also strengthen the autonomy of the judiciary. Such a move, if adopted by the CCP, would contribute to the rule of law.

Alternatively, runaway corruption could accelerate regime decay, induce collapse, and in that way trigger a democratic transition. Uncontrolled corruption could, at some point in the future, conceivably destroy the legitimacy of the CCP, corrode the authority of the state, cause serious economic hardship or even a financial crisis, fuel social unrest, and contribute to environmental degradation. However, a crisis of those proportions may not necessarily spawn a stable liberal democracy. The transition costs would likely be extremely high, and the resulting new democracy could easily fall under the control of China's own oligarchs, whose illicitly acquired wealth could accord them great resources to manipulate an infant democratic system.

NOTES

1. For recent literature on corruption in China, see Yan Sun, *Corruption and Market in Contemporary China* (Cornell University Press, 2004); Shawn Shieh, "The Rise of Collective Corruption in China: The Xiamen Smuggling Case," *Journal of Contemporary China* 14, no. 42 (2005): pp. 67–91; Andrew Wedeman, "The Intensification of Corruption in China," *China Quarterly*, no. 180 (December 2004): 895–921; Xiaobo Liut, "Booty Socialism, Bureau-Preneurs, and the State in Transition: Organizational Corruption in China," *Comparative Politics 32* (April 2000): 273–94.

2. Li Shaoming and Judy Jun Wu claim that corruption has not hurt China's economic growth because of high social trust. But the only empirical evidence they offer is a survey by the World Values project showing that 54 percent of the people in China reported they trust other people. Li Shaoming and Judy Jun Wu, "Why China Thrives Despite Corruption," *Far Eastern Economic Review*, April 7, 2007, pp. 24–28.

3. Chinese press reports show that corruption is frequently behind major environmental accidents, mining disasters, and the sale of counterfeit products, including dangerous, fake pharmaceuticals.

4. In the Chinese context, *crony-capitalism* refers to government officials' practice of giving sweetheart real estate deals, government contracts, and state-bank loans

to companies owned by their children, friends, and bribe-givers. Two high-profile scandals in Shanghai are representative. Zhang Rongkun, a well-connected thirty-five-year-old private entrepreneur from Zhejiang, managed to borrow more than ¥10 billion to invest in toll roads. Most of his loans came from the Shanghai Social Security Fund. Zhou Zhengyi, a Shanghai private real estate developer, made a huge fortune mainly by gaining access to cheap land and easy credit from state-owned banks. *Gaige neican* (Internal reference materials on reform), no. 26 (2006), pp. 14–16.

5. Chinese prosecutors usually get most of their cases from the CCP's in-house discipline and inspection committees, which decide whether to transfer to the courts for criminal prosecution the cases they investigate and conclude.

6. See www.chinanews.com.cn, January 19, 2006.

7. *Gaige neican*, no. 6 (2006), p. 910; in 2006 the number of *difang* officials was 170,000. *China Newsweek*, August, 21, 2006, p. 32.

8. The trend seems to be worsening. In 2001, 51 percent of individuals convicted of *zhiwu fanzui* received suspended sentences; in 2005, 67 percent did. *Gaige neican*, no. 23 (2006), p. 17; www.chinanews.com.cn, July 26, 2006.

9. Corruption was rated the most serious social problem in 2000 and 2002, and the second most serious in 1999,

2003, and 2004. In 2006 the top three issues were crime, income inequality, and lack of access to health care. In 2005 the top three were income inequality, regional income disparities, and declining public morality. In 2004 income inequality was tops; in 2003, unemployment. The number of midlevel officials who participated in each survey ranges from 100 to 150. *Blue Book on Chinese Society* (Beijing: Shehui kexue chubanshe, various years); *Gaige neican*, no. 35 (2006), p. 19.

10. *Banyuetan* (Fortnightly Discussion Forum), August 15, 2006, p. 4.

11. *DRC Research Report* 285, December 13, 2006.

12. Such violations include overstating the number of staff, setting up slush funds, misappropriating special funds, and collecting illegal fees. See www.chinanews.com.cn, October 16, 2006, and December 26, 2005.

13. Xu Sitao, "Shengzhi Jiasu nan," *Caijing* (Finance), July 24, 2006, p. 68; I decided to use the on-budget expenditures in 2000 as a reference point because this happened to be the midpoint for this period. See *Zhongguo tongji nianjian 2004* (Chinese Statistical Yearbook 2004) (Beijing: Zhongguo tongji nianjian chubanshe, 2005), p. 291.

14. Huang Genglan, "Gaige neican pinglun ban," *Gaige neican*, no. 15 (2006), p. 46.

15. *Zhongguo tongji nianjian* 2004, pp. 53, 293.

16. Xiao Hua, "6000 Yi xingzheng shoufei jingle sheide yaobao?" *Beijing wanbao* (Beijing Evening News), May 9, 2007, p. 16.

17. *Zhongguo tongji nianjian 2004*, p. 187.

18. Hu Angang, *Zhongguo: Tiaozhan fubai* (China: Challenging corruption) (Hangzhou: Zhejiang renmin chubanshe, 1999), p. 61.

19. Minxin Pei, "Will China Become Another Indonesia?" *Foreign Policy*, Fall 1999, pp. 94–109.

20. Xie Shan, "Shangye huilu shida paixingbang," *Fanfubai daokan* (Anti-Corruption Herald), no. 4 (April 2006), pp. 7–16.

21. "Zhanwang 2006: Liuda yaoan cheng fangfu zhongdian," *Jiancha fengyun* (Prosecutorial Storm), no. 2 (2006), p. 8.

22. See www.chinanews.com.cn, April 29, 2007.

23. Xie Shan, "Shangye huilu shida paixingbang," *Fanfubai daokan*, no. 4 (April 2006), pp. 7–16.

24. See www.chinanews.com.cn, October 17, 2006.

25. These officials include Zhao Zhanqi, director of the provincial transportation department of Zhejiang. Reported by *Jiancha ribao* (Prosecutors' Daily) (www.chinanews.com.cn, April 12, 2007).

26. Ibid.

27. Ibid., April 29, 2007.

28. Ibid., February 7, 2007.

29. Ibid., June 20, 2006.

30. Ibid., March 27, 2007.

31. Ibid., August 4, 2006.

32. Xie Shan, "Shangye huilu shida paixingbang," *Fanfubai daokan*, no. 4 (April 2006), pp. 7–16.

33. Wang Yuanfu, "Fanfu zaixian," *Fanfubai daokan*, no. 5 (May 2006), p. 5.

34. Lu Lei, "Guatou zhimeng—fangdichan paomo yu jinrong anliu," *Caijing*, September 4, 2006, pp. 39–70.

35. See www.chinanews.com.cn, September 25, 2006.

36. Xieping and Lu Lei, "Jinrong fubai qiujie," *Caijing*, January 10, 2005, p. 48.

37. Xie Shan, "Shangye huilu shida paixingbang," *Fanfubai daokan*, no. 4 (April 2006), pp. 7–16.

38. See www.chinanews.com.cn, April 12, 2007.

39. Li Qing and Hu Jiao, "Fantan guanyuan shetan," *Caijing*, no. 4 (2006): pp. 39–58.

40. Xie Shan, "Shangye huilu shida paixingbang," *Fanfubai daokan*, no. 4 (April 2006), pp. 7–16.

41. Nicholas Zamiska, "China's Probe Vindicates Drug Critic," See www.chinanews.com.cn, April 7, 2007; *Wall Street Journal*, April 5, 2007, p. B2.

42. See www.chinanews.com.cn, March 27, 2007.

43. Wang Heyan, "Wuhan zhongyuan zaimeng yinying," *Caijing*, September 4, 2006, p. 126; www.chinanews.com.cn, May 3, 2007.

44. Ren Jianming, "2005 Fangfubai Zhanwang," *People's Daily Online*, May 11, 2005; Xiao Zhong, "Zhuoyang zhongyuan sanren yuanzhang qi shoushen," *Jiancha fengyun* (Prosecutors' Storm), no. 22 (2006), pp. 22–25.

45. See www.chinanews.com.cn, November 10, 2006.

46. Bao Yonghui, "Guo Bensheng, Toushi guanchang 'quanzhi bing,'" *Liaowang xinwen zhoukan* (Outlook News Weekly), no. 2 (2005), p. 8.

47. "Zhonggong zhongyang guowuyuan guanyu shishi keji guihua ganyao, zhengqiang zizhu cuangxin nengli de jueding," *Xinhua yuebao* (Xinhua Monthly), March 2006, p. 43.

48. Huang Shan and Xia Lin, "Shengwei zuzhi buzhang de 'qinpeng maiguan tuan,'" *Xiangzhen luntan* (Township and Village Forum), no. 4 (2006), p. 30.

49. *Gaige neican*, no. 6 (2006), p. 9.

50. See www.chinanews.com.cn, May 3, 2007.

51. Ibid.

52. Minxin Pei, *China's Trapped Transition: The Limits of Developmental Autocracy* (Cambridge, MA: Harvard University Press, 2006), p. 160.

53. *Gaige neican*, no. 6 (2006), pp. 9–10.

54. See www.chinanews.com.cn, March 27, 2007.

55. *People's Daily Online*, May 11, 2005; Xiao Zhong, "Zhuoyang zhongyuan sanren yuanzhang qi shoushen," *Jiancha fengyun*, no. 22 (2006), pp. 22–25. The following Fuyang officials have been arrested or sentenced for serious corruption: the director of the Bureau of State Security, who collected ¥10 million in bribes; the deputy police chief, sentenced to life in prison for taking ¥5.5 million in bribes; a former Party secretary responsible for law enforcement, arrested for accepting "huge" bribes; the head of the traffic division of the local police, found guilty of pocketing ¥14 million in bribes; Wang Huaizhong, a former Party secretary and vice governor, executed for taking tens of millions of yuan in bribes; Wang Zhaoyao, another former party secretary and vice governor, arrested; and Xiao Zuoxin, a former mayor, executed for corruption. Other corrupt officials included a party chief and the city's police chief. Altogether, eight members of the city CCP Standing Committee and 11 *ting*-level officials were brought down by corruption over the years.

56. See www.chinanews.com.cn, November 21, 2005, and April 29, 2007.

57. See He Qinglian, "Zhongguo zhengfu xingwei de heishehui hua" (The criminalization of the behavior of the Chinese government), *Report for Human Rights in China* (New York: 2007).
58. See www.people.com.cn, January 12, 2007.
59. Ibid., March 27, 2007.
60. Ibid.
61. Ibid., September 1, 2006.
62. The new provincial discipline chiefs in Henan, Shanxi, Chongqing, Shanghai, and Beijing were from the CDIC; the newly appointed discipline chiefs in Guangdong, Zhejiang, Anhui, Fujian, and Tianjin were from other provinces; www.chinanews.com.cn, April 18, 2007.
63. See ibid.
64. Ibid.
65. *Gaigen neican*, no. 35 (2006), p. 47.
66. Zong Jian, "Fanfu liqi: gongbu xinghui 'heimingdan,'" *Jiancha fengyun*, no. 1 (2006), p. 4.
67. See www.thebeijingnews.com, October 25, 2005.
68. Xu Shuiya, "Lu Dingyi: Chengzhl fubai lingyou waili," quoted in *Beijing ribao* (Beijing Daily); www.chinanews.com.cn, May 5, 2007.

MURDER MYSTERIES[*]

The Economist

Official figures showing a sharp drop in China's murder rate are misleading. For a country under so many social stresses, with millions of rural migrants pouring every year into cities and a widening gap between rich and poor, China boasts a remarkable achievement: a sharp fall since the turn of the century in murders and gun crimes. Official surveys suggest citizens feel increasingly safe from violence.

Reality is a bit more complicated.

Last May a newspaper run by the Ministry of Public Security said China's murder rate had fallen below those of Switzerland and Japan, countries which it said were "acknowledged to have the best public order in the world." In fact, figures compiled by the UN Office on Drugs and Crime (UNODC) show that in 2009, the latest year with data from all three countries, China had a murder rate of 1.1 per 100,000 people, compared with 0.7 in Switzerland and 0.4 in Japan. Yet even by the UN agency's count, China outperforms Australia and Britain (1.2 in 2009) and, easily, America (5.0). Official figures show that the number of murder cases rose from fewer than 10,000 in 1981 to more than 28,000 in 2000. Since then it has dropped almost every year, to about 12,000 in 2011. China's statistics bureau does not disclose which crimes are included in its murder data. Chinese scholars say that a single case might include several deaths, and that some killings which occur in the course of other violent crimes such as rape or robbery might be excluded. In a 2006 report, the World Health Organization estimated that in 2002, when 26,300 murder cases were recorded in China, 38,000 people died from "homicide-related injuries."

But some of China's other crime statistics appear to bolster the claim that murders have been much reduced. Robberies are down more than 40% since 2002, and rapes by nearly 18% from a peak in 2001. Gun-related crimes fell from around 5,000 cases in 2000 to a mere 500 in 2011, and bombings from 4,000 to about 200 over the same period. Gun ownership has long been tightly controlled in China. But the authorities have difficulty policing porous borders, such as the one with Myanmar, across which guns (and drugs) are often smuggled. If accurate, the data point to surprising success by the police in preventing these weapons from being used for criminal purposes.

The numbers also seem to counter what many would expect in a country undergoing such rapid social change. As China began to cast off the economic shackles of Maoism in the late 1970s, crime rates rose rapidly. Greater freedom of movement and rising unemployment appear to be factors. But since the early years of this century, China appears to buck a tendency observed by the UNODC in a global study of murder published in 2011: that countries with high levels of income inequality have much higher murder rates than more equal societies. China's wealth gap is not far off that of some of Latin America's most crime-ridden countries.

The data, however, are so suspect that it is difficult to say with certainty what the trends really

[*] This article was published in *The Economist* on April 6, 2013.

are. Some Chinese scholars believe the murder numbers are indeed falling, though not as dramatically as the official figures appear to show. If they are right, it might help disprove the widely held notion in China that executions act as deterrent: it is generally believed that China has become more cautious in recent years in applying the death penalty. Figures about murder are especially prone to manipulation by local governments. This is because of political pressure to solve such crimes. A campaign launched in 2004 demanded, at the very least, an 85% success rate in murder cases in the first year, and higher rates from then on. The central government's motive was commendable. Local police forces had begun to pay more attention to solving crimes involving money, in the hope of getting a share of any recovered cash. But the campaign boosted incentives to falsify results. By 2005 more than two-fifths of China's counties were claiming 100% success rates in solving new murders. Even the official media carried reports of police forces failing to register murder cases unless they were confident of cracking them, or had already done so. Only registered cases are recorded in the published statistics.

Not So Fast, Wise Guy

The campaign made wrongful arrests and torture even more common. "Wouldn't it be even more persuasive if we were to announce the number of unjust and fabricated cases that have been overturned at the same time as we announce the rate at which murder

cases are solved?" asked *Southern Daily*, a newspaper, in 2007. Its rare plea went unheeded.

Local governments continue to issue claims of high murder-solving rates. Last year Zhengzhou, the capital of Henan province in central China, reported that it had solved 98.9% of its murders, a record high for the city (including rural hinterland) of more than 7 million people. Such apparent achievements have helped bolster the government's claims to be creating a "harmonious society," an objective declared by China's then-president, Hu Jintao, in 2005. Government researchers have produced many surveys purporting to show that citizens feel safer than ever before (even as sellers of home-security equipment appear to be doing a roaring trade, and the incidence of non-fatal violence has continued to rise). The Chinese Academy of Social Sciences said in December that the citizens of Lhasa, the capital of Tibet, felt happier and safer than those of any other city in China. The omnipresence of armed troops has seemingly helped boost their joy. The port city of Shanghai came in second.

Skepticism about the authorities' handling of murder cases has been fueled by the most notorious one in recent years: the killing in November 2011 of Neil Heywood, a British businessman, in a hotel in Chongqing in southwestern China. The wife of Chongqing's Communist Party chief, Bo Xilai, was given a suspended death sentence last August for her role in this. But had a police chief not tried to defect to America, her connections might easily have helped her get away with it. The trial of Mr. Bo, expected soon, is likely to reinforce the public's cynicism.

III. Human Rights

World Human Rights Report 2014: China[*]

Human Rights Watch

Rapid socio-economic change in China has been accompanied by relaxation of some restrictions

on basic rights, but the government remains an authoritarian one-party state. It places arbitrary curbs on expression, association, assembly, and religion; prohibits independent labor unions and human rights organizations; and maintains Party control over all judicial institutions.

[*] This report was first published as part of Human Rights Watch annual *World Report* (2014), available at: http://www.hrw.org/world-report/2014/country-chapters/china.

The government censors the press, the Internet, print publications, and academic research, and justifies human rights abuses as necessary to preserve "social stability." It carries out involuntary population relocation and rehousing on a massive scale, and enforces highly repressive policies in ethnic minority areas in Tibet, Xinjiang, and Inner Mongolia. Though primary school enrollment and basic literacy rates are high, China's education system discriminates against children and young people with disabilities. The government obstructs domestic and international scrutiny of its human rights record, insisting it is an attempt to destabilize the country.

At the same time, citizens are increasingly prepared to challenge authorities over volatile livelihood issues, such as land seizures, forced evictions, environmental degradation, miscarriages of justice, abuse of power by corrupt cadres, discrimination, and economic inequality. Official and scholarly statistics, based on law enforcement reports, suggest there are 300–500 protests each day, with anywhere from ten to tens of thousands of participants. Despite the risks, Internet users and reform-oriented media are aggressively pushing censorship boundaries by advocating for the rule of law and transparency, exposing official wrongdoing, and calling for political reforms.

Civil society groups and advocates continue to slowly expand their work despite their precarious status, and an informal but resilient network of activists monitors and documents human rights cases as a loose national *weiquan* (rights defense) movement. These activists endure police monitoring, detention, arrest, enforced disappearance, and torture.

The Xi Jinping administration formally assumed power in March 2013, and proposed several reforms to longstanding policies, including abolishing one form of arbitrary detention, known as "Re-education Through Labor" (RTL), and changes to the household registration system. It staged high-profile corruption investigations, mostly targeting political rivals. But it also struck a conservative tone, opposing constitutional rule, press freedom, and "western-style" rule of law, and issuing harsher restrictions on dissent, including through two legal documents making it easier to bring criminal charges against activists and Internet critics.

Bo Xilai, once a rising political star, was sentenced to life imprisonment in September after a show trial that captured public attention but fell short of fair trial standards and failed to address widespread abuses of power committed during his tenure in Chongqing.

Human Rights Defenders

China's human rights activists often face imprisonment, detention, torture, commitment to psychiatric facilities, house arrest, and intimidation. One of the most severe crackdowns on these individuals in recent years occurred in 2013, with more than 50 activists put under criminal detention between February and October. Human rights defenders are detained for ill-defined crimes ranging from "creating disturbances" to "inciting subversion" for organizing and participating in public, collective actions. In July, authorities detained Xu Zhiyong, who is considered an intellectual leader of the New Citizens Movement, a loose network of civil rights activists whose efforts include a nationwide campaign that calls on public officials to disclose their assets. In September, Beijing-based activist Cao Shunli was detained after she was barred from boarding a flight to Geneva ahead of the United Nations Human Rights Council (HRC) review of China on October 22. Cao is known for pressing the Chinese government to include independent civil society input into the drafting of China's report to the HRC under a mechanism called Universal Periodic Review (UPR). Another activist, Peng Lanlan, was released in August after she spent one year in prison for "obstructing official business" for her role in the campaign.

Nobel Peace Prize winner Liu Xiaobo continues his 11-year jail term in northern Liaoning province. His wife Liu Xia continues to be subjected to unlawful house arrest. In August, Liu Xiaobo's brother-in-law, Liu Hui, was given an 11-year sentence on fraud charges; it is widely believed the heavy sentence is part of broader effort to punish Liu Xiaobo's family.

Legal Reforms

While the government rejects judicial independence and prohibits independent bar associations, progressive lawyers and legal scholars continue to be a force for change, contributing to increasing popular legal awareness and activism.

The Chinese Communist Party maintains authority over all judicial institutions and coordinates the judiciary's work through its political and legal committees. The Public Security Bureau, or police, remains the most powerful actor in the criminal justice system. Use of torture to extract confessions is prevalent, and miscarriages of justice are frequent due to weak courts and tight limits on the rights of the defense.

In November, the government announced its intention to abolish re-education through labor (RTL), a form of arbitrary detention in which the police can detain people for up to four years without trial. There were about 160,000 people in about 350 camps at the beginning of the year, but numbers dwindled rapidly as the police stopped sending people to RTL. The official press, however, reported that some of these facilities were being converted to drug rehabilitation centers, another form of administrative detention. At time of writing it was unclear whether the government would fully abolish administrative detention as a way to deal with minor offenders, or whether it would instead establish a replacement system that continued to allow detention without trial.

China continues to lead the world in executions. The exact number remains a state secret, but experts estimate it has decreased progressively from about 10,000 per year a decade ago to less than 4,000 in recent years.

Freedom of Expression

Freedom of expression deteriorated in 2013, especially after the government launched a concerted effort to rein in micro-blogging. The government and the Party maintain multiple layers of control over all media and publications. Internet censors shape online debate and maintain the "Great Firewall," which blocks outside content from reaching Internet users in China. Despite these restrictions, the Internet, especially microblog services known as *Weibo* and other social media tools, are popular as a relatively free space in which China's 538 million users can connect and air grievances. However, those who breach sensitive taboos are often swiftly identified and their speech deleted or disallowed; some are detained or jailed.

In January, *Southern Weekly,* a Guangzhou-based newspaper known for its boundary-pushing investigative journalism, was enveloped in a censorship row after the paper's editors found that their New Year's special editorial was rewritten on the censors' orders and published without their consent. The original editorial had called for political reform and respect for constitutionally guaranteed rights, but the published version instead praised the Chinese Communist Party. The paper's staff publicly criticized the provincial top censor, called for his resignation and went on a strike; the paper resumed printing a week later.

In May, the General Office of the Chinese Communist Party's Central Committee issued a gag order to universities directing them to avoid discussions of "seven taboos," which included "universal values" and the Party's past wrongs, according to media reports.

Since August, authorities have waged a campaign against "online rumors." The campaign has targeted influential online opinion leaders and ordinary netizens. The authorities have detained hundreds of Internet users for days, closed down over 100 "illegal" news websites run by citizen journalists, and detained well-known liberal online commentator Charles Xue.

Also in August, the government official in charge of Internet affairs warned Internet users against breaching "seven bottom lines," including China's "socialist system," the country's "national interests," and "public order." In September, the Supreme People's Court and the Supreme People's Procuratorate (state prosecutor) issued a new judicial interpretation applying four existing criminal provisions to Internet expression, providing a more explicit legal basis for charging Internet users.

Freedom of Religion

Although the constitution guarantees freedom of religion, the government restricts religious practices to officially approved mosques, churches, temples, and monasteries organized by five officially recognized religious organizations. It audits the activities, employee details, and financial records of religious bodies, and retains control over religious personnel appointments, publications, and seminary applications.

Unregistered spiritual groups such as Protestant "house churches" are deemed unlawful and subjected to raids and closures; members are harassed and leaders are detained and sometimes jailed. The government classifies Falun Gong, a meditation-focused spiritual group banned since July 1999, as an "an evil cult" and arrests, harasses, and intimidates its members. After releasing a new documentary about a labor camp in which Falun Gong practitioners were detained and tortured, filmmaker and photographer Du Bin was detained in May. He was released after five weeks in detention. In April, a court in Henan province sentenced seven house church leaders to between three and seven years in prison on charges of "using a cult to undermine law enforcement"; evidence suggested they had only attended meetings and publicized church activities.

Health and Disability Rights

The government has developed numerous laws, regulations, and action plans designed to decrease serious environmental pollution and related threats to public health, but the policies are often not implemented. In February, a lawyer's request under the Open Government Information Act to reveal soil contamination data was rejected; according to the authorities, such data was a "state secret." Also in February, after years of denial and inaction, the Ministry of Environmental Protection finally acknowledged the existence of "cancer villages," those with abnormally high cancer rates. Victims had long pressed for justice and compensation and domestic media had written extensively on the issue.

Despite a review in 2012 under the Convention on the Rights of Persons with Disabilities (CRPD), protections of the rights of persons with disabilities remain inadequate. These individuals face serious discrimination in employment and education, and some government policies institutionalize discrimination. In February, the State Council's Legislative Affairs Office announced amendments to the 1994 Regulations of Education of Persons with Disabilities in China. While welcome, the amendments do not ensure that students with disabilities can enroll in mainstream schools or mandate appropriate classroom modifications ("accommodations") enabling them to participate fully in such schools.

In May, China's first Mental Health Law came into effect. It filled an important legal void but does not close loopholes that allow government authorities and families to detain people in psychiatric hospitals against their will. In July, after the law came into effect, Gu Xianghong was detained for five weeks in a Beijing psychiatric hospital for petitioning the authorities about her grievances.

Women's Rights

Women's reproductive rights and access to reproductive health remain severely curtailed under China's population planning regulations. While the government announced in November that Chinese couples will now be allowed two children if either parent was a single child, the measure does not change the foundations of China's government-enforced family planning policy, which includes the use of legal and other coercive measures—such as administrative sanctions, fines, and coercive measures, including forced abortion—to control reproductive choices.

The government's punitive crackdowns on sex work often lead to serious abuses, including physical and sexual violence, increased risk of disease, and constrained access to justice for the country's estimated 4 to 10 million sex workers, most of whom are women. Sex workers have also documented abuses by public health agencies, such as coercive HIV testing, privacy infringements, and mistreatment by health officials. In January, the Supreme People's Court upheld a death sentence against Li Yan, a woman convicted of murdering her physically abusive husband. Domestic violence is not treated as a mitigating factor in court cases. In May, Ye Haiyan, China's most prominent sex worker rights activist, was detained by police for several days after being assaulted at her home in Guangxi province over her exposure of abusive conditions in local brothels.

Although the government acknowledges that domestic violence, employment discrimination, and gender bias are widespread, it limits the activities of independent women's rights groups working on these issues by making it difficult for them to register, monitoring their activities, interrogating their staff, and prohibiting some activities.

Migrant and Labor Rights

The official All-China Federation of Trade Unions (ACFTU) continued to be the only legal representative of workers; independent labor unions are forbidden. Despite this limitation, workers have become increasingly vocal and active in striving for better working conditions across the country, including by staging protests and strikes. In September, Shenzhen dock workers went on strike to demand better pay and working conditions. Ten days later, the workers accepted a government-brokered deal that met some of their demands.

In May, the official All-China Women's Federation issued a new report revealing that the number of migrant children, including those living with their parents in urban areas and those "left behind" in rural areas, had reached 100 million by 2010. Migrant workers continue to be denied urban residence permits, which are required to gain access to social services such as education. Many such workers leave their children at home when they migrate so that the children can go to school, rendering some vulnerable to abuse.

Although China has numerous workplace safety regulations, enforcement is lax, especially at the local level. For example, in June, a fire at a poultry farm killed 121 workers in Jilin province. Subsequent investigations revealed that the local fire department had just days before the fire issued the poultry farm a safety certificate even though it failed to meet a number of standards.

Sexual Orientation and Gender Identity

The Chinese government classified homosexuality as a mental illness until 2001. To date there is still no law protecting people from discrimination on the basis of sexual orientation or gender identity, which remains common especially in the workplace. Same-sex partnership and marriage are not recognized under Chinese law. In February, a lesbian couple attempted to register at the marriage registry in Beijing but their application was rejected. On May 17, the International Day against Homophobia, Changsha city authorities detained Xiang Xiaohan, an organizer of a local gay pride parade, and held him for 12 days for organizing an "illegal march." In China, demonstrations require prior permission, which is rarely granted.

Tibet

The Chinese government systematically suppresses political, cultural, religious and socioeconomic rights in Tibet in the name of combating what it sees as separatist sentiment. This includes nonviolent advocacy for Tibetan independence, the Dalai Lama's return, and opposition to government policy. At time of writing, 123 Tibetans had self-immolated in protest against Chinese policies since the first recorded case in February 2009. Arbitrary arrest and imprisonment remains common, and torture and ill-treatment in detention is endemic. Fair trials are precluded by a politicized judiciary overtly tasked with suppressing separatism. Police systematically suppress any unauthorized gathering. On July 6, police opened fire in Nyitso, Dawu prefecture, on a crowd that had gathered in the countryside to celebrate the Dalai Lama's birthday. Several people were injured. The government censored news of the event.

In an apparent effort to prevent a repetition of the popular protests of 2008, the government in 2013 maintained many of the measures it introduced during its brutal crackdown on the protest movement—a massive security presence composed largely of armed police forces, sharp restrictions on the movements of Tibetans within the Tibetan plateau, increased controls on monasteries, and a ban on foreign journalists in the Tibetan Autonomous Region (TAR) unless part of a government-organized tour. The government also took significant steps to implement a plan to station 20,000 new officials and Party cadres in the TAR, including in every village, to monitor the political views of all residents.

The government is also subjecting millions of Tibetans to a mass rehousing and relocation policy that radically changes their way of life and livelihoods, in some cases impoverishing them or making them dependent on state subsidies, about which they have no say. Since 2006, over two million Tibetans, both farmers and herders, have been involuntarily "rehoused"—through government-ordered renovation or construction of new houses—in the TAR; hundreds of thousands of nomadic herders in the eastern part of the Tibetan plateau have been relocated or settled in "New Socialist Villages."

Xinjiang

Pervasive ethnic discrimination, severe religious repression, and increasing cultural suppression justified by the government in the name of the "fight against separatism, religious extremism, and terrorism" continue to fuel rising tensions in the Xinjiang Uyghur Autonomous Region.

In 2013, over one hundred people—Uyghurs, Han, and other ethnicities—were killed in various incidents across the region, the highest death toll since the July 2009 Urumqi protests. In some cases, heavy casualties appear to have been the result of military-style assaults on groups preparing violent attacks, as in Bachu prefecture on April 23, and in Turfan prefecture on June 26. But in other cases security forces appear to have used lethal force against crowds of unarmed protesters. On June 28, in Hetian prefecture, police tried to prevent protesters from marching toward Hetian municipality to protest the arbitrary closure of a mosque and the arrest of its imam, ultimately shooting into the crowd and injuring dozens of protesters. On August 8, in Aksu prefecture, police forces prevented villagers from reaching a nearby mosque to celebrate a religious festival, eventually using live ammunition and injuring numerous villagers. After each reported incident the government ritualistically blames "separatist, religious extremist, and terrorist forces," and obstructs independent investigations.

Arbitrary arrest, torture, and "disappearance" of those deemed separatists are endemic and instill palpable fear in the population. In July, Ilham Tohti, a Uyghur professor at Beijing's Nationalities University published an open letter to the government asking for an investigation into 34 disappearance cases he documented. Tohti was placed under house arrest several times and prevented from traveling abroad.

The government continues to raze traditional Uyghur neighborhoods and rehouse families in planned settlements as part of a comprehensive development policy launched in 2010. The government says the policy is designed to urbanize and develop Xinjiang.

Hong Kong

Despite the fact that Hong Kong continues to enjoy an independent judiciary, a free press, and a vocal civil society, freedoms of the press and assembly have been increasingly under threat since Hong Kong returned to Chinese sovereignty in 1997. Prospects that election of the territory's chief executive starting in 2017 would be genuinely competitive dimmed after Beijing indicated that only candidates who did not "oppose the central government" would be able to run.

Hong Kong has witnessed slow erosion of the rule of law in recent years, exemplified by increasingly strict police controls on assemblies and processions, and arbitrary Immigration Department bans on individuals critical of Beijing, such as members of the Falun Gong and exiled dissidents from the 1989 democracy spring.

Chinese Foreign Policy

China has become more engaged with various United Nations mechanisms, but has not significantly improved its compliance with international human rights standards or pushed for improved human rights protections in other countries. In a notable exception, shortly after it was elected to the UN Human Rights Council in November, China publicly urged Sri Lanka "to make efforts to protect and promote human rights."

Even in the face of the rapidly growing death toll in Syria and evidence in August 2013 that the Syrian government used chemical weapons against civilians, Beijing has continued to object to any significant Security Council measures to increase pressure on the Assad regime and abusive rebel groups. It has opposed referral of the situation to the International Criminal Court (ICC) and an arms embargo against forces that commit widespread human rights or laws of war violations. China has also slowed down Security Council–driven efforts to deliver desperately needed humanitarian assistance across the border to rebel-controlled areas in northern Syria.

In a minor change of tactics, if not of longer-term strategy, Chinese authorities have become modestly more vocal in their public and private criticisms of North Korea, particularly following actions by Pyongyang that increased tensions between members of the Six Party Talks aimed at addressing security concerns posed by North Korea's nuclear weapons program.

Both private and state-owned Chinese firms continue to be a leading source of foreign direct investment, particularly in developing countries, but in some cases have been unwilling or unable to comply with international labor standards.

Key International Actors

Most governments that have bilateral human rights dialogues with the Chinese government, including the United States, European Union, and Australia, held at least one round of those dialogues in 2013; most acknowledge they are of limited utility for promoting meaningful change inside China. Several of these governments publicly expressed concern about individual cases, such as those of Xu Zhiyong or Liu Hui, or about trends such as restrictions on anti-corruption activists. Ambassadors from the US and Australia, as well as the EU's special representative for human rights, were allowed to visit the TAR or other Tibetan areas. None of these governments commented on the denial of Chinese people's political rights to choose their leaders during the 2012–2013 leadership transition, and few successfully integrated human rights concerns into meetings with senior Chinese officials.

China participated in a review of its compliance with the Convention on the Rights of Persons with Disabilities by the international treaty body charged with monitoring implementation of the convention and a review of its overall human rights record at the UN Human Rights Council, but it failed to provide basic information or provided deeply misleading information on torture, arbitrary detention, and restrictions on freedom of expression. There are eight outstanding requests to visit China by UN special rapporteurs, and UN agencies operating inside China remain tightly restricted, their activities closely monitored by the authorities.

IV. CIVIL SOCIETY

Chinese Civil Society: Beneath the Glacier[*]

The Economist

Against a powerful alliance of factory bosses and Communist Party chiefs, Zeng Feiyang cuts a frail figure. Mr. Zeng, who is 39, works from a windowless office in Panyu, on the edge of the southern city of Guangzhou, where he runs a non-governmental organization (NGO) called the Panyu Migrant Workers' Service Centre. For

more than a decade his organization has battled against the odds to defend the rights of workers in the factories of Guangdong province. For his troubles, Mr. Zeng has been evicted from various premises, had his water and electricity cut off, and been constantly harassed by local officials and their thugs. Then last autumn he received a call from one such official. "The man asked if I wanted to register the NGO," he says. "I was very surprised." Over the past three

---

[*] This article was published in *The Economist* on April 12, 2014.

years other activists at unregistered NGOs have received similar phone calls from the authorities about the sensitive issue of registration, an apparently mundane bit of administrative box-ticking which in fact represents real change. China has over 500,000 NGOs already registered with the state. The number comes with a big caveat. Many NGOs are quasi-official or mere shell entities attempting to get government money. Of those genuine groups that do seek to improve the common lot, nearly all carry out politically uncontentious activities. But perhaps 1.5 million more are not registered, and some of these, like Mr. Zeng's, pursue activism in areas which officials have often found worrying.

These unregistered NGOs are growing in number and influence. They are a notable example of social forces bubbling up from below in a stubbornly top-down state. The organizations could be a way for the Communist Party to co-opt the energy and resources of civil society. They could also be a means by which that energy challenges the party's power. And so their status has big implications. Guo Hong of the Sichuan Academy of Social Sciences in Chengdu calls the liberalization of NGO registration laws "the partial realization of freedom of association." Just as economic liberalization in the early 1980s had a profound material effect, so these latest moves could have a profound social one.

We (Some of) the People

The new rules apply only to some types of NGOs, notably those providing services to groups such as the poor, the elderly, and the disabled. Those engaged in any kind of political advocacy continue to be suspect. Human-rights organizations remain banned, as do most groups promoting religious, ethnic or labor rights. Yet Mr. Zeng's experience in Guangzhou suggests the authorities are looking for new ways to deal at least with some labor groups whose activities would once have been seen as unquestionably subversive.

Until 2012, any NGO that wanted to register—and so be legal—had to have a sponsoring official organization, typically a government agency that worked in the area of the NGO's interest. This ensured firm government control over all NGOs, or "social organizations," as the party likes to call

them (in Chinese, "non-government" carries a whiff of "anti-government"). Foreign NGOs could operate in China only under strict conditions.

It was a rigid regime, but it actually represented a liberalization compared with what went before. When it seized power in 1949 the Communist Party eliminated anything that stood between the state and the individual, including churches, trade unions, and independent associations of all sorts—it even tried to break traditional family bonds. In other words, what elsewhere came to be known as civil society was shut down completely in China, at least until after the death of Mao Zedong in 1976. The only groups allowed to function were state entities parading as non-state ones. They go by the Orwellian name of government-operated non-governmental organizations, GONGOs. One is the China Youth Development Foundation; another is the China Foundation for Poverty Alleviation.

After the 1989 protests in Tiananmen Square, and their subsequent bloody put-down, the deal China's leaders offered the country changed: stay out of politics and you can do almost anything else you want. Most of the new quasi-freedom was economic, but social space expanded, too.

There were clear limits. The collapse of the Soviet bloc, which trade unions, churches, and other groups in Poland, Czechoslovakia and elsewhere helped precipitate, reinforced the idea among Chinese rulers that NGOs had to be kept away from issues that were or could become political. Still, local NGOs with limited, mostly charitable concerns were allowed to develop in some areas, provided they submitted to control by the state through the process of registration. Environmental protection and HIV/AIDS were among the first areas to benefit from a new toleration of some NGOs. Even so, on the ground their freedoms were often hard won, and much official persecution persisted.

Running Away

The growth of NGOs since has not always been a smooth one. In 2005—spooked by "color" revolutions in Ukraine, Georgia, and Kyrgyzstan—Chinese leaders clamped down on NGOs, especially in their more activist manifestations. But in recent years that tight control has relaxed again, largely out of necessity. Rapid urbanization and a more complex society mean that the party can no longer provide everything for its citizens as once it did, or claimed to. Anger over inadequate social services could put at risk the domestic stability that underpins the party's rule. Nor does it help that the central government has pushed responsibility for health, education, and other services onto local governments that are unwilling or unable to pay for them.

The array of unofficial NGOs that have sprung up over the past decade is remarkable. Some are inspired by religious faith: Christian doctors setting up a local clinic to fill gaps left by the health care system, or Buddhists caring for the elderly. Others involve, for instance, parents of autistic children forming support groups through the Internet or a website showing the location of needy schools around a city that urges people passing the neighborhood to pack a bag of books or pencils to donate. Idealism is far from dead, as the Communist Party increasingly appreciates. When party leaders sent out researchers to look into NGOs, they realized, as He Jianyu of the NGO Research Centre at Tsinghua University in Beijing puts it, that "NGOs are not all revolutionaries who want to overthrow the party—as they had thought."

A big boost to China's growth in NGOs—double the number of a decade ago—seems to have been a huge earthquake in Sichuan in 2008, which killed 70,000 people. Thousands of volunteers converged on Sichuan to lend a hand to the rescue. Ordinary people found out what it was like to get organized and join in. "We all saw the NGOs at work, and saw that they were much more effective than the government," says the Sichuan Academy's Ms. Guo. The government drew similar conclusions and allowed more NGOs to register through state organizations.

Behind the growth is the irrepressible rise of a new middle class. It shares the party's desire for stability. But some members, at least, also want new ways to participate in society. Party leaders, now only vaguely constrained by Communist ideology, have a new sense that something is to be gained by co-opting such activist citizens rather than suppressing them. It may, they think, offer a way of providing some of the social support that the party can no longer supply on its own. Thus the easing of the rules—not just allowing NGOs

to register without a state sponsor, but actually encouraging them to do so.

Since 2011 four types of groups have been able to register directly in a number of provinces: industry associations, science and technology organizations, charities and outfits providing social services. Later this year, the changes are expected to apply nationwide. Karla Simon, an American academic and author of *Civil Society in China*, says that the number of NGOs could double again in just a couple of years as registration is further eased.

It is telling, however, that these changes come at a time of increased political repression, including against those who simply call upon an overweening party to abide by China's own (Communist Party–written) constitution. Since Xi Jinping became party chief in 2012, the state has cracked down on freethinkers. The sentencing in late January of Xu Zhiyong, a prominent academic, to four years in jail, and the constant harassment of other activists, show that even those, like Mr. Xu, who have tried a less confrontational approach will not be tolerated. The approaching 25th anniversary of the Tiananmen Square massacre means control will continue to be tight. The party appears to believe that it can encourage the expansion of NGOs without relaxing its political grip. Perhaps it is the Leninist chameleon changing color again, developing a clever new brand of "consultative authoritarianism," in the phrase of Jessica Teets at America's Middlebury College, that leaves the realities of power unchanged and room for dissent constrained. But many who work for NGOs suggest the opposite: allowing new freedoms for civil-society groups will slowly transform the party from the inside—just the kind of "peaceful evolution" that party hardliners have always warned against. Though moves towards meaningful political reform remain glacial at best, activists say these new regulations are part of an unseen river of social change that is starting to erode the glacier from below.

From Comrades to Citizens

Belatedly, the party realizes that NGOs have a number of things it lacks: ideas, a hard-won understanding of the issues on the ground, and trust from the local community. Few people believe the party on anything. Most think NGOs approach problems with knowledge and sensitivity. For example, they treat drug-users or prostitutes with AIDS as a health issue to be met with care and counselling rather than as a criminal one. A long-awaited party blueprint for urbanization, issued in March, spoke of the need to "arouse the energy" of such groups. One Beijing academic says the challenge is now as much to help the government learn how to delegate some areas of social policy as it is to increase the capacity of NGOs to do the work.

Philanthropy is re-emerging as a social force as expectations have risen. Some are prompted by religious teachings: Buddhism and Daoism are enjoying a renaissance, and there are now some 80 million Christians in China, many of whom want to do good works. Volunteering and working in the non-profit sector is becoming more popular. Charity and philanthropy, says Shawn Shieh, the American editor of *China Development Brief*, a Beijing-based publication that covers NGOs, have become buzzwords among the wealthy.

The nascent sector has a long way to go. The biggest problem is funding. Some local governments finance NGOs directly: the government of Guangdong province gave 466 million *yuan* ($75m) in 2012; Yunnan spent 300 million *yuan*. Those numbers are expected to increase. But, although many groups no longer need an official sponsor and are free to receive public donations, they are not allowed to raise money publicly. Fundraising activities must go through a dreaded GONGO, which means the government can control how much publicity an NGO receives and therefore its sources of income. Control over foreign funding has even been tightened.

All of this offers new opportunities for corruption. Some local governments have set up shell NGOs to tap into the new official funding. Real NGOs often fail to hear of tenders for service-provision contracts they could fulfil. The jobs go to well-connected insiders, who sometimes subcontract, taking a cut on the way.

Here, though, as elsewhere, the Internet is changing things. China's Twitter-like microblogs enable like-minded people to hook up and rally public support for a cause. It is now possible to complain about things online without being seen as subversive—though there are limits you would be wise to observe: you can tweet about air pollution, but not necessarily about a specific noxious factory with links to certain leaders. Urban middle-class types tweet furiously about food safety, water shortages, the treatment of migrants, education, and health care—core NGO issues. NGOs that spread the word about their work online can see significant donations come their way even without actively raising funds.

Working the System

The emerging civil society is not a clear-cut story of stooges and heroes. The action is in the middle ground, where lines are blurred and both sides negotiate for space. The temptation for activists to compromise and tap into government money is great. Still, says a Western diplomat in Beijing, if you are prepared to play within the system you can get a lot done.

Zhicheng, a legal-services organization which helps the disadvantaged, is an example of how to do just that. It was established in 1999 by Tong Lihua, a lawyer from a poor village, who first set out to protect the rights of rural children. He impressed local-government officials, who were persuaded to give him their support. Mr. Tong then began to advise workers who had not been properly paid. Government officials leave him alone, he says, because, although he is dealing with sensitive areas, he is enhancing social stability not damaging it. He says his aim is to promote legal and social reform from the inside. Though sometimes derided by other activists for being too close to the party, Mr. Tong says that 99.9% of what he does is independent. He bristles when asked if he is just an agent of the government. He says Zhicheng has provided up to 400,000 people with free legal advice, helping them claim overdue wages and work-related injury compensation totaling 400 million *yuan*.

By contrast, Yirenping works on the fringes, an advocacy NGO staffed by lawyers who take on legal cases with an eye to the precedents they might set. One of its recent cases was that of a girl who was not allowed to take the national high-school exam because she is blind. It has helped people with hepatitis B and AIDS who have been fired from their jobs. One of its lawyers, Huang Yizhi, says the group will probably not try to register. Like many NGOs unable to find an official sponsor, it is currently registered as a business. If it registered as an NGO, says Ms. Huang, it might receive government money but it would have to tone down its advocacy. The ambiguity of its status suits it as it chooses its cases carefully, engages in advocacy on issues, such as social equality, that the party says it cares about too and tries not to tweak the dragon's tail enough to risk being squashed by it.

Ma Jun takes an approach somewhere between the two. A former reporter, in 1999 he published a notable book on the environment, *China's Water Crisis*. Mr. Ma runs the Institute of Public and Environmental Affairs (IPE), which operates legally. Like Mr. Tong, he sees co-operation with the government as essential. "We are all in this boat, and we don't want the boat to capsize," he says. But he is less cooperative with official GONGOs. With many demonstrations now arising from environmental issues, the party is growing ever more worried about green activism. And Mr. Ma is at the forefront of inter-provincial NGO co-operation, another former taboo. The party is afraid of like-minded people, bound by a common cause, linking up around the country. NGOs are not allowed to register branch offices in different provinces. But the IPE is part of a network of 50 environmental groups called the Green Choice Alliance which can speak with one voice. Mr. Ma walks a fine line, and fine lines can move. Just a few years ago officials lauded Mr. Xu, the recently jailed academic, just as they praise Mr. Ma now.

The government is by no means consistent in its approach to NGOs. Last July the environment ministry held a workshop in Beijing to which it invited groups like Mr. Ma's for the first time. That would have been unthinkable ten years ago. According to one startled participant, officials encouraged the NGOs to be strong in order to "confront powerful authorities"—meaning local vested interests. Yet at the same time there are moves to withdraw the ability of environmental NGOs to bring court cases against local governments. And a Party brief known as Document Number 9, circulated to all government offices in 2013, accuses NGOs of cultivating "anti-China forces." The situation is "schizophrenic," says Mr. Shieh. Mr. Zeng, the labor activist, says that even after being asked to register his NGO, he still gets harassed.

After loosening the restraints on NGOs, the party could easily tighten them again. And Chan Kin-man at the Chinese University of Hong Kong says that NGOs have exploded in number but not in influence. The space in which civil society may operate is actually shrinking, he argues. Aspects of the current political clampdown, such as a law against "rumor-mongering," would seem to bear him out. Yet others say that space for action that is won through negotiation, not confrontation, is space nonetheless. Meanwhile, many feel that the party's distinction between service provision and advocacy will erode. "There is no way to deliver services to the elderly without becoming an advocate for the elderly," says a foreign NGO worker in Beijing.

Whither China?

Some activists still worry that by allowing themselves to be co-opted, they are strengthening the Communist Party's dictatorial hold on power because they are helping it to solve its biggest problems of governance. The Chinese head of an NGO says his friends tell him he should let the whole system "rot until it collapses." His organization provides funding and support to injured workers, a tricky area. Yet as soon as the NGO received publicity for its work through microblogs, the government donated several million *yuan* to the cause. "Once you highlight an issue, the government has to act," he says.

It is not clear that the party believes in civil society. More likely it sees NGOs as a useful tool to achieve its own ends. But with politics directed from on high unable to meet social needs, and a new generation that wants more participation, some increased role for civil society is unavoidable. So a strange, unspoken pact has evolved, where both sides accept the compromise as a way of furthering their goals in the short term, while hoping future developments work in their favor.

Limitations and frustrations are legion. Changes to the registration procedure will be slow to affect the day-to-day life of ordinary Chinese. And other social or financial problems could multiply, negating any progress towards a broader civil society. Yet, in their way, NGOs are starting to provide "glue" that can help knit society together as the state retreats, family structures change and the social fabric is stretched to the point of tearing. Today's NGOs are backed by a new generation of Chinese who feel better off and more empowered. The party will not find it easy to slap them back down.

CITIZEN CONTENTION AND CAMPUS CALM: THE PARADOX OF CHINESE CIVIL SOCIETY[*]

Elizabeth J. Perry

Civil society in contemporary China presents a perplexing paradox. Despite the brutal suppression of the 1989 Tiananmen uprising, social contention and associational activism swelled over the ensuing years. One might have expected the ruthless June Fourth repression of the massive student movement to have deterred subsequent dissent, but in fact the frequency of protest has steadily escalated in the past 25 years. Moreover, China today is host to countless grassroots (as well as government-sponsored) nongovernmental organizations (NGOs), foundations, and charities—not to mention a vibrant sphere of online public debate. In contrast to 1989, a nascent civil society can now be said to exist.

Nowhere is this organizing and societal engagement more evident than among college students. There are, however, few signs of another student-led "democracy movement" looming on the horizon. Instead, university campuses in the People's Republic of China (PRC) these days form a critical component of an apparently effective web of support and stability for the existing political system.

The scope and spread of protest in post-1989 China have been impressive. The early 1990s witnessed a wave of violent tax riots by farmers complaining of "unfair burdens." When the central government responded to the rural unrest with a historic decision to abolish China's centuries-old agricultural tax, the locus of protest shifted from the countryside back to the cities. In the late 1990s, the privatization and bankruptcy of many state enterprises prompted laid-off and retired workers to lodge petitions and stage sit-ins at factories and government offices in opposition to plant closures and paltry pensions.

In the 2000s, as the negative side effects of rapid economic reform became increasingly visible, environmental pollution sparked "not-in-my-backyard" rallies among a growing middle class anxious to protect its newly acquired property and its health. State-sanctioned infrastructure development and commercial real estate projects ignited angry remonstrations by displaced residents. Labor disputes erupted with calls for higher wages and better working conditions. Migrant workers demanded that their children be permitted to sit for university entrance examinations in the cities where their parents labored. And yet, amid the explosion of protest activity by seemingly all manner of aggrieved citizens, China's university campuses have remained remarkably quiet.

Threat Averted

Averting campus unrest in China is no mean feat. Over the course of the twentieth century, every generation of Chinese university students played a catalytic role in a cycle of protest movements that transformed the country's political trajectory. The Chinese Communist Party (CCP) traces its own origins to the May Fourth Movement of 1919, when nationalist students streamed out of college campuses onto the streets to denounce Japan's threat to

---

[*] This article was published in *Current History* (September 2014).

Chinese sovereignty. Two years later, a small band of intellectuals—led by the dean and librarian of Peking University—founded the CCP to spearhead a revolution intended to restore China's national pride. In the 1930s and 1940s, thousands of college students suspended their studies to participate in the Communist revolution and its front organizations—first in the war against Japan (1937–45) and then in the Civil War against the Nationalist Party (1945–49).

Just a few years after the establishment of the People's Republic in 1949, students rallied to Chairman Mao Zedong's injunction to "let a hundred flowers bloom" by offering spirited criticisms of the new socialist system; shocked by the depth of dissent, the PRC leadership unleashed a draconian "anti-rightist campaign" in the summer of 1957. A decade later, campus protest again augured radical change when Mao called on student Red Guards to jumpstart his Great Proletarian Cultural Revolution.

In 1966, Beijing's leading universities served as launching pads for Mao's final revolutionary quest. For the better part of the Cultural Revolution decade (1966–76), mass criticism and "class struggle" supplanted classroom instruction as the main campus activity. When the Tiananmen Uprising erupted only 13 years after the conclusion of the Cultural Revolution, it looked as though China's university students were once again poised to spark a major political transformation.

But the bloody suppression of June Fourth not only stymied the call for fundamental political reform on the part of millions of protesters; it also stemmed the generational tide of politically influential student protest that had punctuated China's entire twentieth century. For the past 25 years now, Chinese campuses have remained uncharacteristically tranquil. The anomaly appears even starker in light of the cascade of momentous events, invigorated if not always instigated by restive students, that occurred elsewhere in the world during this same period: Eastern Europe's revolutions of 1989, the fall of the Soviet Union, the Color Revolutions in former Soviet states, and the Arab Spring, for example.

In the immediate aftermath of June Fourth, journalistic and scholarly consensus in the West ascribed the disappointing failure of the Tiananmen uprising—in contrast to the stunning success of anticommunist movements across Eastern Europe later that year—to the relative weakness of Chinese civil society. On the one hand, Poland's Solidarity, Czechoslovakia's Charter 77, and Hungary's Danube Circle were applauded as part of an emerging urban civil society whose rise spelled the demise of Communist regimes from Bucharest to Budapest. On the other hand, the absence of a comparable level of autonomous associational activity in Beijing was blamed for the durability of the PRC's authoritarian political system.

It is certainly true that the Tiananmen uprising occurred in the absence of a robust and independent urban civil society of the type that is often presumed to be a prerequisite for democratization. Although so-called democracy salons had sprouted up on a number of Chinese university campuses in the 1980s, these were small and nebulous entities, closely monitored by the state's security apparatus. The millions of protesters who marched in Beijing and other major Chinese cities in the spring of 1989 were for the most part mobilized not by new civil society associations, but instead via preexisting socialist institutions: public universities, state-owned enterprises, official mass associations, and even government and party agencies. When central leaders finally issued an unambiguous directive to demobilize the movement, these organizations quickly fell into line and the protest crumbled almost overnight.

Tracing the failure of Tiananmen to the weakness of Chinese civil society heightens the paradox of post-1989 developments, however. For the past quarter-century has not only seen a torrent of popular protest in virtually all corners of Chinese society outside of academia; recent years have also witnessed an unprecedented growth in volunteerism and activism—that is, fledgling civil society—which is particularly pronounced on college campuses.

Students and professors are at the forefront of an extraordinary surge in associational participation and community service. Yet, further deepening the paradox of post-1989 trends, applications to join the CCP are also at an all-time high among university students and instructors. Contrary to conventional predictions, the growth of protest and civil society in contemporary China seems more conducive to the resilience of authoritarianism than to imminent democratization.

At the center of the PRC's anomalous situation is the compliance of its academics. The causes of this complicity are multiple. First, and most obvious, is the array of control mechanisms that the party-state deploys to maintain order on university campuses. Second is a range of more subtle techniques of cultural governance designed to produce political allegiance and regime loyalty among citizens in general and students in particular. Third, and arguably most important, are the various opportunities for regime-supportive civic engagement and service afforded by the recent expansion of civil society. Ironically, the increased associational activity among Chinese students today is working to underpin, rather than to undermine, the authority of the Communist party-state.

Compounding this irony is the fact that the very term "civil society" (gongmin shehui) is one of seven topics (along with universal values, freedom of speech, civil rights, crony capitalism, judicial independence, and historical errors of the CCP) that the current regime has officially banned from public discourse on grounds that the concept reflects "dangerous Western influences."

Campus Control

Let us consider first the control mechanisms. Acutely aware of the potential threat of campus turmoil, China's Communist party-state has developed a battery of methods to monitor and restrain student behavior. College students are organized by "homeroom" (banji) as well as by class year (nianji), with these units headed by politically reliable peers who convey information both from and to university administrators. Peer surveillance and pressure are embedded within a professional oversight hierarchy.

Forming the mainstay of the control regimen are so-called guidance counselors (fudaoyuan)—trained personnel tasked with keeping close tabs on their student charges to ensure that their beliefs and behavior do not violate approved boundaries. Although a system of guidance counselors was originally introduced at Tsinghua University as early as 1953, it assumed renewed and enlarged significance after 1989.

Some of the counselors' duties are similar to those of resident tutors on many Western college campuses: helping to resolve personal problems, offering academic advice, and generally serving as older role models for undergraduates. Unlike resident tutors at Oxford or Harvard, however, the chief responsibility of the fudaoyuan is ideological and political. Typically young instructors in their late 20s or early 30s, the guidance counselors (assisted by student informants) report directly to the deputy Party secretaries responsible for student work at all levels of the university structure.

In recent years these control methods have been "modernized" with the aid of new techniques and technologies. For example, as in the United States, mental health facilities are now a staple feature of Chinese college campuses. But in the PRC the definition of "mental illness" is broadly construed to include ideas and inclinations that the state deems politically dangerous, and the results of mandatory mental health screening for freshmen are forwarded to political cadres for analysis and possible preventive or punitive action.

Another "modernized" means of gauging (and guiding) student opinion is afforded by the spread of the Internet and social media. In 2008 China passed the United States as the world's biggest Internet user, with microblogging via Weibo (the Chinese equivalent of Twitter) and messaging via WeChat (an alternative to Facebook) especially popular among college students. Blog postings, text messages, and other electronic and cellular communications facilitate the growth of (both virtual and actual) civil society among Chinese university students. But they also enable the state to better monitor this burgeoning activism. Counselors and cadres combat subversive or suspicious content not only through censorship, but also by commissioning counter-posts that promote the officially prescribed point of view.

The party-state deploys proactive as well as reactive measures in the effort to channel student sentiment in directions favorable to the CCP's agenda. Since the 1990s, ideological and political education (sixiang zhengzhi jiaoyu) and military training (junxun) have been standard components of the university curriculum. Such classes and exercises are designed to inculcate regime-supportive dispositions and deportment. Of growing importance in recent years has been instruction in "cultural proficiency" (*wenhua suzhi*) and "national character" (*guoqing*), which presents Chinese history, art, philosophy, and literature in ways that postulate an organic connection and essential compatibility between the splendors of China's ancient "tradition" and its contemporary "socialist" system.

This instruction is an extension of the "Patriotic Education Campaign," launched in the aftermath of the Tiananmen uprising, which highlighted both China's national cultural heritage and its modern revolutionary experience as twin sources of legitimacy for the CCP. Cultural proficiency—thanks to generous funding from the Central Propaganda Department—is promoted not only in the classroom, but also in theaters, museums, field trips to ancient and revolutionary historical sites, invited lectures by distinguished scholars and public intellectuals, research projects by renowned teams of social scientists and humanists, and so forth. The universities constitute a key node in a massive party-state initiative in cultural governance intended to convince citizens that CCP rule is endowed with "Chinese characteristics" that render the Party's authority both natural and necessary.

While overt control mechanisms and formal ideological instruction are a common cause for complaint among Chinese university students, the more subtle and sophisticated modes of cultural governance appear to enjoy considerable success. To be sure, one hears many criticisms of the contemporary political system on Chinese campuses; seldom, however, do these critics suggest that the system is in any way "un-Chinese." Under the banner of patriotism, the Propaganda Department's grafting of China's ancient heritage onto its twentieth-century revolutionary legacy to fashion an allegedly seamless "socialism with Chinese characteristics" (as Deng Xiaoping dubbed the post-Mao system) seems to have taken firm root. For a political system whose basic ideology and institutions were imported almost wholesale from the Soviet Union, this level of cultural recognition and acceptance (at least among those who identify as Han Chinese, if not among

ethnic minorities such as Tibetans or Uighurs) is a significant achievement.

Student Volunteers

Even more effective in eliciting campus compliance than either control mechanisms or cultural governance, I would submit, are the expanded opportunities for voluntarism and community service that have developed apace in recent years—especially since the Wenchuan earthquake and the Beijing Olympics of 2008.

Student clubs of various sorts had been a feature of Chinese college life since the 1980s. The past few years, however, have seen a mushrooming of organizations whose missions extend beyond conventional campus recreational and educational activities to the provision of social services outside the academy. Although the Xi Jinping administration has blacklisted "civil society" as a dangerous Western notion, its emergence is actually an important contributor to campus calm in the contemporary PRC. The space for meaningful participation afforded by the growth of grassroots NGOs encourages college students (and their professors) to concentrate on varieties of activism that directly and indirectly benefit Communist rule—relieving the state of a portion of its social welfare burden while at the same time channeling youthful energy away from potentially disruptive behavior.

Many of the associations that have sprung up in recent years enjoy close connections to the party-state and its official "mass associations." The Chinese Communist Youth League (CYL) plays a particularly prominent role on university campuses, not only as a training camp for prospective party members but also as sponsor for a range of volunteer and philanthropic activities. The best known of these CYL endeavors, Project Hope, mobilizes a steady stream of college student volunteers to help staff the thousands of elementary schools that it has recently constructed in impoverished areas of the country.

While a disproportionate share of financial and political resources is concentrated in such GONGOs, or government-organized nongovernmental organizations, they by no means monopolize the field of associational activity either on or off campus. The Chinese Academy of Social Sciences, a government think tank, reported an official figure of over 800,000 "social organizations" and "social associations" in 2013. Unofficial estimates, which include a multitude of unregistered groups, put the total number of grassroots NGOs of various sorts at several million.

Thanks to recent reforms making it easier for social service organizations to register with local municipal bureaus of civil affairs, grassroots groups have been able to enlarge their fundraising efforts. Since the catastrophic 2008 Wenchuan earthquake, when both government and social media encouraged citizens to dig deep into their own pockets to aid the disaster victims, the practice of private giving has spread rapidly in Chinese society. Charitable foundations and philanthropic venture funds have proliferated, now numbering in the thousands, and affording ever expanding opportunities for community activism.

The Wenchuan quake not only encouraged the rise of private philanthropy; it also triggered a massive volunteer movement when concerned citizens from across the country, especially college students, flocked to Sichuan to offer their personal assistance to the rescue effort. The trend of youthful voluntarism for public causes accelerated a few months later when the government (via the CYL, the Confucius Institute, and other official agencies) mobilized large numbers of student volunteers to help out at the Beijing Olympics. The experiences of 2008 were clearly transformative for the current generation of young Chinese, some of whom went on to establish private charities of their own. Many others have continued the practice of devoting generous amounts of personal time and money to support their favorite causes.

While battling HIV/AIDS and environmental pollution animated the first generation of China's grassroots NGO activists, both the issues and the motives that drive today's activists are remarkably wide-ranging. A variety of religious faiths—from Christianity to Buddhism—is inspiring the establishment of privately operated medical clinics and nursing homes, for example.

A secular sense of social responsibility is fueling donation drives for everything from books for school libraries to winter coats for the poor. And the influence of socialist ideals can be detected in the rapid growth of labor NGOs that provide legal and welfare services for downtrodden workers.

A Worried State

Under some pressure to live up to its own officially espoused socialist ideology by upgrading the provision of social services, the party-state is anxious to reap the positive dividends of this flourishing of community activism. In some cases, local governments even contract with civic organizations to facilitate the implementation of mandated welfare policies and other social services.

But the state's top priority remains that of "stability maintenance" (weiwen), or the perpetuation of Communist Party rule. Fearful that networks of social activists could pose an existential threat similar to what transpired in Eastern Europe in 1989, the government keeps close tabs on NGOs and makes it difficult (through registration rules as well as public security surveillance and harassment) for local groups to forge links with counterparts in other parts of the country. The party-state pays special attention to constraining the involvement of intellectuals—college students included—in order to prevent their serving as bridges between groups operating in different locations or composed of disparate social classes or interests.

An outside observer might suspect PRC authorities of betraying a streak of paranoia by devoting so much concern to combating the supposed political threat of university students. After all, rapid expansion in higher education enrollments, combined with the growth of professional and technical training at the expense of liberal arts education, has rendered college students in China today—as in many other countries—more focused on securing a job than on sabotaging the system. But in fact the party-state's worries are hardly groundless. In addition to the historic cycles of Chinese student protest, there is ample contemporary evidence of the challenge posed by student power in those parts of Greater China where campus controls are less stringent than on the mainland.

As the PRC keenly appreciates, the possibility of college students' acting as sparkplugs of political protest certainly did not disappear on June 4, 1989. Twenty-five years after the suppression of the Tiananmen uprising, events in both Taiwan and Hong Kong have demonstrated the continuing capacity of Chinese students—in concert with civil society allies—to trigger mass movements with unwelcome political implications for Beijing. In Taiwan, the Sunflower Student Movement (*taiyanghua xueyun*) occupied the Legislative Yuan for the first time in its history and forced the ruling party to reconsider a cross-strait service trade agreement with the PRC. In Hong Kong, students spearheaded some of the largest demonstrations in the island's history to register dissatisfaction with the PRC's stipulated process for nominating the city's chief executive.

It is too soon to assess the long-term impact of either of these two protest movements, but the events in Taiwan and Hong Kong this spring and summer have surely reinforced PRC authorities' worries about the dangers of an alliance between politicized student activists and an awakened civil society. Instead of resorting to crackdowns by riot police, as occurred in both Taipei and Hong Kong, Beijing would obviously far prefer to prevent the emergence of student-inspired protest in the first place. Ensuring that college campuses are tightly monitored and that student energies are channeled into system-supportive rather than system-subversive modes of activism is therefore a critical element in the regime's comprehensive scheme for "stability maintenance."

The Upper Hand

Like so many features of the contemporary Chinese scene, the role of civil society would seem to challenge conventional wisdom concerning the relationship between socioeconomic development and political change.

Counterintuitively, the recent increase of popular protest and associational activity in the PRC has proved more of a help than a hindrance to the perpetuation of Communist party-state rule. Rather than providing a platform for political agitation and democratization, the burgeoning of civil society in mainland China has offered an outlet for public service that relieves the state of some of its own onerous welfare burden while also fulfilling citizens' growing desire for social engagement.

The pervasive contestation that takes place outside the gates of university campuses, while sometimes sparked by grassroots NGOs, has concentrated on economic and environmental issues that do not directly challenge CCP authority. And the campuses themselves, the cradle of political ferment in twentieth-century China, have remained uncharacteristically quiet for the past 25 years.

To be sure, the PRC is not the only case where a rising civil society failed to produce democratization. Interwar Germany and Japan present examples of another, more disturbing, scenario in which the development of vociferous protest and vibrant associations in the 1920s and '30s presaged a turn toward right-wing militarism. Both Weimar Germany and Taisho Japan lacked the robust political institutions necessary to channel the activism of an aroused citizenry in ways productive of political liberalism. The result in those cases was not democracy, but fascism and the scourge of World War II.

In stark contrast to interwar Germany and Japan, however, the PRC today does not lack for strong political institutions. The CCP retains a tight grip on both government and society. Thus, while a turn toward aggressive militarism is not beyond the realm of possibility, a more likely trajectory for the PRC is that of continued Communist Party rule. To date, the party-state has shown a deft ability to keep the upper hand amid an extraordinary explosion of citizen contention.

A key pillar of this successful strategy has been the prevention of campus unrest. Thanks in no small part to new opportunities for volunteerism provided by the dramatic development of civil society, China's university students are at present devoting more energy to community service than to political mobilization. Hostile as the top leadership is toward the whole idea of civil society, the Communist party-state's survival has actually been prolonged by its emergence.

Still, one cannot help but wonder: If China's authoritarian polity is so resilient, why are its leaders so anxious about the system's durability? Why do they feel compelled to lavish such extravagant resources on the quest for "stability maintenance"? Judging by recent events in Taipei and Hong Kong, the advent of an independent Chinese civil society—aroused by impassioned university students—could indeed at some future point pose a serious threat to the endurance of the Communist party-state.

Media and Culture

Editorial Introduction

China's rise has also impacted the intellectual and cultural spheres in China—for better and for worse. Public discourse has certainly opened and become more pluralistic since the Maoist era and even during the early reform years (addressed in previous editions of *The China Reader*). The commercialization of the media, a dynamic process that has occurred since the turn of the century, has contributed to the increased openness and variety of topics publicly discussed in China. The advent of social media has further fueled this discourse diversity, despite the fact that major global platforms like Facebook and Twitter are blocked in China. Permitted platforms like WeChat (*Weixin*) now connect hundreds of millions of Chinese people. China's intellectuals have also been exposed to the outside world as never before—with millions of students going abroad for study and many professors having opportunities as visiting scholars at foreign institutions. At the same time, foreign students now populate Chinese campuses as never before (400,000 in 2014), while Chinese students are taught by a growing phalanx of foreign teachers. Despite this progress, Chinese media and intellectual life remain severely constricted. State censorship permeates the public and educational spheres—enforced by a large army of Internet monitors, censors, and propaganda apparatchiks. The following selections illustrate this dichotomy between increased openness simultaneously occurring amidst extreme controls on information and thought.

The first selection by Oxford University scholar Rachel Murphy concerns the changing media landscape in China. She first contextualizes and frames the discussion in terms of civil society, but then focuses on the interactive relationship between the propaganda authorities and censors, on the one hand, and the media on the other. This delicate relationship is under *constant* interaction and negotiation between the two—what is known as "playing line balls" (查遍球) in Chinese. In this constant to-and-fro process, journalists constantly "push the envelope" until the propaganda state pushes back, setting the parameters of the permissible; then the process begins all over again. Over time, the "space" for media discussion gradually broadens—although the party-state maintains very tight (and since 2009 *increased*) controls. Professor Murphy describes this process very well. She shows how journalists have become "agenda setters" in that their reports are forcing social issues of concern to the public on to the government's agenda. She also describes the rise of investigative and "compassionate" journalism, as well as the rising importance of the Internet and other instant communications technologies. She finds that the Internet and social media are not only means for instantaneous dissemination of information and personal views, but that they have also significantly contributed to the development of "associational life" in communities. All in all, Professor Murphy sees society changing the media in China more than vice-versa.

The next entry by Beina Xu of the Council on Foreign Relations delves more specifically into the issue of media censorship in China. She cites numerous examples of state censorship—both subtle and unsubtle—and provides examples of how the authorities control information. She also discusses the conditions under which foreign journalists must operate in China, a working environment that has steadily worsened in recent years.

The most major change in how Chinese get their information is, of course, the advent of the Internet. The next selection is a special report by *The Economist* magazine on the Internet in China. An estimated 600 million Chinese are now online. To be certain, the government attempts to strictly control what reaches the populace—by erecting its "Great Firewall." Most foreign search engines are blocked—including Google, Yahoo!, Bing, MSN, and others. So are foreign social media platforms like Twitter and Facebook. Nonetheless, users enjoy considerable latitude in what they discuss in these mediums. Certain boundaries should not be crossed, however. Incitement, attacks on party leaders by name, and other acts deemed seditious by the state result in retribution by government authorities. As a result, *The Economist* observes, "Dissidents in China say that freedom is knowing how big your cage is."

Intellectuals have always struggled in communist China. But, like many aspects of society, their lot has generally improved during the reform era. Nonetheless, severe restrictions on freedom of thought, speech, research, and publication exist. The next entry by Boston University Professor Merle Goldman, one of the world's leading experts on the Chinese intelligentsia, explores their current conditions. She discusses the role of public intellectuals, professional intellectuals, and political intellectuals. The first two communities have generally found their lives and working conditions improved, while the third group continues to experience the hard fist of the state. Nonetheless, brave ones like Liu Xiaobo have challenged the state. As a result, Liu is serving an eleven-year prison term in Liaoning Province for his role in organizing *Charter '08*. Goldman concludes by noting that, since 2008, the political atmosphere for intellectuals and public discourse has deteriorated markedly.

The next two entries concern China's search for "soft power" (a term first coined by Harvard professor Joseph Nye). Since 2008, when President Hu Jintao first used the term (软实力) in his speech to the 17th Party Congress, the Chinese government has been investing huge sums into promoting propaganda and cultural activities abroad in an attempt to improve China's international image. This massive effort has involved a number of institutions, resources, and activities.[1]

The first selection is drawn from former President Hu Jintao's speech to the 18th Party Congress in 2012. In it Hu discusses the need to build a "strong socialist culture"

---

[1] See David Shambaugh, "China's Soft Power Push: The Search for Respect," *Foreign Affairs* (July–August 2015).

inside China. This includes, in his description, the need to "vigorously foster China's national character and promote the underlying trend of the times, intensify education in patriotism, collectivism and socialism, and enrich people's cultural life and enhance their moral strength." Hu also called for the improvement of civic morality and ethics, clean business practices, integrity of government, and improved intellectual life. If all of this is carried out, according to Hu, Chinese culture and society will flourish at home and appeal abroad.

The final selection is by the "father" of the concept of soft power, Joseph Nye. In this newspaper op-ed, Nye is critical of Chinese government efforts to build (and buy) soft power abroad. He observes that the overt propagandistic nature of much of Beijing's efforts abroad undercut the potential viability of China's cultural appeal. "The best propaganda, Nye says, is not propaganda." Nye also takes China to task for the inconsistency of its benign-sounding propaganda abroad the harsh realities of China's political system at home. He provides a number of examples of the government's attempts to silence some of its most talented artists and writers. In the end, the father of soft power is not at all optimistic about China's accrual of it.

I. The Mainstream Media

Civil Society and Media in China[*]

Rachel Murphy

Civil society is conventionally understood to be an intermediate space between the state and the private realm of the family. Three overlapping aspects of civil society include the *public sphere* (public spaces where people can meet and exchange views); *associations* such as churches, hobby groups, and networks of friends and former classmates, which are the vehicles through which people participate in the public sphere; and *autonomous individuals* with their rights, views, and participation in associations and the public sphere. China has experienced dramatic transformations in the public sphere, associational life, and individual lifestyles and perspectives, and these have in turn interacted with recent changes in the form and content of the media. This contribution looks at the interactions between each of these three components of civil society and changes in the media.

The Public Sphere

In the social sciences, the concept of the public sphere is strongly associated with the ideas of Jürgen Habermas, who examined the conditions in seventeenth- to nineteenth-century Europe and found that private people came together in public domains such as tea houses and parks. He explored the ways in which their discussions helped to establish a public consensus about what is moral, rational, true, just, and beautiful. Habermas thought people could contribute in a genuine way to such discussions because they had experience of genuine feelings within the private realm of the family, and they could use the world of letters to make their personal feelings public, thereby facilitating shared understandings of the human condition. The sociologist John Thompson has argued that a key limitation of Habermas's analysis is that he defines "public" in terms of people being physically together and talking. Thompson objects to this limited definition of "public" because it does not capture the

---

[*] This article was originally published in David Shambaugh (ed.), *Charting China's Future: Domestic & International Challenges* (Abingdon, UK and New York: Routledge, 2011).

nature of information exchange and conversation in the twenty-first century.

Alongside these developments was the emergence of capitalism, long-distance trading, and technological innovations which allowed for the establishment of social networks and journals as corollary institutions of the public sphere. Trading and the spread of capitalism involved a shift away from reliance on family-based production, with the family unit meeting most of its own consumption needs, to a situation where people moved outside the home and into public places of work and information exchange. In the present era we can use information-communication technologies to interact with others and to witness persons and events without even meeting them. So we can feel empathy for others whom we do not know personally but whom we nevertheless see to be part of our community. For instance, at Spring Festival in China there is a variety show broadcast on China Central Television (CCTV) station that everyone in every corner of the country watches—in this example, by watching a television program, vast numbers of strangers share a common identity and a sense of purpose across a wide area.

Orwell Lives in China

In the case of China the party-state apparatus has explicitly used the media to cultivate a public consensus about what is a good way to live. Specifically, it has regarded the media as an instrument that educates individuals in building a particular vision of a prosperous, harmonious, and civilized society. Strict control over media employees has been exercised in no small part through ideological education coordinated by the Publicity Department and its subordinate departments at provincial, prefectural, county, and township levels.

This control by the Central Publicity (Propaganda) Department of the Communist Party has been so penetrating that it has been described by a former Chinese professor of journalism as "a dark empire in which the rays of law do not shine" and "the stumbling block in the cultural development of Chinese society."[1] The executive complement to the Publicity Department in the print sector is the State Press and Publications Agency (SPPA), a ministerial-level agency established in 1987 with corresponding agencies at provincial and municipal levels. The SPPA issues guidelines about news management and occupational codes and requires the registration of all publications and all journalists. This bureaucratization enables publishers to be regulated by the apparently impartial logic of professionalism and procedures, a handy pretext for reining in unruly editors. The Party control is pervasive precisely because it does not involve simple censorship. Rather it involves mobilizing editors, journalists, publishers, and producers in regulating their own behavior to ensure that the media serves national interests in accordance with laid-down guidelines. Indeed journalists seldom dare to report on controversial issues until a "line" (policy) has been decided on—hence many stories, such as the tainted blood scandal in rural Henan province or the river pollution in Heilongjiang, were not reported until widespread coverage in the international press forced the domestic media also to report.

Yet even though in the conventional media strong state control continues, there has in recent years been an important shift from "propaganda" to "agenda-setting" approaches to reporting. Propaganda involves telling people what to think, featuring mainly successful stories and model people, and working out how to report bad news that cannot be kept quiet. Agenda-setting involves the more nuanced approach of bringing issues to the fore, exploring possible explanations and perspectives, and gently encouraging the viewers to side with a favored perspective.

Establishing Journalistic Space

Some of the new agenda-setting approach to exploring social problems has taken the form of investigative journalism. Programs such as *Focus* (*Jiaodian Fangtan*) and *Legal Report* (*Jinri Shuofa*) often expose dark sides of society and politics. However, in doing so, these programs may actually strengthen rather than weaken the system. By focusing on a few bad apples at the local level these programs reinforce the idea that the "Center" (term for Beijing) is good. By giving an impression of an open media they create a space in which people feel they can vent their grievances and see the culprits exposed and punished. By highlighting problems and shaming those who are corrupt or inept, the programs generate pressures for those at lower levels to improve their governance practices. Lastly, the programs inculcate certain norms, and promote the idea that rule of law, filial piety, and national virtue are characteristics of China's public sphere.

Television has also been "guiding public opinion" through what the scholar Sun Wanning has called "compassionate journalism." Such journalism portrays the suffering of individuals, thereby generating public consensus about a rightful moral order that may have been violated. Yet, as Sun argues, the "us" in the consensus is usually an urban middle class. Sun further argues that, while such programs admittedly draw attention to the plight of selected "weak" and "poor" individuals, they also reinforce a paternalistic order whereby an elite invested in the system claims the moral authority that comes with bestowing charity and compassion.

Some media exposés of conditions in the countryside have pushed beyond the boundaries of compassionate journalism and into the realm of social and economic policy debate. A prime example of this is public discussion about hardship in the countryside. The catalyst for this came in March 2000 when Li Changping, a Party secretary from a rural township in Hebei province, wrote a letter to the then Chinese Premier Zhu Rongji entitled "Heartfelt Words from a Township Party Secretary." In his letter Li identified three inter-related aspects of the rural problem: the fall in peasant incomes, the decline in agriculture, and social disintegration in rural areas. According to the political scientist Lei Guang (2010), after Li's book was published in 2002 the number of articles published in the official newspaper *People's Daily* associated with *san nong wenti* (the "three rural problems") increased dramatically. The politically sanctioned public focus on *san nong wenti* led to major measures to improve the condition of farmers. Most notably, after 2004 officials were no longer permitted to levy taxes and fees on farmers, and in 2006 all rural taxes were banned—the idea was to eradicate the so-called farmers' burden that crippled so many and underpinned considerable unrest. Rather than extract local fees and

taxes, grassroots governments were instead to obtain their revenue from central government fiscal transfers, and they were to encourage investment in county-based industry and commerce development zones in order to build up an off-farm tax base.

The widespread media discussion of the *san nong* problems was politically palatable in part because it appealed to the Party as a caring entity that would bring forth a solution. By contrast, journalists who have highlighted the abuses that peasants have faced on account of systemic failures and the unsupervised power of party-state officials at the lower levels have been vulnerable to having their works banned. Such was the case with *Will the Boat Sink the Water?*, a book by the journalists Chen Guidi and Wu Chuntao which aimed to "give a voice to the voiceless" in rural Anhui province during the early 2000s.

Aside from the emergence of investigative and compassionate reporting, a further dynamic that has diversified the content of media is marketization. The example of newspapers lets us see this process at work. Specifically the content of newspapers became more varied after the early 1990s because lower-level party-state institutions across the country were permitted to establish their own media enterprises. This was also the time when fiscal decentralization required that media agencies become financially self-reliant. In the coastal regions these changes pushed cash-strapped Party newspaper agencies to respond to the opportunities presented by the fact that their localities had increasingly diverse social and economic interest groups, and their populations had burgeoning consumer power. The agencies therefore allowed satellite publishers to set up popular newspapers and magazines under their auspices, and this led to the flourishing of a whole range of publications to cater to different kinds of interests: sport, women's magazines, house decoration magazines, stock-market newspapers, and so on. The Party newspaper agencies then faced the challenge of competing with the newspapers of these satellite publishers for the custom of advertisers. This impetus led them to make the content and format of their own newspapers more attractive to readers and to increase their number of pages.

A further locus of diversification in ideas in the public sphere is the Internet. Indeed this is the media domain in which public debate is least amenable to state control. The rise of the green movement is a good example of how the rise of the Internet has enriched debate within China's public sphere. Guo and Calhoun explain that the Internet has created an apparently apolitical "green public sphere" in which discussions about citizens' and governments' rights and responsibilities with regard to the environment can occur in relative safety. As Elizabeth Economy has argued, this public sphere is therefore at the forefront of innovations among China's civil society organizations more generally, with regard to strategies for forging alliances, disseminating information, and engaging in advocacy.

However, protests on the Internet about the environment as well as other topics are not transformative. The protesters use language which shows support for the status quo, and they do not challenge the political order; rather they call upon the government to pay attention to certain issues and injustices, and this enables the government to respond in ways that enable more effective policies to be formulated.

Associational Life

The second component of civil society is voluntary associational life. Examples of associations include religious associations, business associations, environmental groups, friends who meet to share hobbies, elderly men who congregate in the park to display their birds and chat, and networks of former classmates who keep in touch. As stated earlier, ideally, such voluntary associations and social networks are the vehicles through which free individuals step outside the family and participate in the public sphere. Certainly alongside the march of market reforms and social liberalization in China, the numbers and varieties of networks and associations in which people can participate have increased dramatically. Moreover any one individual is likely to participate simultaneously in several networks and associations.

The Internet came into being in China at a time when civic associations were starting to increase in number and diversity. Guobin Yang argues that the civil society and the Internet in China have therefore energized each other. The Internet has invigorated civil society by offering new possibilities for citizenship participation. Meanwhile civil society has facilitated the development of the Internet by providing the necessary social basis: that is, the citizens and the citizen groups who communicate online. Guobin Yang's research provides at least two examples of ways in which civil society associations and the Internet have co-determined each other's emergence.[2] One is that civil society groups have used the Internet to help them carry out their activities. Based on his survey of 129 civic associations Guo explains that younger civic organizations with a commitment to social change have used the Internet much more than older associations that have a business orientation. The Internet provides these newer socially engaged associations with a way to strike out in China's constrained political context. The Internet is a tool that these organizations can use to foster links with government institutions: as several scholars have observed, in the Chinese context complete autonomy from the state equates with powerlessness—one needs a state connection if one wants to be able to influence policy and to have access to certain resources. Additionally, the Internet enables civil society organizations to find out about, and to publicize their activities to, international donors, which are often the main source of funding.

The Internet also facilitates the creation of new forms of associational life among people who have shared life experiences, interests, or objectives. Across China there is the phenomenon of communities who come to know each other through online bulletin boards: for example, those set up and run by people who were sent down to the countryside during the Cultural Revolution. These bulletin boards have provided a virtual place in which people who share a common generational identity talk about their memories and feel that they are understood.

Jens Damm offers further insight into how people use the Internet to form virtual and even real associations that are based on common interests.[3] He makes the important point that, despite a preoccupation amongst Western observers with the potential for the Internet in China to be used for political ends, in reality most usage has to do with lifestyle. These include sites about shopping, sexual orientation, motherhood, hobbies such as poetry, and so on—though creative writing may also have a political inflection, in that these commentaries may refer to human experiences of social change.

Mobile phones are a further kind of communication technology which enables individuals to participate in social networks. Their usage has become ever more widespread as CDMA signal-engineering technology has expanded across the country. Not surprisingly, and as has been noted for the Internet, people mainly use mobile phones for mundane but important daily-life purposes: for instance, sustaining caring relationships and managing economic arrangements.

However, alongside emails and Internet communications, mobile phones also facilitate associational activities in the real world which are not necessarily sanctioned by the party-state. The now outlawed Falun Gong sect has used new communication technologies. As one example, in 1999 10,000 members of the sect assembled outside the headquarters of the Communist Party in Beijing to collectively practice *qigong* breathing activities in protest at earlier attempts to repress their activities. The practitioners came from a range of social backgrounds—retirees, laid-off workers, the unemployed, people in ill health. Many of them had turned to Falun Gong and its transformative promises because market vagaries and the dismantling of state welfare services had left them feeling vulnerable. The Falun Gong members used mobile-phone text messaging to communicate with each other across a wide geographic area to arrange the mass *qigong* event. The capacity of so many diverse people to organize *by* themselves (usually it is the Party that organizes *for* the people) alarmed the party-state, and its efforts to denounce and repress the Falun Gong gained an urgent impetus.

Indeed when public protests occur, the attention of authorities has increasingly turned to the new media communications of mobiles and the Internet. This was certainly the case in July 2009 in the western province of Xinjiang, when the economically and politically disadvantaged Uighurs—prompted by news about the deadly beating of a Uighur in Guangzhou—attacked the shops and business interests of the Han Chinese. The authorities responded by immediately blocking text messaging services as well as Internet services in the region.

Clearly, then, in the reform era there has been a proliferation of the kinds of shared identities and interests that provide a basis for people to associate with each other, and both old and new media have greatly facilitated this aspect of social life. At the same time, though, we see that the party-state's monitoring of associational activities has extended in recent years to include efforts to monitor new media communications.

Citizenship and Individual Identity

The final aspect of civil society is the presence of autonomous individuals who believe that they have the right to express themselves in public forums, the right to associate with others, and the right to participate in civil society, but who at the same time also feel that they have a responsibility to behave in a moral, respectful, and civil way. Certainly much of the rise of civil society as well as much media usage in China has occurred in a context of wider social changes: for example, individuals have become ever more disentangled from state collective institutions, such as the former work units that provided cradle-to-grave security, and set free to find their own neighborhoods and social groups.

It is possible to identify at least two broad dynamics which encourage people to see themselves as individuals with rights. The first has been discussed by Habermas, according to whom the patriarchal head of the household in seventeenth- or eighteenth-century Europe had the status to participate autonomously in the public sphere because he had both family and property, and family and property came to be seen as part of the natural order of things. With the development of markets and the transfer of many aspects of economic work to places outside the home, the state increasingly left the social reproduction of the family and the resources required for this to the family. The state became totally separated out from society, so that the only role of the state was to ensure that appropriate policies and legal regulation were in place to allow the market and free trade to develop across space. Respect for privacy, for private property, and for legal protection for the free control of productive property were seen as natural rights.

This leads us to the question that some external observers have asked about China: with marketization and the rise of a middle class, will members of this class demand legal protection—in other words, rights for their property? Surely they will start to speak out publicly when the food they buy is contaminated with pollutants and when developers want to build a super-rail outside their home? One instance of such protest was that waged in Xiamen in 2007 by media-savvy citizens' groups and bloggers against the building of a paraxylene plant. Yet can such issue-focused calls for rights lead to calls for broader systemic changes?

In the present era, the urban middle classes in China seem to prefer to use their personalized connections to advance their own interests and to protect their "own back yard" rather than to mobilize for any wider institutional change or common good: a practice that among peasants has been lamented by China's educated elite as an expression of a parochial mentality and the reason for the absence of social democracy, which is the precursor to political democracy. This lack of middle class political activism in China may be explained by a lack of requisite "social infrastructure"—in other words, lack of a striving civil society to support organization around democratic ideas and demands. A related explanation is that China's capitalist development has been an artifact created by the Communist state, and the middle class must rely heavily on its arbitrary power to prosper.

Another dimension to understanding how marketization fosters people's awareness of their individual aspirations pertains to the right to consume. Individuals buy goods not just to support their families' basic subsistence, as was often the case in China's not too distant past, but also to express their individual identities and pursue their preferred lifestyles. The mobile phone and the proliferation of associated products such as personalized carriers, covers, and ring tones are but one instance of this. Yet, it is not always possible for so-called marginalized individuals to consume and express their own identities in ways that transform their lowly status. For example, Tiantian Zheng notes how the attempts of rural migrant women to use make-up and clothes to imitate the urban women whom they saw on television

seldom enabled them to transform their lot; indeed some were mocked as bumpkins in fancy dress.[4] Despite inequalities in the possibilities for different people to transform their lives through consumption, however, the consumer market does offer promises of change and progress that entice many individuals.

The second dynamic which encourages people to see themselves as individuals who have rights is state civic education. In some investigative journalism programs marginalized people are shown to have lost out in their dealings with other individuals or institutions, and the explanation given is usually that their legal consciousness is too low. Yet, as noted by Kevin O'Brien and Lianjiang Li,[5] the content of such media reporting not only suggests to marginalized people that they should be law-abiding, it also suggests to them that they have rights. Such people—be they laid-off workers, unpaid migrant workers, or farmers whose land has been expropriated for urban construction—often use the slogans and the policies of the central government to "rightfully resist" unfair practices and to lay claim to their entitlements. As with the protests of the urban middle classes, however, these calls for rights by marginalized individuals are not politically transformative: they fit within a permitted tradition of protest and of bargaining with an authoritarian state which can bestow justice.

Among people who are more educated and have access to the Internet, a sense of individual right to free expression and of individual obligation to uphold morality can lead to more challenging forms of protest. This includes expressions of criticisms in the public domain that involve the co-ordination of protest movements across space (something the state tries to prevent with explicit regulations that restrict the activities of civil society organizations to particular administrative districts) and across social groups (something the state bans by forbidding the members of potentially disaffected groups, such as ex-soldiers or migrant workers, from setting up their own associations).

People have devised strategies for dealing with the political and technological blocking and censorship constraints that get in the way of online expression and co-ordination. For instance, people disguise their online identities, use homonyms for controversial words, and express their criticisms in ways that will not result in their bulletin board sites being shut down. Indeed there are numerous instances of nationwide Internet petitions led by outraged individual crusaders that eventually helped to bring perpetrators of particular injustices to account. We do therefore see a gradual pushing of the boundaries of permissible protest and activism by individuals in the public sphere—even as both the state and individuals enforce those boundaries.

Outlook for the Future

The diversification and the expansion of media form and content interacts with and in many ways supports the emergence of civil society in China. In particular, the media helps to make the public sphere more dynamic and vibrant by enabling more topics to be discussed and by creating more spaces in which conversations among different "publics" can be held. The Internet, in particular, enables more associations to emerge, thereby creating new vehicles through which people can participate in the public sphere. The media also creates more possibilities for individuals to become aware of their rights, to express their own identities, and to pursue certain lifestyle choices.

There are, though, two types of limitation which should temper our enthusiasm with regard to the "empowering" potential of a mediated civil society in China: inequalities and party-state dominance. With regard to the former, there are inequalities in access to the media, new media in particular. For instance, in 2003, while 69 percent of China's population held rural residency, only 1 percent of Chinese Internet users worked in agriculture, forestry, husbandry, and fishery. Further, there are inequalities across social groups in access to opportunities for producing one's own media content and for speaking in one's own voice in public debates. Even with the rise of compassionate journalism, marginalized individuals are generally spoken about in ways that buttress a paternalistic social and political order, rather than in ways that let them speak for themselves.

The second set of limitations pertains to the ongoing party-state dominance of civil society and the media, and here there are several factors to consider. First, the party-state maintains a firm grip on the parameters of permissible conversations in the public sphere—Charter 08's calls for China to adhere to the International Covenant on Civil and Political Rights and the official crackdown on its principal authors and supporters provide a clear instance of the limits. Liu Xiaobo was dealt a harsh eleven-year prison sentence for "inciting state subversion," before he was awarded the 2010 Nobel Peace Prize. Second, the party-state constrains the activities of civil society associations. It is difficult for them to register, and if they do manage to register it is often difficult for them to operate without interference and the appropriation of resources and employment opportunities by their state "mothers-in-law"—that is, the state agencies with which they must register. Finally, the party-state continues to exert control over the kinds of information that individuals can obtain, and over what they can express in public. Certainly, uncivil spheres—such as those involving pornography or Internet-based public vigilantism—legitimate party-state intervention. But it is always easy to use extreme cases to justify intrusive surveillance over public conversation more generally. That said, we need to recall that the vast majority of Chinese individuals who participate in associations, both real and virtual, do so to pursue lifestyle interests.

These interests appear apolitical. Importantly, though, these dimensions of civic life—for instance, hobby groups and lifestyle bulletin boards—are integral to a development trajectory that draws ever more people, albeit unequally, into the communications and consumption grid of an expanding marketplace. Furthermore, the members of social groups who are doing particularly well from this market-based development enjoy most privileges for participating in associations where their voices can be heard: for instance, elite consultative social organizations, municipal government online forums, popular Internet bulletin boards, and participatory television programs. Through such forums these more privileged people help to shape public conversations about China's future development and to secure their stake in this future.

NOTES

1. For more on the CCP Publicity Department, see Anne-Marie Brady, *Marketing Dictatorship: Propaganda and Thought Work in Contemporary China* (Lanham, MD: Rowman & Littlefield, 2008); and David Shambaugh, "China's Propaganda System: Institutions, Process & Efficacy," *The China Journal*, No. 57 (January 2007).

2. See Guobin Yang, "Online Activism," *Journal of Democracy*, Vol. 20, No. 3 (2009), pp. 33–6; Guobin Yang, "How Do Chinese Civic Associations Respond to the Internet: Findings from a Survey," *The China Quarterly*, No. 189 (2007), pp. 122–43; Guobin Yang, "The Co-Evolution of the Internet and Civil Society in China," *Asian Survey*, Vol. 43, No. 3 (2003), pp. 405–22; Guobin Yang and Craig Calhoun, "Media, Civil Society and the Rise of a Green Public Sphere in China," *China Information*, No. 21 (July 2007), pp. 211–36.

3. Jens Damm, "The Internet and the Fragmentation of Chinese Society," *Critical Asian Studies*, Vol. 39, No. 2 (2007), pp. 273–94.

4. Tiantian Zheng, "Performing Media-Constructed Images for First-Class Citizenship: Political Struggles of Rural Migrant Hostesses in Dalian," *Critical Asian Studies*, Vol. 39, No. 1 (March 2007), pp. 89–120.

5. Kevin O'Brien and Lianjiang Li, *Rightful Resistance in Rural China* (Cambridge: Cambridge University Press, 2006).

MEDIA CENSORSHIP IN CHINA[*]

Beina Xu

The Chinese government has long kept tight reins on both traditional and new media to avoid potential subversion of its authority. Its tactics often entail strict media controls using monitoring systems and firewalls, shuttering publications or websites, and jailing dissident journalists, bloggers, and activists. The severity of media censorship grabbed headlines in early January 2013 when *Southern Weekly,* a liberal-leaning paper based in Guangzhou, staged a week-long confrontation with the government after local propaganda authorities rewrote a front-page proreform editorial. Google's battle with the Chinese government over Internet censorship in China, and the Norwegian Nobel Committee's awarding of the 2010 Peace Prize to jailed Chinese activist Liu Xiaobo, have also increased international attention to media censorship in the country. At the same time, the country's burgeoning economy has allowed for greater diversity in China's media coverage, and experts say the growing Chinese demand for information is testing the regime's control.

Official Media Policy

China's constitution affords its citizens freedom of speech and press, but the opacity of Chinese media regulations allows authorities to crack down on news stories by claiming that they expose state secrets and thus endanger the country. In April 2010, the Chinese government revised its existing *Law on Guarding State Secrets* to tighten control over information flows. The amendment strengthens requirements for Internet companies and telecommunications operators to cooperate with Chinese authorities in investigations into leaks of state secrets. But the definition of state secrets in China remains vague, facilitating censorship of any information that authorities deem harmful to their political or economic interests. Council on Foreign Relations (CFR) Senior Fellow Elizabeth C. Economy says the Chinese government is in a state of "schizophrenia" about media policy as it "goes back and forth, testing the line, knowing they need press freedom and the information it provides, but worried about opening the door to the type of freedoms that could lead to the regime's downfall."

In May 2010, the government issued its first White Paper on the Internet that emphasized the concept of "Internet sovereignty,"

[*] This article was first published online by the Council on Foreign Relations on September 25, 2014: http:www.cfr.org/china/media-censorship-china/p11515. Isabella Bennett contributed to it.

requiring all Internet users in China, including foreign organizations and individuals, to abide by Chinese laws and regulations. Chinese Internet companies are now required to sign the "Public Pledge on Self-Regulation and Professional Ethics for China Internet Industry," which entails even stricter rules than those in the white paper, according to Jason Q. Ng, a specialist on Chinese media censorship and author of *Blocked on Weibo*.

How Free Is Chinese Media?

The watchdog group Reporters Without Borders ranked China 173 out of 179 countries in its 2013 worldwide index of press freedom. Reporters face harassment and jail time for violating rules, and are effectively pressured into "self-censorship." Former CFR Edward R. Murrow Press Fellow Matt Pottinger says that Chinese media outlets usually employ their own monitors to ensure political acceptability of their content. Censorship guidelines are circulated weekly from the Communist Party propaganda department and the government Bureau of Internet Affairs to prominent editors and media providers. A leaked March 2010 version lists some of the prohibitions.

In the past, only state agencies could own media in China, but today there is increased private ownership. China News Network Corporation (CNC), a twenty-four-hour global news network launched in July 2010, for example, is reportedly half privately financed. Although the government claims that the number of publications has proliferated in recent years, Pottinger argues that the increase has not necessarily delivered plurality to the media landscape in China. The new publications remain "a populist, socialist media, just as controlled by the government," he says. "The seemingly chatty, freewheeling press is not really freewheeling at all. The Chinese Communist Party is just more cunning about how it controls public opinion."

Certain websites that the government deems potentially dangerous—like Wikipedia—are blocked during periods of controversy, such as the June 4 anniversary of the Tiananmen Square massacre. Specific material considered a threat to political stability is also banned, including controversial photos and search terms. In June 2013, the censorship around the Tiananmen anniversary reached new heights, with Chinese social media blocking even vague, tertiary references to the incident.

The government is particularly keen on blocking reports of issues that could incite social unrest, like official corruption and ethnic strife. The websites of Bloomberg and the *New York Times* were blacked out in 2012 after each ran reports on the private wealth of Party Secretary Xi Jinping and Premier Wen Jiabao. Restrictions were also placed on microblogging services in April 2012 in response to rumors of a coup attempt in Beijing involving the disgraced former Chongqing party chief Bo Xilai. Online media companies Sina Corp. and Tencent Holdings Ltd. were forced to shut down the commenting function—a key feature for discussions—for three days. Censors were also swift to block any mention of an October 2013 attack on Tiananmen Square by individuals from Xinjiang province, home to the mostly Muslim Uighur minority group.

The Censorship Groups

More than a dozen government bodies review and enforce laws related to information flow within, into, and from China. The most powerful monitoring body is the Communist Party's Central Propaganda Department (CPD), which coordinates with General Administration of Press and Publication (GAPP) and State Administration of Radio, Film, and Television (SARFT) to ensure content promotes party doctrine. Xinhua, the state news agency, is widely considered a propaganda tool. Ng says that the various ministries once functioned as smaller fiefdoms of control, but have recently been more consolidated under the State Council Information Office, which has taken the lead on Internet monitoring.

The CPD gives media outlets editorial guidelines as well as directives restricting coverage of politically sensitive topics. In one high-profile incident involving liberal Guangdong magazine *Southern Weekly*, government censors rewrote the paper's New Year's message from a call for reform to a tribute to the Communist Party. The move triggered mass demonstrations by the staff and general public, who demanded the resignation of the local propaganda bureau chief. While staff and censors reached a compromise that would theoretically relax some controls, much of the censorship remained in place, and the calls for resignation were ignored.

China's government also tightens censorship in times of political transition; before its Eighteenth National Congress power handover in late 2012, it issued new rules requiring Internet users to provide real names to service providers, while assigning Internet companies greater responsibility for reporting forbidden postings to the authorities.

Exerting Control

The Chinese government deploys myriad ways of censoring the Internet. Experts say it includes technical methods like bandwidth throttling, keyword filtering, as well as the wholesale blocking of access to websites. Google, after a protracted battle with Chinese authorities over the banning of search terms, quietly gave up its fight in early 2013 by turning off a notification that alerted Chinese users of potential censorship. But as Ng points out, the government also employs a diverse range of methods to induce journalists to censor themselves. Such tactics include dismissals and demotions, libel lawsuits, fines, arrests, and the shuttering of news outlets.

Journalists and activists who overstep boundaries can also face prison; as of February 2014, thirty journalists and seventy *netizens*—bloggers, online journalists, or cyber-dissidents—are imprisoned, according to Reporters Without Borders. In 2009, Chinese rights activist Liu Xiaobo was sentenced to eleven years in prison for advocating democratic reforms and freedom of speech in Charter 08, which earned him the Nobel Peace Prize. Censors quickly blocked news of the prize within China. A year later, journalist Tan Zuoren was sentenced to five years in prison for drawing attention to government corruption and poor construction of school buildings that collapsed and killed thousands of children during the 2008 earthquake in Sichuan province. The Chinese government blocked all inquiries into the issue, and Tan's volunteers were harassed and

beaten. Early 2014 saw the government hand a four-year prison sentence to human rights activist Xu Zhiyong, who observers say was targeted due to his growing presence on Chinese social media platforms.

The Xi administration, in power since March 2013, has further tightened the reins on journalists. A new July 2014 directive on journalist press passes bars reporters from releasing information from interviews or press conferences on social media without permission of their employer media organizations. The government also said it would not grant press passes to those who failed to sign the secrecy agreement.

Publicizing the CPD guidelines also invites punishment, as they may be classified as "state secrets." Such was the case of Shi Tao, a journalist who served eight years in jail for detailing, in a Yahoo! email, the CPD's instructions for how to report the fifteenth anniversary of Tiananmen Square. Matt Pottinger adds that on top of such national restrictions, local officials also release their own directives. Some of these have restricted information at the cost of public health, as in early 2014, when China's national poultry association requested provincial governments to stop reporting individual cases of H7N9 bird flu infections, fearing damage to profits.

Foreign Media

All inbound data from foreign Internet sources are filtered through one of three computer centers in Beijing, Shanghai, and Guangzhou, where keywords alert authorities to provocative content. The Foreign Correspondents Club of China reported 178 cases of interference with foreign media in 2008, but it has since stopped publishing figures on its website to ensure its continued operation.

Although foreign media can't be censored, international journalists face government intimidation, surveillance, and restrictions on their reporting, writes freelance China correspondent Paul Mooney, who was denied a visa in 2013. The government's propaganda bureaus have also cracked down on reporters' involvement with foreign media outlets; veteran journalist Gao Yu was detained in May 2014 for allegedly leaking a Party document to the foreign press, and two months later, *China Fortune* reporter Song Zhibiao was forced to resign for writing commentaries for the Hong Kong–based Oriental Press Group. In August 2014, authorities released Xiang Nanfu, a contributor to the US-based Chinese language news website Boxun.com, after detaining him on charges of fabricating stories that disparaged the Chinese government ahead of the twenty-fifth anniversary of the Tiananmen Square massacre.

China requires foreign correspondents to obtain permission before reporting in the country and has used this as an administrative roadblock to prevent journalists from reporting on potentially sensitive topics like corruption. Austin Ramzy, a China reporter for *Time* magazine, relocated to Taiwan in early 2014 after failing to receive his accreditation and visa. *New York Times* reporter Chris Buckley was reported to have been expelled in early January 2013—an incident China's foreign ministry clarified as a visa application suspension due to improper credentials. China observers were most notably shaken by the 2013 suspension of Bloomberg's China correspondent, Michael Forsythe, after Bloomberg journalists accused the news agency of withholding investigative articles for fear of reprisal from Chinese authorities. "Taken together, this is the Chinese government's broadest effort in decades to roll back unwelcome foreign coverage—and that raises the stakes for news organizations that are struggling to figure out how to handle China" writes Evan Osnos, a former China correspondent for *The New Yorker*.

The treatment of foreign reporters has become a diplomatic issue. In response to the Arab Spring protests in early 2011, then Secretary of State Hillary Clinton pledged to continue US efforts to weaken censorship in countries with repressive governments like China and Iran. In response, China warned Washington to not meddle in the internal affairs of other countries. On a December 2013 trip to Beijing, Vice President Joe Biden pressed China publicly and privately about press freedom, directly raising the issue in talks with Chinese President Xi Jinping and meeting with US journalists working in China. In the wake of Ramzy's denied visa, White House spokesman Jay Carney also issued a statement urging China to unblock US media websites and eliminate travel restrictions on journalists.

Circumventing the Censors

Despite the systematic control of news, the Chinese public has found ways to get news past censors through proxy servers and virtual private networks (VPNs), as well as through microblogging sites like Weibo that have become the primary spaces for Chinese netizens to voice opinion or discuss taboo subjects. "Over the years, in a series of cat-and-mouse games, Chinese Internet users have developed an extensive series of puns—both visual and homophonous—slang, acronyms, memes, and images to skirt restrictions and censors," writes Ng.

Google's chairman, Eric Schmidt, said in early 2014 that encryption could help the company penetrate China. But such steps experienced a setback in March 2014 when authorities cracked down on social networking app WeChat (known as *Weixin* in China), deleting prominent, politically liberal accounts. Soon thereafter, the government announced new regulations on "instant messaging tools" aimed at mobile chat applications such as WeChat, which has more than 270 million users and was increasingly seen as replacing Weibo as a platform for popular dissent that could skirt censors. Elizabeth Economy says that the Internet has increasingly become a means for Chinese citizens to ensure official accountability and rule of law, noting the growing importance of social network sites as a political force inside China despite government restrictions.

China had roughly 618 million Internet users as of December 2013. Although there have been vocal calls for total press freedom in China, some experts point to a more nuanced discussion of the ways in which the Internet is revolutionizing the Chinese media landscape and a society that is demanding more information. "Some people in China don't look at freedom of speech as an abstract ideal, but more as a means to an end," writes Emily Parker. Rather, the fight for free expression fits into a larger context of burgeoning citizen attention to other, more pertinent social campaigns like environmental degradation, social inequality, and corruption—issues for which they use the Internet and media as a means of disseminating information, says Ng.

II. THE INTERNET AND SOCIAL MEDIA

China's Internet: A Giant Cage*

The Economist

Thirteen years ago Bill Clinton, then America's president, said that trying to control the Internet in China would be like trying to "nail Jell-O to the wall." At the time he seemed to be stating the obvious. By its nature the web was widely dispersed, using so many channels that it could not possibly be blocked. Rather, it seemed to have the capacity to open up the world to its users even in shut-in places. Just as earlier communications technologies may have helped topple dictatorships in the past (for example, the telegraph in Russia's Bolshevik revolutions in 1917 and short-wave radio in the break-up of the Soviet Union in 1991), the Internet would surely erode China's authoritarian state. Vastly increased access to information and the ability to communicate easily with like-minded people round the globe would endow its users with asymmetric power, diluting the might of the state and acting as a force for democracy.

Those expectations have been confounded. Not only has Chinese authoritarian rule survived the Internet, but the state has shown great skill in bending the technology to its own purposes, enabling it to exercise better control of its own society and setting an example for other repressive regimes. China's party-state has deployed an army of cyber-police, hardware engineers, software developers, web monitors, and paid online propagandists to watch, filter, censor and guide Chinese Internet users. Chinese private Internet companies, many of them clones of Western ones, have been allowed to flourish so long as they do not deviate from the party line.

If this article were about the Internet in any Western country, it would have little to say about the role of the government; instead, it would focus on the companies thriving on the Internet, speculate about which industries would be disrupted next and look at the way the web is changing individuals' lives. Such things are of interest in

China too, but this report concentrates on the part played by the government because that is the most extraordinary thing about the Internet there. The Chinese government has spent a huge amount of effort on making sure that its Internet is different, not just that freedom of expression is limited but also that the industry that is built around it serves national goals as well as commercial ones.

Walls Have Ears

Ironically, the first e-mail from China, sent to an international academic network on September 14th, 1987, proclaimed proudly: "Across the Great Wall we can reach every corner in the world." Yet within China's borders the Communist Party has systematically put in place projects such as the Great Firewall, which keeps out "undesirable" foreign websites such as Facebook, Twitter, and YouTube, while Golden Shield monitors activities within China. It has also worked closely with trusted domestic Internet companies such as Baidu (a search engine), Tencent (an Internet-services portal), Renren (China's leading clone of Facebook) and Sina, an online media company that includes Weibo, a Twitter-like microblogging service.

Of all these newcomers, microblogging has had the biggest impact on everyday life in China. It has allowed the spread of news and views in ways that were not previously possible, penetrating almost every Internet-connected home in China. The authorities, having blocked Twitter and Facebook early on, allowed Chinese microblogs and social-media services to develop as trusted and controlled alternatives. They grew exponentially, far beyond anything that Twitter achieved in the Chinese market.

Google, the West's foremost search company, hesitantly tried to play by China's rules for a while, introducing a self-censored search engine there in 2006, but eventually withdrew that service in 2010, not so much because of the restrictions imposed on it but because it was being hacked

---
* This article was published in *The Economist*, April 6, 2013.

by the Chinese. China's cyber-hackers continue routinely to break into the e-mails of dissidents as well as into the computer systems of foreign media that report sensitive stories on China's leaders. They have recently made headlines by stealing the technology of American defense firms and probing critical American infrastructure for vulnerabilities. Numerous hacking attacks abroad have purportedly provided Chinese firms with sensitive commercial information and given the People's Liberation Army valuable insights into other countries' defense apparatus.

The party has achieved something few had thought possible: the construction of a distinct national Internet. The Chinese Internet resembles a fenced-off playground with paternalistic guards. Like the Internet that much of the rest of the world enjoys, it is messy and unruly, offering diversions such as games, shopping and much more. Allowing a distinctly Chinese Internet to flourish has been an important part of building a better cage. But it is constantly watched over and manipulated.

Sometimes the authorities' efforts at controlling it are absurd, even ridiculous, but the joke is on the users. Government agencies across the country have invested heavily in software to track and analyze online behavior, both to gauge public opinion and to contain threats before they spread, and the authorities deal ruthlessly with those who break the rules. In 2009 Liu Xiaobo, a Chinese writer, was sentenced to 11 years in prison for co-writing an online manifesto calling for an end to authoritarian rule and asking for signatures in support. At the time few in China had heard of Mr. Liu, a much-jailed democracy activist, and not many saw the declaration. He became famous outside China when he was awarded the Nobel Peace Prize in 2010 but is still largely unknown within the country because of strict censorship (his name is among a huge and growing number of "sensitive keywords" which are blocked online).

Also in 2009, after riots in Xinjiang, a remote north-western region, the authorities shut off the area's Internet from both the rest of China and from the world. By flipping an Internet "kill switch," they isolated the area for almost a year. And in March 2012, when social media carried rumors of an attempted coup in Beijing, the government temporarily shut down some of the Internet's microblogging services and detained six people.

Wobbling Jell-O

Will the Chinese state be able to go on controlling, manipulating and hacking the Internet indefinitely? There are reasons to think it will not. When Mr. Clinton made his famous remark about nailing Jell-O to the wall, only 20 million people in China were online. Now the cage strains to hold in excess of 560 million, almost as many as the online population of North America and Europe combined. The fastest growth in Internet use is in China's poorer, more rural provinces, partly because of a surge in users connecting via mobile devices, which now outnumber those connecting from computers. The Internet is no longer confined to an urban, educated and relatively well-off public. Most farmers are getting online to listen to music, play mobile games, and check the weather, not blog dissent. But even casual users can be drawn into political debates online, and the Internet is one place where people can speak their minds and criticize the government relatively freely.

In private they have always grumbled, and families at their dinner tables have scoffed at the propaganda served up on state-run television. But being able to express diverging views collectively online is new. Millions of users are low-grade subversives, chipping away at the imposing edifice of the party-state with humor, outrage, and rueful cynicism. Only those deemed to be threatening the state—on a very broad definition that can include being critical of a leader, or airing some grievance—are singled out for punishment.

Sometimes online complaints do produce results, swiftly bringing offenders to book. When an army political commissar got abusive with a flight attendant, she posted photographs of the incident. Internet users soon ferreted out his name, job title, and location, and he was eased out of his job. When an official was photographed smiling at the scene of a gruesome accident, the online crowd noticed he was wearing a luxury watch and quickly came up with more photographs of the same official wearing other luxury watches. "Brother Watch," as he came to be known, was fired.

Small victories like this are becoming increasingly common, to the dismay of millions of Communist Party cadres. Many web users believe that the balance of power has shifted: in a survey conducted in 2010 by a magazine affiliated to the *People's Daily*, the party mouthpiece, more than

70% of respondents agreed that local Chinese officials suffered from "Internet terror."

Yet for the party as a whole the Internet holds much less terror than it does for local officials. The online mob can gorge itself on corrupt low-level officials because the party leaders allow it. It can make fun of censorship, ridicule party propaganda and mock the creator of the Great Firewall. It can lampoon a system that deletes accounts and allows them to pop up again under a new name, only for the new accounts to be deleted in turn. It can rattle the bars of its cage all it likes. As long as the dissent remains online and unorganized, the minders do not seem to care.

At the same time, though, the more sensitive tweets and blog posts, attacking senior party leaders by name or, most serious of all, calling for demonstrations in the real world, are quickly deleted, sometimes before they even make it onto the web. Activists who directly challenge the central party organization or attempt to organize in numbers (like Mr. Liu) are crushed long before they can pose a threat. (Pornography is also officially censored, though it proliferates nonetheless.) The rest of the chaotic Internet that takes up people's time, energy and money carries on, mostly undisturbed. Dissident activity plays only a small but potent part in the overall mix.

Adaptive Authoritarianism

For the party leaders the Internet has created more subtle challenges. Collective expression on the web, led by civic-minded microbloggers with millions of followers, is focusing attention on recurring problems such as food safety and pollution, showing up the gap between expectations and performance. That means the authorities now have to try to come up with credible responses to crises such as the huge spike in air pollution in January and February. In short, the Internet requires the Party Center to be more efficient at being authoritarian.

This is the online blueprint for what scholars call "adaptive authoritarianism," and there is an international market for it. China sells its technological know-how abroad, including tools for monitoring and filtering the Internet. Huawei and ZTE, two big Chinese companies, are leading suppliers of Internet and telecoms hardware to a number of states in Central and Southeast Asia, Eastern Europe and Africa, including Kazakhstan, Vietnam, Belarus, Ethiopia, and Zambia. Many of these would like to increase online access while retaining tight political and technological control. China has aligned itself with these countries and dozens of others, including Russia, in a global dispute with Western democracies over how the Internet should be governed.

Dissidents in China say that freedom is knowing how big your cage is. It could be argued that with their Internet the Chinese authorities have built one of the world's largest, best-appointed cages. It could equally be said that they have constructed an expensive, unwieldy monstrosity, a desperate grab for control to buy time for the party.

III. THE INTELLIGENTSIA

China's Beleaguered Intellectuals*

Merle Goldman

Political scientists have long differentiated between totalitarian and authoritarian regimes.

The distinction is particularly relevant in contrasting the reform era in the People's Republic of China with the period that preceded it. Under Mao Zedong, who ruled from 1949 until 1976, China was governed by a totalitarian system in which Mao and the Communist Party dominated

---

* This article was first published in *Current History* (September 2009).

not only the country's political life but also the intellectual, artistic, economic, and personal lives of their subjects.

After Mao died in 1976 and was succeeded by his former Long March comrade Deng Xiaoping, China moved from a totalitarian to an authoritarian regime. The party still dominated the political system and, except for elections at the village level, it determined the political hierarchy. But the government's economic reforms and its loosening of controls over nonpolitical activities, together with the country's opening to the outside world, allowed a degree of freedom into people's personal, economic, cultural, and intellectual lives. The post-Mao period has witnessed a proliferation of ideas, activities, and artistic endeavors outside the party's control.

Of course, there is risk in giving too much weight to the totalitarian-authoritarian distinction. China's government today remains under the control of the Communist Party, and so do most Chinese citizens. A new generation of party leaders, led by former Shanghai Mayor Jiang Zemin, came to power after the violent crackdown on prodemocracy demonstrators in Tiananmen Square on June 4, 1989. That leadership—and particularly the current generation of leaders headed by President Hu Jintao and his associates, who came to power in 2002—have sought to re-indoctrinate party cadres in Leninist ideology. While strengthening the government's capacity to deal with the increasing inequalities and rampant corruption unleashed by China's move to a market economy, the country's leaders have also recentralized political authority.

Perhaps nowhere are the limits of freedom in the post-Mao era more conspicuous than in the party-state's treatment of public intellectuals. While a degree of pluralistic discourse and openness to foreign ideas exists in China's universities, academic journals, and think tanks, particularly in the sciences, these institutions are still under the control of party officials. And the Hu regime has detained, put under surveillance, and thrown out of the academic establishment scholars who dissent politically and criticize the party's policies publicly.

Nevertheless, public intellectuals in post-Mao China have found ways to promote political reform. In the Mao era, any intellectual who dissented not only from the party's political views, but also from its scientific, artistic, historical, or economic views, generally lost his or her job, was unable to make a living, and was literally banished from the intellectual community. In the post-Mao era, China's economic reforms and opening to the outside world have made it possible for dissident intellectuals to publish abroad and in Hong Kong and to support themselves and their families with freelance jobs.

In short, while China's movement from a totalitarian to an authoritarian polity has not protected public intellectuals from reprisals and detention, it has made it possible for them at times to speak out publicly on political issues and to have an impact beyond their immediate intellectual circles.

Heirs of Confucius

Public intellectuals are not unique to Western civilization. Indeed, although they were repressed during most of the Mao era, they have played a significant role in China throughout the country's history. China's pre-modern intellectuals, the Confucian literati, not only ran the governmental bureaucracies but were also viewed as the conscience of society. Their commitment to improving the human condition led them to assume responsibilities comparable to those of public intellectuals in the modern West. They were generalists who publicly discussed and contended with political, economic, and social issues. They organized philanthropic efforts and supervised education. Most important, the Confucian literati regarded it as their responsibility to criticize officials and even the emperor when official policies or practices diverged from the Confucian ideals of morality and fairness.

Public intellectuals helped to bring about the end of China's dynastic system and prepared the way for the 1911 revolution, whose leader Sun Yat-sen personified the public intellectual. Even though the Kuomintang government of Chiang Kai-shek (1928–1949) attempted to stifle criticism and dissent, it was too weak to silence intellectuals, who publicly criticized repressive officials and Kuomintang policies and advocated political reforms. But under Mao's totalitarian leadership—with the exception of brief interludes such as the

"Hundred Flowers" period in 1956 and 1957—public intellectuals were silenced and unable to play their traditional role.

Unlike in the West, no laws afforded protection to intellectuals in China during the dynastic, Kuomintang, and Mao eras. When critics said something that displeased the leadership, they could be silenced with impunity. In the 1980s, virtually all of the intellectuals whom Mao had persecuted were rehabilitated, and most found positions in the political and intellectual establishments. Public space for political discourse and pluralistic views opened up in book publishing, the media, universities, and research centers. Even then, however, no laws were enacted to protect political and civil rights; thus public intellectuals remained vulnerable to the whims of party leaders. Most of the intellectuals rehabilitated in the post-Mao era became members of the establishment and the party, but when a small number of them called for reform of the party-state, they were purged once again, particularly in the aftermath of the Tiananmen protests.

And yet, even though critics were silenced for a while, China's move to the market made it possible for them in the 1990s to make a living, speak out periodically, and publish on political issues. They were able to do so by means of new Internet technologies, private publishing, and contact with foreign media outlets such as Voice of America, the BBC, and Radio Free Asia, which would beam back their views into China.

websites to discuss political issues. Scores of cyber-dissidents have been imprisoned as a warning to others regarding how far they can go in discussing political reforms on the Internet. Public intellectuals who speak out and publish essays on controversial issues have been briefly detained as well.

One example is Jiang Yanyong, a military doctor who had treated victims of the violent June 4 crackdown and contradicted the party's assertion in 2003 that the SARS epidemic had been brought under control. He was detained and then put under surveillance in 2004 when he called on the party to change its designation of the 1989 Tiananmen demonstrations from a "counterrevolutionary" to a "patriotic" movement.

In addition to suppressing a number of well-known independent intellectuals and imposing a ban on the discourse of public intellectuals, the Hu government has tightened controls over the media and various outlets for dissent. Media reports on growing protests against corruption, abusive officials, property confiscation, and job conditions have been banned. Jiao Guobiao, a journalism professor who criticized—on the Internet—the party's repressive control of the media, was no longer allowed to teach at Peking University. Another public intellectual, Wang Yi, a Chengdu University law lecturer who called for a system of checks and balances in public life, was also barred from teaching. The journal *Strategy and Management,* which had been an outlet for intellectuals of a liberal persuasion, was closed down.

The Hu Crackdown

When the generation of leaders led by Hu came to power in 2002, it was expected that this younger group of officials—many of whom had roots in the China Youth League, an organization supposedly less doctrinaire than the party itself—would continue the opening up of public space for political discourse, even if it remained circumscribed within certain limits. That, however, has not proved to be the case. The public space for political discourse in fact has contracted since the late 1990s, when Jiang headed the party.

The Hu regime has cracked down on a number of people who use new communications technologies—for example, those who set up

Finding a Way

Despite the continuing crackdown on critical voices and the media, and despite censorship of the Internet, the role of public intellectuals in China has nonetheless changed significantly as a result of policy differences between the Mao and post-Mao eras, as well as because of changes in the critics' own strategies. Millions were harshly persecuted in the Anti-Rightist campaign (1957–1958) and during the Cultural Revolution (1966–1976), though only a small number had engaged in criticism and protests. By contrast, in the post-Mao era, persecution for public dissent has not reached far beyond the accused and their immediate associates. Moreover, although they might lose their jobs in academia or the media, and may be briefly detained, public critics have been able to find employment and outlets for their views in China's expanding market economy.

Thus, unlike during the Mao era, public intellectuals have not been completely silenced. Some still try to function as citizens, either on their own or along with others, and they continue to express their political views in unofficial publications, and in increasingly organized petitions and protests. Although their writings may be officially banned, they have found ways to distribute their views on street corners, through private publication, and over the Internet by means of connections to outside servers. In addition, for the first time in the People's Republic, a number of lawyers have been willing to defend those accused of political crimes, and journalists have reported on the party's repressive policies in some media outlets, such as the *Southern Weekend,* based in Guangdong province.

There are also differences between intellectuals' behavior in the 1980s and in the first decade of the 21st century. A number of public intellectuals in the 1980s called themselves "Marxist humanists" and pointed out how the party's policies diverged from the ideals of Marxist doctrine. Since then, because of the increasing bankruptcy of Marxism-Leninism as a governing philosophy, most public intellectuals have moved away from a focus on ideology and instead emphasize the establishment of new institutions to achieve political reforms.

Moreover, until the 1989 Tiananmen demonstrations, public intellectuals considered themselves an elite and did not join with other social classes in political actions. But starting with the 1989 protests, a small number began to join with workers and operators of small businesses in petition drives and in organizing groups to bring pressure on the government for political reforms. Thus, in the first decade of the 21st century, despite continuing repression, a qualitative change has occurred in the thinking and actions of China's public intellectuals: They have become increasingly independent political actors and have shown a willingness to join with other social groups in advocating reforms.

China's increasing interaction with the rest of the world, particularly with the West, has been another factor promoting a degree of liberalization in the intellectual environment. China signed the United Nations Covenant on Civil and Political Rights in October 1998, having already signed the UN Covenant on Economic, Social, and Cultural Rights in 1997.

Although China's rubber-stamp National People's Congress has confirmed the Covenant on Economic, Social, and Cultural Rights, it has not done the same with the Covenant on Civil and Political Rights. Nevertheless, the party's endorsement of the UN rights covenants as well as the easing of political controls at home has been part of China's effort to create goodwill abroad, particularly with the United States and other Western countries. At the same time, thousands of Chinese students have gone abroad to study at Western universities. China's relaxation of ideological controls at home has correlated with its engagement with the international community.

The 1998 Spring

Intellectuals and students have periodically made demands for political reform in post-Mao China. In addition to the best-known such effort—the Tiananmen protests in the spring of 1989—two later episodes, occurring 10 years apart, help illustrate public intellectuals' evolving role in society and relationship with the state. Perhaps the most broad ranging public discourse on political reforms since Tiananmen occurred in 1998—a century after China's Hundred Day Reforms, a movement that led to later political change and the fall of the Qing dynasty in 1911.

Like the Hundred Day reformers, and indeed like the major exponents of political reforms throughout the late twentieth and early twenty-first centuries, public intellectuals in 1998 were establishment intellectuals—academics, writers, journalists, lawyers, and ex-officials—who were not at the center of power. They worked at think tanks, universities, newspapers, and law offices, or were retired; yet they managed to promote their reformist ideas in books, scholarly journals, academic forums, and other channels in the public arena. At times, they even joined with those outside the establishment to call for political change.

Although none of China's establishment intellectuals publicly proposed a multiparty system or direct elections of the political leadership by universal suffrage, a small number advocated the establishment of other institutions associated with liberal democracy. Some emphasized the rule of law; others stressed freedom of expression and association; still others called for more competitive elections. Some were concerned with intraparty democracy; others with grassroots democracy. Virtually all, however, called for a political system based on some form of checks and balances. All emphasized the need for political reform in order to deal with the rampant corruption and accelerating economic and social inequalities accompanying China's economic reforms.

Those expressing liberal political views in 1998 differed from the Marxist humanists of the 1980s in that they were relatively more independent of political patronage—not only because of China's accelerating market economy and openness to the outside world, but also because of their desire to acquire more intellectual autonomy. Also, with the fall of the Berlin Wall in 1989 and the collapse of the Soviet Union and the communist states of Eastern Europe in 1991, intellectuals no longer called for reforms within a Marxist-Leninist framework. The younger generation of liberals cited a range of Western thinkers from Adam Smith to Karl Popper to support their arguments.

Liberal Forums

In 1998 economists, political scientists, philosophers, and historians spoke out publicly on the need for democratic reforms in two journals—*Reform (Gaige)* and *The Way (Fangfa)*—which became major forums for liberal views. On the occasion of its tenth-anniversary issue in January 1998, *Reform* published a speech given by Li Shenzhi, a former policy adviser to Prime Minister Zhou Enlai, entitled "Also Push Forward Political Reform" (*"Ye yao tuidong zhengzhi gaige"*). Li, born in 1923 to a wealthy merchant family in Wuxi city, Jiangsu province, had received a Western-style education and graduated in economics from Yenching University, the precursor of

Peking University, before joining the Communist Party in the early 1940s.

Li was labeled a "rightist" in 1957 for questioning one-party rule and as a result was ostracized for almost two decades. After Mao's death, however, he was rehabilitated to advise on foreign policy. Li became a vice president of the Chinese Academy of Social Sciences and established the Institute of American Studies there in 1981.

After June 4, 1989, he was dismissed from his positions because of his criticism of the Tiananmen crackdown. Yet, in the late 1990s, Li was still one of the most public and eloquent advocates of liberalism and political reform. Li's essays in *Reform* and *The Way* unreservedly proclaimed a liberal political agenda.

Also in the tenth anniversary issue of *Reform,* the well-known economist Mao Yushi emerged as an outspoken advocate of political reform. Mao Yushi, born in 1928, had like Li been branded a rightist in 1957. His works were banned from publication, and he was stripped of his job. Although Mao was from a revolutionary family, when he was invited to join the Communist Party during the 1980s, he refused. As an economist at the Chinese Academy of Social Sciences, he established an independent economics think tank called Unirule. He also organized a forum to discuss a new Chinese translation of *The Constitution of Liberty* by Friedrich Hayek. (Hayek, the philosopher and economist who was one of socialism's harshest critics and a proponent of individualism and property rights, is widely read by liberal Chinese intellectuals.) Mao Yushi wrote a long essay entitled "Liberalism, Equal Status, and Human Rights" in 1998, in which he praised Western liberalism and called for human rights. He argued that market economies require a loosening of political controls in order to develop fully.

Even a revolutionary elder, Mao Zedong's former secretary Li Rui, published an article in *Reform's* January 1998 issue calling for political reform. His article was an abridged version of a letter he had written to an unidentified comrade in the central government on September 10, 1997, in which he complained of continuing leftist influence in the party. Citing an August 18, 1980, speech by Deng, Li Rui pointed out that "after

17 years, problems criticized by Deng's speech, such as ... overconcentration of power ..., the inability to separate the functions of the party from government administration, the substitution of the party for the government, the abnormal inner-party democratic life, and the imperfection of the legal system have not been solved well."

Many of the articles calling for political reform that were published in *Reform* and *The Way*—as well as in several other journals and newspapers in1997–1998, even including a few in the official *People's Daily*—were collected in two major volumes that appeared in July and September 1998 respectively: *Political China,* subtitled *Facing the Era of Choosing a New Structure,* and *Liberation Literature 1978–1998.* The concentration of articles advocating political reforms in these two volumes, written by a number of academics, journalists, and members of think tanks, helped increase the impact of the liberals' proposals.

Particularly significant, the funding sources for these volumes revealed that a few members of China's new business class were beginning to use their profits to sponsor debate on political issues and to advocate political change. Most of China's rising entrepreneurs have colluded with local officials in order to improve their own economic status (though there have been a few exceptions, such as Wan Runnan, head of the Stone Group, which Wan set up as a think tank in the 1980s to study political reform and which supported the 1989 demonstrators in Tiananmen Square). Consequently, most businesspeople have stayed away from efforts to engender political change.

Yet these two volumes were funded by private businesspeople, some of whom, because of their previous participation in political activities in the 1980s, had been excluded from the intellectual establishment and had gone into business instead. By the late 1990s, they were willing and able to fund such political and intellectual endeavors.

Charter '08

A more recent episode in China's public discourse points to a new phenomenon that has emerged in the past decade: public intellectuals and other citizens calling on the government to live up to principles to which it has given written approval. On December 10, 2008, the 60th anniversary of the Universal Declaration of Human Rights, a group of people from all walks of life launched a movement called Charter '08. It presented a blueprint for fundamental legal and political reforms with the goal of achieving a democratic political system.

Patterned on Vaclav Havel's Charter '77 movement in the former Czechoslovakia, Charter '08 criticized China's government for failing to implement human rights provisions that its leaders had signed on to such as the UN Covenant on Political and Civil Rights, signed in 1998, and 2004 amendments to China's constitution that include the phrase "respect and protect human rights." Charter '08 pointed out that "Unfortunately, most of China's political progress has extended no further than the paper on which it is written." The political reality, it declared, "is that China has many laws but no rule of law; it has a constitution but no constitutional government." Charter '08 called for a political system based on democratic institutions of checks and balances.

Again, intellectuals and students in China have periodically made such demands. What made Charter '08 qualitatively different from most previous protests is that it became a political movement that crossed class lines. Past demonstrations were usually carried out by specific classes focused on particular economic issues, such as peasants' protests against confiscation of their land by local officials or workers' protests against nonpayment of salaries. Even during the 1989 demonstrations in Tiananmen Square, students at first linked arms to keep workers and other urbanites from participating, because they knew that the party feared an alliance between intellectuals and workers. By late May 1989, when other social classes had forced their way into the protests and the movement had spread to other cities and classes, Deng feared a threat to the party's rule. That is why he ordered the army to suppress the movement.

Another feature making Charter '08 unusual in China is that, although originally it was signed by just 300-plus intellectuals, very quickly ordinary Chinese citizens from all walks of life—entrepreneurs, professionals, local officials, workers, farmers, housewives, and street vendors—added their names as it circulated on the Internet and elsewhere. Also new to grassroots political movements in the People's Republic was the participation in Charter '08 of a number of lawyers who have defended those accused of political crimes.

Despite the detention of Charter '08's originator, the writer Liu Xiaobo, and despite the government's harsh denunciation of the movement, just before the Party completely shut down the Charter '08 website in mid-January 2009, more than 8,000 people had managed to sign their names.

The Charter '08 episode reveals that it is not only intellectuals who are expressing dissatisfaction with China's authoritarian system; it is also farmers, workers, and small entrepreneurs who are the supposed beneficiaries of China's political model. Their participation in the Charter '08 movement may be attributed in part to worsening economic conditions in late 2008. Factories in many of China's export industries were closed because of slackening demand for consumer goods in the West, and many college graduates, for the first time in the post-Mao era, were having difficulty finding jobs.

More fundamentally, the Charter '08 movement questioned a political system that bases its legitimacy on the Communist Party's ability to deliver economic growth. Despite the crackdown, and the detention of Liu and a few other signers, Charter '08 represented a multi-class movement for political change that is likely to continue.

Such a movement needs the support of the international community, including the United States, to succeed. International outcries over a crackdown on the Charter '77 movement in Czechoslovakia marked the beginning of the unraveling of the communist system in Eastern Europe. China's leaders, like the leaders of the former Soviet Union, are not immune to foreign pressure on political issues.

It is hoped that the Barack Obama administration can be a catalyst in efforts to achieve more academic and intellectual freedom for China's intellectuals by continuing and increasing academic exchanges and international discourse on political as well as scientific and economic issues. In this endeavor, increased international engagement with China's intellectuals, as well as China's political leaders, can play a role in protecting those who call for political reforms. Such engagement could influence the party's treatment of public intellectuals.

Toward Democracy?

In the spring of 2009, during the run-up to the 20th anniversary of the Tiananmen crackdown, [the CCP's] Propaganda Department censored the foreign media's discussion of the events of 1989. It blocked pages of the *International Herald Tribune* and the Hong Kong newspaper *South China Morning Post,* as well as discussion on the BBC, YouTube, and Twitter. Yet those in China's population who cared about what happened at Tiananmen found ways to find out about it through their Blackberries and Internet access to foreign servers.

As seen in the Charter '08 episode, the post-Mao era has seen a growing consciousness of citizenship and an increase in organized efforts to assert political rights, among both ordinary people and intellectuals. These developments do not necessarily imply movement toward democracy, but they are indeed prerequisites for a freer intellectual environment and for the eventual establishment of democratic institutions.

Democracy depends on the desire of organized citizens to participate in the political process in order to hold political authority accountable for its actions and to improve the public welfare. Therefore, although efforts to assert political rights in China are quickly suppressed, and although few political reforms have been introduced, it would be wrong to discount the impact of such efforts.

Unlike in the Mao era, when any dissent was brutally and utterly suppressed, China's public intellectuals today are experiencing intellectual pluralism, vigorous debate, and engagement with the international community. Just as remarkably, they are joining with other classes and social groups in calling for political reforms. While China's movement from a totalitarian to an authoritarian regime has not ended the repression of political discourse, neither has it prevented intellectuals from periodically performing their historic role as public critics or from seeking a broader impact on Chinese society.

IV. Soft Power

Developing a Strong Socialist Culture in China

Report to the 18th National Congress of the Communist Party of China [Excerpts]*

Hu Jintao

Culture is the lifeblood of a nation, and it gives the people a sense of belonging. To complete the building of a moderately prosperous society in all respects and achieve the great renewal of the Chinese nation, we must create a new surge in promoting socialist culture and bring about its great development and enrichment, increase China's cultural soft power, and enable culture to guide social trends, educate the people, serve society, and boost development.

To develop a strong socialist culture in China, we must take the socialist path of promoting cultural advance with Chinese characteristics. We should adhere to the goal of serving the people and socialism, the policy of having a hundred flowers bloom and a hundred schools of thought contend, and the principle of maintaining close contact with reality, life, and the people. We should fully promote socialist cultural and ethical progress and material progress, and develop a national, scientific, and people-oriented socialist culture that embraces modernization, the world, and the future.

To develop a strong socialist culture in China, it is critical to inspire the cultural creativity of the whole nation. We should deepen reform of the cultural sector, release and develop cultural productive forces, foster a democratic atmosphere in both academic research and artistic pursuit, create a vast cultural arena for the people, and encourage the free flow of cultural inspiration from all sources. By doing so, we will open up a new horizon in promoting China's cultural advance: The Chinese nation's cultural creativity will continuously burst forth; China's

cultural life will flourish as never before; people's basic cultural rights and interests will be better protected; the ethical and moral standards as well as the scientific and cultural standards of the people will be fully raised, and the international influence of Chinese culture will steadily increase.

Strengthen Core Socialist Values

Core socialist values are the soul of the Chinese nation and serve as the guide for building socialism with Chinese characteristics. We should carry out thorough study of and education in these values and use them to guide social trends of thought and forge public consensus. We should continue to adapt Marxism to China's conditions in keeping up with the times and increase its appeal to the people, work hard to equip the whole Party with the system of theories of socialism with Chinese characteristics, and educate the people in these theories. We should further implement the national project to study and develop Marxist theory, build an innovation system in philosophy and the social sciences, incorporate the system of theories of socialism with Chinese characteristics into the curriculum, and make it a way of thinking. We should carry out extensive education about our ideal and conviction, and rally the people under the great banner of socialism with Chinese characteristics. We should vigorously foster China's national character and promote the underlying trend of the times, intensify education in patriotism, collectivism, and socialism, and enrich people's cultural life and enhance their moral strength. We should promote prosperity, democracy, civility, and harmony, uphold freedom, equality, justice, and the

* This speech was published by the Communist Party of China on November 8, 2012 (http://www.china.org.cn/china/18th_cpc_congress/2012-11/16/content_27137540.htm).

rule of law and advocate patriotism, dedication, integrity, and friendship, so as to cultivate and observe core socialist values. We should maintain leadership and initiative in theoretical work, provide correct guidance, enhance our ability to guide public opinion, and strengthen the influence of the underlying trend of thought in our country.

Improve Civic Morality in an All-Around Way

This is the basic task for strengthening socialist morals. We should integrate the rule of law with the rule of virtue, intensify education in public morality, professional ethics, family virtues, and individual integrity, and advocate traditional Chinese virtues and new trends of the times. We should press ahead with the program for improving civic morality, exalt the true, the good, and the beautiful and reject the false, the evil, and the ugly. We should encourage people to willingly meet their statutory duties and obligations to society and family. We should create a social atmosphere in which work is honored and creation is lauded, and cultivate social trends of recognizing honor and disgrace, practicing integrity, encouraging dedication, and promoting harmony. We should carry out thorough education to address serious ethical problems, and step up efforts to enhance government integrity, business and social ethics and judicial integrity. We should strengthen and improve education in values, provide compassionate care and psychological counseling, and cultivate self-respect, self-confidence, a sense of being rational, composure, and a desire to excel oneself among the people. We should conduct more public activities to promote cultural and ethical progress, encourage volunteer service, and carry out regular activities to learn from paragons of virtue such as Lei Feng and publicize their exemplary deeds.

Enrich People's Intellectual and Cultural Lives

Enabling the people to lead healthy and rich intellectual and cultural lives is an important part of our efforts to complete the building of a moderately prosperous society in all respects. We should pursue people-centered cultural creation, and create better cultural products to provide the people with more and better nourishments for the mind. We should be community- and people-focused in our cultural work, carry out at a faster pace key cultural projects that benefit the people, increase support for promoting cultural progress in rural areas and underdeveloped areas, and open more public cultural service facilities to the public free of charge. We should develop a system for carrying forward fine traditional culture and promote outstanding traditional Chinese culture. We should extend and standardize the use of the standard Chinese language. We should promote the development and flourishing of cultural activities of ethnic minorities. We should carry out public cultural activities and guide the people to express, educate, and serve themselves in the course of developing culture. We should launch reading programs for the general public. We should improve the contents of online services and advocate healthy themes on the Internet. We should strengthen social management of the Internet and promote orderly network operation in accordance with laws and regulations. We should crack down on pornography and illegal publications and resist vulgar trends. We should extend scientific knowledge, foster respect for science, and make the whole nation better educated in science. We should carry out fitness activities across the country and fully promote both recreational and competitive sports.

Enhance the Overall Strength and International Competitiveness of Chinese Culture

The strength and international competitiveness of Chinese culture are an important indicator of China's power and prosperity and the renewal of the Chinese nation. We should promote rapid development and all-around flourishing of the cultural industry and cultural services and ensure both social effect and economic benefits, with priority on the former. We should develop philosophy and the social sciences, the press and publishing, radio, television and films, and literature and art. We should launch more major public cultural projects and programs, improve the public cultural service system, and make such services more efficient. We should promote integration of culture with science and technology, develop new forms of cultural operations, and make cultural operations larger in size and more specialized. We should develop a modern communications network to improve our capacity for communications. We should invigorate state-owned non-profit cultural institutions, improve corporate governance of profit-oriented cultural entities, and create a thriving cultural market. We should open the cultural sector wider to the outside world and draw on cultural achievements of other countries. We should foster a fine environment that enables a large number of talented cultural figures, particularly eminent cultural figures and representatives of Chinese culture, to distinguish themselves in artistic pursuit. We should honor cultural personalities with outstanding contributions. We must adhere to the goal of advancing socialist culture, deepen our awareness of and confidence in Chinese culture, and strive to meet the grand goal of developing a strong socialist culture in China.

CHINA'S SOFT POWER DEFICIT[*]

Joseph S. Nye

I was recently invited to lecture at several Chinese universities about "soft power"—the ability to get what one wants by attraction and persuasion rather than coercion or payment. Since the 1990s, thousands of essays and articles have been published in China on the topic, and the lectures drew large crowds.

Over the past decade, China's economic and military might has grown impressively. This has frightened its neighbors into looking for allies to balance China's increase in hard power. But if a country can also increase its soft power of attraction, its neighbors feel less need to balance its power. For example, Canada and Mexico do not seek alliances with China to balance US power the way Asian countries seek a US presence to balance China. In 2007, understanding this, President Hu Jintao told the 17th Congress of the Chinese Communist Party that China needed to invest more in its soft power resources. That's a smart power strategy, but Beijing is having difficulty implementing it.

China is spending billions of dollars to increase its soft power. Its aid programs to Africa and Latin America are not limited by the institutional or human rights concerns that constrain Western aid. The Chinese style emphasizes high-profile gestures, such as building stadiums. Meanwhile, the elaborately staged 2008 Beijing Olympics enhanced China's reputation abroad, and the 2010 Shanghai Expo attracted more than 70 million visitors. China has also created several hundred Confucius Institutes around the world to teach its language and culture. The enrollment of foreign students in China increased to 240,000 last year from just 36,000 a decade ago, and China Radio International now broadcasts in English around the clock. In 2009–10, Beijing invested $8.9 billion in external publicity work, including 24-hour cable news channels.

But for all its efforts, China has had a limited return on its investment. A recent BBC poll shows that opinions of China's influence are positive in much of Africa and Latin America, but predominantly negative in the United States, everywhere in Europe, as well as in India, Japan, and South Korea.

Great powers try to use culture and narrative to create soft power that promotes their national interests, but it's not an easy sell when the message is inconsistent with their domestic realities. As I told the university students, in an Information Age in which credibility is the scarcest resource, the best propaganda is not propaganda.

---

[*] This article was originally published in the *Wall Street Journal* on May 8, 2012.

The 2008 Olympics was a success abroad, but shortly afterward China's domestic crackdown on human rights activists undercut its soft power gains. The Shanghai Expo was also a great success, but it was followed by the jailing of Nobel Peace Laureate Liu Xiaobo. His empty chair at the Oslo ceremony was a powerful symbol. And for all the efforts to turn Xinhua and China Central Television into competitors for CNN and the BBC, there is little international audience for brittle propaganda.

Now, in the aftermath of the Middle East revolutions, China is clamping down on the Internet and jailing human rights lawyers, once again torpedoing its soft-power campaign. No amount of propaganda can hide the fact that blind human rights attorney Chen Guangcheng recently sought refuge in the US Embassy in Beijing.

Rather than celebrate the heroes of today in civil society, the arts and the private sector, the Communist Party has taken to promoting the greatness of Chinese culture in general and the historical significance of the Middle Kingdom. Pang Zhongying, a former Chinese diplomat who teaches at Renmin University, says this reflects "a poverty of thought" in China today. When Zhang Yimou, the acclaimed director, was asked why his films were always set in the past, he replied that films about contemporary China would be "neutered by the censors."

I read the students a recent statement by Ai Weiwei, the acclaimed Chinese artist who's suffered from state harassment. He warned that censorship is undermining creativity. "It's putting this nation behind in the world's competition in the coming decades. You can't create generations just to labor at [electronics manufacturer] Foxconn. Everyone wants an iPhone but it would be impossible to design an iPhone in China because it's not a product; it's an understanding of human nature." Slight waves of nervous laughter swept through the audience when I mentioned Ai Weiwei's name. But from their questions, it seemed that some students agreed with his view that it's not possible for Chinese leaders "to control the Internet unless they shut it off—and they can't live with the consequences of that."

After I finished speaking, a party official told the students that the Chinese approach to soft power should focus on culture, not politics. I hope this changes. The development of soft power need not be a zero-sum game. If Chinese soft power increases in the US and vice versa, it will help make conflict less likely.

All countries can gain from finding attraction in each other's' cultures. But for China to succeed in this, its politics must unleash the talents of its civil society.

THE MILITARY AND SECURITY

Editorial Introduction

One of the most noticeable, and most written about, dimensions of China's rise has been its sustained military modernization program over the past two decades. Of course, military capabilities are directly related to a nation's security environment. In this section we assess both dimensions.

It is always important to understand how a nation's leaders and security specialists define their *own* security concerns and environment. As such, the first selection is a speech by then Vice President Xi Jinping (now president and China's preeminent leader). Xi begins by noting the complexities and dynamism of the global environment in which China lives. He specifically notes regional "hot spot" challenges, nonproliferation issues, global financial instability, terrorism, and other challenges. This security menu produces multiple uncertainties for China. Still, Xi optimistically notes that "peace, development, and cooperation" continue to be the dominant trends of the times. Xi notes that security must be based on five elements: development, equality, mutual trust, cooperation, and innovation. Xi concludes by noting several priorities for China's security policy: continued peaceful development; building a "new type of relations" among major powers; upholding peace and stability in the Asia-Pacific; and fulfilling China's international responsibilities and obligations.

The second selection focuses specifically on China's military capabilities and military modernization program. Written by one of the world's leading experts, Professor Richard Bitzinger of the Rajaratnam School of International Studies in Singapore, this selection is a rather recent (2012) extensive assessment and overview of China's military. He examines both the "inputs" and the "outputs" of China's military modernization. The former includes China's defense budget (now No. 2 in the world) as well as the defense industrial and science and technology base (a subject on which Bitzinger is one of the world's leading experts). Turning to capabilities, he details the dramatic progress the People's Liberation Army (PLA) has made in recent years: achieving stealth capabilities for its planes and ships, long-range precision strike, advances in submarines, upgrading of ballistic missiles, a robust space and satellite program, cyber capabilities, unmanned aerial vehicles (UAVs), and other hardware. On the "software" side, the PLA has achieved breakthroughs in computer networking, command, and control. Despite these advances—many of which have surprised foreign analysts—Bitzinger correctly points to several ongoing weaknesses in the Chinese military: a stove-piped Soviet-style force structure; corruption in the officer corps; weak logistics lines; no foreign bases; no real long-range power projection; lack of "jointness" among services on the battlefield; lack of real-time intelligence for operations; problems with readiness and repair of equipment; low-grade domestically produced engines for planes and ships; and other deficiencies (which includes not having fought an actual war since 1979). Thus, despite the remarkable progress the PLA has achieved over the past two decades, China's military still has numerous gaps vis-à-vis the state-of-the-art.

The next selection turns from China's external to internal security posture. Written and published in 2004, Murray Scot Tanner describes the rising tide of social and ethnic unrest across China. The number of "mass group incidents" of unrest reported by the Ministry of Public Security has only risen since Tanner's article was published—rising from 30,000 in 2000 to approximately 200,000 per year 2014. These incidents range from dozens to tens of thousands of protestors. Tanner describes the multiple catalysts for the rising epidemic of unrest—the majority being local grievances arising from land seizures, factory working conditions, wage arrears, unemployment, environmental damage, ethnic and religious oppression, and other sources. He then details the various methods the government, public security, and paramilitary authorities use to deal with the unrest—methods known as "stability maintenance" (*wei wen*). These modalities range from monetary to lethal. The seriousness with which the party-state takes the issues is reflected in the startling fact that China's *domestic* security budget *surpassed* the *military* budget in 2010 (RMB 624 billion vs. RMB 601 billion)! Chinese society remains highly volatile and this is a matter of regime survival.

The next selection from *The Economist* further explores the issue of internal security. Specifically, it discusses the regime's nervousness about a potential political uprising. This fear is ever-extant, but spiked in March 2011 in the wake of the "Arab Spring" when it was thought there was potential for a similar "jasmine revolution" in China.

The final selection in this section concerns China's growing and changing roles in global security. Although China does not have any military bases abroad or security alliances with other countries, this does not mean that it does not have international security concerns or a role to play in multinational contributions to global peace and security. I begin by noting that China's role in global security is tied to its general role in contributing to global governance. But I also note that the security sphere is one of the most challenging areas for China—simply because its capabilities are more limited than in other areas. China possesses greater capacities to contribute to global financial and economic stability and growth; to development assistance in developing countries; to global climate change through its own industrial growth; to global public health through its domestic as well as international actions; to global innovation and technological development through its indigenous innovation; and to global energy consumption through its own appetite for natural resources and investments in new energy technologies. In all these areas, China's capacities to influence global patterns and global governance are greater than in the security sphere. Nonetheless, Beijing has a growing stake in global security because issues such as access to energy sources and terrorism, for example, are daily potential threats for China. So too is the rising threat of Chinese citizens working abroad being in harm's way when civil conflicts break out or if they are kidnapped or killed. China successfully evacuated 35,800 of its citizens from Libya in 2011 and another 900 in

2014, while evacuating 600 more from Yemen in 2015. I also discuss China's growing military footprint (mainly naval) abroad, as well as its contributions to United Nations Peacekeeping Operations (UNPKO), disaster relief operations, military-to-military exchanges, bilateral and multilateral security dialogues, and arms transfers to other nations. In all of these areas, China's global security and military roles have increased in recent years. China is also a party to many international security treaties and agreements. Finally, China has become much more active in contributing to combatting "non-traditional" security threats, for example counter-terrorism; monitoring financial institutions for money laundering; strengthening controls against human and drug trafficking; tracking down financial fugitives and cracking down on organized international crime networks.

I. China's Security Calculus

Work Together to Maintain World Peace and Security[*]

Xi Jinping

Address at the Opening Ceremony of the World Peace Forum
7 July 2012

Distinguished Guests,
Ladies and Gentlemen,
Dear Friends,

I am very glad to attend the opening ceremony of the World Peace Forum held at my alma mater, Tsinghua University. First of all, I would like to offer my warm congratulations on the opening of the forum and sincere greetings to the honorable guests, experts and scholars.

The World Peace Forum is the first high-level non-governmental forum on international security hosted by China. Its theme "win–win for all: peace, security, cooperation" has a major significance that bears on the future and destiny of the world and happiness and well-being of people in all countries. In-depth discussion and exchange of views over this important subject will offer new perspectives, approaches, and make new contributions to world peace and security.

Ladies and Gentlemen,

Today, the world is in a period of major development, change and readjustment. The international situation is experiencing very deep and complex changes. The trend towards a multipolar world and economic globalization are gaining momentum. Scientific and technological revolutions hold the promise for new breakthroughs. Information is exerting greater influence on the society. Members of the international community are more interconnected and interdependent. Emerging market economies and developing countries continue to grow in strength. All of this has changed the international landscape profoundly and exerted far-reaching impact on the development of all countries and international relations.

Despite new developments in the current international situation, peace and development remain the main trend of our times. This is reflected in the following aspects. The exchange, dialogue and cooperation among countries are deepening. Peace, development, and cooperation represent the common aspirations of people in all countries. On the other hand, the international community is also facing increasingly complex and diverse security challenges. Regional "hot spot" issues keep cropping up. Terrorism is

---

[*] This article was published in *Foreign Affairs Journal,* Issue 105 (Autumn 2012), published by the Chinese People's Institute of Foreign Affairs.

rampant. Non-proliferation still faces grave challenges. The underlying impact of the international financial crisis continues to be felt. To maintain world peace and promote common security remains an arduous task.

It is important to recognize that in today's world, the interests of countries of different systems, types and development stages are intertwined. Their interdependence is growing. Countries have shared interests and a common stake in security. Under such new circumstances, security goes far beyond the security based on confrontation and balance of power during the Cold War, military security in the traditional sense, or security of just one country or one region. In face of complex and diverse security challenges, no country can stay immune or achieve the so-called absolute security on its own. A country which pursues its own development, security and well-being must also let other countries pursue their development, security, and well-being. All countries must take a cooperative approach with an innovative spirit and responsible attitude, stand together and seek win-win cooperation to resolve various problems and challenges, and foster a harmonious and stable international and regional security environment.

To this end, we need to be committed to the following ideas and principles.

First, we must seek security on the basis of development. Economic development and prosperity provides a strong guarantee for security. Many of the world's conflicts and chaos are closely related to the issue of development. Development is what matters most. Only when all countries develop, can we better maintain world peace and stability. With the lingering impact of the international financial crisis, the issue of economic and financial security becomes more acute. All countries are facing the pressing task of economic development and improvement of people's lives. We need to continue to give serious attention to and well address the major issue of achieving all-round, balanced, and sustainable development, make continued efforts to grow ourselves, actively support the progress of developing countries, endeavor to narrow the growth gap between the North and the South, and achieve common development and prosperity.

Second, we must seek security on the basis of equality. Treating each other as equals is essential for maintaining security. Countries, rich or poor, strong or weak, are equal members of the international community. The rich and the strong bullying the poor and the weak can only lead to endless cycle of hatred and revenge. Only by respecting each other and treating each other as equals can countries live in harmony and contentment. It is important to respect all countries' sovereignty, territorial integrity, and national dignity, their people's independent choice of social system and path of development, as well as their legitimate security concerns. At any time and under any circumstances, countries should adhere to the Five Principles of Peaceful Coexistence, refrain from interfering in other's internal affairs and imposing their own will on others, and bring about security for all through dialogue on an equal footing and mutually beneficial cooperation.

Third, we must seek security on the basis of mutual trust. Increasing mutual trust is indispensable for maintaining security. A person without credibility cannot stand. Mutual trust, not mutual suspicion and mutual respect, not mutual confrontation, are what countries need to transcend differences, manage crisis, understand each other, seek common ground, and resolve divergence, and live together in peace and harmony. As countries differ in history, culture, social system, and development stage, it is natural for them to have differences and disputes. Therefore, we should make continuous efforts to increase strategic and political mutual trust among countries, properly handle differences and sensitive issues, respect core and vital interests of other countries, expand strategic consensus, and consolidate the foundation for the maintenance of security.

Fourth, we must seek security on the basis of cooperation. Dialogue and cooperation is fundamental to maintaining security. Today, traditional and non-traditional security challenges to human survival and sustainable economic and social development are more pronounced. Only through candid and in-depth dialogue and consultation and comprehensive and sustained exchanges and cooperation can countries effectively respond to these challenges. Countries should seek peaceful solutions to international disputes and oppose the use or threat of force. Countries should abandon the zero-sum mentality, the notion that one's rise means the others' fall. They should always work for peace, security and settlement of disputes through cooperation, expand converging interests, and commit themselves to win–win and all-win outcome.

Fifth, we must seek security on the basis of innovation. Security issues in today's world are diverse, are easy to spread and have a domino effect, and are difficult to predict. Security factors, internal and external, domestic and international, traditional and non-traditional, are intertwined. New issues and challenges are emerging one after another. We must abandon those mindsets and approaches that are rendered obsolete, keep pace with the times, forge ahead with innovation, foster a new security concept featuring mutual trust, mutual benefit, equality, and coordination, cultivate a new approach of comprehensive security, common security, and cooperative security. We must find new answers to old questions and good solutions to new issues to successfully tackle development and security challenges facing mankind.

Ladies and Gentlemen,

China is experiencing rapid industrialization and urbanization. China is committed to economic development, world peace and common development of mankind. China pursues peaceful, open, cooperative, and win–win development. After the outbreak of the international financial crisis and the European sovereign debt crisis, China has been working with the international community to tide over the difficulties and made important contribution to the stability and recovery of the world economy. On major international and regional hotspot issues, China is committed to promoting peace and encouraging talks and has played a constructive role in this regard. China has taken an active part in peace-keeping missions and is the largest contributor of peace-keepers among the permanent members of the UN Security Council. We have sent a total of 21,000 personnel to 30 peace-keeping missions of the United Nations. China has worked with the international community to actively tackle terrorism, proliferation of weapons

of mass destruction, climate change, food and energy security, major natural disasters, and other global challenges. China has acceded to over 100 international intergovernmental organizations and signed over 300 international conventions and covenants. Facts have shown that China has actively participated in and contributed to the building of the international system. The sustained and fast development of China would not have been possible without peace and development of the world. At the same time, China's development has provided valuable opportunities and broad space for the common development of all countries.

China will stay committed to the path of peaceful development. China pursues its own development by upholding world peace and helps maintain world peace through its own development. It works with the international community to push for the building of a harmonious world of lasting peace and common prosperity. This is a strategic choice that follows the trend of the times and serves China's fundamental interests. It is also what China needs to achieve sustained development. The Chinese nation values good faith and pursues harmonious relations. China adheres to the foreign policy of peace. Even when China becomes more developed in the future, it will never seek hegemony. China consistently and firmly pursues a defense policy that is defensive in nature to firmly safeguard its sovereignty, security, and development.

China will stay committed to the building of a new type of relations between major countries. Major country relations are important factors in the evolvement of the international situation. China and the United States are actively exploring a new type of relations between major countries featuring mutual respect and win–win cooperation. This is in the shared interests of China, the United States and the world. It will be a pioneering effort in the history of international relations. China will continue to encourage all major countries to see each other's strategic intentions objectively and rationally, respect each other's interests and concerns, and strengthen coordination and cooperation on major international and regional issues, and strive to build a new type of major country relations and international relations in the 21st century.

China will continue to firmly uphold peace and stability of the Asia-Pacific region. China has a vast land territory, vast sea area, and many neighboring countries. China has always been committed to building good neighborly relations. China is committed to the principle of building amicable relations and partnerships with neighboring countries, in an effort to foster a regional environment featuring peace and stability, equality, and mutual trust, and win-win cooperation. In the future, China will continue to deepen bilateral and regional cooperation, vigorously develop friendly relations with neighboring and other countries in the Asia-Pacific, and contribute, through its own development, to the development of its neighbors. At the same time, China will continue to seek appropriate settlement of the differences and frictions with relevant countries and, on the basis of firmly defending national sovereignty, security, and territorial integrity, work together with neighboring countries to maintain the stability of their relations and of the region.

China will continue to fulfill its due international responsibilities and obligations. To endeavor to contribute China's due share to the progress and development of mankind is the long-standing and solemn commitment of the Chinese government. We are of the view that for China, the biggest developing country in the world, the most important way to be responsible to the world is to manage its own affairs well. China will continue to bear in mind the interests of its own people and the common interests of mankind,

follow the principle of responsibility consistent with rights, interests, and capability, and undertake more international responsibilities within its capability. China will actively participate in the reform of the international system and global governance, with a view to moving towards a more just and equitable international political and economic order. China will continue to play a constructive part in resolving, through political means, major international and regional hotspot issues and the handling of global challenges. We will strive to make fresh and bigger contribution to world peace, security, and stability. China will continue to take an active part in the global development undertaking, and work with all countries for the realization of the UN Millennium Development Goals (MDGs) and global prosperity and progress.

Ladies and Gentlemen,

Today's world is in general peaceful and stable, despite conflicts and turbulence in some regions. There are both opportunities and challenges for development and security. We must meet the challenges together, pursue win-win cooperation and gradually achieve peace and security in the whole world so that all countries will be able to enjoy peace, security, common development, and prosperity in the 21st century.

To conclude, I wish the World Peace Forum a full success!

Thank you very much.

II. MODERNIZING THE MILITARY

Modernizing China's Military, 1997–2012[*]

Richard A. Bitzinger

For the past fifteen years, China has been engaged in a concerted effort to modernize and upgrade its armed forces. These modernization activities have

several objectives. For one thing, as China strives to become a global power, it is increasingly seeking "hard" power, i.e., military strength, commensurate with its growing economic, diplomatic, and cultural "soft" power. Second, Beijing appears to be more prone to use military force (or the threat of

---

[*] This article was published in *China Perspectives*, No. 4 (2011).

military force) to defend and promote its regional interests, such as its territorial claims in the South China Sea or protecting local sea lanes of communication (SLOCs) vital to its energy supplies and trade; consequently, building up that military wherewithal is instrumental to this strategy. Third, it aspires to increase its military capacities in order to keep the pressure on Taiwan not to declare independence *and* to eventually accept some kind of reunification with the mainland; at the same time, China wants to reduce the willingness of the United States to intervene on behalf of Taiwan in case of a cross-Strait military clash by raising the costs of involvement for the US. Fourth, China wants to increase its capacities for military operations other than war (MOOTW) so as to defend its growing interests around the world, to which end it is participating more in activities such as peacekeeping operations, humanitarian assistance and disaster relief operations, and anti-piracy operations. Finally, China overall seeks military power to mitigate the rising American military presence in the Asia–Pacific, and to establish itself as a credible rival to the United States in this region.

These efforts have paid remarkable dividends, and since the late 1990s the People's Liberation Army has made substantial progress in transforming itself into a modern fighting force; in many areas, it is practically unrecognizable compared to the PLA that existed before 1997. The impact of this transformation has been particularly noticeable in the past few years in the form of a much more assertive, even aggressive, China, increasingly willing to use its military to protect and advance its national interests. Prominent examples of this increased use of the PLA as an instrument of national policy include the dispatch of PLA Navy vessels to fight piracy in the Gulf of Aden, and the PLAN's recent launching of an aircraft carrier. What the end result of this military modernization process will be, or how China may further use its growing military power, is still an open question.

1997 is a good place to start when addressing the current modernization of the PLA, as this was a watershed year in the history of the Chinese military. Starting that year, for instance, Chinese defense spending began its remarkable (and, except for one year, unbroken) run of double-digit real annual growth (after adjusting for inflation), which underwrote the process of military

modernization that was to follow. Also in 1997, the decision was made by the central government to force the PLA to divest itself of the bulk of its commercial activities so as to concentrate on its primary functions—deterrence, compellence, and if necessary, war-fighting.[1] At the 15th Party Congress in September 1997, the Chinese Communist Party (CCP) decided to radically reform the state-owned enterprise (SOE) sector, which marked the beginning of the current process of restructuring and upgrading the Chinese defense industry. Finally, 1997 was also around the time the PLA officially adopted the strategic concept of fighting "limited local wars under high-technology conditions" (and later, "under conditions of informatization," or the addition of computers and information-sharing networks to military platforms), which still drives current operational and hardware requirements for military modernization.

This article traces the process of Chinese military modernization over the past 15 years (1997–2012), focusing on its drivers and enablers, the recapitalization of the armed forces with more advanced military hardware, and changes in PLA training, recruitment, and retention. It then assesses the progress that the PLA has made over this period in transforming itself into a more modern military force, where it still faces challenges, and how, in the end, a more powerful PLA may impact the regional military balance.

Tying Military Modernization to Requirements: Chinese Defense Strategy in the Twenty-first Century

In 2011 China allocated RMB 601 billion (US$91.5 billion) for defense, an increase of 12.7 percent over 2010. Indeed, the 2010 defense budget of RMB 532.1 billion (US$81 billion) was itself 7.5 percent greater than 2009's RMB 481 billion (US$70.3 billion) defense budget, which was in turn 14.9 percent larger than the 2008 defense budget.[2] Overall, since 1997, Chinese military expenditures have increased at least 600 percent in real terms. As a result, since the late 1990s, China has moved from having a military budget smaller than Taiwan's to being the second-largest defense spender in the world, outstripping

314 THE CHINA READER

Japan, France, Russia, and the United Kingdom. Today, only the United States spends more than China on defense.

Its dramatically expanded commitment to funding defense expenditures has allowed China to devote considerable resources to procurement and defense industrial research and development (R&D). While all categories of Chinese military spending, including personnel, training, and operations, have increased significantly over the past fifteen years, nowhere has Beijing's munificence been more notable, or more alarming to its neighbors, than in the PLA's budget for equipment acquisitions. According to its biannual defense white papers, Beijing has consistently allocated approximately one-third of its military expenditures over the past decade and a half to equipment purchases. This compares very favorably with most other countries. France, for example, apportioned 27 percent of its 2009 defense budget to equipment and R&D, while the United Kingdom dedicated 26 percent, and Germany only 17 percent.[3] In 2010, only 17.5 percent of all Japanese defense-related expenditures went to buying equipment, along with only 2.5 percent for defense R&D.[4] In real terms, PLA annual spending on equipment procurement has increased from around US$3.1 billion in 1997 to an estimated US$30.5 billion in 2011; of this, perhaps US$4 to 6 billion is dedicated to defense R&D. This likely makes China the second highest spender in the world in terms of spending on procurement, and at least the third highest when it comes to defense R&D.[5]

If anything has supported China's recent expansion in military power, it is this explosion in defense spending, which has permitted the PLA to acquire new surface combatants and submarines, modern fighter jets, air-to-air refueling aircraft, satellites, unmanned aerial vehicles, and a host of ballistic, cruise, and tactical missile systems. Additionally, expanding defense budgets have allowed China to fund an array of new military R&D projects, such as its J-20 fifth-generation fighter, its DF-21D anti-ship ballistic missile (ASBM), and its nuclear submarine program.

As noted above, most expert observers believe that the official budget released by the Chinese every year accounts for only a fraction of actual defense spending. In particular, whole categories of military expenditure are believed to be missing from official figures, including arms imports, expenses for the People's Armed Police (PAP) and militia/reserve forces, state subsidies to China's military-industrial complex, and earnings from PLA-run businesses. How much all this extra-budgetary spending actually amounts to has been the subject of considerable debate and analysis in Western literature on the PLA, and unofficial estimates of "real" Chinese defense expenditures have ranged from anywhere between one-and-a-half to as high as ten times greater than the official budget.[6] The US Department of Defense (DoD), for example, has asserted that China's actual military expenditures are at least twice the officially stated figure (though the DoD provides no methodology or criteria for arriving at this figure).[7] In fact, the actual amount of extra-budgetary spending may actually be quite small compared to the publicly announced defense budget—perhaps $2 billion to $4 billion. Nevertheless, even such a small amount could be significant when it comes to underwriting certain Chinese military activities, particularly internal security, which is normally the purview of the PAP.

This upward trend is likely to continue for some time. In May 2006, for example, Beijing approved a 15-year national development plan (2006–2020) for defense science and technology, with the goal of "transforming the PLA into a modernized, mechanized, IT-based force" by 2020.[8] This program is intended to boost military R&D spending, focusing on high-technology weapons systems (and specifically on "IT solutions"), supporting advanced manufacturing technologies, and cultivating collaborative international defense R&D efforts.[9]

Enabler of Chinese Military Modernization #2: Defense Industrial Base Reforms

Since the establishment of the People's Republic, Beijing has striven to become self-reliant in the development and production of armaments, and accordingly it has created the largest military-industrial complex (MIC) in Asia. The Chinese MIC comprises more a thousand SOEs, employing at least one million workers, including several thousand scientists, engineers, and technicians. In particular, China is one of the few countries in the world to produce a full range of military equipment, from small arms to armored vehicles to fighter aircraft to warships and submarines, in addition to nuclear weapons and ballistic missiles.

Nevertheless, despite its ambitions and scope, China's MIC has shown, for most of its history, an unimpressive record of performance. As recently as the late 1990s, China still possessed one of the most technologically backward defense industries among the major powers of the world. Most indigenously developed weapons systems were at least 15 to 20 years behind those of the West, and quality control was consistently poor. Moreover, China's defense R&D base was deficient in several critical areas, including aeronautics, jet propulsion, microelectronics, computers, and new materials.

Since around the turn of the century, however, China has made significant progress in turning around its long-ailing defense sector. This is evident in the growing number of new types of weapons, increasingly of a quality and capability comparable to Western systems. These include the J-10 fighter, the *Yuan*-class diesel-electric submarine, the Type-052C destroyer, and the HQ-9 long-range surface-to-air missile (akin to the US Patriot). At the same time, China appears to have produced the world's first working anti-ship ballistic missile (ASBM), and it has test-flown a purportedly fifth-generation combat aircraft. Additionally, production and sales are up throughout the Chinese MIC.

After decades of false starts and fitful progress, Beijing appears to have finally hit upon the right formula to reform and revitalize its MIC. Beginning in the late 1990s, Beijing launched several initiatives intended to inject more market-oriented incentives into the defense industrial sector, including the introduction of Western management techniques, a new emphasis on quality control, and greater oversight by the Chinese military when it comes to procurement and program management. Efforts were also made to rationalize the country's bloated military-industrial complex, laying off excess workers and consolidating production. China even injected a modicum of competition, breaking up giant defense SOEs into smaller, contending firms, particularly in the aviation and shipbuilding sectors.

In addition, China has aggressively pursued a dual-use R&D strategy that stresses the development of advanced civilian technologies—particularly in the areas of electronics and information technologies, aviation, space launch vehicles, satellites, and advanced manufacturing—that can be spun-on to defense products and production. Over the past decade, Beijing has worked hard both to encourage further domestic development and growth in these sectors and to expand linkages and collaboration between China's MIC and civilian high-technology sectors. And this approach appears to be paying dividends.[10]

Finally, the reform of the defense industry must be seen as building on the expansion of state funding committed to defense modernization more broadly. Arguably, simply throwing more money at the problem may have had the greatest impact on the local defense industry, by increasing procurement and therefore production; by expanding R&D spending; and by subsidizing the upgrading and modernization of arms-manufacturing facilities. Consequently, China's MIC is better suited than ever to absorb and leverage advanced, militarily relevant technologies and therefore provide the PLA with the advanced military systems it requires. In fact, in recent years Beijing has greatly reduced its once-sizable arms purchases from Russia, an indicator that China is getting closer to realizing its long-cherished goal of self-sufficiency in arms acquisition.

At the same time, critical weaknesses remain. China's MIC still appears to possess only limited indigenous capabilities for cutting-edge defense R&D, and Western armaments producers continue to outpace China when it comes to most military technologies, particularly in areas such as propulsion and defense electronics. Overall, it is still more of a "fast follower" and niche innovator when it comes to military R&D, though this may be irrelevant if China is only looking to gain asymmetric niche advantages such as using an ASBM to attack aircraft carriers. Nevertheless, the Chinese defense industrial base has made undeniable advancements over the past decade and a half in terms of manufacturing new, relatively modern military systems, and this pace of defense development and production could even quicken in the decades ahead as the lessons of these reforms are incorporated further.

China's Military Build-Up, 1997–2012

With constantly expanding defense resources, the PLA has been engaged in a concerted effort to replace and upgrade its military hardware since at least the late 1990s. Initially, Beijing relied heavily on foreign suppliers, particularly Russia, Ukraine, and to a lesser extent Israel, to meet its immediate requirements for advanced armaments. Since the turn of the century, however, the PRC has increasingly turned to its own indigenous defense industry to provide the PLA with modern weaponry—supplementing this capacity with technologies that have either been reverse-engineered (for example, the J-11B fighter, a clone of the Russian Su-27) or stolen outright from foreign suppliers (e.g., stealth and information technologies).

Consequently, it is reasonable to argue that Beijing has been engaged in something more than the "mere" modernization of its armed forces over the past decade and a half. The PLA has not just undergone certain qualitative improvements, but in many cases it has added capabilities that it did not possess before, such as stealth, standoff precision-strike, long-range airborne and undersea attack, and expeditionary warfare. In addition, these new war-fighting capabilities have been further enhanced by significant improvements in Chinese military C4ISR infrastructure, including satellites, unmanned aerial vehicles (UAVs), and computer networking. For this reason, it is fair to describe China's military improvements as a "build-up" rather simply a "modernization drive."

Recent Chinese military thinking has been particularly influenced by the so-called revolution in military affairs (RMA) and concepts of network-centric warfare (NCW). Many in the PLA see considerable potential for force multipliers in such areas as information warfare, the digitization of the battlefield, and networked systems.[11] At the same time, adversaries who are highly dependent on advanced technology—such as the United States—are seen as susceptible to low-tech countermeasures or attacks on their own command, control, and communications capabilities. Consequently, the PLA has devoted increasing attention to the development of asymmetric responses aimed at enabling "the inferior to defeat the superior."

In particular, China's military is increasingly focused on the information-technologies side of the RMA. According to PLA expert You Ji, the Chinese military is currently engaged as part of an ambitious "generation-leap" strategy in a twin transformational effort to simultaneously pursue both the mechanization and informatization of its armed forces.[12] Thus, even as it is attempting to upgrade its current arsenal of conventional industrial age weapons, it is also seeking to incorporate improved communications systems and other high technology capabilities that will enable it to fight "informationalized" conflicts by leveraging net-centric concepts of integration and rapid information exchange.

Of particular note over the past decade and a half has been the PLA's pursuit of weapons for asymmetric warfare, sometimes referred to as "assassin's mace" or "trump card" capabilities.[13] Some of these weapons are designed to strike an enemy's vulnerabilities, such as using computer-network attacks to knock out overhead C4ISR capabilities. Others are basically "old wine in new bottles," that is, existing programs such as fighter-bombers, missiles, submarines, and smart mines that are nevertheless regarded as the most effective weapons in the PLA's arsenal and whose development or deployment has therefore been accelerated. Finally, this category of weapons also includes so-called "new concept" arms, such as kinetic energy weapons (e.g., railguns), lasers, radiofrequency and high-powered microwave weapons, and anti-satellite (ASAT) systems. Most military systems in this last category are still in development, although China did successfully test an ASAT device in 2007.[14]

With regard to its naval forces, China built six destroyers of three different types between 2000 and 2011, including one class (the Type-052C *Luyang-II*) outfitted with an Aegis-type air-defense radar and fire-control system; additional Type-052C destroyers are currently under construction. These vessels are equipped with the indigenous YJ-83 or YJ-62 anti-ship cruise missile (ASCM) and the HN-2 land-attack cruise missile (a variant of the Russian Kh-55 missile). The Type-052C also carries several Chinese-built HHQ-9 surface-to-air missiles (SAM), housed in vertical launch systems (VLS). China has also added at least a dozen new frigates to its forces, including the Type-054

Jiangkai-class, which features a stealthy design and is armed with ASCMs and VLS-deployed SAMs, as well as the new-generation Type-022 *Houbei*-class catamaran-hulled missile fast attack craft (outfitted with YJ-83 ASCMs), of which at least 60 have been built.

Rounding out its modern surface fleet, in the late 1990s and early 2000s, the PLA Navy (PLAN) also acquired four *Sovremenny*-class destroyers from Russia. Of particular note, these ships are outfitted with the 3M-80E *Moskit* (NATO designation: SS-N-22 Sunburn) ramjet-powered, supersonic ASCM, which has a range of 120 kilometers; later-model Sunburns have a 200-kilometer range.

China has also greatly expanded its submarine fleet over the past 15 years. Since the late 1990s, the PLAN has acquired 13 Type-039 *Song*-class diesel-electric submarines. The *Song-class* is the first Chinese-built submarine to feature a modern "Albacore" (or teardrop-shaped) hull and a skewed propeller (for improved quieting), and to carry an encapsulated ASCM capable of being fired while submerged (through a regular torpedo tube), as well as an antisubmarine rocket. The PLAN further upgraded its capabilities by fielding the Type-41 *Yuan*-class in 2005. The *Yuan*-class also carries both torpedoes and ASCMs, and some or all of the boats in this class may be equipped with an as-yet unidentified engine (perhaps the Stirling engine, which has been outfitted to Swedish and Japanese submarines) for air-independent propulsion (AIP). So far, four *Yuan-class* submarines have been built, with at least three more under construction. On top of these indigenously-produced vessels, beginning in the mid-1990s, the PRC acquired 12 *Kilo*-class diesel-electric submarines from Russia. Some of these are armed with the 3M-54E *Klub* (SS-N-27) ASCM and the 53-65KE wake-homing torpedo. According to some reports, some of the features found in the *Kilo* were incorporated into the *Yuan*-class submarine.

Furthermore, the PLAN has begun replacing its small and aging fleet of nuclear-powered submarines, i.e., five *Han*-class nuclear-powered attack boats (SSN) and one *Xia*-class nuclear-powered ballistic missile-carrying submarine (SSBN). The first in a new class of SSNs, the Type-093 *Shang*-class was launched in 2002 and commissioned in 2006; one additional Type-093 has

since also entered service, and some sources estimate that up to eight boats in this class could be built, though other analysts expect that the PLAN will field more advanced Type-095s instead.[15] The PLAN has also launched two new SSBNs of the Type-094 *Jin*-class, each intended to carry 12 JL-2 submarine-launched ballistic missiles (SLBMs) with a range of 7,000 kilometers (three times greater than that of the JL-1 SLBM carried by the *Xia*) once the JL-2 enters operational readiness.[16]

China is also in the process of expanding its capacities for force projection and expeditionary warfare, in particular involving the acquisition of platforms capable of operating fixed-wing aircraft. China has recently launched two Type-071 17,000–20,000 ton LPD (landing platform dock) amphibious warfare ships, capable of carrying two helicopters and two air-cushioned landing craft (LCAC) each, as well as carrying up to 800 troops. Up to eight Type-071s are likely to be built, and some observers have speculated that these may be complemented by a new larger LPH (landing platform helicopter) amphibious assault ship.[17]

In perhaps its most dramatic development, the PLAN has recently taken delivery of China's first aircraft carrier: the rebuilt Soviet carrier ex-*Varyag*. A casualty of the Cold War's end, the *Varyag* was laid down in the early 1980s, but construction was halted in 1992 when the vessel was only 70 percent complete. Ukraine, which inherited it after the breakup of the Soviet Union, stripped the ship bare and left it exposed to the elements for several years. When the *Varyag* was finally sold and delivered to China in 2001—ostensibly to be turned into a Macao casino—it was a rusted shell without engines, a rudder, a weapons systems, or electronics. In addition, the process of removing sensitive equipment from the vessel had resulted in damage to its structure, so that even its seaworthiness was questioned by some. In mid-2005, however, the Chinese moved the *Varyag* to dry-dock at the Dalian shipyard in northeast China, where it underwent substantial repairs and reconstruction, along with the installation of new engines, radars, and electrical systems. The rebuilt ex-*Varyag* carrier underwent its first sea trials under PLAN colors in August 2011.

At the moment, China still lacks carrier-capable fixed-wing aircraft. At one time, the PLAN was rumored to be interested in purchasing 50

Su-33 fighter jets from Russia, which are flown off Moscow's lone remaining carrier, the *Admiral Kusnetzov*; this sale never materialized, however. Currently, it is believed that the ex-*Varyag* will fly either the so-called J-15 fighter jet (reportedly reversed-engineered from a Su-33 acquired surreptitiously from Ukraine) or a naval version of the indigenous J-10 combat fighter.

The ex-*Varyag* vessel will likely initially be used more as a research and training platform for future Chinese carrier designs and crews rather than as a fully functioning carrier (although it could be pressed into military service in a limited capacity). China is expected by most naval power analysts to begin construction of several indigenous carriers soon. At one time, Jane's Information Group speculated that the PLAN could build up to six aircraft carriers. If that happens, it would likely mean the reorientation of the PLAN around Carrier Battle Groups (CVBGs), with the carrier at the heart of a constellation of supporting submarines, destroyers, and frigates—an amalgamation of power projection capabilities such as China has never before possessed. Such CVBGs are among the most impressive instruments of military power in terms of sustained, far-reaching, and expeditionary offensive force, and such a development would constitute a major shift in the PLAN's strategic direction away from mere near-coast defense.

Modernization efforts for the PLA Air Force (PLAAF) and the naval aviation forces of the PLA Navy (often referred to as the PLA Navy Air Force, or PLANAF) have focused on the acquisition of modern fighter aircraft with advanced air-to-air missiles (AAMs) and air-to-ground weapons, as well as long-range surface-to-air missile systems (which the PLAAF manages as a part of its overall responsibilities for China's air defenses). The PLAAF and PLANAF have, over the past 15 years, acquired a large number of so-called fourth-generation or fourth-generation-plus fighter aircraft, capable of firing stand-off active radar-guided medium-range air-to-air missiles or delivering precision-guided air-to-surface munitions. Beginning in 1992, for example, China began to import the Russian-built Su-27 *Flanker* fighter jet; this was subsequently complemented by the purchase of the more advanced Su-30MKK version (first for the PLANAF and

later for the PLAAF), and Beijing and Moscow eventually agreed to an arrangement to license-produce the Su-27 (designated the J-11A) at the Shenyang Aircraft Company. All together, the PLAAF and PLANAF have acquired approximately 300 Su-27s and Su-30MKKs, including around 100 J-11As. Additionally, since the early 2000s, the Chinese have been manufacturing a reverse-engineered version of the Su-27 (designated the J-11B), albeit still relying on a Russian-supplied engine.

China is also currently manufacturing its first indigenous fourth-generation-plus combat aircraft, the J-10. The J-10 is an agile fighter jet in roughly the same class as the F-16C, and it features fly-by-wire flight controls and a glass cockpit (but nevertheless equipped with the Russian AL-31 engine, underscoring China's continuing difficulties with developing a usable jet engine). The J-10 first flew in the mid-1990s, and production started around the turn of the century. At least 150 J-10s have been delivered to the PLAAF since the early 2000s, with production continuing at a rate of about 30 aircraft a year; estimates are that the Chinese air force will buy upwards to 300 of these aircraft. Altogether, by 2020, the PLAAF and PLANAF will likely have between 600 and 700 combat aircraft of the fourth-generation or later type.

All of these modern aircraft can fire advanced air-delivered weapons. The PLAAF has purchased the RE-77E (AA-12) active-radar guided air-to-air missile (AAM) for its Su-27s, while the Su-30s can be equipped with the Russian-made Kh-31P anti-radiation missile (for use against radars). The J-10 carries the Chinese-designed PL-12 active-radar AAM and the short-range PL-8, a licensed-produced version of the Israeli Python-3 infrared-guided AAM, as well as laser-guided and satellite-guided bombs, high-speed anti-radar missiles, and air-launched cruise missiles.

In a move comparable to the launching of the country's first aircraft carrier, China has recently unveiled a purportedly "fifth-generation" combat aircraft, the J-20. The J-20, which had its first flight in January 2011, nominally resembles the US F-22, although the actual details of this aircraft—how stealthy is it, how advanced its radar and other avionics are, what kind of sophisticated weaponry it carries, etc.—are sketchy.

Consequently, one should be careful not to read too much into this program.[18] At the same time, the J-20 demonstrates China's ambitions to enter the vanguard of advanced fighter-jet producers.

More than most countries, the Chinese military relies heavily on ballistic missile systems for long-range precision-strike, although these are increasingly being supplemented by new land-attack cruise missiles (LACMs). Beginning in the mid-1990s, for example, China began acquiring conventionally-armed short-range ballistic missiles (SRBMs, missiles with ranges of less than 1,000 kilometers), mostly CSS-6/DF-15s and CSS-7/DF-11s, at a rate of about 50 to 75 missiles a year. By late 2010, the PLA's Second Artillery (the arm of the Chinese military that controls the country's nuclear and conventional missile forces) was estimated by the US DoD to have deployed approximately 1,000 to 1,200 SRBMs, most of which were arrayed opposite Taiwan.[19] China's conventional ballistic missile capabilities, moreover, have expanded into the medium-range category—that is, those missiles with ranges between 1,000 and 3,000 kilometers. The more recent versions of these missiles, such as the GPS-guided CSS-5/DF-21C, are believed to be accurate enough to hit targets such as airfields and ports, and can carry a variety of warheads, including conventional high explosive, anti-armor sub-munitions, and fuel air explosives.[20] In addition, China's Second Artillery has fielded around 150–350 conventional, ground-launched LACMs, such as the DH-10, with a range of 2,000 kilometers or more, that are even more accurate.[21]

Considerable attention has been paid of late to the DF-21D anti-ship ballistic missile (ASBM). The first of its kind, the DF-21D ASBM combines a maneuverable re-entry vehicle (MARV) with a terminal guidance system, has a range of 1,500 kilometers, and is capable of hypersonic (Mach 5 and above) speeds.[22] This makes the missile potentially effective against slow-moving carrier battle groups, and has earned the DF-21D the nickname "the carrier-killer." According to the US DoD, the DF-21D appears to be a "workable design" and has been deployed in small numbers, having achieved "initial operating capability."[23]

Regarding China's nuclear strategic forces, the Second Artillery currently operates approximately 55–65 intercontinental ballistic missiles (ICBMs),

up from around 20 ICBMs a decade ago.[24] These systems include the silo-based SS-4/DF-5 Mod 2, as well as the solid-fuelled, road-mobile CSS-10/DF-31. Improved versions of these ICBMs are expected to be deployed by the middle of this decade.[25] Additionally, China's land-based ICBMs are complimented by a growing number of sea-launched missiles, particularly the JL-2 SLBMs, of which 24 are currently deployed on two *Jin-class* SSBNs.

Finally, the PLA has paid considerable attention over the past 15 years to expanding and improving its capabilities for C4ISR (command, control, communications, computing, intelligence, surveillance, and reconnaissance) and for information operations/information warfare. Developing an advanced C4ISR system is a high priority for the Chinese military; accordingly, the PLA has created a separate military communications network using fibre-optic cable, satellites, microwave relays, and long-range high frequency radio. The PLA has also acquired several types of unmanned aerial vehicles and expanded its constellation of space-based systems, including the *Haiyang Yaogan*, and *Huanjin* remote-sensing satellites, the *Beidou* navigation satellite system (which just came online in late 2011), and the *Fenghuo* military communications satellite.[26] In addition, similar to the US Army's "Future Force Warrior" program, the PLA is reportedly experimenting with digitizing its ground forces, right down to outfitting the individual soldier with electronic gadgetry in order to provide him with real-time tactical C4ISR.

Concurrently, the PLA is expanding its capabilities to wage "offensive information warfare" (OIW). OIW is intended to disable or degrade an enemy's C4ISR system to such an extent that he is either deterred from fighting or, once at war, that his ability and resolve to fight back is weakened to the brink of capitulation. OIW is seen as a critical new development in the PLA's emerging war-fighting capabilities. The PLA is developing operating concepts of "integrated network electronic warfare," an amalgam of operations including electronic warfare (such as jamming the enemy's communications and intelligence-gathering assets), computer network operations (such as hacking or disrupting the enemy's computers and cyberspace operations), and even physical attacks on the enemy's C4ISR infrastructure (strikes against sensors such as AWACS and satellites, or against information nodes such as command posts).[27] The PLA has established special information warfare units to carry out attacks on enemy computer networks, in order to blind and disrupt an adversary's C4I systems.

In many instances, the PLA's efforts at "informatization" have benefited from leveraging advances and improvements in China's rapidly expanding commercial information technology sector. China's military telecommunications satellites, its *Beidou* navigation satellite system, and its *Yaogan* series of reconnaissance satellites are all based on commercial satellite technologies, for example. In particular, many of the technologies being developed for commercial remote sensing satellites, such as charge-coupled device cameras, multispectral scanners, and synthetic aperture radar imagers, have obvious applications for military systems. Similarly, much of the hardware and skill base for conducting information warfare is dual-use in nature, and the Chinese military has benefited from piggy-backing on developments and growth in the country's commercial IT industry.

Professionalization and Training of PLA Personnel

China is combining its force modernization efforts with actions intended to increase the professionalization and "jointness" of the PLA.[28] PLA officers and non-commissioned officers (NCOs) are receiving increased training and education, while recent military exercises have emphasized amphibious warfare with limited multi-service participation. PLAAF and PLANAF training regimens increasingly devote more time to supporting amphibious operations, while PLA ground forces are increasingly integrating training and exercises with maritime, airborne, and special operations forces.[29]

China has been improving personnel quality along several dimensions. One is improving the educational background of new officers and enlisted personnel. Today, to be inducted into the PLA as an enlisted person, recruits from rural areas must have at least graduated from middle school, and those from urban areas must have graduated

from a vocational high school or three-year technical college, or be enrolled in a four-year college.[30]

Officers in the PLA used to be drawn from the ranks of enlisted personnel. Some were promoted directly to become officers while others were sent to one of the PLA's 30 or so military academies. Direct promotions have ended, however, and those remaining officers who were directly promoted have been required to attend military academies. More importantly, approximately half of the PLA's officers are now recruited from civilian universities, which are regarded as providing higher quality education than the PLA's academies.[31]

Another aspect of the PLA's efforts to improve the quality of its personnel is the creation of an NCO corps. The vast majority of these are enlisted personnel who volunteer to reenlist after the end of their initial two-year commitment. As of 2008, all NCOs must have at least a high-school education and a "certificate of professional qualification." Diplomas from vocational high schools and technical colleges are considered acceptable, but those NCOs who are not high school graduates or who do not have a diploma from a vocational high school or technical college are sent to PLA academies or to civilian colleges, research institutes, and industrial colleges to receive the requisite training. In addition to satisfying these minimum education requirements, NCOs receive further education and training throughout their careers in the PLA, and senior NCOs (those who reach the top two of six total NCO grades) are required to have a degree from a three-year technical college.[32]

In addition to improving the quality of its soldiers and officers, the PLA is attempting to improve the quality of its training by increasing the realism, complexity, and "jointness" of its exercises. Traditionally, training was conducted in small units belonging to a single branch (e.g., infantry, frigates, or fighter aircraft), and was performed in benign conditions that included familiar terrain, daylight, and good weather. Moreover, training exercises were done either without an opposing force or with opposing forces whose actions were predetermined and briefed to the force being trained ahead of time. Now, however, training is routinely conducted on unfamiliar terrain, at night or in bad weather, and against opposing forces whose actions are not predetermined. The frequency of combined-arms (different branches within a single service) and joint (different services training together) training has also increased, as has the scale of the exercises. Some training areas now have dedicated opposition forces that simulate the tactics of potential adversaries and are even allowed to defeat the visiting unit. Finally, rigorous evaluation and post-exercise critiques have become an integral part of PLA training, with units required to meet standardized performance benchmarks or else undergo remedial training.[33]

Conclusions

China has been engaged in an ambitious, concerted, and methodical transformation of its armed forces since the late 1990s. China's recent military acquisitions, as well as its current R&D efforts, particularly its emphasis on "trump card" weapons for asymmetric warfare, have been critical developments in the upgrading of its warfighting capabilities. At the same time, the PLA has made considerable progress over the last 15 years in enhancing the professionalism of its military personnel, and in expanding its training and making it both more realistic and more joint. Consequently, China has noticeably improved its military capabilities in several specific areas—particularly missile attack, precision-strike, power projection at sea and in the air, and joint operations. The Chinese armed forces have also made significant advances in exploiting informatization, in promoting the development of advanced weaponry, and in accelerating the pace of military modernization, all of which create new levers of military power for the PLA. Ultimately, the PLA seeks to turn itself into a modern, network-enabled fighting force, capable of projecting sustained power throughout the Asia-Pacific region. If successful, China's military modernization drive will give the country the potential, in the estimation of the US Department of Defense, to "pose credible threats to modern militaries operating in the region."[34]

At the same time, the PLA continues to suffer from a number of deficiencies and weaknesses that limit its ability to constitute a major military

threat to advanced militaries such as the United States armed forces. In the first place, for all of its talk of becoming a more networked military, the PLA is still decidedly a *platform-centric* force that is still in the process of becoming more network-enabled. Second, despite more than fifteen years of continuous defense spending increases and at least a decade of aggressive acquisitions on the part of the PLA, the bulk of the Chinese military remains relatively backward. Overall, barely 25 percent of the PLA's fighter aircraft, 25 percent of its surface combatants, 40 percent of its surface-to-air missiles, and 55 percent of its submarine fleet are deemed by the US Department of Defense to be modern.[35] Even many of the PLA's most recently acquired systems, such as the J-10 fighter jet, the Yuan-class submarine, and the *Luyang-II* destroyer, although advanced by the PLA's standards, are basically 1980s-era weapons systems. The J-10 fighter jet, for instance, is basically equivalent to the F-16C, which entered service in the mid-1980s. Even equipment that China has acquired from Russia—such as Su-30MKK fighters, *Sovremenny-class* destroyers, and *Kilo*-class submarines—are hardly transformational, game-changing systems. Finally, it is worth remembering that the bulk of the PLA ground forces are still equipped with old or obsolete weaponry; only about a third of the PLA's 7,500 main battle tanks are the relatively modern Type-96 and Type-99—the remainder being Type-59 and Type-69 tanks based on the 1950s-era Soviet T-54. Other types of modern ground systems—including infantry fighting vehicles, self-propelled artillery gun systems, helicopters, anti-tank guided missiles, and surface-to-air missile systems—are only gradually being introduced in modest numbers.[36] In sum, the capabilities gap between the PLA and the US military remains wide, even as the PLA is posing new problems for regional militaries that do not have the aggregate power or budget of the US armed forces.

Moreover, the technology gap between China's defense industry and the leading Western arms producers remains significant in several critical areas. This is particularly apparent in China's continued reliance upon foreign suppliers for propulsion systems, especially engines for its naval forces, as well as turbofan jet engines used to power modern military aircraft and transports.

China's largely indigenously-built J-10 fighter, for example, still uses AL-31FN engines imported from Russia.[37] One should also keep in the mind that many advanced weapons programs, such as its aircraft carrier or its J-20 combat aircraft, are still in the developmental stage, and actual deployment remains years, perhaps even a decade or more, away. Additionally, the US DoD has reported that the JL-2 SLBM has experienced a "number of problems," and that its in-service date remains "uncertain."[38] Finally, China continues to lag far behind the West in areas such as C4I architectures and surveillance and reconnaissance capabilities.

Operationally, it is important to note that the PLA remains overwhelmingly a ground forces–dominated military. Top leadership positions in the Chinese armed forces are dominated by the Army—and the Army is made up mostly of modestly-armed infantry troops, at that. In short, large segments of the PLA today remain incapable of much in the way of mobility or expeditionary capacities. The PLA still lacks the logistical and lift capacity, either by sea or by air, required for projecting force far beyond its borders or immediate ocean areas. It still has the capability to sea- and airlift only two or three regiments of soldiers and marines at any given time, and the PLA still possesses little in the way of sustained logistical abilities, particularly over long distances (although the PLA Navy continues to expand its fleet of amphibious and logistics vessels, including the launch of its first hospital ship in 2010). Finally, the PLA "continues to face deficiencies in inter-service cooperation and actual experience in joint exercises and combat operations," making the attainment of a joint operations capability—let alone an integrated joint operations capability—rather remote for the time being.[39]

All these problems aside, however, it is undeniable that the Chinese military has made impressive gains in upgrading and improving its military capabilities over the past 15 years. Moreover, the pace of this modernization process does not yet appear to have abated. And while PLA modernization has not been across-the-board, it may also not be necessary for it to constitute a modern fighting force. Many have speculated that the Chinese are basically engaged in building an "army within an army," that is, a relatively small force—approximately a dozen division- or brigade-sized rapid reaction units, including three airborne and four amphibious or marine divisions, as well as special operations forces—equipped and trained to carry out rapid attacks. The forces will be supported in turn by the more advanced elements of the rest of the PLA, such as precision-strike missile forces, fourth-generation fighters, modern surface and submarine forces, and surface-to-air missiles systems, all backed up by an increasingly capable C4ISR network and an offensive information warfare capability. Such a force would mostly likely be used to attack and defeat Taiwan, while also deterring or defeating US intervention on Taipei's behalf. Such capabilities could also be applied to other regional contingencies, such as territorial disputes in the South China Sea.[40]

So while Chinese military power may still pale in comparison to the US armed forces, the strength of the PLA relative to its likely local competitors in the Asia-Pacific region has increased significantly, and will likely continue to grow over the next ten to twenty years. As a result, China is definitely gaining an edge over other regional militaries in the Asia-Pacific, particularly Taiwan and perhaps even Japan and India.[41]

Naturally, many of Beijing's neighbors have looked upon China's growing hard power and its "creeping assertiveness" in the South China Sea with a certain amount of trepidation. Some are attempting to hedge against a rising China by engaging in their own military build-ups. In particular, India and several nations in Southeast Asia have over the past decade or so been engaged in their own often intensive efforts to modernize their armed forces. As a result, these countries have added new or expanded military capabilities that can be directed against any potential "China threat." India is in the midst of upgrading its navy, acquiring several large surface combatants—including two aircraft carriers—and more than a dozen new submarines (both nuclear- and conventionally powered), as well as buying hundreds of new fighter jets. Singapore, Malaysia, Indonesia, and Vietnam are all acquiring submarines and new warships, modern anti-ship cruise missiles, fourth-generation-plus fighter jets, and stand-off air-launched weapons. The challenge to Beijing, of course, is that it may be instigating an arms race where it does not seek one, especially with regard to India, which increasingly sees itself in a rivalry with China for great-power status in the Asia-Pacific. And even if the smaller states in Southeast Asia cannot hope to match China's military force, they at least aspire to blunt this power, particularly when it comes to their own claims in the South China Sea.

In sum, it is readily apparent that China has made significant—perhaps even unexpected—progress in building up its military power over the past fifteen years. And because China's rise is so recently tainted with a growing self-assertiveness (both verbally and policy-wise) bordering on belligerence, its growing military capabilities have injected new uncertainties into the regional security calculus. At the same time, Chinese military power still possesses several weak links that mitigate its effectiveness. It could be argued that China is growing in hard power just enough to potentially destabilize regional security—particularly if it chooses to use military power to press its claims and interests; at the same time, it is not yet powerful enough militarily to actually resolve these issues. This is, to say the least, a delicate balance that is fraught with peril and the potential for conflict.

NOTES

1. James Mulvenon, *Soldiers of Fortune* (Armonk, NY: M.E. Sharpe, 2001), p. 177.
2. "China Plans to Boost 2009 Military Spending by 14.9%," *Bloomberg*, March 4, 2009.
3. European Defense Agency (EDA), Defense Data of EDA Participating Member States in 2009 (Brussels: EDA), p. 9.
4. *Defense of Japan 2009* (Tokyo: Ministry of Defense, 2009), pp. 164–166; Jon Grevatt, "Japan Proposes Defense Cut for 10th Year," *Jane's Defense Industry*, December 18, 2009.
5. In 2009, for example, France spent approximately US$14 billion on procurement and US$5.8 billion on defense R&D; that same year, the United Kingdom spent US$10.9 billion and US$4.2 billion, respectively, on procurement and R&D EDA. See *Defense Data of EDA Participating Member States in 2009*, p. 11.
6. See Richard A. Bitzinger, "Just the Facts, Ma'am: The Challenge of Analyzing Chinese Military Expenditures," *China Quarterly* (March 2003).
7. Office of the Secretary of Defense (OSD), *2011 Report to Congress: Military and Security Developments Involving the People's Republic of China*, (Washington, DC: US Department of Defense, 2011) p. 41.
8. Ben Vogel, "China Embarks on 15-Year Armed Forces Modernization Program," *Jane's Defense Weekly*, July 1, 2006.
9. Ibid.; OSD, *2011 Report to Congress*, op. cit., p. 45.
10. See Tai Ming Cheung, *Fortifying China* (Ithaca, NY: Cornell University Press, 2009); and Evan Medeiros et al., *A New Direction for China's Defense Industry* (Santa Monica, CA: The RAND Corporation, 2005).
11. You Ji, "Learning and Catching Up: China's Revolution in Military Affairs Initiative," in Emily O. Goldman and Thomas G. Mahnken (eds.), *The Information Revolution in Military Affairs in Asia* (New York: Palgrave Macmillan, 2004), pp. 97–123.
12. You Ji, "China's Emerging National Defense Strategy," *China Brief*, November 24, 2004; see also "Chapter III: Revolution in Military Affairs with Chinese Characteristics," *China's National Defense in 2004*.
13. Jason E. Bruzdzinksi, "Demystifying *Shashoujian*: China's 'Assassin's Mace' Concept," in Andrew Scobell and Larry Wortzel (eds.), *Civil-Military Change in China* (Carlisle, PA: US Army War College, 2004), pp. 309–364; OSD, *2011 Report to Congress*, op. cit., p. 22.
14. Mark A. Stokes, *China's Strategic Modernization: Implications for the United States* (Carlisle, PA: US Army War College, 1999), pp. 195–213; Craig Covault, "Chinese Test Anti-Satellite Weapon," *Aviation Week & Space Technology*, January 17, 2009.
15. "Type 093 (Shang Class) Nuclear Powered Missile Submarine," Sinodefense.com, www.sinodefence.com/navy/sub/type093shang.asp.
16. Ronald O'Rourke, *PLAN Force Structure: Submarines, Ships, and Aircraft*, paper presented to the CAPS-RAND-CEIP-NDU conference on "The Chinese Navy: Expanding Capabilities, Evolving Roles?," pp. 4–9, 13–18, "Type 094 (Jin Class) Nuclear Powered Missile Submarine," www.sinodefence.com/navy/sub/type094jin.asp.
17. O'Rourke, *PLAN Force Structure*, p. 19; "Type 071 Landing Platform Dock," www.sinodefence.com/navy/amphibious/type071.asp.
18. "J-20 vs. F-35: One Analyst's Perspective," http://defensetech.org/2010/12/31/j-20-vs-f-35-one-analysts-perspective.
19. OSD, *2011 Report to Congress*, op. cit., p. 30.
20. "Dongfeng 21," http://www.sinodefence.com/space/missile/df21.asp.
21. "DF-11 (CSS-7/M-11)," *Jane's Strategic Weapon Systems*, June 26, 2009; "DF-15 (CSS-6/M-9)," *Jane's Strategic Weapon Systems*, June 26, 2009; "DF-21 (CSS-5)," *Jane's Strategic Weapon Systems*, June 26, 2009; Office of the Secretary of Defense, *Annual Report to Congress: Military Power of the People's Republic of China 2009* (Washington, DC: US Department of Defense, March 2009), p. 66.
22. Wendell Minnick, "China Developing Anti-Ship Ballistic Missiles," *Defense News*, January 14, 2008.

23. Tony Capaccio, "China Has 'Workable' Anti-Ship Missile Design, Pentagon Says," *Bloomberg*, August 26, 2010.

24. OSD, *2011 Report to Congress*, op. cit., p. 34.

25. Ibid.

26. "China's Satellite Program," www.sinodefence.com/space/satellite.

27. Jacqueline Newmeyer, "The Revolution in Military Affairs with Chinese Characteristics," *Journal of Strategic Studies* 33, no. 4 (August 2010), pp. 488–490; OSD, *2011 Report to Congress*, p. 25; You Ji, "China's Emerging National Defense Strategy"; Wendell Minnick, "China Shifts Spending Focus to Info War," *Defense News*, September 11, 2006.

28. This section draws in part on Richard A. Bitzinger and Roger Cliff, "PLA Modernization: Motivations, Directions, and the Revolution in Military Affairs," in Mingjiang Li and Dongmin Lee (eds.), *China and East Asian Strategic Dynamics* (Lanham, MD: Lexington Books, 2011), pp. 31–32.

29. See, for example, Dennis J. Blasko, *The Chinese Army Today* (New York: Routledge, 2006), pp. 91–120, 144–170; OSD, *2011 Report to Congress*, op. cit., p. 24.

30. David E. Johnson, et al., *Preparing and Training for the Full Spectrum of Military Challenges: insights from the Experiences of China, France, the United Kingdom, India, and Israel* (Santa Monica, CA: The RAND Corporation, 2009), p. 29.

31. Ibid., pp. 32–33.

32. Ibid.

33. Ibid., pp. 46, 50–51.

34. Office the Secretary of Defense, *Annual Report on the Military Power of the People's Republic of China 2006* (Washington, DC: US Department of Defense, 2006), p. i.

35. OSD, *2011 Report to Congress*, op cit., p. 43.

36. "Ground forces," www.sinodefence.com/army/.

37. Evan S. Medeiros et al., *A New Direction for China's Defense Industry* (Santa Monica, CA: The RAND Corporation, 2005), p. 170.

38. OSD, *2011 Report to Congress*, op. cit., p. 34.

39. Ibid., p. 27.

40. Timothy Hu, "China—Marching Forward," *Jane's Defense Weekly*, April 25, 2007.

41. China now outspends Japan on defense by a factor of nearly two to one.

III. THE INTERNAL SECURITY STATE

China Rethinks Unrest*

Murray Scot Tanner

A June 2003 dispatch in a preeminent US newspaper described a "rare and short-lived demonstration" by more than 100 enraged Shanghai apartment dwellers protesting their forced eviction to make way for luxury condos. The one discernible error of the tightly researched report was its characterization of such protests as "rare." Public protest in China is now anything but, with such incidents numbering in the tens of thousands each year, far more than most foreign analysts seem to acknowledge, according to an unprecedented new wave of internal data from China's own police forces. A raft of recent police reports also indicate that protests are not only growing in number but also are increasing in size and becoming better organized.

The histories of China and other developing societies unfortunately provide no yardstick for

gauging how serious a threat such levels of protest pose to the Chinese Communist Party's (CCP) grip on power, let alone a basis for confidently predicting a "coming collapse" of China.[1] Social unrest has sparked a tremendous policy debate among the guardians of the state in Beijing. In their internal discussions, the analysts and officials of China's public security system are fundamentally rethinking the sources of unrest in a changing society as well as strategies for coping with it. Many among China's police now frankly concede that economic, cultural, and political changes, not enemy conspiracies, underlie this emerging crisis of order. Some security specialists even cautiously assert that, unless China undertakes serious institutional reform, neither coercion nor rapid economic growth will be sufficient to contain unrest.

As China's new leadership under General Secretary Hu Jintao struggles to find a more realistic and sophisticated strategy to manage unrest and strike an effective balance between reform

---

* This article was published in *The Washington Quarterly* (June 2004).

and social control, these internal police debates will form a pivotal part of the counsel they receive. As these analyses underscore, the struggle to control unrest will force Beijing's leaders to face riskier dilemmas than at any time since the 1989 Tiananmen Square demonstrations. Experiments with less violent police tactics, economic concessions to demonstrators, and more fundamental institutional reforms all risk further encouraging protest in an increasingly restive society. Nevertheless, these challenges must be navigated if the party wants to avoid the ultimate dilemma of once again resorting to 1989-style violence or reluctantly engaging in a more fundamental renegotiation of power relations between the state and society.

The United States also needs to rethink social unrest in China and recognize its potential systemic impact on the Sino-US bilateral relationship. Underlying Beijing's emerging new diplomacy of self-confidence and international cooperation, quiet fears of instability are increasingly limiting and complicating the relationship by raising Beijing's perception of the risks involved in a full range of strategic and economic issues. Inevitably, Beijing will face major social-control crises as it struggles to find a new and hopefully less repressive strategy to ensure social order. Meanwhile, within the limits of our influence, the United States and its allies must now start crafting responses that will encourage Beijing to accelerate institutional reform rather than revert to the violence of 1989.

Protests Rising

Newly published internal statistics from China's police leadership, the Ministry of Public Security (MPS), confirm a dramatic increase in public protests, officially labeled "mass group incidents." These incidents take various forms, from peaceful small-group petitions and sit-ins to marches and rallies, labor strikes, merchant strikes, student demonstrations, ethnic unrest, and even armed fighting and riots.[2]

The official rate of increase is truly striking. Police admit to a nationwide increase of 268 percent in mass incidents from 1993 to 1999 (from 8,700 to 32,000). In not a single year during this period did unrest increase by less than 9 percent. The rate spiked upward by 25 percent and 67 percent, respectively, in the financial crisis years of 1997 and 1998 and grew by another 28 percent in 1999. China witnessed more than 30,000 mass incidents during January–September 2000, a rate that yields an annual projected estimate of more than 40,000 incidents and an increase of 25 percent over 1999, according to Chinese police sources cited in the Hong Kong press.[3]

Despite the unavailability of nationwide figures after 2000, all evidence indicates that unrest in China remains high to the present day, although it is unclear whether the total number of incidents has continued to increase, diminished somewhat as the economy began to recover, or declined in frequency, while increasing in size. In any case, the problem clearly remains serious. In April 2001, a widely publicized study by the CCP's Organization Department characterized mass unrest as still on the rise, although it provided no statistics. Police in one central Chinese province reported a 40 percent increase in protests during 1999–2001; in another central province, authorities declared a 35 percent increase in the first four months of 2000 compared to the same period in 1999. In the spring of 2002, although focused attention was on massive, prolonged worker demonstrations in the northeastern industrial cities of Liaoyang and Daqing, a harried Premier Zhu Rongji told visitors that his office was being flooded with hundreds of reports of labor unrest. Finally, a late September 2003 MPS press communiqué claimed that several forms of protest, including "collective petitions and road and building blockades," were "continuing to increase" nationwide.[4] This increase has been widespread throughout China, yet the levels and rates of increase vary greatly from province to province.

Clearly, no region has been hammered harder than China's aging northeastern industrial region, where free-market reforms have badly hurt workers in inefficient state enterprises. For several years in the mid-1990s, even before the financial crisis, police in Jilin province annually confronted an average of more than 500 "relatively large-scale incidents"—those involving at least 50 protestors. These numbers, however, pale in comparison with those in Liaoning province, where protests have exploded since the mid-1990s. In a recent report, the province's public security chief claimed a stunning 9,559 incidents between January 2000 and September 2002—an average of about 290 per month, or nearly 10 per day for almost three years. Even more astonishing, these numbers reportedly represent a partial decline from those reported in 1999.[5]

Changing Protest Styles

For those concerned about China's internal stability, the raw numbers of protests are less important than an escalation in their size, level of organization, severity of demands, or degree of violence. The CCP's remarkable capacity thus far to avoid the fate of its late Leninist brethren in Europe owes much to the party's skill not only in preventing large-scale, well-organized protests with broad anti-regime demands but also in suppressing organized opposition or civil society groups that can mobilize such protests. Having absorbed the brutal lessons of the Tiananmen demonstrations, Chinese protestors throughout the mid- to late 1990s self-consciously restrained their actions. Most disgruntled citizens declined to establish permanent underground organizations that might have threatened the party. Their protests rarely included more than a few dozen people, usually from the same work unit or village. Protest tactics remained scrupulously peaceful, and demands focused on concrete local issues rather than broad systemic changes. Indeed, to avoid official wrath, many petitioners took pains to reaffirm their support for the party's central leadership, claiming that they only wanted local officials to obey Beijing's laws. Political scientist Kevin O'Brien has thoughtfully dubbed this style of protest "rightful resistance," pointing out that it not only presented little threat to CCP authority but also offered Beijing the chance to portray itself as a savior for citizens plagued by lawless, predatory, local party officials.[6]

Recent reports indicate, however, that, even though most protesters' demands remain limited and concrete, in many other ways unrest is starting to outgrow the self-restrained rightful-resistance model. The most obvious signs are reports by security officials indicating a clear trend toward larger and larger demonstrations, many involving hundreds, thousands, or even tens of thousands of protestors.[7] During 2002–2003, the thousands of factory strikers in Liaoyang and Daqing as well as student demonstrators in Anhui province highlighted this trend. Even though the MPS claimed that police nationwide handled only 125 incidents involving more than 1,000 persons during 1999, provincial police reports make clear that these figures greatly understate the situation. In the same year, for example, the small southwestern province of Guizhou alone reported 21 incidents with more than 1,000 participants—one-sixth of the declared national total—even though Guizhou accounted for less than 1 percent of the reported 32,000 total protests nationwide. Police in coastal Fujian province reported that the number of protests in the first half of 2001 was not much higher than the number for the same period in 2000, but the number of protestors had increased by 53 percent.[8] Again, however, Liaoning's problems dwarfed those of other provinces, with police estimating that more than 863,000 citizens took part in the 9,000-plus protests that occurred between 2000 and 2002—an average of more than 90 people per incident and more than a tenfold increase in average size over previous years. Inevitably, the raw size of such incidents greatly increases the risk that they will get out of control, no matter the extent to which protest leaders try to restrain the demands and tactics of the participants.

Chinese police and Western observers also concur that the level of organization among protestors is gradually improving. Despite determined efforts to undermine organized links, police report that many of the protests they face—indeed a majority in some places—now boast an elaborate organization, complete with designated leaders, "public spokespersons," "activists," and "underground core groups."[9] To circumvent tough laws against "illegal organizations," many of these groups reportedly piggyback on legally registered industrial associations; official trade unions; family and clan associations (especially in the countryside); and nominally apolitical social, recreational, and even athletic groups. One frustrated officer complained that local protestors now show up "having already raised funds for petition drives, hired lawyers, and invited news reporters" to the event.[10]

Increasingly, demonstrators are overcoming one of Chinese communism's signature devices for curbing dissent: the country's vast web of self-contained, cellular neighborhoods and work units (*danwei*). Historically, these units controlled unrest both passively and actively by allowing workers and peasants little regular contact with potential sympathizers in other units. Instead, protests traditionally focused on local officials, and their demands remained manageably narrow. Security officials reinforced these obstacles to broader organization by harshly punishing efforts to link up with other units, treating these attempts as prima facie evidence of hostile intent toward CCP rule. In conversations with foreigners, disgruntled workers and peasants frequently testified to the success of this divide and rule system, stressing their careful efforts to avoid linking up.[11] Nevertheless, many recent police reports concur that linking up is becoming more common in recent years.[12] Police in the central province of Anhui, for example, reported that 11 local construction groups jointly organized a series of protests in January 2002 that blocked access roads to government offices in the provincial capital.[13]

China's protestors are also proving astute learners, exhibiting impressive tactical and technical sophistication. Cellular telephones, text messaging, the Internet, and e-mail enable faster and more flexible organization. Police complain that protests now spring up more suddenly, with simultaneous, coordinated actions breaking out in distant locations and quickly overtaxing the capacity of the police to respond adequately. Displaying a keen grasp of political street theater, many protest leaders now routinely place senior citizens, women, and children in the front lines of demonstrations, thereby shaming the targets of their protests and paralyzing the police. Police frustration over this tactic is palpable, as evidenced by a recent report by two officials of the paramilitary People's Armed Police (PAP) on the Muslim protests in Xinjiang. With masterful euphemism, they complained that, "because the rioters were mixed in among . . . many ethnic minority women and children, the Public Security and PAP forces were unable to adopt *appropriate measures* for handling the protest."[14]

Finally, even though Chinese police insist that the vast majority of protests have remained peaceful, violent resistance is clearly on the rise. In 1999, for example, Guizhou police reported a 42 percent increase in protests involving physical attacks on party and state officials, resulting in 17 deaths and 282 injuries. In part, this increase reflects a dramatic rise in violence generally throughout Chinese society. Police deaths in the line of duty, which averaged a remarkably low 36 per year between 1949 and 1978, have skyrocketed to 450–500 annually, several times more than the number of police deaths in the United States, which has a far more heavily armed society. Although most police fatalities are the result of traffic accidents and ill-advised struggles with better-armed criminals, evidence suggests that protestors, too, are increasingly responding to suppression with violence.

Reevaluating Causes

In the face of a rapidly increasing number of protests, top Chinese internal security specialists and many in the police community are reassessing the causal factors behind social unrest in China as well as strategies for coping with it, embracing views that diverge markedly from the official lessons imposed after the Tiananmen demonstrations. More specifically, many are now quietly deemphasizing shopworn conspiracy theories that blame mass protests primarily on the CCP's foreign and domestic enemies, reflecting the classic Leninist insistence that social protest in a Communist country cannot just happen, it must be instigated.

In the days after the Tiananmen demonstrations, this Leninist conspiratorial worldview was typified in a report on the protests issued by Gu Linfang, the Chinese vice minister of public security who was in charge of "political security."[15] To document a conspiracy in 1989, Gu painstakingly listed dozens of allegedly nefarious contacts among protest leaders; reformist Communist officials; foreign academics; and, of course, Western and Taiwanese intelligence agencies. The vice minister railed against party reformers for coddling schemers who fomented rebellion. A Leninist to his marrow, Gu refused to concede any acceptance of what social scientists have known for decades, that whenever a society grows and changes as rapidly as China has, an increase in political protests is a normal development.

By the late 1990s, however, many analysts from the MPS's own think tanks and universities recognized that subsequent efforts to deter social unrest or limit it to very low levels were failing. They have responded with a flurry of unprecedentedly frank scholarship on social protest that reconsiders the official lessons of 1989 on the sources of protest and the best strategies for handling it. To be sure, limits remain. No security official has dared publicly to question one-party rule or to open a historical can of worms by reassessing the official verdict that the Tiananmen demonstrations themselves were a "counterrevolutionary riot." Yet, in new analyses of unrest, reliance on social science is increasingly supplanting paranoia.

Although the extent to which analysts suspect enemy instigation of protests today still differs widely, it is increasingly difficult to find analyses that even approach Gu's obsession with conspiracy. (The principal exception is the probably excessive blame heaped on the Falun Gong and Muslim separatist organizations.) Even relatively traditional analysts list "international enemy forces" as only one among many major sources of unrest.[16] Most available police analyses now blame unrest primarily on approximately the same list of social, economic, and political forces that Western scholars invoke, implicitly relegating enemy instigation to the role of a secondary catalyst. One provincial deputy police chief, for example, rather candidly downplayed "enemy forces" in his region, noting that "there have only been a few sprouts or trends toward these, though we cannot permit ourselves to overlook them."

A powerful ideological consequence of this view is that most analysts now claim that the vast majority of protests results from disagreements "among the people" ("non-antagonistic contradictions"), not from conflicts "between the people and their enemies" ("antagonistic contradictions"). An internal MPS document prepared in 2000 reportedly made this verdict on protests official.[17] In terms of internal security strategy, this characterization typically, though not always, reduces reliance on coercion. Reflecting this judgment, since 1999 the MPS and its think tanks have adopted as the new standard phrase for protests "mass group incidents," a term whose assumption that the protestors are "the masses" suggests powerful sympathetic overtones.

The New Orthodoxy:
It's the Economy, Shagua!

In lieu of conspiracy theories, most security analysts now embrace the classic economic explanations of unrest, with some even claiming that economic conflicts ultimately underlie all social protest. Like most Western analysts, Chinese analysts emphasize the problems accompanying Beijing's painful 20-year reform of its state-owned enterprises, including layoffs, unemployment, improperly withheld wages, housing allowances, health care payments, and pensions. Police experts concede that 50–80 percent of all medium- and large-sized state-owned enterprises are now in serious financial trouble, a situation that by 2001 had affected the jobs of more than 27 million workers.[18]

Surprising numbers of analysts in the public security system display an undisguised sympathy for the very worker and peasant protestors the police are supposed to suppress. In their writings, they characterize laid-off demonstrators as "exploited," "marginalized," "socially disadvantaged," "victims," and "losers" in economic competition, driven to protest by social distrust and the "heartlessness" of the free market. They frankly concede that many protestors are victims of crooked managers who drove their factories into bankruptcy through illicit dealings or who absconded with company assets. One Shanghai analyst recently claimed that 55 percent of the protests there were attributable to illegal actions by enterprise managers.[19]

Many police experts hold a special contempt for China's increasingly unequal income distribution. They suggest, almost humorously, that, even after 25 years of market-oriented reform, China's police force remains riddled with "Communist sympathizers." Some invoke comparative development studies to claim that such widening inequality places China in a "zone of genuine danger" of instability. With undisguised judgmentalism, one provincial police report argues that inequality exacerbates unrest primarily because most citizens realize that many of China's *nouveaux riches* attained their wealth through corrupt, illegal enterprises that made "explosive profits."

Beijing hopes that it can grow its way out of social unrest before it threatens the regime's survival. As former premier Zhu stated in his March 2003 valedictory, "Development is the fundamental principle, and the key to resolving all problems China is facing. We must maintain a comparatively high growth rate in our national economy." Zhu also argued that the pace of reform had to be balanced against the risks of unrest.[20]

Even the MPS's own data, however, suggests that Beijing may be kidding itself if it believes economic growth alone will bring unrest under control. The rapid spike in protests in 1997–1998 suggests that social unrest may be correlated to decelerating economic growth and rising unemployment, and the underlying sustained increase in incidents is at least consistent with long-term, persistent economic changes, such as rising inequality. Yet, declining economic growth and increasing inequality are only part of the story. The data demonstrate that unrest began rising rapidly no later than 1993–1995 when the rate of economic growth exceeded 10 percent. Protests also show a ratchet effect, remaining quite high (and continuing to rise in at least some provinces) even as the rate of economic growth revived.

Moreover, stepping back from the 1993–2000 data, unrest also flared up during a period of rapid economic growth between 1986 and 1989, as double-digit inflation and corruption spawned resentment among students and workers. Thus, since 1986, social unrest has, at times, risen during periods of inflationary high growth, recession, and recovery—a serious challenge to any simple economic determinist explanation of social unrest. Apparently recognizing these inadequacies, some police analysts contend that social and political forces are also stoking social unrest and this situation is likely to continue regardless of economic conditions.

More specifically, a few analysts attribute rising unrest to deeper shifts in China's political culture. A quarter century of gradual, progressive political reform is forging a new culture that they characterize, rather positively, as one that is more open, assertive, and even "developed." China's citizens are now simply much less willing to tolerate unjust, corrupt bureaucrats, and the population is far more willing to take complaints to the streets. In Tiananmen Square in 1989, Deng Xiaoping administered a brutal lesson in social calculus: that the risks and dangers of street protest far outweigh

any potential rewards. Fifteen years later, however, many police see a new social logic gradually taking hold, with disgruntled citizens increasingly convinced that peaceful protest is significantly less dangerous and not only effective but often unavoidable as a means to win concessions. Police sources now routinely quote a popular expression: "Making a great disturbance produces a great solution. Small disturbances produce small solutions. Without a disturbance, there will be no solution."

Institutional Failure

The most far-reaching new police critiques argue that mass protests are to some extent an inevitable product of socioeconomic development, but are exacerbated when political and legal institutions fail to keep up with change. Rapid socioeconomic development causes a rapid expansion in popular economic and political demands. When citizens have not learned how to voice demands through the available political and legal channels, or if those channels are clogged or underdeveloped, frustration inevitably spills over into the streets.[21] Socioeconomic change may generate these underlying demands and clashes of social interest, but it is usually government failures that cause these contradictions to turn antagonistic and dangerous.

Although the Chinese ideological roots behind this analysis and the language used to express it reflect a moderate period in Mao's thinking of the mid-1950s, many Western scholars immediately will recognize this theory of unrest as a central theme in Samuel P. Huntington's 1968 classic, *Political Order in Changing Societies*. The similarities are not accidental, and some Chinese police analysts explicitly claim Huntington as an influence. One such analyst argues that China's increasing unrest results from "imperfect political structures" that provide inadequate avenues for voicing, aggregating, and balancing this surge in popular demands. Lacking "proper channels" to voice their demands, citizens often express them through "improper channels ... such as illegal assemblies, marches, and demonstrations."[22]

These analysts argue that the CCP and the state cannot hope to contain social unrest unless they address its institutional catalysts, including government mishandling of social tensions and bureaucrats who are corrupt, indifferent, or abusive.[23] In strikingly harsh tones, some police officials and analysts lambaste local officials and their law enforcement colleagues for their favoritism, corruption, and tendency to wring illegal fines from defenseless peasants and workers. They also blame China's badly underdeveloped legal institutions for failing to protect the unemployed and disadvantaged from business owners who exploit China's Wild West–style capitalism and illegally divert money from workers' pension and insurance funds. They emphasize that any successful strategy for controlling social unrest in China cannot and should not rely exclusively on repression by the state's law enforcement organs, no matter how professional and effective they may be. Unless coercion is combined with broader legal and democratic reforms that encourage more effective state response to popular demands, protests cannot be handled successfully. Exactly which political reforms police analysts and officials may advocate to senior party leaders in private, however, remains a tantalizing mystery. Certainly, in China's strict one-party system, none have yet dared even to mention publicly the institutional solution that Huntington himself preferred: a competitive two-party system that could peacefully integrate new groups and demands into politics.

Dilemmas of Changing Strategy: From Deterrence to Containment

Regardless of their preferred explanations for the rise in protest, all Chinese police analysts accept another of Huntington's implicit insights: that a key task of security forces in a developing country is to buy time for the regime by containing protests and keeping popular demands from overwhelming the state's governing capacity before it can undertake needed political reforms. In the years immediately after Tiananmen Square, Chinese police strategies for accomplishing this goal focused on trying to deter or quickly squelch demonstrations with overwhelming force. Yet, as police shift from a strategy of deterrence and quick suppression to a more permissive strategy of containment and management, they are facing trickier dilemmas than ever.

Security leaders understand that violent tactics may help if the key goal is to deter protestors. Increasingly, though, they are now conceding that moderate levels of protest are probably inevitable and that protestors enjoy considerable sympathy from the public (indeed, even the police). Once a protest has started, police risk further enraging protestors if they resort to crude, ham-fisted violence. As a result, the predominant concern of police strategists has recently shifted from how best to deter all protests to how to avoid misusing force and accidentally exacerbating popular ire.

The new goal of security forces today is to minimize popular anger through more moderate, professional policing of protests and to limit police use of violent coercive tactics to incidents of imminent mob violence, arson, looting, or attacks on key government buildings. This approach, of course, implicitly means police will allow many low-key illegal protests to continue while they try to maintain order at the scene. Police leaders increasingly discourage officers from plunging into crowds or making mass arrests and urge them instead to maintain containment, carefully gather intelligence, and wait until after crowds have dispersed before quietly detaining protest leaders. The police who handled the previously mentioned factory worker protests in Liaoyang skillfully deployed many of these tactics.[24] Some security analysts go even further, advocating that police act as go-betweens, brokering concessions by managers and government officials to protestors. Although such moderate containment tactics minimize the risk that any given protest will boil over into violence, they also risk encouraging other protests by sending average citizens the message that it is now far less risky and dangerous to take part in demonstrations.

Moreover, Beijing's directives to local police on handling protests are often vague or internally contradictory, with a lot of room for local interpretation—or local error. As a result, many police quite reasonably fear that this change in tactics will trap them in paralyzing, dangerous situations, caught between angry protestors and intransigent, local party bosses demanding that the police decisively restore order. Among the best examples of these vague, contradictory rules are the principles on police use of force, dubbed the "three cautions" and the "three fears." Police are instructed to use police power, weapons, and coercive measures cautiously, but Beijing also insists that using force cautiously does not mean not using it at all. Therefore, national authorities also instruct police to overcome their "three fears": fear that they will be held responsible for botched operations, fear that the masses will surround and attack them, and fear that after the fact the police will suffer either official punishment or popular revenge. Such principles provide little concrete guidance to local police trying to avoid punishment for being either too harsh or too soft. The history of Chinese communism is littered with disasters caused by local officials who tried vainly to balance such contradictory orders.

A favorite anti-protest tactic of many local government officials—buying off demonstrators with lump-sum payments of part of their back wages and pensions—creates enormous dilemmas for police. Some police endorse such payoffs and regard them as efforts by local officials to solve real problems for angry citizens who deserve the money anyway. These buy-offs, of course, also spare police from carrying out unpopular repressive actions. One police analyst indicates that some types of worker protests in Shanghai declined significantly after officials strengthened health care and pension guarantees. Other police officials reject such buy-offs as shortsighted, counterproductive, and even dangerous. Although buy-offs may help local officials prevent Beijing from finding out about an embarrassing local protest in their jurisdiction, the tactic creates a dangerous incentive structure and risks contagion to other areas by showing citizens that they too could win concessions by taking their complaints into the streets.

The Leadership's Responses

Unfortunately, despite the significant new issues addressed by these police debates on unrest, several important and intriguing questions remain unanswered. We do not know, for example, how widespread these more sophisticated views of unrest and the strategies for dealing with it are within the public security system, especially among top police leaders and working-level members of the police force. If sympathy for worker protestors

becomes strong and widely shared within the force, it could gravely undermine police morale and discipline in confronting protestors. There is, for example, strong evidence that police sympathy played a role in allowing the protests in Tiananmen Square to grow beyond control.[25] The analyses also raise questions about whether or not China's security services, notwithstanding their concern for social order, are really a unified bloc against political reform, as is often assumed in the West. As usual, the crucial unknowable remains: What advice are Beijing's security gurus privately giving top party leaders, and how might such thinking affect China's strategies for reform and domestic security?

Since becoming CCP general secretary in November 2002, Hu Jintao has not yet elaborated a clear strategy for reform and internal security. Does Hu share the hope of his predecessors that the CCP can ride out social unrest and avoid tough institutional reforms through some combination of sustained economic growth, buy-offs, and tougher but more professional police forces? Alternatively, will Hu insist on implementing significant political reforms that would offer would-be protestors better legal channels for voicing dissent? There is evidence to support both interpretations. Before his accession, Hu often publicly embraced the conservative dictum espoused by Deng and Jiang Zemin—"Stability overrides everything"—but he has also made occasional cryptic calls for "new thinking" in dealing with popular tensions.[26] During the Severe Acute Respiratory Syndrome (SARS) debacle, Hu shrewdly advocated more open flows of information and policy discussion. In September 2003, he also called for "active" but "stable" progress toward unspecified "judicial structural reforms," "village elections," and other legal and quasi-democratic reforms that could further open institutional channels for disgruntled citizens to voice their views.[27]

Yet, for the time being, instead of elaborating on any sort of comprehensive internal security strategy, Hu Jintao is sending disgruntled citizens the same dangerous mixed messages that his predecessors did: organizing protests is still an extremely risky undertaking, but protest itself is often rewarded with concessions. For example, in May 2003, several workers who had organized the

Liaoyang protests were sentenced to long prison terms. On the other hand, in response to protests in the winter of 2003 by several thousand students in Anhui, Hu reportedly ordered local officials to meet one of their demands by stiffly punishing a driver who had killed a fellow student.

Hu sits atop an ill-defined power structure that is hardly conducive to taking risks. Despite a promising start, he is still far from consolidating his leadership over a Politburo full of Jiang's former associates, and Jiang still lurks over his shoulder as head of the CCP's Central Military Commission. It is unclear how much power Jiang still wields and how far he might permit Hu to go toward revising the highly risk-averse strategy toward unrest that the CCP has embraced since the Tiananmen demonstrations. From Hu's perspective, however, this ambiguous hierarchy must still seem eerily reminiscent of the 1980s, when Deng twice stormed out of official retirement to remove successors whom he felt were too soft on student protestors. Hu could surely strengthen his public legitimacy by seizing on a few populist reform issues, as he did with his open information policy on SARS, but even Hu's very modest calls for institutional reform are fueling rumors that there are serious disagreements between Hu and the more hard-line Jiang. As in Tiananmen Square in 1989, such popular perceptions of leadership disagreement could dangerously embolden some protestors to think they have a closet ally in the Politburo. For the reflexively cautious Hu, even appearing to condone or back down before mass protests would be a very high-risk strategy.

Whether or not there are real disagreements among the leadership over handling unrest, their options may be narrowing. As these police debates demonstrate, security officials are recognizing that the old strategy of deterring and demonizing protest movements is failing. Low- to medium-intensity protest is an increasingly normal part of China's political bargaining game.[28] Many in the security forces are trying to respond to this change by forging a new safety-valve strategy of containment and management, which focuses on preventing large-scale organized opposition or violence and protecting the key cities and institutions that are essential to the regime's survival.

The erosion of repressive regimes during the 1980s and 1990s in Taiwan, Indonesia, the Philippines, South Africa, and especially South Korea suggests that such safety-valve containment strategies are neither static nor sustainable. When the regime can no longer prevent chronic, low-level demonstrations, social protest often ceases to be a safety valve that can protect the regime. Instead, protest escalates until the regime must either reassert its dominance through extreme repression or enter a prolonged renegotiation with society over more fundamental issues of power, policy, and institutional change. Ultimately, it seems likely that China's leaders will once again be forced to confront the wrenching choice of trying to re-teach the lessons of Tiananmen Square or entering into those negotiations with society. Although the police debates over institutional reform discussed above might suggest that some of Beijing's security experts have already made up their minds on that question, there is simply no way of knowing how they might respond at the height of a genuine, 1989-style social order crisis, especially if CCP leadership once again united behind a decision that claimed that violence is necessary to suppress another imaginary conspiracy.

Unrest and the Limits of the New Diplomacy

In sum, China's internal security officials are now recognizing with growing frankness the expansion of unrest in their society—not just the raw numbers of demonstrations but also their size, social scope, level of organizational sophistication, and occasionally their level of violence. Increasingly, police experts and officials are backing away from narrow Leninist interpretations and acknowledging that most protest reflects not anti-Communist conspiracies (the official claim regarding Tiananmen) but rather a largely legitimate popular reaction to genuine economic, social, and political problems in Chinese society. By acknowledging both the magnitude of unrest and many of its true causes, however, China's security leaders have set themselves a much greater challenge as they seek more sophisticated strategies to contain and manage protests they can no longer entirely prevent. They also force Beijing to acknowledge more openly that an enormous array of policy issues—both domestic and foreign—have implications for China's growing social order crisis. Because the implications of China's growing unrest cannot be limited to China, the United States and its allies would also benefit from rethinking the state of China's social unrest and particularly its widening influence on Sino-US relations. For example, as a number of Western analysts have correctly observed, in the past several years China has begun to engage in a new style of diplomacy marked by greater international activism, self-confidence, and engagement, especially with selected multilateral economic and security institutions.[29] At the same time, China's pervasive fear of unrest, like a systemic illness with few obvious symptoms, has quietly insinuated itself into almost every issue in China's major bilateral and multilateral relationships and, in many ways, will set the limits on how far China can go in its new diplomacy. Unlike their colleagues in China's internal security forces, Chinese diplomatic interlocutors have been loath to concede the growing latent impact of protest on Beijing's foreign relations, probably for fear of appearing to admit that their government's legitimacy may be increasingly challenged. Yet, as unrest continues to raise the risks of major reforms and concessions, relations with China are likely to become much trickier and the recent era of good feelings between China and the United States is likely to become much more complicated.

For example, the economic theory of unrest that currently dominates in Beijing, that social stability and regime survival hinge on the CCP's ability to deliver economic growth and to save jobs, imposes a negotiating asymmetry in trade relations between China and the United States. That is to say, many economic issues that Washington might consider mere horse trading, Beijing sees as intimately related to social stability or even regime survival. Beijing's concerns lend a deadly seriousness to its handling of such issues as liberalizing *renminbi* exchange rates or the pace of implementing World Trade Organization (WTO) agreements that could threaten to increase unemployment in China's highly protected state-owned enterprises, particularly in the increasingly unstable northeast. Rather than risk further loss of social control by implementing systemic reforms, China can be expected to offer quick fixes and face-saving gestures, such as the recent promise to purchase large numbers of US airplanes and other exports. Beginning in the late 1990s, even before WTO accession, China's Public Security

researchers began publishing hundreds of openly circulating forecasts of the industries and regions that would be hardest hit by WTO-related reforms in China as well as the likely consequences for internal security. From the standpoint of Western trade negotiators, the MPS's conclusions will constitute a virtual playbook of WTO implementation issues on which China is most likely to drag its feet. Western commercial officials would benefit from detailed analyses of these MPS studies.

Similarly, more than any other factor, fear of unemployment and domestic instability explains China's persistent unwillingness to confront the country's increasingly insolvent state banks and to open up the financial sector to foreign competition. To keep functioning, state enterprises that are operating at a loss rely on loans from state banks; as a result, perhaps 50 percent or more of these loans are now nonperforming loans. As Beijing negotiates further opening of its financial sector to foreign competition, the leadership knows that, by allowing its citizens more alternatives to keeping their savings in state banks, it risks depleting the pools of capital that underwrite both these loans and the jobs of millions of factory workers.

Fear of unrest also complicates China's full range of strategic as well as economic relations. The tremendous concentration of protests in Jilin, Liaoning, and other regions near the North Korean border ultimately means that Washington and Beijing will diverge in where they rank preferred outcomes as well as tactics in the six-party talks over North Korea's nuclear program. There is little love lost between Beijing and Pyongyang these days, and the United States and China clearly share a strong desire for negotiations leading to a nuclear-free North Korea. Whereas many US officials may prefer more coercive tactics and ultimately hope for regime change in North Korea, however, Beijing can only shudder at the prospect that a collapse of North Korea might unleash even greater swarms of refugees streaming into China's most restive region. Some of Beijing's senior military analysts have openly argued that, partly because of the fear of unrest in the northeast, China should explicitly rank peace and stability on the Korean peninsula ahead of denuclearization.[30] Such scenarios even complicate Beijing's willingness to use food and fuel as levers because China must weigh the value of exerting pressure on Pyongyang against the risk of hastening its collapse. The further the United States and China get into negotiations with North Korea, the more China's fear of unrest is likely to expose deep differences in Washington's and Beijing's respective preferences.

The nexus between the US war on terrorism and Beijing's struggle to repress ethno-religious dissent places Washington in an especially ticklish position. In one of the few remaining spheres in which the old conspiratorial theory of unrest clearly still predominates, Beijing's official analyses insist on treating terrorism, ethnic separatism, and extremism as a single phenomenon, refusing to concede that both violent and peaceful minority nationalists live within its borders. For the United States to gain Beijing's cooperation against real terrorism without turning a blind eye to ethnic repression, Washington must vastly improve the on-the-ground information it gathers about ethnic groups in western China and then not be afraid to draw clear distinctions for Chinese interlocutors.

Differing assumptions about social unrest also have a powerful impact on Western interpretations of Beijing's strategic buildup. One of the central debates among US analysts concerns whether a CCP regime that feels threatened internally is more likely to become more cautious while confronting international security threats or resort to a Chinese version of wagging the dog, engaging in bellicose external behavior to rally nationalist support. China's modern history does not reveal many cases of initiating such "diversionary wars" at times of internal strife. At the same time, increased Taiwanese moves toward independence probably present a special case, because Beijing's concern over unrest and its high dependence on nationalist appeals for legitimacy would almost certainly make it regard concessions to Taipei as very risky.

A second debate concerns the magnitude of the burden that social unrest imposes on China's national security system and the subsequent perception of the potential China threat. Amid all the attention paid to China's rapid increase in defense expenditures, few analysts have explicitly tried to estimate what might be called the "political instability deflator," that is, what percentage of the resources that China devotes to national security (broadly defined) support increasing internal security forces, buy off disgruntled workers, keep insolvent defense factories afloat, or simply ensure the military's loyalty.

As Beijing debates the dilemmas of handling social unrest and seeks new strategies focused on managing protests rather than deterring them, China's foreign partners must prepare as well. Both the demonstrations in Tiananmen Square and Beijing's violent reaction caught the West off guard. The United States and its allies need franker and fuller discussions about the range of potential crises that CCP leaders may encounter, the way Beijing might respond, and what might result, from renewed repression to reform to chronic low-level instability to state erosion. While recognizing their limited capacity to influence a regime that may see its very survival at stake, China's partners must also begin to think creatively about ways to encourage Beijing to see balanced institutional reform, rather than coercion and accusations of conspiracy, as its best response to social unrest should it flare out of control.

NOTES

1. Gordon Chang, *The Coming Collapse of China* (New York: Random House, 2001).
2. The nationwide data are from a report by the Ministry of Public Security's (MPS) Guards Bureau published in a larger June 2001 collection of national and local reports on "mass incidents." See MPS Fourth Research Institute, ed., *Quntixing Shijian Yanjiu Lunweiji* (Collected Research Essays on Mass Incidents) (Beijing: Chinese People's Public Security University Press, 2001) (hereinafter MPS Fourth Research Institute essays). Unless otherwise noted, all data and commentary in this article are from this volume.
3. Xiao Tangpiao, "Ershi yu lai Dalu Nongcun de Zhengzhi Wending Zhuangkuang," *Ershiyi Shiji* (Hong Kong), October 21, 2003. The fact that Xiao reports MPS mass-incident statistics for several other years in the 1990s that are the same as the MPS Fourth Research Institute figures greatly enhances the credibility of Xiao's claim that this is the Central Political-Legal Committee's official 2000 estimate.
4. Available at www.mps.gov.cn.
5. Li Wenxi, "Development Forges New Glory," Liaoning Public Security Bureau, November 2002.
6. Kevin O'Brien, "Rightful Resistance," *World Politics* 49, no. 1 (October 1996): 31–55. See Ching Kwan Lee, "Pathways of Labor Insurgency," in *Chinese Society: Change, Conflict, and Resistance*, eds. Elizabeth Perry and Mark Selden (London and New York: Routledge and Kegan Paul, 2000).

7. Fu Yongkun, "Jiji yufang, tuoshan chuzhi quntix-ing shijian, quanli weihu shehui wending" (Actively prevent and appropriately handle mass incidents, make full efforts to maintain social stability), 44–46; *Gong'an Yanjiu* (Policing Studies), no. 3 (2002): 12–13.

8. Fu, "Jiji yufang," pp. 44–46.

9. MPS Fourth Research Institute essays, pp. 94–95.

10. Ibid., p. 287.

11. See Lee, "Pathways of Labor Insurgency."

12. Ibid., p. 287.

13. *Gong'an Yanjiu,* no. 3 (2002): 12–13.

14. Zhao Jianxin and Sun Liwen, "Some Problems to Be Grasped in Handling Mass Incidents in Nationality and Religious Areas," MPS Fourth Research Institute essays, p. 318 (emphasis added).

15. Gu Linfang, "Drawing on the Turmoil and Riot to Examine Class Struggle in Socialism's Initial Stage," *Renmin Gong'an* (People's Public Security), October 5, 1989, pp. 3–9. This article is concluded in the maga-zine's subsequent issue.

16. Zhang Shengqian, *Shehui zhi'an shijian chuzhi* (Handling social order incidents) (Beijing: People's Public Security University Press, 2001), pp. 21–23.

17. See generally MPS Fourth Research Institute essays.

18. Zhang, *Shehui zhian shijian chuzhi,* pp. 32–34.

19. Zhang Min, *Shanghai Gong'an Gaoke Xueyuan Bao* (Shanghai Public Security Academy Journal) (April 2001): 33–35.

20. Zhu Rongji, "Report on the Work of the Government," speech, March 5, 2003 (transcript in Xinhua, March 19, 2003).

21. Zhou Guangyang, MPS Fourth Research Institute essays, pp. 14–17.

22. Zhang, *Shehui zhi'an shijian chuzhi,* pp. 24–36.

23. MPS Fourth Research Institute essays, p. 58.

24. Phillip P. Pan, "Three Chinese Workers: Jail, Betrayal and Fear," *Washington Post,* December 28, 2002, p. A1.

25. On police behavior in 1989, see Murray Scot Tanner, "The Institutional Lessons of Disaster: Reorganizing China's People's Armed Police After Tiananmen," in *The People's Liberation Army as Organization,* ed. James Mulvenon (Washington, DC: RAND Corp., 2002), pp. 587–635; "Chinese Bureaucratic and Leadership Battles over Public Security, 1989–1990: Dissecting an Organizational Disaster," paper presented to the Association for Asian Studies, March 1997. See also Andrew J. Nathan and Perry Link, eds., *The Tiananmen Papers* (New York: PublicAffairs, 2001) (police reports).

26. On Hu's statements, see Murray Scot Tanner, "Hu Jintao's Succession: Prospects and Challenges," in *China's Leadership in the 21st Century: The Rise of the Fourth Generation,* eds. David M. Finkelstein and Maryanne Kivlehan (Armonk, N.Y.: M.E. Sharpe, 2002), pp. 45–65.

27. "Hu Jintao Stresses Building 'Political Civilization' at Politburo Study Session," Global News Wire, September 30, 2003 (translation of Xinhua article).

28. For a superb study of local government manipulation of the threat of unrest, see William J. Hurst, "The Forgotten Player: Local State Strategies and the Dynamics of Chinese Laid-Off Workers Contention" (n.d.).

29. Two of the best analyses of this trend are found in Evan S. Medeiros and M. Taylor Fravel, "China's New Diplomacy," *Foreign Affairs* 82, no. 6 (November/December 2003): 22–35; David Shambaugh, "Commentary: China's New Engagement with the Region," *Asian Wall Street Journal,* February 19, 2004.

30. Xu Weidi, "Resolving the Korean Peninsula Nuclear Crisis and Moving the Korean Peninsula Out of the Cold War," *Shijie Jingji yu Zhengzhi* (World Economics and Politics), September 14, 2003, pp. 59–64.

CHINA'S SECURITY STATE: THE TRUNCHEON BUDGET*

The Economist

Among the misleading and ill-explained details that, as usual, spiced up China's annual budget, unveiled on March 5, were some especially eye-catching numbers for security. The surprise was not just that China's military budget had resumed double-digit growth after a one-year hiatus, but that spending on internal security was higher and growing even faster. The state sees an abundance of threats within.

The risk that turmoil in the Middle East will spread to China is one of them, though the

premier, Wen Jiabao, studiously avoided men-tioning events there in his two-hour address to the country's legislature, the National People's Congress (NPC). Mr. Wen did, however, speak of the need to "solve problems that cause great resentment among the masses," such as the illegal demolition of housing and the forced appropria-tion of farmland.

The NPC session, an annual rubber-stamp affair lasting a few days, was full of measures intended as crowd-pleasers. Central-government spending on education, health care, and social security is to increase by more than 16%, and on

---

* This article was published in *The Economist,* March 12, 2011.

subsidized housing by more than a third. Two days before the session began Chinese media published a surprising survey indicating that only 6% of citizens felt happy. More welfare spending, perhaps, is to keep unhappy people off the streets.

Officials are less eager to draw attention to their preferred option for keeping the peace, namely beefing up security. The budget presented to the NPC calls for spending of 624 billion yuan ($95 billion) this year on items related to law and order, 13.8% more than in 2010. Military spending is to increase by 12.7%, to 601.1 billion yuan. This follows an unexpected easing of its growth last year to 7.5%. But for a second consecutive year it will be less than the outlay on internal security.

The authorities' horrified response to anonymous calls on the Internet for a "jasmine revolution" in China will add to the cost of policing. For three Sundays in a row central areas of several Chinese cities have been saturated with uniformed and plainclothes officers. They have staked out shopping streets where the Internet messages have urged protesters to "stroll" (a euphemism often used in China for demonstrating, which the police hardly ever permit). The messages have said these protests, which have yet to materialize, should continue every Sunday indefinitely. The police clearly worry that if they scale back their deployments people will converge at the appointed places.

A day after the latest such security operation, the foreign minister, Yang Jiechi, blandly told journalists that he had noticed no kind of tension in China. He also denied that police had beaten foreign journalists trying to report in the designated areas, even though one had been kicked and hit by goons and others roughed up less severely in full view of uniformed officers. The authorities have decided to rescind—at least partially—their 2007 decision to give foreign correspondents freer rein. Now correspondents "must apply for approval" to conduct interviews in Beijing.

Antagonism towards the foreign press, and a sweeping round-up of Chinese dissidents, could also signal concerns about tension within the leadership as it prepares to hand over power to a younger generation next year. Power struggles in China have a habit of going hand-in-hand with street protests (the Tiananmen Square unrest in 1989 broke out amid fierce confrontation at the top). On March 5th–6th the state media, which had kept silent about the "strolls," published editorials stridently denouncing them. The *Beijing Daily* called for "constant vigilance against these people with ulterior motives" who wanted to "throw China into turmoil" (echoes of hardline language at the time of Tiananmen).

A rare criticism of the government's approach appeared this week on the website of the state-run news agency, Xinhua, in an article by a scholar in Singapore. China, it said, would enhance its stability far more if it were to turn its "colossal expenses on stability maintenance" to improving people's livelihoods instead. The leadership is beefing up spending on both, but seems not to know which one will work better.

IV. GLOBAL SECURITY

China's Roles in Global Security[*]

David Shambaugh

* This selection was originally published in David Shambaugh (ed.), *Charting China's Future: Domestic and International Challenges* (New York: Routledge, 2011), 95–104.

How will China's global security role evolve over the next few years, and what will be the major factors affecting its international security role? To address this question requires, first, an understanding of China's conceptualization of its general global role(s) and international expectations of it. Second, it requires an understanding of China's existing international security presence and trends in recent years. This analysis will proceed to address these two variables in turn, and then will conclude with a summary of future prospects.

Will China Be a "Responsible Global Power?"

China's capacity to contribute to meeting global security challenges is inextricably linked with its own conceptualization of its growing global role as well as the world's growing expectations of it. In other words, security is simply a subset of the broader question of China's contributions to global governance more generally. In fact, the security sphere is one of the most challenging areas for China—simply because its *capabilities* are more limited than in other areas. China possesses greater capacities to contribute to global financial and economic stability and growth; to development assistance in developing countries; to global climate change through its own industrial and consumer growth; to global public health through its domestic as well as international actions; to global innovation and technological development through its indigenous innovation; and to global energy consumption through its own appetite for natural resources and investments in new energy technologies. In all these areas, China's capacities to influence global patterns and global governance are greater than in the security sphere. Yet, in *all* of these areas, the degree and intensity of China's global involvement and contributions will be heavily influenced by a combination of external expectations and internal debates.

One thing is certain: the international community—particularly the developed countries in North America and Europe—will expect a continually growing Chinese contribution to international challenges and global governance commensurate with China's new power, size, and growing global footprint. In recent years, successive American administrations have called on China to be a "responsible international stakeholder," while the European Union has repeatedly called on China to be a "responsible power" and increase its multilateralism and contributions to global governance. But, just as these governments will expect more from China, two other things are equally certain.

First, there will remain substantial unease in some of these countries—particularly the United States and in Asia—about China's growing global role, and particularly its military profile. Nascent angst over an emerging China "threat" will continue to exist, and will likely grow proportionately to China's increased military capabilities and global power-projection capabilities. There already exists considerable unease in the West about China's rapidly growing global economic presence and, most notably, its voracious appetite for energy and raw materials. Once a larger military/security footprint is married to an already robust economic/energy footprint, the cacophony of anti-China voices in Washington and elsewhere will only rise. China's new diplomatic assertiveness and increased combativeness on the world stage in 2009–10 stunned many observers and may presage increased tensions over the next few years.

While the developed world wants China to be a constructive global partner, it has recently been met with truculence and hubris by Beijing. Observers wonder: is this a cyclical trend or a secular trend? How long will it last? Will Beijing return to a softer and more cooperative posture—or will it continue to harden its positions, bully its neighbors, and prove increasingly difficult to work with? China can, of course, help its own image and case for global multilateral security cooperation by reverting to a more cooperative posture, continually enhancing its military transparency, acting in non-provocative ways towards its neighbors (including Taiwan), and by continually expanding participation in multilateral and bilateral peace-keeping activities and security forums. China has, in fact, become quite active in addressing "non-traditional" security threats in recent years, and is making a positive contribution in several areas. To its credit, China *has* become involved in recent years in disaster-relief operations (the 2004 Southeast Asian *tsunami,* the 2005 Pakistani earthquake, the 2007 Philippines typhoon, and 2010 Haitian and Chilean earthquakes): it has joined an expanding number of UN peacekeeping operations (see below); it is involved in fighting organized crime, drug smuggling, and terrorism; and it has been active in controlling the spread of pandemic diseases. Thus, China's global security involvement has grown in some (non-traditional) areas, but remains quite limited in other missions (like Afghanistan).

This raises the second certainty—namely that China itself is conflicted about its international role and contributions to global governance generally, and international security cooperation specifically. There exists a profound ambivalence within the Chinese government, society, and expert community concerning the wisdom of external entanglements and contributing to global governance. Robust subterranean debates rage in Beijing over several aspects of China's international involvement. At one end of the spectrum are "nativist isolationists" who seek total international autonomy and view international multilateral obligations as "traps" laid by the West to embroil China in costly commitments overseas. At the other end of the spectrum are those "global multilateralists" who both view the international system through an interdependent lens and believe that China must shoulder an ever-greater responsibility for addressing a wide range of global governance issues commensurate with its size, power, and influence. Between these two ends of the spectrum lie several intermediate positions. One predominant group are the "hard realists," who argue that China should only become involved in issues that *directly* affect it, and its priorities should concentrate on "core" issues like Taiwan, Tibet, economic growth, and social and political stability at home. Another group, the "selective multilateralists," believe that China should expand its global involvements gradually, but only on issues where China has a direct national (security) interest—particularly on China's immediate periphery in Asia. There are several variations and splinter factions of this group: one argues China should only engage in UN-mandated activities, while another believes it should not thus hold back from getting involved in multinational (as distinct from multilateral) actions together with other major powers.[1]

Thus, when considering the potential for China's involvement in the international security arena, the above-mentioned factors will all influence, constrain, and embolden China's choices and involvements. Most likely, the world will witness exactly what it has been witnessing over the past five years: a China that is progressively more involved in global security at a diplomatic level and on low-cost non-traditional security issues, but a China that remains internally deeply conflicted about the wisdom of deeper involvement in global governance. Thus we can expect a China that emphasizes protecting its own (narrow) national interests before making a greater contribution to broader international cooperation (especially when it involves the use of force and intervention), and a China that continues to emphasize domestic strengthening over international commitments.

China's Global Security Footprint

When considering China's global security presence to date, there are several dimensions to consider. The first is China's rapidly growing military capabilities. This dimension is clearly the one with the most direct impact abroad.

Military Modernization For the past twenty years, since 1989, China has pursued a steady and sustained comprehensive military modernization process. It has been strategic in conceptualization, with a clear sense of purpose and capabilities to be attained. Military modernization is seen as one element of comprehensive modernization of the Chinese state and nation. While priority has been devoted to broader economic and technological modernization since 1978, the People's Liberation Army has been garnering a greater share of resources over the past two decades. The 1995–96 Taiwan Strait crises further focused the PLA's attention on acquiring a wide spectrum of capabilities needed to fight and win a war over Taiwan if necessary. The military modernization program has been extremely well resourced, with annual budget allocations increasing on average 15 percent per year and now totaling $91.7 billion. In addition to this official budgetary figure, the PLA now probably benefits from an additional $20 billion in funds buried in other central, provincial, and local state budgets—bringing its entire expenditure for 2011 to somewhere around $110 billion.

Over the past twenty years every dimension of China's military capabilities has been significantly upgraded. This includes, importantly, not only weaponry, but also "software": the professionalization of personnel, logistics, mobility, training, computerization, communications, surveillance, and intelligence. China's electronic, space, and cyber capabilities have made particularly notable progress. Its weapons systems and "hardware"—from tanks to ballistic missiles, aircraft to ships—have all enjoyed significant upgrading. Many of these new weapons systems were on impressive display in Tiananmen Square on October 1, 2009, to commemorate the sixtieth anniversary of the People's Republic of China. Since then, important new weapons systems have been tested—such as the new stealthy J-20 fighter/bomber. It is also quite likely that in 2011 China will finally put to sea (at least in sea trials) its first aircraft carrier, the refitted *Varyag* (purchased from Ukraine).

Qualitative advances have been made throughout the armed forces, new weapons systems have been deployed, important new ones are under development, the training regime has intensified, the fighting capacity of all services has been increased, and the command, control, and "jointness" of PLA forces (the ability to operate ground, air, naval and electronic forces in conjunction) have been improved. PLA forces are now undertaking certain types of exercises and are displaying certain capabilities that many foreign analysts and intelligence agencies did not think were likely just a few years ago.

The relatively rapid and comprehensive modernization of China's military is affecting the balance of power in the Asia–Pacific region. With the exception of the United States, China now has the region's largest navy and air force, by far the largest ballistic missile arsenal, the largest standing army, and the most sophisticated space-based communication and reconnaissance system. The PLA's area of operation (AOR) is expanding further and further into the western Pacific, South China Sea, and Indian Ocean. Although China's military actions have not been aggressive to date, the sheer size and improved quality of its forces are changing calculations in governments and strategic-studies communities through Asia.

Despite this impressive progress, China's global military footprint remains limited. Other

than cyber warfare and intercontinental ballistic missiles, it has no true global power-projection capabilities. While the PLA Navy (PLAN) is beginning to operate further and further from continental China, the scope and duration of these operations and the numbers of deployed vessels remain very limited, and deployment has gone no further than the Gulf of Aden (although one ship did pass through the Suez Canal to assist in the evacuation of Chinese and foreign nationals from Libya in February 2011). The PLA actually evinces little evidence of attempting to acquire a power-projection capability beyond its periphery in the western Pacific. It has no bases abroad (although it is beginning to acquire refueling rights for ships). It has no deployed aircraft carriers (although apparently one or two are being built). It has no truly intercontinental bombers and possesses only a very small fleet of in-flight refueling tankers and airborne command-and-control aircraft. It has a small number of truly blue-water-capable naval surface combatants. And it has no global network of command-and-control or other elements that one would expect to see from a nation seriously trying to develop a global power-projection capability or to become a global military power. Even a close reading of Chinese military doctrinal manuals gives little, if any, evidence that power projection beyond China's immediate periphery is a priority.

Thus, China's global military footprint remains limited—and can be expected to remain so over the next five years. While presently the PLA does not seem to be developing globally deployable forces, China's growing international economic presence and energy needs may dictate that it begins to develop such capabilities. As Peter Ferdinand's chapter in this volume illustrates, China's global commercial footprint grows by the day—and, along with it, Chinese nationals may come to be at risk. Kidnappings of Chinese workers in Africa have already occurred and the 2011 political unrest in North Africa resulted in large-scale evacuations. The Chinese government and military are thus contemplating the further development of marine and special-operations forces and are beginning to develop the naval assets necessary to deploy them.

While its global military capacities remain relatively limited, the PLA's regional military posture is becoming more and more robust and will continue to impact the balance of power in Asia. The PLAN is increasingly operating throughout the western Pacific, is exercising on its own and in tandem with some regional navies, and China has become more assertive in pressing its territorial claims in the East and South China Seas.[2] Its air forces are also increasingly operating over water. China's "defense perimeter" is ever-expanding—much to the consternation of some of its neighbors and the United States.

Peacekeeping Operations Another dimension of China's global security presence is in UN peacekeeping operations (UNPKO). In recent years China has increasingly contributed military, paramilitary, police, medical and other assistance personnel to UNPKO.[3] The origins of China's PKO involvement date to the 1989–92 period, when it first dispatched military observers to Namibia and the Middle East, and a military engineering corps to Cambodia. Since that time China's contributions of personnel (but not budget, where it is the seventh-largest assessed financial contributor) to UNPKO operations has grown dramatically and positively. By late 2009 China had 2,155 peacekeepers serving on the ground in eleven of the UN's nineteen PKO missions worldwide. These deployments are primarily in Africa, although in the past they have included the Middle East, Southeast Asia, Central and Latin America. This ranks China as the fourteenth-largest national contributor of personnel (out of 119 contributing countries), but first among permanent members of the UN Security Council. Over time, since 1990, China has contributed more than 12,000 personnel to UNPKO missions. These have been mainly in the form of logistical, engineering, transport, or medical personnel—although China has also contributed military combat forces, paramilitary People's Armed Police, military observers, civilian police, and land mine clearing personnel.

China has received very high marks and positive evaluations for the quality and integrity of its personnel and contributions to UN peacekeeping operations (although their general inability to speak languages other than Chinese is seen as a detriment). They are increasingly involved in mission leadership and decision-making. China has also contributed to the delivery (mainly by sea) of equipment and personnel of other contributing nations' PKO forces. This has improved other countries' capacity to take part in peacekeeping—a not insignificant factor when considering that, with the exception of India, none of the top ten contributors to UNPKO operations has a blue-water navy or long-range transport capabilities. China has thus enabled a number of Asian and African countries to contribute to such missions.

Beginning in 2009, China has made a visible contribution to anti-piracy operations off Somalia in the Gulf of Aden by contributing several naval vessels to a multinational flotilla patrolling the area. The PLAN has undertaken a number of rotations and deployments as part of the multinational anti-piracy force. In July 2010 the PLAN's largest vessel was dispatched to the Gulf of Aden—the 17,000-ton *Kunlun Shan* (Mount Kunlun)—which, for the first time ever, carried a platoon of PLA marines. The *Kunlun Shan* also carries two Z-8 helicopters and small landing craft—thus demonstrating, for the first time, China's capacity to deploy its own forces so far from home. The marines engaged three separate groups of pirates, repelling potential attacks.

All in all, China's contributions to UNPKO have been a definite "net plus" for the UN, for China and for the recipient countries. It is a tangible—perhaps *the* most tangible—indication of China's contribution to global governance. China's overseas development assistance (ODA) is also a significant contribution. As noted above, since the 2004 Asian *tsunami,* China has also begun to contribute personnel and resources to disaster relief in Asia and other parts of the world (even as far away as Latin America).

Joint Exercises Finally, China has begun to increase its joint bilateral and multilateral military exercises in recent years. These have been primarily of the nature of naval search-and-rescue and ground-based counter-terrorism operations, although some maritime exercises are for patrolling and surveillance. In 2010 the PLAN began, for the first time, to undertake live-fire exercises at sea (including an unprecedented large-scale exercise in the South China Sea in July 2010). China and Russia also held two large-scale ground and air exercises in 2006–7.

Military Exchanges and Assistance China is also stepping up its military diplomacy, strategic, dialogues, training programs and arms sales. Today China maintains "strategic dialogues" with eighteen countries.[4] These usually, but not always, include PLA personnel. Their content varies by partner country, but generally comprises surveys of regional and global security and foreign-policy trends. In terms of bilateral military-to-military exchanges, China's biannual defense White Papers show that the PLA sent out official delegations to visit sixty countries every year from 2001 to 2007 (then it dipped to forty in 2007–8) while receiving foreign military delegations from 60 to 90 countries per year. Many of these visits are fairly routine—for consultations, visiting military academies, occasionally observing an exercise, and exchanging views on regional and global strategic issues.

The PLA has also been stepping up both the number of officers it sends to study in foreign institutions and those hosted in Chinese military academies. From 2006 to 2008, the PLA dispatched over 900 military students abroad, while training about 4,000 military personnel in China.[5] Some of the latter take part in the international officers' course run twice a year by the PLA National Defense University in Beijing, but several hundred also study in 68 service academies around the country (the PLA Air Force Command College is particularly active). The PLA maintains military educational exchange agreements with over twenty countries. A number of lower-level exchanges also take place in the areas of military medicine and hygiene, defense science and technology, arts and sports. A final form of military diplomacy is port calls and ship visits. In 2010, for example, China dispatched its 10,000-ton *Peace Ark* hospital ship on an 87-day mission to West Africa. As the PLA Navy's blue-water capability

expands, these exchanges can all be expected to increase.

Some military personnel exchanges accompany China's arms sales abroad. Beijing is not a major seller of weapons, ranking No. 9 internationally according to the Stockholm International Peace Research Institute (SIPRI), selling approximately $824 million worth of weapons and equipment in 2008.[6] For the most part, China no longer engages in the export of large platforms of conventional weapons, and it has curtailed assistance to missile and nuclear weapons programs, so as to comply with its obligations under the Non-Proliferation Treaty and its *de facto* adherence to the Missile Technology Control Regime (MTCR). Most of its exports are light weapons and mortars, ammunition, trucks and transport equipment, radar, ship-to-ship and surface-to-air missiles. On occasion China sells armored personnel carriers and light tanks, and it is trying to market the export version of its J-10 fighter and light training aircraft. Chinese arms are relatively cheap, so they appeal to developing countries in Africa and South Asia. Pakistan remains China's largest arms client, followed by Iran, Sri Lanka, Namibia, Bangladesh, Egypt, Cambodia, and Venezuela.

Harder to track, but of growing importance, is China's military-industrial and dual-use-technology assistance to these countries—which helps recipients to modernize their own indigenous defense industrial capacities. We can expect this modest assistance to expand in the next few years, as China looks for more export markets while its generally low cost appeals to developing countries.

Non-Proliferation and Arms Control China used to be a serial proliferator of nuclear-weapons-related technologies and missile delivery systems. However, over the past decade China has come into full compliance with the relevant international treaties and regimes.[7] Now Beijing stands firmly opposed to the enlargement of the international nuclear weapons club. To this end, it has served a vital role in convening the Six-Party Talks on North Korea's nuclear program, opposed the exception made for India within the Non-Proliferation Treaty regime, and has worked with the UN Security Council to curtail Iran's nascent nuclear weapons program. But Beijing has also been particularly allergic to toughening and enforcing sanctions against Tehran, given its large commercial, energy and military interests there. With respect to both North Korea and Iran, we can expect to see a China that is not as cooperative as the other stakeholder nations would like, but nonetheless will remain engaged.

With respect to nuclear arms control, China has been involved in the UN Conference on Disarmament in Geneva for many years, calling in particular for a ban on all nuclear weapons, a Fissile Material Cut-Off Treaty (FMCT), as well as the non-militarization of outer space. But, other than this, Beijing has not entered into nuclear arms-control reductions bilaterally or multilaterally. It has long argued that the two major nuclear-weapons states—the US and Russia—must bring their arsenals down to China's level before Beijing will consider joining such discussions. If Washington and Moscow can indeed agree to a new strategic arms treaty that (perhaps in two phases) brings their warheads down to 1,000 or less on each side, then pressure will mount for China to enter into multilateral (with France and Britain) and multinational negotiations. At present, China is thought to have approximately 500 nuclear warheads (only a small portion of which, perhaps one-tenth, are deployed on long-range intercontinental or submarine-launched ballistic missiles).

China's nuclear arsenal has long been based on a doctrine of minimum deterrence and second-strike capability, and Beijing publicly adheres to a No First Use (NFU) policy.[8] Thus it possesses a relatively small *deployed* nuclear arsenal: approximately 30–40 intercontinental ballistic missiles (ICBM). What is not known is how many of these missiles are now fitted with multiple warheads. Over the past decade the PLA's Second Artillery (which controls the nuclear force) has been engaged in an assertive modernization program for these missiles—arming them with multiple warheads of increasing accuracy and moving from liquid- to solid-fuelled rockets (in order to improve its reaction time). Another leg of China's small nuclear deterrent has been

its two *Han*-class nuclear submarines (each of which carries about a dozen missiles). These two boats will soon be phased out as several new *Yuan*-class (095 and 096) nuclear-powered and nuclear-armed submarines join the fleet in the next few years. Each carries 18–20 intercontinental nuclear-tipped missiles. Thus, when these new subs go to sea, China's intercontinental nuclear strike *launch* capability will roughly double to approximately sixty missiles—but its *strike* capability could increase to a total of 150–180 depending on how many missiles are fitted with multiple warheads.

China's Future Global Security Role

China's future global security footprint will likely be a combined function of the political considerations outlined in the first section above, as well as the growing capabilities and lessons drawn from its experiences to date outlined in the second section.

As China grows more and more comfortable with its involvement in UNPKO operations, this involvement in particular is likely to expand. China will likely move into the top ten or five PKO-providing states during the period 2010–15, and it is well in the realm of possibility that China could contribute 7,000–12,000 personnel per annum within a few years (if the international demand exists). China clearly recognizes the positive international political capital it accrues from such contributions, and it is a good way to deflect Western pressures in other areas of global governance. Although its 2,100-plus deployed peacekeepers have been a tangible investment in Beijing's contributions to global governance and public goods, China still ranks No. 14 internationally in such deployments. Much smaller nations contribute considerably more personnel than China. Nonetheless, Beijing gains a lot from such involvement— with the United Nations, with the US and EU, and with the recipient countries. As the Chinese like to say, it's "win-win."

Increased Chinese contributions to disaster relief, poverty alleviation, public health and a broad range of other "non-traditional" security challenges/threats will also gain Beijing international prestige, while making tangible contributions. After all, the international security agenda is increasingly of a "non-traditional" nature, and China is increasingly comfortable with this agenda. Even the People's Liberation Army now frequently discusses "military operations other than war" (MOOTW)—code words for the non-traditional security agenda. China already is quietly contributing to intelligence-sharing and in the area of counter-terrorism; monitoring financial institutions for money laundering; strengthening controls against human and drug trafficking; and cracking down on organized international crime networks. In the latter areas, China is an increasingly active member of INTERPOL. This whole area of "non-traditional security" will not only continue to grow in importance on the international security agenda—but China's contributions in these areas can also be expected to improve and increase.

China's military exchanges will probably follow the numerical pattern and formats of recent years, but it will become increasingly involved in bilateral and multilateral exercises. Its arms sales will remain negligible as compared with major suppliers, but Beijing will continue to find niche markets in the developing world and will likely increase its sales to $1.0–1.5 billion per year.

We can also expect to continue to witness continued and deepened modernization of China's military forces and capabilities. Over the period 2010–15, it is quite conceivable that China will advance to possessing the second most comprehensively capable military in the world after the United States (it already is the second largest in terms of defense spending). While it will remain *far* behind the capabilities of the United States military, the PLA is likely to pull ahead of Russia, the UK, Japan, Germany, and France—all roughly clustered together in terms of military spending and capabilities. In some areas, China's capacities have already pulled ahead—but over the next five years it will comprehensively do so (unless Russia undertakes a large-scale modernization program). Its nuclear weapons arsenal, in particular, will increase in number and improve in quality.

All in all, I would expect to see a continuation but *acceleration* of the trends evident over the past five years. China will steadily increase its contributions to global security—largely within a multilateral context with regard to United Nations PKO operations, anti-piracy operations, and INTERPOL cooperation, but also in the area of non-traditional security. It would also be nice if China would see the way to contribute tangibly, on the ground, in crisis countries like Afghanistan—where it has large vested national security interests and *could* be doing a lot in the areas of police training, infrastructure building, public health and education development (China is presently not one of the 48 nations with deployed military personnel as part of the International Security Assistance Force, or ISAF, in Afghanistan). But such involvement requires a different mindset in Beijing.

In the end, however, all of China's involvement in global security will be shaped by its own calculations of its national interests (no matter what the inducements and pressure from the international community). Here, Beijing's continuing ambivalence over international involvements and its preoccupation with domestic development and protecting its irredentist interests (e.g., Taiwan, Tibet, maritime claims) will continue to have a limiting effect on China's global security role.

NOTES

1. For a fuller elaboration of this spectrum of views see David Shambaugh, "Coping with a Conflicted China," *The Washington Quarterly*, Vol. 34, No. 1 (Winter 2011).
2. See "China's Three-Point Naval Strategy," IISS *Strategic Comments*, Vol. 16, No. 37 (October 2010).
3. Two excellent recent studies of China's PKO involvement are: Bates Gill and Chin-Hao Huang, *China's Expanding Role in Peacekeeping: Prospects and Policy Implications* (Stockholm: SIPRI Policy Paper No. 25, 2009); International Crisis Group, *China's Growing Role in UN Peacekeeping* (Beijing, Brussels, New York: Asia Report No. 166, 2009). Much of the data cited above is drawn from these two reports.

4. Interview at China's Ministry of Foreign Affairs, March 24, 2010.

5. State Council Information Office, *China's National Defense in 2008* (Beijing: State Council Information Office, 2009), p. 74.

6. SIPRI Arms Transfer Database. See http://www.sipri.otg/contents/armstrad/output_types_ TIV.html.

7. For the best study of China's evolution, see Evan S. Medeiros, *Reluctant Restraint: The Evolution of China's Nonproliferation Policies and Practices, 1980–2004* (Stanford, CA: Stanford University Press, 2007).

8. For an excellent study of the evolution of China's nuclear doctrine and weapons capabilities, see M. Taylor Fravel and Evan S. Medeiros, "China's Search for Assured Retaliation: The Evolution of Chinese Nuclear Strategy and Force Structure," *International Security*, Vol. 35, No. 2 (Fall 2010), pp. 48–87.

FOREIGN RELATIONS

Editorial Introduction

As China has risen it has also become more deeply involved in world affairs. While Deng Xiaoping's post-1978 "reform and opening" (改革与开放) policies were intended to bring the world *into China* (引进来) through investment, trade, tourism, and a wide range of exchanges, the policies of Jiang Zemin and his successors have been intended for China to *go out* (走出去) into the world. As a result, since the 1990s China has "gone global" to an unprecedented degree.[1]

China has now established a presence on every continent (including Antarctica and in outer space) and in virtually every functional domain in international affairs. After spending its first three decades cut off from the international community of nations, China is now fully embedded in the multilateral institutional architecture and enjoys bilateral diplomatic relations with all but 21 nations (which still maintain ties to Taiwan). Its relationships with the major powers are balanced by a continuing emphasis on its fraternal ties with developing countries. As China has become more of a status-quo actor it has abandoned its former revolutionary ideology and support for "national liberation" movements in favor of solidifying ties with governments around the world.

China's ideology today is simply development—China's own development—and many countries can contribute to that goal. Among other things this means that China scours the globe in search of energy supplies and raw materials that can (quite literally) fuel its economic development. But China is increasingly exporting to, and investing in, countries all around the world (trade with developing countries is now growing rapidly). China's diplomacy is also extremely active on a global basis—in 2014, for example, President Xi Jinping and Premier Li Keqiang visited fifty countries on five continents while receiving a steady stream of visiting heads-of-state and other officials in Beijing.

This section explores different dimensions of China's foreign relations. It begins with two selections on how China views the world. It is vitally important to understand the *perceptions* within China in order to understand and anticipate Beijing's external behavior.

The first is by China's leading scholar on international relations, Professor Wang Jisi of Peking University. Professor Wang explores the question of whether China has a "Grand Strategy" that guides its interactions with the outside world. After noting that China's past experiences continue to shape its current perspectives—such as hypersensitivity to encroachments on China's borders and the belief that domestic unrest will be manipulated by hostile outsiders—he describes how in 2009 China's leader Hu Jintao defined three core features of China's grand strategy: sovereignty, security, and development. Wang also describes how, around this time, Chinese strategists began to debate the continuing efficacy of Deng Xiaoping's 1989 admonition that China should "bide its time and hide its brightness" (韬光养晦)—a euphemism for laying low and not taking risks in world affairs while building China's strength. Some Chinese strategists argued that this guidance was outdated and China should start to become more active in world affairs. Indeed, 2010 became known as China's "year of assertiveness"—a period when Beijing managed to simultaneously irritate virtually all of its neighbors as well as the United States and European Union. China's nationalistic hubris was on display, and the global financial crisis that year further contributed to the Chinese sense that tectonic plates of geoeconomics were tipping from the West to China. Wang concludes by suggesting "four transformations" that are shaping China's evolving grand strategy—in the realms of security, diplomacy, economic development, and values—and he offers some astute observations about the subtle yet important changes underway in China's approach to the world.

The second selection in this section is my own assessment of the spectrum of opinion in China's foreign policy community concerning the nation's role in the world. I happened to be living in China on an academic sabbatical during 2009–2010, when the "strategic debate" that Wang Jisi mentions occurred. But in discussions with Chinese officials and scholars during that year I discovered that the debate ran far deeper than whether China should continue to lay low (following Deng's admonition) or be more active in international affairs—I discovered that there actually existed a broad spectrum of opinion. This ranged from those I label the "Nativists" who advocated that China essentially withdraw from the world, to the "Globalists" who argued that China should become deeply involved in global governance. In between I further identified five other distinct strains of thought: Realists; Major Powers; Asia First; Global South; and Selective Multilateralism. The fact that such an animated and contested debate occurred within China's international relations community is itself an interesting indication of both the diversity in China's foreign relations and within Chinese society. China has, I argue, a profound "identity crisis" in its international persona. This diverse discourse may help to explain the apparent contradictions and different emphases in China's foreign relations in recent years.

The next section focuses on China's relations with its Asian neighbors. It offers three perspectives.

The first selection by Phillip Saunders, a leading expert from the US National Defense University, offers a thorough examination of China's "sweet and sour" relations within the region since the 2009–2010 "year of assertiveness" and post-2011 efforts by Beijing to reassure its neighbors. He also discusses four instruments of power in China's toolbox that it uses vis-à-vis its neighbors: economic, diplomatic, military, and cultural. Saunders concludes by identifying a series of factors that will shape the evolution and interaction of China's relations with its neighbors in the years to come.

The second selection is a Chinese perspective on China's relations with the Association of Southeast Asian Nations (ASEAN). Written by China's former ambassador to Thailand, Zhang Jiuhuan, on the 20th anniversary of China becoming a formal "dialogue partner" of ASEAN (China established formal diplomatic relations with the ten members of ASEAN in different years). Zhang is upbeat about China–ASEAN ties. He notes the dramatic increase in commercial relations, with two-way trade now topping $300 billion. This surging trade has been facilitated, in no small part, by the 2010 China–ASEAN Free Trade Area (FTA) agreement. China and ASEAN have also signed a swath of other agreements over the years, including a Strategic Partnership agreement and China's accession to ASEAN's Treaty of Amity and Cooperation in 2003. Ambassador Zhang also details the many other elements of China's deep and extensive interactions with Southeast Asia. He also notes, however, that the history of the People's Republic of China's interactions with Southeast Asia have not always been so positive—he candidly admits that regional governments feared China was trying to usurp them while China was in its Cultural Revolution phase during the 1960s. While a certain lingering residue of this period remains in the minds of Southeast Asians, Zhang's article is testimony to the dramatic transformation and development in China's ties with the region over the past two decades.

The next selection similarly elucidates China's burgeoning ties with Central Asia. Written by the French China specialist Valérie Niquet, the article describes how China has cultivated relations with the newly independent states of Central Asia following the collapse of the Soviet Union in 1991. Written before Xi Jinping and China unveiled its "One Road, One Belt" initiative in 2012, Niquet nonetheless traces the considerable development in cross-border trade and other interactions between China and its northwestern neighbors in recent years. She also describes the political sensitivity in the region, owing to Uighur separatism and their ethnic ties across the border. This has resulted in several uprisings and loss of life. It has also resulted in a security dragnet by the Chinese People's Armed Police and security services in Xinjiang. She also describes the burgeoning energy and infrastructure linkages between China's northwest and its adjacent neighbors.

The next sub-section considers China's relations with the United States. It is no understatement, as government officials in both countries frequently note, that the US–China relationship is the most important bilateral relationship in the world. These are the world's two most important powers by many measures.

The first selection by leading American China specialist Kenneth Lieberthal of the Brookings Institution looks at the increasingly global nature of the Sino-American relationship. It has always been both a bilateral and regional (Asia) relationship, but as China has gone global so too has the US–China relationship become globalized. Writing in 2009, Lieberthal found grounds for growing concern. He notes that deep distrust exists in both capitals. This pervasive and deepening distrust is not only a psychological condition, but has practical effects on a series of pressing issues on the agenda between the two sides. He notes North Korea, Taiwan, military relations, the regional Asian multilateral architecture, and other issues. But he also notes how China and the US are increasingly interacting—and bumping up against each other—in the Middle East, South Asia, and Latin America. There is also a broad menu of transnational and international functional issues in which both powers have a major stake: energy supplies, climate change, the global economy, and so on. Lieberthal discusses in depth the climate change challenge. In all of these areas, Washington and Beijing have overlapping interests and growing imperatives for cooperation—yet, at the same time, competition is growing is all spheres of the relationship.[2]

The next selection is by one of China's leading America specialists, Professor Wu Xinbo of Fudan University. Wu describes the "new type of major country relations" (新型大国关系) that President Xi Jinping and the Chinese government seek to build with the United States (and other powers). Based on "no conflict, no confrontation, mutual respect, and win–win cooperation," Beijing seeks to build a long-term functional relationship with Washington. In contrast to Lieberthal's assessment that deep distrust stands in the way of Sino-American relations, Professor Wu is much more optimistic— arguing that, "This new vision of 'global partners' provides the backbone to the new model of a major power relationship." In order to achieve this, though, Wu argues that the United States must "adjust its thinking" away from "realist thinking about things such as power balance, geopolitics, military alliances, and zero-sum games. Washington manifests a proclivity for overemphasizing national security concerns, seeking superior military might, and securing hegemony." While criticizing the United States for these "Cold War tendencies," Wu argues that "China values liberal ideals such as peaceful development, mutual trust, mutual benefit, equality and coordination. It repudiates forging military blocs and seeking military superiority as obsolete Cold War mentality." He then proceeds to offer a catalog of issues (not dissimilar from Lieberthal's) on which the US and China should cooperate. Wu ends on the optimistic note that achieving long-term cooperation between the two powers is not only essential, it is also feasible.

The next sub-section turns to China's' relations with the two other global powers— Russia and the European Union. As China's relations with the United States have encountered strains in recent years, its relations with Russia have developed positively and rapidly. China–Europe ties have fluctuated more—basically positive before 2007, then strained until 2011, stabilizing in 2012–2013, and improving again in 2014–2015.

The first selection is by respected Russia scholar Andrew Kuchins of the Center for Strategic and International Studies, and was written in 2007. Since the time of publication, Sino-Russian ties have continued to develop positively—although Kuchins notes that underlying suspicions and tensions persist. Kuchins traces in detail the historical evolution as well as the positive developments and the under-lying frictions. In essence, he finds a great deal of common convergence between Moscow and Beijing strategically and tactically today. This is good news for both nations, the Asian region, and indeed the world. One must only recall the tensions and dangers caused by the decades of Sino-Soviet enmity. Nonetheless, given the long history of frictions between Russia and China, one wonders when past patterns will reemerge?

Diplomatic historian Odd Arne Westad, formerly of the London School of Economics and Political Science and now at Harvard's Kennedy School of Government, assesses China–EU relations in the next selection. Professor Westad notes that China ranks far higher in Europe's list of priorities than vice versa. He illustratively quotes a Chinese diplomat as saying, "The EU is about as important for China as is Australia." This quotation highlights Beijing's frequent frustrations with Brussels, and its disap-pointment that the EU has not materialized as a full-fledged "pole" in China's wished-for multipolar world. Nonetheless, China–EU relations have developed remarkably since the end of the Cold War.[3] Westad notes, in particular, the dramatic expansion of trade and investment. China has been the European Union's largest trading partner since 2004, while the EU ranks second for China. But there are also irritants in the relationship—human rights, the EU arms embargo, cyber security, climate change, and the trade imbalance. Looking to the future, Westad envisions huge potential syn-ergies between the EU and China—but he questions whether they can be realized.

The next sub-section (V) considers China's relations with the developing world (the "Global South"). It contains four articles that unpack China's complicated rela-tionship with developing Asia, Africa, the Middle East, and Latin America.

This section opens with an overview by British scholar Peter Ferdinand of Warwick University. He begins by demonstrating the increased importance that the developing world plays in China's global trade profile. From 1990–2008, China's trade with less-developed-countries (LDCs) grew *twice* as fast as trade with the OECD countries. This is the case both on the import and export side of the ledger—China is importing huge amounts of natural resources, raw materials, and energy while exporting a range of manufactured goods and low-end technologies. China's outbound direct investment (ODI) is also rapidly increasing across the Global South, including the building of numerous automotive production facilities. The bulk of both trade and investment remains in Asia, but both Africa and Latin America are rising quickly in China's global profile over the past two decades. China's focus on the Middle East has come more slowly, but is picking up; China is now the largest exporter to the region. Professor Ferdinand also discusses China's aid programs in these regions (primarily in Africa). While still a fraction of OECD aid (10 percent), China is increasing its assistance to LDCs in recent years (approximately $2.5 billion per year now). He also looks at China's diplomacy with these regions, which is extremely active. China also exhibits a strong tendency to vote alongside LDCs at the United Nations. While China's footprint across the Global South has grown quite dramatically, it has not come without its problems. Ferdinand concludes: "Thus, while the Chinese presence in developing countries will grow, so too will the complexity of the challenges China has to confront. Declarations of diplomatic solidarity with developing countries and references to the memory of the injustices of foreign ownership of territory in China will only go so far. Some large Chinese production sites in Africa may not look so different from those of Western multinational corporations."

The next selection focuses specifically on China in Africa. Written by Joshua Eisenman (a scholar at the University of Texas) and Joshua Kurlantzick (Council on Foreign Relations) and published in 2006, they describe China's expansive footprint across Africa (which has only grown subsequently). The authors provide a wealth of detail concerning China's presence in and relations with Africa. But they also focus on Beijing's "strategy" towards the region: "Beijing's motives are clear. China's growing industries demand new energy and raw material suppliers; its exporters want markets; its diplomats require support in international organizations; and its propaganda still seeks support from allies to advance Chinese interests and, when necessary, to counter the United States." But they also take note of the blemishes that tarnish China's reputation: resource extraction; dumping of goods; support for dictators; "no strings attached" aid that violates international donor standards for "good governance"; weapons smuggling; and so on. On the other hand, China's aid programs have done much good for Africans (particularly in public health, tertiary education, agriculture, and capacity training of government officials), while its investment has helped build telecommunications networks and hard infrastructure across the continent. Thus, China's presence in Africa is large and growing while its record is mixed.

The next selection, which is a speech I delivered at the Brazilian Ministry of Foreign Affairs in Brasília in 2013, considers China's presence in Latin America and the Caribbean. To some extent, China's presence and interests in the Western Hemisphere parallels those in Africa—but with two exceptions: (1) China has been involved in Africa far longer (dating to the 1960s, while its presence in Latin America is primarily a post-1990s phenomenon), and (2) its economic footprint is not as dominated by raw materials and energy extraction. Otherwise, there are many similarities. In this selection I trace four dimensions of China's presence: diplomatic, cultural, security, and commercial. I also note that there is one other factor that distinguishes China's relations and presence in Latin America: *geography*. There are two dimensions here. First, Latin America is a *very* long way from China (and vice versa). There are no direct flights and shipping takes more than a week. Distance also begets unfamiliarity—I note that there is a very low level of knowledge and understanding about China in Latin America. The other geographic factor pertains to the United States. Although the Monroe Doctrine is a thing of the past, nonetheless the United States still considers this region as its strategic "backyard." As a consequence, Washington keeps a very close eye on China's presence—particularly military—while Beijing has been careful not to establish much of a security relationship with the countries in the region.

The final selection in this section concerns China's membership in, and relations with, the BRICS organization (Brazil, Russia, India, China, South Africa). Written by Yan Sun, then a visiting scholar at the Brookings Institution, the article shows how the organization embodies, in many ways and on many levels, China's aspirations for empowering the Global South in international relations.

The final sub-section (VI) focuses on China's contributions to global governance. The first selection is a speech given by then Deputy Secretary of State Robert Zoellick in 2005, in which he famously called on China to become a "responsible [international] stakeholder" in global governance and world affairs. Zoellick argued in his speech that China was institutionally now a "member of the club," that is, that since the 1970s China had joined virtually all multilateral regional and international institutions and China's own development had benefitted a great deal from what these bodies had to offer. Now, Zoellick argued, it was time for China to become more active, overcome its relative passivity, taking less and contributing more to the global pool of common resources.

The following selection by Australian scholar Michael Fullilove, who directs the Lowy Institute of International Policy in Sydney, examines Zoellick's thesis in the context of China's participation in the United Nations and other global institutions. He develops an analytical device he calls the "stakeholder spectrum" (a reference to Zoellick's earlier phrase) and investigates the extent to which Beijing has become a greater "stakeholder" in global governance affairs. Not surprisingly, Fullilove finds that it varies by issue area and institution. Within the United Nations, he finds China to have become impressively active and effective. But across a range of issues, Beijing has shown continued reluctance to get deeply involved and very hesitant to back the United States or other Western positions.

Taken together, the following selections offer a comprehensive examination of China's foreign relations since 2000. They are collective testimony to the extensiveness of China's global presence and interactions—which are only likely to grow further over time—but also the complexities and problems that have arisen therefrom.

NOTES

1. See David Shambaugh, *China Goes Global: The Partial Power* (Oxford and New York: Oxford University Press, 2013).
2. See David Shambaugh (ed.), *Tangled Titans: The United States and China* (Lanham, MD: Rowman & Littlefield, 2013).
3. See David Shambaugh, Eberhard Sandschneider, and Zhou Hong (eds.), *China-Europe Relations: Perceptions, Policies, and Prospects* (London: Routledge, 2008).

I. China Views the World

China's Search for a Grand Strategy: A Rising Great Power Finds Its Way[*]

Wang Jisi

Any country's grand strategy must answer at least three questions: What are the nation's core interests? What external forces threaten them? And what can the national leadership do to safeguard them? Whether China has any such strategy today is open to debate. On the one hand, over the last three decades or so, its foreign and defense policies have been remarkably consistent and reasonably well-coordinated with the country's domestic priorities. On the other hand, the Chinese government has yet to disclose any document that comprehensively expounds the country's strategic goals and the ways to achieve them. For both policy analysts in China and China watchers abroad, China's grand strategy is a field still to be plowed.

In recent years, China's power and influence relative to those of other great states have outgrown the expectations of even its own leaders. Based on the country's enhanced position, China's international behavior has become increasingly assertive, as was shown by its strong reactions to a chain of events in 2010: for example, Washington's decision to sell arms to Taiwan, US–South Korean military exercises in the Yellow Sea, and Japan's detention of a Chinese sailor found in disputed waters. It has become imperative for the international community to understand China's strategic thinking and try to forecast how it might evolve according to China's interests and its leaders' vision.

The Enemy Within and Without

A unique feature of Chinese leaders' understanding of their country's history is their persistent sensitivity to domestic disorder caused by foreign threats. From ancient times, the ruling regime of the day has often been brought down by a combination of internal uprising and external invasion. The Ming dynasty collapsed in 1644 after rebelling peasants took the capital city of Beijing and the Manchu, with the collusion of Ming generals, invaded from the north. Some three centuries later, the Manchu's own Qing dynasty collapsed after a series of internal revolts coincided with invasions by Western and Japanese forces. The end of the Kuomintang's rule and the founding of the People's Republic in 1949 was caused by an indigenous revolution inspired and then bolstered by the Soviet Union and the international communist movement.

Since then, apprehensions about internal turbulences have lingered. Under Mao Zedong's leadership, from 1949 to 1976, the Chinese government never formally applied the concept of "national interest" to delineate its strategic aims, but its international strategies were clearly dominated by political and military security interests—themselves often framed by ideological principles such as "proletarian internationalism." Strategic thinking at the time followed the Leninist tradition of dividing the world into political camps: archenemies, secondary enemies, potential allies, revolutionary forces. Mao's "three worlds theory" pointed to the Soviet Union and the United States as China's main external threats, with corresponding internal threats coming from pro-Soviet "revisionists" and pro-American "class enemies." China's political life in those years was characterized by recurrent struggles against international and domestic schemes to topple the Chinese Communist Party (CCP) leadership or change its political coloring. Still, since Mao's foreign policy supposedly represented the interests of the "international proletariat" rather than China's own, and since China was economically and socially isolated from much of the world, Beijing had no comprehensive grand strategy to speak of. Then came the 1980s and Deng Xiaoping. As China embarked

[*] This article was published in *Foreign Affairs*, Vol. 90, No. 2 (March/April 2011).

on reform and opened up, the CCP made economic development its top priority. Deng's foreign policy thinking departed appreciably from that of Mao. A major war with either the Soviet Union or the United States was no longer deemed inevitable. China made great efforts to develop friendly and cooperative relations with countries all over the world, regardless of their political or ideological orientation; it reasoned that a non-confrontational posture would attract foreign investment to China and boost trade. A peaceful international environment, an enhanced position for China in the global arena, and China's steady integration into the existing economic order would also help consolidate the CCP's power at home.

But even as economic interests became a major driver of China's behavior on the international scene, traditional security concerns and the need to guard against Western political interference remained important. Most saliently, the Tiananmen Square incident of 1989 and, in its wake, the West's sanctions against Beijing served as an alarming reminder to China's leaders that internal and external troubles could easily intertwine. Over the next decade, Beijing responded to Western censure by contending that the state's sovereign rights trumped human rights. It resolutely refused to consider adopting Western-type democratic institutions. And it insisted that it would never give up the option of using force if Taiwan tried to secede. Despite those concerns, however, by the beginning of the twenty-first century, China's strategic thinkers were depicting a generally favorable international situation. In his 2002 report to the CCP National Congress, General Secretary Jiang Zemin foresaw a "twenty-years period of strategic opportunity," during which China could continue to concentrate on domestic tasks. Unrest has erupted at times—such as the violent riots in Tibet in March 2008 and in Xinjiang in July 2009, which the central government blamed on "foreign hostile forces" and responded to with harsh reprisals. And Beijing claims that the awarding of the 2010 Nobel Peace Prize to Liu Xiaobo, a political activist it deems to be a "criminal trying to sabotage the socialist system," has proved once again Westerners' "ill intentions." Still, the Chinese government has been perturbed by such episodes only occasionally, which has allowed it to focus on redressing domestic imbalances and the unsustainability of its development.

Under President Hu Jintao, Beijing has in recent years formulated a new development and social policy geared toward continuing to promote fast economic growth while emphasizing good governance, improving the social safety net, protecting the environment, encouraging independent innovation, lessening social tensions, perfecting the financial system, and stimulating domestic consumption. As Chinese exports have suffered from the global economic crisis since 2008, the need for such economic and social transformations has become more urgent.

With that in mind, the Chinese leadership has redefined the purpose of China's foreign policy. As Hu announced in July 2009, China's diplomacy must "safeguard the interests of sovereignty, security, and development." Dai Bingguo, the state councilor for external relations, further defined those core interests in an article last December: first, China's political stability, namely, the stability of the CCP leadership and of the socialist system; second, sovereign security, territorial integrity, and national unification; and third, China's sustainable economic and social development.

Apart from the issue of Taiwan, which Beijing considers to be an integral part of China's territory, the Chinese government has never officially identified any single foreign policy issue as one of the country's core interests. Last year, some Chinese commentators reportedly referred to the South China Sea and North Korea as such, but these reckless statements, made with no official authorization, created a great deal of confusion. In fact, for the central government, sovereignty, security, and development all continue to be China's main goals. As long as no grave danger—for example, Taiwan's formal secession—threatens the CCP leadership or China's unity, Beijing will remain preoccupied with the country's economic and social development, including in its foreign policy.

The Principle's Principle

The need to identify an organizing principle to guide Chinese foreign policy is widely recognized today in China's policy circles and scholarly community, as well as among international analysts. However, defining China's core interests according to the three prongs of sovereignty, security, and development, which sometimes are in tension, means that it is almost impossible to devise a straightforward organizing principle. And the variety of views among Chinese political elites complicates efforts to devise any such grand strategy based on political consensus.

One popular proposal has been to focus on the United States as a major threat to China. Proponents of this view cite the ancient Chinese philosopher Mencius, who said, "A state without an enemy or external peril is absolutely doomed." Or they reverse the political scientist Samuel Huntington's argument that "the ideal enemy for America would be ideologically hostile, racially and culturally different, and militarily strong enough to pose a credible threat to American security" and cast the United States as an ideal enemy for China. This notion is based on the long-held conviction that the United States, along with other Western powers and Japan, is hostile to China's political values and wants to contain its rise by supporting Taiwan's separation from the mainland. Its proponents also point to US politicians' sympathy for the Dalai Lama and Uighur separatists, continued US arms sales to Taiwan, US military alliances and arrangements supposedly designed to encircle the Chinese mainland, the currency and trade wars waged by US businesses and the US Congress, and the West's argument that China should slow down its economic growth in order to help stem climate change.

This view is reflected in many newspapers and on many Web sites in China (particularly those about military affairs and political security). Its proponents argue that China's current approach to foreign relations is far too soft; Mao's tit-for-tat manner is touted as a better model. As a corollary, it is said that China should try to find strategic allies among countries that seem defiant toward the West, such as Iran, North Korea, and Russia.

Some also recommend that Beijing use its holdings of US Treasury bonds as a policy instrument, standing ready to sell them if US government actions undermine China's interests.

This proposal is essentially misguided, for even though the United States does pose some strategic and security challenges to China, it would be impractical and risky to construct a grand strategy based on the view that the United States is China's main adversary. Few countries, if any, would want to join China in an anti-US alliance. And it would seriously hold back China's economic development to antagonize the country's largest trading partner and the world's strongest economic and military power. Fortunately, the Chinese leadership is not about to carry out such a strategy. Premier Wen Jiabao was not just being diplomatic last year when he said of China and the United States that "our common interests far outweigh our differences."

Well aware of this, an alternative school of thought favors Deng's teaching of *taoguang yanghui*, or keeping a low profile in international affairs. Members of this group, including prominent political figures, such as Tang Jiaxuan, former foreign minister, and General Xiong Guangkai, former deputy chief of staff of the People's Liberation Army, argue that since China remains a developing country, it should concentrate on economic development. Without necessarily rebuffing the notion that the West, particularly the United States, is a long-term threat to China, they contend that China is not capable of challenging Western primacy for the time being—and some even caution against hastily concluding that the West is in decline. Meanwhile, they argue, keeping a low profile in the coming decades will allow China to concentrate on domestic priorities.

Although this view appears to be better received internationally than the other, it, too, elicits some concerns. Its adherents have had to take great pains to explain that *taoguang yanghui*, which is sometimes mistranslated as "hiding one's capabilities and biding one's time," is not a calculated call for temporary moderation until China has enough material power and confidence to promote its hidden agenda. Domestically, the low-profile approach is vulnerable to the charge that it is too soft, especially when security issues become acute. As nationalist feelings surge in China, some Chinese are pressing for a more can-do foreign policy. Opponents also contend that this notion, which Deng put forward more than 20 years ago, may no longer be appropriate now that China is far more powerful.

Some thoughtful strategists appreciate that even if keeping a low profile could serve China's political and security relations with the United States well, it might not apply to China's relations with many other countries or to economic issues and those nontraditional security issues that have become essential in recent years, such as climate change, public health, and energy security. (Beijing can hardly keep a low profile when it actively participates in mechanisms such as the BRICs, the informal group formed by Brazil, Russia, India, China, and the new member South Africa.) A foreign policy that insists merely on keeping China's profile low cannot cope effectively with the multifaceted challenges facing the country today.

Home Is Where the Heart Is

A more sophisticated grand strategy is needed to serve China's domestic priorities. The government has issued no official written statement outlining such a vision, but some direction can be gleaned from the concepts of a "scientific outlook on development" and "building a harmonious society," which have been enunciated by Hu and have been recorded in all important CCP documents since 2003. In 2006, the Central Committee of the CCP announced that China's foreign policy "must maintain economic construction as its centerpiece, be closely integrated into domestic work, and be advanced by coordinating domestic and international situations." Moreover, four ongoing changes in China's strategic thinking may suggest the foundations for a new grand strategy.

The first transformation is the Chinese government's adoption of a comprehensive understanding of security, which incorporates economic and nontraditional concerns with traditional military and political interests. Chinese military planners have begun to take into consideration transnational problems such as terrorism and piracy, as well as cooperative activities such as participation in UN peacekeeping operations. Similarly, it is now clear that China must join other countries in stabilizing the global financial market in order to protect its own economic security. All this means that it is virtually impossible to distinguish China's friends from its foes. The United States might pose political and military threats, and Japan,

a staunch US ally, could be a geopolitical competitor of China's, but these two countries also happen to be two of China's greatest economic partners. Even though political difficulties appear to be on the rise with the European Union, it remains China's top economic partner. Russia, which some Chinese see as a potential security ally, is far less important economically and socially to China than is South Korea, another US military ally. It will take painstaking efforts on Beijing's part to limit tensions between China's traditional political-military perspectives and its broadening socioeconomic interests—efforts that effectively amount to reconciling the diverging legacies of Mao and Deng. The best Beijing can do is to strengthen its economic ties with great powers while minimizing the likelihood of a military and political confrontation with them.

A second transformation is unfolding in Chinese diplomacy: it is becoming less country-oriented and more multilateral and issue oriented. This shift toward functional focuses—counterterrorism, nuclear nonproliferation, environmental protection, energy security, food safety, post-disaster reconstruction—has complicated China's bilateral relationships, regardless of how friendly other states are toward it. For example, diverging geostrategic interests and territorial disputes have long come between China and India, but the two countries' common interest in fending off the West's pressure to reduce carbon emissions has drawn them closer. And now that Iran has become a key supplier of oil to China, its problems with the West over its nuclear program are testing China's stated commitment to the nuclear nonproliferation regime.

Changes in the mode of China's economic development account for a third transformation in the country's strategic thinking. Beijing's preoccupation with GDP growth is slowly giving way to concerns about economic efficiency, product quality, environmental protection, the creation of a social safety net, and technological innovation. Beijing's understanding of the core interest of development is expanding to include social dimensions. Correspondingly, China's leaders have decided to try to sustain the country's high growth rate by propping up domestic consumption and reducing over the long term the country's dependence on exports and foreign investment. They are now more concerned with global economic imbalances and financial fluctuations, even as international economic frictions are becoming more intense because of the global financial crisis. China's long-term interests will require some incremental appreciation of the *yuan*, but its desire to increase its exports in the short term will prevent its decision-makers from taking the quick measures urged by the United States and many other countries. Only the enhancement of China's domestic consumption and a steady opening of its capital markets will help it shake off these international pressures.

The fourth transformation has to do with China's values. So far, China's officials have said that although China has a distinctive political system and ideology, it can cooperate with other countries based on shared interests—although not, the suggestion seems to be, on shared values. But now that they strongly wish to enhance what they call the "cultural soft power of the nation" and improve China's international image, it appears necessary to also seek common values in the global arena, such as good governance and transparency. Continuing trials and tribulations at home, such as pervasive corruption and ethnic and social unrest in some regions, could also reinforce a shift in values among China's political elite by demonstrating that their hold on power and the country's continued resurgence depend on greater transparency and accountability, as well as on a firmer commitment to the rule of law, democracy, and human rights, all values that are widely shared throughout the world today.

All four of these developments are unfolding haltingly and are by no means irreversible. Nonetheless, they do reveal fundamental trends that will likely shape China's grand strategy in the foreseeable future. When Hu and other leaders call for "coordinating domestic and international situations," they mean that efforts to meet international challenges must not undermine domestic reforms. And with external challenges now coming not only from foreign powers—especially the United States and Japan—but also, and increasingly, from functional issues, coping with them effectively will require engaging foreign countries cooperatively and emphasizing compatible values.

Thus, it would be imprudent of Beijing to identify any one country as a major threat and invoke the need to keep it at bay as an organizing principle of Chinese foreign policy—unless the United States, or another great power, truly did regard China as its main adversary and so forced China to respond in kind. On the other hand, if keeping a low profile is a necessary component of Beijing's foreign policy, it is also insufficient. A grand strategy needs to consider other long-term objectives as well. One that appeals to some Chinese is the notion of building China into the most powerful state in the world: Liu Mingfu, a senior colonel who teaches at the People's Liberation Army's National Defense University, has declared that replacing the United States as the world's top military power should be China's goal. Another idea is to cast China as an alternative model of development (the "Beijing consensus") that can challenge Western systems, values, and leadership. But the Chinese leadership does not dream of turning China into a hegemon or a standard-bearer. Faced with mounting pressures on both the domestic and the international fronts, it is sober in its objectives, be they short- or long-term ones. Its main concern is how best to protect China's core interests—sovereignty, security, and development—against the messy cluster of threats that the country faces today. If an organizing principle must be established to guide China's grand strategy, it should be the improvement of the Chinese people's living standards, welfare, and happiness through social justice.

The Birth of a Great Nation

Having identified China's core interests and the external pressures that threaten them, the remaining question is, how can China's leadership safeguard the country's interests against those threats? China's continued success in modernizing its economy and lifting its people's standards of living depends heavily on global stability. Thus, it is in China's interest to contribute to a peaceful international environment. China should seek peaceful solutions to residual sovereignty and security issues, including the thorny territorial disputes between it and its neighbors. With the current leadership in Taiwan refraining from seeking formal independence from the mainland, Beijing is more confident that peace can be maintained across the Taiwan Strait. But it has yet to reach a political agreement with Taipei that would prevent renewed tensions in the future. The Chinese government also needs to find effective means to pacify Tibet and Xinjiang, as more unrest in those regions would likely elicit reactions from other countries.

Although the vast majority of people in China support a stronger Chinese military to defend the country's major interests, they should also recognize the dilemma that poses. As China builds its defense capabilities, especially its navy, it will have to convince others, including the United States and China's neighbors in Asia, that it is taking their concerns into consideration. It will have to make the plans of the People's Liberation Army more transparent and show a willingness to join efforts to establish security structures in the Asia-Pacific region and safeguard existing global security regimes, especially the nuclear nonproliferation regime. It must also continue to work with other states to prevent Iran and North Korea from obtaining nuclear weapons. China's national security will be well served if it makes more contributions to other countries' efforts to strengthen security in cyberspace and outer space. Of course, none of this excludes the possibility that China might have to use force to protect its sovereignty or its security in some special circumstances, such as in the event of a terrorist attack.

China has been committed to almost all existing global economic regimes. But it will have to do much more before it is recognized as a full-fledged market economy. It has already gained an increasingly larger say in global economic mechanisms, such as the G-20, the World Bank, and the International Monetary Fund. Now, it needs to make specific policy proposals and adjustments to help rebalance the global economy and facilitate its plans to change its development pattern at home. Setting a good example by building a low-carbon economy is one major step that would benefit both China and the world.

A grand strategy requires defining a geostrategic focus, and China's geostrategic focus is Asia. When communication lines in Central Asia and South Asia were poor, China's development strategy and economic interests tilted toward its east coast and the Pacific Ocean. Today, East Asia is still of vital importance, but China should and will begin to pay more strategic attention to the west. The central government has been conducting the Grand Western Development Program in many western provinces and regions, notably Tibet and Xinjiang, for more than a decade. It is now more actively initiating and participating in new development projects in Afghanistan, India, Pakistan, Central Asia, and throughout the Caspian Sea region, all the way to Europe. This new western outlook may reshape China's geostrategic vision as well as the Eurasian landscape.

Still, relationships with great powers remain crucial to defending China's core interests. Notwithstanding the unprecedented economic interdependence of China, Japan, and the United States, strategic trust is still lacking between China and the United States and China and Japan. It is imperative that the Chinese-Japanese-US trilateral interaction be stable and constructive, and a trilateral strategic dialogue is desirable. More generally, too, China will have to invest tremendous resources to promote a more benign image on the world stage. A China with good governance will be a likeable China. Even more important, it will have to learn that soft power cannot be artificially created: such influence originates more from a society than from a state.

Two daunting tasks lie ahead before a better-designed Chinese grand strategy can take shape and be implemented. The first is to improve policy coordination among Chinese government agencies. Almost all institutions in the central leadership and local governments are involved in foreign relations to varying degrees, and it is virtually impossible for them to see China's national interest the same way or to speak with one voice. These differences confuse outsiders as well as the Chinese people.

The second challenge will be to manage the diversity of views among China's political elite and the general public, at a time when the value system in China is changing rapidly. Mobilizing public support for government policies is expected to strengthen Beijing's diplomatic bargaining power while also helping consolidate its domestic popularity. But excessive nationalism could breed more public frustration and create more pressure on the government if its policies fail to deliver immediately, which could hurt China's political order, as well as its foreign relations. Even as it allows different voices to be heard on foreign affairs, the central leadership should more vigorously inform the population of its own view, which is consistently more moderate and prudent than the inflammatory remarks found in the media and on Web sites.

No major power's interests can conform exactly to those of the international community; China is no exception. And with one-fifth of the world's population, it is more like a continent than a country. Yet despite the complexity of developing a grand strategy for China, the effort is at once consistent with China's internal priorities and generally positive for the international community. China will serve its interests better if it can provide more common goods to the international community and share more values with other states.

How other countries respond to the emergence of China as a global power will also have a great impact on China's internal development and external behavior. If the international community appears not to understand China's aspirations, its anxieties, and its difficulties in feeding itself and modernizing, the Chinese people may ask themselves why China should be bound by rules that were essentially established by the Western powers. China can rightfully be expected to take on more international responsibilities. But then the international community should take on the responsibility of helping the world's largest member support itself.

Coping with a Conflicted China[*]

David Shambaugh

The years 2009–2010 will be remembered as ones in which China became difficult for the world to deal with, as Beijing exhibited increasingly tough and truculent behavior toward many of its neighbors in Asia, as well as the United States and the European Union. Even its ties in Africa and Latin America became somewhat strained, adding to its declining global image since 2007.[1] Beijing's disturbing behavior has many observers wondering how long its new toughness will last. Is it a temporary or secular trend? If it is a longer-term and qualitative shift toward greater assertiveness and arrogance, how should other nations respond?

What the world is witnessing in China's new posture is in part the product of an on-going intensive internal debate, and represents a current consensus among the more conservative and nationalist elements to toughen its policies and selectively throw China's weight around. Although there seems to be domestic agreement at present, China remains a deeply conflicted rising power with a series of competing international identities.

Many new voices and actors are now part of an unprecedentedly complex foreign-policymaking process.[2] Consequently, China's foreign policy often exhibits diverse and contradictory emphases. Understanding these competing identities is crucial to anticipating how Beijing's increasingly contradictory and multidimensional behavior will play out on the world stage. Each orientation carries different policy implications for the United States and other nations.

Open Discourse in a Constrained Environment

No nation has had such an extensive, animated, and diverse domestic discourse about its roles as a major rising power as China has during the past decade. Official, semi-official, and unofficial circles in China all actively debate the opportunities, dangers, risks, and responsibilities of being a major power.[3] To be sure, there is still a segment of official opinion that denies China even *is* a major power, arguing instead that it remains a developing (socialist) country. Another significant segment of opinion denies that China is a

---

[*] This article was published in *The Washington Quarterly* (Winter 2011).

global power, arguing it is only a regional one at best. Although these traditional identities continue to be articulated in official government speeches and documents, the preponderance of domestic discourse recently recognizes that China is a major power, or at least well on the way to becoming one. As a result, the discourse in recent years has shifted to *what kind* of major power should China be.

Few, if any, other major or aspiring powers engage in such self-reflective discourse. There are even a variety of "how to" books published in China on how to become a great power.[4] Although such discussions take place primarily in the semi-official policy and academic communities, they also extended to society at large with the 2006 airing of the 12-part China Central Television (CCTV) documentary series "Rising Powers" (*Daquo Jueqi*). Hundreds of millions of Chinese watched this series, which aired several times and portrayed the conditions that gave rise to other modern great powers (Portugal, Spain, Holland, France, Great Britain, Germany, Russia, the Soviet Union, Japan, and the United States), so that China's own rise could be contextualized and informed by these historical experiences. Although the series focused primarily on the conditions that precipitated the rise (and fall) of great powers, the theme of the concluding episode was how to avoid the historically repetitive "asymmetry trap" between the major established power and the primary rising power, in which the latter challenged the former's hegemonic position in the international system, causing tensions, competition, clashes, and even wars.[5] The CCTV series came after a series of lectures on the subject given by academics to the Chinese Communist Party Politburo during 2005–2006. Thus, both masses and elites in China have been preoccupied in recent years with anticipating the dilemmas of being a rising power.

Despite a somewhat constrained intellectual environment with restrictions imposed by propaganda authorities, China's international identity discourse has nevertheless been robust and diverse, offering important windows into Chinese thinking about other nations, regions, international issues, and particularly China's own evolving role as an emerging major power in world affairs. Most importantly, it reveals the multiple and sometimes conflicting identities that exist in the Chinese worldview as well as contending perspectives on China's role in the world. China has no single international identity today, but rather a series of competing identities.

Understanding the content and spectrum of discourse within the country is central to understanding what Chinese themselves are wrestling with, as their nation has been thrust quickly into the international arena. It is apparent that China is unprepared for its new international status, and the rapidity of its rise has come much more quickly than anticipated. For Chinese, it is quite jarring to all of a sudden be confronted with a whole new set of questions and external demands about China's international status, roles, and responsibilities. So, how do Chinese international affairs experts view the world and China's role in it today?

The Spectrum of Discourse on China's International Identity

Different schools, or "tendencies," of thought and analysis are evident in the Chinese discourse.[6] Although intellectually distinct, it would be incorrect to see these schools as mutually exclusive; they are sometimes contradictory, but also sometimes complementary. Moreover, individual international relations scholars and officials in China are often eclectic thinkers; although strongly rooted in one school of thought, they often voice views associated with other schools. Cognitive complexity prevails. One also finds that groups of thinkers do not correlate with institutions. Although it would be nice to be able to label one institution as "realist" or another as "globalist," it is not so simple. Schools of thought crosscut institutions.

As a consequence of competing international identities, China's foreign policy reflects several elements simultaneously. This is illustrated in the official policy of *daguo shi guanjian, zhoubian shi shouyao, fazhanzhong guojia shi jichu, duobian shi zhongyao wutai* (major powers are the key, surrounding areas are the first priority, developing countries are the foundation, and multilateral forums are the important stage). Although these are clearly different policy orientations, they are not necessarily mutually exclusive. In the author's reading of, and interactions with, China's international relations community, seven distinct

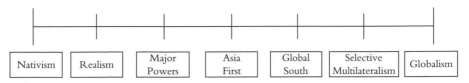

Figure 1 Spectrum of Chinese Global Identities

perspectives are apparent. The spectrum, illustrated in Figure 1, ranges from isolationist tendencies on the left end to full engagement in global governance and institutions on the right end. In between the two extremes, other schools of thought progress from more realist to more liberal orientations.

Nativism At one end of the spectrum is the "Nativist" school. It is a collection of populists, xenophobic nationalists, and Marxists. This school distrusts the outside world, seeks total national autonomy, distrusts international institutions, and thinks China should not be internationally active. It vociferously criticizes the West, especially the United States. The group bears a strong traditional Marxist orientation. The Nativists are a loose coalition spread across a number of institutions; indeed a number of its leading advocates operate as independent pundits. To the extent that they have an institutional home, many work in research institutes under the Central Committee of the Communist Party that are involved in Communist Party history and ideology, and in the Marxism Academy of the China Academy of Social Sciences (CASS).

The Nativists are the twin of the "new left" (*xin zuopai*) in domestic policy debates. Both believe the "reform and opening" policy of the past 30 years has cost China its socialist integrity, corroded its culture with negative foreign influences, and compromised China's sovereignty and autonomy in world affairs. They believe that had China never opened its doors to the world, it would not have lost these elements. They argue that domestic reform (*gaige*) has inevitably led to China's restoration of capitalism, and that "peaceful evolution" (*heping yanbian*)—a policy whereby the West attempts to peacefully evolve China so as to undermine Chinese Communist Party rule—has become the main domestic threat. In this regard, the "color revolutions" in Ukraine

and Central Asia caused great concern among this cohort. Thus they advocate the main policy priority should be to counter peaceful evolution and close China's doors.

Earlier examples of this line of thinking appeared during the 1990s with the "China Can Say No" (*Zhongguo Keyi Shuo Bu*) school. The more recent manifestation has been the upsurge in popular books that might be described as "dissatisfaction literature": *China is Unhappy (Zhongguo bu Gaoxing), Who in China is Unhappy? (Shei zai Zhongguo bu Gaoxing?)*, and *Why is China Unhappy? (Zhongguo Weishenma bu Gaoxing?).*[7] The latter group of authors includes some who contributed to *China Can Say No.*

With respect to international affairs, the Nativists believe that the international system is unjust and favors wealthy imperialist countries. Thus they argue that developing countries cannot eradicate poverty just through hard work—there needs to be a fundamental change in the global order to force a redistribution of income and resources from North to South. In this regard, they share perspectives with the "Global South" school (see below). As good Marxist–Leninists, the Nativists also argue that "globalization" is in fact a process of the internationalization of capital, similar to Lenin's description of imperialism.[8]

The 2008–2010 global financial crisis further emboldened this line of thinking, as many argued that "state-monopoly capitalism" (*guojia longduan zibenzhuyi*) had finally brought the world economy to the brink of disaster, just as Lenin predicted in 1917. Fang Ning, Director of the CASS Institute of Political Science, argues that this phenomenon actually dates to the 2003 Iraq War, which marked the arrival of an era of "new imperialism." For Fang and others, the war indicated that Deng Xiaoping's era of "peace and development" was over.[9] The foreign policy of George W. Bush's administration gave rise to a revival of Marxist—or more accurately neo-Leninist—studies of international relations and a number of articles and books on "new imperialism."[10] Although they regurgitated much of the analysis from the 1980s,[11] the new scholarship went much further in dissecting both the new developments in "state-monopoly capitalism" and the international order. These authors also accuse China's policy toward the United States of being far too soft, and categorize a Sino-US "strategic partnership" as an illusion. The Nativists contain hyper-nationalistic and strongly anti-American elements (although not as vituperative as found on the Chinese Internet).

Realism with Chinese Characteristics China's "Realists" are the dominant group in the discourse on international relations and China's global role today (if not forever). Realism has had deep roots in China's intellectual worldview for several centuries,[12] even during the country's socialist era. Chinese Realists take the nation-state as their core unit of analysis, uphold the principle of state sovereignty above all else, and reject arguments that transnational issues penetrate across borders. Like realists elsewhere, they tend to see the international environment as anarchic and unpredictable, thus placing a premium on building up a strong state that can navigate its own way in the world and resist outside pressures.

China's Realists may be sub-divided into "offensive" and "defensive," as well as "hard" and "soft," camps. Each strand believes that the state has to build its own strength, but what distinguishes them is the purposes for which the state uses its power. Hard-power realists argue for strengthening comprehensive national power (*zonghe guoli*)—particularly the military and economic dimensions—while soft-power realism emphasizes diplomacy and cultural power. The offensive realists argue that China should use its newly built military, economic, and diplomatic influence to essentially coerce others toward the ends China desires. They believe that power is worth little if it is not used. In their minds, China should, for example, leverage its holding of US treasury bonds to get Washington to stop selling arms to Taiwan, or penalize large US corporations for selling weapons to Taipei. They would like China to establish a much broader military (particularly naval) presence in the western Pacific

to force the United States to stop operating close to China's coastline. Defensive realists agree that China should possess strong military might, but should "keep its powder dry" and use it essentially to deter aggression and Taiwanese independence.

Discussions with Realists reveal a certain frustration: they want China to use its new-found power, but feel constrained in doing so. Said one: "As China's posture abroad grows, our investments and interests abroad are growing. We need to think about how to protect our nationals, investments, and interests. One way is to behave as an imperialist country with gunboat policies—but given our past history, this is not feasible."[13]

There also is a certain element of retribution in their thinking. Many Realists harbor a strong sense of aggrievement from China's long period of weakness, and believe that now that China is strong, it should retaliate against those countries that have done China wrong in the past. Shen Dingli, Dean of the Institute of International Studies at Shanghai's Fudan University and a leading security expert, explained that, "In 10 to 20 years, China will be a major exporter of high-technology—it may impose restrictive sanctions on those that previously imposed them on us!"[14] On another occasion, Shen asserted that "China is a big power, we can handle any country one-on-one. No one should try to lead us, no one should tell us what to do."[15]

The Realists are found throughout the military and in some universities and think tanks. People's Liberation Army (PLA) journals and books are rife with hard realist rhetoric. Some civilian scholars, such as Yan Xuetong of Tsinghua University and Zhang Ruizhuang of Nankai University (both Ph.D. students of leading American realist Kenneth Waltz of the University of California–Berkeley), are self-proclaimed staunch realists. Yan holds a hawkish position on a variety of issues. To him, "peaceful rise" is a dangerous theory because it gives potential adversaries (including Taiwan) a message that China will not act forcefully to protect its national sovereignty and interests. In the past, Yan argued that China should resort to the use of force, when necessary and without hesitation, to counteract Taiwan's move toward legal independence.[16] Yan's 1997 book *China's Rise* was a manifesto for building and using China's comprehensive and hard power.[17]

For Zhang Ruizhang, the "peaceful development" view, taken together with the "multipolar world" and "US–China strategic partnership" theses, represent mistaken ideas which misjudge the international situation and could lead to policy errors for China. Zhang argues for a much more assertive policy toward the United States, saying "the United States has been damaging China's interests for a long time. China should be *dis*satisfied, not satisfied, with the state of US–China relations. It is not a relationship in good condition. If China does not oppose the United States, the US will abuse China's interests and China will become America's puppet."[18] Zhang also thinks multipolarity is an overly optimistic view of the post–Cold War order, underestimating the daunting challenges China faces from US hegemony, and weakens China's vigilance.[19]

In these respects, Realists are pessimists about China's external environment, cross-strait relations, and the United States. Above all, they take a narrow and self-interested definition of China's national interests, rejecting concepts and policies of globalization, transnational challenges, and global governance. Advocates of Chinese realism tend to argue (like Nativists) that Western attempts to enlist greater Chinese involvement in global management and governance is a dangerous trap aimed at tying China down, burning up its resources, and retarding its growth. However, Realism is not an isolationist school—it simply argues for a very hard-headed definition and defense of China's narrow national interests.

The Major Powers School Another group may be identified as the "Major Powers" school. Its members tend to argue that China should concentrate its diplomacy on managing its relations with the world's major powers and blocs—the United States, Russia, perhaps the European Union—while paying relatively less attention to the developing world or multilateralism: "*Daguo shi shouyao*" (major powers are of primary importance) is their watchword. Not surprisingly, scholars in this school are specialists on the United States, Russia, and the European Union. Interestingly, these analysts do not identify India, Japan, or the Association of Southeast Asian Nations (ASEAN) as "major powers," although they certainly identify China as one.

This school argues that not having strong and stable ties with the major powers will be detrimental to a range of Chinese interests and will complicate China's other regional relationships. China's modernization drive is one obvious reason for a major-power orientation—the Western powers (the United States and the European Union) are the major source of advanced technology as well as of capital and investment. Russia is a separate case, but it is seen as a significant supplier of energy resources and military equipment, a place for investment, and of importance to China's national security. Analysts in this group often identify the Sino–US relationship as the "key of the keys" (*zhongzhong zhi zhong*), thus arguing that maintaining harmonious ties with Washington should be the top priority in Chinese diplomacy. Most members of this school are in China's American Studies community, individuals such as Wang Jisi (Peking University), Jin Canrong (Renmin University), Wu Xinbo (Fudan University), and Cui Liru (China Institutes of Contemporary International Relations). This group was dominant during Jiang Zemin's tenure as China's president, as he practiced an "America-first" policy, but is not as influential under Hu Jintao, who has practiced a more diversified foreign policy.

Some in this school believe, however, that China's foreign policy should emphasize Russia. Pan Wei of Peking University sees the United States as a dead end for China and says it is wishful thinking to seek a Sino–US strategic partnership, which has more disadvantages than advantages.[20] Pan and likeminded thinkers argue that China's foreign policy should be adjusted and geared toward a closer relationship with Moscow. These critics call for a tougher policy toward the United States (thus sharing a perspective in common with the Nativists and Realists). They are similarly skeptical of the line of thinking first suggested by Deng Xiaoping and adopted for the last 30 years, i.e., putting emphasis on opening up to the developed powers in the West.[21]

A contingent of this school argued until a few years ago that China should emphasize the European Union in its diplomacy, as the EU was a key pillar in a multipolar world, but their voices have disappeared since 2008 given the disorganization in Brussels and the impotence of EU foreign and security policy. Chinese analysts have been disappointed and have become disillusioned and dismissive of the EU, after having hoped for a long time that the EU would become a "new emerging power" (*xinxing daguo*) in world affairs.

Although scholars and pundits debate the wisdom of a major-power orientation, they point out that the majority of senior Chinese leaders and policymakers are pragmatic about China's national needs and interests and thus still adopt a major-power orientation. Their logic is that it would be too costly for China to have strained ties with any of the three major powers noted above. Nevertheless, it is apparent that there has been a reorientation away from an "exclusive" focus on the United States (as was practiced during the Jiang Zemin period) toward a more balanced and global policy under Hu Jintao.

Asia First There is a group in the middle of the spectrum which argues for concentrating China's diplomacy on its immediate periphery and Asian neighborhood. The "Asia First" school believes that if China's neighborhood is not stable, it will be a major impediment to the country's development and national security. Priority should thus be placed on building ties and a stable environment all around China's periphery. As one scholar put it, "Every power must protect its own backyard."[22] In this context, Chinese scholars discuss a variety of regional trends, including the evolving regional multilateral architecture, the role of the United States, the role of India, the North Korean issue, the role of ASEAN, non-traditional security issues, and other Asian topics. These discussions occur without significant cleavages and lines of debates. Not surprisingly, this school is largely composed of Asia specialists (and not those who work on other parts of the world or international relations).

The Asia First school initially made an impact on Chinese foreign policy in the late 1990s. Following the 1997 Asian Financial Crisis and the 1999 "Peace and Development Debate," which concluded that China had been too passive on its periphery, China began to emphasize its neighborhood diplomacy (*zhoubian waijiao*) much more.[23] Beijing embarked on a sustained period of proactive and cooperative regional diplomacy under the rubric of "establish good neighborliness, make neighbors prosperous, and make them feel secure" (*mulin, fulin, anlin*). This "Asia First" strategy produced much fruit for more than a decade after 1997, as China managed to dramatically improve and stabilize relations all around its periphery. Since 2009, however, various strains have emerged between China and its regional neighbors as Beijing has adopted a more assertive, and occasionally belligerent and demanding, tone and posture. Increased friction with ASEAN over the South China Sea and regional multilateral institution building, sharpened tensions with India over territorial disputes and politics, the September 2010 dust-up with Japan over a fishing boat intrusion into disputed waters, and the aggravation of Sino–South Korean ties after the Cheonan incident have all strained Beijing's relationships with its neighbors. These recent strains have significantly damaged China's regional image and have undone much of the positive relationship-building of the previous decade.

Those who push for "multilateral regionalism" and East Asian community building, as distinct from a more state-based strategy, are an important sub-group of the Asia First school. These individuals are "constructivists with Chinese characteristics" drawing their intellectual inspiration from international relations constructivism abroad. They emphasize normative behavior rather than international law, and push for institutionalizing cooperative and collective behavior. Professor Qin Yaqing of China Foreign Affairs University and Zhang Yunling of the China Academy of Social Sciences (CASS) have been at the forefront of this movement, and have each contributed significantly to building regional institutionalism in Asia, and increasing China's involvement in such institutions.

Those who emphasize China's ties within Asia do not do so to the exclusion of relations with other regions or nations; for them it is a question of balance. They argue in favor of not neglecting Asia relative to the major powers or China's relations with the developing world.

The Global South School The "Global South" school believes that China's main international identity and responsibility lies with the developing world. This group's perspective has much to do with China's longstanding self-identification as a developing country (*fazhanzhong guojia*). Its members argue for prioritizing China's longtime partners and client states among developing countries (or at least a more balanced foreign policy which takes them into account), and advocates for their interests. This reasoning appears in China's strong support for the UN Millennium Development Goals, the Forum on China–Africa Cooperation (FOCAC), reform of international financial institutions, developing countries' interests in the G-20, granting "no strings attached" aid programs and debt relief, and placing the climate-change burden on developed countries.

Within China's international relations community, there has always been a tension between those whose work focuses on the developed countries of the North and those who work on the South. Since the 1990s, the latter group of Chinese analysts has increasingly taken notice of the differentiation and fragmentation occurring in the developing world. They have realized that there are various kinds of developing countries, and often it is hard to simply lump them together. Developing countries may maintain a good, ordinary, or in some cases adversarial relationship with China. Although cooperation between China and those countries is sound on balance, new frictions are also emerging.

Economically, analysts in this school argue that the developing countries have broken into three groups. The first is newly industrializing economies, such as Brazil, Chile, South Africa, South Korea, and Turkey. The second is average-income developing countries such as Mexico or Thailand, with per capita GDP varying from $800 to $7,000. The third group is the least developed countries (generally in sub-Saharan Africa and South Asia). Since the countries are considerably differentiated, these analysts argue that China needs to formulate more targeted policies toward at least these three groups of developing countries to replace a more general approach.[24] Nevertheless, for proponents of this school of thought, China should continue to see itself as a developing country, and it is therefore obliged to work with developing countries for common development and common international positions, even after China rises to global power status.[25]

From this perspective, China needs to continue its self-identity and South–South solidarity, as it offers indispensable diplomatic support to fend off the West on issues such as Tibet, Taiwan, human rights, climate change, and so on. Not surprisingly, this school is a staunch advocate of the Brazil-Russia-India-China (BRIC) group, and also strongly supports the G-20 as an instrument to redistribute power and resources from the North to the South. In these ways, China is a revisionist, not status quo power.

Selective Multilateralism Moving along the spectrum to the right, the "Selective Multilateralist" school believes that China should expand its global involvements gradually but selectively, and only on issues in which China's national security interests are directly involved. There are several variations and splinter factions of this school. One argues that China should only engage in UN-mandated activities, another argues that China should only become involved on its periphery and not far away, while another believes China should not constrain itself from getting involved in multinational (as distinct from multilateral) actions together with other major powers.

Within this school, the issue of global governance has been highly contentious. Many question whether it is China's obligation and within its ability to contribute. Many simply argue that China is not ready and does not possess the capabilities to become fully engaged in global governance. A leading expert bluntly asserted, "China can't even manage itself—how can it manage the world?"[26] Many are deeply suspicious of doing too much abroad. Most Chinese analysts believe (and there is virtual consensus across the spectrum) that the whole concept of global governance is a Western trap which tries to undermine China's sovereignty and lure it into a variety of foreign entanglements where China does not belong.[27] There is a widespread perception that US and EU calls for China to be a "responsible major power" (*fuzeren de daguo*) or "responsible international stakeholder" are just the latest ruse for retarding and undermining China's power. As one official put it: "During the 1980s, you [the US] tried to subvert us politically; during the 1990s, you tried to contain us strategically; in this decade, you are trying to overextend us internationally."[28] Another scholar noted that, "Global governance is a Western concept. The West emphasizes 'governance,' while China emphasizes the 'global' dimension. We care more about equality of participation than about governance." This is what China means by "international democracy." Not only do many see global governance as a trap for China, they also question the concept of responsible power: "Responsible to whom? To whose standards? The United States? Never!" shouted one analyst.[29]

Despite their skepticism, the Selective Multilateralists believe China should do more to contribute to global governance, commensurate with its newfound position and power, but do so selectively. This strand of selective multilateralism maintains that China should continue to adhere to Deng Xiaoping's 1989 instructions to "maintain a low profile, hide brightness, not seek leadership, but do some things" (*taoguang yanghui, bu dang tou, yousuo zuowei*). Deng's dictum has attracted much attention in the West as a blueprint for stealth development of Chinese power. More than 20 years later, Deng's canon continues to cause intense debate among international relations experts in China, as scholars and officials wrestle with exactly how much China should do on the world stage. Says one scholar, "At the strategic level, everyone agrees we should continue to follow Deng's *taoguang yanghui* concept, but tactically there are many different views. Some think China is too reactive, while others think China should be more proactive."[30] Some Chinese scholars have challenged the current relevance of Deng's views, arguing that they are out of date and not appropriate to China's newfound international status. They argue that China should "do *more* things" (*duosuo zuowei*), while a few say China should "do nothing" (*wusuo zuowei*). Ye Zicheng of Peking University, for example, argued in the early 2000s that *taoguang yanghui* was too vague to serve as a master (or grand) strategy for China; it suggested a sinister intention to many abroad, and a better plan was for China to improve its transparency rather than conceal its capabilities. Others countered by arguing that ambiguity was precisely the wisest strategy for China at this stage of development.

Yet, the mainstream consensus holds that the phrase remains an appropriate guiding strategic principle for Chinese diplomacy.

At the 2010 annual meeting of China's Association of International Relations in Lanzhou, participants heatedly debated the continuing efficacy of this paradigm and concluded that it was still a good guide for China's diplomacy. As a result of this macro conclusion, participants came to nine other principal policy recommendations: do not confront the United States; do not challenge the international system in general; do not use ideology to guide foreign policy; do not be the chief of the "anti-Western camp"; do not conflict with the majority of countries, even when we are right; learn to make compromises and concessions, and learn the game of reciprocal interests; do not compromise China's core interests concerning unification of the country; provide public goods in needed areas of international affairs; and change China's international image by taking advantage of important global events.[31]

Such a strategy fits with the core of Chinese diplomacy throughout the post-1978 period. As China Institutes of Contemporary International Relations (CICIR) President Cui Liru explained, "For most of the past 30 years, China's diplomacy has been defensive and passive in most respects—China's foreign policy has been to make compromises, avoid confrontations, seek common ground, and reserve differences. But a weak country has no foreign policy, so we have been seeking to build our country so as to strengthen our diplomacy."[32]

Concerning global governance, Chinese scholars also use the term multilateralism (*duobianzhuyi*), but have a very different concept of it than is commonly used in the West. Observed one scholar: "For Chinese, multilateralism is a *tool* and a *tactic*, not an intergovernmental mechanism or institutional arrangement. China also worries that multilateralism is a tool for others to contain China. Since the 1990s, China has used multilateralism to solve bilateral issues—to this end, multilateral meetings are a useful platform (*wutai*) to negotiate bilaterally. But we are still uncomfortable with multilateralism, and prefer bilateralism and multipolarity."[33] The official view on global governance, from Foreign Minister Yang Jiechi, is that:

> A more developed China will undertake more international responsibilities and will never pursue interests at the expense of others. We know full well that in this interdependent world, China's future is closely linked to that of the world. Our own interests and those of others are best served when we work together to expand common interests, share responsibilities, and seek win-win outcomes. This is why while focusing on its own development, China is undertaking more and more international responsibilities commensurate with its strength and status.[34]

In the context of this animated debate over global governance, the Selective Multilateralism school generally avoids increasing China's global involvements, but realizes that China must be *seen* to be contributing to global governance. Thus contributing to global governance is a *tactic*, not a *philosophy*. Proponents are not Liberal Institutionalists, but are more an internationalist version of realists. Selective Multilateralism is wary of foreign entanglements, but recognizes that China must not be perceived to be free riders on the international community. Actually, Selective Multilateralism tends not to favor multilateralism per se, in the sense of international institutions, as its proponents are more comfortable working within small ad hoc groups of nations, reflecting China's general discomfort with global institutions or regimes as potentially inhibiting China's independence and freedom of action.

As such, the Selective Multilateralism school has advocated increasing China's participation in UN peacekeeping operations (China at present has 2,155 peacekeeping personnel deployed in 11 of the UN's 19 current global operations), contributing to disaster relief (the 2004 Southeast Asian tsunami, the 2005 Pakistani earthquake, the 2007 Philippines typhoon, the 2010 Haiti earthquake, the 2010 Chile earthquake), fighting international piracy in the Gulf of Aden, and being diplomatically involved in the North Korean and Iranian nuclear issues, but they eschew deeper involvement in sensitive and risky areas such as Iraq and Afghanistan. And they essentially reject the entire transnational

non-traditional security agenda. There remains a strong reluctance to engage in international security operations for humanitarian reasons.

Globalism At the far end of the spectrum is the "Globalism" school, which tends to believe that China must shoulder the responsibility for addressing a range of global governance issues commensurate with its size, power, and influence. This is the equivalent of the Liberal Institutionalism school in the West. In China, this is a very eclectic group comprised of individuals adhering both to "Constructivism" as well the "English School" of international relations. Advocates are more philosophically disposed toward humanitarianism, embrace globalization, place less emphasis on state sovereignty, and believe that transnational challenges require transnational partnerships. They are interested in soft—not hard—power, and put their faith in diplomacy and pan-regional partnerships. They are more supportive and trusting of multilateral *institutions* than the Selective Multilateralists.

The Globalist school thinks that it is incumbent upon China, given its global rise, to contribute much more to global governance and act as a responsible power (*fuzeren de daguo*) in the international arena. Globalists are "interdependence institutionalists" in essence, who adopt globalization and transnationalism as their analytical foundation. As with their Western counterparts, they recognize that in the era of globalization, sovereignty has its limits as various "non-traditional" challenges regularly cross sovereign borders and must be dealt with in a multilateral manner. Much of their analytical focus therefore is on non-traditional security such as human security, economic security, counterterrorism, public health, organized crime, smuggling, cyber hacking, piracy, and so on. Interestingly, there is a growing community inside China's military who work on these subjects, which are euphemistically described as "military operations other than war."

Globalists are strong advocates of the UN and an active Chinese role in the Security Council. They are also strong proponents of China's participation in regional diplomatic groupings all over the world. China has been centrally involved in initiating the formation of new dialogue groupings, such as the Forum on China–Africa

Cooperation, the China–Arab Cooperation Forum, and the East Asia–Latin America Forum, and has become an observer or full member of many existing ones. In Latin America, China has held 17 dialogue rounds with the Rio Group and has established a dialogue mechanism with the Mercosur common market group, the Caribbean Community, and the Latin American Conference among others.

The Globalists attract odd bedfellows. For example, Yan Xuetong, the noted Realist and Director of the Institute of International Studies at Tsinghua University, believes that China should become much more involved in international institutions and should throw its weight around in them, commensurate with its new global status.

Globalists also show a predilection toward soft power. This line of thinking tends to argue that China has much to contribute to international norms from its traditional culture and philosophy. Men Honghua of the Central Party School, the "Dean" of soft-power studies in China, argues that four key Confucian and Mencian values are particularly pertinent: *he* (harmony); *de* (morality); *li* (ritual); and *ren* (benevolence).[35]

Although the Globalists continue to have a public voice, their resonance has diminished considerably. By the end of 2009 and into 2010, this group seemed to be being eclipsed both in the Foreign Ministry and academic circles, as distrust of global governance grew across the spectrum and China began to pursue a much more realist and self-interested global policy.

Implications

Collectively, these schools of thoughts also have policy implications. The international community must grasp that China's international identity is not fixed. It is fluid and a work-in-progress that remains contentious and constantly debated. As such, the United States and others can influence the ongoing debates (as well as policy outcomes) through both actions and words, both negatively and positively. Harsh words and tough actions from the United States are likely to have a reinforcing effect on China, producing more truculent and troubling behavior from Beijing as domestic voices push the government to stand firm against Washington. However, more conciliatory statements and encouragement for China to act as a "responsible international stakeholder" and become more deeply involved in global governance will also exacerbate Chinese suspicions and not likely produce the intended outcome. Thus, Washington and the West are caught in a real conundrum: to get tough with China is likely to produce more Chinese toughness in response, but to be conciliatory will only strengthen the Realists' self-interested "China first" orientation.

China's realist posture plays directly into the realist and conservative camps in the United States, which tend to view China as a rising military power, a mercantilist economic power, a more assertive regional power, and a less cooperative global partner. Even those US analysts who have tended to view China in a more benign fashion, and hope that a more cooperative and internationalist nation would mature on the world stage, are growing disillusioned by Beijing's recent behavior. But China specialists should not be entirely surprised by such behavior, as it just reflects the six-decade-long single-minded mission of the Chinese Communist Party, government, military, and society to strengthen itself comprehensively and become a major world power.

NOTES

1. See "Views of China's Influence," World Public Opinion.org, January 2009, http://www.world-publicopinion.org/pipa/images/feb09/BBCEvals/BBCEvals2.htm; and "Global Views of United States Improve While Other Countries Decline," BBC News, April 18, 2010, http://news.bbc.co.uk/2/shared/bsp/hi/pdfs/160410bbcwspoll.pdf.

2. In this regard, see Linda Jakobson and Dean Knox, "New Foreign Policy Actors in China," *SIPRI Policy Paper*, no. 26 (Stockholm: Stockholm International

Peace Research Institute, 2010), http://books.sipri.org/files/PP/SIPRIPP26.pdf.

3. For another recent assessment, see Zhu Liqun, "China's Foreign Policy Debates," *Chaillot Papers* (Paris: Institute for Security Studies European Union, September 2010); for an earlier assessment, see Daniel Lynch, "Chinese Thinking on the Future of International Relations: Realism as the *Ti*, Rationalism as the *Yong*?," *The China Quarterly* 197 (March 2009): pp. 87–107.

4. See, for example, Xue Yong, *Zenmayang Zuo Da Guo?* [How to be a Great Power] (Beijing: Zhongxin chubanshe, 2009); and Yu Defu, *Daguo Faze* [The Rules for Great Nations] (Beijing: Zhongguo Huaqiao chubanshe, 2009).

5. Also see Robert Gilpin, *War and Change in Global Politics* (Cambridge: Cambridge University Press, 1983).

6. It is better to think of these cohorts as "tendencies of analysis" than rigid schools of thought. The pioneering work on "tendency analysis" is H. Gordon Skilling and William Griffiths, *Interest Groups in Soviet Politics* (Princeton: Princeton University Press, 1973).

7. Wang Xiaodong et al., *Zhongguo bu Gaoxing* [China Is Unhappy] (Beijing: Jiangsu renmin chubanshe, 2009); and He Xiongfei, *Zhongguo Weishenma bu Gaoxing?* [Why Is China Unhappy?] (Beijing: Shijie zhishi chubanshe, 2009).

8. Zhang Wenmu, "Shijie lishi zhong de qiangguo zhilu yu Zhongguo de Xuanze" [The Road of Great Powers in World History and China's Choice], in *Zhanlue yu Tansuo* [Strategy and Exploration], ed. Guo Shuyong (Beijing: Shijie zhishi chubanshe, 2008), pp. 33, 54.

9. Fang Ning, "Xin diguozhuyi yu Zhongguo de zhanlue xuanze" [The New Imperialism and China's Strategic Choice], in *Zhanlue yanjianglu* [Lectures on Strategy], ed. Guo Shuyong (Beijing: Peking University Press, 2006), pp. 132–133.

10. See Wang Jinsong, *Diguozhuyi Lishi de Zhongjie: Dangdai Diguozhuyi de Xingcheng he Fazhan Qushi* [Imperialism Is the Final Stage of History: Contemporary Imperialism's Formation and Development Trends] (Beijing: Shehui kexue wenzhai chubanshe, 2008).

11. See David Shambaugh, *Beautiful Imperialist: China Perceives America, 1972–1990* (Princeton: Princeton University Press, 1990).

12. See Alastair Iain Johnston, *Cultural Realism: Strategic Culture and Grand Strategy in Chinese Culture* (Princeton: Princeton University Press, 1998).

13. Scholar at China Reform Forum, interview with author, Beijing, January 20, 2010.

14. Shen Dingli, presentation at the New Zealand Institute of International Affairs, June 28, 2010.

15. Shen Dingli, presentation at Roundtable with China Foreign Policy Experts, Wellington, New Zealand, June 29, 2010.

16. Yan Xuetong, "An Analysis of the Advantages and Disadvantages of Containing Legal Taiwan Independence by Force," *Strategy and Management* 3 (2004): pp. 1–5.

17. Yan Xuetong, *Zhongguo Jueqi* [China's Rise] (Tianjin: Tianjin renmin chubanshe, 1997).

18. Zhang Ruizhang, statement at conference at Zhongshan University, Guangzhou, May 7, 2010.

19. Zhang Ruizhang, "Chonggu Zhongguo waijiao suochu zhi guoji huanjing—heping yu fazhan bingfei dangdai shijie zhuti" [Reassessing the International Environment of China's Foreign Affairs—Peace and Development Are Not the Main Theme of Today's World], *Strategy and Management* 1 (2001): pp. 20–30.

20. See Pan Wei, "Yetan heping jueqi" [Again Discussing Peaceful Rise], http://www.360doc.com/content/07/0831/17/41440_708164.shtml; and Pan Wei, "Diqiushang conglai mei fasheng guo 'heping jueqi' zhezhongshi" [There Was Never Such a Thing as 'Peaceful Rise' in the World's Past], http://www.360doc.com/content/09/1102/17/346405_828157.shtml.

21. See Wang Yizhou, *Zhongguo Waijiao Xin Gaodi* [High Land over China's Foreign Affairs] (Beijing: China Academy of Social Sciences Press, 2008), p. 7.

22. Scholar interview with author, Beijing, March 25, 2010.

23. See David Shambaugh, "China Engages Asia: Reshaping the Regional Order," *International Security* 29, no. 3 (Winter 2004/2005): pp. 64–99.

24. Yu Xintian, "Zhongguo ying zhuanbian dui dui fazhanzhong guojia de zhanlue" [China Should Change Its Strategy Toward Developing Countries], *Strategy and Management* 3 (2003): pp. 40–45.

25. Huanqiu, ed., *Baiwen Zhongguo Weilai: Zhongguo Jingying Duihua Quanqiu* [A Hundred Questions on China's Future: Dialogues with Chinese Elites] (Beijing: Xinhua Press, 2009), p. 12.

26. Scholar, interview with author, Guangzhou, May 7, 2010.

27. See, for example, statement by Chen Hanxi of Guangdong Foreign Studies University at conference at Zhongshan University, Guangzhou, May 8, 2010.

28. Communist Party official, interview with author, Beijing, July 7, 2010.

29. Scholar at CICIR, interview with author, Beijing, April 19, 2010.

30. Jin Canrong, interview with author, Renmin University, January 29, 2010.

31. "Zhongguo Guoji Guanxi Xuehui 2010 nian nianhui zai Lanzhou zhaokai" [China's International Relations Society 2010 Annual Meeting in Lanzhou Review], *Waijiao Pinglun* 4 (2010): p. 157.

32. CICIR President Cui Liru, presentation at conference on "Sixty Years of China's Foreign Policy," Fudan University, Shanghai, October 21, 2009.

33. Song Xinning, statement at conference at Renmin University, Beijing, May 3, 2010.

34. Yang Jiechi, "A Changing China in a Changing World" (speech, Munich Security Conference, February 5, 2010).

35. Men Honghua, interview with author, Beijing, May 2, 2010.

II. THE ASIAN NEIGHBORHOOD

China's Role in Asia: Attractive or Assertive?*

Phillip C. Saunders

After decades of exerting only modest regional influence, China now plays an active and important role in Asia. Market-oriented economic reforms and China's subsequent integration into regional and global production networks have produced thirty-five years of rapid economic growth that have dramatically increased China's national power. Aggressive Chinese behavior toward Taiwan and in the South China Sea from 1994 to 1996 created alarm about a "China threat," but more restrained behavior and assurance measures adopted over the period from 1997 to 2008 helped to ease regional concerns about a stronger China. During this period, Asian views largely shifted from regarding China as a potential threat to regarding China as an opportunity; this shift was widely interpreted as an indicator of the success of China's Asia policy.[1] Beginning in 2009, however, more "assertive" Chinese behavior on maritime territorial disputes and other issues dissipated much of the goodwill built by China's charm offensive and revived regional concerns about how a strong China might behave.[2]

This article examines China's Asia strategy, the sources of Chinese power and influence, and the assurance measures Beijing has employed to try to reconcile the region to a dominant Chinese regional role without antagonizing the United States or destabilizing the region. It considers the impact of China's more assertive recent behavior on the regional security environment and discusses how Chinese leaders have adapted their Asia policy in light of the new circumstances. Chinese leaders will have to strike a balance between restrained policies to preserve a stable regional security environment and the desire to use China's new power to make progress on long-standing territorial disputes. The conclusion considers key variables and potential developments that might alter China's regional policy.

China's Asia Strategy

China's regional strategy derives in part from its global grand strategy.[3] The top domestic concern of Chinese leaders is maintaining political stability and ensuring the continued rule of the Chinese Communist Party (CCP). China's leaders have tried to build new sources of political support by raising living standards through rapid economic growth and by appealing to nationalist sentiment.[4] Throughout the reform era, Chinese leaders have focused on maintaining a stable international environment that supports economic modernization. This objective requires China to avoid a hostile relationship with the United States, the dominant power in the current international system. Given the high costs of confrontation, Beijing seeks stable, cooperative relations with Washington. Yet many Chinese elites believe that the United States seeks to subvert the Chinese political system and to contain China's economic and military potential. China therefore seeks to build positive relationships with current and potential great powers to facilitate the emergence of a multipolar world order and to deny the United States the opportunity to construct a coalition to contain China and prevent its continued rise.[5] By properly managing relations with the United States, other great powers, and developing countries, Chinese leaders hope to take advantage of a "period of strategic opportunity" in the first two decades of the twenty-first century to build China's comprehensive national power and improve China's international position.

This grand strategy defines the international and domestic context in which China formulates and pursues its Asia policy. Asia is the most important region of the world to China in economic, security, and political terms. It serves as a

* This article was published in David Shambaugh and Michael Yahuda (eds.), *International Relations of Asia* (Lanham, MD: Rowman & Littlefield, 2014, second edition), 147–72.

source of raw materials; as a supplier of components, technology, and management expertise for production networks operating in China; and as a market for finished Chinese products. The Asia-Pacific region is the most important destination for Chinese exports and for Chinese direct investment. Investment from other Asian countries played a critical role in fueling China's economic takeoff and export boom. Much of China's economic success can be attributed to the operations of multinational companies that import components from Asia, assemble goods using Chinese workers, and export the finished products to markets in the United States, Europe, and elsewhere. Approximately 50 percent of Chinese exports are produced by foreign-owned or foreign-invested companies, with the figure rising as high as 80 percent in sophisticated sectors such as electronics.[6] China's economic growth has produced increasing dependence on oil imported from the Middle East and Africa and on secure sea lanes to support its maritime trade. Most of this traffic passes through Asian waters, including through potential choke points such as the Strait of Malacca.

Geography also makes Asia critically important to China from a security perspective.[7] China shares land borders with fourteen East Asian, South Asian, and Central Asian countries. Chinese leaders worry that neighboring countries could serve as bases for subversion or for military efforts to contain China. This is of particular concern because much of China's ethnic minority population, which Chinese leaders view as a potential separatist threat, lives in sparsely populated border regions such as Xinjiang and Tibet. Chinese concerns about threats posed by "terrorism, separatism, and religious extremism" have prompted increased efforts at security cooperation with its Central Asian and South Asian neighbors. China's unresolved territorial claims are all in Asia, including claims to the Spratly Islands and the South China Sea, the Diaoyu/Senkaku Islands and parts of the East China Sea, a disputed land border with India, and China's self-described "core interest" in unification with Taiwan. China also worries about the possibility of encirclement and threats from conventional military forces based on its periphery. In the 1960s, the United States had significant military forces based on Taiwan, the Philippines, Japan, South Korea, and Thailand, all within striking distance of Chinese territory. Chinese strategists are highly sensitive to recent US actions to improve its military power projection capability in the Pacific and the possibility that US alliances in Asia might someday be turned against China, concerns that have strengthened with the US "rebalance to Asia."[8]

Asia is also important politically. The broader Asia-Pacific region is home to major powers such as China, Japan, and India and to advanced economies such as Korea and Singapore. East Asia alone has 31 percent of the world's population and produces about 28 percent of global GDP.[9] If Asia were able to act collectively, it could rival the geopolitical weight of North America and Europe. Asia has historically lacked the web of regional institutions that produced economic and security cooperation in Europe and which supported the regional integration process that led to the creation of the European Union. The political, ethnic, and cultural diversity of the region and the tendency of Asian states to jealously guard their sovereignty have impeded the creation of strong regional institutions. Over the last 15 years, new regional institutions have emerged to promote regional cooperation between Asian states in the economic, security, and political domains. A robust set of non-governmental organizations and people-to-people contacts have also emerged at the societal level. Some see these processes as promoting greater regional integration, which would greatly alter the political dynamics in Asia. China has a strong stake in influencing the political evolution of the region in ways that advance Chinese interests, and in blocking developments that might work against Chinese goals.

China's preferred outcome is a stable environment in Asia that permits rapid Chinese economic growth to continue and supports increased Chinese regional influence. Many Western analysts believe that China's ultimate (but unstated) goal is to eventually displace the United States as the dominant power in Asia.[10] Chinese officials and analysts acknowledge that the US role in supporting regional stability and protecting sea lanes of communication makes a significant contribution to regional stability and supports Chinese interests. The US security alliance with Japan also exerts a degree of restraint on Tokyo, although Chinese analysts believe this restraining influence has been reduced in recent years with the transformation of the alliance, the easing of constitutional and legal constraints on Japanese military activities, and the election of right-wing Japanese governments such as that of Prime Minister Shinzo Abe. The potential for US power and alliances to be turned against China makes Chinese analysts uneasy at the prospect of an enduring American security role in the region. China disclaims any desire to dominate Asia, declaring that it will never seek hegemony and talking about cooperation on the basis of equality, mutual respect, and non-interference in the internal affairs of other nations. But Chinese elites also appear to expect that weaker countries will defer to Chinese wishes as the country grows more powerful.[11] In formulating Asia policy, Chinese leaders must manage the tensions between official foreign policy principles and a foreign policy firmly grounded in realpolitik concerns. Chinese leaders are acutely sensitive to trends in the global and regional balance of power, which are closely monitored by Chinese intelligence agencies and research institutes.

Chinese leaders are aware that China's increasing economic and military power is viewed as a potential threat by other countries in the region.[12] This wariness partly reflects the legacy of earlier support for communist parties and national liberation movements in Asian countries. Beijing ended such ideologically based support by the early 1980s, but Asian countries have residual concerns that China could build relationships with their ethnic Chinese citizens that could undermine their sovereignty. Asian countries also worry about China's potential to use coercion and force to resolve territorial disputes and to employ its superior power against smaller and weaker countries in Asia using "divide-and-conquer" tactics.

China's strategic dilemma is finding a way to reconcile the rest of Asia to a dominant Chinese regional role without antagonizing the United States or destabilizing the region. This task is greatly complicated by China's claims to territories it does not currently control. Chinese actions to "safeguard sovereignty and territorial integrity" are viewed by neighboring states as efforts to use intimidation and the threat of force to strengthen Chinese territorial claims. Beijing would greatly prefer to resolve the Taiwan issue peacefully but has refused to rule out the use of force. China's military is developing capabilities that could be used to coerce Taiwan (including efforts to deter and raise the costs of US military intervention), but which could also be used in other territorial disputes. The need to preserve a peaceful regional environment for economic development—a necessity for internal stability—is thus in tension with the desire to use China's newfound power to achieve nationalist territorial goals at the expense of China's neighbors. Efforts to manage these tensions in China's Asia policy are further complicated by the US rebalance to Asia, which has altered regional strategic dynamics and increased US-China competition for regional influence.

Sources of Chinese Power in Asia

Economic Power China's rapid economic growth, and the increasing economic ties with Asia that it has produced, is the most important source of China's power and influence in Asia. Chinese officials regularly use free trade agreements, trade-facilitation agreements, and non-binding bilateral trade targets to leverage access to China's market as a diplomatic tool in bilateral relations. One important pattern in China's trade relations is that other East Asian countries are becoming more dependent on exports to China, but China's relative dependence on East Asian markets is staying the same. The volume of Chinese trade with East Asia has increased dramatically over the last decade, but the share of Chinese exports going to East Asia (excluding Hong Kong) has declined from 34 percent in 1996 to 21 percent in 2012.[13] Conversely, China has become the first- or second-largest trading partner of almost every country in the region since the turn of the millennium (see tables 1 and 2). Despite periodic political tensions, Japan's trade with China now exceeds Japan's trade with all ten members of the Association of Southeast Asian Nations (ASEAN) and surpassed US-Japan trade levels in 2007. ASEAN exports to China have grown rapidly in recent years; China is now the second most important export market for ASEAN products.

These changes in Asian dependence on the Chinese market reflect both the shift of export

Table 1 Percentage of Imports from China (China's Rank as Import Source)

	Japan	South Korea	Taiwan[a]	ASEAN 6[b]	India[c]
1986	4.7% (4)	0.0% (—)	0.28% (33)	4.0% (6)	0.55% (27)
1996	11.6% (2)	5.7% (3)	3.0% (7)	3.0% (5)	1.9% (18)
2006	20.4% (1)	15.7% (2)	12.2% (2)	11.0% (3)	9.4% (1)
2012	21.3% (1)	15.6% (1)	15.0% (2)	13.2% (2)	11.1% (1)

Source: UN Comtrade Database.

[a] Taiwan Trade Statistics: Taiwan figures are from Taiwan's Bureau of Foreign Trade, available at cus93.trade .gov.tw/ english/FSCE/FSC0011E.ASP; 1989 data (the earliest available) are used for the 1986 figure.

[b] ASEAN 6 is Singapore, Malaysia, Indonesia, Thailand, Philippines, and Brunei. ASEAN 6 data for Brunei use 1985 data and 1998 data to substitute for unavailable 1986 and 1996 data. ASEAN 6 rankings consider intra-ASEAN 6 trade with other ASEAN 6 members (e.g., ASEAN 6 exports to Singapore) as trade with other countries for ranking purposes.

[c] 1986 India data are from the *IMF Direction of Trade Statistical Yearbook 1990*.

Table 2 Percentage of Exports to China (China's Rank as Export Market)

	Japan	South Korea	Taiwan[a]	ASEAN 6	India
1986	4.7% (4)	0.0% (—)	0.0% (—)	2.3% (12)	0.74% (28)
1996	5.3% (5)	8.8% (3)	0.54% (23)	2.9% (12)	1.8% (14)
2006	14.3% (2)	21.3% (1)	22.7% (1)	8.8% (3)	6.6% (3)
2012	18.1% (1)	24.5% (1)	26.7% (1)	11.4% (2)	5.1% (3)

Source: UN Comtrade Database.

[a] Taiwan Trade Statistics.

production from other East Asian economies to tap inexpensive Chinese labor and the Chinese domestic market's appetite for imports from Asia. Chinese leaders and analysts believe that trade dependence can generate significant political influence as groups that benefit from trade with China mobilize to protect their economic interests. In recent years, China has shown a greater willingness to use economic coercion against other Asian countries over political or territorial disputes.[14] This tactic has produced alarm among foreign business groups but has not necessarily produced the desired outcomes. For example, Japanese business groups have called for better Sino-Japanese relations, but their influence has not outweighed other Japanese voices seeking a tougher policy toward China.

China has also emerged as a significant source of foreign direct investment in Asia, which is the most important destination for Chinese FDI. Chinese statistics indicate that Chinese enterprises have invested at least $55 billion in East Asia as of 2012, while Chinese investment in ASEAN

passed $10 billion in 2011.[15] This investment makes a significant contribution to Southeast Asian economies.

China's foreign aid is also significant. China does not publish a detailed breakout of its foreign aid programs, but poorer countries in Southeast Asia and Central Asia are significant recipients of Chinese development assistance.[16] Much of this assistance goes to improve transportation infrastructure connecting Southeast Asian and Central Asian countries to China. This infrastructure contributes to these countries' economic development, but it also links them more closely to the Chinese economy and will produce greater trade dependence in the future.[17] China's role as a production site in regional production networks serves as an important link between Asian producers of capital goods and production inputs and developed country markets in the United States and Europe. This ties together the economic interests of Asian companies and countries in a positive-sum manner.

Military Power China's military, the People's Liberation Army (PLA), is also becoming a more effective policy tool, both in terms of its combat potential and its role in security cooperation. The PLA has historically been a large land force with very limited ability to project and sustain power beyond China's borders. China's military power has increased significantly over the last decade, creating both newfound respect and heightened concerns in other Asian countries.[18] The "three pillars" of PLA reform and modernization include (1) development, procurement, and fielding of new weapons systems and capabilities; (2) institutional and systemic reforms to improve the professionalism and quality of Chinese military personnel; and (3) development of new war-fighting doctrines for employing these new capabilities.[19] China's military modernization has been supported by significant increases in defense spending, with the PLA receiving double-digit real budget increases every year since 1997. The official 2013 defense budget was approximately $114 billion, but Stockholm International Peace Research Institute (SIPRI) estimates that include military-related and off-budget spending suggest that the total may have been about 1.5 times the official budget, or $166 billion.[20] This funding has underwritten higher salaries, expanded training and facilities, and the development and acquisition of advanced indigenous and Russian arms.

Many of the new weapons systems the PLA is acquiring appear to be focused primarily on deterring Taiwan independence and on deterring or delaying possible US intervention. These include development of more accurate short-range and medium-range conventional ballistic missiles, acquisition of Russian Kilo-class submarines and *Sovremenny* destroyers and development of an anti-ship ballistic missile that can target US aircraft carriers, modernization of China's strategic nuclear arsenal, and deployment of anti-ship and land-attack cruise missiles. Chinese military strategists are exploring tactics such as attacks on US military computer systems and space assets as means of deterring or delaying the arrival of US military forces in the event of a Taiwan crisis. China's January 2007 test of a direct-ascent antisatellite weapon illustrates one aspect of these efforts. To the extent that these "anti-access strategies" are actually able to hold US military forces

in the Western Pacific at risk, they may begin to shift regional perceptions of the military balance of power in Asia.[21]

Some of the new military capabilities China is developing will significantly expand the PLA's ability to project power within Asia. In addition to the capabilities listed above, China is also deploying tankers and air-refueling technology that will extend the range of Chinese fighters. The PLA is improving the capabilities of its airborne and amphibious forces capable of expeditionary operations and making efforts to improve its airlift and sealift capability. China has refurbished a Soviet-era Ukrainian aircraft carrier, now commissioned as the training carrier *Liaoning*, and is expected to build an indigenously designed carrier in the future. The PLA already performs some power projection missions such as responding to natural disasters, contributing to deterrence, and enhancing regional stability. Although lack of overseas bases constrains PLA power projection capability, the PLA is increasing its "presence deployments" through naval visits and port calls and participation in joint and combined military exercises with other militaries.[22] China also has extensive naval paramilitary forces that nominally handle tasks such as maritime surveillance and enforcing fishing laws, but which have been used regularly to reinforce China's maritime claims.[23]

Soft Power China is also seeking to expand its "soft power," defined as China's ability to persuade others to pursue its goals and values or to emulate its behavior. One important trend is increasing contact between Chinese citizens and people in other Asian countries. Flows of tourists and students between China and other Asian countries have increased dramatically in recent years as China has loosened restrictions on overseas travel. Chinese tourists have flocked to Asia, with about 4 million visiting other East Asian countries in 2012.[24] Many Chinese tourists visit Asian countries as part of large tour groups, which do not always leave positive impressions on their hosts. Educational contacts between China and Asia have also increased significantly. China sent about 240,000 students to Asia-Pacific countries in 2010 and hosted more than 160,000 students from the region in 2012, with South Korea and Japan sending the most.[25] The Chinese government has supplemented student exchanges by establishing "Confucius Institutes" in foreign countries to teach Chinese language and promote Chinese culture. As of 2012 ten East Asian countries and India hosted some 63 Confucius Institutes, with Thailand, South Korea, and Japan hosting at least ten apiece.[26]

The Chinese government also actively supports the participation of Chinese scholars and experts in academic and unofficial "Track II" policy conferences in Asia. Much of this activity occurs via Chinese government think tanks or government-operated non-governmental organizations (GONGOs) created to interact with foreign non-government organizations. The Chinese government has sought to increase contacts between Chinese and East Asian think tanks—and to exert some degree of control over the regional agenda—by providing financial and organizational support for participation of Chinese experts and by sponsoring the establishment of the Network of East Asian Think-Tanks (NEAT), which includes members from all the ASEAN + 3 countries.[27] Chinese scholars and experts increasingly have the language skills and expertise to function effectively in these types of meetings. However, the perception that Chinese participants often deliver approved government talking points and cannot fully express their individual viewpoints probably limits their influence.

Appeals to cultural and linguistic affinities have been important in dealing with countries with significant ethnic Chinese minorities. Malaysia and Indonesia, which previously viewed their ethnic Chinese populations with considerable suspicion, now regard them as an asset in building economic relations with China. Beijing found some sympathy in Southeast Asia for appeals to "Asian values" during its efforts to resist Western human rights pressure in the 1990s, but this has been tempered by the deepening of democracy in Japan, South Korea, Taiwan, and some Southeast Asian countries. Cultural and linguistic diversity in Asia is likely to limit China's ability to harness purported common "Confucian values" as a diplomatic tool. Few Asian elites are attracted to Chinese values or desire to emulate China's system of government.[28]

In the cultural sphere, talented China artists are beginning to win regional and international recognition. Some Chinese cultural products reflect traditional Chinese culture in ways that resonate within East Asia, but most have limited appeal due to their focus on Chinese domestic concerns, their derivative nature, political constraints on content, and language barriers. Films have arguably been China's most successful cultural exports. Some of these constraints may ease as China becomes richer, but for now other Asian countries are producing work with more regional impact and influence. It is worth noting that many of the most successful Chinese artists achieved their fame with work done outside China, including Nobel Prize–winning novelist Gao Xingjian.

Chinese companies have sought, with limited success, to build internationally recognized brand names. Haier (refrigerators) and Huawei (routers and communications products) have been most successful. However, most Chinese products compete on the basis of price rather than quality. Nevertheless, if goods are cheap enough, Chinese products can promote a positive image. For example, Chinese motorcycles that sell at about a quarter of the price of those produced in Japanese-owned factories in Thailand have become affordable for poor villagers in Laos. The resulting access to transportation has literally saved lives and has had a major improvement in the quality of life for Laotian villagers in remote areas.[29]

Many Asian elites look at China's economic success with envy and admiration. The pace of construction in China's major cities—and the number of architecturally ambitious new buildings in Beijing and Shanghai—is striking. Beijing built an impressive set of facilities and infrastructure improvements to support the 2008 Olympics. China's manned space program is regarded by some Asian elites as an important technological achievement of the Chinese system.[30] Yet these impressive accomplishments have a darker side. China's breakneck growth has been accompanied by rampant environmental degradation that has severely damaged China's air and water.[31] Rapid growth and construction in China's major cities has destroyed many of their most distinctive features and displaced poorer citizens to distant suburbs with limited compensation. Poor urban planning and rapid growth in the number of automobiles are making traffic a nightmare in many Chinese cities.

Some believe the Chinese approach of reforming the economy while limiting political freedom represents a new development model with considerable appeal to authoritarian leaders in developing countries.[32] China's development model actually draws heavily on orthodox development economics and benefits from special factors such as a large domestic market and large labor supply that cannot readily be replicated by most other countries.[33] Domestic problems, social inequality, environmental degradation, and periodic political clampdowns limit China's attractiveness as a model for others to emulate. Within Asia, Vietnam has clearly been influenced by China's approach to economic development, but the country Chinese leaders have tried hardest to influence—North Korea—has proved reluctant to embrace a Chinese-style opening. A significant slowdown in growth, a widespread financial crisis, or a major internal security crackdown would highlight the downsides of the Chinese model and significantly reduce China's ability to employ soft power as a diplomatic tool.

China's Reassurance Efforts

Regional concerns about Chinese power were aggravated in the mid-1990s by China's aggressive efforts to pursue its territorial claims, including its 1994 seizure and subsequent fortification of Mischief Reef, a small island in the South China Sea claimed by the Philippines. In late 1995 and March 1996, China used military exercises (including firing ballistic missiles into waters near Taiwan) to express its concerns about the Taiwan independence movement and its displeasure at a US decision to permit Taiwan president Lee Teng-hui to visit the United States and speak at Cornell University. These actions prompted numerous articles and books highlighting China's military modernization and growing nationalism and asking whether China posed a threat to the Asia-Pacific region.[34] Chinese officials, scholars, and the party's propaganda apparatus launched repeated attacks on what they labeled the "China threat theory," but Chinese leaders also recognized the need for actions to address regional concerns.

China has employed a variety of diplomatic, economic, and military means to reassure its Asian neighbors that a stronger China will not threaten their interests. China's diplomatic efforts in Asia rest upon a foundation of well-trained and capable diplomats able to convey Chinese messages effectively.[35] The content of China's diplomatic messages also changed to increase their appeal in Asia. In 1997–98 China advanced the "New Security Concept," a reformulation of its five principles of peaceful coexistence that called for mutually beneficial cooperation on the basis of equality, mutual respect, noninterference in the internal affairs of other countries, and resolution of conflicts through dialogue.[36] This concept meshed reasonably well with the principles and preferred methods of operation of ASEAN states.[37] (The so-called ASEAN Way emphasizes decision making by consensus, respect for national sovereignty, non-interference in internal affairs, and a gradual pace to security cooperation.) Chinese pledges of non-interference and respect for sovereignty provide assurances that Beijing will not support separatist groups or intervene on behalf of ethnic Chinese outside its borders.

China has sometimes sought to reassure ASEAN states by engaging and negotiating with them on a multilateral basis, forgoing the bargaining advantages a stronger country enjoys in bilateral negotiations. Beijing's willingness to negotiate in the "ASEAN + China" framework offered some reassurance that China would not pursue a "divide and conquer" strategy, although China has repeatedly ruled out multilateral negotiations to resolve the dispute over the Spratly Islands. China also launched a series of annual summits with ASEAN, began participating more actively in the ASEAN Regional Forum and its unofficial counterpart the Council for Security Cooperation in the Asia Pacific (CSCAP), and signed the Declaration of Conduct on the South China Sea, a non-binding pledge to resolve territorial disputes peacefully. This pledge was an important confidence-building measure because four ASEAN countries (Vietnam, the Philippines, Brunei, and Malaysia) claim parts of the disputed Spratly Islands, At the 2003 Bali summit, China became the first non-ASEAN member to sign the Treaty of Amity and Cooperation (TAC), which codified ASEAN's preferred principles of international conduct such as non-aggression, non-interference, and peaceful resolution of disputes.

Beijing also signed a strategic partnership agreement with ASEAN, giving the organization a status equal to its partnerships with other major powers.

China has also participated substantively in multilateral regional organizations such as the Asia-Pacific Economic Cooperation (APEC) forum; ASEAN + 3 (Japan, China, Korea); the ASEAN Regional Forum; and the East Asia Summit. China was historically reluctant to participate in multilateral forums due to fears that other countries would gang up on it and because multilateral norms and procedures could constrain its ability to pursue its interests. Increased multilateralism is a means of channeling Chinese power in ways that make it more acceptable to its neighbors.[38] Some analysts argue that China now views multilateral and regional organizations as important political venues and has become more active in these organizations as a means of pursuing its national interests.[39] China's establishment of the Shanghai Cooperation Organization (SCO) as a means of combating terrorism and expanding its influence in Central Asia is compatible with this view, as is China's effective use of bilateral diplomacy to influence the agenda of multilateral organizations such as ASEAN and the SCO in directions that advance Chinese interests.

China has taken some concrete measures to address Asian security concerns, such as its efforts in the 1990s to resolve most outstanding land border disputes. These agreements eased concerns about potential conflicts and paved the way for increased cross-border cooperation against terrorism and organized crime.[40] To handle maritime disputes in a less confrontational way, China revived Deng Xiaoping's approach of setting aside sovereignty concerns and pursuing joint development of resources in disputed areas. This approach yielded a 2004 agreement between China and the Philippines to conduct seismic exploration for energy resources in parts of the South China Sea. Vietnam joined the effort in 2005, but exploration efforts did not identify promising areas for development and the agreement ended when the Philippines withdrew in 2007.[41] China made another joint development attempt in the East China Sea in 2008, reaching an agreement with Japan to jointly develop one bloc in disputed waters and to allow Japanese investment in the Chunxiao gas fields in Chinese waters. However, the agreement reportedly sparked intense nationalist opposition within China, and Beijing has not implemented it. China has also pursued military confidence-building measures with some of its neighbors, especially in the context of land border agreements.

China's accelerated military modernization has been accompanied by efforts to reassure its Asian neighbors that a more powerful PLA will not threaten their security. China has sought to demonstrate that its growing military and paramilitary forces can make useful contributions to regional security. The 2013 Chinese *Defense White Paper* states, "China's armed forces work to promote dialogue and cooperation on maritime security; participate in UN peacekeeping missions, international counter-terrorism cooperation, international merchant shipping protection and disaster relief operations; conduct joint exercises and training with foreign counterparts; conscientiously assume their due international responsibilities; and play an active role in maintaining world peace, security and stability."[42] Starting in 2002, China began to observe and then participate in bilateral and multilateral military exercises with neighboring countries as a confidence-building measure. Although most are simple search-and-rescue exercises, they provide an opportunity for Asian militaries to interact with the PLA. China has also improved the quality of its participation in official and unofficial multilateral security dialogues and established bilateral security dialogues with most major countries in Asia. Although Chinese participants remain reluctant to talk about Chinese military capabilities and often repeat official talking points, these dialogues still have some value.

In the economic realm, China has sought to persuade Asian countries that they will share in the benefits of China's rapid growth, while simultaneously advancing Chinese interests through commercial diplomacy. "Win-win" and "mutual benefit" are the watchwords of China's economic diplomacy. Demand from China helped shield Asian countries from the 2008 global financial crisis and is credited with helping to revive the Japanese economy from its decade-long slump. China's increasing role in world trade and expectations of future growth make it an attractive market and give Beijing leverage in dealing with trade partners. A relatively new element in China's economic diplomacy involves negotiation of regional and bilateral free trade agreements (FTAs). The 2002 China-ASEAN FTA is the most significant example, but China has also signed bilateral FTAs with New Zealand and Singapore and begun negotiations or feasibility studies with Australia, South Korea, India, and others.[43] In the China-ASEAN FTA negotiations, China let individual ASEAN states determine their own comfort level with the coverage and pace of trade liberalization commitments and included "early harvest" provisions that offered additional benefits to ASEAN agricultural producers. Southeast Asian diplomats note that China has often been willing to adapt its proposals for regional cooperation to build consensus, deferring contentious issues or delaying proposals that are moving too fast for ASEAN sensibilities.[44] China is also a participant in a 2012 ASEAN-led initiative to negotiate a Regional Comprehensive Economic Partnership (RCEP), which seeks to establish an FTA between the ten ASEAN states and Australia, China, India, Japan, South Korea, and New Zealand by 2015.[45]

China's Relations in Asia Since 2009

From 1998 to 2008, China achieved remarkable success in improving relations with its neighbors in Asia by employing the diplomatic, military, and economic assurance measures described in the previous section. Their effectiveness was predicated on a patient approach to territorial disputes and restraint in the employment of Chinese military forces (even as PLA budgets grew and military modernization efforts accelerated). However, in 2009 a more assertive Chinese posture emerged on a wide range of bilateral, regional, and global issues.[46] Within the space of eighteen months, Chinese diplomatic bullying, assertive military and paramilitary actions, and disregard for foreign reactions undid many of the gains from Beijing's decade-long charm offensive. In particular, the means used to advance Chinese maritime sovereignty claims in the South China Sea and East China Sea did considerable damage to Beijing's efforts to persuade others that China's rise would be peaceful.[47]

The shift in the tone and substance of Chinese policy had both international and domestic causes. Chinese officials initially feared that the 2008 global financial crisis would severely damage China's economy, but these concerns eased as China's massive 4 trillion RMB economic stimulus (proportionately about four times the size of the US stimulus) took effect. As Chinese growth resumed and the United States and Europe remained mired in a recession, Chinese officials and analysts appear to have exaggerated the negative impact of financial problems on US global leadership and mistakenly concluded that a fundamental shift in the global balance of power was under way. Chinese officials also appear to have misinterpreted Obama administration efforts to increase bilateral cooperation and expand China's role in global institutions as a sign of US weakness and an opportunity to press Washington for concessions.[48] An exaggerated sense of Western decline was coupled with overconfidence in China's international position following the successful hosting of the 2008 Olympic Games. This assessment played into a nationalist mood in China, where many commentators (including retired military officers) argued that a more powerful China should take a hard line on challenges to Chinese territorial claims and use its economic leverage to punish the United States for arms sales to Taiwan. Chinese officials and scholars began to regularly cite nationalist public opinion as a reason China could not compromise on territorial and sovereignty issues.[49] Finally, senior Chinese leaders appear to have been preoccupied with domestic concerns and not focused on foreign policy. High-level policy coordination mechanisms such as the Foreign Affairs Leading Small Group reportedly did not meet for more than a year during 2009–10, allowing the PLA and China's paramilitary forces more autonomy in implementing policy on maritime disputes.

Chinese officials and scholars deny that Beijing changed its foreign policy goals, expanded its territorial claims, or adopted a more assertive attitude toward maritime disputes. They argue that other countries, emboldened by passive or active US support, stepped up their challenges to China's long-established territorial claims. The May 2009 deadline for submissions to the United Nations Convention on the Law of the Sea (UNCLOS) did spur many Asian countries (including China) to reinforce their claims to disputed islands and waters. Sometimes China initiated contentious actions, such as increased patrolling in disputed waters and arrests of fishermen; other times Chinese nationalists clamored loudly for strong reactions to actions by countries such as Vietnam, the Philippines, and Japan that challenged Chinese sovereignty claims. Chinese officials and military officers argued that restraint in response to provocations was misinterpreted as weakness; Beijing could either allow others to infringe on Chinese sovereignty and territorial integrity or take appropriate measures in response.[50] Beijing employed economic coercion in some of the sovereignty disputes, including a temporary ban on exports of rare earths to Japan following the 2010 arrest of a Chinese fishing boat captain and import restrictions on Philippine bananas in 2012. China also took a tough line on military activities in its exclusive economic zone, acting to interfere with US ships (including a March 2009 incident off Hainan Island when Chinese paramilitary vessels attempted to snag the towed sonar array of the USNS *Impeccable*).[51]

Chinese officials, academics, and military officers all stress that China's domestic policy–making environment has changed, and that leaders must now be more responsive to the concerns of Chinese citizens, including nationalists who advocate a tough line on sovereignty disputes.[52] Chinese officials insist that China has not taken any actions that violate legitimate freedom of navigation and that its policies of seeking to resolve territorial disputes through peaceful dialogue and its willingness to set aside sovereignty and pursue joint exploitation of resources in disputed areas remain unchanged. China's self-image as a peace-loving principled country that has been reluctantly forced to respond to provocations contrasts with the views of neighboring countries that Beijing is systematically using coercion and intimidation to expand its effective control of disputed territories.

Whatever the motivation, China's actions caused widespread concerns that a stronger China, driven by popular nationalism and a misperception of US weakness in the aftermath of the global financial crisis, was seeking to dominate the region and intimidate its neighbors. For a US administration emphasizing the importance of unimpeded access to the "global commons" for economic growth, Beijing's actions represented a

clear threat to regional peace and stability, freedom of navigation, open sea lines of communication, and commerce. For China's neighbors, these assertive actions raised concerns about increasing vulnerability to Chinese coercion as PLA power projection capabilities improved and Chinese economic power increased relative to the United States.[53]

Heightened concerns about Chinese behavior found political expression in the July 2010 ASEAN Regional Forum (ARF) meeting in Hanoi, when twelve Asian states joined US Secretary of State Hillary Clinton in expressing concerns about freedom of navigation in the South China Sea, despite the efforts of Chinese diplomats to discourage them from raising the issue. Chinese foreign minister Yang Jiechi gave an angry speech during the meeting in which he wagged his finger at the Singapore representative and pointedly stated that "China is a big country and other countries are small countries, and that's just a fact." This meeting highlighted the negative impact of assertive Chinese actions on China's position in Asia and may have prompted Beijing to adjust its approach. State Councilor Dai Bingguo, the senior Chinese foreign policy official, gave a speech in fall 2010 reiterating China's continued commitment to "peaceful development" and began discussing the need for a "new type of great power relationship" with Washington, measures intended to reassure foreign audiences.

Perceptions of a more assertive China prompted policy shifts throughout Asia and in the United States. Asian countries (especially those involved in territorial disputes with China) began to improve their military capabilities to reduce their vulnerability to Chinese pressure. ASEAN members tried to engage China multilaterally in order to reduce Beijing's power advantage in dealing with individual states, with a particular focus on negotiating a legally binding code of conduct governing behavior in the South China Sea. ASEAN members also sought to increase the involvement of major powers such as Japan, India, Russia, and the United States in regional affairs in order to offset China's power and influence. (This is one reason the East Asia Summit included India, Australia, and New Zealand and later added Russia and the United States.) US treaty allies and partners such as Singapore, Malaysia, and Vietnam increased security cooperation with the United States (including allowing greater base access to US forces) and urged Washington to reinforce its long-term commitment to the region.

This political context formed the backdrop for the US "rebalance" to Asia announced in November 2011. Although primarily a response to expanding US economic, political, and security interests in Asia, the rebalance also reflected regional demands for concrete evidence of US long-term commitment.[54] The Obama administration coupled the rebalance with efforts to build a more cooperative and stable Sino-US relationship. The broad US strategy of seeking to integrate China more fully within the current global order, while discouraging any efforts to reshape that order by force or intimidation, remained in place. Washington sought to make the rebalance robust enough to reassure US allies and partners of its capability and will to maintain a presence in Asia over the long term while not alarming Chinese leaders to the point where they abandoned bilateral cooperation. Nevertheless, the rebalance is widely viewed as evidence of increasing US-China competition for regional influence.

The official Chinese reaction to the US rebalance has been to express concern and skepticism about the stated US rationale, lament the "lack of strategic trust" between Washington and Beijing, urge greater respect for Chinese "core interests," and stress the negative consequences of the rebalance for Asian security (especially its supposed role in emboldening US allies and partners to challenge Chinese maritime territorial claims). Chinese officials have also expressed concerns about Washington's support for the Transpacific Partnership (TPP), a proposed regional trade agreement with high-quality labor, environmental, and intellectual property standards that Beijing would have difficulty meeting. These views are echoed in the description of the regional security environment in China's 2013 *Defense White Paper*: "The Asia-Pacific region has become an increasingly significant stage for world economic development and strategic interaction between major powers. The US is adjusting its Asia-Pacific security strategy, and the regional landscape is undergoing profound changes." The white paper continues, "Some country has strengthened its Asia-Pacific military alliances, expanded its military presence in the region, and frequently makes the situation there tenser. On the issues concerning China's territorial sovereignty and maritime rights and interests, some neighboring countries are taking actions that complicate or exacerbate the situation, and Japan is making trouble over the issue of the Diaoyu Islands."[55]

China's Balancing Act

Chinese leaders have responded to the US rebalance and their perception of an altered regional security environment with both assurance measures and enhanced efforts to deter challenges to Chinese sovereignty claims. One aspect of China's response has been to redouble efforts to stabilize Sino-US relations, most notably through efforts to build a "new type of great power relations" with Washington. Chinese leaders were initially suspicious of Obama administration efforts to build a partnership, but Beijing has subsequently taken the lead in trying to build a US-China strategic relationship.[56] A second element is to recalibrate China's bilateral approach to countries in Asia to pay closer attention to each country's relations with Washington and the overall state of US-China relations. This "triangular approach" has generally produced more restrained and cooperative policy, with Beijing leaning more heavily on assurance measures to avoid driving countries into Washington's arms. Increased cooperation with the United States also offers potential leverage over third countries (if Beijing can persuade Washington to restrain its allies and partners from actions that challenge Chinese claims). This approach appears patterned on how China dealt with the pro-independence Taiwan government led by Chen Shui-bian in 2000–8. By portraying Chen as an irresponsible leader whose actions threatened regional stability, China sought (and to some degree obtained) US cooperation in preventing Chen from engaging in pro-independence actions that might cross Beijing's red lines for the use of force.

At the same time, China has continued its harder line on territorial disputes. Chinese leaders have defined sovereignty and territorial integrity as a "core interest" where compromise is impossible.[57] New top leaders President Xi Jinping and Premier

Li Keqiang have emphasized their refusal to sacrifice China's core interests and steadfast determination to uphold national sovereignty and territorial integrity.[58] One scholar argues that Beijing's approach is focused on consolidating its maritime territorial claims and deterring other states from strengthening their claims at China's expense. Beijing has employed a range of diplomatic, administrative, and military tactics to expand its effective control over disputed territories.[59] Beijing has expanded and reorganized its naval paramilitary forces to improve their ability to patrol disputed waters and reinforce China's territorial claims. Chinese leaders have also accelerated military modernization efforts with a focus on limiting the US ability to operate close to Chinese territory and gradually extending the PLA's power projection capability.

In 2012 and 2013, China engaged in a series of heated territorial disputes with the Philippines, Vietnam, Japan, and India in which an even tougher Chinese approach became evident. In April 2012, a tense standoff occurred between a Philippine navy frigate investigating illegal fishing and China Marine Surveillance and an armed Fishery Law Enforcement Command ship around Scarborough Shoal/Huangyan Island. Both sides eventually agreed to withdraw their ships, but Chinese paramilitary ships later returned, set up a barrier at the entrance to the shoal, and have maintained a presence ever since. The outcome redefined the status quo in a way that expanded China's effective control over the disputed territory. Chinese officials, military officers, and scholars blamed the Philippines for starting the incident and argued that the outcome would deter future challenges. China subsequently applied the "Scarborough model" to the Senkaku/Diaoyu Islands in September 2012 after the Japanese government purchased several of the islands from a private Japanese owner. China argued that the Japanese action altered the status quo and initiated air and maritime patrols near the island to reinforce China's sovereignty claim and to challenge Japan's position that there is no dispute over the sovereignty of the islands.[60] In both cases, China used the opportunity provided by another claimant's actions to alter the status quo in its favor.

The more assertive approach to territorial disputes described above is in tension with efforts to persuade China's neighbors of Beijing's commitment to "peaceful development." A hard line on territorial disputes raises tensions with other claimants, including major regional powers such as Japan and India. Chinese leaders are therefore trying to strike a careful balance between maintaining a peaceful and stable security environment and gradual efforts to strengthen control over disputed territories. In a July 2013 Politburo study session on maritime issues, President Xi reiterated China's uncompromising position on sovereignty, but also highlighted the importance of simultaneously "maintaining stability" and "safeguarding [maritime] rights."[61] A senior PLA officer privately described one of China's major challenges as "the balance between pursuing national interests and maintaining world peace."[62]

China's policy includes a number of elements designed to make this tension more manageable. One is to rely primarily on paramilitary forces and coercive tactics while minimizing employment of military assets and the use of force. This reduces the political cost of aggressive tactics and limits the risk of escalation into a broader military conflict. A second is to try to deter challenges by ensuring that countries that challenge China's claims wind up in a worse position. Beijing hopes that improved relations with Washington may limit US support for other claimants or even restrain them from challenging China's claims. Beijing's insistence on bilateral resolution of territorial disputes allows it to differentiate and adjust its policies to individual claimants, preventing rivals from uniting to resist Chinese tactics. China successfully pressured Cambodia not to include concerns about Beijing's behavior in the chairman's statement at the November 2012 ASEAN summit, casting doubts about ASEAN unity on the issue. China's proclaimed willingness to pursue joint development in disputed areas is also intended to soften Beijing's hard-line approach to territorial disputes and offer "win-win" solutions. Chinese leaders hope that these measures, coupled with liberal use of reassurance measures, will allow China to gradually expand its effective control of disputed territories without the need to use force.

Ultimately, Beijing's patient approach is based on the belief that the regional balance of power is moving in China's favor and that other countries will eventually have to compromise in order to maintain good relations with a dominant China. This belief allows Chinese leaders to avoid the difficult compromises that would be necessary to settle maritime territorial disputes. However, other claimants also face nationalist publics and are unlikely to simply abandon their claims to disputed territories. If they adopt equally uncompromising policies, Beijing's efforts to gradually extend its control of disputed territories are likely to have an increasingly corrosive impact on China's relations with its neighbors and the regional security environment.

Conclusion

China's future role in Asia will be shaped by a number of variables. The first important variable is China's own power trajectory. China is facing a difficult transition to an economy driven less by exports and more by domestic demand, a transition complicated by opposition from politically powerful state-owned enterprises, a weakened financial system, and adverse demographic trends. Growth will slow considerably under the best-case scenario, and a major financial crisis or protracted political infighting could derail China's growth trajectory. A weaker China whose leaders are distracted by domestic problems is likely to improve economic cooperation with other countries and to seek to stabilize its regional environment by following more restrained policies on territorial disputes. (However, some analysts believe Chinese leaders might divert attention from a lagging economy by picking fights with neighboring countries.) Conversely, a stronger China will have more military power projection capabilities and may be less restrained in its international behavior.

Because power is relative, a second important factor will be the power of other regional and extraregional actors. One critical question is the US ability to sustain the rebalance to Asia. If financial problems or reduced willingness to deploy military forces overseas compels US strategic retrenchment, China would have a freer hand. Conversely, a more powerful and engaged United States would increase the competitive dynamics between Washington and Beijing in the region. The relevance of Russia and the European Union to regional political and security affairs is also uncertain. Within Asia, the economic fortunes of Japan and India and their political ability to sustain an active regional role will be critical variables. Assertive Chinese policies on territorial disputes would increase tensions with both countries, impeding regional integration and potentially beginning to unwind regional economic interdependence. No single ASEAN country can stand up to China alone, so the ability of ASEAN to engage the support of outside powers and maintain a degree of internal unity will also be an important factor.

A third variable will be the relative weight Chinese leaders place on legitimacy derived through economic growth versus legitimacy derived by achieving nationalist goals. In the reform era, Chinese leaders have prioritized growth to raise living standards and maintain the Communist Party's leading position. Given China's economic interdependence with its neighbors, Chinese leaders have been highly sensitive to the economic consequences of assertive actions and have generally shifted to more restrained policies when military or nationalist actions threatened economic cooperation. This is still the most likely outcome, but nationalist sentiment among Chinese leaders (and in the Chinese population) may lead to greater weight on nationalist goals. The balance could also be affected if political support for the Communist Party continues to erode or if leadership factions within the party begin to use nationalist goals to compete for power.

A fourth variable involves the ability of Chinese leaders to adapt policy smoothly to maintain the right balance between a stable regional environment and expanding control of disputed territories. China's national security policy-making apparatus is relatively weak and uncoordinated. It has difficulty recognizing and responding rapidly to changed circumstances, especially when responses require politically difficult compromises. Heightened nationalism or leadership disagreements could make it harder for China to adjust policies and pursue effective reassurance measures to maintain stability. Moreover, territorial disputes (and increased US-China military interactions within Asia) may increase the likelihood of an accident or an incident escalating into a larger military confrontation. China's relatively underdeveloped crisis-management capabilities could be put to the test and fail.

Finally, unexpected regional security problems could produce fundamental changes in Chinese policy. A North Korean collapse or a military conflict precipitated by Pyongyang's nuclear weapons ambitions could lead to Chinese military actions to control the situation, which could heighten conflicts with Seoul, Tokyo, and Washington. Despite China's efforts to paint Taiwan as a "domestic issue" qualitatively different from its approach to international security concerns, Asian countries still view Beijing's approach to Taiwan as a litmus test. A decision to use force or coercion against Taiwan (more likely if a pro-independence Taiwan leader is in power) would alarm East Asian countries and could shift both US policy and that of China's neighbors.

During the reform era, China has sought to preserve a stable international environment that supports continued economic growth that can help maintain domestic stability, build its national wealth and power, and expand its influence. These principles have also guided China's Asia policy, which has emphasized the need to reassure Asian countries that a stronger China will not threaten their interests. However, a more assertive approach to territorial disputes is in tension with efforts to persuade China's neighbors of China's commitment to "peaceful development." If Beijing cannot maintain the right balance, the result will be increasingly strained relations with its neighbors and the United States and the creation of a more hostile regional security environment.

NOTES

The views expressed in this chapter are those of the author and do not necessarily represent those of the National Defense University, the Department of Defense, or the US government. The author thanks Joseph Kettel and Katrina Fung for research assistance.

1. See Robert Sutter, *China's Rise in Asia: Promises and Perils* (New York: Rowman & Littlefield, 2005); Evelyn Goh, ed., *Betwixt and Between: Southeast Asian Strategic Relations with the U.S. and China* (Singapore: Institute of Defence and Strategic Studies, 2005); David Shambaugh, ed., *Power Shift: China and Asia's New Dynamics* (Berkeley: University of California Press, 2006); David Shambaugh, "China Engages Asia: Reshaping the Regional Order," *International Security* 29, no. 3 (2004–5): 64–99; Bronson Percival, *The Dragon Looks South: China and Southeast Asia in the New Century* (Westport, CT: Praeger Security International, 2007).
2. See David Shambaugh, "The Chinese Tiger Shows Its Claws," *Financial Times*, February 17, 2010; and Michael Swaine, "Perceptions of an Assertive China," *China Leadership Monitor*, no. 32 (May 2010).
3. For assessments of China's grand strategy, see Michael D. Swaine and Ashley J. Tellis, *Interpreting China's Grand Strategy: Past Present and Future* (Washington, DC: RAND Corporation, 2000); Avery Goldstein, *Rising to the Challenge: China's Grand Strategy and International Security* (Stanford, CA: Stanford University Press, 2005); and David Shambaugh, *China Goes Global: The Partial Power* (New York: Oxford University Press, 2013).
4. Erica Strecker Downs and Phillip C. Saunders, "Legitimacy and the Limits of Nationalism: China and the Diaoyu Islands," *International Security* 23, no. 3 (Winter 1998/1999): 114–46.
5. For a useful overview from a Chinese scholar, see Ye Zicheng, *Inside China's Grand Strategy: The Perspective from the People's Republic* (Lexington: University Press of Kentucky, 2011).
6. Robert Koopman, "How Much of Chinese Exports Is Really Made in China?," US International Trade Commission, March 2008, http://www.usitc.gov/publications/332/working_papers/ec200803b_revised.pdf.
7. For a comprehensive analysis of Chinese security concerns, see Andrew J. Nathan and Andrew Scobell, *China's Search for Security* (New York: Columbia University Press, 2012).
8. Phillip C. Saunders, "The Rebalance to Asia: U.S.-China Relations and Regional Security," *INSS Strategic Forum*, no. 281 (2013).
9. World Bank, "Key Development Data and Statistics," http://www.worldbank.org. The East Asia percentage of global GDP is based on 2012 World Bank purchasing power parity estimates at http://data.worldbank.org/data-catalog/GDP-PPP-based-table.
10. Sutter, *China's Rise in Asia*; Aaron L. Friedberg, *A Contest for Supremacy: China, America, and the Struggle for Mastery in Asia* (New York: Norton, 2011).
11. See Denny Roy, "More Security for Rising China, Less for Others?," *AsiaPacific Analysis*, no. 106 (January 2013).
12. For accounts of how Chinese leaders and analysts came to this realization, see Shambaugh, "China Engages Asia: Reshaping the Regional Order"; and Yong Deng, "Reputation and the Security Dilemma: China Reacts to the China Threat Theory," in *New Directions in the Study of China's Foreign Policy*, ed. Alastair Iain Johnston and Robert S. Ross (Stanford, CA: Stanford University Press, 2006), 186–214.
13. Calculated from Chinese export statistics as reported in the UN Comtrade database.

14. Bonnie S. Glaser, "China's Coercive Economic Diplomacy: A New and Worrying Trend," *PacNet*, no. 46 (Honolulu: Pacific Forum CSIS, July 23, 2012).

15. Chinese 2012 outbound investment data are from the CEIC China database; "China-ASEAN FDI Surpasses $10 BLN," Bermana Media, April 8, 2011, http://my.news.yahoo.com/china-asean-fdi-surpasses-us-10-bln-201104G8-063544-436.html.

16. *China's Foreign Aid* (Beijing: Information Office of the State Council, 2011).

17. John W. Garver, "Development of China's Overland Transportation Links with Central, Southwest and South Asia," *China Quarterly*, no. 185 (March 2006): 1–22; Phillip C. Saunders, *China's Global Activism: Strategy, Drivers, and Tools* (Washington, DC: National Defense University Press, 2006), http://www.ndu.edu/inss/Occasional_Papers/ OCP4.pdf (accessed January 15, 2008).

18. Important studies include David Shambaugh, *Modernizing China's Military: Progress, Problems, and Prospects* (Berkeley: University of California Press, 2004); Dennis J. Blasko, *The Chinese Army Today: Tradition and Transformation for the 21st Century*, 2nd ed. (New York: Taylor & Francis, 2012); Phillip C. Saunders, Christopher Yung, Michael Swaine, and Andrew Nien-Tzu Yang, eds., *The Chinese Navy: Expanding Capabilities, Evolving Roles* (Washington, DC: NDU Press, 2011); Richard P. Hallion, Roger Cliff, and Phillip C. Saunders, eds., *The Chinese Air Force: Evolving Concepts, Roles, and Capabilities* (Washington, DC: NDU Press, 2012); and Ashley J. Tellis and Travis Tanner, eds., *China's Military Challenge* (Seattle, WA: National Bureau of Asian Research, 2012).

19. David M. Finkelstein, "China's National Military Strategy: An Overview of the 'Military Strategic Guidelines,'" in *Right-Sizing the People's Liberation Army: Exploring the Contours of China's Military*, ed. Roy Kamphausen and Andrew Scobell (Carlisle, PA: Strategic Studies Institute, 2007), 70–72.

20. Estimate is from the SIPRI Military Expenditure Database, accessed October 4, 2013. The US defense department estimates that Chinese defense spending in 2012 was in the range of $135 to $215 billion. Office of the Secretary of Defense, "Annual Report to Congress: Military and Security Developments Involving the People's Republic of China 2013," 45, http://www.defense.gov/pubs/2013_China_Report_FINAL.pdf.

21. Roger Cliff, Mark Buries, Michael S. Chase, Derek Eaton, and Kevin L. Pollpeter, *Entering the Dragon's Lair: Chinese Antiaccess Strategies and Their Implications for the United States* (Arlington, VA: RAND Corporation, 2007); Sam J. Tangredi, *Anti-Access Warfare: Countering A2/AD Strategies* (Annapolis, MD: Naval Institute Press, 2013).

22. Roy D. Kamphausen and Justin Liang, "PLA Power Projection: Current Realities and Emerging Trends," in Michael D. Swaine, Andrew N. D. Yang, and Evan Medeiros, ed., *Assessing the Threat: The Chinese Military and Taiwan's Security*, ed. (Washington, DC: Carnegie Endowment for International Peace, 2007), 111–150.

23. See Lyle J. Goldstein, *Five Dragons Stirring Up the Sea: Challenge and Opportunity in China's Improving Maritime Enforcement Capabilities* (Report No. 5, China Maritime Studies Institute, US Naval War College, Newport, RI, April 2010).

24. "Everyone Wants a Chinese Tourist in 2013," January 8, 2013, http://skift.com/ 2013/01/08/everyone-wants-a-chinese-tourist-in-2013.

25. Figures for 2010 outbound Chinese students are from the UNESCO Institute for Statistics, http://www.uis.unesco.org/Education/Pages/international-student-flow-viz.aspx (accessed September 30, 2013); figures for Asia-Pacific students in China are from *China's Foreign Affairs 2013*, table 10 (Beijing: World Affairs Press, 2013): 403–8.

26. Office of Chinese Language Council International, "Confucius Institutes: Asia," http://english.hanban.org/node_10971.htm (accessed September 11, 2013).

27. Network of East Asian Think-Tanks, "About Us," http://www.neat.org.cn/english/ zjdyen/index.php?topic_id = 001001 (accessed October 8, 2013).

28. See David Shambaugh, *China Goes Global*, chap. 6.

29. Thomas Fuller, "Made in China: Cheap Products Change Lives," *New York Times*, December 27, 2007.

30. Other Asian countries also view their space programs as an indicator of national achievement. See James Clay Moltz, *Asia's Space Race: National Motivations, Regional Rivalries, and International Risks* (New York: Columbia University Press, 2011).

31. See Elizabeth C. Economy, *The River Runs Black* (Ithaca, NY: Cornell University Press, 2004). One useful resource is the Wilson Center's "China Environment Forum" website, http://www.wilson-center.org/program/china-environment-forum.

32. Joshua Cooper Ramos, The Beijing Consensus (London: Foreign Policy Centre, 2004), http://fpc.org.uk/fsblob/244.pdf (accessed January 18, 2008); Stefan Halder, *The Beijing Consensus: How China's Authoritarian Model Will Dominate the Twenty-First Century* (New York: Basic Books, 2010); Randall Peerenboom, *China Modernizes: Threat to the West or Model for the Rest?* (New York: Oxford University Press, 2007). For more skeptical views, see Minxin Pei, *China's Trapped Transition: The Limits of Developmental Autocracy* (Cambridge, MA: Harvard University Press, 2006); and Scott Kennedy, "The Myth of the Beijing Consensus," *Journal of Contemporary China*, 19, no. 65 (2010): 461–77.

33. Chinese labor costs have risen rapidly, especially in major cities in Southeast China. Labor-intensive production is beginning to move to countries with lower labor costs such as Bangladesh and Vietnam.

34. Denny Roy, "Hegemon on the Horizon? China's Threat to East Asian Security," *International Security* 19, no. 1 (Summer 1994): 149–68; Richard Bernstein and Ross H. Munro, *The Coming Conflict with China* (New York: Knopf, 1997). For a survey of regional views and strategies, see Alastair Iain Johnston and Robert S. Ross, eds., *Engaging China: The Management of an Emerging Power* (New York: Routledge, 1999).

35. Evan S. Medeiros and M. Taylor Fravel, "China's New Diplomacy," *Foreign Affairs* 82, no. 6 (2003): 22–35.

36. David M. Finkelstein, "China's New Security Concept: Reading Between the Lines," *Washington Journal of Modem China* 5, no. 1 (1999): 37–50.

37. The ten ASEAN members are Brunei, Cambodia, Indonesia, Laos, Malaysia, Myanmar (Burma), the Philippines, Singapore, Thailand, and Vietnam.

38. On the role of multilateral organizations in legitimating and constraining power, see John Gerard Ruggie, ed., *Multilateralism Matters* (New York: Columbia University Press, 1993); and G. John Ikenberry, "Institutions, Strategic Restraint, and the Persistence of American Postwar Order," *International Security* 23, no. 3 (Winter 1998/1999): 43–78. On China's changing attitude and increasing participation in these institutions, see Elizabeth Economy and Michel Oksenberg, eds., *China Joins the World: Progress and Prospects* (New York: Council on Foreign Relations, 1999); Alastair Iain Johnston, "Socialization in International Institutions: The ASEAN Way and International Relations Theory," in *International Relations Theory and the Asia-Pacific*, ed. G. John Ikenberry and Michael Mastanduno (New York: Columbia University Press, 2003), 107–62; and Bates Gill, *Rising Star: China's New Security Diplomacy* (Washington, DC: Brookings Institution, 2007).

39. See Marc Lanteigne, *China's Engagement with International Institutions: Alternate Paths to Global Power* (New York: Routledge, 2005); Guoguang Wu and Helen Lansdowne, eds., *China Turns to Multilateralism: Foreign Policy and Regional Security* (New York: Routledge, 2008); and Mingjiang Li, ed., *China Joins Global Governance* (New York: Lexington Books, 2012).

40. M. Taylor Fravel, "Regime Insecurity and International Cooperation: Explaining China's Compromises in Territorial Disputes," *International Security* 30, no. 2 (Fall 2005): 46–83.

41. See Ian Story, "Trouble and Strife in the South China Sea—Part II: The Philippines and China," *China Brief* 8, no. 9 (2008).

42. "The Diversified Employment of China's Armed Forces" (Beijing: Information Office of the State Council, 2013).

43. See the Ministry of Commerce website page, "China FTA Network," http://fta.mofcom.gov.cn/english/index.shtml (accessed October 2, 2013); and Guoyou Song and Wen Jin Yuan, "China's Free Trade Agreement Strategies," *Washington Quarterly* 35, no. 4 (2012): 107–19, http://csis.org/files/publication/twql2FallSongYuan.pdf.

44. Author's interviews with Southeast Asian diplomats, 2004–7.

45. See Murray Hiebert and Liam Hanlon, "ASEAN and Partners Launch Regional Comprehensive Economic Partnership," CSIS, December 7, 2012, http://csis.org/publica tion/asean-and-partners-launch-regional-comprehensive-economic-partnership.

46. See Jeffrey A. Bader, *Obama and China's Rise: An Insider's Account of America's Asia Strategy* (Washington,

DC: Brookings Institution Press, 2012), chap. 7; and the discussion in Michael D. Swaine, "Perceptions of an Assertive China," *China Leadership Monitor* 32 (2010).

47. Michael D. Swaine and M. Taylor Fravel, "China's Assertive Behavior—Part Two: The Maritime Periphery," *China Leadership Monitor* 35 (2011).

48. For an insider's perspective on Obama administration thinking about building a partnership with China, see Bader, *Obama and China's Rise*, chap. 1. Chinese overconfidence in Western decline and the increasing power of the developing world is evident in the shifting language used to describe the trend toward a multipolar world in the 2008, 2011, and 2013 defense white papers. Also see Andrew Scobell and Scott W. Harold, "An 'Assertive' China? Insights from Interviews," *Asian Security* 9, no. 2 (2013): 111–31.

49. Suisheng Zhao, "Foreign Policy Implications of Chinese Nationalism Revisited: The Strident Turn," *Journal of Contemporary China* 22, no. 82 (2013): 535–53.

50. Author's interactions with Chinese officials, military officers, and scholars, 2009–13.

51. Mark E. Redden and Phillip C. Saunders, "Managing Sino-U.S. Air and Naval Interactions: Cold War Lessons and New Avenues of Approach," *China Strategic Perspectives* 5 (2012).

52. See Linda Jakobson and Dean Knox, "New Foreign Policy Actors in China" (Stockholm International Peace Research Institute [SEPRI] Policy Paper No. 26, September 2010), http://books.sipri.org/product_info2c_product_id—410.

53. See Ashley J. Tellis, Travis Tanner, and Jessica Keough, eds., *Asia Responds to Its Rising Powers* (Seattle, WA: National Bureau of Asian Research, 2011).

54. Saunders, "The Rebalance to Asia."

55. "The Diversified Employment of China's Armed Forces." This assessment is the party's official view and closely parallels the description in the Eighteenth Party Congress work report.

56. See David Shambaugh, ed., *Tangled Titans: The United States and China* (Lanham, MD: Rowman & Littlefield, 2013).

57. See Michael D. Swaine, "China's Assertive Behavior—Part One: On 'Core Interests,'" *China Leadership Monitor*, no. 34 (2011).

58. Robert Sutter and Chin-hao Huang, "China's Growing Resolve in the South China Sea," *Comparative Connections* 15, no. 1 (2013).

59. M. Taylor Fravel, "China's Strategy in the South China Sea," *Contemporary Southeast Asia* 33, no. 3 (2011): 292–319; Michael Yahuda, "China's New Assertiveness in the South China Sea," *Journal of Contemporary China* 22, no. 81 (2013): 446–59.

60. M. Taylor Fravel, "China's Island Strategy: 'Redefine the Status Quo,'" *Diplomat*, November 1, 2012.

61. M. Taylor Fravel, "Xi Jinping's Overlooked Revelation on China's Maritime Disputes," *Diplomat*, August 15, 2013.

62. Author's interview, Beijing, September 2013.

FRUITFUL RESULTS AND BROAD PROSPECTS: A REVIEW OF TWENTY YEARS OF CHINA–ASEAN RELATIONS*

Zhang Jiuhuan

The year 2011 marks the 20th anniversary of China–ASEAN dialogue relations. Built on the past achievements, China's relations with Southeast Asian countries have made tremendous progress over the past 20 years. Over the past two decades, the friendly relations between China and ASEAN have enjoyed all-round and rapid development and the mutually beneficial cooperation has yielded remarkable results, which has attracted world attention.

The two sides have worked together to maintain regional peace and stability, achieve social and economic progress and ensure the well-being of the people.

In 2010, the trade volume between China and ASEAN countries stood at approximately $292.8 billion, representing a 36-fold increase over the 1991 figure of $7.96 billion. According to Chinese statistics, China became ASEAN's largest trading partner and ASEAN became China's fourth largest trading partner. In 2010, the mutual investment between China and ASEAN amounted to over $70 billion in cumulative terms, 180 times bigger than the 1991 figure of $382 million. In 2010, China and ASEAN exchanged more than 100,000 students, of which, over 40,000 were from ASEAN and over 70,000 from China. In 2010, people from various sectors made over 11 million visits between China and ASEAN. All of the ten ASEAN countries become approved destinations for Chinese tourists.

China and ASEAN have worked jointly to respond to difficulties and challenges, such as the SARS outbreak in 2003, the Indian Ocean tsunami in 2004 and the international financial crisis in 2008. Braving together in times of difficulty, the two sides have built stronger mutual understanding and trust and further promoted the long-standing traditional friendship.

---

* This article was published in *Foreign Affairs Journal*, Chinese People's Institute of Foreign Affairs (Spring 2011).

Accomplishments

Over the past two decades, China and ASEAN together have accomplished the following. The two sides have defined their political relations. In July 1991, the then Foreign Minister Qian Qichen was invited to the opening ceremony of the 24th ASEAN Foreign Ministers' Meeting and he announced the official launch of China–ASEAN dialogue relations. In July 1996, China became a full dialogue partner of ASEAN. In December 1997, President Jiang Zemin attended the first China–ASEAN leaders' meeting and, together with ASEAN leaders, issued a joint statement, identifying a partnership of good neighborliness and mutual trust oriented towards the 21st century between China and ASEAN. In October 2003, Premier Wen Jiabao and ASEAN leaders signed a joint declaration, putting in place the China–ASEAN strategic partnership for peace and prosperity. In December 2008, China appointed its first ambassador to ASEAN.

The two sides have signed a regional treaty and a declaration. In October 2003, at the request of ASEAN, China signed the Treaty of Amity and Cooperation (TAC) in Southeast Asia, marking a new level of political mutual trust between China and ASEAN. China has also signed with ASEAN member states the *Declaration of Conduct (DOC) of Parties in the South China Sea*, which reaffirms that relevant disputes over the South China Sea should be resolved by peaceful means through friendly consultation and negotiation. Pending the settlement of disputes, the parties undertake to exercise self-restraint and refrain from taking actions that may complicate or expand disputes. The signing of the document is of great significance for maintaining peace and stability in the South China Sea region.

The two sides have established the China–ASEAN Free Trade Area (FTA). At the China–ASEAN Summit in Singapore in 2000, the then Chinese Premier Zhu Rongji put forward the proposal of establishing China-ASEAN FTA, which received positive response from ASEAN countries. At the meeting in Brunei in 2001, leaders of China and ten ASEAN member states agreed to establish the China-ASEAN FTA within ten years. In 2002, the two sides signed the Framework Agreement on Comprehensive Economic Cooperation in Phnom Penh, followed by the signing of the Agreement on Trade in Goods, the Agreement on Trade in Services and the Agreement on Investment successively. In January 2010, the two sides held a ceremony in Nanning to officially launch the China-ASEAN FTA. It covers 11 countries, with an area of 14 million square kilometers, a population of 1.9 billion, a total GDP of $6 trillion and $4.5 trillion in trade combined. It is the world's largest free trade area of developing countries. Its establishment has made positive contribution to tackling the global financial crisis, promoting regional economic development and driving world economic recovery.

The two sides have promoted regional cooperation. China has participated in and facilitated the formation and operation of such cooperation mechanisms as 10+1, 10+3, the ASEAN Regional Forum (ARF), and the East Asia Summit (EAS). China advocates and supports the leading role of ASEAN, the main channel of 10+3 and the nature of EAS as a forum. China has worked with ASEAN to advance regional cooperation step by step. One thing commendable in the process of regional cooperation is the Chiang Mai Initiative and its multilateralization, through which a $120 billion regional foreign exchange reserve pool was established. It will play a positive role in enabling regional countries to assist each other in helping themselves to counter financial risks.

Retrospect and Prospect

Since the founding of the People's Republic of China, the Chinese government has responded to the changing situation and the call of the times and actively brought about three rounds of great development of China's relations with Southeast Asian nations. In the 1950s, American imperialism and its followers carried out an encirclement policy against China in an attempt to strangle the newly founded People's Republic in the

cradle. China established diplomatic ties first with Vietnam, Indonesia, Myanmar, and Cambodia and then with Laos. China, together with Myanmar and other countries, initiated the Five Principles of Peaceful Coexistence. China, together with Indonesia and other countries, formulated the Ten Principles of Bandung and developed the Asian and African spirit of seeking common ground while shelving differences and fighting in solidarity against imperialism and colonialism. China and Myanmar, enjoying eternal friendship and sharing water from the same river, formed a "Pauk-Phaw" (meaning full brothers) relationship. China and Vietnam, enjoying a brotherly friendship, are comrades-in-arms. The development of China's relations with Southeast Asian nations in their early days helped to break a key link in the imperialist blockade against China.

In the mid-1970s, the United States withdrew its troops from Vietnam, the Soviet Union carried out a strategy of southward expansion and regional hegemony was rampant. Southeast Asian countries, one after another, called for strengthened cooperation with China and China responded positively and established diplomatic relations with Malaysia, the Philippines, and Thailand and improved relations with Singapore and other countries. China collaborated with Southeast Asian countries in reining in hegemony in various forms and upholding regional peace and stability.

The late 1980s and early 1990s witnessed the collapse of the former Soviet Union and the end of the Cold War. The international socialist movement was at a low ebb while "socialism with Chinese characteristics" stood as the only exception after undergoing the test of political turbulence. Indonesia, which suspended diplomatic ties with China in 1965 after the "September 30" incident, eventually restored it in 1990. Singapore and Brunei established diplomatic relations with China soon afterwards. The once deteriorating China-Vietnam relations were also normalized during this period of time. Up to that point, China had established or restored diplomatic ties with all the ten Southeast Asian countries. The establishment of relationship between China and ASEAN was only a matter of time.

ASEAN had no diplomatic relations with China for 24 years after its establishment in 1967.

The lack of mutual understanding and trust was a key reason. As ASEAN's predecessor the Southeast Asia Treaty Organization (SEATO) was anti-Communist and anti–China, we were not sure about the nature of this newly established ASEAN. Later, with the United States drawing back its military presence in the region, ASEAN countries were gradually moving away from the US and becoming more positive toward China. They began to adopt policies of peace, neutrality, and "balance of major powers." The Chinese nation, after experiencing the turbulent Cultural Revolution, presented a new image of reform and opening up to the outside world. The conditions were then ripe for China and ASEAN to establish diplomatic ties.

In the early days of the People's Republic, Western imperialists framed overseas Chinese as the "fifth column." Therefore, Southeast Asian countries' governments were afraid that China would make use of its overseas Chinese to overturn them. The Chinese government's timely promulgation of a law on "single nationality" revealed the lies created by imperialists and dispelling misgivings of relevant countries. This played a positive role in facilitating the establishment of diplomatic ties with countries like Indonesia and Myanmar.

In the 1960s and 1970s, the Communist anti-government armed forces were active in Southeast Asian countries and the governments of these countries feared that these forces would get support from China. The Chinese government made it clear that Communist-related problems were the internal affairs of other countries that China would never interfere in. What China stated and did helped remove misgivings of those countries. It also helped facilitate the establishment of diplomatic ties with Malaysia, the Philippines, and Thailand.

With China's economy developing rapidly and the Western countries preaching "China threats," Southeast Asian countries, from time to time, have been skeptical about whether China would seek hegemony. To alleviate their worries, we have in turn pursued a "harmonious world" and the policy of building friendship and partnership with neighboring countries with a view to enhancing mutual trust and promoting the development of bilateral relations.

What has happened shows that it is a long-term task to enhance trust and dispel misgivings and it should be integrated into each step of the development of bilateral relations. During this process, efforts can never be slackened and it can never be accomplished once and for all.

Second, mutually beneficial and win-win spirit provide inexhaustible driving force for bilateral cooperation. Immediately after the introduction of the reform and opening up policy, China began to actively pursue business cooperation with ASEAN countries. Back then, there were some people worrying that as both sides were developing countries, their products might overlap with each other and it would be impossible to conduct business cooperation. However, what happened shows that as long as both sides fully recognize the similarities and differences existing in each other's development level, structure, and products, follow the principles of equality and mutual benefit, draw on each other's strengths, and strive to be pioneering and innovative, business cooperation was not only made possible in a short period of time but also kept growing and expanding. Therefore, broad vistas opened up before us.

In the late 1990s, a financial crisis hit Southeast Asia. Bearing in mind the greater picture, China kept its RMB exchange rate stable and offered effective assistance to crisis-affected countries in a timely manner. As a result, China's economy maintained sound and fast growth, giving Southeast Asian countries a "free ride" that shortened their recovery period. Cooperation in difficult times brought real benefits to both sides and subsequently heightened each other's expectation for and confidence in closer cooperation. That is why China's proposal for the establishment of China-ASEAN Free Trade Area in 2000 was warmly and unanimously welcomed by ASEAN countries.

In the process of building of the free trade zone, thanks to the implementation of the Early Harvest Program, some less developed countries were among the first beneficiaries of the zero-tariff treatment on vegetables and fruits. The signing and implementation of the treaties on trade in goods and trade in services in 2004 and 2006 gave strong boost to two-way trade between China and ASEAN countries. In 2008 when the financial storm from Wall Street swept the whole world, ASEAN countries suffered from a sudden shrinking in their export markets. The only exception was their smooth and flourishing trade with China.

Investment cooperation between China and ASEAN has also made enormous headway. Southeast Asia is a region linking the East with the West, and through this region, China can not only attract surplus local capital but also introduce in capital, advanced technologies and managerial expertise from the West indirectly. One of the best examples is the Suzhou Industrial Park, which has been jointly developed by China and Singapore starting from 1994. For the past few years, there used to be more investment from Southeast Asian countries to China. However, with its rapid development, China's investment to the region has increased by a big margin. A strong two-way investment flow pattern is taking shape. Only mutually beneficial cooperation can encourage both sides to keep the bilateral cooperation growing flourishing and lasting.

Third, harmony in diversity is the basic model for the two sides to interact and coexist. Both China and the ASEAN countries suffered invasions of Western powers in history, and they are both developing countries today with a common desire for peace and development. But the two sides differ greatly in many areas, including social systems, development patterns, and cultural backgrounds. There also exist differences among ASEAN countries themselves. Some of them (such as Vietnam and Laos) are socialist countries, while some (the original ASEAN countries for instance) are capitalist countries. Among those capitalist countries, the Philippines practices parliamentary democracy, which is regarded as the "showcase of American democracy," while Singapore's parliamentary democracy is actually a one-party rule. Countries like Thailand and Cambodia pursue constitutional monarchy, while Myanmar is a country that is administered by the military. In terms of development levels, there are countries like Myanmar, Cambodia, and Laos whose people's per capita annual income is less than $1,000. There are also middle-income countries such as Malaysia, Thailand, Indonesia, the Philippines, and Vietnam whose per capita annual income ranges from $1,000 to several thousand US dollars. There are also high-income ones like Singapore and Brunei whose per capita annual

income is about $30,000. The ASEAN culture is a perfect blend of the native, Chinese, and Western elements.

Since modern times, Western colonialists once vainly attempted to "Westernize" Southeast Asia. Japanese invaders' "Great East Asia Co-Prosperity Sphere" ended in failure. Meanwhile, the US attempts to preach the "universal" values and democracy model produced little result. Due to the impact of the ideological trend of "limited sovereignty" and the pressure imposed by the West, ASEAN once collectively intervened in the internal affairs of Myanmar, and made demands on its democratic process. It caused great discontent from Myanmar and eventually went nowhere.

China always upholds equality among all countries, big or small, and respects ASEAN countries' different national conditions and independent choices. We believe that these countries have the best understanding of their own situation and have the ability and wisdom to manage well their own affairs. When a *coup d'état* took place in Thailand in 2006, Western countries one after another expressed condemnation and announced sanctions. ASEAN countries had to express regret. Only China adhered to the principle of non-interference in other countries' internal affairs, stressing that it was up to the Thai people to seek a solution, and keeping to our friendly policies towards Thailand. What we have said and done has won wide acclaim and appreciation from the general public of Thailand. Despite the political turbulences and frequent changes of government in Thailand over the past few years, China-Thailand friendly relations and cooperation has kept the momentum of sound development.

The world is diversified and colorful. Countries, big or small, strong or weak, all have their respective strengths and weaknesses. Mutual respect, co-existence, and common prosperity are the natural choice. We have many favorable conditions. Long-term efforts of the two sides have helped lay a quite solid foundation for China-ASEAN relations. Fast and sustained economic growth in China and the rise of its overall national strength provide a strong buttress for China-ASEAN cooperation. Geographical proximity offers advantages for contacts and cooperation between the two sides. Cultural similarities and links make it easy for the two sides to communicate with and understand each other. However, there are also some unfavorable conditions. Western countries such as the United States have increased attention and input in this region and from time to time sow discord between China and ASEAN countries. ASEAN countries have mixed feelings about China's rise, wanting to benefit from China's economic growth while relying on the United States to "balance" China's influence. To bear in mind the overall picture, bring out advantages, and take well-targeted measures is key to further development of China-ASEAN relations.

There are several prominent matters in China-ASEAN relations that merit our special attention. First, we must attach great importance to and manage well relations with the United States. After the end of World War II, the United States increased its presence in Southeast Asia and viewed this region as its sphere of influence. In the mid-1970s, the United States lost the Vietnam War, shifted to strategic contraction, and withdrew from the military bases in Thailand and the Philippines. But it still kept a strong military presence in the region. After the 9/11 incident in 2001, the United States reduced its attention to Southeast Asia. After it took office in 2009, the Obama administration announced a high-profile "return" to Southeast Asia. Such a "return" is part of the adjusted Asia-Pacific strategy and is, to some extent, targeted at the fast growth of China-ASEAN relations. We welcome a constructive role of the United States in maintaining regional peace and stability and strive for more cooperation with the US in handling regional affairs on the basis of mutual respect and mutual benefit. At the same time, we need to exercise caution and keep vigilant against US hegemonist actions.

ASEAN countries pursue a diplomatic "balance between major countries" and seek to survive in between them. This is a normal mentality and policy direction of small and medium-sized countries. These countries do not want to see another Cold War, nor do they want to offend the United States or China. We should understand their position and try not to put them in an awkward situation where they have to take sides.

Second, we should continue to develop the Free Trade Area (FTA). The China-ASEAN FTA has provided a broad platform for China and ASEAN countries to carry out economic cooperation and trade and offered great convenience. The success of China and ASEAN countries in tackling the global financial crisis in the past two years was attributable to the FTA. It is necessary to strengthen coordination of FTA development, help enhance industrial connection, and address in a timely manner some sensitive matters that may come up. The two sides enjoy fast growth in trade, but investment is the "weak link." This situation, if not changed soon, will constrain further development of China-ASEAN business ties. Some cooperation projects that have been implemented or are being implemented, including Mekong River Sub-regional Cooperation, Pan-Beibu Gulf Cooperation, China-ASEAN Expo, and Business and Investment Summit, should be incorporated into the FTA framework and make full use of favorable conditions of the FTA for greater development. "Connectivity" is a major engineering plan of enhancing connection and cooperation among ASEAN countries and between China and ASEAN. Some projects such as China-Myanmar oil and gas pipeline and Kunming-Bangkok highway are under construction. Some plans such as high-speed rail through the Indochina Peninsula and Sunda Strait bridge are still in the making. All of them are important to regional development and stronger China-ASEAN relations. It is necessary to attach great importance to these projects and try to facilitate them.

Third, we should pay close attention to regional cooperation and guide its development. In recent years, regional cooperation has had diversified forms and rich contents. China, ASEAN countries, Japan, the ROK, and India have participated in and promoted the inception and operation of these cooperation mechanisms. The United States kept the attitude of an onlooker until last year when it turned active and even tried to play a "leadership" role in some way.

The direction of regional cooperation bears on China's major interests in this region and deserves our high attention. It is advisable to continue to support ASEAN's leading role, uphold 10+3 as the main channel, maintain the nature of East Asia Summit as a strategic forum, and adhere to the operational principle of openness, inclusiveness, consensus building and gradual progress, and guide the region in moving forward on a sound and stable track.

Fourth, we attach importance to cultural and people-to-people exchanges and do a good job in promoting them. Human resources are the most valuable among all resources. The basis of China-ASEAN friendly relations and cooperation is the general public. Only by enhancing understanding and friendship between the people and bringing real benefit to them can bilateral relations have solid basis and lasting driving force. We will continue to run well China-ASEAN personnel exchange and training cooperation projects covering both elites and youth, Confucius Institutes and Overseas Volunteer Chinese Language Teachers Program to sustain "Chinese language fever" in Southeast Asia, and China Culture Centers and the Chinese Culture Week in Spring Festival. We should actively conduct public diplomacy with ASEAN countries, encourage people from various sectors to get widely involved and learn from each other through exchanges. The driving force of China-ASEAN friendly relations and cooperation comes from the general public.

This year (2011) is China-ASEAN Friendship and Exchange Year. On 23 January, foreign ministers of ASEAN countries traveled to Kunming by car along the Kunming-Bangkok highway, which was still under construction. At the China-ASEAN Foreign Ministers' Meeting held in Kunming, the two sides reviewed the remarkable development of China-ASEAN relations in the past 20 years and envisioned broader prospects for development. The meeting serves as a prelude to the celebrations in this year.

What has happened has proved that the development of China-ASEAN relations follows the trend of the times and people's aspirations, and is conducive to regional and world peace, stability, development, and cooperation. We have every reason to believe that with the joint efforts of the two sides, China-ASEAN relations will usher in an even brighter future in the next 20 years.

China and Central Asia[*]

Valérie Niquet

The interest of the People's Republic of China in Central Asia is not new. It has always been related to issues concerning the extension and control of the country's territory as well as its territorial security. A sign of this complex interest, official visits to the Central Asian republics since their independence have succeeded each other at a sustained rhythm following Premier Li Peng's first tour in 1994.

The guiding thread of Chinese policy with regard to Central Asia is thus essentially one of "stability" on a continuum that runs from internal stability, that of the traditionally restless regions such as Xinjiang, to the stability of the frontier zones and of the periphery, from where may emerge a whole new series of risks.[1]

Since the collapse of the Soviet system and the independence of the Central Asian republics, which has led to a fragmentation and a relative autonomy of the region, the stakes and the opportunities for the People's Republic of China have been greatly complicated, and this movement is far from concluded today. In 1989, the first fruits of the end of communism in the USSR—greater liberty granted to the Soviet republics of Central Asia—had coincided in China with the resurgence of a democratic movement that found expression in Beijing around the students in Tiananmen Square—but also in the autonomous region of Xinjiang, which has since experienced numerous periods of unrest.[2]

Following the end of the Cold War and the disappearance of the Soviet threat, it seemed that the bilateral dimension of relations between China and Central Asia would win the day, in an initially rather positive direction involving the development of exchanges, with the opening of frontier posts allowing traditional ties to be rewoven and with the themes surrounding

---

[*] This article is excerpted from, and was originally published in, *China Perspectives* (September–October 2006).

the "New Silk Road." This was also the period in which the final stretch of the Yili-Yining railway linking Xinjiang with Kazakhstan was constructed; it had been interrupted because of the Sino-Soviet conflict. Following the violent pro-independence incidents in Yining in 1997, the Chinese government reinforced its control over cross-frontier exchanges. More recently, the emergence of concerns related to the role of NATO and the United States has added a more global dimension to this consideration of the risks, while today the new ambitions asserted by a more self-confident Russia—even if the means for Moscow to take action remain limited—have again complicated the stakes.[3]

The Internal Stability Dimension

The stability of Xinjiang lies at the heart of the concerns surrounding the security of the People's Republic of China, and it constitutes one of the primary factors determining China's policy towards Central Asia. The problems of economic development and political control are in fact far from resolved in Xinjiang, a province that was only officially integrated into the Qing Empire in 1884, and which remains a "disputed periphery," to use the expression coined by Thierry Kellner, despite the implementation since the end of the 1980s by the central authorities of multiple strategies of both repression and development.[4] These strategies can be summarized in two slogans: that of the "strike hard" campaigns, launched in 1996, which are not solely targeted at Xinjiang but which become heightened repression in the province,[5] and that of the "western development" intended to extend the benefits of growth to this province far removed from the large centers of development. However, since the ascension to power of Hu Jintao, it seems that this campaign has become the object of some disaffection on the part of the central authorities in the face of multiple social tensions, also in the more developed regions.

At the economic level, Xinjiang is in fact not only confronted with a differential in development that remains significant in relation to the national average, but, even more destabilizing, with a persistent and increasing inequality

between the population of Chinese Han, which today comprises almost 50 percent of the local population, and the indigenous population characterized ethnically and culturally by an identification with all of the Turkic populations of Central Asia.

This identification has, of course, played its part in the resumption of exchanges with the reopening of the frontiers and the large communication flows following the collapse of the USSR, but the development of exchanges and the period of relative liberalization that China has experienced since the beginning of the 1980s has also encouraged the reemergence of autonomist currents. The strategy of control by occupation, which has been translated in a considerable increase in the population of Han origin in the region—accelerating from 6 percent of the total population of Xinjiang in 1949, with 300,000 people, to 40.6% of the total in 2000, with 7.5 million people, an increase of more than 2,200% in 50 years—also constitutes a subject of resentment.

In this objective of controlling territory at the marches of the empire (which, moreover, resumes a model initiated in the Han dynasty [202 BCE–220 CE] with the institution of peasant soldiers), the role played by the production and construction units in Xinjiang entrusted with exploiting the agricultural land and controlling the frontiers is far from marginalized, in contrast to what has happened in the rest of the country where the people's communes have disappeared. Following a period of opening up that had characterized the end of the 1980s, the central government has put the emphasis back on the control and the reconstitution of the frontiers.[6]

In terms of strategic priority, the defense of the frontiers and the control of the borderlands still constitute an essential mission of the People's Liberation Army (PLA), even though they attract less attention than the "external" targets of projection of the Chinese strategy, for example overseas or in the direction of Taiwan. Thus it has recently been decided to reinforce the technological standards of the People's Armed Police units entrusted, together with the PLA, with the defense of the frontiers. The improvement of the infrastructure for the defense of the frontiers in Xinjiang, such as the road network and the control barriers, also represent a priority that shows a tendency to be reinforced rather than reduced.[7]

Although the factors of internal destabilization do exist, for Beijing it is equally evident that control of Xinjiang entails control of the periphery and of cross-border contacts. Thus, while Beijing has insisted on good relations with all the new republics of Central Asia, a directive from the Central Committee of the CCP underlined the necessity of obtaining a promise from Kazakhstan and Kyrgyzstan not to give support to the Uighur or Kazakh independence movements originating in Xinjiang.[8]

Internal Control and "Border Stability"

Internal control and the maintenance of order depend in fact, for the Chinese authorities, on control of the border and preventing any "contamination" or any external support for the independence movements. Indeed, while the internal destabilizing factors are frequently noted, in particular those linked to the inequalities of economic development, the indications of discontent that are regularly expressed in Xinjiang are real. Yet they are denounced by the central authorities as originating from outside and are aimed to weaken China and put a brake on its emergence as a superpower. The strategy of stabilizing the periphery, which forms part of the "border policy" put in place by China, is linked to the theory of the "peaceful rise," and constitutes the theoretical foundation of this strategy. All of this is termed "the principal challenge and objective of China's foreign policy."[9]

This strategy is also based on a "new concept of security" intended to promote "mutual trust, equality, mutual benefits and coordination," a kind of non-binding Chinese-style multilateralism. As far as Central Asia is concerned, this strategy of border stabilization has been to resolve all of the frontier questions inherited from the Soviet era more favorably to the new Central Asian republics with which Beijing wished to establish good relations. China then put in place a strategy of alliance against separatism, which has gradually taken the more established form of the fight against the "three evil forces"—terrorism, extremism, and separatism.

These elements have similarly incorporated a commitment on the part of the Asian republics not to support the separatist movements originating in Xinjiang, a commitment that, ideally, should lead to active cooperation in terms of repression and repatriation of the "separatists elements" sought by Beijing.[10] This element was all the more important given that more than 400,000 Uighurs have settled in Central Asia, over 300,000 of which in Kazakhstan alone, where family ties are tight. Moreover, a dozen or so Uighur organizations have been tolerated in Kazakhstan despite agreements signed with Beijing.[11] China has in fact put in place a cross-border cooperation network in the military realm and for the maintenance of order. For China, this was essentially a question of breaking an evident cultural, linguistic, ethnic and religious community that exists between Xinjiang and the Central Asian republics. But while reinforcing the "strategic" links between China and Central Asia, it was simultaneously necessary for Beijing to deny or minimize the natural and historical integration of Xinjiang with this whole region of Central Asia.

The Shanghai Five, set up in 1996 and which brought together the People's Republic of China, Kazakhstan, Kyrgyzstan, Tajikistan, and Russia, had as its official mission the resolution of frontier questions, the reduction of military tensions, and the implementation of confidence-building measures; more generally, it aimed to move from a status of confrontation to one of cooperation in a zone still profoundly marked by the Sino-Soviet conflict.[12] In a sign of goodwill on the part of China, it was during his trip to Central Asia in 1996 that Jiang Zemin announced the suspension by China of its nuclear testing program, while the question of the tests and the risks of radiation was particularly sensitive in Kazakhstan and also represented an element of the dispute in Xinjiang itself.

At the bilateral level, China has similarly instituted a series of "strategic partnerships" with all the Central Asian countries, the full titles of which nevertheless bear witness to the evolution in relations. With Kazakhstan, the partnership is termed "strategic" (this is the highest level), as Kazakhstan is the most sensitive state for reasons relating to its geographic proximity to Xinjiang, but also, as we will see, to the potential for cooperation in the field of energy. With the other republics, on the other hand, the terms are much less "strategic." With Kyrgyzstan, there is a "partnership of good neighborliness and friendly cooperation," with Uzbekistan a "partnership of friendly cooperation," with Tajikistan a "partnership of good neighborliness and friendly cooperation directed towards the 21st century," and with Turkmenistan "relations of friendly cooperation for the 21st century on the basis of equality and the common interest." But beyond the concern for stability, for Beijing, there is also the question in this sensitive region of expanding its sphere of influence or privileged interests.

The Dream of Expanding the Sphere of Chinese Influence

Reflecting this sensitivity, a Chinese analyst wrote recently that "China will never attempt to draw Central Asia into its zone of influence and does not have the intention of bringing its resources under its control." If the second part of the phrase very specifically mentions resources, the first part reiterates virtually in the same terms the declarations Li Peng made during his first tour of the region in 1994 following the proclamations of independence.[13] The reiteration indicates in fact that the conviction of these statements is undoubtedly not as strong as Beijing might have hoped for. Indeed, for an initial period, it seemed that the collapse of the USSR would offer China an unimagined opportunity to expand its sphere of influence or, at least, of "benevolent neutrality" in a region that had until then been inaccessible to it. While in the 1990s this strategy of reinforcing Chinese influence was limited to the strategic-diplomatic realm, since the beginning of this century, and particularly following the terrorist attacks of September 11, 2001, which brought with them a real disruption in the strategic situation in Central Asia, Beijing has also placed emphasis on reinforcing cooperation in the economic field.

The economic strategy that China is pursuing in Central Asia can be analyzed at several levels. It appears to be a prolongation of the development strategy for western China, with one aim being the opening up of Xinjiang and the economic development of the province in order to cool tensions there. But Beijing applies the same analysis to the republics of Central Asia, the economic backwardness of which is denounced as one of the causes of the social tensions and of the rise of Islamic terrorism.[14] Moreover, and this is a relatively new element, Central Asia appears today to be both a market for Chinese products, but also a source of energy supplies, the importance of which has grown considerably for China. China is thus encouraging, with nevertheless qualified success, the development of infrastructure intended to facilitate the trade with Central Asia as well as the opening up of Xinjiang. The transport network, in particular the road and air network, has been considerably strengthened with trans-Central Asia motorway projects linking Andijan Osh and Kashgar and passing via the strategic route of Karakorum in order to open up the southern part of Xinjiang. The last agreement signed in 2005 with Pakistan provides for the Karakorum highway to be open to traffic throughout the year.

The strategic and security dimension of these projects is obviously not absent, but the newer economic dimension is also essential. Since 1986, the year of its reestablishment, and in particular since 1992, border trade has developed considerably. In 2003, it accounted for 50 percent of the province's total trade.[15] More than 28 crossing points have been opened, and in 2004 an agreement with Kazakhstan was signed to open a free trade zone centered in Khorgos.

However, the role of Xinjiang appears essentially to be that of a transit route for products that are exported to Central Asia, the vast majority of which come from China's more developed neighboring provinces. This fact means, however, that the development of trade, which largely remains in the hands of the Han community, constitutes another source of frustration. On the other side of the border, it is the invasion of the markets by the Han traders, such as has happened in Almaty, that provokes a sense of unease. Chinese economic dynamism thus plays a part in reinforcing a common feeling of exclusion that affects the local populations both in Xinjiang and in Central Asia.

Beyond access to a new market for the less sophisticated of Chinese products, Central Asia, and Kazakhstan in particular, represent for China a major interest in energy. In 1994, the China National Petroleum Company (CNPC) acquired 60 percent of the shares in the Kazakh company Aktobemunaj Gaz, which has been exploiting the Aktyubinsk field. In 1997, a joint venture agreement was signed with the company Uzemunigaz to exploit the Uzen field. In August 2005, CNPC also initiated the acquisition of Petrokazakhstan, and was supported in this project by the Kazakh authorities. On the other hand, the pipeline projects required heavy investments, which foreign— in particular Japanese—companies, have not been prepared to make for both economic and strategic reasons. In December 2005, a first 998 kilometer-long section linking the oil fields of Kazakhstan to Xinjiang's northeast via the Alashan Pass was completed; the aim was to extend this network in the direction of eastern China towards Shanghai. With the construction of this pipeline, China is increasing Kazakhstan's room for maneuver and negotiation, with the latter thus gaining an additional partner alongside Russia and the United States. On the other hand, the gas pipeline projects linking Xinjiang to Turkmenistan have still not gone anywhere.[16]

In economic terms, the aim of supplying energy to China's coastal regions, which are the most developed and the heaviest consumers, failed to materialize given the very high costs of exploitation and transport. The stakes have recently changed, however, for reasons that are both economic, with the increase in the cost of oil, and strategic, with the strengthening of the American military presence in the Middle East, China's primary source of oil imports. But beyond these preoccupations, Chinese policy with regard to Central Asia possesses a more global dimension related to the reinforcement of the American presence in the region.

The Shanghai Cooperation Organization: The Instrument of Pragmatism

In order to respond to these complex challenges, which have evolved considerably over time, China has relied on a mechanism that is itself evolutionary: the Shanghai Cooperation Organization (SCO). Although it no longer corresponds today to what it was at the time of its creation in 1995 under the name of the "Group of Five," the SCO's fundamental objectives remain as they were at its establishment. For Beijing, these are to counter the penetration of the United States in the region; to promote the reinforcement of Chinese influence; to play a part in the stabilization of the frontier zones; and possibly to be able to present it as a "new model for international relations" that could be extended to the rest of Asia.

At the time of its creation in 1996, the Shanghai Group (which was to be expanded in 2001 to include Uzbekistan and adopt the new name of the SCO) was intended to reinforce the cooperation and define a new framework for relations between China and the former Soviet republics of Central Asia following the disappearance of the Soviet Union. On the other hand, China's overriding strategic interests were heavily emphasized: opposition, at that time, to any reconsideration of the ABM treaty; support for the Chinese positions concerning Taiwan and Tibet; and opposition to any "separatist" attacks. With regard to these, for China, the attacks of September 11th represented a genuine turning point and a reason for disappointment when faced with the fragility of the structure built up since 1996. All of the member countries demonstrated their support for the United States, Russia accepted the abrogation of the ABM treaty and the Central Asian republics authorized the opening of American military bases on their territory.

Having to a large extent lost the initiative within the SCO, China therefore began to reorient its strategy, which from that point on has emphasized the economic and energy cooperation dimension as well as on that of the common fight against the attempts at regime change encouraged by Washington. As one Chinese analyst has recognized, following the attacks of September 11, any frontal opposition to the presence of the United States in the region had no chance of succeeding, and China thus had to find divergent means to progressively rebuild its influence in the region. For an initial period, Beijing thus insisted on the fight against terrorism, without obtaining any genuine reorientation of American strategy in its favor. Beijing also highlighted the common fight against non-traditional security.

At the economic level, Beijing proposed in 2003 (in accordance with a strategy that can be found everywhere in Asia) the establishment of a free trade zone based on the potential of the Chinese market and the supposed complementarity of the Chinese and Central Asian economies. China has similarly proposed that a working group on energy be set up with the intention of facilitating large-scale transborder projects such as the construction of pipelines.

At the political level, bilateral visits have been multiplied and several working groups have been set up. During the 2004 SCO summit, a development aid program for the countries of the region based on low-interest loans was also initiated by China. Nevertheless, Beijing remains a minor actor in Central Asia. Its principal partner remains Kazakhstan. But, even in this case, Russia continues to be, by far, Astana's primary commercial partner. In terms of investment, it is the Western countries (72 percent of the total) who have taken the lead, with the United States (40 percent of the total) predominant, followed by Russia and then by China (3 percent of the total).

Despite these initiatives, Beijing's influence within the SCO has been diluted. As we have seen, China is no more than one actor among others, one on which the Central Asian states can rely to buttress their own strategies and defend their interests, but also one on which they are not absolutely dependent.

Conclusion

China's policy with regard to Central Asia thus reveals a capacity for adaptation, a flexibility and pragmatism that contrasts with its policy, for example, towards Taiwan. Beyond the search for alliances with authoritarian states that share Beijing's distrust of the strategies of "regime change" initiated by the United States, the ideological dimension is in effect absent from the relations between China and Central Asia.

The highlighting of multilateralism and of the SCO as a model bears witness to this pragmatism. Since its creation in 2005, the SCO has undergone important evolution; nevertheless, the permanent objective of Beijing has been, with more or less success and more or less room for maneuver, to try to orient the group in the direction of the narrow interests of the Chinese regime both at the strategic as well as at the economic levels.

NOTES

1. Nicolas Becquelin, "Criminalizing Ethnicity: Political Repression in Xinjiang," *China Rights Forum*, (2004), and Dru Gladney, *Dislocating China: Muslim Minorities and other Subaltern Subjects* (Chicago: University of Chicago Press, 2004).
2. Valérie Niquet, "China, Mongolia, Central Asia: China on the Edges of the ex-USSR," *China News Analysis*, No. 1532, April 1, 1995.
3. Zhang Weiwei and Xu Jin, "An Observation of Security Cooperation between China and the Central Asian Countries," *International Strategic Studies* (April 2005).
4. Thierry Kellner, *La Chine et la Nouvelle Asie Centrale* (Brussels: GRP, 2003).
5. According to Marie Holzman, while the population of Xinjiang only represents 0.21 percent of the total population of China, it accounts for 2.1 percent of those sentenced to death.
6. *Research Brief*, No. 9, Australian Parliament, 2005–2006.
7. Taylor Fravel, "Securing China: The PLA's Approach to Frontier Defense," Conference on PLA Affairs, CAPS-RAND-CEIP, November 2005.
8. Document No. 7, "XIV Comite central du Parti communiste chinois," in Thierry Kellner, *la Chine et la Nouvelle Asie Centrale* (Bruxelles: GRIP, 2004).
9. Zhao Gongcheng, "China: Periphery and Strategy," *SIIS Journal*, Vol. 10, No. 2 (May 2003), pp. 24–33.
10. Chien Peng-Chung, "The SCO: Institutionalization, Cooperation and Rivalry," *Japan Focus*, October 17, 2005.
11. During the Cultural Revolution, the Soviet republics of Central Asia served as a refuge for Uighurs who fled the radicalism of the China of Mao and the Gang of Four.
12. Zhang Weiwei and Xu Jin, op. cit.
13. Valérie Niquet, op.cit.
14. Zhang Weiwei, op. cit.
15. Xinhua News Agency, June 17, 2003.
16. Chien Peng-Chung, op. cit.

III. THE UNITED STATES AND CHINA

The China-US Relationship Goes Global*

Kenneth Lieberthal

What should be expected in US-China relations under the administration of President Barack Obama? During the tenure of President George W. Bush, relations developed relatively smoothly. When Bush left office the relationship could reasonably be described as mature, wide-ranging, constructive, and candid. Each of these dimensions of the relationship reflected protracted effort on both sides.

"Mature" conveys that the leaderships of the two countries had gotten to know each other well; had some understanding of each other's goals, operating styles, and major concerns; and recognized the value of maintaining effective ties even when significant problems arose. None of this was true 30 years ago, in the early days after normalization of US-Sino relations. Today, major problems can arise in one part of the relationship without jeopardizing the two sides' capacity to manage other issues of mutual concern.

"Wide-ranging" reflects the reality that the two governments now deal with each other regularly across an extraordinary array of issues, including not only traditional matters of diplomacy, economics, or security, but also such concerns as public health, the environment, science and technology, and education. Accordingly, a broad array of regular meetings occurs between the two governments as a matter of course. For most ministries in each government, it would be unusual for a week to go by without direct contact with counterparts in the other country.

"Constructive" indicates that both countries value development of the relationship and therefore look for ways to reduce tensions, manage differences, and solve problems. Neither side intentionally seeks to undermine US-Sino ties. On many issues, of course, differences between

China and the United States are significant. Such will always be the case in relations among major powers. But in recent years each side has sought to make the relationship work more effectively.

"Candid" highlights that each side has learned how to convey its serious concerns in top-level meetings. Both sides, for example, can make clear their views on human rights. Interest in human rights will not disappear from US foreign policy, and China will express its own views on this topic. Without a capacity to raise and discuss serious and sensitive issues such as this, the US-China relationship inevitably would run into trouble.

Mutually Assured Distrust

If, by themselves, the four adjectives cited above fully defined US-Sino relations, prospects for the relationship's future would be very bright. But the reality is more complex than this, for two reasons. First, the US-China agenda going forward will include important, relatively new issues that will increasingly shape the overall relationship. The most prominent among these today are the worldwide economic downturn and climate change. Indeed, the advance of *global* issues to a prominent role in bilateral affairs marks a significant change in the US-China relationship and presents both opportunities and perils.

Second, the single biggest failure of 30 years of diplomatic ties between Washington and Beijing is that neither side, even today, trusts the long-term intentions of the other toward itself. Close observers of US-China relations constantly hear evidence of this lack of trust as they listen to concerns voiced in each capital.

In Beijing, many believe that the United States is simply too zero-sum in its thinking and too wedded to maintaining its position of global hegemony ever to allow China to realize its aspirations of being wealthy and strong. This belief

---

* This article was published in *Current History* (September 2009).

causes many Chinese rather readily to believe that various American actions conceal a nefarious plot to limit and complicate China's rise.

Some in China believe, for example, that the current global recession not only started in America but was designed by Americans to undermine China's economy. Some see US concerns about climate change, and US pressure on China to make burdensome commitments to reduce carbon emissions, as an American scheme to slow China's economic development. To an American ear such allegations seem outrageous, but that does not make them any less credible to Chinese who distrust America's long-term intentions toward the People's Republic.

Comparable distrust of China's long-term intentions exists on the American side. Many Americans with significant influence on policy making believe that, as China becomes wealthy and strong, Beijing will seek to marginalize the United States in Asia. Because Asia is such a dynamic and important region, an attempt to marginalize America there would directly threaten key US interests. Many Americans are also deeply troubled by China's annual double-digit military budget increases and the growing capabilities the Chinese military is acquiring.

This distrust on both sides is deeply rooted. Moreover, because the distrust concerns long-term (that is, 10-to-20-year) *intentions* rather than immediate goals and policies, it is very difficult to change. And it has serious consequences. It produces behavior—primarily in terms of military planning and development—that is geared toward protecting national interests if things go wrong. Each side has some understanding of the other side's long-term military investments, and each takes this information as confirmation that its distrust is warranted. This situation could, of course, amount to a self-fulfilling prophecy that over time increases the chances of US-Sino relations shifting from constructive to antagonistic, at potentially great cost to both sides.

As both Washington and Beijing look to the future, therefore, they should specifically address attention to a key question: How can each side *credibly* signal that its preferred outcome over the course of the coming decades is that the United States and China maintain a normal big-power relationship, one in which the two sides cooperate when they can and try to manage and mitigate differences when their interests set them apart? This is not an easy task—conspiracy theorists in each country will always be able to develop seemingly plausible stories to "explain" how superficially good intentions in reality mask nefarious goals. But the task is critical.

Flashpoints

The United States and China face a large, difficult, and significant agenda of ongoing issues. Some of these will pose tough challenges that will test the maturity of the Sino-US relationship in the period ahead. North Korea's nuclear program is one important example. China took the lead in the six-party talks meant to address the issue and has played a skillful role in keeping this process going in the face of various obstacles. But the issue remains far from resolved. And now it appears that North Korea may be experiencing internal political difficulties that diminish the chances of Pyongyang's agreeing to and then implementing compromises leading to the full termination of its nuclear program. Indeed, the provocative behavior displayed by North Korea during the spring of 2009 signaled major new difficulties in keeping the nuclear talks moving forward.

The cross-strait issue, of course, also remains unresolved. The past year has witnessed serious progress toward creating a more stable, win-win situation across the Taiwan Strait. Even so, much remains to be done to relieve the concerns of both sides. In particular, both sides have addressed the military and security dimensions of the cross strait situation in principle, but so far there has been no significant concrete progress. The capabilities of the People's Liberation Army (PLA) continue to increase with respect to Taiwan, and the United States remains committed to providing Taiwan with sufficient military capability to address the potential military threat it faces. None of the sides—Beijing, Taipei, or Washington—wants to see military force ever used across the strait, but the status quo inevitably raises periodic tensions—such as when America authorizes additional arms sales to Taiwan.

Military-to-military relations between US forces and the PLA have developed to some extent but still remain far below the level necessary to develop mutual understanding and trust. The PLA's ongoing modernization and expansion of its capabilities predictably raise issues for the US military, just as ongoing US weapons systems development, and changes in deployments in Asia, attract serious attention in the PLA. It is thus becoming more important for the two militaries to increase the frequency, depth, and scope of their contacts and to address issues such as arms control and mutually understood operational rules, especially as the two countries' navies increasingly work in the same spaces.

The multilateral architecture in the Asia-Pacific region is undergoing rapid development and change. New multilateral forums and combinations of countries gathering for various types of consultations seem to proliferate like bamboo shoots after a spring rain. It is important for the United States and China to welcome each other into any wide-ranging Asian multilateral forum in which either one participates. This would increase mutual trust and reduce the chances of polarization in the region, but it has not always happened to date (witness the East Asia Summit and the Shanghai Cooperation Organization).

A voluminous literature treats each of the above issues and most articles on Sino-US relations deal with one or more of them. Notably, all are bilateral concerns or problems that concern China's periphery. These are the types of issues that have traditionally shaped US-China relations. In the past, the United States and China have sometimes taken up more general issues or issues that concerned places farther from China's shores—such as nonproliferation and developments in the greater Middle East—but these until now have remained at the margins of the US-China relationship. Given China's rapidly growing power and global engagement, some of these issues will now become more significant in Sino-US relations. For example, opportunities now exist for China and the United States to engage much more fully on problems across the Middle East—from Pakistan and Afghanistan, to Iran, to the Arab-Israeli question, to energy security in general. These challenges are all interrelated; America's approaches to this vast region are changing; and China's own interests in the area have grown to the point that systematic Sino-US engagement is warranted.

But even more important, the most critical *global* issues are for the first time moving to a central place in the US-China relationship. The prominence on the agenda of both the global economic downturn and the issues of clean energy and climate change is relatively new: The economic crisis only developed in the final months of the Bush administration, while the climate change issue stayed at the margins of US-China relations until President Bush left office.

If the two sides can engage effectively on these issues, Sino-US relations will enter a new stage in which ties will become deeper, stronger, more stable, and more important for the international system than ever before. The resulting cooperation could, in turn, reduce the mutual distrust about each country's long-term intentions.

The Dollar Trap

The global economic difficulties now at the center of international attention began with a financial crisis brought on by failures in regulation and management in the US financial services system. Other countries and institutions had fully participated in that system to reap its benefits, and as a consequence when problems developed the contagion proved extremely rapid and widespread.

The resulting economic problems directly involve the United States and China on both bilateral and multilateral levels. The two countries' economies are highly interdependent in ways that go far beyond the bilateral trade relationship. China holds the vast majority of its foreign currency reserves in US dollars, primarily in various debt instruments in the United States. Economic recovery plans have included issuing a large amount of new sovereign debt, and it is important to the United States that China continues to purchase a portion of these new debt obligations. Beijing, in turn, views US economic recovery as critical to China's own prospects for returning quickly to the growth rates to which it has grown accustomed.

The United States needs to consult closely and work cooperatively with China to address both the bilateral issues that are related to economic recovery and also multilateral issues concerning a restructuring of the global financial system's regulatory framework and substance. It is too early to ascertain how effective this effort at consultation and cooperation will be. This is in part because it is still unclear exactly how deep and long-lasting the global downturn will prove to be.

It is not too early, though, to highlight some of the difficult issues and contradictions with which the United States and China have to wrestle. President Obama adopted bold fiscal and regulatory measures to get ahead of the crisis and limit its scope and severity. But this required running a high budget deficit (exactly how high will depend on the pace of economic recovery). The president's economic calculations include an assumption that China will continue to purchase US debt instruments at a significant level. Otherwise, the cost of US borrowing—and therefore the size of the US deficit—will grow significantly larger.

But China is nervous about how much it has already invested in US debt instruments, and it fears that the US government will resort to printing dollars as one way to reduce its real debt burden. A mildly cheaper dollar could be in China's interests because it would make Chinese exports somewhat more competitive, as long as China kept the value of the renminbi (RMB) roughly fixed in relation to the dollar. But a major decline in the value of the greenback would cost China many billions of dollars in the value of its foreign exchange holdings. Other countries, moreover, would object strongly to the RMB's following the dollar all the way down, thus making it difficult for China to respond to major dollar depreciation by allowing its own currency to depreciate as well. China thus wants the United States to spend enough to restore economic growth but also to manage its expenditures wisely so as to maintain the basic value of the dollar—a difficult balancing act.

Many Chinese are advising that China is already too heavily invested in dollar assets and should stop buying US debt. (Indeed, some believe China should start selling off US debt and move its funds into RMB or other currencies.) But China is caught in what might be called a "dollar trap." It holds so many dollars that if it tries to sell enough of them to make a serious impact on its exposure, the sale itself will weaken the dollar and increase the value of the currencies China is purchasing instead. China in that case would lose a great deal of money simply by trying to reduce its dollar exposure. If, on the other hand, China holds onto its dollars, then US treasuries provide a source of debt that is deep, flexible, and secure (except for the exchange rate risk)—a very desirable set of qualities in a time of uncertainty.

Nothing will completely eliminate the contradictions and tensions in this set of monetary issues. But at a minimum, the United States and China should maintain consultations that are more in depth, frequent, and transparent than they have ever been before. This could help ensure that each side is sensitive to the requirements of the other, understands the other's strategy and concerns, and is not surprised by developments as they occur. All of this should contribute to increasing confidence and stability.

A Consuming Problem

The United States and China also need to consult closely over macroeconomic adjustments. Fundamentally, China realizes that it needs to increase personal consumption as a component of gross domestic product. Currently, China's level of personal consumption as a percentage of GDP is close to the lowest in the world. Beijing has recognized the need to change this situation for several years, but during this time personal consumption has actually declined as a percentage of GDP, despite government efforts. Now that exports have dropped off significantly, the need to increase domestic consumption demand has proportionately become even more pressing.

In terms of stimulating demand in the short run, the largest single item in the $586 billion stimulus package that China's government announced in November 2008 is infrastructure development. This spending will increase domestic demand but also production capacity, and puts China at risk of massive overcapacity if exports do not revive substantially in the next two years and domestic demand otherwise remains low. At that point, additional infrastructure investment as a way to keep stimulating the economy would be far more difficult to sustain.

The United States has the opposite problem. It permitted personal consumption to rise to such a level that the country for the past several years had no net personal savings. This high consumption model became possible because of a mistaken presumption that housing prices would continue to rise, which led banks to extend excessive credit to homeowners based on the (inflated) imputed value of their houses. The United States now needs to transition to a positive rate of personal savings—and the transition seems to be occurring extraordinarily rapidly. In the months since the initial acceleration of the economic crisis, Americans have suddenly remembered their traditional ethic of thrift, and the personal savings rate has leaped to about 5 percent.

The problem is that high American personal consumption and high Chinese personal savings are directly linked, each enabling the other. Effectively, the United States has borrowed China's savings to finance personal consumption. At the same time, China has accumulated the money to maintain high savings and make loans to the United States by producing goods that Americans buy with their consumer dollars. The complexities, moreover, do not end there.

While the United States wants to increase personal savings over the long run, it wants to foster personal consumption now in order to get out of a short-term economic crisis. And while China wants to increase personal consumption for the sake of domestic demand, it must also build institutions and capabilities to enhance its social safety net. Doing the latter involves long-term investments that do not produce the short-term stimulating effects that new infrastructure investments provide. But without social safety net enhancements, most Chinese will still want to save for unexpected expenses or bad times, and personal consumption is unlikely to rise significantly.

The necessary adjustments are thus truly society-wide in each country. At least three to five years will be required to make these changes and put them on a sustainable footing. During this time, it makes enormous sense for the United States and China to consult closely on their macroeconomic adjustment policies and plans, as each side can reduce its own problems by being more sensitive to developments in the other country. This is one of the major issues that is a focus of the new Strategic and Economic Dialogue, to which President Obama appointed Secretary of State Hillary Clinton and Treasury Secretary Timothy Geithner as special representatives.

Trade and Trouble

Another potentially serious matter is the issue of Chinese exports of goods and capital. China is now trying to increase exports in order to bolster employment. To do so, it is enhancing various forms of assistance to exporters. At a time when the US unemployment rate has approached double digits, such Chinese policies could engender a very strong and negative political response from America—and this is especially true if China also increases nontariff barriers to US imports.

Chinese firms at the same time may seek to purchase undervalued real manufacturing assets in the United States. If they do this, they need to be sensitive to the importance of presenting their efforts to Americans as high-quality deals—deals that seek to grow the US firms, create jobs, and produce win-win situations. If Chinese merger and acquisition efforts instead appear to be "vulture" investing—that is, using takeovers to acquire brands and technology, strip assets, and undermine jobs—then such investing could become a source of major US-China tensions.

Meanwhile, if America's long-term personal saving rate is at 5 to 8 percent, sufficient demand for US goods and services can be created only if exports increase. But China's recovery and growth strategies depend on a revival of its own exports. The potential for trade frictions is obvious.

Multilaterally, the United States and China are critical participants in reshaping the global financial regulatory system. As recently as late 2008, it seemed unclear whether China would play a proactive role in suggesting new idea and promoting new policies. But in the run-up to the Group of 20 meeting in April 2009, when Beijing began to take initiative on the issue of a global supersovereign reserve currency, it became apparent that China might play a more active role in the global talks than previously expected.

The United States will, as always, be very active in putting forward ideas and working to shape revisions to the global financial system's architecture and rules. And US and Chinese interests will not be identical. China wants over the long term to reduce the role of the US dollar as the global reserve currency, while the United States has little interest in seeing that occur. Given the array of issues in international finance and financial regulation that China and the United States face, and given the complex connections among many of these issues, close Sino-US consultation is a necessary part of reaching global consensus on how to move forward.

The issues revolving around financial uncertainties and the global recession are of core national importance to each country. Tremendous room for cooperation exists—as does tremendous room for disagreement and misunderstanding. If the latter becomes the dominant story, the chances of mutually destructive protectionism will rise, and it will be harder for everyone to emerge from the current downturn. Close consultation could lift US-China relations to a new level both bilaterally and in terms of global impact. But failure to consult closely, and to find ways to reduce problems, could produce profoundly negative effects on mutual trust, expectations, and outcomes.

The Hot Topic

Alongside the global economic situation, climate change now ranks as an equally significant issue on the bilateral agenda. Climate change played a relatively minor role in US-China relations until the end of the Bush administration. President Bush himself did not believe the government should play a substantial role in addressing the climate change threat. His treasury secretary, Henry Paulson, by contrast, believed deeply that global warming posed a threat to future civilization, and he sought to develop cooperation with China to address the issue. In mid-2008 the United States and China signed a 10-year framework agreement on the environment and clean energy. This pact provides one basis for future cooperation, but relatively little was accomplished under it before Bush left office.

The centrality of climate change in Sino-US relations is growing rapidly for four reasons. First, President Obama's view of the issue is the opposite of President Bush's. For Obama, shifting to a low-carbon economy—both domestically and globally—must be one of America's most important goals, and the government has a serious role to play in this project. Indeed, the development of clean energy ranks with resolving the economic crisis and addressing domestic health care and education as his highest priorities.

Second, the Chinese government has greatly increased its own attention to climate change in the past two years. As reflected in the government's white paper on the issue in October 2008, China now views itself as one of the countries most vulnerable to the ravages of climate change, and this requires major efforts in China at both adaptation and mitigation.

Third, the scientific community's understanding of the speed, scope, and consequences of climate change is improving rapidly. Almost every new major scientific study of the phenomenon makes clear that previous studies underestimated the degree of global warming's danger and overestimated the amount of time available to take strong remedial action.

Fourth, a meeting is scheduled for Copenhagen in December 2009 to adopt a new climate framework agreement as a successor to the Kyoto Protocol. As a result, the international community is paying enormous attention to the issue this year, and everyone is looking particularly at the American and Chinese postures. Yet, in both the United States and China, taking strong domestic measures to reduce carbon emissions is very difficult because it affects powerful interests.

The way the United States and China handle the issue of clean energy within their own borders affects, moreover, the ability of the other country's leadership to adopt effective measures. China's leaders find it harder to take rigorous measures when the United States, a richer and more technologically advanced country that is also a major carbon emitter, does not itself take a leadership role. Similarly, China's record on carbon emissions plays into the domestic debate in the United States. Obama wants the Congress to adopt legislation that effectively puts a cap on overall carbon emissions and imposes a price on carbon. But the opponents of such "cap-and-trade" legislation point to China and argue that making carbon emissions costly in the United States will simply provide Chinese enterprises (and foreign investors in China) with a competitive advantage because China is not imposing a comparable cost on its carbon emissions. The result, they argue, would simply be an increase in American unemployment and no reduction in global emissions.

Each side, therefore, wants the other to do more—partly in order to create a better environment for advancing its own efforts to restrain carbon emissions. This presents a natural environment in which to foster cooperation, but it also presents another arena in which failure to achieve cooperation might increase mutual suspicion and tension.

After You Please

The Obama administration is anxious to avoid repeating Bill Clinton's experience with the Kyoto Protocol—the Clinton administration signed the document but was unable to win enough domestic support to implement it. Thus the administration hopes, before Copenhagen, to achieve real progress on domestic actions, laws, and regulations in order to instill international confidence that the United States can follow through on what it agrees to do. If Obama can honestly say to the US Congress that China is very concerned about the issue of climate change; is taking strong measures to deal with it; and is willing to work with the United States and others to advance the goal of reducing emissions of greenhouse gases—the president's chances of legislative success increase considerably.

In the past, American and Chinese officials, technical specialists, firms, and nongovernmental organizations have interacted quite extensively on issues related to global warming. But their interactions have lacked the momentum, direction, and support that would result from an explicit agreement between the two countries' presidents and governments to form a clean-energy partnership to promote better outcomes on carbon emissions. The United States and China in fact can identify many aspects of the climate change issue in which cooperation would provide mutual benefits. An overall partnership agreement would greatly enhance prospects for capitalizing on this.

The issue of clean energy goes to the heart of both countries' economies, and it is inherently

an issue that will remain on the agenda for many decades to come. Large-scale cooperation around this issue could, therefore, greatly enhance the range of serious working relationships between the two societies, and the long-term nature of the cooperation could instill greater trust in each other's long-term intentions.

When it comes to the problem of carbon emissions, of course, serious disagreements exist over issues of principle. These center (from the Chinese perspective) on cumulative historical emissions, per capita emissions, and the two countries' stages of development—or (from the US perspective) on current emissions and future trajectories, total national emissions, and legacy structures and styles of life. These differences reflect the perspectives of developing and industrialized countries.

The reality, though, is that sea level rise will submerge Los Angeles at the same time it submerges Shanghai, and cooperation cannot wait until all participants agree on the "correct" perspective. China and the developing countries are raising issues that are accurate and have merit—and the same is true of the issues raised by industrialized countries. No progress is likely to be made on cooperation if each side makes the other side's capitulation on these issues a condition for moving forward.

Therefore each side, while reserving differences, needs to seek common ground, acknowledge that the perspective of the other side reflects serious realities, and achieve pragmatic cooperation on an issue that threatens both sides and will not wait. In this way US-Sino cooperation on this vital global issue—involving the world's most important developed country and the world's most important developing country—could help bridge the divide between industrialized and developing nations in global negotiations over how to respond to the threat of climate change.

Two Roads

The climate change challenge highlights both the global nature of the key issues that are moving to the center of Sino-US relations and the very high stakes in how these issues are handled. Finding a way to enhance serious consultation and cooperation would strengthen US-China relations and move the relationship to a new stage. Cooperation on this issue would inherently be so long-term and so central to each society, moreover, that it could contribute significantly to reducing the distrust that each side currently harbors concerning the willingness of the other to maintain a cooperative relationship over the long run.

Both the United States and China want a cooperative, productive relationship, and the two countries already have extensive experience in managing the ongoing issues that have shaped their relationship to date. But the critical global issues now moving to the center of Sino-US relations will significantly affect ties going forward.

How America and China deal with each other regarding these new global challenges will to a significant extent determine the relationship's prospects over the long term. Will Beijing and Washington overcome their mutual distrust over long-term intentions and create the "positive, cooperative, comprehensive" twenty-first-century relationship touted by Presidents Obama and Hu Jintao at their April meeting in London? Or will Sino-US relations instead enter very troubled territory? The long-term consequences of the introduction of global issues into the bilateral agenda may be very large.

AGENDA FOR A NEW GREAT POWER RELATIONSHIP[*]

Wu Xinbo

"Well begun is half done," Aristotle once said, meaning that beginning a project well makes it easier to do the rest. Yet, this may not be true of China-US relations during Obama's presidency. Although the Obama administration secured a smooth transition from the George W. Bush years and attached high priority to relations with China during its first year in office, bilateral relations turned downward over the rest of Obama's first term, leaving a legacy of growing mutual suspicion and rising competition between the two countries, especially in the Asia-Pacific region. In spite of the November 2009 bilateral agreement to build a "positive, cooperative, and comprehensive relationship,"[1] the two sides missed opportunities for more cooperation while mishandling and even misguiding bilateral ties on some points.

The next several years are crucial for China-US relations. Beijing is now under a new leadership that is more self-confident and more attentive to its public opinion. The further narrowing of the power gap between China and the United States will inevitably generate more anxiety in Washington. The competition between

the two countries in the Asia-Pacific may pick up momentum. At the same time, the world's two largest economies will need to coordinate to promote global governance in an era when regional and global challenges are only getting more complicated. It is indeed high time to reset China-US relations—for the long-term interests of both countries as well as the entire world.

There are definite opportunities as the Obama administration's second term proceeds. China's new leader Xi Jinping feels comfortable in dealing with Washington, striving for "a new type of major power relationship" with the United States. Xi first put forward this idea when he visited the United States in February 2012 as the Chinese Vice President. In May 2012 during the fourth Strategic and Economic Dialogue (S&ED) held in Beijing, the Chinese side further elaborated on this concept to the US interlocutors. Finally, in June 2013, President Xi fully expounded his optimism for building such a relationship to President Obama during their informal meeting in California—both sides have the political will to construct a new type of relationship between great powers; cooperation between the two countries over more than 40 years constitutes a solid foundation for the further cooperation between them; over 90 dialogue and communication mechanisms

[*] This article was published in *The Washington Quarterly* (January 2014).

set up between China and the United States provide a guarantee for the pursuit of that goal; the robust exchanges and bonds forged between two societies and peoples have laid a profound foundation of public opinion favorable to the construction of such a relationship; and finally, there exists enormous space for further cooperation between China and the United States. Xi also stressed that the way to construct such a new great power relationship is to strengthen dialogue, enhance mutual trust, develop cooperation, and manage differences.[2]

From the Chinese perspective, the core elements of this relationship are "no conflict, no confrontation, mutual respect, and win-win cooperation."[3] Although the full policy implications have yet to be explored, the idea reflects an honest desire on the part of Beijing to avoid the tragedy of major power conflicts given the contemporary era's rapid development of globalization and deepening interdependence among countries. The US side was initially cautious and even dubious of the idea, but during the meeting in California, President Obama agreed to make joint efforts along with China to advance this goal. This agreement not only sends a good signal to the other side about their respective intentions, but also helps set a positive tone for internal policymaking on both sides.

It is quite common that US presidents usually devote more time and energy to foreign policy in their second term, trying to establish their political legacy on major international issues. Without the pressure of getting reelected, President Obama can pay more attention to relations with Beijing and provide necessary leadership in his China policy. Fortunately, US Secretary of State John Kerry understands China's growing importance to US interests as well as global affairs and supports the development of close and cooperative relations with China. From the Chinese perspective, his team appears more credible than "the Clinton-Campbell axis" during Obama's first term, which appeared to dislike China ideologically and oppose China strategically.

Since 2013, both sides have made serious joint efforts to get bilateral relations back on track. As mentioned, in June 2013 Xi and Obama held an informal meeting in Sunnylands, California. This unprecedented summit meeting, less formal but more substantive and candid, established a new type of interaction between Chinese and US presidents, reflecting the overlapping expectation from both sides for better Sino-US ties. With this positive tone set, the fifth S&ED, held in Washington, DC one month later, allowed diplomatic and economic teams from both countries to meet and make progress on a wide range of issues.

Despite these positive developments, both Beijing and Washington have room for growth as 2014 begins. As China is becoming a hub for regional economic links, it should also play a central role in regional security; therefore, Beijing needs to demonstrate both the willingness and capacity to work with others, including the United States, to effectively deal with security challenges to the region. Meanwhile, Beijing should also assure others that it can peacefully manage and resolve maritime disputes with some of its neighbors, just as it did over land territorial disputes with countries such as Russia and Vietnam during the past two decades.

For its part, the United States should treat China as an important global partner not just rhetorically and with diplomatic gestures, but in its actions. This will require Washington to adjust some of its long-held practices such as arms sales to Taiwan, the US president's meeting with the Dalai Lama, and frequent and intrusive air and maritime surveillance on China in its vicinity. Moreover, US policymakers should avoid responding to China's rising power and influence from a zero-sum perspective, where it aims to check China's growing capability and international clout, rather than fostering a mutually beneficial ascent.

New Vision

Forging a new model of relationship between China and the United States requires both new vision and new thinking. Without a new vision, both sides may lose direction in steering through an increasingly complex bilateral agenda. From a historical perspective, bilateral ties have experienced several major changes since Sino-US reconciliation in the early 1970s. With Nixon's visit to China, Beijing and Washington became strategic partners with the aim of checking Soviet expansion. A generation later, with the end of the

Cold War and acceleration of globalization, China sought to fully join the international economic architecture—and the United States welcomed and facilitated this process. Now in the early 21st century, with developments such as China's rapid rise amidst growing global challenges and multipolarization in international politics, Beijing and Washington are destined to become global partners in enhancing global governance, no matter the hurdles that must be overcome. This new vision of "global partners" provides the backbone to the new model of a major power relationship.

For China and the United States to become genuine global partners, both sides need to adjust their respective thinking. Given its history from World War II through the collapse of the Soviet Union, the United States' perspective is saturated with realist thinking about things such as power balance, geopolitics, military alliances, and zero-sum games. Washington manifests a proclivity for overemphasizing national security concerns, seeking superior military might, and securing hegemony. It is this thinking and ensuing practices that have given rise to Beijing's distrust of Washington. To be sure, the United States is an established power, yet it should not obsolesce by sticking to outmoded thinking and practices. Rather, it should cast itself as a progressive power, embracing the thinking commensurate with the international politics of the 21st century.

China has naturally more easily embraced such new thinking as it has emerged as a major power in the post–Cold War era, benefitting from economic globalization and international cooperation. Therefore, China values liberal ideals such as peaceful development, mutual trust, mutual benefit, equality, and coordination.[4] It repudiates forging military blocs and seeking military superiority as obsolete Cold War mentality.

On the other hand, as a country that has suffered at the hands of the Western powers and Japan in "the century of humiliation" dated from the Opium War in 1840 to the founding of the People's Republic of China (PRC) in 1949, China carries a bitter legacy of the past and possesses a weak state mentality. As a result, Beijing has insisted on stricter adherence to the concept of sovereignty and the principle of non-interference in the internal affairs of others, which constrains its role in promoting regional and global governance. Also, as a traditional regional power rather than global power to date, China lacks real global thinking in its foreign policy and worldwide diplomatic activism. These limitations have from time to time frustrated Washington when its expectations of Beijing's cooperation have gone unfulfilled. The challenge for China is that as its material power expands, so should its ideational power, thus allowing it to keep up with the times and play its role as a responsible global power.

An Agenda for a New Type of Relationship

Forging a new model for a major power relationship between China and the United States should start with expanding cooperation and managing differences over a handful of key issues: the Korean issue, maritime disputes in East Asia, military-to-military ties, economic relations, and cyber security.

The Korean Issue North Korea's third nuclear test in February 2013 indicated that Pyongyang continues to develop its nuclear capability, and the denuclearization of the Democratic People's Republic of Korea (or DPRK) thus becomes more urgent. However, the ultimate solution of North Korea's nuclear issue depends on Pyongyang's policy transformation on two fronts: domestically, from putting its military first to its economy first, and externally, from a posture of confrontation to one of reconciliation and cooperation. While external pressure may help prevent Pyongyang from conducting further nuclear tests aimed at enhancing its nuclear capability, denuclearization will only occur as a result of these transformations.

Evidence suggests that since Kim Jong Un's accession to power, North Korea has been shifting its national agenda to economic development and improving people's welfare. The recent execution of his uncle and ensuing political reshuffling might serve to consolidate Kim's power rather than alter his current policy agenda. On the other hand, after the DPRK's third nuclear test, the international pressure mounted as China emphasized the need for DPRK's denuclearization and curtailed North Korea's access to articles that may be used for its nuclear and missile program. As a result, Pyongyang has been softening its posture towards the Republic of Korea (or ROK) and the United States. At the same time, the new ROK President, Park Geun-hye, is pushing a process of trust-building on the peninsula. Under these circumstances, there seems to exist a good opportunity for Beijing, Washington, and Seoul to work together to facilitate Pyongyang's policy transformation.

From 2003 to 2008, China hosted the Six-Party Talks (among China, Japan, North Korea, South Korea, Russia, and the United States) in an attempt to solve North Korea's nuclear issue, yet it failed to prevent Pyongyang from developing its nuclear capability. Why? Because this approach didn't effectively address North Korea's core security concern. As long as hostility drags on between North Korea and South Korea as well as the United States, Pyongyang will remain concerned about its survival and will continue to develop its nuclear capability. It is time to try an alternative.

Instead of restarting the Six-Party Talks aimed at solving the DPRK nuclear issue, the four parties to the Korean War—China, the United States, and the two Koreas—should restart the "Four-Party" process that ran from December 1997 to August 1999.[5] Aimed at reducing tension and building a permanent peace mechanism on the Korean peninsula, the Four-Party Talks enhanced dialogue among the related parties over security issues and explored ways to address them. In fact, it was the Four-Party process that facilitated the summit between North and South in 2000 and the adjustment of US policy towards the DPRK in the late Clinton years.

The reconstituted Four-Party Talks would restart the efforts to reduce the tension on the peninsula and replace the 1953 truce treaty with a formal peace mechanism. Such an instrument, formally terminating the state of war and renouncing the use of force to solve disputes on the peninsula in the future, would provide Pyongyang the incentive to adopt a more reconciliatory posture and abandon its nuclear program.

China and the United States have important roles to play in the process, from providing re-start initiatives to helping set the agenda to navigating the negotiations to finally signing the new peace treaty.[6] Effective Sino-US cooperation in solving the DPRK nuclear issue and burying the Cold War legacy in Northeast Asia will certainly contribute to forging a new model of major power relations between the two countries.

Maritime Disputes The flare-up of old disputes over the Diaoyu/Senkaku Islands between China and Japan in the East China Sea, and over the Nansha Islands among China, Vietnam, the Philippines, Malaysia, and Brunei in the South China Sea, have posed challenges to Sino-US relations. These will only continue. Some of the disputants, such as Japan and the Philippines, are US allies—thus they expect US support for their positions and have tried to drag the United States deeper into the disputes. Moreover, many observers suspect that, against the background of China's growing sea power and more active naval activities in the Western Pacific as well as the Obama administration's rebalance to Asia strategy, the United States may be tempted to make use of these disputes to check China.

However, Washington should understand the limits of its role in these disputes. As the United States is not a claimant to those islands/islets/reefs, it cannot get involved in the entanglements as a direct party, nor can it support the sovereignty claim of any side. But it also doesn't want to see a military conflict over these islands. Therefore, the United States should help defuse the situation in the East and South China Sea and facilitate a peaceful solution by encouraging mutual restraint, dialogue, and creative diplomacy, while discouraging provocative rhetoric or actions as well as the use of force. Also, Washington has to be careful in extending support to the Philippines and Japan based on their alliance relations, as Manila and Tokyo may regard such support as a blank check that they can use to take a stronger or more assertive position in these disputes. The United States must also understand that the growth of China's naval power and the expansion of its activities do not mean China is competing with the United States for supremacy in the Pacific; therefore, Washington should resist the temptation to turn the East and South China Seas into a battlefield for Sino-US strategic rivalry.

China has successfully solved most of its land border disputes through negotiation and has accumulated rich experiences in this regard. It should have the wisdom and capacity to prevent maritime disputes from escalating into conflicts with its neighbors. On disputes over Nansha Islands, Beijing should further clarify its sovereignty claims over the area with regards to the nine-dash line, which was drawn in the 1940s and laid the basis for China's claim to rights in the South China Sea. It should also conduct more flexible and creative diplomacy; for instance, instead of insisting on dealing with other claimants only bilaterally, Beijing could engage in multilateral efforts to develop agreements conducive to managing and even solving the disputes. Even if such a multilateral approach may not ultimately work, it can still demonstrate Beijing's willingness to find a peaceful and reasonable solution.

Before achieving such a solution, efforts should be made to calm the situation and avoid crisis. In this regard, Beijing's agreement to start negotiation on a Code of Conduct (COC) with Association of Southeast Asian Nations (ASEAN) members in the South China Sea is a useful step in the right direction. A Code of Conduct is mandated to govern behaviors of China and ASEAN countries and prevent conflicts, accidental or deliberate, in the South China Sea. On the Diaoyu/Senkaku Islands dispute, as China continues to conduct regular boat patrols in the waters around the islands so as to assert its sovereignty claim, it should help reduce the risk of inadvertent conflict with Japan. Meanwhile, Beijing should work to secure an agreement with Tokyo that either re-freezes the disputes, or allows the two countries to pursue joint development of the islands and resources in adjacent water.

Military-to-Military Ties Over the past several years, as Obama's rebalancing strategy has given more preeminence to the security dimension of US Asia-Pacific policy and the Pentagon formally adopted the Air-Sea Battle doctrine, which is designed to counter the People's Liberations Army's (PLA) growing missile and submarine capabilities (or so-called anti-access and area-denial [A2AD] capabilities) in the Western Pacific, the US military posture in the Western Pacific has focused on China. Also, in the face of defense budgetary constraints, the US military (Navy and Air Force in particular) is using China as a convenient pretext for securing resources. Meanwhile, as the PLA drives its modernization, dealing with US military pressure in the Western Pacific has become a major task, which is partially reflected in the PLA's pursuit of A2AD capabilities. As a result of these developments, military rivalry has grown in the Western Pacific in recent years. This bodes ill for the overall Sino-US relationship.

Even though the two militaries are preparing for a worst-case scenario, a major military conflict between China and the United States is highly unlikely. First, the Taiwan issue—the most likely source of serious military confrontation between the two powers—is well under control as relations across the Taiwan Straits have improved since 2008. This is when the Kuomintang (KMT) came to power and adopted a new agenda for cross-strait relations, namely, forging closer economic ties with the Chinese mainland and building political trust with Beijing. Second, the economic interdependence between the United States and China is so high that neither side can afford a rupture in bilateral ties. Third, the two sides have the political wisdom to control the negative strategic dynamics and avoid a major conflict. Given this, the real challenge is how to secure more positive and cooperative bilateral military relations and reduce factors that give rise to distrust and frictions.

In an era when war between major powers is increasingly unlikely, the Chinese and US militaries should devote more resources to providing international public goods—such as protecting sea lanes of navigation, offering disaster relief, and providing humanitarian assistance. Rising non-traditional security challenges like natural disasters, transnational crimes, and terrorism offer plenty of potential areas of cooperation between them. Once the PLA and US Army pay more attention to expanding cooperation, rather than posturing for a conflict with each other, the mood between the two will surely improve.

Meanwhile, as the PLA expands its parameter of activities, its ships and aircraft will encounter those of the US military more and more frequently. To reduce misjudgment and avoid inadvertent conflicts between two militaries, it is important and urgent that they cultivate good habits of communication, establish effective mechanisms for consultation, and work out clear rules of interactions.

On another front, the lasting and frequent military surveillance on China by the United States from both air and sea in China's vicinity stands as an irritant to bilateral military relations.

The intensity of such surveillance, according to a Chinese source, has outrun that conducted by the United States against the Soviet Union during the Cold War years. For the Chinese, it is simply provocative and intolerable. In fact, it not only gives rise to the PLA's suspicion of US strategic intentions toward China, but also runs the risk of causing unintended incidents between the two militaries in the air or on the sea, as occurred in April 2001 when a US spy plane collided with an intercepting Chinese jet fighter in the air close to Hainan Island. US political leaders should rethink whether they really need to conduct so many intrusive surveillances on China for the sake of US national security interests, especially as Sino-US military exchanges grow and increase the transparency surrounding China's military development.[7]

Economic Relations At a time when both China and the United States are working to secure robust and sustainable growth, cooperation between the world's two largest economies is all the more important. To ensure that economic ties will steadily grow and continue to underpin the overall relationship, the next several years should address a couple of areas. In terms of trade, the Chinese side has long complained about the discriminatory treatment it receives in US technology export control in areas such as high-fledged computers, numerical machines, and aerospace engineering. Although the Obama administration signaled its intention over the past several years to lessen controls of high-tech exports to China, so far there has been no real progress. Even though China is the United States' third-largest export market, and also the fastest growing one, it is not treated on par with many other US trading partners, such as India, in high-tech trade.

This suggests that Washington still views China as a strategic rival even though bilateral economic ties are only getting stronger and closer. At the 5th S&ED held in Washington in July 2013, the US side committed to "give fair treatment to China during its export control reform process and to consider China's concerns seriously by promoting and facilitating bilateral high-tech trade with China of commercial items for civil end uses and civil end users."[8] But how far and fast the Obama administration will move forward remains questionable. If Washington can deliver something substantive on this issue in the years to come, it will not only enhance US exports to China and reduce the trade imbalance, but will send a positive signal to China that the United States is willing to address legitimate Chinese concern in the spirit of reciprocity. China, for its part, should do a better job in protecting intellectual property rights; hopefully, doing so will facilitate US export control policy adjustments.

The second area of concern is investment. As Chinese direct investment in the United States grows, so does Beijing's concern over the political and security influence behind the US opposition to Chinese investment, or so-called investment protectionism. From the failed bidding by China National Offshore Oil Company (CNOOC) for US oil company Unocal in 2005, to the fuss over Chinese steel company Anshan Iron & Steel Group's investment plan in a US steel plant, and to the failed attempt by Huawei (a Chinese telecommunications equipment manufacturer) to buy a small American company, the Chinese concern is only getting stronger.[9] Such concern is further deepened not only by often unreasonable and irrational voices from Capitol Hill, but also by the lack of transparency of the review process of the Committee on Foreign Investment in the United States (CFIUS).

At the 5th S&ED, both sides agreed to start the negotiation for a Bilateral Investment Treaty (BIT), which should help address China's concerns. Yet this negotiation may take time, and before the conclusion of the BIT, Washington should do its best to avoid letting unwarranted security concerns block Chinese investment. Otherwise, it will not only discourage the inflow of Chinese direct investment, which is important to US economic growth and job opportunities, but it will provoke Chinese retaliation against US investment in China.

For the Chinese side, it is important to overcome local protectionism as well as the monopoly of state-owned enterprises, and further improve the environment for foreign direct investment. In this regard, the ambitious reform agenda unveiled at the Third Plenary Session of the 18th Central Committee of the Communist Party of China, held in November 2013, suggests that Beijing is determined to provide a more level playing field for both Chinese private sector investors as well as foreign companies, which means more opportunities for the US business community in China.

The third focus is Sino-US economic interactions in the Asia-Pacific. As the United States pushes the Trans-Pacific Partnership Agreement (TPP)—a regional free-trade arrangement that includes Australia, Brunei, Canada, Chile, Japan, Malaysia, Mexico, New Zealand, Peru, Singapore, the United States, and Vietnam but excludes China—while China promotes East Asian cooperation such as the Regional Comprehensive Economic Partnership (RCEP)—a regional free trade architecture that includes China, Japan, South Korea, 10 Southeast Asian countries, Australia, New Zealand, and India but excludes the United States—it seems the United States and China are engaging in geoeconomic competition in addition to their geopolitical rivalry in the region. Given their economic importance to each other as well as to the entire region, it is crucial that China and the United States pursue serious economic cooperation in the region, even while pushing separately for their respectively favored FTA arrangements. The Asia-Pacific Economic Cooperation (APEC) forum is the right venue for such cooperation, as it includes both China and the United States and advocates trans-Pacific, rather than just East Asian, cooperation.

Fortunately, at the 5th S&ED, China and the United States agreed to "further strengthen coordination and cooperation in the APEC forum, in order to jointly promote economic growth and prosperity in the Asia-Pacific region."[10] As China is going to host the 2014 APEC Economic Leaders Meeting, both sides committed to "seek a closer partnership" at the forum to promote trade and investment liberalization and facilitation, strengthen regional economic integration and coordination, and carry out capacity building.[11] Should concrete and effective Sino-US cooperation occur along these lines, it would send an encouraging message throughout the Asia-Pacific region, which has witnessed the most vibrant economic growth over the past several decades.

Cyber Security The United States has long accused China of launching cyber attacks against its national security as well as commercial targets, while China has repeatedly denied such accusations and claims itself also a victim of cyber attacks from other countries, among which the United States ranks first. The Snowden revelation suggests that the US National Security Agency (NSA) conducted many cyber attacks against Chinese targets,[12] confirming Chinese complaints. While neither Beijing nor Washington would openly acknowledge their cyber espionage on each other, the Snowden episode could provide an opportunity to convert a cause for conflict into the basis for a dialogue that takes place on a more equal footing.

In July 2013, China and the United States held the first meeting of the bilateral Cyber Working Group. The two sides discussed issues of mutual concern and decided to take practical measures to enhance dialogue on international norms and principles in order to guide action in cyberspace, and to strengthen the Computer Emergency Response Team (CERT), a mechanism that deals with computer security incidents. With the first meeting of the Cyber Working Group described as "candid, in-depth, and constructive," the two sides agreed to hold sustained dialogue on cyber issues.[13]

Given the fact that cyberspace is a new field in which international rules and an international oversight mechanism do not exist, many state and non-state actors have taken advantage of the situation to pursue their respective goals. This not only hurts the national interests of many countries, China and the United States alike, it also undermines the stability of cyberspace—a new but increasingly important global commons in the 21st century. It is therefore desirable that Beijing and Washington not only exercise self-restraint in their respective cyber activities, but also help promote the establishment of international rules and international oversight mechanisms, a vital public good that the great powers should provide in the era of information.

New Opportunities

As the rise of China is rapidly changing the power balance between China and the United States, relations between them have entered a decade of major transformation. The continuing evolution of this relationship affects not only the two countries, but also the Asia-Pacific region and the entire world. While Sino-US ties are largely driven by their respective national interests, leadership in both countries also plays an important role in shaping their pace and direction of developments. It seems that both President Xi and President Obama have a good vision about this relationship, while the challenge is whether such a vision can be translated into effective actions on both sides. Given lost opportunities over the last several years, it is high time to grasp new ones.

It is worth noting that constructing a new great power relationship between China and the United States does not require this relationship to be restarted all over. Rather, what should be done is to increase the momentum for cooperation, reduce the dynamics for competition, and avoid the possibility of conflicts. Hence, this article focuses mainly on how to expand areas of cooperation while curtailing and eliminating elements that affect adversely bilateral ties. Although the above agenda may not guarantee that a new great power relationship will grow between Beijing and Washington, it can shape a positive posture of bilateralism at a crucial juncture and generate more benign momentum for its future development, thus laying a solid foundation for realizing the goal that both sides have committed to.

Needless to say, both China and the United States have a big stake in forging a new great power relationship—and both should make serious efforts, jointly or unilaterally, to enhance this goal. To be sure, due to the asymmetry of their respective positions and influences, the United States has more resources than China to shape bilateral ties. Therefore, Washington should take more initiatives and actions to positively guide relations with Beijing. China, as a rising power, should reassure the United States and others that it is willing to reasonably define and seek its national interest objectives, play by the rules commonly agreed upon, and exercise its growing power responsibly.

Only by demonstrating that it is a new type of rising power—one that differs from many historical rising powers who pursued their interests through war and confrontation—can China work effectively with the United States to write a new logic about the relationship between a rising great power and an established great power.

Notes

1. In the joint statement released during President Obama's visit to China, the two countries promised that "they are committed to building a positive, cooperative and comprehensive China-U.S. relationship for the 21st century, and will take concrete actions to steadily build a partnership to address common challenges." Office of the Press Secretary, The White House, "U.S.-China Joint Statement," November 17, 2009, http://www.whitehouse.gov/the-press-office/us-china-joint-statement.

2. Ministry of Foreign Affairs of the People's Republic of China, "Xi Jinping and U.S. President Obama Hold Joint Press Conference," June 8, 2013, http://www.fmprc.gov. cn/eng/topics/xjpttcrmux/t1049545.shtml.

3. Ministry of Foreign Affairs of the People's Republic of China, "Exploring the Path of Major-Country Diplomacy With Chinese Characteristics," Remarks by Foreign Minister Wang Yi at the Luncheon of the Second World Peace Forum, June 27, 2013, http://www.fmprc.gov.cn/eng/wjdt/zyjh/t1053908.shtml.

4. "China's Peaceful Development," Information Office of the State Council, The People's Republic of China, September 2011, http://www.gov.cn/english/official/2011-09/06/content_1941354-htm.

5. C.S. Eliot Kang, "The Four-Party Peace Talks: Lost Without a Map," *Comparative Strategy* 17, no. 4 (1998): 327–344

6. For more details, see Wu Xinbo, "Forging Sino-US Partnership in the Twenty-First Century: Opportunities and Challenges," *Journal of Contemporary China 21*, issue 75 (2012): pp. 397–398.

7. For further discussion, see Wu Xinbo, "Beijing's Wish List: A Wiser China Policy in President Obama's Second Term," *Brookings Asia Commentary*, no. 59/69, The Brooking Institution, December 2012, http://www.brookings.edu/research/opinions/2012/12/11-china-obama-wu.

8. Press Center, US Department of the Treasury, "Joint U.S.-China Economic Track Fact Sheet of the Fifth Meeting of the U.S.-China Strategic and Economic Dialogue," July 12, 2013, http://www.treasury.gov/press center/pressreleases/Pages/jl2010.aspx.

9. Doug Palmer, "U.S. Lawmakers Cheer as China Steel Firm Backs Out," August 19, 2010, http://cn.reuters.com/article/companyNews/idCNN1926784020100819; Adam W. Goldberg and Joshua P. Galper, "Where Huawei Went Wrong in America," March 3, 2011, *Wall Street Journal*, http://online.wsj.com/article/SB1

000142405274870355960457617569259833356. html?KEYWORDS = huawei +.

10. "Joint U.S.-China Economic Track Fact Sheet of the Fifth Meeting of the U.S.-China Strategic and Economic Dialogue," op. cit.

11. Ibid.

12. Te-Ping Chen, "Snowden Alleges U.S. Hacking in China," *Wall Street Journal*, June 23, 2013, http://online. wsj.com/article/SB10001424127887324577904578562483284 884530.html; Barton Gellman and Greg Miller, "U.S. Spy Network's Successes, Failures and Objectives Detailed in 'Black Budget' Summary," *Washington Post*, August 29, 2013, http://www.washingtonpost.com/world/national-security/black-budget-summary-details-us-spy-networks-successes-failures-and-objectives/2013/08/29/7e57bb78-10ab- 11e3-8cdd-bcdc09410972J tory.html.

13. Office of the Spokesperson, US Department of State, "U.S.-China Strategic and Economic Dialogue Outcomes of the Strategic Track," July 12, 2013, http://www.state. gov/r/pa/prs/ps/2013/07/211861.htm.

IV. Russia and Europe

Russia and China: The Ambivalent Embrace*

Andrew Kuchins

Russia's perspective on China is shaped by a complex amalgamation of geopolitical, economic, historical, and cultural factors that add up to a profound ambivalence. Despite this ambivalence, Russian policy toward China over the past 15 years under Presidents Boris Yeltsin and Vladimir Putin has been driven mainly by pragmatic considerations, resulting in a gradual rapprochement and thickening of the relationship. The "strategic partnership" established in 1996 by Yeltsin and Chinese President Jiang Zemin, though it appeared long on rhetoric and short on substance when Putin assumed power in 2000, has taken on considerable weight as economic and political cooperation has deepened.

Moscow has no desire to establish an alliance with Beijing, but growing irritations in US-Russia and Europe-Russia relations have redounded to the benefit of the China-Russia relationship. One still hears Russians express concerns about ending up as China's "junior partner," or as nothing more than a natural-resource appendage (*pridatka*). These worries surface less frequently, however, as Russian confidence continues to increase, thanks to the virtual macroeconomic revolution that has taken place in that country in recent years. Russian leaders and foreign policy experts recognize, as does China's political elite, that their countries' unbalanced alliance in the 1950s, followed by the total breakdown of relations in the 1960s and 1970s, constituted a tremendous strategic mistake.

Moscow's attitude toward China in some ways reflects Russia's sense of identity and its view of its own place in the world as a uniquely Eurasian power. Occupying the massive geographical space between Europe and Asia, Russia has often in its history experienced a split identity—between, on one hand, the Asiatic legacy of the Mongol period that began in the thirteenth century; and, on the other, Westernizing reforms, attempted intermittently by Russian leaders from Peter the Great to Catherine the Great to Alexander II to Mikhail Gorbachev and Yeltsin.

Historically, Asia has occupied a special place in Russians' imagination and in their version of Manifest Destiny. It has been viewed as a vast region critical for Russia's development and global role. Fyodor Dostoevsky famously expressed this view in 1881 after Russian forces defeated the Turkmens in their quest to conquer Central Asia:

What is the need of the future seizure of Asia? What is our business there? This is necessary because Russia is not only in Europe, but also in Asia; because the Russian is not only a European, but also an Asiatic. Not only that: In our coming

---

* This article was published in *Current History* (October 2007).

destiny, perhaps it is precisely Asia that represents our way out. . . . In Europe we were hangers-on and slaves, whereas to Asia we shall go as masters. In Europe we were Asiatics, whereas in Asia we, too, are Europeans. Our civilizing mission in Asia will bribe our spirit and drive us thither. It is only necessary that the movement should start. Build two railroads: Begin with the one to Siberia, and then to Central Asia, and at once you will see the consequences.

Of course, for much of its history, especially during the nineteenth and twentieth centuries, when interaction between China and Russia grew significantly during a first wave of globalization, Russia viewed itself as the superior country. During the brief period of the Sino-Soviet alliance in the 1950s, the Soviets described themselves as the "elder brother." Today Russia finds itself the weaker partner with China, a situation unprecedented since the Russians first began to settle Siberia in the seventeenth century.

Tilting for Leverage

China currently represents the dominant counterpoint to Russia's political, economic, and cultural orientation toward the United States and Europe. Shortly after becoming president in 2000, in his first tour of Asia, which included a visit to China, Putin elegantly summarized the importance of balance in his country's foreign policy. "Russia," he said, "is both a European and an Asiatic state. It is like a bird and can only fly well if it uses both wings."

More broadly speaking, Russian perspectives on China and international relations tend toward traditional realpolitik considerations of the dynamics between rising and falling great powers. In this realist framework, Russian views of China often depend on the status of US-Russian relations and Moscow's ties with the West. In the 1990s—when Russia was unhappy about US support for NATO expansion, the war in Kosovo, and the development of national missile defense—the Yeltsin administration gravitated closer to Beijing. In recent years, the United States' support for democracy promotion, as well as its increased influence in the post-Soviet states, has also driven

the Putin administration to seek closer ties with China.

Yeltsin nicely captured China's position as a leverage point with the West when he said in 1995:

China is a very important state for us. It is a neighbor, with which we share the longest border in the world and with which we are destined to live and work side by side forever. Russia's future depends on the success of cooperation with China. Relations with China are extremely important to us from the global politics perspective as well. We can rest on the Chinese shoulder in our relations with the West. In that case the West will treat Russia more respectfully.

Like Yeltsin before him, Putin has repeatedly invoked an improvement in ties with China as an alternative to a more pro-Western foreign policy if Washington does not pay greater attention to Moscow's interests.

For the most part, the United States and its allies through the 1990s remained fairly relaxed about the gradual rapprochement between Russia and China. Those skeptical that Moscow and Beijing would engage in a real alliance against the United States pointed to their long and complicated history, which has involved intense competition and occasional conflict along their extensive border. They also cited current-day competitive instincts in Central Asia and elsewhere. NATO Secretary General George Robertson expressed this view in a lecture in Uzbekistan in 2000. "The relationship between Russia and China," he said, "is a matter for Russia and China, but [such an alliance] has been tried before and has not always worked." In us policy circles, more suspicious views of the Sino-Russian relationship have tended to come from the right wing of the political spectrum.

Predictably, the impulse in both Moscow and Beijing to use each other for balance increased in response to exercises of US power such as the Kosovo war in 1999 and the invasion of Iraq in 2003. It also has increased in response to policies or developments that appear to augment US power, such as NATO expansion, missile defense, and support of the "color" revolutions in Eurasia. This balancing impulse has been constrained both by the absence of a sufficiently compelling threat to either Russia or China, and by the reality that, at least militarily, a Sino-Russian alliance would not be capable of balancing US power in the near term or medium term.

However, Russian arms sales to China have raised increasing concern among some in the US military. They worry about the capacity of Moscow to increase China's ability to hurt the US Seventh Fleet in a showdown over Taiwan. China has been Russia's number one weapons customer for the past 15 years. In the 1990s, arms sales to Beijing averaged $1 billion to $2 billion per year. In the past seven years they have run about $2 billion to $3 billion annually—representing about 30 percent to 40 percent of Russian arms sales overall.

Sick Man No More

Concern in US policy circles over closer relations between Russia and China grew considerably in 2005 in response to Chinese and Russian support for Uzbek President Islam Karimov's brutal suppression of rioting in Andijan in May; the subsequent eviction of US forces from the base at Karshi-Khanabad; and, in November 2005, the signing of a Russian-Uzbek security agreement. Many Russian analysts viewed these developments in Central Asia as a real turning point for Moscow's influence in the region, as well as for the role of the emerging Sino-Russian axis. One Kremlin-connected analyst told me: "There is an impression that US foreign policy expansion has reached its limits and now there begins an epoch of the gradual decline of American empire."

With Russia's resurgence after the modern-day *Smutnoe Vremya* ("Time of Troubles") that it experienced during the traumatic 1990s, the country's confidence grew tremendously in 2005 and 2006. Indeed, the magnitude and the rapidity of Russia's revival have been as unexpected as they have been impressive. The numbers are staggering. According to the Moscow-based investment bank Troika Dialog, between 1999 and 2006 Russia's nominal GDP grew nearly fivefold—from less than $200 billion to more than $900 billion— and it is poised to exceed the $1 trillion mark in 2007. Russia's foreign exchange reserves over this period have grown 20 times, from about $20 billion when Putin became president to more than

$400 billion today. The Russian stock market has consistently been one of the fastest growing in the world for the past seven years, increasing in value about 1,000 percent. Meanwhile, average wages have increased fourfold. With economic numbers like this, it is not a big surprise that Putin continues to enjoy popularity ratings above 70 percent.

In 1999–2000, my standard public talk on Russia was entitled "Russia: The Sick Man of Eurasia." That is no longer the case. On whatever issue we look at in 2007—Iran, the Middle East peace process, gas and oil supplies to Europe and Asia, foreign investment in the energy sector— Russia is asserting its interests far more confidently than ten years ago, five years ago, even one year ago. It is Russia's changing fortunes, along with US foreign policy, that have had the most significant influence on Russia's perception of and policy toward China.

The Brief Honeymoon

After the terrorist attacks against America on September 11, 2001, Putin decided to align Russia with the US-led war in Afghanistan, agreeing to allow US military bases in Central Asia. He also seemed to accept quietly both a second round of NATO expansion and the United States' withdrawal from the Anti-Ballistic Missile (ABM) Treaty. This approach caused a great deal of concern in Chinese foreign policy and security policy circles in 2001 and 2002, with many worrying that Putin was fundamentally altering Russia's balanced foreign policy in order to embrace Washington instead.

In May 2002, this second honeymoon of US-Russia relations reached its apex when President George W. Bush traveled to Moscow, where he signed the Strategic Offensive Reduction Treaty that places limits on operationally deployed nuclear warheads. The United States also awarded Russia "market-economy" status, improving bilateral trade relations and bringing Moscow a step closer to membership in the World Trade Organization.

However, like the first US-Russian honeymoon in 1992, the post–9/11 embrace would prove short-lived. Putin had made a bold decision to support the United States unequivocally in

Afghanistan, going against the recommendations of the majority of the Russian foreign policy elite. But he and his colleagues in the Kremlin quickly came to believe that his decision went underappreciated and virtually unrewarded by the Bush administration. Moscow's public protests over the US decision to withdraw from the ABM treaty, as well as to support further NATO expansion, may have been muted at the time. But Washington's actions in the fall of 2001, coming so soon after Putin had extended support to his "friend George," left the Russians disappointed and feeling that they were receiving very little in return for their support.

As 2002 wore on, it became increasingly evident that the Bush administration would take military action against Iraq in defiance of Putin and much of the international community, including China. Although Putin disagreed with the US administration's decision to invade Iraq, both Washington and Moscow sought to prevent a major falling-out in the US-Russian relationship. A series of other events and trends, however, threw the relationship into a tailspin from which it has yet to escape.

Indeed, the past four years of deterioration in US-Russian ties contrast sharply with the continued improvement of Sino-Russian economic, security, and political relations. While Putin has said on several occasions in recent years that Sino-Russian ties have never been better, US-Russian relations are chillier today than at any time since the collapse of the Soviet Union.

Alarm in the West about rising authoritarianism in Russia, and about Russia's growing influence on its periphery, increased with Ukraine's Orange Revolution at the end of 2004. The causes of the Orange Revolution—following the Rose Revolution in Georgia, which brought pro-Western Mikheil Saakashvili to power; and preceding the Tulip Revolution in Kyrgyzstan, which toppled the Askar Akayev regime—were seen differently in Moscow and Washington. The Russian explanation for the "color" revolutions tended to emphasize the role of nongovernment organizations and politicians supported by the United States and other Western countries. The United States and its European allies argued that the upheavals came about primarily because of falsified elections and the public's dissatisfaction with corrupt governments and officials.

The positions of Washington and Moscow on these events became increasingly polarized as officials and opinion leaders in Washington argued that Putin's authoritarian inclinations led him to support dictatorship over democracy in countries on Russia's periphery. The quasi-official Russian view held that the United States was interfering in countries that Moscow considered part of its sphere of influence. The US position was seen as hypocritical because Washington, in Moscow's view, only cared about regime changes that would bring in pro-US governments like those of Saakashvili in Georgia and Viktor Yushchenko in Ukraine—not about real democracy.

A Beijing-Moscow Consensus?

The Chinese for the most part remained on the sidelines during this growing dispute between Washington and Moscow—until the specter of color revolutions arrived in Central Asia, first in Kyrgyzstan in March 2005 and then with civil unrest in Uzbekistan and the brutal crackdown in the city of Andijan in May of that year. Chinese sensitivities about the potential for unrest in Central Asia to spill over to its Muslim groups across the border in Xinjiang province moved Beijing to clearly back Karimov in Uzbekistan, and to defend the principles of order and sovereignty over the right of any outside power to interfere in a country's domestic affairs. After the events in Andijan, the first places to which Karimov traveled, and where he received full support for his actions, were Beijing and then Moscow. The dividing lines were sharpening between the West's support for democracy and human rights and, in Eurasia, the interests of an emerging "authoritarian intenationale" led by Moscow and Beijing.

It is unclear at this point how far Moscow and Beijing are prepared to go together to contest the interests of the United States in Eurasia, but what appeared as mainly rhetorical support for a "multipolar world" in the 1990s is now assuming greater substance. One example is Russia and China's cooperation in the United Nations Security Council on an increasing number of issues. The Chinese have followed Russia's lead on sanctions on Iran, and are likely to follow Russia on the status of Kosovo. In January 2007, Russia and China for the first time jointly vetoed a UN resolution, this one having to do with sanctions on Burma.

Another example of Sino-Russian coordination was the decision in 2005 by the Shanghai Cooperation Organization (SCO)—the intergovernmental group consisting of Russia, China, Kazakhstan, Kyrgyzstan, Tajikistan, and Uzbekistan—to request clarification from the United States about its plans for withdrawing from military bases established in Central Asia after 9/11. The gathering of the SCO's foreign ministers in Moscow in 2005 also included representatives of states that had recently acquired observer status—India, Iran, Mongolia, and Pakistan. In his opening remarks, Putin crowed about the fact that 3 billion people, virtually half the planet, were represented at the gathering. Putin noted that the "SCO has gone far beyond the framework of the tasks initially set for it."

Russian attitudes toward the SCO reflect the broader ambivalence with which Moscow views Beijing. This is natural, since the China-Russia relationship is at the heart of the SCO. The mainstream Russian view is that the SCO is essentially a Chinese project, as the name of the organization makes clear. Russians would prefer that a group like the Collective Security Treaty Organization, in which Russia is the clear hegemonic leader and from which China is excluded, act as the main multilateral organization with security responsibilities in Central Asia. Even so, the Russian leadership is pragmatic and realist. It understands that Chinese influence in Central Asia, in the realms of both economics and security, is a natural outgrowth of geography and expanding Chinese power. With this the case, Moscow figures it benefits if Chinese regional engagement is undertaken through an organizational format that includes Russia, and the SCO serves this purpose.

The Shifting Global Balance

There are striking similarities between the maturing ideological foundations that underpin Russia's and China's respective outlooks on the world and on their global roles. The Putin administration promotes an emerging ideology often described by Russians as "sovereign democracy." The starting point for understanding sovereign democracy is Russia's perception of the 1990s as a contemporary equivalent to the Time of Troubles—the years of turmoil that preceded the establishment of the Romanov dynasty in 1613, when the country was in chaos and foreign powers and organizations exerted considerable authority. According to this narrative, Putin has restored stability and set Russia on the road to recovery, and he has done so not by abandoning democratic values and institutions, but by adapting them to Russian values and traditions.

Foreign Minister Sergei Lavrov described the foreign policy analog to sovereign democracy in a January 2007 speech:

> The fundamental principles of Russia's foreign policy—pragmatism, multiple vectors, and consistent but nonconfrontational protection of national interests—have gained broad international recognition. . . . Many countries have come to realize that a new, safer, fair, and democratic world order, whose foundations we are laying together, can only be multipolar, based on international law, and regulated by the UN's unique legitimacy and central role.

To be sure, this kind of rhetoric is hardly new. One can easily imagine a variant of it coming from the mouth of Evgeny Primakov when he was foreign minister in the 1990s or Andrei Gromyko when he held the same position for more than a quarter-century under the Soviet government. But Lavrov's rhetoric also has much in common with Chinese ideological formulations.

The rhetorical and operational foundations for Chinese foreign policy have been described, tellingly, as the "Beijing Consensus." As described by Joshua Cooper Ramo, the Beijing Consensus is principally a socioeconomic development model that the Chinese have successfully implemented, a model that differs considerably from the so-called Washington Consensus as promoted by the US government and multilateral organizations like the IMF and the World Bank. The Beijing Consensus has significant implications for foreign policy and international relations that resonate with the Kremlin's sovereign democracy.

First, there is not just one correct path to development. A country must experiment to find the path best suited to its culture and traditions, and no other country or organization should seek to impose external models. Most Russians today view the advice of Western advisers and multilateral organizations as having failed and exacerbated Russia's socioeconomic problems. The typical Chinese interpretation of Russian development over the past 15 years suggests that Moscow took the wrong path in the 1990s, but that the Putin administration has learned from the Chinese reform experience and has begun to correct mistakes that devolved too much power away from the state.

The other commonality between Moscow's view of the world and Beijing's concerns the ongoing shift in the global power balance from the unipolar moment of the 1990s to a genuinely multipolar world. Rhetoric supporting such a change is not new, but today there is evidence to support the conclusion that the global balance of power is indeed shifting—and the Russians consider themselves among the emerging powers. For several years now the financial and investment community has used the term BRICs to describe four large emerging economic world powers: Brazil, Russia, India, and China. Putin himself alluded to the emergence of the BRICs as a powerful stimulus toward the reordering of the world in a speech in Munich in February of this year:

> The combined GDP, measured in purchasing power parity, of countries such as India and China is already greater than that of the United States. Similarly calculated, the GDP of the BRIC countries—Brazil, Russia, India and China—surpasses the cumulative GDP of the EU. And according to experts this gap will only increase in the future. There is no reason to doubt that the economic potential of the new centers of global economic growth will inevitably be converted into political influence and will strengthen multipolarity.

Political circles in Washington have been slow to come around to an appreciation of Russia's recovery and increased international confidence. The dominant view today is to see it as a malign phenomenon, with a more authoritarian Russia increasingly brandishing its energy "weapon," as Vice President Dick Cheney referred to it last year in Vilnius, Lithuania. But erosion of America's worldwide influence is also part of the equation. On the basis of many discussions in 2006 with Chinese and Russian scholars and analysts, my

sense is that there is a reasonably broad consensus in Russian and Chinese policy circles that the United States made a grave mistake by overextending itself in Iraq, and that it has overplayed its hand in Central Asia and elsewhere in efforts to promote democracy.

Pushed Together

Despite the perceptions of a shifting balance of power and the evident cooling in US-Russian ties, Russian elites remain at best ambivalent about the emerging Chinese superpower. The official line from Putin and members of his administration tends to accentuate the positive—and it is probably true that China-Russia relations today are better than ever. But the history of China-Russia relations does not set the highest of bars, so to speak.

In the 1990s, Russia engaged in lively debates about China, centering on whether it was a potential friend or foe, and the advisability of selling Beijing arms and technology. These kinds of debates, whether undertaken from ideological or regional perspectives, have largely disappeared. But this does not tell us much, since public debate about even the most important domestic and foreign policy issues has been muted during the Putin years. Moreover, much of the community of China experts established during the Brezhnev years and still active in the 1990s has now retired, died, or gone into business—and there is no sizeable generation of younger experts and scholars in international relations or area studies to replace them.

Russian public opinion about China tends to be quite positive, but this is probably for the most part a reflection of the fact that most Russians get their information from national television. Essentially controlled by the Kremlin, it promotes the sunny outlook on China touted by Putin and company.

Research conducted by the VTSIOM public opinion research center in July 2005 noted that, although 56 percent of Russians view China as either a strategic partner or ally, 62 percent believe the increasing Chinese economic presence in Russia is negative, and 66 percent see the involvement of Chinese companies and workers in the development of mineral resources in Siberia and the Russian Far East as dangerous for Russia.

These results at first appear to signify cognitive dissonance. In reality, they probably reflect Russia's strategic view of China as a partner with whom to contain the United States, combined with a sense of economic and demographic vulnerability experienced in the Russian regions bordering China.

Despite deep-seated wariness toward China on the part of the Russian leadership and people, ties with Beijing have significantly advanced under the leadership of both Yeltsin and Putin. The economic relationship, which has led to trade volume increasing nearly fivefold since Putin became president—to just under $35 billion in 2006—is likely to continue to grow rapidly as major oil and gas sales finally get on track in the next few years. It is possible the two countries could reach their announced targets for annual trade volume of $60 billion by 2010 and $100 billion by 2020.

What will happen in the strategic relationship, from the Shanghai Cooperation Organization to cooperation in the UN to arms sales, is harder to predict. Such developments will be contingent to a considerable extent on the actions of the United States. If, for example, the United States were to undertake military action against Iran that was not sanctioned by the United Nations, this would undoubtedly push Russia and China closer together strategically. A US-China military conflict over Taiwan would place Russia in an awkward position, but I think Moscow would choose not to take sides. If the Europeans or the Americans removed their boycott on arms sales to China, this would over time undercut Russian companies' dominant position as a supplier. A more aggressive US posture in the name of democracy promotion and human rights, if it confronted Russian interests in the post-Soviet space, would also likely push Russia and China closer together.

Another important driver in the Russian-Chinese strategic relationship will be the development of the Russian oil and gas sector. China, the fastest-growing petroleum consumer in the world, has viewed Russia as an important alternative source of oil—and to a lesser extent gas—for the past decade or so. To date, the Chinese have been mostly frustrated by the slow development of the Sino-Russian energy relationship, and they are competitors for Central Asian resources (notably in Turkmenistan, but also Kazakhstan). Yet, aside from money, which Moscow is not short of now, Chinese companies have little to offer the Russians in the development of Russian greenfields. This development will entail some of the largest capital expenditures and greatest technical challenges ever undertaken. Western companies have useful management experience and technical expertise. Therefore, to the extent foreign companies are allowed to participate in the development of the Russian hydrocarbon sector, Western businesses likely will have a significant advantage over Chinese firms. Of course, if Russia's political relations with the West deteriorate further, or the legal and business environment becomes more corrupt, this equation could change.

For historical, cultural, geographic, and economic reasons, Russia's preferred option is to lean West—while also improving ties with China, for intrinsic reasons and to gain leverage with the United States and Europe. Only events of quite a significant magnitude could alter Russia's trajectory, which has been fairly consistent for nearly 15 years after the brief lurch to the West that followed the Soviet Union's collapse.

CHINA AND EUROPE: OPPORTUNITIES OR DANGERS?*

Odd Arne Westad

Just when parts of the European integration project seem to be in significant amounts of

* This article was published in the LSE IDEAS Reports series, London School of Economics & Political Science (2013).

trouble, Chinese leaders are beginning to open their eyes to the need for more in-depth cooperation with both the Union itself and with individual European countries. After years of relative neglect, when China's main priorities have been the United States, the eastern Asian region, and the main developing economies (roughly in that order), Europe is now coming into fashion for discussion in Beijing, both as opportunity and threat.

There are two main reasons for this. The first is that the global financial crisis of 2008 and the recession that followed have shown how dependent the Chinese economy is on European markets. The second reason is that some Chinese analysts have begun believing that Europe, in spite of its internal instability, may serve as a genuine balancer in international affairs during a period of US decline, helping smooth the transition to a more multipolar world. There are both possibilities and challenges in these perceptions, but there is little doubt that for some time at least China's interest in Europe will be at an all-time high.

China and the European Union

While the first generation of Chinese revolutionaries looked to Europe for inspiration, the post-revolutionary generation has been looking to the United States. Those who concentrate on the rivalry that now exists for power and influence between the two powers tend to forget how deeply China has been influenced by the United States over the past generation. Ideas, technologies, and products have tended to come from across the Pacific—the routes to Europe have been much less trafficked. Analysts in Beijing have—correctly it seems—described Sino-American ties as a love-hate relationship: just as Americans like to take credit for introducing capitalist markets to China, they also fear the purposes to which the Chinese are putting their new-found wealth. And just as the Chinese prefer American products and view the United States as much more "advanced" than any other part of the world, they also resent the US role in East Asia and its "hegemonic" approach to world politics.

Europe has, until quite recently, lagged far behind in the developing Chinese consciousness about the outside world. In the 1980s the countries of the European Community (with Britain as a partial exception) were mainly important to China to the degree that they were willing to confront the Soviets and export technology to China. In the 1990s, as China's remarkable economic transformation took off, Europe's market significance increased, but not its political relevance. In the decade that has just ended, economic relations have become crucial and the institutionalization of political and diplomatic contacts has improved, but Europe is still not seen as relevant for the bigger picture in China's foreign relations. Even on a good day, the Chinese Foreign Ministry spends more than twice the hours and the manpower on dealing with Southeast Asia than it does with Europe. "In diplomatic terms," a top Chinese diplomat recently confirmed, "The EU is about as important for China as is Australia."[1]

Part of the Chinese difficulty in interacting with Europe has been the remarkable slowness with which Beijing has caught on to the centrality of the EU in European and world politics. Despite having inherited an empire, the Chinese leadership believes in nation-states, not unions or federalism. Far too often Beijing has come up short by interpreting the EU simply as a vehicle for the interests of the key states, and not as an integrationist project. In diplomatic terms, China has had some small-scale success with its consistent attempts at dealing with individual states rather than the Union as such. But it has failed on big issues, such as trade and environmental policies, where the EU has become more integrated and more consistent. (Much the same pattern can be seen with regard to Beijing's policy towards the Association of Southeast Asian Nations—ASEAN—where China has had state-to-state influence on minor matters, but has failed disastrously in understanding basic ASEAN cohesion on trade and security matters.)[2]

The lack of a more comprehensive reorientation in the Chinese approach to Europe is also influenced by Beijing's view of the continent as a zone of instability after the Cold War ended. The images created by the fall of Communism in Eastern Europe and, especially, of the wars in Yugoslavia, still loom large in China, both among the leadership, as well as the general public. The extraordinary lack of specific knowledge even at higher levels in China about smaller European countries and their international and EU role plays into this sense of shakiness and unpredictability. In this sense, the sovereign debt crises of 2011 play into a pattern already set by the past.[3]

The increasing Chinese concentration on Germany does not help, either, in a broader policymaking sense. Though the Chinese often attach great significance to the fact that roughly half of EU exports to China are German in origin, Germany does not have the influence on the Union's foreign policy-making towards the outside world that Beijing often expects. In Europe, as we know, being bigger, richer, and more populous does not necessarily translate into the kind of foreign policy prowess that the Chinese expect. Looking at Chinese policymaking in a wider context, this parochial misapprehension is in many ways a symbol of how difficult it has been for Beijing to develop a more sophisticated foreign policy towards Europe.[4]

Although Europe as a whole is doing better in terms of knowledge about China than vice-versa, neither of the two sides show any of the well-developed mutual comprehension that exists between China and the United States. Without significant improvement in this regard, both through contacts between policymakers and within academia, it is unlikely that the issues in the Sino-European relationship that are dealt with below will move towards a more broad-based resolution. Both sides need to realise that for closer relations to develop, more knowledge—much beyond the pro forma—is essential.

Economic Issues

At present, the economic interaction between Europe and China is by far the most important aspect of the relationship. Since 2004 the European Union has been China's largest trading partner, and overall economic relations have been expanding rapidly. EU foreign direct investment in China is at an all-time high, reaching €17.7 billion in 2011, and EU exports to China are growing faster than its imports.[5] Chinese investments in Europe have grown rapidly, tripling 2009 and 2011 to €7.4 billion, across an increasingly wide range of sectors.[6] The sovereign debt crises have led China to invest in European bonds, both for political and economic reasons. Nonetheless, even these investments are fewer and further apart than Eurozone governments would like to see.[7]

The present situation provides Europe with great opportunities in its economic relations with China. European products have substantial market potential in China, and the Chinese have the funds needed to invest in Europe. But the EU needs to prove that it is capable of developing a trade policy that responds to the present situation. As Francois Godement has correctly argued, the EU should respond to China's interest-driven economic policy with an interest-driven policy of its own. It should demand access on equal terms for European companies in bidding for large public projects in China; it should attempt to stimulate Chinese investment to where it is needed in Europe; and it should work with the emerging economies (and not just the United States) in developing trade policy with regard to China.[8]

In order to be successful, such a realistic approach to dealing with China's growing economic influence will depend on the development of the necessary instruments and on a high degree of inner cohesion. Europe today seems to be found wanting in both respects. Chinese observers marvel over the fact that the Eurozone is dependent on bonds issued by the various governments rather than by the European Central Bank. They know, of course, that Europe would be in a much stronger position vis-à-vis China if there were Eurobonds covering the whole common currency area (and they also suspect that some of the current crises could thereby have been ameliorated, if not avoided). Beijing also benefits from the lack of coordination between member states and between them and Union officials on issues related to China. Although steps have been taken to improve the EU's international coherence on Asian matters, the current set of crises within the EU structure will not help in creating a more coherent and coordinated EU policy.

In addition to realistic aims, however, the EU also needs to grasp what is the deeper background for Chinese policies on trade and investment. The Chinese Communist Party (CCP) needs to deliver growth in order to stay in power. In order to do so, it must have access to foreign markets, of which the EU at the moment is the largest. But the CCP does not want to be seen as giving up political positions in the process of acquiring what it needs. On the contrary, the EU needs to be prepared for a China that does not always act in strict conformity with its immediate economic aims, as the country has shown in its recent relations with ASEAN and the Southeast Asian region. Issues concerning human rights, the environment, and especially its relationship to the United States in international organizations, may all affect China's economic policies. As a result, it is important to have enough knowledge to be able to identify China's political preoccupations and—if need be—turn them to Europe's advantage with regard to trade and investment.

As history often shows, the challenge for a realistic economic policy will be handling the middle-term perspective, five years or so down the road. As China's economic power grows, so will its appetite for getting political concessions in return for economic cooperation. But such policies will not necessarily be something that China gains from. On the contrary, one of China's bigger problems will be how to integrate its immediate interests with its growing global power in Europe and elsewhere.

Human Rights

Current European policy on human rights in China is in a shambles. Instead of having a positive effect in China, it is seen by the CCP and its critics as inconsistent and self-serving, neither of which are far from the truth. In practice, the EU is split down the middle on how to deal with the issue, with France and Germany having given up its public criticism of China's human rights violations in the late 1990s in favor of "quiet diplomacy." Other European countries are taking the lack of elementary rights in China seriously, but are proceeding in a largely uncoordinated manner.[9]

In practice, member states are very happy to leave the heavy lifting on human rights issues with regard to China to the common EU institutions. In spite of efforts made recently by the European External Action Service (EEAS), there is neither the capacity nor the power within that department to deal with both policy development and coordination. Instead, a further harmonization between EEAS and the human rights units

in the Council Secretariat and the European Commission's China desk is needed to present a viable policy and help convince member states to adopt it.

The political core of such a policy must be that all member states should speak with one voice on the Chinese government's violations of international norms and of its own laws. Such practices have not disappeared with the overall strengthening of the Chinese legal system that has taken place over the past several years. If the EU is not seen as being consistent and honest on the issue, it will be very easy for Beijing to conclude that its government's lack of respect for citizens' rights is a matter of no consequence as far as its relations with Europe are concerned. Such a mistaken conclusion will necessarily lead to further difficulties in the European-Chinese relationship at a later stage.

The Arms Embargo

The arms embargo that the EU imposed on China after the Tiananmen events of 1989 has become an embarrassing example of the EU's political impotence. While the embargo had a political effect in the 1990s, it is very doubtful whether that is the case today. On the contrary, it has come to undermine parts of the EU's political leverage with regard to China, having become a prime exhibit in the CCP's domestic presentation of the outside world's hostility. Because of the different positions taken by member states, however, it has been impossible for the EU to achieve what Cathy Ashton has suggested—namely, to remove the embargo in return for the deepening of cooperation with China on security issues, including those that relate to China's policies towards its neighbors in Korea and Southeast Asia, and its policies on Taiwan.[10]

The most important link that the EU could make to such a lifting of the embargo would be Chinese compliance with international efforts to prevent Iran from becoming a nuclear weapons power. Although China's support of Iran is not in itself at this stage crucial for the Iranian nuclear program, such a change in Chinese policies would send a very strong signal to the regime in Teheran. And even if it would slow down rather than end

Iran's efforts, it would still give EU external policies a new relevance, both in the Middle East and
in East Asia.

Removing the embargo would also be a way
for the EU to get out from the shadow of the
United States on its China policy. This is no aim
in itself—on the contrary, US-European cooperation with regard to many China-related issues
is important and wise. But the sense that has
developed over the past five years—that individual European governments are keeping the
embargo in place first and foremost to please
the United States—is unhealthy. Americans and
Europeans can only truly cooperate on China if
each acts out of political conviction rather than
expediency.

At present, the embargo does not serve
Europe's own security interests. Europe does
not want to see a closer Sino-Russian partnership on advanced weapons' systems, which seems
to be in the making in part because of the US
and European embargos. Between 1991 and 2010,
over 90 percent of the heavy conventional weapons imported into China came from Russia, as
the EU embargo created a windfall for Russian
companies.

With the modernization of China's defense
industry one of the main goals of the PRC's
new Five-Year Plan, Beijing is set to increase its
imports of state of the art equipment.[11] While
nobody believes that China will turn to European
arms manufacturers for imports immediately after
the embargo comes to an end, such a decision
would at least prevent Russia from getting unnat-
ural advantages in terms of its arms industry.

Climate Change EU leaders know that if
Europe's global position is going to become
more significant, they need to play a leading
role on key issues, such as climate change policies. They also know that dealing with China is
currently the main arena within this sector, and
it will remain so, as long as the United States
remains gridlocked internally. In spite of its lack
of leadership during the Copenhagen summit,
the EU has real opportunities to influence China
on environmental issues, both in technological as
well as policy terms. What remains to be seen is
whether European leaders are willing to invest

enough in their direct relations with China on
this issue in order to make use of its advantages.[12]

While still being the world's largest polluter,
China has come a long way in realizing the need
for energy efficiency and a reduced use of fossil
fuels. The new five year plan from 2011 sees sustainable growth as a real priority, and the potential for working with Europe—and European
companies—in furthering this aim will be seen
by Beijing as very large indeed. In technological
terms, the European shift towards decarboniza-
tion has now led to China looking much more to
Europe than to the United States for the means to
further its own goals.

There are, of course, significant difficulties in
the relationship between the two in this field as
well. China will not give up its main polluting
energy production or industries, as long as the
United States is not willing to reach reasonable
and comprehensive international deals. The EU is
rightly critical of Chinese double-talk, in which it
pledges long-term support for lofty international
aims, while opening new coal power stations
every day. Also, the EU still has internal problems
with support for some of the aims that the Union
has already signed up for.

Even so, climate change policy is an almost
unique field in which Sino-European cooperation may lead the way towards broader international deals. While the US position shows how
impotent the Americans have become on some
global issues, Beijing and Brussels are increasingly
leaning in similar directions, both in terms of their
view of the current situation and on at least some
of the remedies. There is reason to believe that
further progress may be made in direct talks over
the next two years, unless other bilateral issues get
in the way. And if European negotiators dealing
with China (and to a lesser degree, India) are able
to arrive at measures that will later become binding targets for multilateral solutions, then some
of the experience of the EU as an integrationist
project will have come to use on a global scale.

Conclusions and Uncertainties

Some of the development of the relationship between China and Europe will be not

be decided by either of the two. A key role in Sino-European relations over the next decade will—perhaps ironically—be played by the United States. How Washington behaves towards both regions during a time in which its political leadership will be tested, and its relative economic position weakened, will be of crucial importance for the future. But American behavior will also define much of the room for maneuver between the two other main poles in world politics. If the United States attempts to reassert its hegemony in Europe in wake of the economic crisis, the institutions of the EU may be further weakened, and differences within the Union—including on foreign policy—exacerbated. If, on the contrary, leaders in Washington will try to build more cooperative relations with the EU as an institution, both on economic and political issues—and avoid any whiff of protectionism, currency wars, and limiting access to technology, as the situation currently stands in light of the crisis—then a more coherent European approach to the rise of China may be expected.

Internal factors will, of course, also play key roles. How the sovereign debt crises in Europe are solved will set some of the pattern of interaction with China for the next decade or more, especially given the Chinese predilection for viewing the continent as a crisis zone. The solution to the Chinese government's problems with a lack of internal political legitimacy will also be crucial. If the CCP allows a gradual introduction of political pluralism and participation, then its interaction with Europe will be much easier to develop in the medium term. While these obstacles are key to the future, however, neither of them should stand in the way for the kind of deepening interaction that the two sides need over the coming decade both in political and economic terms.

The global shift in wealth and power from West to East seems at the moment to be happening faster than most experts believed only a year ago. For Europe, even more than for the United States, such a change is an immense challenge to its future prosperity and stability. The solution will be found in developing, on a global scale, the knowledge in terms of growth and technology that Europe has accumulated over generations. But for such an approach to be fully implemented, the EU will need a much larger direct engagement with China, and with other emerging economies, than it has had up to now.

NOTES

1. For an overview from a Chinese perspective, see Guan Chengyuan, ed., *Lingjulijie du Oumeng: waijiaoguan de qianyan baogao* [Studying the EU Up Front], (2009).
2. I am grateful to the LSE's Marie-Julie Chenard for discussions of this matter.
3. Natalia Chaban, Martin Holland, and Peter Ryan, eds., *The EU Through the Eyes of Asia* (2007).
4. Massimiliano Andretta and Nicole Doerr, "Imagining Europe: Internal and External Non-State Actors at the European Crossroads," *European Foreign Affairs Review* vol. 12, no. 3 (2007), 385–400.
5. http://ec.europa.eu/trade/creating-opportunities/bilateral-relations/countries/china/.
6. Kenneth Rapoza, "Chinese Companies Inching Into Europe," *Forbes*, June 10, 2012.
7. See Bernadette Andreosso-O'Callaghan and Francoise Nicolas, "Complimentary and Rivalry in EU-China Economic Relations in the Twenty-First Century," *European Foreign Affairs Review*, no. 12, 13–38.
8. See, for instance, Francois Godement and Jonas Parello-Plesner, *The Scramble for Europe*, European Council on

Foreign Relations Brief, 2011. http://www.ecfr.eu/page/-/ECFR37_Scramble_For_Europe_AW_v4.pdf.
9. For a general overview of the human rights issue, see Jing Men and Giuseppe Balducci (eds.), *Prospects and Challenges for EU-China Relations in the 21st Century: The Partnership and Cooperation Agreement* (2010).
10. For an excellent overview of the arms embargo issue, see Nicola Casarini, *Remaking Global Order: The Evolution of Europe-China Relations and Its Implications for East Asia and the United States* (2009).
11. Richard Rousseau, "The Tortuous Sino-Russian Arms Trade," *CESRAN Analysis*, June 8, 2012. http://cesran.org/index.php?option=com_content&view=article&id=1462%3Athe-tortuous-sino-russian-arms-trade&catid=57%3Arussiaeurasiaanalysis&Itemid=312&lang=en.
12. For an overview of the issues, see Constantin Holzer and Haibin Zhang, "The Potentials and Limits of China-EU Cooperation on Climate Change and Energy Security," *Asia Europe Journal* vol. 6, no. 2 (2008), 217–227.

V. THE GLOBAL SOUTH

China and the Developing World*

Peter Ferdinand

China has long considered itself a developing country and a presumptive leader of the developing world, but it was not until recently that China's global footprint had actually extended to the developing world. Previously, Beijing's role with the developing world was more rhetorical than real—now it is being felt in many ways. This chapter will consider, first, China's growing economic ties with developing states, then its evolving diplomacy towards them, and finally the impact of these changes on China's place in global governance.

Trade and Aid Intertwined

Over the past decade China's involvement with the developing world has gathered momentum, especially in economic terms. As table 1 shows, the developing world has grown as a destination for Chinese exports in both absolute and relative terms. Equally importantly, the developing world now supplies China with ever-growing quantities of imports. This growth has accelerated in recent years. This table, however, does not capture the rapidity in the growth of trade in absolute volumes in recent years, especially over the past decade. Table 2 illustrates this.

Two elements are particularly striking about these figures. The first are trends in the overall growth rates. In the period 1990–2008 China's total world trade grew 22 times in nominal terms, but trade with the developing world grew 43.6 times: almost exactly twice as fast. Within the latter category, trade with developing Asia grew slightly more slowly (39.5 times), but trade with Africa grew 65.6 times, with the Western Hemisphere 72.6 times, and with the Middle East 74.9 times. When considering exports and imports separately, the most striking changes were an increase of 108.9 times in exports to the Western Hemisphere, and increases of 151.3 times in

imports from Africa and of 170 times in those from the Middle East. These are astounding increases.

Through ramping up its trade with the developing world, China has become much more integrated into global trade patterns as a whole. It no longer is so overwhelmingly focused on exports to the US and Europe.

Second, China has moved from being a net exporter of goods to the developing world in 1990, to being a net importer of them in 2000, and back again to a net exporter in 2008. Yet, whereas in 1990 China was a net exporter to most areas of the developing world (with the exception of the western hemisphere), by 2008 it was a net importer from most of them. In that way China is contributing demand that stimulates economic growth in the developing world. This trend seems set to continue. According to the Ministry of Land and Resources, China will increasingly need to import 19 out of the 45 key minerals needed for maintaining economic growth over the next twenty years, and eleven of these are considered "vital." By 2020, 40 percent of China's iron ore demand, 60 percent of crude oil consumption and 70 percent of its copper and potassium needs will have to be imported. Nor are minerals the only material resources that will need to be imported. China has also started spending significant sums of money on agricultural products from abroad, e.g., soya beans from Brazil. So concerns over food security will also drive China into greater trade.

Despite its many natural resources, China is confronted by the need to obtain natural resources from abroad to maintain economic development and the welfare of its people. What is clear from its strategy is that the government in Beijing is reluctant to allow itself to become too dependent upon global commodities markets to ensure the adequate and timely supply of vital energy and mineral supplies. What China would like to do is to tie up supplies as far as possible through long-term contracts, wherever possible at fixed prices. It has been most successful at this in completing deals over energy, but less so over iron ore.

---
* This article was published in David Shambaugh (ed.), *Charting China's Future: Domestic & International Challenges* (New York: Routledge, 2011).

Table 1 Regional Distribution of China's Trade with the Developing World (as percent of total trade)

	Exports			Imports		
	1990	*2000*	*2008*	*1990*	*2000*	*2008*
Developing Africa	1.89	1.67	3.02	0.65	2.40	4.67
Developing Asia	5.80	6.48	9.01	5.00	8.58	10.57
Central Asia	N/A	0.31	1.50	N/A	0.47	0.73
Developing Middle East	2.28	2.52	4.30	0.89	4.34	7.17
Developing western hemisphere	1.02	2.77	4.88	2.41	2.36	6.21
Developing countries total	15.49	16.28	28.60	15.15	21.55	32.33

Source: Based on data in IMF *Direction of Trade Statistics Yearbook* (various years).

Table 2 Regional Distribution of China's Trade with Developing World (US$ million)

	Exports			Imports		
	1990	*2000*	*2008*	*1990*	*2000*	*2008*
Developing Africa	1,187.25	4,151.51	43,293.50	349.63	5,41 3.03	52,884.40
Developing Asia	3,644.76	16,149.60	129,795.00	2,666.11	19,318.20	119,622.00
Central Asia	N/A	767.2A	22,593.50	N/A	1,052.07	8,226.50
Developing Middle East	1,430.38	6,305.22	61,627.70	477.43	9,767.27	81,167.10
Developing Western Hemisphere	640.18	6,908.33	69,740.80	1,287.33	5,321.51	70,276.20
Developing countries total	9,719.89	40,566.10	410,206.00	8,083.60	48,514.30	365,984.00

Source: Based on data in IMF *Direction of Trade Statistics Yearbook* (various years).

Of course, while the share of developing countries in China's foreign trade profile is rising significantly, trade with developed economies continues to be more important. In 2008, 71 percent of China's exports went to "advanced economies," and 59 percent of its imports came from there. Nevertheless in 2008 China was only a little way behind the US as top exporter to emerging and developing markets. China is now the largest exporter to the Middle East, to Africa, and the second largest to Latin America.

The developing world is more important to China in one other respect. It accounts for a higher proportion of Chinese foreign direct investment (FDI) than of Chinese trade. According to analysis by the Hang Seng Bank, 39 percent of China's global FDI in the period 2004–8 went into mining ventures alone. In addition, China developed a strategy of lending to African governments for production or infrastructural development that will be repaid with guaranteed supplies of minerals or oil. This was first formulated in a deal with Angola, but the principle has spread more widely. Under this scheme African governments retain ownership of their natural resources and therefore also greater control over profit distribution, whilst acquiring improved infrastructure that helps to make their economies more efficient in general. In this way both sides benefit. The biggest deals have been with countries that can offer large quantities of oil and minerals that China needs—Sudan, Nigeria, Angola, Zambia, Democratic Republic of Congo, Mozambique, Ethiopia. At present, China accounts for 10–16 percent of the African oil market, while Europe and the US account for 33 and 36 percent of it. But oil reportedly accounts for 80 percent of China's trade with Africa and about one-third of its oil imports.[1] And two-thirds of Sudan's oil exports and one-third of Angola's go to China.

What this means is that China has also become much more heavily involved in large-scale construction projects in developing countries. By 2006 China had already risen to second place among countries supplying large construction work in Africa, with 21 percent of the market, only marginally behind the then market leader, France (24 percent).[2] Back in 2000 its work amounted to $540 million; by 2006 this had risen to $3.23 billion, a six-fold increase. It seems likely that China has already become the market leader. Whilst many of these contracts were with African governments, some are with international aid agencies and were won through competitive tendering. Some of the biggest have been to build hydro-electric dams and transport infrastructure, especially railways and roads.

This means that large numbers of Chinese workers are deployed to Africa. There have been complaints that this has prevented the employment of Africans, and there have been protests within these states. There have also been reports of numerous sporadic attacks on Chinese nationals in at least twelve African countries, some lethal.[3] It has also led to reports of greater Chinese protection for their construction sites, and no doubt the numbers of security personnel will increase. Sometimes this creates the impression of Chinese territorial enclaves overseas. Yet other reports suggest that China has already become sensitive to accusations that they are discriminating against local nationals, so they predominantly employ Chinese with skills that are locally in short supply. It has also been suggested that the proportion of expatriate labor in these projects is minimal.

Given predicted future shortages in key resources, this pattern of increased involvement in infrastructural projects will spread. In addition to opening doors to deals over oil and minerals, Chinese corporations seek profitable deals involving construction. Not only does this apply to national corporations; some provincial corporations have also targeted this business. So China's physical presence in the developing world will become proportionately greater, especially if it continues to face difficulties in securing agreement for investments in deposits of natural resources in more developed economies.

The bulk of these projects have a commercial logic and are financed through the Chinese Export-Import Bank. But some of China's activities fall more appropriately into the category of development aid. It is difficult to establish precise figures on this for two reasons. First, China does not report its aid contributions in the same format as other states. Second, there is no single national agency responsible for coordinating aid efforts. This means that there is no single figure for the national aid effort. Estimates vary wildly. The Chinese Academy of Social Sciences stated that by May 2006 China had extended over $5.7 billion to Africa in over 800 projects, but a senior Chinese official estimated that $4.5 billion had been disbursed in 2006 alone. By comparison, the OECD Development Assistance Committee (DAC) member states were allocating $43.4 billion in 2006, which would mean that China's aid added about 10 percent to that figure. These figures, however, omit debt relief that China has granted to developing states, where official announcements suggest that several billion dollars have also been written off. But also, according to Davies, most of China's aid goes to Asia, with about one-third going to Africa.[4]

At the same time, China has been forced to offer loans to some developing states that are shunned by other potential investors because of poor governance, human rights abuses, etc. Such examples include Sudan, Equatorial Guinea and Zimbabwe. This has been criticized by international agencies and other aid donors as undermining their efforts to encourage better governance.

So far we have suggested that the main reason for China's increasing involvement in the developing world is national commercial advantage. More recently, however, two other factors have emerged. The first is a growing partnership between China and the World Bank to develop infrastructure in Africa. There are two dimensions to this. The first is a proposed program to develop health-care services there, together with the World Health Organization and the Gates Foundation. The second is recently revealed negotiations between China and the World Bank to help selected African states develop their versions of China's Special Economic Zones, which played a big part in integrating China into the world economy in the 1980s. This would aim at constructing low-cost factories which would begin to increase Africa's share of world trade. It would be part of what Chinese economists have dubbed China's "Marshall Plan for Africa," i.e., using some of China's huge foreign exchange reserves to stimulate the global economy, focusing particularly on the developing world.

To some extent, these zones would serve as customers for Chinese export industries, which would help to maintain international demand for Chinese products at a time when demand from the developed world would slow down. Also, some of the loans would be in *renminbi* (RMB), so they would gradually contribute to the internationalization of China's currency. And it would diversify China's overseas investments and financial holdings away from excessive reliance upon the US. So, Chinese commercial interests are involved; nevertheless it would also represent an attempt by China to contribute leadership in resolving the international economic crisis, whilst not simply following Western prescriptions.

Towards Multipolarity

All of this economic evidence confirms China as a rising world power, probably the most important one. But it is not alone. The international economic order is in flux, especially since the global financial crisis of 2008–10. Commentators and analysts have begun competing to identify new poles of economic attraction. Already in the early part of this decade Goldman Sachs popularized the idea of new rising world economic powers with the acronym BRIC (Brazil, Russia, India, China). More recently the OECD has produced a study of six rising economic powers, which consisted of the BRIC states as well as South Africa and Indonesia. There have been various speculations on other combinations of potential "winners."

Then, in 2008, the global financial crisis drove the West to make use of the G-20 group of countries to try to devise a coherent global response, rather than the G-8. This includes all the G-8 and BRIC states, Argentina, Australia, Indonesia, Saudi Arabia, South Africa, South Korea, and Turkey, as well as the EU. Although their per capita GDP varies considerably, it is the size of their economies that matters for the system of global trade. The potential economic weight of the newcomers is strengthened in the current crisis by the size of their foreign-currency reserves. At the end of September 2009 the four BRIC states held roughly one-third of the world's declared foreign-exchange reserves, six times as much as those of the Eurozone, and nearly twenty-five times those of the US. China alone held almost one-quarter. Recently think tanks in China have been considering the greater deployment of China's reserves in investments in BRIC states, as a way of stimulating economic growth there. It would enhance China's diplomatic clout, as well as encourage non-Western-oriented growth strategies.

More generally, the shape of world governance is mutating quite rapidly. The unipolar global position of the US, which has existed since the collapse of the USSR in 1991, is eroding. The recent US National Intelligence Council report *Global Trends 2025* envisages as a "relative certainty" that a global multipolar system is emerging, so that by 2025 a "single international community" composed of nation-states will likely no longer exist.

One symbol of the change has been the growing diplomatic interaction among the BRIC states. The chief thing that these states had in common when Goldman Sachs highlighted them was that they were predicted to have a bright future and offered good prospects for potential international investors. However, over time the leaders of these states also began to see opportunities for diplomatic co-operation—from 2006 their foreign ministers began to meet on an annual basis, and then in June 2009 their heads of state or government met for their first summit in Yekaterinburg, Russia. To some extent the G-7/8 group of countries began to try to involve these states in their activities as a way of reaching out to the developing world. In 2007 five such states (Brazil, India, China, South Africa, Mexico) plus Russia (BRICSAM) were invited to exchange views on international affairs at the G-8 summit in Heiligendamm, Germany, thus initiating what was termed the "Heiligendamm Process." China had refused invitations to attend G-8 summits in 1999 and 2000. Now it could accept, since it would not be alone.

Since 1949 China, like many developing states, has cherished an aspiration for greater South-South co-operation as part of its foreign policy. It sees itself as a leader there. On many international issues they share common instincts. This is reflected in table 3, which compares China's voting in the General Assembly of the UN with that of the other BRICSAM countries on the one hand, and the other permanent five (P-5) members of the Security Council on the other. It shows that China has voted the opposite way to France, the UK, and above all the US far more often than it has where the BRICSAM states are concerned.

This is the background to China's growing diplomatic activity in the developing world. The Forum on China–Africa Co-operation (FOCAC) is the body that has attracted most Western attention. It held its fourth summit in 2009 and announced a $10 billion fund of low-cost loans for economic assistance to Africa, twice the amount committed at the previous summit in 2006. In addition, $1 billion was pledged to help small and medium businesses in Africa, as well as a number of other educational and public health joint measures. Already by 2006 China's loans to Angola, Nigeria, and Mozambique exceeded

loans to the whole of sub-Saharan Africa by the World Bank, the US and France combined. Then in 2007 China established the China–Latin American Business Summit, which has held annual meetings. As for the Middle East, China's growing energy needs have also led to a more active enhancement of its economic links, which have stimulated Arab investment in China as well as the reverse. And in general Chinese leaders—all the members of the Politburo, not just President Hu Jintao and Prime Minister Wen Jiabao—criss-cross the world regularly on missions to develop Chinese influence.

Of course the fact that many developing states share such a common general orientation in international relations does not mean that they will escape conflicts of interest, or even violent conflicts. For example, despite the warmth of the BRIC summit, border tensions between China and India over Kashmir and Arunachal Pradesh have been rising again. Security rivalries still disturb the harmony. Trade disputes, too, can have the same effect, e.g., those between India and China, and Brazil and China. There is no united front from the developing world.

It would be wrong to take BRIC summits, or G-20 summits, as already robust new agents of international governance. They are harbingers of multipolarity, not yet the reality itself.

Table 3 Voting Records of Rising World Powers (BRICSAM) and Other P-5 Members in UN General Assembly Compared with PRC's, 1974–2008 (as percent of total votes cast)

	Identical with PRC (yes/no/abstain)	*1 yes/no + 1 abstain*	*1 yes + 1 no*
Brazil	77.83	11.35	1.86
India	77.36	10.85	2.60
Mexico	78.58	11.02	2.07
Russia	65.99	17.64	6.53
South Africa*	80.38	15.12	1.83
France	36.26	34.84	17.32
UK	33.42	32.57	22.70
US	13.21	23.20	50.80

*1994–2008; N = 3,384 votes cast

Source: Erik Voeten and Adis Merdzanovic, United Nations General Assembly Voting Data (available at: http://hdl:1902.1/12379UNF:3:Hpf6qOkDdzzvXF9m66yLTg=).

Note: Figures do not total 100 because of absences of one of the states from individual votes.

Nevertheless, the current global financial crisis may endow them with a greater effectiveness. It will certainly give countries like China greater self-confidence in proposing changes in international governance. The BRIC summit called for greater voice and representation for developing and emerging economies in general in decision-making in international financial institutions. The participants presented themselves as spokesmen for the developing world. And four of the BRICSAM countries (Brazil, India, China, and South Africa) co-ordinated their negotiating positions in preparation for the climate change conference in Copenhagen. Indeed the outcome of the conference, however disappointing, demonstrated the growing significance of the BASIC group of countries (Brazil, South Africa, India, and China), since it was they who met with President Obama to achieve some consensus over international commitments which involved the developing world and which formed the basis for such international agreement as was achieved. It was they who subsequently again met to co-ordinate their voluntary commitments to reduce greenhouse emissions to try to maintain momentum for implementation. Deng Xiaoping's injunction in 1989 that China's leaders should "keep a low profile and bide their time" seems increasingly anachronistic.

Forecast: Back to the Future?

This chapter has suggested that the next few years will see a heightened Chinese profile in the developing world. This will be for reasons of commercial advantage through trade, and also for reasons of diplomatic advantage. The Chinese government will link this change to its earlier professions of ideological decolonizing solidarity with African, Asian, and Latin American countries in the Non-Aligned Movement from the 1950s, and even earlier. But they will be reinforced by "pull" factors. South Africa is one of the BASIC group of countries that wants to leverage its ties with China so as to become a more important diplomatic player on the global stage itself. And many developing states will hope for financial support in the middle of a global economic crisis from the state with the largest foreign-exchange reserves

in the world. China is now a much more economically powerful state than it was, and so it is able to offer much more material assistance. Its aid budget is a significant attraction for the governments of developing states in Africa and Asia, both in terms of potential quantities and also because China does not insist upon the same preconditions of human rights observance, etc., as Western aid donors.

Nevertheless it should not be assumed that China is indifferent to issues of good governance. China, no less than Western governments, does not want its aid siphoned off into corruption and private bank accounts. It has already begun redesigning projects so that they minimize opportunities for venality. Those aspects of good governance programs which focus on preventing corruption will gain Chinese support. Nor will China be indifferent to issues of illegality if people in host countries protest about domestic abuses and target Chinese projects that they associate with them, especially if they feel that their projects do not employ enough Africans. The sporadic but repeated attacks on Chinese citizens living and working in Africa will be likely to continue, and Chinese companies may well respond by increasing the security protection on large projects. Some of their responses may not differ from those of Western companies targeted by local protests: e.g., security perimeters and professional security teams.

Thus, while the Chinese presence in developing countries will grow, so too will the complexity of the challenges China has to confront. Declarations of diplomatic solidarity with developing countries and references to the memory of the injustices of foreign ownership of territory in China will only go so far. Some large Chinese production sites in Africa may not look so different from those of Western multinational corporations.

How do these changes affect the overall picture of Chinese foreign relations? Relations with the developing world used to be regarded as important in China, but as a lower priority than relations with the superpower(s) and with Asian neighbors. This hierarchy will not change any time soon. Nevertheless, the distance between these priorities is diminishing. Relations with the developing world are becoming more closely bound with China's "peaceful rise" in general, both economically and diplomatically.

More than one commentator has drawn analogies between China's rise and that of Wilhelmine Germany at the end of the nineteenth century, indicating parallels between Anglo-German and Sino-American relations. In fact the parallels between the two eras should be extended. It is not just the case of one newcomer state challenging the existing hegemonic powers. Both periods have witnessed the rise of several new powers. Their dynamism and rivalry in the nineteenth century added to the turmoil, as newcomers jostled not only to assert themselves in Europe but also to seize economic assets or colonies in other regions of the world. Ultimately the rivalry between all these powers, reinforced by diplomatic miscalculations, culminated in the catastrophe of the First World War. Today's world is challenged by the same turbulence. If a calamity like the First World War is to be avoided, then all the parties will need to display greater diplomatic skill.

All of this highlights the growing importance of diplomatic finesse that China will need to display in the pursuit of this complex set of objectives. On the one hand, China will want to keep good relations with the developed world, especially the US. On the other hand, it will want to develop closer ties with developing states. To some extent this ambiguity has been inherent in China's external relations for decades. And the skill of the country's diplomacy can be seen in China's behavior at the United Nations. In the UN Security Council, China has generally maintained good and co-operative relations with the other P-5 members. China has very rarely cast a veto, despite its objections to any attempt by states to intervene in the internal affairs of a sovereign nation, e.g., Kosovo and Iraq. In fact, it was striking that at the end of the Bush administration the Chinese government commented that relations with the US had never been better. On the other hand, as can be seen from table 2, China has often voted contrary to the US in the General Assembly of the UN, and this trend was most pronounced during the George W. Bush presidency.

The good news is that China has demonstrated impressive diplomatic adroitness since the 1980s. But will other states show equal diplomatic skill? And will China and its partners accept the responsibilities, as well as the prestige, of international leadership? How will China cope with the end of its low international profile? That remains to be seen.

NOTES

1. Thomas Lum, "China's Assistance and Government-Sponsored Investment Activities in Africa, Latin America, and Southeast Asia," Congressional Research Service, November 25, 2009, available at: http://www.fas.org/sgp/crs/row/R40940.pdf.
2. Chuan Chen et al., "An Empirical Analysis of Chinese Construction Firms' Entry into China," available at: http://crgp.stanford.edu/publications/conference_papers/Chen_Chiu_Orr_Goldstein_Emp_analysis_Chinese_Africa.pdf.
3. Jerker Hellström, "China's Emerging Role in Africa," May 2009, available at: http://www.foi.se/upload/Kinaiafrika.pdf.
4. Martyn Davies, "How China Delivers Development Assistance to Africa," February 2008, available at: http://www.dfid.gov.uk/Documents/publications/china-dev-africa.pdf.

CHINA'S AFRICA STRATEGY*

Joshua Eisenman and Joshua Kurlantzick

The streets of Maputo, the capital of the former Portuguese colony of Mozambique, look little different from those of other sub-Saharan African cities. Open sewers overflow with rotting fruit, beggars harass pedestrians for 1,000 meticals (the equivalent of less than 10 cents), and young mothers walk past in dirty rags, carrying emaciated

---

* This article was published in *Current History* (May 2006).

children. Yet Maputo is also hopeful. After decades of brutal civil war, Mozambique has enjoyed peace since the early 1990s and has built a nascent, if fragile, democracy. Mozambican entrepreneurs have reconstructed the shattered economy of their capital, whose business district has even sprouted a small skyline.

Amid the pink and green Mediterranean-style buildings on Maputo's oceanfront, signs of its Portuguese colonial heritage, one structure stands out—an enormous, blocky building with an Asian pagoda roof that hardly resembles the surrounding architecture. It is the Ministry of Foreign Affairs, and it has been built, as part of a larger initiative, with Chinese aid. Indeed, in recent years China has become a major provider of aid to Mozambique, launching an investment-and-trade-promotion center in Maputo, offering debt reduction, and promising significant other economic assistance.

Perhaps unsurprisingly, Mozambique now regards China as one of its most important allies outside of Africa. On one visit to Beijing, Mozambique's prime minister announced that his country supports China's "independent foreign policy"—a term Beijing uses to denote independence from American power—and called for China to play a larger role on the African continent.

Mozambique is hardly unique. Over the past decade, while the United States has too often ignored sub-Saharan Africa policy other than counterterrorism cooperation and aid initiatives, Beijing has quietly established relationships with the continent's political and business elites. And Beijing has enjoyed considerable success in Africa, building close ties with countries from Sudan to South Africa, becoming a vital aid donor in many African nations, signing trade initiatives with more than 40 African states, and developing military relationships with many of the continent's powers.

Into Africa

A decade ago, China's influence in Africa was limited. Its aid programs were hardly significant, its diplomats relatively unskilled. And many Chinese were unsure about their country's role as an international actor. In most international forums, China did little other than defend core interests, like the "one China" principle. Recently, however, continued strong economic growth, a more sophisticated generation of Chinese leaders, better scholarship in China on Africa, and a domestic population more confident in China as a global actor have encouraged Beijing to take a more proactive approach to foreign affairs.

Beijing's motives are clear. China's growing industries demand new energy and raw material suppliers; its exporters want markets; its diplomats require support in international organizations; and its propaganda still seeks support from allies to advance Chinese interests and, when necessary, to counter the United States.

Africa has become central to these strategies. In part, China's courtship of Africa is a resource grab. Rapid Chinese economic growth coupled with dwindling domestic Chinese petroleum and mineral deposits have encouraged Beijing to look abroad for resources. Last year, China became the world's second-largest consumer of petroleum products, and its imports of natural gas, copper, cobalt, and other key resources are rising by as much as 20 percent annually.

Within the next decade, China's domestic oil production is likely to continue diminishing, and the country will surpass the United States as the largest global consumer of oil. And China possesses no significant strategic petroleum reserve. According to energy analysts such as Erica Downs of the Brookings Institution, who follows the debate on oil within the Chinese leadership, Beijing is convinced that it must become less dependent on market-dictated pricing in case of a global crisis or a deliberate US attempt to cut China's energy supply lines.

This search for resources takes Chinese officials to commodity-rich Africa, home to major oil producers, including Nigeria, Sudan, Angola, and Gabon, as well as some of the richest deposits of minerals in the world. China already imports about 28 percent of its oil and gas from sub-Saharan Africa, compared with about 15 percent for the United States, and it has made sizable copper purchases in Zambia, the Democratic Republic of Congo, and other African states. Although Zimbabwe lacks oil, it has the second-largest deposits of platinum in the world; those riches remain largely untapped, as do Zimbabwe's deposits of more than 40 other minerals, including ferrochrome, uranium, gold, silver, and copper.

But China's Africa strategy is about more than resources. As in other parts of the developing world, Chinese businessmen are looking to open new markets for their products. They have been surprisingly successful: according to Chinese government reports, trade between China and Africa jumped over 35 percent between November 2004 and 2005.

In fact, Chinese merchants may have been too successful. In 2004, Chinese exports to Ethiopia made up over 93 percent of the two nations' bilateral trade, and in the first half of 2005, Chinese purchases from Djibouti, Eritrea, and Somalia/Somaliland were negligible, an imbalance that could alienate these countries in the long run, as Beijing's trade imbalance has already begun to alienate Latin American states. In an attempt to ease the lopsided trade relationship, this year Beijing scrapped tariffs on 190 commodities from 25 African nations.

Yet, despite claims by Beijing that this initiative marks an "important commitment to help African countries develop their economies," the decision is unlikely to dramatically change China's trade relationships in the region. Meanwhile, aided by its undervalued currency, China's unparalleled competitiveness in developed international markets like those of the United States and Europe have hurt African exports, such as textiles.

China's efforts to win friends across Africa also are aimed at safeguarding its interests in international forums and institutions, such as the UN Commission on Human Rights. The commission is to be replaced by the Human Rights Council in part because China helped fill it with Africa's worst human rights abusers, including Zimbabwe, Sudan, and Eritrea. At every turn these African nations then have supported Beijing's efforts to sideline attempts to redress abuses throughout China and Africa. In the case of Sudan, China has used its status as a member of the UN Security Council to block real measures intended to address genocide in Darfur. By leveraging its seat, China has driven a further wedge between Sudan and the West, a move that only bolsters Beijing's importance to the oil-rich Khartoum regime.

Africa is one of two parts of the world, along with Latin America, with sizable numbers of states that still recognize Taiwan. Taiwan's remaining allies are vital to preventing the island from becoming isolated diplomatically, and Beijing clearly wants to reduce Taiwan's influence on the continent. In late 2005, China lured Senegal, one of the most important West African states, back to its camp. African rulers affirm their support for the "one China" principle at nearly every official meeting with their Chinese counterparts. Earlier this year, Ethiopia's parliament even approved a resolution in support of Beijing's anti-secession law.

How to Win Friends

Since at least the 1980s, US scholars on Africa have focused primarily on developments within the continent, or on Africa's relations with Western nations and international aid and financial institutions. American China scholars, by contrast, tend to focus on Chinese domestic developments, US-China relations, and China's relations with the Asian region. As a result, there has been limited research on how China has pursued influence in Africa over the past two decades. Understanding these tools of influence offers a window into China's strategies on the continent, and whether they could be replicated in other parts of the developing world.

How does China obtain resources, build trade, and win African nations to its side? In January, Beijing released an official China-Africa policy white paper, a document remarkable for the broad range of issues it covers. The white paper offers some clues into Beijing's strategy in Africa. First, China is dramatically boosting its aid and economic support to Africa—aid it can provide with few strings, at the same time as international financial institutions, like the World Bank, increasingly link aid disbursements in the developing world to good governance and anticorruption initiatives.

Chinese aid to the continent has become more sophisticated. While China once focused on large buildings—sports stadiums in Gambia and Sierra Leone, for example—it has increasingly used aid to support infrastructure creation that then also helps Chinese companies, and to directly woo African elites. In 2002, China gave $1.8 billion in development aid to its African allies. (Beijing has since then stopped officially reporting its aid, making a complete and accurate tally impossible.)

China has also used debt relief to assist African nations, effectively turning loans into grants. Since 2000, Beijing has taken significant steps to cancel the debt of 31 African countries. In 2000, China wrote off $1.2 billion in African debt; in 2003 it forgave another $750 million. Ethiopian Prime Minister Meles Zenawi has proclaimed that "China's exemplary endeavor to ease African countries' debt problem is indeed a true expression of solidarity and commitment." Debt relief has been an excellent public relations tool for Beijing because it not only garners popular support but also allows for two positive press events: the first to provide the loan, the second to relieve the debt.

In addition to increased aid, China's outreach includes efforts to boost its soft power in Africa. This is evident in a growing focus on promoting Chinese cultural and language studies on the continent. In 2003, 1,793 African students studied in China, representing one-third of total foreign students that year. Indeed, China plans to train some 10,000 Africans per year, including many future African opinion leaders who once might have trained in the West.

Beijing also seeks to establish "Confucius Institutes" in Africa—programs at leading local universities, funded by Beijing and devoted to China studies and Chinese language training. Already, in Asia, Confucius Institutes have proved effective in encouraging graduate students to focus on China studies and, ultimately, to study in China. Meanwhile, Chinese medical schools and physicians train African doctors and provide medicine and equipment free of charge to African countries.

Through these programs and exchanges, China develops trust by investing in long-term relationships with African elites that formerly might have been educated in London or Washington. Beijing is also working to encourage tourism in Africa, partly in an effort to develop cultural ties. The government has approved 16 African countries as outbound destinations for Chinese tourists, including Ethiopia, Kenya, and Zimbabwe. This pushed the number of Africa's Chinese tourists to 110,000 in 2005, a 100 percent increase over 2004, according to Chinese government figures.

Trade Summits and Arms Deals

On the trade front, Beijing has enacted policies to encourage greater Chinese investment in Africa. It has launched centers for "investment and trade promotion," providing business and consultation to Chinese enterprises in Africa. Beijing has also created special funds and simplified procedures to promote Chinese investment.

As Chinese investment in the continent has grown, some 80,000 migrant workers from China have moved to Africa, creating a new Chinese diaspora that is unlikely to return home. (In some cases, this diaspora, along with imports of cheap Chinese goods, has sparked anger in Africa. Many African businesspeople believe that Chinese goods are unfairly undercutting them, and fear the diaspora is remitting nearly all of its money back to China rather than reinvesting it into local economies. These are the kinds of concerns that once led to anger against Indian populations on the continent.)

In a strategy Washington would be wise to emulate, China uses summits and informal meetings to reach out to African business leaders. The first Sino-African business conference was held in Ethiopia in December 2003. It resulted in agreements on 20 projects with a total value of $680 million. In August 2004, China held a China-Africa Youth Festival in Beijing, and in 2006 Beijing will host the third ministerial meeting of the China-Africa Cooperation Forum. Events like these provide a venue for rolling out Beijing's technical assistance, and where the idea of China as a benign actor in Africa can be tacitly emphasized.

Finally, Beijing increasingly views Africa as a center for military-military cooperation and a market for China's growing arms industry. Today, Chinese firms rank among the top suppliers of conventional arms in Africa. Between 1996 and 2003, Chinese arms sales to Africa were second only to Russia's. In particular, China has developed close military ties with Zimbabwe, Sudan, and Ethiopia, three of Africa's most strategically important states.

In April 2005, Zimbabwe's air force received six jet aircraft for "low-intensity" military operations. The year before, a Chinese radar system was installed at President Robert Mugabe's mansion in the Harare suburbs. Most important, in June 2004, Zimbabwe reportedly purchased 12 jet fighters and 100 military vehicles, worth an estimated $240 million. This order, which had been kept secret, was also reported to have circumvented the state procurement board tasked with appropriating Zimbabwe's $136 million defense budget.

China has become the largest supplier of arms to Sudan, according to a former Sudanese government minister. Chinese-made tanks, fighter planes, bombers, helicopters, machine guns, and rocket-propelled grenades supplied Khartoum's forces in the north-south civil war.

And even as world leaders remain fearful of new conflict between Ethiopia and Eritrea, China has extended arms sales to both nations. (During the war between Ethiopia and Eritrea from 1998 to 2000, China bypassed a UN arms embargo and sold over $1 billion in weapons to both states.) Ethiopian Prime Minister Meles Zenawi and Chinese Lieutenant General Zhu Wenquan met in Addis Ababa in August 2005. They agreed that "Ethiopia and China shall forge mutual cooperation in military training, exchange of military technologies, and peacekeeping missions, among others." The previous week, Zhu had met with the commander of the Eritrean Air Force. At that gathering, Zhu had said it was China's desire "for the armies of the two sisterly countries to cooperate in various training."

"Number 1 Friend"

These tools and strategies have proved effective. China has gained access to sizable resources across the continent. It has been offered exploration rights to important Nigerian oil fields. Beijing already dominates Sudan's oil industry and has the inside track to Angola's and Algeria's oil industries. More Chinese companies, too, are proving successful in mining African markets. The Chinese telecommunications giant Huawei, for instance, now holds contracts worth $400 million to provide mobile phone service in Kenya, Zimbabwe, and Nigeria. In Zambia, Chinese investors are working on a $600 million hydroelectric plant at Kafue Gorge. They are also active in South Africa and Botswana's hotel and construction industries. Chinese firms dominate

the recovering economies of Sierra Leone and Angola, and China has become an increasingly close trade partner with South Africa, the region's largest economy.

African leaders are increasingly treating China like a great power on the continent, affording Chinese officials and businesspeople the type of welcome and access once reserved for Western leaders. Beijing's outreach has been well received by many African leaders, who welcome China's rhetoric of noninterference and constant inveighing against American "hegemonism."

Just as Gabon, Sudan, Angola, and other nations now look to China first, so too Mugabe now calls China his "number one friend," while the leaders of Rwanda, where the government is accused of rigging polls and locking up opposition leaders, have lavished praise on Beijing. "It's a different way of doing business," Rwanda's finance minister told reporters, pleased that China has offered aid without any preconditions, such as improving Rwanda's human rights record. Sudanese officials, too, give thanks to Beijing: "We have our supporters," the deputy head of Sudan's parliament said wryly after Washington attempted, with little luck, to sanction Sudan at the United Nations. As Mugabe put it, China is becoming "an alternative global power point."

This growing influence comes at some US expense. Africa has not been a priority for US foreign policy, other than counterterrorism cooperation with states in North and East Africa. Meanwhile, in some democratic African nations, the war in Iraq, the use of the term "empire" in relation to elements of US foreign policy, and the American focus on transparency, sometimes seen as meddling, genuinely anger average citizens. The White House has held few bilateral meetings with the continent's most important players, and, according to a report on West Africa by the Center for Strategic and International Studies, it has cut back on American energy attachés to the continent, even as African oil becomes more important to the United States. At the same time, restrictive US policies on student visas have led many Africans studying abroad, historically a vanguard of pro-American sentiment, to look outside the United States for their education.

Yet the fact that some African leaders welcome Beijing does not mean that average Africans will always benefit from China's influence. Although much of Africa has rid itself of dictators, the continent is still left with fragile, poor pseudodemocracies that lack strong civil societies, independent media, and other important pillars of democracy. These nations could go either way. Like Benin and Botswana, they could blossom into consolidated, mature democracies. Or, like Zimbabwe and Rwanda, they could deteriorate into one-party states that hold elections but lack other essential elements of a democracy.

Setting a Poor Example

In this fragile environment, Chinese influence could complicate democratic consolidation and good governance. It might also undermine China's own efforts to be seen as a responsible global power. In Zimbabwe last year, the country held a dismal election; before the vote, candidates and poll workers from the Movement for Democratic Change, the leading opposition party, were threatened, beaten, and even killed. Mugabe had gerrymandered parliament so he would be guaranteed to start with more seats than the MDC before votes were even counted. On Election Day, when Mugabe unsurprisingly won a smashing victory, and the MDC unsurprisingly cried foul, no major international power would endorse the outcome—except China.

In the run-up to the election, China had delivered to Zimbabwe agricultural equipment, electricity transformers, and planeloads of T-shirts bearing the insignia of Mugabe's party. Chinese businesses also reportedly offered the government jamming devices to be used against Zimbabwean opposition radio stations, and Beijing is said to have sent Harare riot control gear, in case of demonstrations. Mugabe was ecstatic at his good fortune. "The Chinese are our good friends, you see," he told a British interviewer.

Beyond Zimbabwe, Beijing has been criticized for blocking Western efforts to isolate and punish the Sudanese government. In the fall of 2004, when the United States submitted draft resolutions to the United Nations that would have called for tough action against ethnic cleansing in Darfur, China's UN ambassador quietly defanged the drafts, rendering them useless.

Chinese support also has helped African leaders maintain controls on information. Beijing aids African regimes with training on press and Internet monitoring. Tracing China's efforts in this area is difficult, but China's official press even alluded to these media initiatives. On November 11, 2005, the *People's Daily* proclaimed, "In the information sector, China has trained dozens of media from 35 African countries for the past two years." The day before, the group Reporters without Borders released an analysis of Mugabe's media activities, finding that "the use of Chinese technology in a totally hypocritical and non-transparent fashion reveals the government's iron resolve to abolish freedom of opinion in Zimbabwe."

China's unwillingness to put any conditions on its assistance to Africa could undermine years of international efforts to link aid to better governance. Already, international corruption watchdogs like Global Witness have warned that China's $2 billion aid to Angola, given in advance and without pressure for poverty reduction, will allow the Angolan government to revert to its old habits, skimming the petroleum cream for itself. Today, the majority of Angola's roughly 13 million people still live in poverty, while elites have siphoned off much of the nation's oil wealth. Yet in November 2005, José Pedro de Morais, Angola's finance minister, said he expected future Chinese loans would exceed $2 billion. "When we ask our Chinese counterparts if they are willing to provide more loans, they say yes," he remarked.

More generally, the state-led business model that China suggests to visiting African leaders could prove problematic in Africa. Chinese firms with state links often have poor standards of corporate governance, including a lack of transparency. In Africa, Chinese firms, many of them owned by the Chinese state, have been known to submit bids below cost in an effort to break into a market. Examples include Asmara's Oratta Hospital in Eritrea and a $300 million hydroelectric dam and power plant on Ethiopia's Tekeze River.

Notably, the Tekeze project is behind schedule and the Ethiopian government is insisting the Chinese construction firm pay for the delays. Because of below-cost bids and a desire to save money, some of the buildings Chinese firms have built in Africa are already crumbling, leading to fears about whether much of the new

Chinese-built infrastructure will stand the test of time.

In China, this poor corporate governance has led to fiscal meltdowns. Yet the Chinese government, constrained by its need to demonstrate some rule of law to foreign investors, has managed to prosecute the most egregious white-collar criminals, including some corrupt officials. In Africa, where the rule of law often does not exist, China's state-led business model could prove a disaster, an invitation for rapacious governments and companies.

Competing Values

Ultimately, Africa will provide a test of whether Beijing can be a successful great power, exerting influence far from its borders. In some respects, China's influence may prove benign, as China shares burdens in Africa with other nations like the United States, becomes a greater source of investment in the continent, and funds much-needed aid programs.

Even as the United States has largely ignored African nations in UN forums, China has supported a range of proposals favored by African countries on UN Security Council reform, peace-keeping, and debt relief. In so doing, Chinese officials often portray Beijing as a champion of the developing world that listens to other countries, drawing an implicit contrast with the United States, which China portrays as uninterested in developing nations' needs. As Chinese Prime Minister Wen Jiabao put it, "As a permanent member of the UN Security Council, China will always stand side by side with developing countries in Africa and other parts of the world."

Yet Beijing's influence must be weighed in light of the fact that China, at least for now, does not share American values of democratization and good governance—in Africa or anywhere else. Because China's influence might constrain the existing powers in Africa, including the United States and France, the temptation may be to match some of China's efforts on the continent in order to win resources. But it is more important that the United States leverage its values, which are still more appealing to average Africans.

For the United States, China's growing role in Africa should be a wake-up call. Washington needs to convince both average Africans and their leaders that their future is better served, over the long term, by working more closely with the United States, the European Union, and international financial institutions. After all, a Chinese victory on the continent could come back to haunt the struggling residents of Maputo and other African capitals.

ASSESSING CHINA'S IMPACT IN LATIN AMERICA[*]

David Shambaugh

Latin America is a good prism through which to view several important features of China's global presence and activities. China's global engagement can be seen and measured along at least four dimensions, in the *diplomatic, commercial, cultural,* and *security* domains. China's presence and engagement in Central and Latin America and the Caribbean are really dominated by the commercial and diplomatic elements.

In other regions of the world the mix is slightly different: in Africa and Asia China's presence is more balanced among the other elements, as China is more present in the military/security arenas, its diplomacy is more active, and its "soft power" has greater appeal than in Latin America. China's presence in the Middle East, Central Asia, and Africa—as it is in Latin America—is driven to a large extent by commerce and its insatiable hunger for raw materials and energy supplies. In these

[*] Lecture delivered for Fundação Alexandre de Gusmão, Brazilian Ministry of Foreign Affairs (Itamarichy), Brasília, May 14, 2013.

regions, China's foreign policy is, to a large extent, a *function* of its economic needs. Other factors—such as multilateral diplomacy and China's soft power appeal—do play roles in these regions, but the dominant impetus for China's policy and presence is commercial and energy driven. In Europe, China's presence is largely diplomatic and commercial, while in the United States it has a combination of diplomatic, commercial, and security elements. In East Asia, China's presence is characterized by all four elements.

Thus, while China is now a global actor along these different dimensions, the actual mix of these elements varies by region. Let us take a look at each element in the case of the Latin American region.

China's expanded relations with Latin America and the Caribbean began in earnest in the late 1990s. Prior to that time, they were primarily based on a combination of diplomatically correct relations, minimal trade and reciprocal investment, and support for "liberation movements" and leftist states. Since the 1990s, though, they have taken off! China's approach, in my view, has been quite systematic, comprehensive, and rapid. It has also been strategic and coordinated. To my mind, China definitely does have a Latin American strategy. The question is: does Latin America have a China strategy? The answer is definitely "no." Indeed, Latin governments, the business communities, academia, and research institutes seem thoroughly unprepared for the complex challenges of coping with China's offensive into the region. Such an awareness is *beginning* to take shape in some of the larger Latin countries. As a result, Chinese is now being taught in universities, some more Confucius Institutes have opened, and the media is beginning to report on China.

Let us now turn to examine the several components of China's position in the region.

Diplomacy

Diplomatically, it must first be noted that Central America, the Caribbean, and Latin America still represent an area of nascent diplomatic competition with Taiwan. Eleven of the twenty-three nation-states in the world that still diplomatically recognize Taiwan lie in the region. Even though Beijing and Taipei have declared an unofficial "truce" in their diplomatic competition over the last few years as relations across the Taiwan Strait have improved, it is still an essential element of Beijing's regional strategy.

Another important element to bear in mind is that, like its ties in Africa and the Middle East, the Latin American region represents China's solidarity with developing countries as well as its desire to foster a multipolar world—so both sides tout their so-called South-South cooperation. Brazil is a key actor in both respects for Beijing, and vice versa. There is a real identity of international interests between Brasília and Beijing. This is manifest in the BRICS, but also G-77 bloc and elsewhere.

China has forged a variety of diplomatic "strategic partnerships" (no fewer than eight types!) with most countries in the region, and this designation provides an overarching framework to develop bilateral ties. Brazil's ties with China are particularly strong—perhaps the strongest of all Latin countries. In 2010, during a state visit by former Brazilian President Luiz Inacio Lula da Silva to Beijing, the two governments signed a Joint Action Plan 2020 to guide their "strategic partnership." Yet China has also managed to build sound relations with most other regional states—notably Argentina, Chile, Peru, Venezuela, Mexico, and Cuba.

High-level bilateral diplomacy is surprisingly active (if not always reported in the international media). During 1997–2010, more than 110 Latin American heads of state and government leaders visited China, while its president visited the region five times and a steady stream of Politburo-level leaders toured various Latin countries.

Multilaterally, Beijing is also active in a range of organizations in the region. In 2008 China became a full member of the Inter-American Development Bank, it joined the Caribbean Development Bank in 1997, and it has held permanent observer status in the Organization of American States (OAS) since 2004. China has held numerous rounds of dialogues with the Rio Group since 1990 and established a dialogue mechanism with the MERCOSUR common market group, as well as the Caribbean Community and Latin American Conference. China is a full member of the Asia-Pacific Economic Cooperation organization (APEC), and Beijing has initiated a series of separate forums with the region, including the China–Latin America Forum, the China-Caribbean Economic and Trade Cooperation Forum, the China–Latin America Common Market Dialogue, the China-Andean Community Consultation Forum, and the China–Latin American Business Summit. Through all of these multilateral mechanisms, China is now extensively linked multilaterally to the region. Thus, both bilaterally and multilaterally, China has built strong diplomatic and political ties throughout the Western Hemisphere.

In addition to state-to-state diplomacy, the CCP/International Department is also extremely—albeit quietly—active in exchanges with a range of political parties across the region (even in countries that diplomatically recognize Taiwan). The CCP now has working relations with more than eighty political parties in more than thirty countries in the region. This ties China not only to ruling parties but perhaps more importantly to opposition parties and politicians in waiting, so that when they come to power Beijing is already familiar with them (and vice versa). Party-to-party exchanges also give Beijing a good mechanism for intelligence collection. China engages as well in parliamentary exchanges with a number of Latin countries, although this is not nearly as widespread as party-to-party diplomacy.

Culture

China's cultural presence is also rising in the region. Chinese tourists are beginning to arrive in large numbers, a result of Beijing having signed group tourism accords with nineteen countries.

China is trying to raise its profile through several media initiatives. For example, the Spanish-language edition of China Daily (China Hoy) was launched in November 2011. There are also more than 100 pairs of sister province and city relationships between Chinese and Latin localities. Immigration is also growing. There are now, for example, thirty thousand ethnic Chinese living in Argentina, and a large number in Peru. Another element in China's attempts to increase its cultural exchanges in the region has been the establishment of 24 "Confucius Institutes" across the

region (out of 350 worldwide), while the Chinese government provides one thousand university scholarships for Latin students to study in China every year.

Numerous government-to-government cultural exchange accords have been agreed, and a variety of universities are beginning to sign their own MOUs as well. Nonetheless, the level of understanding in the academic world and throughout Latin societies remains abysmally low, and China has little real "soft power" attraction in the region.

Security

China's military-security presence in the Latin American region is not large, but it is growing. As US Deputy Assistant Secretary of Defense for Western Hemisphere Affairs said in a recent speech at the US National Defense University (April 30, 2013), "China's defense engagement appears at first glance to be a minor component . . . However, upon closer inspection, one finds that China's defense activities have grown over the past few years and now encompass a wide range of activities from weapons sales to defense dialogues, to ship visits, as well as exercises, and professional military education."[1] Beijing is very aware that there are already concerns in Washington concerning China's growing presence in the region and the military dimension is particularly sensitive, but this has not stopped China from gradually building up its security ties throughout the region. While this is occurring on a truly hemispheric basis, it seems to particularly be the case with the leftist ALBA countries (Bolivarian Alliance for the Americas): Venezuela, Cuba, Bolivia, Ecuador, as well as Argentina.

There are two main levels of this military-security presence in the region. The first is professional military exchanges, some of which are very high-level. For example, four members of China's Central Military Commission visited the region between 2008 and 2010—more than any other region of the world—while a steady stream of Latin defense ministers and service chiefs visit Beijing annually. Another example was the November 2012 first-ever "China–Latin America High-Level Defense Forum," which brought together officials from Bolivia, Cuba, Columbia, Ecuador, Peru, and Uruguay. China also trains Latin officers in its staff academies.

China's arms sales to, and imports from, the region are a second type. It sells a relatively small amount of weaponry and military equipment to Latin America—helicopters, artillery, armored personnel carriers, vehicles, K-8 trainer fighter aircraft, transport aircraft, radars and command and control equipment, anti-ship missiles (man portable), anti-aircraft missiles, night vision equipment, and light assault weapons—while buying avionics and antitank and anti-air missiles from Brazil. Some of the Sino-Brazilian aerospace cooperation is also military-related.

It is alleged that China may also have some access to former Soviet-built military intelligence communications facilities in Cuba, but this has not been established.

All in all, China's military-security presence in Latin America is gradually growing. As it does so, it is increasingly drawing the attention of the United States and its Central Command. Make no mistake: Washington is carefully monitoring China's security (and other) moves in the hemisphere!

Commerce

Commerce is by far the most important dimension of China's presence in Latin America. Trade has been growing almost exponentially, reaching $242 billion in 2011. This is a dramatic increase of more than twenty times since 2000, and the growth seems to be accelerating. It jumped 31.5 percent from 2010 to 2011. China is now the No. 1 trading partner of many Latin nations, having supplanted the United States. In 2010 China surpassed the United States as Brazil's largest trading partner ($56 billion). Brazil dominates regional trade with China, accounting for almost 40 percent of the total, while Mexico, Chile, Venezuela, and Argentina comprise Beijing's Top Five trade partners. Two-way trade has grown dramatically in recent years, but Latin America still accounts for only about 4 percent of China's total foreign trade. Although Brazil is China's largest export market in Latin America, it ranks only as China's number twenty trading partner.

In terms of trade composition, though, it is heavily concentrated and not well diversified. The trade is dominated by Chinese purchases of raw materials and agricultural commodities (70 percent). China imports large amounts and a wide range of minerals, energy supplies, and raw materials from Latin America. China's voracious appetite for raw materials has contributed to high global prices for these commodities (and has provided a significant revenue stream for Argentina, Brazil, Chile, and Peru). Today China consumes about 40 percent of the world's coal, 25 percent of the nickel, 25 percent of iron ores, 20 percent of copper ores, and 14 percent of aluminum. China is the world's leading importer of iron ore and number two of copper. It also buys large amounts of agricultural products, fish, and wine from the region, along with accounting for 40 percent of global soybean imports. About 80 percent of China's imported fish meal comes from Peru and Chile, while 80 percent of its sugar comes from Cuba. Argentina is also a significant source of meats and leather goods for the Chinese market.

In return, Latin countries purchase a range of manufactured goods, especially electronics (largely cell phones and computers). Large Chinese exports of textiles, footwear, and other low-end consumer goods have hit several Latin economies hard, particularly Mexico and Argentina. There is also evidence of China's dumping these goods on Latin markets, taking advantage of Market Economy Status (MES) accords China has managed to sign with fifteen Latin countries. Many of these countries signed these accords unwittingly, as Chinese diplomats told them they were a "normal" part of bilateral "strategic partnerships." In fact, MES status exempts China from countervailing dumping duties. As a result, Mexico and Argentina have had to institute unilateral safeguards against the flood of Chinese goods since 2007.

Gradually, China is beginning to move up the technological ladder in its regional trade in Latin America, trading in autos, motorcycles, aircraft and aircraft parts, electronics, and agro-, bio-, nano-, and information technologies. As it does so, it may begin to alleviate the competitive dynamic in low-end manufactured goods.

To facilitate trade, China has signed bilateral FTAs with Chile, Peru, and Costa Rica. Creative trade financing is also an interesting new area. Beijing struck a $10 billion arrangement with Buenos Aires that permits Argentina reliable access to Chinese currency to pay for its imports from China. This deal follows similar ones Beijing has struck with South Korea, Indonesia, and Belarus.

China is also increasing its direct investment in the region (16 percent of worldwide ODI), becoming the second-largest destination for Chinese ODI after Asia. The Ministry of Commerce reported $7.3 billion in 2009, of which the vast majority of the financial flow was into tax havens in the British Virgin Islands ($1.61 billion) and the Grand Cayman Islands ($5.36 billion). The total stock of Chinese ODI in the region at the end of 2009 was $30.5 billion. The Economic Commission for Latin America and the Caribbean (ECLAC) provides higher figures, however, reporting that Chinese ODI into the region was $15 billion in 2010. This represents approximately 10 percent of the total foreign investment in the region.

To date, most of China's non-financial ODI has been in the mining, energy, and agricultural sectors. Given China's hunger for natural resources, and Latin America's fairly well-developed infrastructure, there is also potential for joint ventures in manufacturing. China's purchase of real estate—particularly farmland—is also likely to grow. As a result of these synergies, ODI into the region is likely to continue to grow at a steady pace in future years.

Finally, China's overseas development assistance (ODA)—or aid—in the region is relatively miniscule. It is estimated at 10 percent of China's estimated $2.5 billion worldwide. But the line between ODA and ODI is a fine one for China, as its construction companies are very active in Caribbean nations and elsewhere.

Conclusion

In all of these dimensions, China's footprint in Latin America and the Caribbean is growing, and growing quickly. China's regional diplomacy is fully in service of its commercial interests. This cannot be overstated.

Despite this rapidly expanding footprint, though, Beijing remains wary of Washington—and Washington is keeping a close eye on China's activities in the region.

Beijing is aware of Washington's scrutiny of its activities in the region and has gone out of its way not to establish a military presence in the region or draw too close to certain regimes. For example, it kept its distance from the Chavez regime in Venezuela; has not been directly involved in supporting insurgencies, socialist movements, or far-left-leaning governments; has maintained a very low level of arms sales in the region; has not established any kind of military presence in the region; and, while being supportive of Havana, has kept its ties with Cuba at a relatively low profile.

Irrespective of US concerns, China's presence in Latin America is only going to continue to grow over time. Whether Beijing's burgeoning foothold will continue to be welcomed, though, remains an open question. What Washington and Beijing can usefully do is to increase and deepen their bilateral dialogue on the region (it currently occurs about once every two years, while it should be twice *per year*).

Public opinion polls show a steady decline in China's favorability ratings in the region since 2007. In 2011, the BBC found that only 55 percent of Brazilians and a paltry 23 percent of Mexicans polled held positive views of China. Its image in Mexico has long been negative, owing to economic competition and unbalanced trade (in 2009 Mexico imported $31.9 billion in goods from China, while exporting only $2.2 billion), and similarly mixed views are now commonplace in Argentina, Chile, Peru, and Colombia. As in Africa, China's declining image is largely the result of its investments in the natural resource and raw materials sectors, and dumping of low-end manufactured goods on Latin markets. The growing impression across the developing world of China as a mercantilist trader and neocolonial extractor is going to be a difficult image for Beijing to cope with.

Recent polling data from the Latin American Public Opinion Project at Vanderbilt University, however, provides both a broader sampling and a more upbeat image of China in the America's. I commend this recent survey to you, as it provides some nuanced and interesting findings. Still, however, the United States is seen as twice as influential as China by a cross-section of Latin publics.

This "snapshot" of different dimensions of China's rapidly growing presence and activities in the western hemisphere clearly indicates that China's presence is growing quickly in many dimensions. This trend can only be expected to continue in the years to come.

NOTES

1. Walter E. Earle, "China's Strategic Engagement in the Americas: Implications for U.S. and Partner Nation Interests," Speech at the National Defense University, Washington, DC, April 30, 2013.

THE BRICS AND CHINA'S ASPIRATION FOR THE NEW "INTERNATIONAL ORDER"[*]

Yun Sun

The destinations of new Chinese leader's first foreign tour are always carefully chosen and reflect two things. First, they are important countries and represent certain foreign policy priorities for China. Second, they are China-friendly, therefore the new leader will be met with open arms and a warm welcome rather than difficult questions or a long list of demands. Russia, China's close neighbor and former ally, fits the profile and has been the first destination for both former President Hu Jintao in 2003 and for Xi Jinping this year. However, a decade ago, Hu focused on China's periphery—Russia, Kazakhstan, and Mongolia—while today Xi is taking China's agenda further away. With the exception of Russia, Xi's foreign tour focuses on Africa: specifically Tanzania, South Africa, and the Republic of the Congo. The highlight is the fifth BRICS (Brazil, Russia, India, China, and South Africa) summit in Durban, South Africa from March 26–27, 2013.

The unprecedented level of emphasis the new Chinese leader is attaching to the BRICS nations reflects the profound changes in China's perceptions of itself and of the outside world. In the past decade, China has grown into the second largest economy in the world. However, this economic muscle is yet to be translated into comprehensive national power and the United States, despite its relative decline, remains the sole superpower in China's foreign policy lexicon. As the US rebalances to Asia, China feels a heightened pressure in its immediate periphery from Washington's enhanced military deployment, alliances and "interference" in China's territorial disputes. As the new Chinese leaders contemplate how to break away from this new "containment and encirclement of China," the reliance on and cooperation with non-Western, rising economic powers are of high importance for China.

China sees natural common ground with emerging economies, especially in the pursuit of a new international economic order and the democratization of international relations. In Beijing's view, the 2008 financial crisis dramatically changed the mapping of the world economy, deeply damaging the strength of the traditional developed countries. The economic recovery of the US and Japan has been sluggish, while the eurozone crisis has lingered on for years. The relatively impressive momentum for growth comes from emerging economies, especially the BRICS nations.

[*] This article was published on the Brookings Institution website, March 25, 2013: http://www.brookings.edu/blogs/upfront/posts/2013/03/25-xi-jinping-china-brics-sun.

For China, since the BRICS countries' share and importance in the world economy has been growing but has not yet surpassed the developed countries', the next step, naturally, would be for them to act as one group to increase their collective voice and bargaining power against traditional developed countries. In China's view, this momentum would democratize international relations by offering developing counties more voice and rights. As Xi pointed out in his interview with journalists from BRICS nations right before his trip on March 19, the international economic governance system must reflect the profound changes of the global economic reality, and emerging markets/developing countries deserve more representation and bigger voices. The reform of voting rights at the IMF and World Bank signifies the direction to which China aspires—in Beijing's dictionary, more responsibility is only justified when it is accompanied with more rights.

China also wishes to strengthen its identity as an emerging economy and a developing country by enhancing its contribution to the BRICS nations and their international status. Xi pledged to deepen the cooperative partnership and improve the cooperation mechanism among the BRICS nations. One possible major move would be the potential plan for the BRICS countries to establish their own development bank to provide funding assistance to Africa's infrastructure development. If this plan transpires, it would demonstrate a major advancement by China in the field of international development assistance. By forming a *de facto* alliance among themselves, BRICS nations will gain more legitimacy and increase competitiveness for their development assistance, which is often criticized and even marginalized by traditional donors.

Xi's first overseas trip reveals the international quagmire China is in. The past 10 years witnessed unprecedented growth of Chinese economy, but it was also accompanied by unparalleled foreign policy challenges. As many Chinese analysts observed, China's external environment did not improve as a result of China's rise; instead, it has worsened. China has become richer, but less respected. It has more transactions with the world than ever, but less friends.

Therefore, Xi's trip to Russia, Africa, and the BRICS summit genuinely reflects China's strategic moves to break away from this predicament. It seeks to reconsolidate friendship with a Russia also antagonized by the West, with Africa to reinforce its developing-country identity and solidarity with the developing world, and with other emerging economies to align their collective power against the traditional developed countries. China learned its lesson that it is yet to be strong enough to challenge the existing international order (and the supremacy of the US) alone. Alignment with other rising powers, like the BRICS countries, and reinforcement of its friendship base among developing countries will be a new emphasis for China's foreign policy in the foreseeable future.

VI. GLOBAL GOVERNANCE

Whither China: From Membership to Responsibility?[*]

Robert B. Zoellick

Earlier this year, I had the pleasure of making the acquaintance of Mr. Zheng Bijian, Chair of the China Reform Forum, who over some decades

[*] Remarks by the Deputy Secretary of State to National Committee on US-China Relations, New York City, September 21, 2005.

has been a counselor to China's leaders. We have spent many hours in Beijing and Washington discussing China's course of development and Sino-American relations. It has been my good fortune to get to know such a thoughtful man who has helped influence, through the Central

Party School, the outlook of many officials during a time of tremendous change for China.

This month, in anticipation of President Hu's visit to the United States, Mr. Zheng published the lead article in *Foreign Affairs*, "China's 'Peaceful Rise' to Great Power Status." This evening, I would like to give you a sense of the current dialogue between the United States and China by sharing my perspective.

Some 27 years ago, Chinese leaders took a hard look at their country and didn't like what they saw. China was just emerging from the Cultural Revolution. It was desperately poor, deliberately isolated from the world economy, and opposed to nearly every international institution. Under Deng Xiaoping, as Mr. Zheng explains, China's leaders reversed course and decided "to embrace globalization rather than detach themselves from it."

Seven US presidents of both parties recognized this strategic shift and worked to integrate China as a full member of the international system. Since 1978, the United States has also encouraged China's economic development through market reforms.

Our policy has succeeded remarkably well: the dragon emerged and joined the world. Today, from the United Nations to the World Trade Organization, from agreements on ozone depletion to pacts on nuclear weapons, China is a player at the table.

And China has experienced exceptional economic growth. Whether in commodities, clothing, computers, or capital markets, China's presence is felt every day. China is big, it is growing, and it will influence the world in the years ahead. For the United States and the world, the essential question is—how will China use its influence?

To answer that question, it is time to take our policy beyond opening doors to China's membership into the international system: We need to urge China to become a *responsible stakeholder* in that system.

China has a responsibility to strengthen the international system that has enabled its success. In doing so, China could achieve the objective identified by Mr. Zheng: "to transcend the traditional ways for great powers to emerge." As Secretary Rice has stated, the United States welcomes a confident, peaceful, and prosperous China, one that appreciates that its growth and development depends on constructive connections with the rest of the world. Indeed, we hope to intensify work with a China that not only adjusts to the international rules developed over the last century, but also joins us and others to address the challenges of the new century. From China's perspective, it would seem that its national interest would be much better served by working with us to shape the future international system.

If it isn't clear why the United States should suggest a cooperative relationship with China, consider the alternatives. Picture the wide range of global challenges we face in the years ahead— terrorism and extremists exploiting Islam, the proliferation of weapons of mass destruction, poverty, disease—and ask whether it would be easier or harder to handle those problems if the United States and China were cooperating or at odds.

For fifty years, our policy was to *fence in* the Soviet Union while its own internal contradictions undermined it. For thirty years, our policy has been to *draw out* the People's Republic of China. As a result, the China of today is simply not the Soviet Union of the late 1940s:

- It does not seek to spread radical, anti-American ideologies.
- While not yet democratic, it does not see itself in a twilight conflict against democracy around the globe.
- While at times mercantilist, it does not see itself in a death struggle with capitalism.
- And most importantly, China does not believe that its future depends on overturning the fundamental order of the international system. In fact, quite the reverse: Chinese leaders have decided that their success depends on being networked with the modern world.

If the Cold War analogy does not apply, neither does the distant balance-of-power politics of 19th Century Europe. The global economy of the 21st Century is a tightly woven fabric. We are too interconnected to try to hold China at arm's length, hoping to promote other powers in Asia at its expense. Nor would the other powers hold China at bay, initiating and terminating ties based on an old model of drawing-room diplomacy. The United States seeks constructive relations with all countries that do not threaten peace and security.

So if the templates of the past do not fit, how should we view China at the dawn of the 21st Century?

On both sides, there is a gulf in perceptions. The overwhelming priority of China's senior officials is to develop and modernize a China that still faces enormous internal challenges. While proud of their accomplishments, China's leaders recognize their country's perceived weaknesses, its rural poverty, and the challenges of political and social change. Two-thirds of China's population—nearly 900 million people—are in poor rural areas, living mostly as subsistence farmers, and 200 million Chinese live on less than a dollar a day. In China, economic growth is seen as an internal imperative, not as a challenge to the United States.

Therefore, China clearly needs a benign international environment for its work at home. Of course, the Chinese expect to be treated with respect and will want to have their views and interests recognized. But China does not want a conflict with the United States.

Nevertheless, many Americans worry that the Chinese dragon will prove to be a fire-breather.

There is a cauldron of anxiety about China. The US business community, which in the 1990s saw China as a land of opportunity, now has a more mixed assessment. Smaller companies worry about Chinese competition, rampant piracy, counterfeiting, and currency manipulation. Even larger US businesses—once the backbone of support for economic engagement—are concerned that mercantilist Chinese policies will try to direct controlled markets instead of opening competitive markets. American workers wonder if they can compete.

China needs to recognize how its actions are perceived by others. China's involvement with troublesome states indicates at best a blindness to consequences and at worst something more ominous. China's actions—combined with a lack of transparency—can create risks. Uncertainties about how China will use its power will lead the United States—and others as well—to hedge relations with China. Many countries hope China will pursue a "peaceful rise," but none will bet their future on it. For example, China's rapid military modernization and increases in capabilities raise questions about the purposes of this buildup and China's lack of transparency. The recent report by the US Department of Defense on China's military posture was not confrontational, although China's reaction to it was. The US report described facts, including what we know about China's military, and discussed alternative scenarios. If China wants to lessen anxieties, it should openly explain its defense spending, intentions, doctrine, and military exercises.

Views about China are also shaped by its growing economic footprint. China has gained much from its membership in an open, rules-based international economic system, and the US market is particularly important for China's development strategy. Many gain from this trade, including millions of US farmers and workers who produce the commodities, components, and capital goods that China is so voraciously consuming.

But no other country—certainly not those of the European Union or Japan—would accept a $162 billion bilateral trade deficit, contributing to a $665 billion global current account deficit. China—and others that sell to China—cannot take its access to the US market for granted. Protectionist pressures are growing. China has been more open than many developing countries, but there are increasing signs of mercantilism, with policies that seek to direct markets rather than opening them.

The United States will not be able to sustain an open international economic system—or domestic US support for such a system—without greater cooperation from China, as a stakeholder that shares responsibility on international economic issues. For example, a responsible major global player shouldn't tolerate rampant theft of intellectual property and counterfeiting, both of which strike at the heart of America's knowledge economy. China's pledges—including a statement just last week by President Hu in New York—to crack down on the criminals who ply this trade are welcome, but the results are not yet evident. China needs to fully live up to its commitments to markets where America has a strong competitive advantage, such as in services, agriculture, and certain manufactured goods. And while China's exchange rate policy offered stability in the past, times have changed. China may have a global current account surplus this year of nearly $150 billion, among the highest in the world. This suggests that China's recent policy adjustments are an initial step, but much more remains to be done to permit markets to adjust to imbalances. China also shares a strong interest with the United States in negotiating a successful WTO Doha agreement that opens markets and expands global growth.

China's economic growth is driving its thirst for energy. In response, China is acting as if it can somehow "lock up" energy supplies around the world. This is not a sensible path to achieving energy security. Moreover, a mercantilist strategy leads to partnerships with regimes that hurt China's reputation and lead others to question its intentions. In contrast, market strategies can lessen volatility, instability, and hoarding. China should work with the United States and others to develop diverse sources of energy, including through clean coal technology, nuclear, renewables, hydrogen, and biofuels. Our new Asia Pacific Partnership on Clean Development and Climate—as well as the bilateral dialogue conducted by the US Department of Energy and China's National Development and Reform Commission—offer practical mechanisms for this cooperation. We should also encourage the opening of oil and gas production in more places around the world. We can work on energy conservation and efficiency, including through standards for the many appliances made in China. Through the IEA we can strengthen the building and management of strategic reserves. We also have a common interest in secure transport routes and security in producing countries.

All nations conduct diplomacy to promote their national interests. Responsible stakeholders go further: They recognize that the international system sustains their peaceful prosperity, so they work to sustain that system. In its foreign policy, China has many opportunities to be a responsible stakeholder.

The most pressing opportunity is North Korea. Since hosting the Six-Party Talks at their inception in 2003, China has played a constructive role. This week we achieved a Joint Statement of Principles, with an agreement on the goal of "verifiable denuclearization of the Korean peninsula in a peaceful manner." But the hard work of implementation lies ahead, and China should share our interest in effective and comprehensive compliance. Moreover, the North Korea problem is about more than just the spread of dangerous weapons. Without broad economic and political reform, North Korea poses a threat to itself and others. It is time to move beyond the half-century-old armistice on the Korean peninsula to a true peace, with regional security and development. A Korean peninsula without nuclear weapons opens the door to this future. Some 30 years ago America ended its war in Vietnam. Today Vietnam looks to the United States to help integrate it into the world market economic system so Vietnam can improve the lives of its people. By contrast, North Korea, with a 50-year-old cold armistice, just falls further behind.

Beijing also has a strong interest in working with us to halt the proliferation of weapons of mass destruction and missiles that can deliver them. The proliferation of danger will undermine the benign security environment and healthy international economy that China needs for its development. China's actions on Iran's nuclear program will reveal the seriousness of China's commitment to non-proliferation. And while we welcome China's efforts to police its own behavior through new export controls on sensitive technology, we still need to see tough legal punishments for violators.

China and the United States can do more together in the global fight against terrorism. Chinese citizens have been victims of terror attacks in Pakistan and Afghanistan. China can help destroy the supply lines of global terrorism. We have made a good start by working together at the UN and searching for terrorist money in Chinese banks, but can expand our cooperation further. China pledged $150 million in assistance to Afghanistan, and $25 million to Iraq. These pledges were welcome, and we look forward to their full implementation. China would build stronger ties with both through follow-on pledges. Other countries are assisting the new Iraqi government with major debt forgiveness, focusing attention on the $7 billion in Iraqi debt still held by Chinese state companies.

On my early morning runs in Khartoum, I saw Chinese doing *tai chi* exercises. I suspect they were in Sudan for the oil business. But China should take more than oil from Sudan—it should take some responsibility for resolving Sudan's human crisis. It could work with the United States, the UN, and others to support the African Union's peacekeeping mission, to provide humanitarian relief to Darfur, and to promote a solution to Sudan's conflicts.

In Asia, China is already playing a larger role. The United States respects China's interests in the region, and recognizes the useful role of multilateral diplomacy in Asia. But concerns will grow if China seeks to maneuver toward a predominance of power. Instead, we should work together with ASEAN, Japan, Australia, and others for regional security and prosperity through the ASEAN Regional Forum and the Asia Pacific Economic Cooperation forum.

China's choices about Taiwan will send an important message, too. We have made clear that our "One China" policy remains based on the three communiques and the Taiwan Relations Act. It is important for China to resolve its differences with Taiwan peacefully.

The United States, Japan, and China will need to cooperate effectively together on both regional and global challenges. Given China's terrible losses in World War II, I appreciate the sensitivity of historical issues with Japan. But as I have told my Chinese colleagues, I have observed some sizeable gaps in China's telling of history, too. When I visited the "9.18" museum at the site of the 1931 "Manchurian Incident," I noted that the chronological account jumped from 1941 to the Soviet offensive against Japan in August 1945, overlooking the United States' involvement in the Pacific from 1941 to 1945! Perhaps we could start to ease some misapprehensions by opening a three-way dialogue among historians.

Clearly, there are many common interests and opportunities for cooperation. But some say America's commitment to democracy will preclude long-term cooperation with China. Let me suggest why this need not be so.

Freedom lies at the heart of what America is ... as a nation, we stand for what President Bush calls the non-negotiable demands of human dignity. As I have seen over the 25 years since I lived in Hong Kong, Asians have also pressed for more freedom and built many more democracies. Indeed, President Hu and Premier Wen are talking about the importance of China strengthening the rule of law and developing democratic institutions.

We do not urge the cause of freedom to weaken China. To the contrary, President Bush has stressed that the terrible experience of 9/11 has driven home that in the absence of freedom, unhealthy societies will breed deadly cancers. In his Second Inaugural, President Bush recognized that democratic institutions must reflect the values and culture of diverse societies. As he said, "Our goal . . . is to help others find their own voice, attain their own freedom, and make their own way."

Being born ethnically Chinese does not predispose people against democracy—just look at Taiwan's vibrant politics. Japan and South Korea have successfully blended a Confucian heritage with modern democratic principles. Closed politics cannot be a permanent feature of Chinese society. It is simply not sustainable—as economic growth continues, better-off Chinese will want a greater say in their future, and pressure builds for political reform:

- China has one umbrella labor union, but waves of strikes.
- A party that came to power as a movement of peasants now confronts violent rural protests, especially against corruption.
- A government with massive police powers cannot control spreading crime.

Some in China believe they can secure the Communist Party's monopoly on power through emphasizing economic growth and heightened nationalism. This is risky and mistaken. China needs a peaceful political transition to make its government responsible and accountable to its people. Village and grassroots elections are a start. They might be expanded—perhaps to counties and provinces—as a next step. China needs to reform its judiciary. It should open government processes to the involvement of civil society and stop harassing journalists who point out problems. China should also expand religious freedom and make real the guarantees of rights that exist on paper—but not in practice.

Ladies and Gentlemen: How we deal with China's rising power is a central question in American foreign policy. In China and the United States, Mr. Zheng's idea of a "peaceful rise" will spur vibrant debate. The world will look to the evidence of actions.

Tonight I have suggested that the US response should be to help foster constructive action by transforming our thirty-year policy of integration: We now need to encourage China to become a responsible stakeholder in the international system. As a responsible stakeholder, China would be more than just a member—it would work with us to sustain the international system that has enabled its success. Cooperation as stakeholders will not mean the absence of differences—we will have disputes that we need to manage. But that management can take place within a larger framework where the parties recognize a shared interest in sustaining political, economic, and security systems that provide common benefits.

To achieve this transformation of the Sino-American relationship, this administration—and those that follow it—will need to build the foundation of support at home. That's particularly why

I wanted to join you tonight. You hear the voices that perceive China solely through the lens of fear. But America succeeds when we look to the future as an opportunity, not when we fear what the future might bring. To succeed now, we will need all of you to press both the Chinese and your fellow citizens.

When President Nixon visited Beijing in 1972, our relationship with China was defined by what we were both *against*. Now we have the opportunity to define our relationship by what are both *for*.

We have many common interests with China. But relationships built only on a coincidence of interests have shallow roots. Relationships built on shared interests *and* shared values are deep and lasting. We can cooperate with the emerging China of today, even as we work for the democratic China of tomorrow.

CHINA AND THE UNITED NATIONS: THE STAKEHOLDER SPECTRUM[*]

Michael Fullilove

In December 2009, representatives of 192 nations—not to mention thousands of journalists, activists, and business executives—assembled in Copenhagen for the 15th Conference of the Parties to the United Nations Framework Convention on Climate Change (UNFCCC). The goal was to strike a new international agreement to replace the Kyoto Protocol, due to expire in 2012—one that would lead to meaningful reductions of greenhouse gas emissions.[1] Expectations were great, and it was evident that one of the key players would be the People's Republic of China. After all, China—the world's largest emitter of greenhouse gases[2]—has taken huge strides in the past decade, toughening up its environment protection laws, fighting pollution, planting forests, and investing aggressively in renewables and energy efficiency. In the lead-up to Copenhagen, China announced it would cut

its carbon intensity by 40–45 percent below 2005 levels by 2020.[3]

In the end, Copenhagen was a flop. No binding treaty covering both developed and developing countries was established, nor was a deadline set for reaching such an agreement. No global target for 2050 was created. Major emitters reached an accord that committed the world to halting the rise in global temperatures to two degrees Celsius, but the measures it contained were insufficient to deliver that outcome.

There were many reasons for the disappointment of Copenhagen, but in the public mind at least, China bore a good deal of responsibility. Beijing's aversion to quantifiable commitments led it to oppose one that didn't even apply to China directly, namely the critical pledge that by 2050 rich countries would cut emissions by 80 percent compared to 1990 levels. China and other high-emitting developing states opposed the principle of international verification, agreeing only to "international consultations and

[*] This article was published in *The Washington Quarterly* (August 2011).

analysis." The Chinese argued for removing references to Copenhagen as a way-stage on the path to a legally binding treaty. China's representatives hardly acquitted themselves well in the conference venue either, with Premier Wen Jiabao dodging important meetings with US President Barack Obama and sending a more junior official instead.[4] Britain's then–Climate Change Minister, Ed Miliband, called China out on its behavior, leading China's Foreign Ministry to reply: "The remarks against China by an individual British politician contained obvious political schemes to shirk responsibilities toward the developing countries and provoke discord among the developing countries."[5] That politician is now Britain's shadow Prime Minister. A widely cited article in *The Guardian* was headed: "How do I know China wrecked the Copenhagen deal? I was in the room."[6]

China's predicament in Copenhagen illustrated in miniature many of the features of China's awkward relationship with the United Nations: the high hopes; the genuine, often startling, progress; the continuing disconnect between China's weight and its strategy; the conflicting desires to be seen as a great power and a poor country; the tacking between arrogance and uncertainty; and the hurt feelings on both sides when expectations are crushed. Copenhagen put the following question in front of the international community: how far has China progressed toward achieving the status of a "responsible stakeholder," urged on it by then–US Deputy Secretary of State Robert Zoellick in 2005?[7] Examining China's approach to the UN could help answer that question. The research for this article, which was supported by the Australia–China Council, included two dozen confidential interviews conducted in 2009–2010 in Beijing, New York and Washington, DC.

Is China a Power or a Player?

Any account of recent shifts in Beijing's foreign policy behavior has to begin with its deeply impressive economic performance. In three decades, China has remade its economy, driven extraordinary productivity increases, and in so doing raised hundreds of millions of people out of poverty. Now this country of 1.3 billion people is achieving an economic weight befitting its huge size. In 2009, its gross domestic product (GDP) was the third largest in the world in dollar terms; if measured in terms of purchasing power parity, it was the second largest. Annual GDP growth in the last five years has averaged more than 11 percent. China is the third largest importer and second largest exporter in world merchandise trade. The country is laying roads and high-speed rail, building airports, and expanding shipping at a frenetic pace. In 2011, its hoard of foreign exchange reserves passed the $3 trillion mark—more than double the amount of second-placed Japan. The historian Paul Kennedy has predicted that by the time the UN celebrates its centenary in 2045, "China could well constitute the largest economic and productive force in the world, bigger even than the United States."[8]

China's economic strength is mirrored in its growing military capabilities. The United States' 2010 Quadrennial Defense Review recorded that "China is developing and fielding large numbers of advanced medium-range ballistic and cruise missiles, new attack submarines equipped with advanced weapons, increasingly capable long-range air defense systems, electronic warfare and computer network attack capabilities, advanced fighter aircraft, and counter space systems." These developments boost China's ability to project power within East Asia and around the world.[9]

While China has arrived as a great power, that does not necessarily mean that it is destined for global or even regional hegemony, as some enthusiasts maintain. China's facade conceals some worrying divisions, including those between rich and poor as well as between the coast and interior. As German strategist Josef Joffe observes, China needs to resolve "the pernicious dynamics of authoritarian modernization—war, revolution, and upheaval—that eventually befell imperial Germany, Japan, and Russia." It also needs to manage two awkward demographic realities: the country has become powerful while many of its people remain poor, and it will get old before it gets rich. Still, even if we don't credit straight-line projections, one thing is clear: China is a global player, with vast implications for the international system.[10]

China has a strong hand; how it will play that hand in the future is not so obvious. There is a notable dualism to China's approach. On one hand, Deng Xiaoping bade his countrymen to keep their heads down and their eyes on the prize of economic development. Deng's so-called 24-character strategy was: "Observe calmly; secure our position; cope with affairs calmly; hide our capacities and bide our time; be good at maintaining a low profile; and never claim leadership." Even as this approach has given way to the newer Chinese foreign policy doctrines of "peaceful rise" and "harmonious world," the Chinese leadership remains overwhelmingly focused on domestic issues.[11] One Chinese interviewee told the author: "Beijing is not psychologically ready to be an active global player."[12]

In their recent paper *Global Governance 2025*, the US National Intelligence Council and the EU Institute of Strategic Studies reported: "Many of our Chinese interlocutors see mounting global challenges and fundamental defects in the international system but emphasize the need for China to deal with its internal problems."[13] The Chinese Communist Party's first priority is regime continuity, which rests on a stable society, a viable economy, and GDP growth sufficient to keep unemployment down. One Beijing observer even asserted to this author that "all of the leadership's top ten issues are domestic."[14] For much of the time, China's external preoccupations are to prevent other powers from trespassing on what it regards as its domestic issues—such as Taiwan and Tibet—and to secure the energy and other resources necessary to power growth. Chinese foreign policy is neither expansionist nor extreme; in many ways, China has been slow to claim the influence it clearly deserves.

On the other hand, it is impossible to miss China's rising confidence and international ambition, even if they sit alongside strains of caution and insecurity. In the past decade, China has expanded its clout in Southeast Asia; thickened its ties with US treaty allies such as South Korea and Australia; and extended its influence in Africa, Latin America, the Middle East, and in new Asian institutions such as the East Asia Summit and the Shanghai Cooperation Organization. One American China-watcher observed to this author that global issues such as international architecture and the world economy have moved to the center of discussions between Washington and Beijing.[15]

This may now be the most important bilateral relationship in the world.

Sometimes, Chinese assertiveness spills over into bluster. Some long-time observers are pessimistic about the direction of Chinese foreign policy. Scholar David Shambaugh has noted that in 2010 frictions manifested in many of China's relationships: with Europe and India, with countries in Southeast Asia, Latin America, and Africa—even with Russia. The US relationship has proven bumpy. Beijing stage-managed President Obama's 2009 visit to China in a way that minimized Obama's effect on his Chinese audience and complicated things for him with his American audience. China snubbed Defense Secretary Robert Gates over relatively routine matters such as the president's meeting with the Dalai Lama and Taiwan arms sales. Meanwhile, the relationship with Tokyo suffered a significant setback after Japan's Coast Guard detained a Chinese trawler captain in the East China Sea near the disputed Senkaku/Diaoyu Islands. China's uncompromising response, including the suspension of ministerial talks and (reportedly) halting rare earth exports, elevated a third-order issue to a matter that had to be resolved by the heads of government.[16]

The explanations for this passage of behavior are diverse, including the ongoing leadership transition, Chinese nationalism, and the country's successful navigation of the global financial crisis. A recent Stockholm International Peace Research Institute (SIPRI) policy paper by Linda Jakobson and Dean Knox makes a powerful argument for the increasing pluralization of Chinese foreign policy, as authority over the policymaking process fractures and the leadership is required to accommodate various institutions, factions, and ideologies. Certainly, there is an uneven quality to China's present foreign policy: usually quiet but occasionally strident; usually cautious but occasionally combative; always prickly; and never entirely predictable.[17]

China and the United Nations

The same ambivalence is evident in China's relations with the international organization. China has quickened the pace of its interactions with the

UN in recent decades, exerting increasing influence in UN forums on matters it cares about. Yet, it has so far refused to assume the responsibilities incumbent upon a global power, and to nurture the international system it hopes to help to lead.

The clashes between Chinese and UN forces in the Korean War and the occupation of the China seat at the UN by Taiwan aroused a great deal of hostility in the People's Republic toward the UN. Since Beijing acquired the seat in 1971, however, the acrimony has faded and it has steadily joined specialist organs and acceded to treaties. Samuel Kim charted the progression of its approaches, from "system-transforming" prior to 1971 to "system-reforming" in the 1980s to "system-maintaining" in the 1990s. From the mid-1990s, this progression has accelerated.[18]

The Chinese began to appreciate two particular advantages the UN offers them as an arena for power politics. First, the UN's structural design tends to mitigate unipolarity: in the General Assembly, the United States is one of a multitude; even in the Security Council, it is at best first among equals. Second, the UN is hierarchical—and China is on the top rung of the hierarchy. Professor Rosemary Foot notes that Beijing "values the status benefits it derives from permanent membership of the Security Council, and especially the influence that comes with the privilege of the veto."[19]

The Stakeholder Spectrum

How should we assess China's current mode of engagement with the UN? The approach differs depending on the issue. One can draw a continuum of China's UN behavior, on which the position of a policy or tool is determined by the degree of openness to, engagement with, and burden-sharing on behalf of the international organization. Let's call it China's "stakeholder spectrum."

Diplomats At the end of the spectrum denoting maximum engagement, we can place the issue of the caliber of China's UN diplomats. There is no question that the quality of people China sends to New York, both as diplomats and officials, has improved markedly. Thirty years ago, argues

Shambaugh, "China's representatives rarely said a word—and when they did speak it was pure propagandistic rhetoric carefully prepared in Beijing. No press conferences were offered to foreign media, at home or abroad." Kim quoted one UN representative describing the old approach like this: "They come. They smile. They leave."[20] Five years ago, a UN insider told this author: "Beijing's representatives used to be woefully unqualified, faceless apparatchiks. Now they are very sharp. China used to take a prophylactic approach to placing people in the UN, asking 'how can we protect our people from outside influence?' Now they want to spread their influence." This year, another remarked that China's diplomats are "extraordinarily sophisticated and capable," with "a clear strategic vision." A diplomat from a Permanent Five (P5) country told this author "they will ride their instructions from Beijing" in order to strike deals they believe are in the Chinese interest.[21]

Elements of the old mentality still persist. In September 2010, China's most senior UN official, Under-Secretary-General for Economic and Social Affairs Sha Zukang, was forced to apologize after a toast he offered to Secretary-General Ban Ki-moon at an alpine retreat descended into a drunken tirade against the UN, Americans, and Ban himself.[22] Yet Sha's behavior was the exception that proved the rule. In general, China's representatives have become much more skillful at promoting their country's interests at headquarters and contributing to the organization's work.

Whether the newer generations have noticeably different views on foreign policy is another question, and one on which interviewees differed. Several think-tankers expressed the view that younger officials are less orthodox in their thinking and more likely to recognize "the legitimacy quotient" in being a global power. But P5 officials interviewed by this author thought otherwise. One volunteered that "a generational divide does not show up in meetings. Junior and mid-level Chinese diplomats are often franker than their elders but they are also well-trained and obedient."[23]

Peacekeeping Also toward the engagement end of the spectrum is China's contribution to UN peacekeeping. This may be the field in which

Beijing has moved the furthest toward engagement with the organization. Prior to admission and even into the 1970s, Beijing was apt to characterize peacekeeping operations as imperialist adventures. A government publication claimed that the establishment of the Special Committee for Peacekeeping Operations, for example, aimed to turn the UN into a "U.S.-controlled headquarters of international gendarmes to suppress and stamp out the revolutionary struggles of the world's people."[24] The ice began to crack in the 1980s, as Deng Xiaoping led China to work toward peaceful relations with the West, including through participation in international organizations. China first voted for peacekeeping operations, then began to support them financially, then joined the Special Committee, and finally deployed its first personnel to peacekeeping operations, in Africa and the Middle East.[25] In the past two decades, the Chinese contribution has grown further, notwithstanding China's traditionally rock-solid commitment to the concept of state sovereignty and the norm of non-interference in the internal affairs of other states.

Beijing's support for UN peace missions has not been limited to traditional peacekeeping operations. It has included post-conflict multi-dimensional peacekeeping—such as in Darfur, Sudan, and the Democratic Republic of Congo—and transitional administrations such as in Cambodia (despite China's association with the Khmer Rouge) and East Timor. Beijing has traditionally referred to three principles, derived from UN peacekeeping history and its own foreign policy theories, when deciding whether to authorize and participate in peacekeeping operations: host-country consent; use of force only in self-defense; and the involvement of regional actors. However, these are being applied flexibly and pragmatically, rather than uniformly. For example, China has voted for resolutions authorizing the use of military force and participated in peacekeeping missions involving the use of force.[26] China has also partly overcome its allergy toward peacekeeping missions in countries that recognize Taiwan. In the 1990s, for instance, China vetoed or threatened to veto proposed missions in Haiti, Guatemala, and Macedonia on this basis; now China supports the current UN operation in Haiti despite that country's continuing diplomatic ties with Taipei.[27]

Beyond generally supporting peace missions, China has begun to staff them, and in increasing numbers. Over the past two decades, Chinese supporters have overcome internal objections based on history, ideology, and concerns from some Chinese military officers about casualties. China now deploys more military and police personnel to UN peacekeeping operations than any other permanent member of the Security Council, and it is the 15th-largest contributor overall. Furthermore, China has invested substantially in training facilities for its peacekeepers who are, according to SIPRI, "among the most professional, well-trained, effective and disciplined contingents in UN peacekeeping operations."[28] This increase—achieved in the absence of external pressure—was an adroit move. Peacekeeping is a prominent UN activity, and China's preparedness to take on more of it has added to its prestige within the organization.

Nevertheless, progress made in Chinese peacekeeping should not be overstated. China's Security Council votes on peacekeeping are still conditioned by its traditional regard for state sovereignty and, to some extent, the principles of host-country consent, minimum use of force, and regional involvement. Although the number of Chinese personnel deployed in UN missions is high relative to the past and to other P5 countries, it remains small in absolute terms: 1,995 people as of September 2010. (There are well over two million personnel in the Chinese armed forces.) Finally, rather than deploying combat troops, Beijing has so far focused on enablers, military observers, and police.[29] Nevertheless, the shift is important.

Responsibility to Protect A little further down the continuum is China's treatment of the concept of "the responsibility to protect" (R2P). R2P is the emerging norm that after Somalia, Bosnia-Herzegovina, Rwanda, and Kosovo, a collective international responsibility exists in cases of genocide, ethnic cleansing, and widespread violations of human rights. The idea is that while states retain the primary responsibility for protecting their citizens, in the event that states are unwilling or unable to protect their people, then sovereignty must yield to the international responsibility to protect them.

Given R2P's potential to violate the traditional concept of state sovereignty, China has exhibited discomfort about some of its ramifications, but it has not opposed it outright. Former foreign minister Qian Qichen sat on the UN panel that endorsed R2P, and China supported the concept at the 2005 World Summit and in Security Council Resolution (SCR) 1674 (2006). However, Beijing has taken a very limited view of its application, emphasizing the importance of building capacity within states to prevent atrocities. It is, says analyst Sarah Teitt, "wary of competing interpretations of R2P, and resists attempts to expand R2P and initiatives to 'invoke' R2P in Council proceedings." Beijing regularly stresses the need for the Council to act "prudently" in the case of emerging crises, and comments that "states must refrain from using R2P as a diplomatic tool to exert pressure on others."[30]

Many believed that, in light of the imbroglios in Afghanistan and Iraq, the high-water mark for humanitarian intervention had passed. Nevertheless, the occurrence of significant popular protests and armed resistance this year against the Qaddafi regime in Libya, and the regime's violent response, has brought the concept of R2P back to the fore in New York. In February, China joined the rest of the Security Council in adopting SCR 1970 (2011), which imposed an arms embargo on Libya as well as a travel ban and assets freeze on the Libyan leadership, while referring the situation to the International Criminal Court. The following month, China abstained from voting on SCR 1973 (2011), which imposed a no-fly zone over Libya's territory and tightened sanctions against the regime. Both resolutions invoked the responsibility to protect civilians.

China's willingness to support the first resolution and not to veto the second represents, on the face of it, a significant advance. This is, as Alex J. Bellamy has noted, the first time in history that the Council has "authorized force against a functioning government to protect civilians." On the other hand, China's behavior was the product of very particular circumstances. The support of the Arab League and African Union for a no-fly zone was plainly critical to China's willingness not to block SCR 1973. Indeed its permanent representative Li Baodong stated that China "attached great importance" to the positions of the two regional organizations. The resolutions had broad international, as well as regional, support, which made them harder to veto.[31] We can also speculate that China was reluctant to be isolated on the Libya issue in a way that would draw attention to the heavy hand it applies to its own citizens. The Arab Spring has proven to be highly infectious. To stand with Qaddafi against international sanctions might have had unpredictable consequences. Far better to present a small target internationally and get on with the business of keeping a lid on any unrest at home.

It would be wrong, then, to see China's recent performance as indicating a significant change of heart on R2P. (Indeed, Beijing has gone out of its way to criticize Western-led air strikes against Libyan government targets.)[32] China was boxed in on this occasion, but its essentially skeptical approach remains. Whether the passage of these two resolutions has created a lasting precedent, with repercussions for China as well as the rest of the world, will depend in large part on the outcome of the conflict in Libya.

Security Council Behavior The extent and limits of China's shift toward UN engagement can be discerned in its general behavior on the Security Council, on which it is the only Asian member of the P5, as well as the only developing country. Historically, China was a passive Council member, rarely seeking to shape the agenda. China used its veto significantly less than any other permanent member, casting only four between 1971 and 2002, for example, compared to the United States' 75. It generally abstained from or did not participate in voting unless the issue touched on sovereignty questions, especially if they might influence Taiwan or Tibet. Votes that were registered were usually preceded by a pro forma statement that no precedent was thereby established. In the past decade and a half, however, Beijing's representatives have displayed much greater confidence in the Council chamber. China is increasingly willing to take the lead on issues and behave more like a normal great power.[33]

The PRC is adamant about the "One China" policy. But at the UN, there are now two Chinas: General Assembly China, which is more rigid and doctrinaire; and Security Council China, which is more pragmatic and flexible. P5 diplomats and UN officials observe that China's Security Council diplomacy is smarter and more subtle than the Russians' and that "the Chinese are more reliable in sticking to deals they have struck."[34] China has developed a good working relationship in the Council with the United States, although it is far from the vaunted "P2" (the P2 being the UN version of the much-discussed "G2"). Day-to-day diplomacy in the Security Council is still coordinated between China and Russia on one hand and among the United States, the United Kingdom, and France on the other. China has partly overcome its instinctive opposition to resolutions passed under Chapter VII of the UN Charter, which empowers the Council to take measures to maintain international peace and security. For example, China voted for resolutions to support the Australian-led INTERFET force in East Timor in 1999 and to establish the UN Transitional Administration in East Timor later that year.[35] On September 12, 2001, it joined with the rest of the Council to condemn the 9/11 attacks as a threat to international peace and security and recognize the right of self-defense against such attacks (SCR 1368 [2001]).

On the other hand, China remains disengaged from many issues of importance where they do not trespass directly on its core interests. Notwithstanding its support for SCR 1368, for instance, it is not active on Afghanistan, being mainly concerned to keep Pakistan happy with the Council's deliberations. To the relief of Sri Lanka, China refused to allow the Security Council to discuss the bloody denouement of that government's operations against the Tamil Tigers in 2009.[36] The majority of the action on the most difficult issues comes from the United States, the United Kingdom, and France. China is as uncomfortable as ever at being isolated (except on sovereignty issues), which limits its negotiating power. In other words, it is occupied largely with protecting its interests and those of its allies rather than projecting its influence—much less doing too much to strengthen the international system. In the words of a P5 diplomat, "China is mostly in defensive mode, intent on preventing things that hurt it, rather than achieving things that help it."[37]

China has a mixed record on the treatment of so-called pariah states in the Council, as analysts Stephanie Kleine-Ahlbrandt and Andrew Small

have previously chronicled.[38] After the Tiananmen Square massacre of 1989 and the Soviet Union's fall two years later, Beijing strengthened its relationships with dictatorships. The connections with energy-rich outcasts such as Sudan and Burma further deepened in the 1990s, as China's growth surged and its appetite for resources grew. "By late 2004 and early 2005," argue Kleine-Ahlbrandt and Small, "China's support for pariah regimes had taken a defensive—even ideological—turn."[39] In 2005, Beijing praised Uzbekistan's violent handling of anti-government protests and welcomed President Robert Mugabe of Zimbabwe for a state visit in the middle of his government's campaign to demolish the homes of opposition supporters. In the Security Council, it consistently resisted, diluted, or abstained from supporting resolutions that threatened real consequences for the government of Sudan over the horrors occurring in the Darfur region.

Since then, however, concerned about the fragility of some of the regimes it supports and conscious of its international reputation, China has begun to condition its support in some cases. During its 2007 Security Council presidency, for example, it prodded Khartoum into accepting a joint UN–African Union mission to support the implementation of the 2006 Darfur Peace Agreement. No doubt China was keen to polish its international reputation in the lead-up to the Beijing Olympics, as well as to prevent the spread of instability in a region in which it had substantial investments.[40] Yet its record remains patchy, as demonstrated by the October 2010 draft report of an expert panel which revealed that Chinese bullets had been used in attacks on UN peacekeepers in Darfur. (Chinese diplomats in New York reportedly threatened to veto the renewal of the panel's mandate unless the language of the report was modified.)[41]

In the Security Council, China has edged up the spectrum in the direction of engagement with the international community. Yet it has not gone far enough. China's larger interests should dictate a more pronounced move. Beijing's economic and political interests with pariah states are significant, but they are dwarfed by its ties with Western countries and the reputational cost of cozying up to the Mugabes of the world. P5 diplomats see little evidence that their Chinese colleagues share this view, especially in relation to the country's reputation. One told this author that "there is a certain amount of fatigue at always being the defender of unpleasant regimes—but it should not be overstated and it is rarely decisive."[42]

A senior UN official characterized shifts in China's Security Council behavior as important, but "incremental, not tectonic."[43] China has become a more skillful and effective player, but it has not developed a policy that is consonant with its expanded interests. This tension is evident in its approach to the two critical issues of the Iranian and North Korean nuclear programs.

Iran There is no definitive proof that Iran is engaged in a program to develop nuclear weapons. However, there is widespread international concern that Tehran's effort to gain mastery of the nuclear fuel cycle through its civilian nuclear program will put it within easy technical reach of a nuclear weapon at some point in the future. Because Iran has been caught lying about the full extent of its nuclear effort, there are also real concerns about the existence of parallel, covert programs to produce such weapons.[44]

China's performance on this issue has been unimpressive; one senior UN official, otherwise complimentary about Beijing, says "the Chinese think they can play fast and loose on Iran."[45] Under sustained pressure from Western powers, China supported three rounds of Security Council resolutions in 2006–2008 imposing sanctions on Iran for violating its obligations to the International Atomic Energy Agency (IAEA) and the UN, but only after working with Russia to dilute the sanctions and drain them of effect. The two countries pursue what the Crisis Group has called "a delay-and-weaken" strategy.[46]

The latest iteration of this took place in 2009–2010, after the revelation of Iran's underground uranium enrichment facility near Qom. In June 2010, after months of haggling, China and Russia signed on to the most comprehensive Security Council sanctions package yet, targeting Iran's financial system in particular. Analyst Michael Swaine argues that China surprised many observers by agreeing to the latest resolution, but it did so only after receiving various incentives and assurances, and to avoid isolation in light of Russia's anticipated shift to support the sanctions.[47] The

financial sanctions appear to be having a greater effect on the regime in Tehran than anticipated. That has not stopped the wrangling, however. In October 2010, the Obama administration concluded that Chinese firms were assisting Iran to develop its missile technology and nuclear weapons, and asked Beijing to get the companies to desist.[48]

Beijing's interests on the Iranian nuclear issue are not, of course, identical to Western ones. China is a significant consumer of Iranian energy, receiving 11 percent of its crude oil from Iran (its third-largest supplier after Saudi Arabia and Angola) and taking a keen interest in the country's oil and gas reserves. It sees Iran as an important partner in the Middle East and something of a counterweight to US dominance in the region, as well as a potential partner in Central and Southwest Asia. With its strong historical attachment to the principle of state sovereignty, China is more prone to rest on Iran's right under the Nuclear Non-Proliferation Treaty to develop nuclear technology for peaceful purposes. Given China's own experiences as the target of sanctions—especially the Western sanctions imposed after Tiananmen Square and the revelations of missile sales to Pakistan—it is most reluctant to agree to sanctions and far more inclined to the diplomatic track.[49] (Almost every Chinese interviewee reminded this author of the history of sanctions directed against China.)

However, this approach seems short-sighted given what is at stake for the world, and for China, as a key player in the international system. An Iranian bomb would embolden a regime with links to Hezbollah and other terrorist groups, endanger strategic waterways, threaten regional states (including, importantly, other key suppliers of energy to China in the Persian Gulf), and contribute to regional and global nuclear proliferation. The idea of a powerful state balancing the United States in the Middle East may seem superficially attractive to Beijing, but as one Chinese strategist commented to this author, "a nuclear-armed stronghold of anti-Americanism in the region would presage a bleak future for China, not least because of rising oil prices."[50] Swaine notes it would also degrade "China's status as one of only a handful of nuclear powers, undermine the NPT, and (perhaps most importantly) add to the number of nuclear armed powers in close proximity to China ... This would reduce China's relative influence as a major power, worsen its immediate threat environment, and arguably destabilize the larger global security environment."[51]

In the long term, China's approach is risky; in the short term, it is undermining its relationships with the West and its international reputation. Surely, if it is opposed to the development of Iranian nuclear weapons and also keen to minimize the use of force to this end by the United States or Israel, then it should maximize its diplomatic solidarity with Western powers in the Security Council. China has legitimate national interests to protect, but it could take a larger view of those interests.

North Korea The North Korean nuclear weapons program is, in the words of a UN official, "much more dangerous for the Chinese" than the Iranian program.[52] During the Cold War, China was North Korea's chief protector and quartermaster, in an alliance that was said to be as "close as lips and teeth."[53] Much of the ideological camaraderie has evaporated since Deng's reforms, but history and personal ties remain—as a Chinese interviewee told this author, "many Chinese lost their lives in the Korean War, and most Chinese people would be reluctant to give up their old friends."[54]

Political and security interests are, naturally, dominant. China is loath to see a collapsed state on the Korean peninsula—with resulting refugee flows and security implications—or reunification with South Korea that would mean China had to suffer American GIs on its eastern border. On the other hand, how comforting is it to suffer a highly unpredictable, not to say unhinged, family-owned regime on your eastern border? There is also the question of the thickness of China's economic ties with the two Koreas: there are 25 times as many commercial flights between China and South Korea as between China and North Korea, and 50 times as much total trade.[55]

Chinese frustration with North Korea emerged at the time of Pyongyang's 2006 nuclear test, which President Hu Jintao was reportedly notified about only 20 minutes in advance. Publicly, Beijing criticized the move as "brazen"; in the Council, it supported sanctions against the hermit kingdom.[56] In 2009, Pyongyang mounted another series of provocations, launching a rocket, walking out of the Six-Party Talks, and testing a second nuclear device. Again Beijing was critical of its ally, yet this time it was determined not to damage its bilateral relationship (or, perhaps, expose its own lack of influence over Pyongyang) with the kind of overt rhetoric it had employed three years earlier. The Crisis Group reports that there is an unusually public debate in Beijing over ties with North Korea between "traditionalists," who propose the continued provision of support to North Korea, and "strategists," who propose a harder line.[57] Strategists even go so far as to say (as one did to this author): "North Korea is the bad guy and South Korea is the good guy. China has to be on the right side of history."[58]

This debate became more prominent in 2010, against the backdrop of an awkward political transition in Pyongyang and North Korea's sinking of the South Korean corvette *Cheonan* in March, with 46 fatalities. China's response—that North Korea's role was unproven—lacked credibility and was characterized by President Obama as "willful blindness."[59] US and South Korean naval maneuvers off the Korean peninsula followed, but Chinese diplomatic maneuvers in New York confined the Security Council's response to a weak statement from its president. Thus, the international organization's response to the unprovoked sinking of a warship with substantial loss of life—a clear threat to international peace and security, one would have thought—was a presidential statement that did not name the attacker and was labeled by the *New York Times* as "absurdly, dangerously lame."[60] Similarly, China refused to allow the Council to condemn North Korea's further provocations in late 2010, when it revealed the existence of a new uranium enrichment facility and launched a deadly artillery barrage at South Korea.[61]

Human Rights The issue at the very end of China's stakeholder spectrum, on which it is the most disengaged, is human rights. Beijing is largely hostile to independent international scrutiny of its own deeply flawed human rights record, as seen in its reaction to the awarding of the Nobel Peace Prize to dissident Liu Xiaobo. China is a member of the UN's Human Rights Council (HRC), and it allows itself to be subjected to the Universal

Periodic Review (UPR) mechanism, by which the HRC assesses the human rights records of all member states every four years. China's participation in the UPR is to be welcomed, and it is right that the resulting reports praise the country's remarkable achievements in poverty reduction. However, human rights groups note that China takes a highhanded and defensive approach to the process.[62]

China Wants Respect, but not Responsibility Beijing is equally obstructionist when it comes to the scrutiny of other countries' human rights records, especially its friends and allies. In 2007, for instance, China was the strongest advocate of proposals to curtail the ability of the HRC to monitor human rights in individual countries, only relenting in exchange for the withdrawal of its special rapporteurs on Belarus and Cuba. In the Security Council, China usually works with Russia to prevent the consideration of human rights violations in places such as Zimbabwe and Darfur. Burma is a good example: in 2007, Beijing and Moscow vetoed a draft Security Council resolution critical of the military junta; in the last few months of 2010, China mounted "a high-octane, Western-style diplomatic effort" to oppose US moves to pressure the country's leaders by launching a commission of inquiry into possible war crimes they may have committed.[63]

Through the approach it has taken in the HRC, the old Commission on Human Rights, the Security Council, and the General Assembly, China has played a critical role in wearing down Western capitals on human rights issues and pushing human rights further to the periphery of UN debate.

Two Steps Forward, One Step Back

In Western countries, there is sometimes a tendency to lay the blame for any friction in the China relationship on our own politicians. No doubt this is sometimes justified. But China, too, has a choice as to how it comports itself. Its behavior helps determine how other states react to it. Its approach to the international organization helps determine its influence over the organization—and in the world.

In the past quarter-century, China has become a far more active and effective player in the UN, sometimes even outperforming the United States. It has changed the way it does business (through its diplomats and on the Security Council) and the business it does (for example, in the areas of peacekeeping and the responsibility to protect). Yet, the last five years have defined more clearly the limits of Beijing's conversion. Some of the items on China's UN agenda (for example North Korea) that were previously moving up the stakeholder spectrum have now stabilized and even slipped down a little. China continues to define its national interests narrowly and pursue them with an uncompromising resolve. China wants respect, but not responsibility. It is reluctant to bind its own freedom of movement and subsume it within international institutions in the way the United States did after the Second World War, even though Washington's relative power was far greater then than Beijing's is now.

Some analysts will say that a rising China will want to reshape the UN in coming years. It may well. However, one should not underestimate either the extent to which the structures and practices of the organization already accord with China's interests, or the difficulty of altering those structures and practices to favor China further over the certain objections of the rest of the P5, other important powers such as Japan and India, and other member states.

There are debates in China over these issues, and in some ways they mirror Western debates: there are "idealists" who study and promote the UN, and "realists" who scold them for neglecting Chinese power or compromising Chinese values.[64] But the Chinese debate is heavily tilted toward UN skeptics and away from UN groupies—"there are not many John Ikenberrys in China," observed one academic to this author.[65] Many foreign policy actors in Beijing regard the West's "responsibility" agenda as an attempt to retard China's rise. In the aftermath of the Copenhagen debacle, for example, the debate in China was less about whether Wen Jiabao's concessions went far enough and more about whether they went too far.

None of this is to say that China's interests coincide exactly with Western interests. They do not, and we should not expect China to act exactly as the West does. Nor should we ask

China to advance global interests at the expense of its national interests. But as China's wealth and power grow, so will its interests expand. A middle-power foreign policy is inadequate for a great power.

If China is to help run the international system, then it has a stake in strengthening it. Beijing needs to strike a new balance between its traditional economic as well as security concerns and the broader imperatives it must now satisfy, including stable great-power relations, non-proliferation, and developing its international prestige. China's UN performance has largely escaped scrutiny in the last two decades, with the world's head turned first by US power and then by US overreach. That pattern will not hold. The old principle—that with power comes responsibility—requires China to move up the stakeholder spectrum.

On the other hand, the West needs to be careful what it wishes for. Western countries want Beijing to be more responsible and active, but they don't like it when Beijing is more assertive. China's version of "stepping up" is not necessarily the same as the West's. Professor Pan Zhongying of Renmin University has argued that a stronger China may be less anxious about external powers intervening in China's domestic affairs, but also less fussy about observing the principle of noninterference in *other* states' domestic affairs.[66] How would the West feel about China involving itself in the Middle East peace process, for example, or participating in "coalitions of the willing" that intervened in other countries?

In other words, the responsibilities—and prerogatives—of a stakeholder are open to interpretation. In the future, Beijing may put forward its own, quite different, stakeholder spectrum.

NOTES

1. Greg Picker and Fergus Green, "Comprehending Copenhagen: A Guide to the International Climate Change Negotiations," Lowy Institute for International Policy, 2009, p. 4): http://www.lowyinstitute.org/Publication.asp?pid=1177.

2. "Comparison of Carbon Dioxide Emissions, 1965–2009: United States and China," http://www.instituteforenergyresearch.org/wp-content/uploads/2010/06/carbon-dioxide-emissions-1965-2009-US-China.jpg; "Carbon Dioxide Emissions (CO2), thousand metric tons of CO2 (CDIAC)," Millennium Development Goals Indicators, http://mdgs.un.org/unsd/mdg/SeriesDetail.aspx?srid=749&crid=.

3. James Fallows, "China's Silver Lining," *The Atlantic*, June 2008, http://www.theatlantic.com/magazine/archive/2008/06/china-8217 -s-silver-lining/6808/; Deborah Seligsohn, Rob Bradley, and Jonathan Adams, "Fact Sheet: Energy and Climate Policy Action in China (Update)," World Resources Institute, November 5, 2009, http://www.wri.org/stories/2009/11/fact-sheet-energy-and-climate-policy-action- china-update; Thomas Friedman, "The New Sputnik," *New York Times*, September 26, 2009, http://www.nytimes.com/2009/09/27/opinion/27friedman.html; Michael Fullilove and Fergus Green, "Talks Should at Least Be a Big Step on the Way," *Sydney Morning Herald*, December 8, 2009, p 11.

4. "Climate Change after Copenhagen: China's Thing About Numbers," *The Economist*, December 30, 2009, http://www.economist.com/node/15179774?story_id=15179774; "Copenhagen Accord Faces First Test," International Institute for Strategic Studies, *Strategic Comments* 16, January 2010, http://www.iiss.org/EasySiteWeb/GatewayLink.aspx?alId=40511; Fareed Zakaria, "Clash of the Titans: How the Democratic Republic of Google is Testing China's Appetite for Democracy Itself," *Newsweek*, January 15, 2010, http://www.newsweek.com/2010/01/14/clash-of-the-titans.html; Jonathan Watts, "Speculation Over Change in Role for Chinese Climate Negotiator," *The Guardian*, January 5, 2010, http://www.guardian.co.uk/environment/2010/jan/05/he-yafei-china-climate-negotiator.

5. Ed Miliband, "The Road from Copenhagen," *The Guardian*, December 20, 2009, http://www.guardian.co.uk/commentisfree/2009/dec/20/copenhagen-climate-change-accord; for Foreign Ministry Spokesperson Jiang Yu's response to the British accusation that China "hijacked" negotiations at the Copenhagen Climate Change Conference, see http://www.fmprc.gov.cn/eng/xwfw/s2510/t647058.htm.

6. Mark Lynas, "How Do I know China Wrecked the Copenhagen Deal? I Was in the Room," *The Guardian*, December 22, 2009, http://www.guardian.co.uk/environment/2009/dec/22/copenhagen-climate-change-mark-lynas.

7. Robert B. Zoellick, "Whither China: From Membership to Responsibility?" (speech to the National Committee on US-China Relations, New York, September 21, 2005), http://www.kas.de/wf/doc/kas_7358-544-1-30.pdf.

8. Xiaochao Li, "Further Expanding Momentum of China's Economic Recovery in the First Quarter of 2010," National Bureau of Statistics of China, April 15, 2010; "Gross Domestic Product 2009," World

Bank, December 15, 2010, http://siteresources. world-bank.org/DATASTATISTICS/Resources/GDP.pdf; "Gross Domestic Product 2009, PPP," World Bank, December 15, 2010, http://siteresources.worldbank. org/DATASTATISTICS/Resources/GDP_PPP.pdf; "GDP Growth (Annual %)," World Bank, http://data. worldbank.org/indicator/NY.GDP.MKTP.KD.ZG; "World Trade Developments in 2008," World Trade Organization, http://www.wto.org/english/res_ e/statis_e/its2009_e/its09_world_trade_dev_e.htm; Fareed Zakaria, "The Recession's Real Winner: China Turns Crisis into Opportunity," *Newsweek*, October 17, 2009, http://www.newsweek.com/2009/10/17/ the-recession-s-real-winner.html; Kevin Yao and Langi Chiang, "China FX Reserves Soar Past $3 Trillion, Add to Inflation," *Reuters*, April 14, 2011, http://www. reuters.com/article/2011/04/14/us-china-economy-reserves-idUSTRE 73D1T620110414; Hugh White, "Power Shift: Australia's Future Between Washington and Beijing," *Quarterly Essay* 39, September 2010, pp. 11–13; Paul Kennedy, *The Parliament of Man: The United Nations and the Quest for Global Government* (London: Allen Lane, 2006), p. 245.

9. US Department of Defense, *Quadrennial Defense Review Report*, February 2010, p. 31, http://www.defense. gov/qdr/images/QDR_as_of_12Feb10_1000.pdf; US Department of Defense, *Military Power of the People's Republic of China 2008*, p. i, http://www.au.af.mil/au/ awc/awcgate/dod/china_report_2008.pdf; M. Taylor Fravel, "China's Search for Military Power," *Washington Quarterly* 31, no. 3 (Summer 2008), http://twq.com/ 08summer/docs/08summer_fravel.pdf.

10. Josef Joffe, "The Default Power: The False Prophecy of America's Decline," *Foreign Affairs* 88, no. 5 (September/October 2009): p. 5; Steven Mufson and John Pomfret, "There's a New Red Scare. But Is China Really So Scary?" *Washington Post*, February 28, 2010, http://www.washingtonpost.com/wp-dyn/content/ article/2010/02/26/AR2010022602601.html.

11. Deng Xiaoping quotation from Stephanie Kleine-Ahlbrandt and Andrew Small, "China's New Dictatorship Diplomacy: Is Beijing Parting with Pariahs?" *Foreign Affairs* 87, no. 1 (January/February 2008): p. 41.

12. Confidential interview, Beijing, June 3, 2010.

13. National Intelligence Council (NIC) and the European Union Institute for Security Studies (EUISS), *Global Governance 2025: At a Critical Juncture*, September 2010, p. iii, http://www.dni.gov/nic/PDF_2025/ 2025_Global_Governance.pdf.

14. Confidential interview, Beijing, June 4, 2010.

15. Confidential interview, Washington, DC, October 7, 2009.

16. David Shambaugh, "The Chinese Tiger Shows its Claws," *Financial Times*, February 17, 2009, http:// www.ft.com/cms/s/0/d55d5578-1b62-11df-838f-00144feab49a.html; Michael Fullilove, "Frustrated US Struggles to Open Dialogue with China," *Sydney Morning Herald*, February 22, 2010; Josh Rogin, "Gates Snub Raises Tough Questions about China

Ties," *Foreign Policy*, June 4, 2010, http://thecable. foreignpolicy.com/posts/2010/06/03/gates_snub_ raises_tough_questions_about_china_ties; Sachiko Sakamaki and Takashi Hirokawa, "Kan, Wen Move to Resolve China-Japan dispute," *Bloomberg*, October 6, 2010, http://www.bloomberg.com/news/2010-10-05/kan-wen-meeting-positive-for-japan-   china-s-bilaterial-ties-sengoku-says.html.

17. Linda Jakobson and Dean Knox, "New Foreign Policy Actors in China," Stockholm International Peace Research Institute, Policy Paper 26, September 2010, pp. vi–vii, http://books.sipri.org/files/PP/ SIPRIPP26.pdf; Fareed Zakaria, "The Beijing Blues," *Newsweek*, June 4, 2010, http://www.newsweek.com/ 2010/06/04/the-beijing-blues.html; Zakaria, "Clash of the Titans"; Fareed Zakaria, "Growing Pains," *Newsweek*, February 5, 2010, http://www.newsweek. com/2010/02/04/growing-pains.html; Kerry Brown, "The Power Struggle Among China's Elite," *Foreign Policy*, October 14, 2010, http://www.foreignpolicy. com/articles/2010/10/14/the_power_struggle_ among_chinas_elite.

18. Samuel S. Kim, "China and the United Nations," in *China Joins the World: Progress and Prospects*, eds. Elizabeth Economy and Michel Oksenberg (New York: Council on Foreign Relations Press, 1999); Bates Gill and Chin-hao Huang, "China's Expanding Role in Peacekeeping: Prospects and Policy Implications," Stockholm International Peace Research Institute, Policy Paper, http://books.sipri. org/files/PP/SIPRIPP25.pdf; "China's Growing Role in UN Peacekeeping," International Crisis Group, Asia Report no. 166, April 17, 2009, pp. 3–5, http://www. crisisgroup.org/~/media/Files/asia/north-east   asia/ 166_chinas_growing_role_in_un_ peacekeeping.ashx.

19. Rosemary Foot, "Chinese Strategies in a US Hegemonic Global Order: Accommodating and Hedging," *International Affairs* 82, no. 1 (January 2006): p. 82.

20. David Shambaugh, "Reforming China's Diplomacy," Copenhagen Business School Asia Research Centre, January 31, 2010, http://openarchive.cbs.dk/bit-stream/handle/10398/8013/Hele_discussion_ paper. pdf?sequence=1; Kim's report of representative's quo-tation reproduced in Michel Oksenberg and Elizabeth Economy, *Shaping US-China Relations: A Long-Term Strategy* (New York: Council on Foreign Relations, 1997), p. 29.

21. Confidential interviews, New York, October 1, 2009, and September 30, 2009.

22. Colum Lynch, "Exclusive: China's John Bolton," *Foreign Policy*, September 9, 2010, http://turtlebay.foreign-policy.com/posts/2010/09/08/chinas_john_bolton; "UN Diplomat Sha Zukang Sorry for Rant," *The Australian*, September 15, 2010, http://www.theaustra-lian.com.au/news/world/un-diplomat-sha-zukang-sorry-for-rant/story-e6fr g6so-1225922928310.

23. Confidential interviews, New York, September 30, 2009, and October 1, 2010.

24. Tiewa Liu, "Marching for a More Open, Confident and Responsible Great Power: Explaining China's Involvement in UN Peacekeeping Operations," *Journal of International Peacekeeping* 13, no. 1–2 (January 2009): pp. 121–122. See also International Crisis Group, "China's Growing Role in UN Peacekeeping," pp. 3–5.

25. International Crisis Group, "China's Growing Role in UN Peacekeeping," pp. 5–10; Gill and Huang, "China's Expanding Role in Peacekeeping," pp. 4–5.

26. International Crisis Group, "China's Growing Role in UN Peacekeeping," pp. 2–3, 19–25.

27. Gill and Huang, "China's Expanding Role in Peacekeeping," pp. 13–14; United Nations, "UN Mission's Summary Detailed by Country," September 30, 2010, http://www.un.org/en/peacekeeping/contributors/2010/sept10_3.pdf. China had a sizeable contingent of riot police in Haiti but it withdrew them in the weeks following the January 2010 earthquake: see Colum Lynch, "In Surprise Move, China Withdraws Riot Police from Haiti," *Foreign Policy*, March 25, 2010, http://turtlebay.foreignpolicy.com/posts/2010/03/25/in_surprise_move_china_withdraws_riot_police_from_haiti.

28. United Nations, "Ranking of Military and Police Contributions to UN Operations," September 30, 2010, http://www.un.org/en/peacekeeping/contributors/2010/sept10_2. pdf; Gill and Huang, "China's Expanding Role in Peacekeeping," pp. 5–7 and 26–27.

29. Gill and Huang, "China's Expanding Role in Peacekeeping," p. 11; Xu Weidi, "Yaobai yu Panghuang zhong de Tansuo: Lianheguo Weihe Xingdong Mianlin de Kunnan yu Tiaozhan. [Exploration in vacillation and hesitation: The difficulties and challenges facing UN peacekeeping operations]," *World Economics and Politics*, no. 5, p. 9; United Nations, "Ranking of Military and Police Contributions to UN Operations"; International Institute for Strategic Studies, *The Military Balance* 110 (Routledge, 2010), p. 465; International Crisis Group, "China's Growing Role in UN Peacekeeping," pp. 27–30.

30. Sarah Teitt, "China and the Responsibility to Protect," Asia-Pacific Centre for the Responsibility to Protect, December 19, 2008, pp. 2, 9, 10, http://www.responsibilitytoprotect.org/files/China_and_R2P%5B1%5D.pdf; "Implementing the Responsibility to Protect: Asia-Pacific in the 2009 General Assembly Dialogue," Asia-Pacific Centre for the Responsibility to Protect, October 2009, p. 18, http://www.responsibilitytoprotect.org/index.php/component/content/article/172-asia-pacific/2667-implementing-the-responsibility- to-protect-asia-pacific-in-the-2009-ga-dialogue-.

31. Alex J. Bellamy, "The Responsibility to Protect: Libya and Beyond," *e-International Relations*, March 30, 2011, http://www.e-ir.info/?p=7912; "Security Council Approves 'No-Fly Zone' Over Libya," SC/10200, March 17, 2011, http://www.un.org/News/Press/docs/2011/sc10200.doc.htm; Douglas H. Paal,

"China: Mugged by Reality in Libya, Again," Carnegie Endowment for International Peace, April 11, 2011, http://www.carnegieendowment.org/publications/index.cfm?fa=view&id=43554.

32. "Foreign Ministry Spokesperson Jiang Yu's Remarks on Multinational Military Strike against Libya," Ministry of Foreign Affairs of the People's Republic of China, March 21, 2011, http://www.fmprc.gov.cn/eng/xwfw/s2510/t808094.htm; "Chinese President Says Force Is No Solution to Libyan Issue," March 30, 2011, Chinese Embassy in the United States, http://www.china-embassy.org/eng/zgyw/t811054.htm.

33. Samuel S. Kim, "China in World Politics," in *Does China Matter? A Reassessment*, eds. Barry Buzan and Rosemary Foot (London: Routledge, 2004), pp. 43–46. In his analysis of voting records of the permanent five, Kim excludes a 1981 volley of US and Chinese vetoes during deliberations on nominations for Secretary-General on the grounds that these "behind-the-scenes" votes are not included in official UNSC documentation.

34. Confidential interview, New York, October 1, 2009.

35. Bates Gill, "China Becoming a Responsible Stakeholder," Carnegie Endowment for International Peace, June 11, 2007, p. 5, http://carnegieendowment.org/files/Bates_ paper.pdf.

36. Jenny Page, "Chinese Billions in Sri Lanka Fund Battle Against Tamil Tigers," *The Times*, May 2, 2009; Security Council Report, "Sri Lanka," Update Report no. 1, June 4, 2009, http://www.securitycouncilreport.org/atf/cf/%7B65BFCF9B-6D27-4E9C-8CD3-CF6E4FF96FF9%7D/Update%20Report%204%20June_Sri%20Lanka.pdf.

37. Confidential interview, New York, October 1, 2009.

38. Kleine-Ahlbrandt and Small, "China's New Dictatorship Diplomacy."

39. Ibid., p. 42.

40. Ibid., pp. 46–47. See also Gill and Huang, "China's Expanding Role in Peacekeeping," p. 14; International Crisis Group, "China's Growing Role in UN Peacekeeping," pp. 20–21.

41. Peter Ford, "China Dismisses UN Report that Chinese Bullets Were Used in Darfur," *Christian Science Monitor*, October 21, 2010, http://www.csmonitor.com/World/2010/1021/China-dismisses-UN-report-that-Chinese-bullets-were-used-in-Darfur.

42. Confidential interview, New York, September 30, 2009.

43. Confidential interview, New York, October 2, 2009.

44. Anthony Bubalo and Michael Fullilove, "Iran, the International Community and the Nuclear Issue: Where to Next?" Lowy Institute for International Policy, December 2005, p. 3, http://www.lowyinstitute.org/Publication.asp?pid=330.

45. Confidential interview, New York, October 1, 2009.

46. Willem van Kemenade, "China vs. the Western Campaign for Iran Sanctions," *Washington Quarterly* 33, no. 3 (July 2010): p. 108, http://twq.com/10july/docs/10jul_va nKemenade.pdf; Michael D. Swaine, "Beijing's

Tightrope Walk on Iran," Carnegie Endowment for International Peace, *China Leadership Monitor*, no. 33, June 28, 2010, pp. 7–8, http://carnegieendowment.org/files/CLM33MS.pdf; "The Iran Nuclear Issue: The View from Beijing," International Crisis Group, Asia Briefing no. 100, February 17, 2010, p. 13, http://www.crisisgroup.org/en/regions/asia/north-east-asia/china/B100-the- iran-nuclear-issue-the-view-from-beijing.aspx; "Factbox: EU, U.N. and U.S. sanctions against Iran," *Reuters*, September 23, 2010, http://www.reuters.com/article/2010/09/23/us-thyssen-iran-sanctions-idUSTRE68M26320100923.

47. Swaine, "Beijing's Tightrope Walk on Iran," p. 8.

48. John Pomfret, "U.S. Says Chinese Businesses and Banks Are Bypassing U.N. Sanctions against Iran," *Washington Post*, October 18, 2010, http://www.washingtonpost.com/wpdyn/content/article/2010/10/17/AR2010101703364.html.

49. International Crisis Group, "The Iran Nuclear Issue: The View from Beijing," pp. 5, 11 n. 103; Swaine, "Beijing's Tightrope Walk on Iran," pp. 1–2; van Kemenade, "China vs. the Western Campaign for Iran Sanctions," p. 103.

50. Confidential interview, Beijing, June 3, 2010.

51. Swaine, "Beijing's Tightrope Walk on Iran," p. 3.

52. Confidential interview, New York, October 1, 2009.

53. Marc Lanteigne, *Chinese Foreign Policy: An Introduction* (London: Routledge, 2009), p. 114.

54. Confidential interview, Beijing, June 2, 2010.

55. Korea Airports Corporation aviation statistics, http://www.airport.co.kr/doc/www_eng/info/E040105.jsp; Korea Konsult, International timetables to/from North Korea, http://www.koreakonsult.com/hur-tar-man-sig-dit_eng.html; International Monetary Fund, *Direction of Trade Statistics Yearbook: 2010*.

56. Kleine-Ahlbrandt and Small, "China's New Dictatorship Diplomacy," pp. 44–45.

57. "Shades of Red: China's Debate Over North Korea," International Crisis Group, Asia Report no. 179, November 2, 2009, p. 1, http://www.crisisgroup.org/en/regions/asia/north-east-asia/china/179-shades-of-red-chinas-debate-over-north-korea.aspx.

58. Confidential interview, Beijing, June 3, 2010.

59. Andrew Jacobs and David E. Sanger, "China Returns U.S. Criticism Over Sinking of Korean Ship," *New York Times*, June 29, 2010, http://www.nytimes.com/2010/06/30/world/asia/30korea.html.

60. "Security Council Blinks," *New York Times*, July 10, 2010, http://www.nytimes.com/2010/07/11/opinion/11sun3.html.

61. Peter S. Green and Frances Yoon, "China Declines to Condemn North Korean Shelling as South Prepares Drill," *Bloomberg*, December 19, 2010, http://www.bloomberg.com/news/2010-12-19/china-declines-to-condemn-north-korean-shelling-as-south-prepares- drill.html.

62. Thomas Lum and Hannah Fischer, "Human Rights in China: Trends and Policy Implications," *CRS Report for Congress*, renowned RL34729, January 25, 2010, http://www.fas.org/sgp/crs/row/RL34729.pdf; Human Rights Watch, "UN: Nations Show True Colors at Rights Review," February 13, 2009, http://www.hrw.org/en/news/2009/02/13/un- nations-show-true-colors-rights-review.

63. Richard Gowan and Franziska Brantner, "A Global Force for Human Rights? An Audit of European Power at the UN," European Council on Foreign Relations, 2008, p. 37, http://www.ecfr.eu/page/-/documents/30b67f149cd7aaa888_3xm6bq7ff.pdf; Sarah E. Mendelson, "Dusk or Dawn for the Human Rights Movement?" *Washington Quarterly* 32, no. 2 (April 2009): p. 109, http://twq.com/09april/docs/09apr_ Mendelson.pdf; "Security Council Fails to Adopt Draft Resolution on Myanmar, Owing to Negative Votes by China, Russian Federation," SC/8939, January 12, 2007, http://www.un.org/News/Press/docs/2007/sc8939.doc.htm; Warren Hoge, "U.S. Rebuke to Myanmar is Defeated by U.N. Vetoes," *New York Times*, January 13, 2007, http://www.nytimes.com/2007/01/13/world/asia/13nations.html; Colum Lynch, "U.S. Push for Burmese War Crimes Probe Hits Chinese Wall," *Foreign Policy*, October 24, 2010, http://turtlebay.foreignpolicy.com/posts/2010/10/24/us_push_for_burmese_war_crimes_probe_ hits_chinese_wall.

64. For an excellent analysis of the various schools of Chinese foreign policy thought, see David Shambaugh, "Coping with a Conflicted China," *Washington Quarterly* 34, no. 1 (Winter 2011): pp. 7–27, http://twq.com/11winter/docs/11winter_Shambaugh.pdf.

65. Confidential interview, Beijing, June 3, 2010.

66. Pan Zhongying, "China's Non-Intervention Question," *Global Responsibility to Protect* 1, no. 2 (March 2009): pp. 237–252, especially pp. 249–252.

"Greater" China

Editorial Introduction

Another important aspect of China's rise concerns its peripheral parts: Hong Kong, Macao, and Taiwan. China has *de jure* sovereignty over all three, although no *de facto* control over Taiwan. Although Beijing's grip over Macao is unchallenged locally, Hong Kong's population has been restive ever since its retrocession from Britain to China in 1997. In 2014 this percolating discontent erupted into an unprecedented "Occupy Central" movement that lasted for 79 days, when hundreds of thousands of citizens demonstrated in opposition to what they perceived to be Beijing's reneging on its promises to give Hong Kong universal suffrage and direct election of the Chief Executive in 2017. Not only did the demonstrators anticipate these two electoral elements, they also anticipated that they would be able to self-select the *candidates*. In August 2014 Beijing made it clear that it would remain in full control of the vetting process and selection/nomination slate of candidates. In other words, only screened and pre-selected candidates could stand for the chief executive election. While the demonstrations eventually died out and the encampments were cleared away by police, the discontent continues to simmer in the Hong Kong Special Administrative Region (HKSAR).

Taiwan has its own unique dynamics. Autonomously ruled since 1949, when the Nationalist Party (Kuomintang) fled the Chinese mainland, the island of 23 million inhabitants has lived an ambiguous international status since it was expelled from the United Nations in 1971. Now officially recognized by only 21 nations (mainly in west Africa and Central America), the government is primarily known as "Chinese Taipei." Despite this ambiguity internationally, the island has continued to support a thriving developed economy with a per capita GDP of $23,000 ($37,000 in PPP terms), is one of the top trading nations in the world, has a thriving democracy, diverse culture and society. In recent years, moreover, its estrangement from the mainland has been radically reduced. Between 2008 and 2011 a raft of "cross-strait" agreements were reached in a variety of sectors ranging from direct transportation and postal links to tourism and academic exchanges. An Economic Cooperation Framework Agreement (ECFA), agreed in 2010, opened the doors further to direct two-way trade and investment with the ultimate goal of creating a free trade area (FTA). Never before have the mainland and Taiwan enjoyed such close ties. To be certain, significant differences still—and will always—exist, primarily the differing political systems, the distinct identity of Taiwanese, and the unwillingness of the majority of those on Taiwan to be absorbed into the People's Republic of China.

The three selections in this section address these dynamics. The first is a speech by former Chinese president and leader Hu Jintao, who provides the standard PRC recitation of the "One Country, Two Systems," formula that is Beijing's longstanding vision for limited suzerainty and semi-autonomous rule for Hong Kong, Macao, and Taiwan within a "Once China" sovereign framework—that is intended to lead, over time, to "reunification of the motherland."

The second selection from *The Economist* was published in the midst of the aforementioned 2014 demonstrations in Hong Kong. It provides good insights into the fervor or the demonstrations and the calculations of its youthful organizers.

The final selection, by leading Taiwan expert Richard Bush of the Brookings Institution, traces the protracted process of cross-strait accommodation, and peers into the future of factors that are simultaneously pushing the two together and pulling them apart. The "Taiwan issue" remains far from being resolved, despite the substantial stabilization and progress made between the two sides in recent years.

I. HONG KONG AND TAIWAN

Enriching the Practice of "One Country, Two Systems" and Advancing China's Reunification
Report to the 18th National Congress of the Communist Party of China [Excerpts]*

Hu Jintao

Since their return to the motherland, Hong Kong and Macao have embarked on a broad road along which they and the mainland draw on each other's strengths and pursue common development, and the success of the "one country, two systems" principle has won global recognition. The underlying goal of the principles and policies adopted by the central government concerning Hong Kong and Macao is to uphold China's sovereignty, security, and development interests and maintain long-term prosperity and stability of the two regions. We must fully and faithfully implement the principle of "one country, two systems," under which the people of Hong Kong govern Hong Kong and the people of Macao govern Macao and both regions enjoy a high degree of autonomy. We must both adhere to the One China Principle and respect the differences of the two systems, both uphold the power of the central government and ensure a high degree of autonomy in the special administrative regions, both give play to the role of the mainland as the staunch supporter of Hong Kong and Macao and increase their competitiveness. At no time should we focus only on one side to the neglect of the other.

The central government will act in strict accordance with the basic laws of the special administrative regions, improve work mechanisms for their enforcement, and firmly support the chief executives and governments of the two

---

* This speech was published by the Communist Party of China on November 8, 2012 (http://www.china.org.cn/china/18th_cpc_congress/2012-11/16/content_27137540.htm).

special administrative regions in governing the two regions in accordance with the law. The central government will firmly support them in leading the people from all walks of life in focusing on economic development, taking effective steps to improve the people's well-being, and advancing orderly and phased-in democracy as well as inclusiveness, mutual support and harmony. The central government will increase economic ties and trade between the mainland and the two regions, and promote exchanges and cooperation between them in all fields. The central government will also firmly support the chief executives and governments of the two special administrative regions in promoting the unity of our compatriots in Hong Kong and Macao under the banner of loving both the motherland and their respective regions and in guarding against and forestalling external intervention in the affairs of Hong Kong and Macao.

We are convinced that our compatriots in Hong Kong and Macao not only have the wisdom, ability and resourcefulness to successfully govern and develop the two regions; they can certainly also play an active role in national affairs and share with other people of all ethnic groups in China the dignity and glory of being Chinese.

To resolve the Taiwan question and achieve the complete reunification of China is an irresistible historical process. Peaceful reunification is in the best interests of the Chinese nation, including our compatriots in Taiwan. To achieve peaceful reunification, we must, above everything else, ensure peaceful growth of relations between the two sides of the Taiwan Straits. We must adhere to the principle of "peaceful reunification and one country, two systems" and the eight-point proposal for growing cross-Strait relations and advancing peaceful reunification of the motherland. We must put into full practice the important thought of peaceful growth of cross-Strait relations, consolidate and strengthen the political, economic, cultural and social foundation for such growth, and create even better conditions for achieving peaceful reunification.

We must continue to adhere to the One China Principle. Although the mainland and Taiwan are yet to be reunified, the fact that both belong to one China has never changed. China's territory

and sovereignty have always been indivisible and no division will be tolerated. The two sides of the Taiwan Straits should uphold the common stand of opposing Taiwan independence and of following the 1992 Consensus. Both sides should increase their common commitment to upholding the one-China framework and, on this basis, expand common ground and set aside differences. We are ready to conduct exchanges, dialogue, and cooperation with any political party in Taiwan as long as it does not seek Taiwan independence and recognizes the one-China principle.

We should sustain cross-Strait exchanges and cooperation. We should deepen economic cooperation to increase common interests. We should expand cultural exchanges to enhance a common sense of national identity, and further people-to-people contacts to cultivate mutual goodwill. We should promote consultation on an equal footing and strengthen institutional building. We hope that the two sides will jointly explore cross-Strait political relations and make reasonable arrangements for them under the special condition that the country is yet to be reunified. We hope the two sides will discuss the establishment of a cross-Strait confidence-building mechanism for military security to maintain stability in their relations and reach a peace agreement through consultation so as to open a new horizon in advancing the peaceful growth of these relations.

We should encourage the compatriots on both sides of the Taiwan Straits to unite and pursue a common endeavor. The compatriots on both sides belong to the same Chinese nation and form a community of common destiny bound by blood ties; and we have every reason to care about and trust each other, jointly advance cross-Strait relations, and share in the fruits of development. We will make every effort to do anything that will promote the common well-being of the compatriots on both sides of the Taiwan Straits. We should fully protect the rights and interests of our Taiwan compatriots and work with them to safeguard and build the common home of the Chinese nation.

We resolutely oppose any separatist attempt for Taiwan independence. The Chinese people will never allow anyone or any force to separate

Taiwan from the motherland by any means. Any separatist attempt for Taiwan independence, which undermines the common interests of the compatriots on both sides of the Taiwan Straits, is doomed to fail.

Working hand in hand, we, the sons and daughters of the Chinese nation, will surely accomplish the great cause of China's reunification in the course of our common endeavor to achieve the great renewal of the Chinese nation.

POLITICAL CITY: DEMOCRACY IN HONG KONG*

The Economist

For more than 30 years now, political activists in Hong Kong have been agitating for a more democratic political system. On August 31st China made it plain they will not get their way. "Take it or leave it," is how the *South China Morning Post* summed up China's position. Not wanting to take it, several thousand people attended a rally in protest that rainy Sunday evening. They heard Benny Tai Yiu-ting, a mild and thoughtful academic, declare a new "era of resistance" and civil disobedience. He is one of the organizers of the "Occupy Central" movement, which is planning waves of street protest, culminating in the peaceful "occupation" of Hong Kong island's central business district. "The road of dialogue has come to the end," he said. Months of debilitating confrontation are in prospect.

Britain, as China never tires of reminding it, ruled Hong Kong for 150 years without granting it democracy. But in 1984 its Joint Declaration with China on the transfer of Hong Kong in 1997 promised the territory a "high degree of autonomy." After the Tiananmen Square protests in 1989 fear of China grew; democracy was seen as a way of ensuring Hong Kong's freedom. China, for its part, always insisted that Hong Kong was an "economic city" and should not become a "political" one.

Yet it is by far the most politically galvanized city in China. Its constitution, the Basic Law, promises "one country, two systems" and that the chief executive will eventually be chosen by "universal suffrage," a goal deferred until 2017. On August 31st it became plain that this is to be universal suffrage, China-style: voters can choose

whom they like, provided the party has chosen first. Under proposals put forward by China's parliament, the National People's Congress (NPC), no more than two or three candidates will be allowed, and they will need the endorsement of at least half the members of a "nominating committee." This is to be modeled on the 1,200-strong committee that picked the current chief executive, "C.Y." Leung Chun-ying, in 2012. An elaborately designed construct, it has a very simple purpose: to ensure "pro-China" votes have a built-in majority. The NPC's proposal leaves no chance that a candidate will even need make the ballot against China's will.

Defending the NPC's decision in press conferences in Beijing and Hong Kong, Li Fei, chairman of its Basic Law committee, insisted that "some people in Hong Kong can never be chief executive" because of their "confrontational" stance. The NPC couches the issue as one of China's "sovereignty, security and development interests." A senior Chinese academic has argued, bizarrely for a Communist, that full democracy would endanger that beleaguered minority, Hong Kong's tycoons.

The NPC proposal will fail unless it gains a two-thirds majority in Hong Kong's Legislative Council (Legco). In this body, half of whose 70 members were directly elected, 27 seats are held by "pan-democrats," or "pan-dems," as those from a variety of pro-democracy parties are commonly known. They have pledged to veto it. Many had expected that the NPC would leave negotiating room to win over moderate pan-dems. That now seems unlikely. Claudia Mo Man-ching, a Legco member from the pan-dem Civic Party, says no pan-dem would endorse the NPC plan, for fear of being branded a "sinner of history."

---

* This article was published in *The Economist* on September 6, 2014.

How to Stay Occupied

Mr. Tai and his colleagues in Occupy are also cornered—and faltering. They had been looking for any excuse to stay off the streets. The whole idea had been to use occupation as the very last of last resorts, at the end of a prolonged process of "deliberative democracy" that involved public consultation and a "referendum" in June attracting 800,000 signatures in support of a more open electoral system. Had China wanted to leave the door open for compromise, it could have fudged details such as the nomination threshold. Instead, in Miss Mo's words, "it has shut the door, the window, the fire escape and the back door." China has given Occupy no excuse. Mr. Tai this week admitted that "up to this point, we failed." The movement abhors violence, yet knows that is a risk. Mr. Li was heckled in Hong Kong, and there were scuffles as police used pepper spray to disperse protesters.

In a practice mini-occupation, following on from a 500,000-strong annual pro-democracy march on the July 1st anniversary of Britain's handover of Hong Kong to China in 1997, over 500 people were arrested. But Mr. Tai has admitted that the apparent hopelessness of the cause is eroding support for Occupy among some of Hong Kong's "pragmatic" people. Occupy claims, however, that others have been motivated to join. Now it has to engage in serious planning. Whether acquiring portable lavatories—as it has done—counts is doubtful. It suggests the new era has hardly struck like thunder. Occupy is keeping quiet about its detailed strategy (if any).

The Chinese and Hong Kong governments may still be hoping that the election proposal wins Legco approval. If it is rejected, the 2017 election will be by committee again. So, by urging Legco to "pocket it now"—take the one-man one-vote offer while it is on the table, and try to improve the system later—the government hopes the public will turn against the pan-dems.

Occupy already has many critics. Even some democrats question a strategy that seeks to preserve Hong Kong's uniqueness in China by undermining its very basis: the observance of the rule of law. Others have been swayed by apocalyptic propaganda about the disruption Occupy might entail—though many business leaders seem remarkably sanguine about the risks.

China's Communist Party has always had its supporters in Hong Kong—an odd alliance of business tycoons favoring stability above all and a well-funded, highly organized grass-roots network, including a strong Communist-front party, the Democratic Alliance for the Betterment and Progress of Hong Kong. A petition against Occupy attracted 1.4 million signatures, though many were of dubious origin; similarly an anti-Occupy march on August 17th was well-attended, but many "demonstrators" had been bused in and paid.

The Chinese and Hong Kong governments may be placing too much faith in Hong Kong's famed preference for doing business over political struggle. After their long struggle for democracy, an older generation of activists has had enough and is no longer willing to play by China's rules. They and many ordinary people are furious at the perceived debasement of Hong Kong's institutions.

The Pressure Grows

Legco, never powerful, has degenerated into farce as frustrated radicals resort to rowdyism and filibusters. The press is widely seen as timid in its criticism of the Communist Party; cowed by a combination of pressure from advertisers and crude intimidation, such as a knife attack on a former editor earlier this year. The Independent Commission Against Corruption, the Caesar's wife of Hong Kong law enforcement, was, rightly or wrongly, assumed by some analysts to have a political motive for raiding the home of Jimmy Lai Chee-ying, a pro-democracy media tycoon, and the office of a pan-dem legislator just before the NPC's announcement.

The judiciary is also seen as under threat. In June lawyers marched in protest against a Chinese White Paper which listed Hong Kong's judges as among those who must "love the country." Even the postal service is under fire for refusing to distribute leaflets on civil disobedience. And the government itself hardly even claims to represent Hong Kong's people, so staunch a propagandist has it become for the Communist Party's plans.

This popular anger is in danger of merging with a prejudice against "locusts"—the ever-more-visible mainland-Chinese visitors to Hong Kong who crowd the underground, force shops to keep stocks of baby formula behind bars (so that they are not snapped up by tourists who are distrustful of mainland brands), and scandalize users of social media every time one of their toddlers urinates in public.

The young, impatient of the limitations their parents tolerated, are less "pragmatic" than their elders. A survey earlier this year showed that dissatisfaction with life in Hong Kong was highest among young people, and that those aged 18–29 were most likely to describe themselves as "Hong Kong people," rather than as "Hong Kong Chinese." Chinese sovereignty has made the young especially conscious of Hong Kong's distinctiveness within China. Student groups are among the fiercest proponents of democratic reform. One, "Scholarism," was founded in 2011 by Joshua Wong, who was 14 at the time, to campaign against changes to the curriculum to make it more "patriotic" i.e., pro-Communist. Now Scholarism and student unions are organizing protests and class boycotts. They will not easily be deterred, even by scare tactics such as armored personnel carriers trundling through the streets, as happened late last month, or a warning from a former Chinese official that "blood will be shed" if Occupy goes ahead.

Nor, however, are they likely to succeed. The pan-dems and business leaders alike share the hope that China will make concessions because it badly wants Hong Kong to thrive—as a matter of national prestige, as a model to Taiwan proving that unification with China need not be feared, and because of its huge economic importance. They

point to 2003, an earlier period of turmoil in Hong Kong over the government's attempt to introduce a law against "sedition" at a time of economic crisis caused by the severe acute respiratory syndrome (SARS). At that time China came to the rescue. It saved the economy with a deal giving Hong Kong firms preferential access to its market, and by allowing more Chinese tourists to visit. And it saw to the removal of an unpopular chief executive.

In 2014 Hong Kong's stock market has been faring well, thanks partly to the prospect of new arrangements next month linking the Hong Kong and Shanghai exchanges. But gloomier businessmen note that Hong Kong's importance to China is dwindling. Its economy, 12% the size of China's in 1984, is now just 3% of it. Its port, in terms of tonnage handled, is smaller than five others in China. And as China liberalizes its financial system and internationalizes its currency, the *yuan*, Hong Kong becomes less special.

Moreover Hong Kong's political significance may have changed. Chinese leaders must know that it is already too late to hope that people in Taiwan will look on it as a positive model. So, from being a possible example of how autonomy could work, it may now be a lesson in how nowhere under China's sovereignty can be allowed a political system that might produce a challenge to the Center. China still wants Hong Kong to be a success, and it would prefer stability. But if instability is the price of having the final say, the party seems prepared to pay it.

CHINA AND TAIWAN[*]

Richard C. Bush

Korea, China, Vietnam, and Germany were the four countries that emerged from World War II divided. The two Vietnams became one in 1976

---

[*] This article was published by the Korea Institute of National Unification (Summer 2014). The essay is based on the finding and interpretations of my previous writings on the China-Taiwan relations in *Untying the Knot: Making Peace in the Taiwan Strait* (Washington, DC: Brookings Institution Press, 2005).

after North Vietnam defeated South Vietnam militarily. The two Germanies became one in 1990 after the collapse of East Germany and the rest of the Soviet bloc. On the Korean peninsula, both Koreas aspire for unification, but how and when it will happen remains very unclear, but there is a broad consensus that at the end of the day the Republic of Korea will rule the peninsula.

Even more uncertain is what will happen to the division between the Republic of China on Taiwan and the People's Republic of China on the mainland, and how unification will occur if it is to occur. The aspiration for unification on the mainland is strong, and the expectation there is that it will occur according to the PRC's formula of "one country, two systems." On Taiwan, opinion is very much divided. A significant share of the population believes that Taiwan should be a separate country. A majority hopes for the preservation of the status quo. Even those Taiwan citizens who would accept unification at some point reject Beijing's approach. So if and how any unification would occur is quite opaque. A military solution seems unlikely, and the PRC regularly reaffirms its peaceful intentions. A negotiated solution seems implausible as long as the two sides stick to the positions to which they have held for thirty years. Is there an intermediate option? This essay explores that background of the division across the Taiwan Strait: its past evolution, current state of play, and the near-term and mid-term possibilities.

Background

Taiwan's relationship to mainland China has been long and complex. The island was incorporated into the imperial Chinese system in 1681 but was more ignored than ruled. The Qing dynasty ceded Taiwan to Meiji Japan in 1895, which ruled it for fifty years and fostered significant economic development. Pursuant to the Cairo and Potsdam Declarations but pending a formal peace treaty, the Republic of China government under Chiang Kai-shek accepted the Japanese surrender. That government then imposed an increasingly repressive regime on the long-time residents, who were largely ethnic Chinese. When Mao Zedong's communists defeated Chiang's armies in 1949 and the ROC government retreated to Taiwan, the expectation was that the fall of the island and the ROC was a matter of time. But the North Korean invasion of South Korea led the new People's Republic of China (PRC) government to put off a quick invasion of Taiwan. Thereafter, the US security guarantee and defense assistance to Taiwan deterred any serious action by

Beijing. Cross–Strait relations remained frozen in all respects until the 1980s. The two governments disagreed on most matters but each believed that Taiwan was a part of Chinese territory and it should reunify China (on its terms, of course).

Three trends changed this status quo. The first was in economic relations. China needed external investment to stimulate the Chinese economy and stabilize its political system, and companies in both Hong Kong and Taiwan were the prime candidates to provide it. Taiwan entrepreneurs were increasingly eager to have access to China, not only because it might become a big consumer market but also because of rising wage rates on the island and American pressure to appreciate Taiwan's currency. The ROC government accommodated to this desire, and there thus began an economic migration that has made Taiwan companies important players in the mainland economy. Between 2006 and 2012, China, including Hong Kong, consumed on average around 39 percent of Taiwan's exports (America takes only 12 percent). Not a small number of people in Taiwan have worried about excessive economic dependence on China, but stopping the trend was impossible.

At first it seemed that economic interaction could produce political reconciliation. The first senior-level, semi-official meetings occurred in Singapore in April 1993, facilitated by mutual acceptance of an ambiguous formula later called the "1992 Consensus." China's leaders became more confident that time was on their side and that ultimately Taiwan would accept its formula for unification. But the second trend replaced Beijing's confidence with alarm.

That trend was Taiwan's democratization, which began in 1986 and culminated in the presidential election of 1996. Chiang Ching-kuo, the leader of the ruling Kuomintang, had the counter-intuitive insight that perhaps the regime could govern more effectively by opening up the political system rather than through continued tight control. He also recognized that democracy would give Taiwan a new, values basis for American support. Lee Teng-hui, Chiang's successor, completed the democratization process that he had begun.

For Beijing, an open and democratic Taiwan was problematic. It meant that native Taiwanese like Lee Teng-hui, who didn't identify with the mainland as much as mainlander leaders like Chiang Ching-kuo did, would henceforth dominate Taiwan politics. It also permitted public discussion of ideas that had been previously taboo. First and foremost of these was the proposal of the opposition Democratic Progressive Party that Taiwan should be an independent country rather than a part of China that was awaiting national unification. Democratization was also problematic for China by transforming the context in which Taiwan might negotiate with Beijing. At least metaphorically, Taiwan voters would have a seat at the negotiating table, and most of them opposed China's one country, two systems formula for unification. The opposition DPP was still a minority, but in Beijing's eyes a negative trend had begun.

The third new trend was the end of the Cold War. Specifically the fall of the Soviet Union caused the collapse of the international arms market. Defense contractors everywhere were in trouble and looking for markets. China saw an opportunity to buy Soviet weapons systems and so modernize its arsenal much faster than was possible through indigenous development. Taiwan saw a similar opportunity with the United States and a few European countries.

The United States did not cause any of these trends, but it welcomed the first two: improvements in cross-strait relations and democracy on Taiwan. In general, it welcomed the end of the Cold War but not all of its consequences. A major consequence: the break-up of the former Yugoslavia. A minor one: the buyer's market in arms led the first Bush administration to approve the sale of F-16s to Taiwan, which was a significant upgrade in quality and quantity. It did so both because China's capabilities were increasing and because of domestic pressure. That China was still in global isolation because of Tiananmen was also at play. But approval of the sale deepened the post-Tiananmen deterioration in US-China relations.

Things went from bad to worse for Beijing in the mid-1990s when Lee Teng-hui sought a second full term in Taiwan's first presidential contest by direct elections. The public wanted Taiwan to break out from China's diplomatic quarantine, so Lee engineered a visit to the United States. To appeal to the Taiwanese majority, he emphasized identity politics. And he saw the value of playing upon the public's fears of China. In response, China therefore engaged in coercive diplomacy,

including conducting missile exercises in the days before the election in March 1996. Thereafter, Lee continued to emphasize, as he saw it, the ROC's status as a sovereign entity. But Beijing concluded that his statements and actions indicated that he sought Taiwan independence.[1]

Chen Shui-bian, a leader of the DPP, won the presidency in 2000 by mounting a centrist electoral campaign. His victory deepened China's sense of vulnerability. Early on, it concluded that Chen sought an independent Taiwan when in fact he hoped to find a way to coexist with China. To keep his party in power in 2004 and 2008, he shifted, aligning with his party's pro-independence base—playing up identity politics, baiting China, and proposing provocative initiatives. China's reactions deepened *Taiwan's* sense of vulnerability. It was a situation of mutual fear.

Taiwan's actions and China's response also alarmed the United States. It feared that a negative cross-strait spiral might lead to a conflict in which it would have to intervene. So the Clinton administration and the second Bush administration pursued an approach of "dual deterrence": simultaneously warning Beijing and Taipei against provocative actions and reassuring each of US intentions.

Since 2008

The March 2008 presidential elections were a turning point in Taiwan politics. Many voters were uncertain about their economic future and rattled by the yo-yo of tensions with China. Both the PRC and the Kuomintang worked to present an alternative path to confrontation. First, PRC President Hu Jintao laid out in some detail the benefits that would flow to Taiwan if it eschewed the road of Taiwan independence. Then Ma Ying-jeou, the Kuomintang's candidate, campaigned on the idea that Taiwan could better maintain its freedom, prosperity, security, and dignity by engaging China, not provoking it. On election day, he got 58 percent of the vote.

Ma Ying-jeou moved quickly to carry out his campaign proposals. He first reassured Beijing about his intentions while president by pledging there would be no move to independence during his presidency. He accepted the so-called 1992 Consensus, a formula that the two sides had worked out for the April 1993 meeting noted above. (To reassure the Taiwan public, he also called for no unification and no war.) The two sides agreed that they would focus first on "easy," mainly economic, issues before moving to harder ones in the political and security arenas. Between 2008 and 2011, they rapidly concluded a series of agreements, mostly economic in nature, to remove the obstacles between them and to expand areas of mutual cooperation. The initial accords removed obstacles to normal interactions between the two sides. More ambitious was crafting a process of economic liberalization, the centerpiece of which was the Economic Cooperation Framework Agreement, signed in June 2010. The ECFA's ultimate objective was the creation of a free-trade area across the Taiwan Strait.

Nothing in this process was easy. Each successive negotiation became more difficult than the one before because the issues were more difficult and affected more domestic interests. In the summer of 2009, Beijing got impatient about moving from economic issues to political ones and only backed off when Taipei signaled that the political climate was not right. On the one hand, Ma Ying-jeou had low approval ratings because of some mistakes by his administration. On the other, the opposition DPP emphasized the downside of mainland engagement. It charged that the benefits were going only to the wealthy while average citizens suffered. It also asserted that Ma had started Taiwan down the slippery slope towards unification, selling out Taiwan's sovereignty in the process.

This view, while understandable, was not accurate. Although Ma probably shares his party's long-term goal of "ultimate unification," he also believes that the terms and conditions must be right and that a broad majority of the Taiwan public believes that the terms are right. A reason for that caution is that unification, whatever the terms, probably will require amendments to the ROC constitution. That in turn requires a three-fourths vote in the legislature and approval in a public referendum by 50 percent of all registered voters—a very high bar. When, during Ma's presidency, there were even hints of movement toward unification, there was a strong negative public reaction. So the goal of Ma's mainland policy was to stabilize Beijing-Taipei relations after a long period of turmoil rather than trying to resolve the fundamental dispute between the two sides. Stabilization might lead to resolution, of course, but only if Taiwan chose to go there.

In the 2012 presidential campaign, the DPP again pushed its anti-Ma and anti-ECFA arguments, warning that Taiwan was on a slippery slope. Ma argued that his policies had brought an improvement in economic performance and that a DPP victory would put those benefits at risk. Ma got the better of the argument and won re-election by a safe margin. Still, Taiwan remains a deeply divided polity.

Just as cross-strait relations improved under Ma, so did US-Taiwan ties. Washington both approved of the results of Ma's policies and improved bilateral ties. The conduct of relations improved considerably. The Obama administration approved both visa-waiver treatment for Taiwan visitors to America and $13 billion in arms sales, a record for one, four-year term. After a couple of false starts, the Ma administration removed obstacles to discussions of bilateral economic liberalization. This reflected a linkage in American policy: US relations with Taiwan are a function of Taiwan's policies towards China.

During Ma's second term, even cross-strait stabilization became hard. One reason was on display in the negotiations with Beijing concerning Ma's sensible but modest initiative to allow each side's semi-official cross-Strait organization (Taiwan's Straits Exchange Foundation and the mainland's Association for Relations Across the Taiwan Strait) to open branch offices in the other's capital city. The talks got hung up on the question of whether officers in the SEF's office on the mainland could visit Taiwan residents who had been detained by mainland law-enforcement authorities. Taipei insisted that it had to be able to help its citizens in trouble. Beijing objected because this service looked a lot like the consular function that embassies perform, thus suggesting that Taiwan was a sovereign entity. Deep differences on that question have been the key obstacle to resolving the basic cross-strait dispute, but they also intrude into the stabilization effort.

A second reason for the slow-down in cross-Strait stabilization was domestic politics on Taiwan. Even in the economic sphere, easy issues were destined to become hard. For example, the Service Trade Agreement, which was signed in

June 2013, would open parts of the Taiwan market to mainland service providers, thus threatening their Taiwan competitors. At the same time, some Taiwan service sectors doubted that they would be able to take advantage of the market openings on the mainland side (this was particularly a concern of small and medium enterprises). To make matters worse for the Ma administration, which probably could have done a better job selling the agreement to the public, the DPP chose to fight the agreement in the Legislature rather than allow it to go through.[2] The DPP, knowing that it could not defeat the agreement if it came to a vote in the Legislative Yuan, chose to block its consideration at every turn. When in mid-March 2014, the KMT caucus grew frustrated and tried to abandon article-by-article review and move directly for a vote on the agreement, DPP legislators seized control of the legislature. They were soon joined by students from various Taiwan universities who called themselves the "Sunflower Movement." After several weeks, the Legislative Yuan returned to something like normalcy, but passage of the agreement was even less likely than when the crisis began.

The Service Trade Agreement was only the most recent battle in a long war. That was a general conflict over how to cope with an increasingly powerful China, which has been the central issue of Taiwan politics for two decades. It is a debate that has evoked rival policy approaches (the proper mix of engagement and resistance) and contending definitions of national identity (Chinese? Taiwanese? Some sort of mixture?).

The Sunflower Movement was one example of a new phenomenon in Taiwan politics: the emergence of new, activist social movements that are intensely dedicated to a specific cause and use social media to mobilize followers. These movements lack confidence in the vision of Taiwan's political leaders and in the effectiveness of the island's political institutions to provide effective and accountable governance. The mass media provides these movements with disproportionate coverage. This phenomenon is not totally new, of course: there were social movements on the island in the 1980s and early 1990s. Thereafter, political parties and elections channeled public sentiment. Towards the new movements, parties have an ambivalent perspective. The Kuomintang appears not to know how to cope with them. The DPP has tried to co-opt

them for its own purposes. Indeed, the Sunflower occupation of the Legislative Yuan would not have happened without the DPP's enabling actions.

Prospects for New Progress in China-Taiwan Relations

The progress that occurred after 2008 was the picking of "low-hanging fruit." The two sides purposefully picked "easy" issues on which to conclude agreements. All of these accords were areas on which mutual benefits were possible, thus receiving the support of a majority of the Taiwan public. If even economic issues were becoming "hard" by 2013, political issues were much more difficult. Whether talks on the latter would ever occur has been the key indicator of how far cross-Strait progress would go.

During Ma's first term, Beijing tried on one occasion to push for political talks, but the opposition in Taiwan was quick and strong. Two obstacles that block the two sides from tackling political issues are truly formidable. The first is Taiwan public opinion, which remains unconvinced that the island would benefit from political agreements as it did from most economic agreements. The Ma administration made the cross-Strait progress it did in the first term because the balance of sentiment in society favored his policies. Roughly speaking, 55 percent approved of them to some degree, while 45 percent was skeptical or outright opposed. This was the margin in the 2012 presidential elections by which conservative candidates bested their rivals on the left. But, it is important to emphasize that this balance of sentiment applies only to cross-Strait economic policy. Although it is hard to say what the margin is on the political side, those who constitute the majority certainly oppose talks. Thus, when there were hints both before and after the 2012 elections that political talks might be in the offing, there was a public panic, to the point that Ma had to promise a role for the legislature and the public in approving any agreement.

The second obstacle is a serious conceptual gap between the two sides on political talks. A central issue in any cross-strait political negotiation will be the status of Taiwan and its government within the framework of one China. Is it a sovereign entity, as most on the island believe, or is it merely a regional authority that lacks any sovereign character (as Beijing asserts)? Essentially, this is the question of the Republic of China, on which each side of the Strait has its own answer. For talks to succeed there would need to be at least a provisional consensus between Beijing and Taipei, and a public education campaign to prepare the Taiwan public since the issues involved are esoteric to say the least. So far, there have been no government-to-government discussions of the Republic of China matter, only Track Two exchanges between scholars of each side. These have served only to make the conceptual differences more explicit rather than bridge any gaps.

Recall the distinction that I made earlier between stabilizing cross-strait relations and resolving the fundamental dispute between the PRC and ROC. One of the reasons that political talks are so difficult for each side is that what might be agreed *for the purpose of stabilization* about the status of Taiwan within the context of One-China is likely to define the point of departure for any negotiations *to resolve the fundamental issue.* Neither side will wish to make a concession now that would be acceptable to the other side, if it fears, correctly or incorrectly, that it will put it in a weak position later. As the weaker party and a democracy, Taiwan is particularly prone to such fears.

The question for the near-term future is how the results of the 2016 presidential election will reshape Taiwan's cross-strait policy and Beijing's response. A victory for the Kuomintang candidate (Ma is term-limited from running) would no doubt result in continuity of basic policy, which would be somewhat reassuring to Beijing. The result would indicate that the 55–45 percent balance of sentiment was holding. Ma's successor would likely reaffirm his commitment to the 1992 Consensus as the political basis for cross-strait interaction and cooperation and to *not* pursue de jure independence. Yet even under this new KMT president, the chances for movement towards political talks would remain low. The factors that made it a non-starter in the Ma period—public opposition and the conceptual gap regarding the ROC—would remain. At least some on the mainland would conclude that the ultimate outcome of this incremental process of stabilization would not be realization of Beijing's goal of unification but a permanent preservation of the status

quo—in effect, peaceful separation. Still, Beijing would be unlikely to upset the current status quo.

If the DPP candidate were to win in 2016, it would be a different story. Clearly, the DPP will regain power at some point, if only because the public dissatisfactions with the Ma administration's performance accumulate to the point that it becomes difficult for any KMT candidate to win. The question is when the DPP comes back to power, not if.

What about Beijing's reaction to a DPP victory? Chinese leaders would no doubt worry that the result reflected a change in sentiment and that the new president would, like Chen Shui-bian, pursue policies that it concluded were a challenge to China's fundamental interests. Beijing would then have to formulate a response that would deter such antithetical policies and seek, over time, to reverse the negative trend (from its point of view) in the balance of sentiment. This will be a matter both of facts and perceptions of facts. If the election agenda is domestic in focus, then it is harder to make the case that the balance of sentiment has changed. But the situation is likely to be more complex. In 2012, Ma was able to foster fear about the consequences of a DPP victory; in 2016, the DPP may be able to make the case is what voters should most fear is further integration with China. So subjective perceptions will come into play. Also complex would be any assessment of a new DPP's president's policies and their impact on PRC interests. That Beijing would make an accurate and objective assessment should not be taken for granted.

What Taiwan Should Fear

On the face of it, Taiwan has much to fear. The fundamental objective of the PRC regime is to formally incorporate Taiwan into the People's Republic of China and terminate the regime of the Republic of China, for reasons of national pride and regional strategy. Beijing's growing advantage over Taiwan in terms of both military capability and international political influence has objectively increased the island's vulnerability. Yet this is a fundamentally political dispute with a military aspect. Whether Beijing would ever use its capabilities to achieve its unification objective would be a function of underlying political factors. Since 1979, Beijing's stated preference has been to use peaceful, that is political, means to induce Taiwan to concede. China's build-up of military capabilities really began in earnest to deter *political* initiatives that Beijing feared Taiwan's leaders might undertake that would challenge China's fundamental interests (independence).

Since 2008, the threat of Chinese military action has receded because Ma Ying-jeou successfully reassured Beijing that he would not pursue independence. That allowed the two sides to expand areas of cooperation. Their mode of interaction was one of "mutual persuasion" rather than provocation or coercion. Mutual persuasion requires that each side know its goals; communicate clearly what it needs from its interaction with the other; have a clear understanding of the other's goals; avoid misunderstanding; have a coherent and relatively unified formulation of its position; be willing to explore points of substantive overlap and convergence; and protect political flanks at home and coordinate politics and negotiations. All of this is extremely complicated, of course, but each has seen the value of this approach. As the smaller party, Taiwan has a greater interest in a continuation of mutual persuasion. What it should fear is that Beijing would abandon this approach and resort to something else.

That "something else" is probably *not* the use or threat of force, the imposition of economic sanctions, or the explicit mobilization of "China-friendly" sectors in Taiwan to manipulate the political system in China's favor. Each of these steps entails a significant degree of risk. They will not necessarily succeed and might lead to an outcome that is worse than not acting.

More likely, I believe, is that Beijing might choose to abandon mutual persuasion and exploit the growing power asymmetry between it and Taiwan. In effect, it would engage in a campaign of pressure and intimidation. It would take advantage of Taiwan's need to sustain economic prosperity through globalization, its relative diplomatic isolation, its latent doubts about US support, its desire for peace, and the dysfunction of Taiwan's political system. It would not employ just one kind of leverage, but exert pressure along several different dimensions of its power at the same time (economic, diplomatic, political, and military). China's hope would be that Taiwan's leaders and public would ultimately conclude that its situation is hopeless and then capitulate. In that contingency, actual economic sanctions or threats of force would never be necessary, because the mere *fact* of its military

and economic power would shape the calculus of Taiwan's decision-makers. As Chas Freeman has written, "When Beijing judges that the moment is ripe, it will know how to use inducements as well as implied threats to help Taiwanese rationalize agreement to a long-term cross-strait accommodation that meets the requirements of Chinese nationalism. . . . China's endgame with Taiwan envisages its eventual preemptive capitulation to the inexorable in response to an offer Taiwan cannot refuse."[3]

This is the logic of Sun Zi, who asserted (correctly) that winning without fighting is far preferable to winning through fighting. If, hypothetically, Beijing were to develop a playbook based on Sun Zi's logic, what would it look like? How would it use its various assets in order to contest Taiwan initiatives, exploit its vulnerabilities, and cumulatively guide the island's leaders and people to the conclusion that it has no choice but to accept the offer that cannot be refused? My guess is that some of the following items would probably make the list:

- Increase Taiwan's economic dependence on the PRC economy and so raise the costs of any political challenge;
- Demonize those on Taiwan who seek *de jure* independence as unpatriotic and dangerous;
- Foster the view that unification is inevitable;
- Point out the success of Hong Kong in preserving the territory's way of life without significant cost;
- Show no flexibility on China's fundamental approach to resolving the fundamental dispute, while suggesting that there is flexibility on details;
- Oppose any significant expansion of Taiwan's participation in the international community but grant token concessions;
- Oppose overt moves toward Taiwan independence through political and diplomatic means if necessary and by displays and use of force if necessary; and
- Constrain arms sales and other forms of US support for Taiwan's security and get American help in blocking Taiwan Independence.

In fact, China has done all of these things to a modest degree already; it would only intensify and concentrate them.

It is quite premature to conclude *prima facie* that China is likely to choose to use its growing capabilities to compel its ultimate objective of unification through pressure and intimidation.

China's military posture appears still to be a significant function of what it fears—independence—and of the need to maintain the capacity to deter that outcome. Beijing can cling to a Marxist confidence that as economic interdependence grows, political views on Taiwan will become more China friendly. It can continue to meddle mildly in Taiwan domestic politics. And it can assume that time is on its side and that the "shadow of the future" over Taiwan will continue to darken.

What are the circumstances under which China may be tempted to abandon a stance of strategic patience and the paradigm of mutual persuasion to actively press Taiwan to recognize the need to resolve the fundamental dispute? Several come to mind:

- If it concludes Taiwan will always avoid political negotiations, even under continued KMT rule;
- If it decides that the unification window is closing or that a serious Taiwan independence window is opening;
- If it overestimates the benefits of pressure and underestimates both the resistance such an approach would provoke on Taiwan and other costs; and
- If it believes that the political forces on Taiwan in favor of final resolution are much stronger than those actively against, and that people in the middle no longer see any value of resisting.

For Beijing to come to any of these conclusions is complicated, and there is a danger that it will miscalculate, both about the need to increase pressure and the benefits it will yield. Yet because the PRC system has been prone to misperceptions concerning Taiwan and other actors in the past, the possibility of an intimidation campaign cannot be ruled out. If in this case China were to over-estimate the prospects for success but then face unexpected resistance from Taiwan, it would have to consider carrying out the threats implied in a pressure policy.

Can China and Taiwan Avoid the Worst?

If Taiwan wishes to preserve the mode of mutual persuasion as the best way to protect its fundamental interests; and if it wishes to avoid China's undertaking a campaign of pressure and intimidation, it must make it less vulnerable by strengthening itself. Five areas seem most important.

The first is economic: how to sustain Taiwan's competitiveness as the Chinese economy modernizes. This is not a problem unique to Taiwan; Korea and Japan face the same problem. The objective here should be to transition to an economy that is powered by knowledge and innovation. The pressing task is to reform the education system so that it creates the human capital that a new Taiwan economy requires. It also requires ending regulations that stifle entrepreneurship. Externally, Taiwan, having become more integrated with the Chinese economy and undertaken the liberalization embodied in ECFA, now needs to expand and liberalize its economic relation with its other major trading partners, including the United States, Japan, Korea, and the European Union. These liberalization efforts will stimulate structural reform within Taiwan in the direction of an innovation-intensive economy.

Second, Taiwan needs to strengthen its understanding on a society-wide basis of its negotiating bottom line with the mainland, that the ROC is a sovereign entity. The issue of sovereignty has been the main obstacle to improving political relations and resolving the fundamental cross-Strait dispute. But the meaning of that concept is fairly superficial. It certainly has an international dimension, but also a cross-strait and internal dimension. Without a clearer understanding of sovereignty, neither Taiwan leaders nor citizens will know what aspects are trivial and can be conceded to Beijing and which must be defended until the bitter end.

Third, Taiwan needs to strengthen itself diplomatically, and that means primarily relations with Washington. The United States remains Taiwan's sole protector, so it cannot afford to have a bad relationship with America. Ties with the United States have been good during the Ma administration but were not before that.

Fourth, Taiwan needs to strengthen itself militarily. This refers not just to defense hardware (weapons) systems but also defense software (military institutions and human resources). On the issue of hardware, Taipei must ensure that it uses scarce defense dollars in support of a defense strategy appropriate to its changing threat environment. As the PLA gets stronger, advanced fighter aircraft may not be the most cost-effective way of deterring mainland adventurism.

Finally, Taiwan needs to strengthen its political system, through which all these measures will be processed. Some elements of the political system appear to do a decent job in reflecting the people's will. The electoral system is a case in point. But other elements do not. The Legislative Yuan is beset by conflicts of interest, lack of specialization, a tolerance of behavior outside of institutional norms, and mechanisms that privilege minority power over majority rule. The media focuses on the scandalous and the sensational, with little attention to the serious challenges that face Taiwan. The island's people are not well served by the political system's dysfunction, and that makes more likely the emergence of protest movements.

Is there anything that China might do that would both be attractive to the Taiwan political elite and public and advance its fundamental goals? The main thing would be to address seriously and creatively the issue of the Republic of China (that is, Taiwan's claim that it is a sovereign entity). If Beijing is to move from stabilization to resolution through mutual persuasion, which, objectively, it is in its interest to do, it cannot avoid the issue of the ROC. Second, it could take a more accommodating position on Taiwan's international space, particularly its participation in liberalization arrangements with its major trading partners. To restrict that participation will only undermine Taiwan's prosperity and foster public resentment.

Conclusion

It is sometimes said that Taiwan is already trapped in China's orbit, with no way to escape. The only question then is how fast that orbit will shrink and disappear. "Orbit" is an interesting metaphor because it implies a balance of centripetal and centrifugal forces. The main centripetal factor is the incentive Taiwan has to integrate deeply into the Chinese economy and reap the benefits of that integration. The main centrifugal force is the fear of people on Taiwan—stronger among some parts of the population than in others—that China's goals are contrary to the island's best interests and sense of itself. Among the 45 percent of the public who support the DPP and other like-minded parties, that fear is very strong.

China's centripetal force will likely grow as China's "comprehensive national power," including military power, grows. The issue then is whether and how Beijing might choose to give full play to that growing power. As I suggest above, no one can rule out the possibility that Beijing ever seeks to coerce Taiwan to surrender; it is unlikely to be solely through military means, but through a multifaceted effort that has economic, diplomatic, political, psychological, and the threat of military action. What is more certain is that a Taiwan that is intimidated into submission would not be a happy and accommodating Taiwan. The question for Taiwan, therefore, is whether is willing and able to strengthen itself so that China would not even try to compel an increase in centripetal force. The question for Beijing is whether it would be willing to increase the centripetal force acting on Taiwan through attraction rather than compellence.

NOTES

1. My own view is that Lee, at least during his presidency, was not pursuing de jure independence at all but was in laying out his own concept of unification. But for China, Lee's concept was inconsistent with one country, two systems, and incompatible with the PRC as a unitary state, and therefore unacceptable on both grounds.
2. This approach was different from the one the DPP eventually adopted regarding the initial ECFA pact in 2010. The party initially said that it would revisit that agreement if it returned to power in 2012. Once it saw how popular ECFA was, it dropped that threat.
3. Class W. Freeman, Jr., "The Taiwan Problem and China's Strategy for Resolving It," remarks at the Center for Naval Analysis, September 14, 2011 (www.mepc.org/articles-commentary/speeches/taiwan-problem-and-chinas-strategy-resolving-it).

CHINA FACES THE FUTURE

Editorial Introduction: Whither China?

Estimating China's future trajectory is difficult, and predicting it with any precision is impossible.[1] China is so large and complex, its internal dynamics and external linkages fluid and variable. China's behavior and trajectory has continued to befuddle China experts around the world for more than half a century—frequently shifting abruptly in unforeseen directions. Yet, China is not a complete mystery either. China may be distinct, but it is not unique. The country today bears much in common with other newly industrialized economies (NIEs) and (former) Leninist polities. Each pass through rather predictable phases, from which China and the Chinese Communist Party are not immune. Moreover, in its 3000+ years of history, China has passed through many dynastic transitions, each of which had certain common features. Bearing in mind these uncertainties, the selections in this section present four different perspectives on China's future evolution.

The first is by China's current Foreign Minister, Wang Yi. Published in 2014, it offers a good insight into the current Xi Jinping regime's views of China's future. It is always important to understand China's own official self-assessments, as they surely vary with those of foreign analysts yet provide windows into the language and concepts used in official discourse (propaganda). Wang Yi begins with a reiteration of Xi Jinping's signature concept of the "Chinese Dream," the essence of which is "national rejuvenation." Wang states unequivocally, "Looking into the future, especially the coming three decades, China has every reason to believe that as long as it adheres to a path of peaceful development, its goal of national rejuvenation will be achieved." The term *peaceful development* is not new—its dates to Deng Xiaoping and has long been the guiding principle of the Chinese government, that is, China seeks only to develop itself, requires a peaceful environment to do so, and it seeks peace with all other nations.

Wang Yi acknowledges that foreign perceptions of China do not necessarily accept the Chinese self-perception of peaceful development. He criticizes both "China failure" and "China threat" theories as unjustified. He also acknowledges the so-called Thucydides

Trap of rising powers and established powers clashing in warfare. But he dismisses these possibilities on the basis of China's stated commitment to peaceful development. Foreign Minister Wang then provides a good overview of China's foreign policy priorities circa 2014—surveying China's relations across the globe. His is a very optimistic assessment, and he concludes by observing, "With time and hard work, a better external environment will be created to facilitate the realization of the Chinese dream of national rejuvenation."

The next three selections all assess the Chinese regime's staying power. The first is by Stanford University Professor Andrew G. Walder, one of the world's leading sociologists on contemporary China. Walder begins by appropriately reminding us of the many stresses and deep crises that the CCP and state have weathered over its 65 years in power. The party-state has survived several existential experiences, and overcame the stagnant Maoist era to develop the nation in ways never before witnessed in human history. In evaluating the present and future prospects for China, Walder notes both the stresses as well as the strengths of the society and regime—particularly rapidly rising public protests stimulated by inequality and predatory behavior of local cadres. Yet, overall, he concludes, "There are symptoms of economic conflicts in a vastly transformed society, and in the context of a regime that is more stable and that enjoys greater popular support than was the case during the first decade of economic reforms. Political change in China will remain a protracted affair, driven forward by forces that are fundamentally different from those that toppled so many economically stagnant and illegitimate communist regimes some two decades ago—and that briefly threatened the Chinese regime in 1989."

The next selection, by long-time China observer Orville Schell and historian John Delury, argues that for China to move ahead into the future it needs to shed its self-imposed identity and national narrative of victimization by foreigners. This self-perception is so deeply ingrained in all Chinese, and is reinforced by the regime on a daily basis on media, textbooks, museums, and other instruments of socialization and indoctrination. For China to fully move forward and achieve its intended greatness, Schell and Delury argue, it needs to overcome this backward-looking and aggrieved psychology. Only then, they say, will China be able to truly coexist with the United States and its neighbors.

The final selection is by Columbia University political scientist and distinguished China watcher Andrew Nathan. In it, he too tries to "see the unforeseeable," that is, how nations and political systems collapse. This is not an idle question when looking at China, as so many other authoritarian and Leninist type systems have collapsed over the past two decades. Only five remain: China, North Korean, Vietnam, Laos, and Cuba. Many of those thirty-plus regimes that did collapse after 1989 possessed common features that, in retrospect, help to explain their demise. Yet, despite the similarities, each case is different—and hence the pathways to their collapse and transitions to post-authoritarian and post-Leninist systems varied. As a result, Nathan looks for what he describes as the "tipping points" in these regimes as a means to anticipating China's possible future. He argues that even though such regimes have many characteristics in common and are ready-made for *dénouement*, they all nonetheless require "triggering events." Once triggered, cascades occur and ruling regimes lose control. Identifying the "inflection points" and triggers are thus analytically important, but nearly impossible to forecast with any precision. Even once triggering events take place, a variety of pathways—differing cascade effects that Nathan describes—unfold with no precisely repeated path to collapse for such regimes. He describes many factors in China today that could trigger such a process, but he concludes that: "For change to happen, there will need to be a breakthrough moment."

Thus the selections in this concluding section of *The China Reader* all look forward into the future, but offer strongly different perspectives. I chose this variety of viewpoints intentionally, so that readers could see the range of opinion and uncertainty about China's future today (2015). The only thing that is certain is that China-watching will remain a fascinating enterprise and profession, and that China itself will continue to perplex and surprise the world.

NOTES

1. For some possibilities, see David Shambaugh, *China's Future* (Cambridge: Polity Press, 2016).

I. MUDDLE THROUGH, ADAPTATION, OR THE END OF DYNASTY?

Peaceful Development and the Chinese Dream of National Rejuvenation[*]

Wang Yi

Shortly after the successful convening of the 18th National Party Congress, newly elected General Secretary Xi Jinping put forth the important concept of the "Chinese Dream." Since then, Xi has made various observations on China's path of peaceful development, including remarks that were issued at the collective learning sessions of the Politburo of the Communist Party. These remarks and observations undoubtedly enrich the strategic connotations of peaceful development. As Xi clearly stated, the concept of the Chinese dream and the path of peaceful development are consistent with each other. The former is China's lofty goal, while the latter is the only correct path via which China can achieve this goal.

Looking back at Chinese history since the founding of the People's Republic, it is evident that only socialism was able to save modern China. With the "Reform and Opening" policy, China was blessed with a pathway towards national prosperity. Looking into the future, especially the coming three decades, China has every reason to believe that as long as it adheres to a path of peaceful development, its goal of national rejuvenation will be achieved. In addition, a favorable international environment can be created to facilitate China's achievement of its bicentennial goals and the Chinese Dream.

The Roots of China's Peaceful Development

To understand how China chose its path of peaceful development, two macro perspectives are helpful. First, it is important to grasp the historical positioning of China's own development, and second, it is just as crucial to understand the historical trajectories of world powers during their rises.

A major oriental civilization with a brilliant history, China did not start its decline until the modern era. During the 20th century, especially the six decades after the founding of People's Republic and the three decades after Reform and Opening commenced, generations of outstanding Chinese, including Communist Party members, took strides towards China's national rejuvenation. Now, China is once again at the dawn of a national revival. It is already the world's second largest economy, the largest industrialized nation, the largest exporting country, and the country with the largest foreign exchange reserves. In addition, China is the largest trading partner of 128 countries. According

---

[*] This article was published in *China International Studies* (January/February 2014).

to the latest International Monetary Fund (IMF) forecasts, Chinese economic growth accounted for 27.7 percent of global economic growth in 2013. It is not an exaggeration to say that the performance of the world economy depends on the performance of the Asian economy, while the performance of the Asian economy in large part depends on the performance of the Chinese economy. This statement is especially true if we consider that China accounted for more than half of the economic growth in Asia. As an important driver of the global economic recovery, China has become an indispensable player in international and regional affairs. As such, many people believe that today's China is perhaps closest to the center of the world—fast approaching its goal of national rejuvenation.

A journey that is 90 percent complete is still incomplete. The closer China comes to achieving its goal, the more sober and alert it must be. To the Chinese nation, the coming decades are bound to be full of inspiration and excitement, as well as risks and challenges. One major challenge is how China will alleviate the concerns and worries of the international community over its future development. In other words, how will China deal with the prejudices and misunderstandings of some countries and how will it thwart the provocations and interventions of hostile forces?

There has never been a historical precedent of such an enormous country rising so rapidly. Nor has there ever been a case of such a huge population modernizing so successfully and comprehensively. China's rise and rejuvenation will not only have a profound impact on the world situation. It will also influence the global balance of power and international order. As such, it is quite understandable that countries in the world are paying close attention to China's strategic moves. China will have to become accustomed to living under such close scrutiny during its national revival.

Once upon a time, there were numerous "China failure" theories circulating in the international community, all claiming that China's development would be short-lived and unsustainable. Nowadays, the "China failure" theories have been replaced by various "China threat" theories. For example, in recent books, John Mearsheimer, an American realist international relations scholar, claims that war will be inevitable between China

and the United States. Mearsheimer's pessimism is not strange, for almost all Western countries in the modern era have risen through non-peaceful means. Their upward paths have been characterized either by colonial expansion or by hegemonic struggles. Since Westerners believe that a rising power will inevitably seek hegemony, they will naturally doubt whether China will be able to escape the traditional fate of rising powers.

In his classic book *History of the Peloponnesian War*, the ancient Greek historian Thucydides traced the cause of the war between Athens and Sparta to Spartan fears over the rapid rise of Athens, the emerging power at the time. Wars consequently broke out between the two city-states. This phenomenon spawned the term "Thucydides Trap" to describe the seemingly inevitable clash between emerging and existing powers. According to some statistics, of the 15 modern historical cases in which emerging powers sought to replace existing powers, 11 ended in war.

Historical power shifts that caused worldwide changes have usually been achieved through radical means—and sometimes through war. The Westphalia System was born after the Thirty Years' War in modern Europe, the Vienna System after the Napoleonic Wars, the Versailles System after the First World War, and the Yalta System after the Second World War. The collapse of the Soviet Union in the late 20th century also led to a worldwide power shift—and in this case, the destructive effects on the former Soviet Union and the global repercussions were no less intensive than those of a war.

In short, given China's rapid growth and development, many are concerned that China will challenge the existing power structure and international order, or even cause a war. Against such a backdrop, the Chinese people and the CCP must confront many realistic, significant and urgent questions: Can China elude the Thucydides Trap? Can it escape the historical fate of degrading into a hegemony-seeking country? Will it effectively and innovatively resolve old puzzles and thereby reduce resistance to achieving its goals at a minimal cost?

In the 21st century, the Chinese Communist Party built on historical experiences and lessons, as well as the current *zeitgeist*, and declared that China would unswervingly adhere to a path of peaceful development. The Communist Party has also declared that China will never resort to aggression or expansion, as many other countries have mistakenly done in the past. Instead, China will remain firmly committed to its new path of national development and rejuvenation. As proof of this commitment, the Communist Party wrote the principle of peaceful development into the 17th and 18th National Party Congresses, as well as the constitution.

During a collective Communist Party learning session in early 2013, General Secretary Xi once again stressed the importance of peaceful development as a strategic decision that is in accordance with the *zeitgeist* and China's fundamental interests. As Xi said, there must be a peaceful international environment for China to achieve its goals. Without peace, neither China nor the world will be able to develop smoothly. And without development, there will never be long-lasting peace. Therefore, China must unswervingly adhere to a path of peaceful development.

China's commitment to peaceful development is not only a key decision made by the Communist Party based on domestic and international affairs. It is also a solemn commitment that the Chinese government is making to the rest of the world. By pursuing peaceful development, China is seeking to develop itself while creating a peaceful international environment. The purpose of such a path is to achieve national rejuvenation via peaceful means, while at the same time promoting the prosperity of other countries. The path of peaceful development not only combines peace with development and connects domestic affairs with international affairs. It also links the interests of a single country to the common interests of mankind. It marks a moment of huge progress in human history and an important innovation in international relations.

Scientific Justifications for China's Peaceful Development

Why must China embark on a path of peaceful development? Is it a viable path? In other words, is peaceful development necessary and feasible?

Peaceful Development Is a Necessary Requirement of Economic Globalization Nowadays, economic globalization and the emerging information society are changing people's lives in a fundamental way. Interconnectivity has rendered our world smaller and flatter by bringing nations and people closer to each other. As a result, the world has evolved into a place with interwoven interests and synchronous symbiosis. In a certain sense, the new global situation can explain the differences between the grave recessions that afflicted the 20th and 21st centuries respectively. The great depression of 1930s shattered the United States, Europe and Japan, but had little impact upon other countries in Asia, Africa, and Latin America. In comparison, the international financial crisis that struck in 2008 threatened the whole world, leaving no country spared and no corner insulated. This provides evidence that globalization has already reached an unprecedented depth and breadth.

Similarly, when the US Federal Reserve signaled that it would cease its quantitative easing monetary policy in 2013, this instantly caused turbulence in several emerging countries' financial markets. Likewise, the slow-down of the Chinese economy in the first half of 2013 also triggered some global tensions. It used to be the case that when bigger countries sneezed, smaller countries would cough in reaction. But in today's world, smaller countries can also exercise influence on big countries through "butterfly effects." The latest proof thereof can be found in the recent Eurozone sovereign debt crisis.

If the balance of power between the United States and the Soviet Union that persisted during the Cold War was a "balance of terror" based on nuclear deterrence, then today's world is more characterized by a check and balance of interests via interest fusion. This has grown to influence all countries today, especially major countries. War has become increasingly expensive, and the use of force is subject to more and more restrictions. Moreover, global challenges—such as the international financial crisis, terrorism, and climate change, to name just a few—all entail international cooperation and global governance. It is not an exaggeration to say that the world is gradually evolving into one community of common destiny. Within this macro environment of world peace and opposition to war, the peaceful settlement of international disputes has become an inevitable choice. The Syrian chemical weapons case provides a great example of this new reality. When the Syrian chemical weapons issue first became public, the British parliament vetoed military intervention plans due to growing domestic opposition. Similarly, France chose to support the convention of the second Geneva conference to peacefully settle the crisis. Even the United States changed its idea at the last minute and agreed to solve the problem peacefully within the framework of the United Nations.

In his recent book *On China*, Dr. Henry Kissinger explores whether a confrontation similar to the one between the United Kingdom and Germany in the 19th century will be inevitable between China and the United States in the 21st Century. In the book, Kissinger concludes that the decisive form of competition between China and the United States will be more economic and social than military. Kissinger's reasoning is that the two countries have built a closer community of common interests: an annual trade volume of approximately $500 billion, an annual mutual investment scale exceeding $80 billion and an annual visitor number reaching 3.5 million people. According to forecasts by the China-US Exchange Foundation, by 2022, China is projected to become the largest trade partner of the United States and vice versa. Exports to China are projected to contribute $460 billion to the United States GDP, while also creating 3.34 million jobs. Exports to the United States will contribute $480 billion to China's GDP and create 10.22 million jobs in China. The combined size of the two economies will account for one third of the total global economy, and their combined population and total trade volume will respectively make up one quarter and one fifth of the world totals. As such, if conflict breaks out between the two countries, the whole world will be affected. This is an important reason why the world does not wish to see the two countries in conflict with each other. In this sense, China's path of peaceful development not only conforms to its own long-term and fundamental interests. It is also a viable route that will benefit the whole world.

Peaceful Development is a Necessary Requirement of China's Own Development China, currently the second largest economy in the world, is gradually growing into a major country. For the time being, however, it remains a developing country with per capita income that ranks roughly 80th in the world

and more than 100 million people that live below the poverty line. At present, China's development is still unbalanced, disproportionate and unsustainable. In order to allow 1.3 billion people to have decent lives, China still has a long way to go. Raising the people's living standards through economic development will be a long-term and arduous task. It is also the most important mission of the Communist Party as a ruling party. To accelerate development, China needs a peaceful and stable international environment. This means that China must insist on and practice peaceful development. If others perceive China's development to be peaceful and non-aggressive, and if countries view China's rise as creating mutual benefits and win–win situations instead of zero-sum games, then the international community will increasingly welcome China's development. In return, China will encounter less opposition and friction, fostering a better environment for its own development.

On the other hand, given China's continued opening-up to the outside world, there are more and more Chinese enterprises and citizens venturing abroad. This has caused a new phenomenon in China's development: its raw material supplies and markets are becoming increasingly internationalized and revenues are being shared between China and foreign countries. In 2012, China's foreign trade volume reached $3.87 trillion, the accumulated scale of its foreign direct investment reached $500 billion and the total size of its overseas assets exceeded $2 trillion. More than half of China's crude oil and iron ore supplies were imported from abroad. An integral part of China's aggregate national interest, this emerging "overseas China" is making considerable contributions to China's economic growth. Protecting its legitimate stake and interests overseas has therefore become one of China's top priorities. To protect its expanding stakes and interests overseas, China should not only count on the continued growth of its comprehensive national power, but also on the development of peaceful relations with all countries. It must also better integrate its interests into the world, create efficient conduits of trade and investment and keep international regimes working well.

Peaceful Development Is the Necessary Requirement of China's Social System and Cultural Traditions As a socialist country, China is thought to have an optimal social system and governing philosophy. Internally, China pursues fairness, justice, common prosperity, and social harmony. Externally, China plays fair, insists on equity, respects justice, and always sides with righteousness. Under no circumstances will China follow the West and admire the law of the jungle. Instead, China must fight hegemony of any form. As Comrade Deng Xiaoping once said, "the socialism we are pursuing should facilitate continued growth of productive forces and connote peace." Regardless of how the international situation has changed since the founding of the People's Republic, independence and peace have always been two essential characteristics of China's diplomacy. These two principles not only constitute the cornerstones of China's foreign policy, but also enable China to stand firm on the just and moral high ground among nations.

China's peaceful development is not only an important feature of Socialism with Chinese characteristics, but also a reflection of some fine ideas of Chinese culture and tradition. Benevolent love, humanitarian care, devotion to peace, good neighborliness, and the ideal of harmony centered on peace are examples of fine Chinese cultural traditions. These traditions were developed by China's ancestors in the ancient times and have been adhered to by the Chinese for millennia. These ideas are also what bolster our peaceful development today. Centuries ago, the Silk Road that connected people along a path for common prosperity was exactly such a symbol of peace. As the famous British philosopher Bertrand Russell said, the Chinese people are natural pacifists and peace-lovers. Former German Chancellor Helmut Schmidt also rated China the most peace-loving nation in world history. Viewed in such a light, peaceful development is not only a natural extension of China's culture and traditions. More importantly, it is an inevitable and reasoned choice made by the Chinese people based on their painful memories in the modern era.

Promoting China's Peaceful Development in the New Environment

Since the founding of the People's Republic more than six decades ago, generations of Chinese leaders have led their people to explore, practice, and improve the strategy of peaceful development.

To facilitate China's peaceful development in a new historical setting, the Communist Party's Central Committee, with General Secretary Xi Jinping at its core, has continued to innovate on diplomatic theories and practices by integrating tradition with new developments. As we can see, the further China advances along the path of peaceful development, the more experienced it will become. But at the same time, it will also encounter more and more problems and challenges. As long as the Chinese people maintain full confidence and enough patience in their national strategy, China, under the strong leadership of the Communist Party, will be able to jointly overcome these obstacles and continue along the path of peaceful development.

Integrating China's National Interests into the Common Interests All Nations In today's world, no country can afford to pursue its own national interests alone and totally neglect or ignore the interests of others. Only by collaborating with other countries and creating a bigger pie can a country's own portion grow in size. As President Xi Jinping said, the viability of peaceful development to a large extent depends on whether China can make breakthroughs and progress in effectively utilizing opportunities in the world—not only for China's own benefit but also for the benefit of the world. In other words, whether China can create a broader space for peaceful development depends on whether it can grasp and coordinate opportunities at home and abroad, stay committed to openness and win-win cooperation, expand its common interests with other countries, and integrate itself better into the wider world.

In 2013, President Xi Jinping and Premier Li Keqiang utilized high-level exchanges and visits and signed roughly 800 inter-governmental, inter-departmental, or inter-regional cooperation agreements with international entities. These agreements cover a range of important cooperative initiatives in politics, economic cooperation and trade, energy, culture, and military cooperation, among other areas. These moves undoubtedly enriched the meaning of China's peaceful development strategy. During his visit to Central Asia, President Xi's proposal to build a "Silk Road Economic Belt" on the basis of five links (political, transportation, trade, currency, and cultural links) received positive feedback from the leaders of Central Asian countries. As *The Economist* magazine wrote, the "Silk Road Economic Belt," which connects the infrastructures of Asia and Europe, will become a huge market encompassing billions of people. Likewise, Xi's initiative to create a "21st Century Marine Silk Road" during his visit to Southeast Asia also received extensive support from regional countries and the international community alike.

During Premier Li Keqiang's visit to India and Pakistan, China reached an agreement to construct a China-India-Burma Economic Corridor as well as a Sino-Pakistani Economic Corridor, one running in a North-South direction and the other in an East-West direction. These two economic corridors will connect the enormous markets of China and India, synergize the growth of East Asia and South Asia, and eventually contribute to the Asia's regional integration.

In addition to infrastructural integration, other development plans are being coordinated and integrated. During President Xi's visit to Indonesia and Malaysia, for example, China signed five-year development programs with both countries to help coordinate their developmental strategies. During Premier Li's visit to Germany, China reached an agreement with its host to cooperate in the fields of neo-industrialization, information technology, urbanization, and agricultural modernization, all to enhance and combine the competitive advantages of the two countries. During the 16th meeting between Chinese and European Union leaders, the two sides signed a "2020 Program on Strategic Cooperation" to coordinate China's 12th Five-Year Plan and the EU's 2020 Development Program.

The Third Plenary Session of the 18th Party Congress earmarked the deepening of reforms and the expansion of China's opening-up, with an emphasis on the important task of accelerating the reform of China's foreign trade system. Specific targets include the creation of an ordered environment to attract high-end production, the improvement of China's overall capabilities to integrate world resources and develop international markets, the promotion of China's high-level international economic integration, and the construction of a renewed open economic system.

In the new global situation, China must combine domestic development with opening-up, linking its own growth to world economic growth and increasingly integrating its national interests with the common interests of mankind. Only in this way can China create a broader space for peaceful development.

Coordinating with Other Major Countries to Improve the Strategic Environment of China's Peaceful Development As major countries greatly determine the peace of the world, relations between major countries have a direct effect on peaceful development. In the field of foreign affairs, the Communist Party leadership is focusing on the important task of managing relations with major countries and solidifying and expanding bilateral relations with other major countries.

The rest of the world pays a lot of attention to the Sino-American relationship. With China being the fastest growing country and the United States being the largest developed country in the world, some people fear that the two countries will inevitably fall into conflict—an example of the aforementioned Thucydides Trap. At President Obama's invitation, President Xi met with the Obama administration in June 2013 at the Sunnylands Summit in California. During the summit, President Xi's proposal to build a new type of major-country relations with the United States received positive feedback from President Obama. This signaled an important consensus between the two countries on this issue. Having a Sino-American summit on a specific topic within three months of a Chinese leadership transition is unprecedented in Chinese history. It showed that both countries attach great importance to the development of their bilateral relations.

President Xi incisively summarized the connotations of a "new type of major-country relations" into three points: namely, no conflict or confrontation, mutual respect and cooperation and win-win. These three points may seem to be simple but are in fact rich with meaning. "No conflict or confrontation" aims to reverse people's negative expectations about the long-term prospects of the Sino-American relationship and thereby influence the two countries' current policies in a positive way. "Mutual respect" stresses that the two countries should respect each other's chosen social systems, development paths, core interests, and major concerns—this is the proper way to communicate and conduct exchanges among nations. "Cooperation and win-win" connotes forgoing a zero-sum game and instead seeking one's own interests while caring about others' interests. It also implies the linking of self-development to codevelopment. These three points not only represent common goals that the two countries should strive to achieve; they are also necessary contributions to the world that are expected by the international community. Through this historical meeting, China and the United States clarified the long-term prospects of the Sino-American relationship and sent a very positive signal to the world. Of course, with the United States and China being the largest capitalist and socialist countries in the world, respectively, constructing and realizing a new type of major-country relations is not an easy job. It requires collective exploration and practical efforts from both countries, including their domestic parties and social groups. Similarly, as a long-term objective, it will require political will and persistence from both sides.

Russia is a major country and China's largest neighbor. Because China and Russia are currently at key stages in their national rejuvenations, they share extensive common interests. If the Sino-Russian relationship develops well, Russia will become an important strategic partner in support of China's peaceful development. President Xi's choice of Russia as his first overseas destination after taking office testified to the importance of the Sino-Russian relationship. During his visit, President Xi spent almost eight hours engaged in in-depth exchanges and communications with President Vladimir Putin. An important joint declaration was consequently issued by the two countries in which China and Russia committed themselves to supporting each other on a number of issues, ranging from development and national rejuvenation to the protection of their core national interests and the maintenance of each party's chosen path and social system. In addition, the two countries signed dozens of "Century Contracts" involving huge volumes of oil and gas, nuclear power, electricity, high technology, and aerospace, among other areas. These concrete

measures raised the level of practical cooperation between the two countries to a new height.

The European and Chinese economies are highly complementary. Tapping the potential of Sino-European cooperation will therefore prove beneficial not only to the peaceful development of China, but also to wider global prosperity. During Premier Li Keqiang's visit to Europe in May 2013, China and Switzerland signed a Free Trade Agreement. This was the first FTA ever signed between China and a European country and it marked a great breakthrough in the history of Sino-European relations. Meanwhile, China's practical cooperation with Germany entered an "acceleration period," and the Sino-German relationship continues to lead overall Sino-EU relations. At the end of 2013, summit meetings between China and the Central and Eastern European countries produced fruitful results as well. And the visits to China by more than ten European leaders (including France, the United Kingdom, Greece, Romania, the Netherlands, Finland, and Iceland) in less than one year represented another highpoint in China's diplomatic relations with the European Union.

India is also an important emerging power. In recent years, some Western media have tried to badmouth the Sino-Indian relationship by fabricating a so-called dragon elephant tussle narrative. The Sino-Indian relationship not only concerns China's peaceful development but also the unity of emerging countries. In June 2013, Premier Li Keqiang's visit to India was soon followed by Indian Prime Minister Manmohan Singh's visit to China in October of the same year. The successful visits by the two countries' Premiers in a single year marked the first time that this had happened in the past 52 years. As Prime Minister Singh told President Xi, Asia is big enough to accommodate the common development of both countries and India will never join any group or alliance against China. The two countries' joint efforts have already pushed the Sino-Indian strategic partnership to new heights.

In general, the relationships between China and other major countries all underwent smooth transitions and positive new developments in the first year since the inauguration of China's new leadership. In the future, China will attach more importance to major country relations, strengthen high-level communications, deepen strategic dialogues, expand practical cooperation efforts, and further integrate the interests of all parties to improve the strategic environment of China's peaceful development.

Intensifying Friendship with Neighboring Countries to Secure Support for China's Peaceful Development With the most complicated surroundings in the world, China borders fourteen inland countries and six marine countries. In addition, there are nine countries that can still be classified as China's close neighbors, even though they do not directly border China. These countries are substantially different from one another not only in terms of history, culture, and religion, but also in terms of their political systems and development levels. Those who doubt China's peaceful development can therefore find proof of China's sincerity by looking at how China handles its relations with its neighbors.

China enjoys very close ties and frequent exchanges with its neighbors. These are countries and entire regions in which China's interests are deeply integrated and in which China exerts a direct influence. In 2012, trade between China and its neighboring countries exceeded $1.2 trillion, accounting for roughly 32 percent of China's aggregate foreign trade. Meanwhile, mutual investment between China and its neighbors surged and China imported a considerable portion of its energy resources from neighboring countries. For example, China imported 53 percent of its natural gas supply from Central Asia. In terms of mutual visits, China and its neighbors collectively registered a total of 35.5 million mutual visits in 2012, with around 60 percent of China's visitors coming from Asian countries.

This is why China deems its neighbors to be the cornerstone of its subsistence, development and prosperity. Sticking to peaceful development first and foremost implies the creation of a peaceful, stable, and prosperous environment. To this end, China's peaceful development should not only benefit its neighbors; it should also be able to count on their support.

Under the leadership of Comrade Xi Jinping, the Communist Party has paid great attention to diplomacy with neighboring countries. In October 2013, the Party's Central Committee organized a forum on diplomacy with neighboring countries, an unprecedented event since the founding of the People's Republic. During the forum, Comrade Xi made important remarks on the guidelines, policies, and principles that govern neighborhood diplomacy in the new historical era. He particularly stressed the ideas of amity, sincerity, mutual benefit, and inclusiveness as requisite components of neighborhood diplomacy. These ideas are vivid declarations of China's insistence on peaceful development. They are both brilliant summaries of China's neighborhood diplomacy practices and innovative developments of China's diplomatic philosophy under the new leadership.

Amity involves the strengthening of friendship on the basis of geographical proximity and kinship. China still feels the profound influence of Confucianism, as do other East Asian countries; China still values Buddhist cultural heritage, as do South Asian countries; China cherishes the historical connections brought by the Silk Road, as do other Central Asian countries. Through thousands of years of communicating and exchanging information and culture, China has forged an inextricable link and a natural sense of intimacy with its neighbors. This link extends beyond the social and cultural fields into political domains. Over the years, China and its neighbors have maintained close and frequent exchanges and communication, just like close relatives making frequent visits. As proof, since President Xi and Premier Li were inaugurated in March 2013, less than a year ago, they have visited Russia, Central Asia (Turkmenistan, Kazakhstan, Uzbekistan and Kirghizstan), ASEAN (Indonesia, Malaysia, Thailand, Vietnam and Brunei) and South Asia (India and Pakistan), while also receiving dozens of visits from the state leaders of China's neighbors. Such frequent mutual visits and interactions fully testify to the special and intimate relations between China and its neighbors.

Sincerity requires being sincere and honest with others to win their trust and support. The Chinese nation has always attached great importance to sincerity, honesty, trust, and credibility. China's deep friendship with King Sihanouk of Cambodia is a good example in this type of respect—China's help to the king over the years not only created a profound friendship between China and the king, but also generated favorable feedback and appreciation among the people of Cambodia. China has no shortage of similarly moving stories, anecdotes, and cases. As for its disputes with some neighboring countries, China is willing to adopt a sincere attitude and seek proper solutions through dialogue and friendly consultation, as long as this is preconditioned on the safeguarding of China's national sovereignty and territorial integrity.

Mutual benefit refers to the idea of win-win cooperation between two countries. As a non-ASEAN member more than a decade ago, China initiated bilateral talks with ASEAN countries to set up free trade zones. During these talks, China managed to take care of ASEAN's concerns on a range of different issues. As a result, in 2010 China and ASEAN collectively set up the world's largest free trade zone among developing countries. So far, ASEAN is the largest recipient of Chinese overseas investment, China's third largest trade partner, and a major travel destination for Chinese citizens. In 2013, Chinese leaders once again demonstrated their sincerity to ASEAN by proposing a series of constructive and win-win cooperative initiatives. These include the construction of a community of common destiny with ASEAN, the 2+7 cooperation framework, the upgrading of the China-ASEAN Free Trade Zone, and the launching of an Asian Infrastructure Investment Bank.

Inclusiveness means openness, tolerance, and the pursuit of common ground, all of which are normally associated with broad minded, major countries. As a major country in East Asia, China has always supported ASEAN's leading role in regional cooperation and welcomed non-ASEAN states to play a constructive role in East Asian cooperation regimes. China has also promoted the synergy and complementation of regimes such as the 10+1, 10+3 and East Asia Summit. In addition, China reacted positively to related countries' concerns over the Asia Pacific regional security situation, facilitating exchanges and communications on regional defense and security issues and demonstrating the utmost tolerance, inclusiveness, and open-mindedness.

Of course, China must clearly realize that in its surroundings there are still factors that could disrupt its peaceful development. This is why President Xi proposed that China emphasize the maintenance of peace and stability in its surrounding regions. On the issue of the Korean peninsula, China's basic proposition can be summarized into three points: insistence on the goal of the denuclearization for the entire Korean Peninsula; insistence on resolving disputes through dialogue and consultation; and insistence on maintaining peace and stability on the Korean Peninsula. China is a responsible major country that believes firmly in justice and is willing to play a positive role in the world—it deems all three points listed above to be indispensable and will not allow any parties to make trouble near China. Since the Democratic People's Republic of Korea (DPRK) conducted its third nuclear test, China has made great efforts to urge relevant parties to have talks and consultations that will help alleviate the tensions in the region. This shows China's unique role in addressing the Korean Peninsula issue, as well as China's positive role as a responsible major country. Denuclearization of the Korean Peninsula should not solely be the responsibility of China. Instead, the key lies in dialogues between the United States and the DPRK and the improved relations between the two countries. The Six-Party talks involving both the United States and the DPRK provide an effective mechanism for relevant parties to resolve the Korean nuclear issue. This is why China is actively working with all related parties to create favorable preconditions for the earliest possible resumption of the Six-Party talks. Only in this way can the Korean nuclear issue come to a peaceful resolution as soon as possible.

A stable and improving Sino-Japanese relationship is in the fundamental interests of both countries. The current difficulties between China and Japan are completely due to Japan's mistakes, and this is not a situation that China wishes to see again. To avoid the further deterioration of the situation, the Japanese side must face reality, be cautious in both words and deeds, and commit itself to no longer hurting China's sovereignty and interests. If the Japanese side really wishes to improve Sino-Japanese relations, then it should take concrete actions to prove itself. The historical issue remains a major obstacle to the improvement of Sino-Japanese relations. The Japanese wars of aggression against China plunged China into great disorder and calamity. Only by drawing lessons from history can a better future be forged. And only by choosing peace will Japan be able win the trust of its neighbors. The Japanese side should understand this basic truth and pay due respect to human conscience and justice. China sincerely hopes that intercultural and cross-regional exchanges between the two nations, as well as communications between younger generations, will help steer the Sino-Japanese relationship out of its current state.

Deeper Cooperation and Closer Unity with Developing Countries To better understand China's path of peaceful development, it is important to observe how China handles the balance between common good and its own interests. In recent years, China's growth and development received increased recognition from the international community. Amidst this recognition, however, were some voices that till sought to defame and misinterpret China's efforts. For example, some accused China of carrying out "mercantilism," while others slandered China as a practitioner of "neocolonialism" in Africa.

Based on China's historical experiences and diplomatic practices since the founding of the People's Republic, President Xi proposed that China develop a correct understanding of the relationship between self-interest and common good. He stressed that China should strive for the common good and welfare of all developing countries and provide, within its capacity, necessary assistance to poor countries. Sometimes, Xi said, China should even neglect or completely forgo its own interests for the sake of justice and common good. Stinginess and mercenary-like attitudes will by no means be allowed.

In March 2013, during his visits to Tanzania, South Africa, and Congo-Brazzaville, President Xi confirmed that China would always support and assist Africa's development. This vow resonated strongly with African leaders and their people. During his visit, Xi and his host countries signed more than 40 cooperation contracts that range from investment, trade, and economic assistance to infrastructure construction and agricultural exchanges. In return, African leaders and their people expressed their sincere appreciation for China's long-term assistance and selfless efforts to expand win-win cooperation between China and Africa. For instance, President Sassou of Congo-Brazzaville issued a candid speech criticizing Western prejudices against China at a large ceremony in honor of President Xi. He said: "We completely disagree with the West in their claim that China is practicing Neocolonialism in Africa. What is colonialism? We understand it too well, because our body and soul have both suffered from it. But China is our trustworthy friend. China's path is Africa's hope."

Developing countries are China's partners on the path of peaceful development. In the new historical era, China must adhere to a path of righteousness while increasing its aid and assistance to less developed countries in proportion to its own national strength. By exploring new opportunities and new approaches to win-win cooperation between developing countries, China can help these other countries achieve independent and sustainable development. This will further help consolidate the foundation of China's peaceful development.

Playing the Role of a Responsible Major Country by Providing Public Goods to the Whole World As a permanent member of the United Nations Security Council, China is expected by the international community to play a significant role in international affairs. President Xi has already noted that Chinese are patriotic and have international visions and aspirations. With its growing national power, China will shoulder international responsibilities in proportion to its capacity, thereby making greater contributions to the peace and development of mankind.

China has demonstrated that it is a firm supporter of world peace not only with words but also with actions. For example, China's use of its veto right in the Security Council has primarily been against intervention into the internal affairs of other countries, especially the affairs of small and middle-sized countries. China is not fighting for its own interests. Rather, it is fighting for international justice, the legitimate rights and interests of developing countries, the honor of the United Nations charter, and the fundamental principles of international relations. So far, China has dispatched more than 20,000 people to participate in UN peacekeeping missions worldwide. This makes China the number one personnel dispatcher among all permanent members of the Security Council. Similarly, China's peacekeeping costs rank top among all developing countries. To support

African peace and security, China took an unprecedented step and dispatched a complete rank of peacekeeping forces to Mali.

As an active promoter of the global development agenda, China has lent strong support to the UN Millennium Development Goals and contributed many useful concepts, ideas and wisdom on a series of global issues, including climate change. For instance, China has contributed ideas like innovative development, coordinated growth, and interest integration on the occasions of many important summit meetings. China has also appealed to the international community to cultivate a strong awareness of its ideas the "Community of Common Destiny" and win-win cooperation in spite of competition. China is happy to see many of these ideas and concepts accepted by the international community. At the same time, China has made great breakthroughs in projects like the BRICS Development Bank and foreign exchange reserve pool. These concrete efforts and measures will help the world economy recover, stabilize international financial markets and initiate reforms to the international system.

Nowadays, more and more countries realize that China brings opportunities and not threats to the world. A stronger China that pursues peaceful development will assume greater responsibility in promoting human peace and progress.

Building a Stronger National Defense to Protect China's National Interests and Peaceful Development The achievement of peaceful development depends on action, not waiting. The pursuit of peaceful development will by no means be smooth. Rather, it is bound to be full of risks and challenges. Therefore, to achieve its goal of peaceful development and national rejuvenation, China must consistently reduce and overcome disruptions and opposition. To ensure the comprehensive implementation of peaceful development, China must strengthen its national defense. As stated during the 18th Party Congress, the purpose of strengthening national defense is to protect China's sovereignty, security, territorial integrity, and peaceful development. A stronger national defense will provide better protection for China's core interests while also allowing China to concentrate on peaceful development. Further, it constitutes a powerful deterrent against countries

that threaten China's peaceful development and serves the ultimate purpose of preventing wars.

To judge whether a country is a supporter of peace, one need only study the type of national defense policy that this country adopts. China adopts a defensive national defense policy. This means that the strengthening of China's military power is conducive to world peace. Increasing its capacity to protect national interests, including its military capabilities, is a necessary requirement of China's peaceful development.

As President Xi put it, China should adhere to peaceful development, but it will never give up its legitimate rights and interests and will never sacrifice its core national interests. No foreign country should expect China to trade its core interests, nor should any country expect China to tolerate encroachments upon its sovereignty, security, and development interests. These clear and forceful words clarified the dialectical relationship between peaceful development and China's protection of national interests.

As China's peaceful development progresses, it will have more resources and measures to protect its national interests and become increasingly proactive in doing so. China will neither sacrifice other countries' interests to achieve its own development, nor will it allow other countries to encroach upon China's legitimate rights and interests. Likewise, peaceful development is not something that simply concerns China. Through its own example, China should encourage other countries to accept the concepts of peaceful development, peaceful coexistence and common development so that peaceful development can become a preferred policy option for all.

Sharing the Dividends of Peaceful Development to Secure Continued Support People provide the foundation of a state. The continued progress of China's peaceful development can be attributed both to the growth in China's national power and the support of the Chinese people. Only by remaining rooted in the principles of the people will China's diplomacy be able to win people's support and trust. Only in this way can China's diplomatic work become popular, successful and progressive.

As President Xi said, China's national power should continuously be developed in order to bring more dividends from peaceful development to the people. In return, people will help lay a more solid material and social foundation for China's continued peaceful development.

Bolstered by years of peaceful development, China is now able to better protect the legitimate rights and interests of its citizens abroad. In 2011, it took China only twelve days to evacuate 35,860 besieged Chinese nationals who were in Libya, using sea, land and air transportation resources. The first large-scale overseas evacuation operation in the history of the People's Republic could well be deemed a rare feat in world history.

So far, China has more than 20,000 enterprises operating in close to 200 countries. In 2013 alone, Chinese customs registered a total of roughly 90 million outbound trips by Chinese nationals. It is estimated that by 2020, this annual figure will jump to 150 million. Following political philosophies that are oriented around the people, China

will make concrete efforts to protect the legitimate rights and interests of Chinese nationals overseas and provide them with better services. Meanwhile, whenever possible, China will negotiate with more foreign countries to simplify visa procedures and even obtain visa exemptions on ordinary passports. By increasing the value of Chinese passports, the overseas travels of Chinese citizens will be made easier and more convenient in the future.

China's unprecedented peaceful development requires the wisdom and devotion of all governmental sectors and regional administrations. Only through concerted effort can progress be made. Under the leadership of the Communist Party with Comrade Xi Jinping at its core, China's path of peaceful development will definitely grow broader in the future. With time and hard work, a better external environment will be created to facilitate the realization of the Chinese dream of national rejuvenation.

UNRULY STABILITY: WHY CHINA'S REGIME HAS STAYING POWER[*]

Andrew G. Walder

Some 34 independent nations in the world today were ruled by communist dictatorships when China began its economic reforms three decades ago. Now, only four communist states remain. Two of these are stagnant, unreformed state socialist regimes mired in poverty—North Korea and Cuba. China and Vietnam are the only two that have carried out extensive market reforms without regime change. For almost two decades these two have also been among the world's fastest growing economies. The remaining 30 regimes have taken different paths: They are "post-communist" states with market economies and a wide range of political systems, from harsh dictatorships to liberal democracies.

China's economic record has been remarkable, and it requires little comment here. But in the past decade a wave of protest over economic issues, and a recent resurgence of ethnic unrest

in China's western regions, have contributed to a perception that the regime may be entering a period of heightened instability, one in which a two-decade run of rapid progress and political order may be coming to an end.

To be sure, China today is a relatively contentious society, and the state is seemingly obsessed with measures to ensure political order. It is also true that very little progress has been made in the reform of China's core political institutions, which are essentially the same ones that existed when the 30 years of economic reform began. Nevertheless, the overall political situation in China is far more favorable for the regime than it was during the relatively tumultuous and strife-torn first decade of economic reform.

Exactly 20 years ago, of course, China was in terrible shape. Martial law was in force in Beijing after the military assault on the Tiananmen Square protest movement, the reform coalition in the Communist Party leadership had collapsed, the country was internationally isolated and under

[*] This article was published in *Current History* (September 2009).

fire for its gross abuses of human rights, and the economy was in the midst of a sharp downturn that would last for several years.

We often forget, however, that the massive crisis of 1989 was simply the result of social and political circumstances that existed throughout the 1980s, circumstances that contrast sharply with the present. If we look back at the 1980s, China appears to have been a different country. The economic growth and national resurgence of the past 20 years, and events in the rest of the world in the interim, have put the Chinese regime in a very different position, and have created a very different relationship between the regime and the society that it rules.

In four ways in particular, China is a different place today. First, as is now clear, China's gradual approach to economic reform has worked. During the 1980s, it was not at all clear that the strategy would succeed, at least outside of agriculture. Second, China's overall political trajectory now looks quite favorable in light of the severe problems experienced by many post-communist successor states. In the late 1980s, China's regime appeared gridlocked and reactionary compared to other communist regimes beginning their own political reforms. Third, China's youth and educated public now display a strong sense of national pride, and on occasion a defensive patriotism. Two decades ago, by contrast, deep questioning of the Communist Party and the legitimacy of the system was far more common. Finally, China's party leaders today are fundamentally united in their views about the direction the country should take. Throughout the 1980s, they were deeply divided over both economic reform and political liberalization.

Uncertain Times

We have now become so accustomed to the economic rise of China that it is hard to remember that considerable skepticism regarding the prospects for economic reforms existed during their first decade. By the end of the 1980s China's economic reforms had not really proceeded very far outside of agriculture, where the country had scored striking early successes simply by abandoning Soviet-style collective farms. Rural incomes went up rapidly, as did the supply of food to cities. At this point China's reforms in agriculture were the most radical in the socialist world. Yet it was commonly observed at the time that this was the easy part, just a first step.

The most difficult task of reform had yet to be addressed in any significant way—how to turn around a gigantic and grossly inefficient state industrial sector. It was evident that industrial firms needed to be downsized, reorganized, and subjected to real competitive pressures, but this would involve a loss of state control over key parts of the economy. It would also risk unrest and political opposition due to layoffs and to the violation of socialism's main tenets. Throughout the 1980s it was unclear whether party leaders could even gather the political will to attempt such an unprecedented transformation, and if they seriously tried, it was unclear whether the Chinese Communist Party could outlast the likely political consequences.

There was also the perilous question of price reform. The freeing of consumer and producer prices in an economy of shortage carried the real risk of rapid inflation, and the destabilizing impact of inflation was already evident in urban China in 1988 and early 1989. As China's leaders were painfully aware, steep rises in consumer prices in Poland had bred the Solidarity movement at the beginning of the decade. We should remember that at this point in history no socialist regime had ever attempted a move to a market-oriented economy, and it was far from clear that this was plausible, or that a ruling communist party could survive such a transition.

It is also easy to forget that China's political trajectory by the late 1980s appeared to be lagging well behind progressive change in the Soviet bloc, much to the chagrin of many students, intellectuals, and liberal-minded party members. The party's backlash against "bourgeois liberalization" in the wake of the student democracy movement of late 1986, and the subsequent purge of the liberal-minded General Secretary Hu Yaobang, made China's leadership seem backward and reactionary. The trend toward press freedom, democratization, and even competitive elections was by 1988 already well in evidence in Poland, Hungary, and most importantly the Soviet Union. Many in urban China, and even in the party and government itself, looked on these developments with envy.

We should also recall that this was precisely the period when neighboring East Asian regimes were emerging from long periods of dictatorship: the Philippines in 1986, South Korea in 1987, and Taiwan in 1988. To many in China at the time, the country's political arrangements looked increasingly anachronistic, dysfunctional, and reactionary—and incompatible with the rapid, market-oriented economic growth to which the party leadership apparently aspired.

Troubled Youth

Another hallmark of the 1980s was the deep alienation of many of China's youths and intellectuals. The decade began with a well-publicized "crisis of confidence" in the Communist Party and socialism. Within the universities a liberal atmosphere of questioning flourished, as did curiosity about the democratic philosophies and institutions of Western civilization. A generation of Chinese in their 20s and 30s had emerged from an interrupted education, with many of them having spent time as "sent down youth" in the countryside, in a questioning and rebellious mood. Many liberal intellectuals also participated in the general ferment.

This was a society still recovering from the horrors of the Cultural Revolution, still trying to explain the root causes of that long national catastrophe. Many at the time dissented from the obviously self-serving party line—that the disasters were caused by a handful of evil leaders reviled as the "Gang of Four." Many were convinced that the causes of China's national catastrophe were woven deeply into its unitary political institutions and reigning ideology.

Finally, China's leadership in the 1980s was deeply divided, often bitterly so, about economic reform and political liberalization. Many leaders saw economic reforms as a threat to the regime and a violation of fundamental socialist tenets. These conservatives could not understand why China did not simply return to an updated version of the Soviet-inspired planning practices that had worked relatively well during the 1950s, before everything was thrown into disarray by Mao Zedong's harebrained extremism. And attempts by reformers in the leadership to push political liberalization and openness led to factional warfare within the party's top ranks.

The result of this constant jockeying was a pattern of abrupt policy change, as moves to liberalize and reform were followed by periods of backlash and retrenchment. Party leader Deng Xiaoping refereed the competing factions, moving first one way, then another, hoping to steer the fractious leadership toward a middle course of market reform under firm party rule. These conflicts were obvious to politically aware youths, intellectuals, and party members.

The Perfect Storm

All four of these longstanding features of 1980s China came together in the spring of 1989 to create a political crisis that can be likened to a perfect storm. The alienated youth culture of the 1980s was on full display in the student protests of April and May. The students took the death of the liberal Hu Yaobang as an opportunity to show their dissatisfaction with the post-1986 reaction against student democracy protests, which had culminated in Hu's firing from the top party post.

The students' rhetoric and symbolism showed a keen familiarity with Western models of democracy, and an almost naive faith in the efficacy of those models and their potency as answers to China's problems. The students displayed an awareness that China was lagging behind world democratic trends, and that this was due to the reactionary views of a certain wing of the party leadership. They hoped to influence the political balance in the leadership in the direction of greater liberalization and democratization.

Intellectuals, reporters, editors, and even government functionaries eventually responded sympathetically to the unfolding drama in Tiananmen Square. Many of them were themselves frustrated with the retarded pace of political liberalization. They joined the protests, calling for peaceful dialogue with the student leaders, and many of them made demands for press freedom and other democratic rights on their own. They were aware that press freedoms were already quite extensive in Poland, Hungary, and even the Soviet Union, and that competitive elections were on the agenda in those countries. They thought it natural that China should be in step with these worldwide trends.

Ordinary citizens flooded into the streets to support the student protesters, a response that escalated the crisis when they blocked martial law troops from entering the city. The protests reflected widespread public uneasiness about the impact of economic reforms on urban livelihoods. The official inflation rate exceeded 25 percent in 1988 and early 1989, and episodes of panic buying occurred as rumors spread of the imminent freeing of all prices. The first tentative steps to lay off workers in overstaffed urban firms also generated anxiety, while a perceived rise in corruption and privilege-seeking by party and government officials provoked anger. These concerns resonated deeply as students chanted slogans calling for openness, dialogue, and an end to official corruption.

The pressures created by these events splintered the already-fractious party leadership and prevented it from formulating a coherent and consistent response. The leadership was paralyzed, and it seemed evident that a deadlock had developed between two separate camps—one calling for dialogue, the other for repression. As a result, the official mass media began reporting extensively and even sympathetically on the unfolding protest movement, with many retired and lower-ranking officials speaking out in favor of moderation.

The evident leadership deadlock, and the official media coverage, only encouraged the protesters and the general population to think that there was a chance their actions could succeed. The ultimate resolution of the crisis was the draconian military operation of June 3–4, 1989. As the streets of Beijing were engulfed in flames and gunfire on the dawn of June 4, Poland held its first multiparty national elections, which soon led to the end of communist rule.

China's "Reagan Generation"

If we fast-forward 20 years to the present decade, we observe a very different China. The alienated youth culture is gone, and the political hangover from the Cultural Revolution is two generations in the past. Party membership is now in vogue among the young, especially for the highly educated and upwardly mobile. In a highly competitive environment, party membership is just another credential that opens doors to greater opportunity. And government jobs are often preferred to the greater risks of careers in China's large and dynamic private sector. If China's alienated 1980s generation was similar in many ways to America's "60s Generation," China's current youth generation in many ways resembles the 1980s "Reagan Generation."

Chinese youth today are pragmatic, career oriented, and patriotic in ways that were rare in the 1980s. Most were born after the events of 1989 and have only a vague knowledge of—and little interest in—the conflicts of those years. Over the past decade they have been politically active, but primarily in protests over biased Japanese textbooks, the NATO bombing of China's Belgrade embassy, rival national claims to sovereignty over the tiny Diaoyu islands in the East China Sea, or criticism by foreign governments and media about China's handling of Tibetan protests on the eve of the Beijing Olympics. This is a generation that feels China's rise and the national pride that comes with it.

Strength in Stability

It is no longer as clear to China's intellectuals and other educated urbanites that the nation's political trajectory compares unfavorably to those of its former socialist brethren. In the late 1980s the socialist world appeared on the verge of a dramatic and promising democratic breakthrough, with China's hidebound leaders hesitating to take the plunge. The history of these transitions over the past two decades has prompted a more sober realism today.

Of the 30 post-communist regimes in the world, fewer than half are now reasonably stable multiparty democracies. All of these success stories are in small and ethnically uniform nations and all but one (Mongolia) are on the eastern edge of the European Union. The rest are either harsh dictatorships or deeply corrupt and illiberal regimes whose attempts to move toward democracy have largely fallen short. In some cases, the attempt to democratize led to the collapse of the nation-state: The Soviet Union and Yugoslavia are prime examples. In other cases, the transition touched off years of nationalist violence or civil war.

And in virtually all cases, the attempt to shift to a market economy in the midst of a political revolution ushered in a deep depression that lasted almost a decade. Many of these economies, including Russia's, only recently emerged from their years of hardship. By contrast, the two countries in this group that have had by far the largest sustained increases in per capita GDP are, ironically, both still ruled by their communist parties—China and Vietnam.

The equation of political stability with economic and social progress is a far more appealing argument today than it was in the 1980s. Any zeal for multiparty democracy as a panacea for China's problems is far in the past. It has been replaced with a more sober awareness of the potential costs of a failed lean to a different type of political system.

China's record of rapid, inflation-free economic development since the early 1990s is well known today. Just as important, however, is the fact that what was once viewed as the greatest single obstacle to China's gradual reform strategy is now largely a thing of the past. Since the mid-1990s China has systematically downsized and restructured its bloated state sector. Employing more than 110 million at its height in 1997, the sector now employs fewer than 60 million.

In the course of this restructuring more than 40 million permanent employees were laid off or retired prematurely. This did indeed touch off a wave of protest, but the downsizing is now over. Not only have China's leaders been able to summon the political will to do what so many observers in the 1980s thought was highly unlikely, but they have weathered the consequences with relatively little political fallout.

A Unified Vision

The deep divisions in the national leadership so prominent in the 1980s are virtually non-existent today. China's leaders are remarkably unified around a model of national development that combines single-party rule and limited political liberalization with a highly statist version of market reform, gradual privatization, and deep engagement with the international economy.

The Tiananmen protests and the subsequent collapse of communist regimes around the globe only reinforced this sense of unity. Indeed, it is hard now to find serious policy disagreements at the top, and the sharp policy reversals and abrupt start-and-stop pattern of the 1980s have not been observed for well over a decade. This is a more confident and unified national leadership that is nonetheless still very cautious about ensuring political order.

These are fundamental changes that have strengthened the party-state's position, but noting them is not to assert that all is well in China, or that the regime will last indefinitely in its present form. There are in fact extensive social forces at work in China today that portend future political change. However, these are different forces from the ones at work in the 1980s, and they are very different forces from the ones that brought down communist regimes *en masse* 20 years ago.

These forces can be seen in the large wave of popular protest that has been so widely reported, and so widely misinterpreted, in recent years. China is in fact a much more contentious society in the current decade than in the 1980s, and the protests are today much more deeply rooted in the urban and rural populations.

The protest movements of the 1980s were located in the major cities; they involved students, educated youths, and to some extent intellectuals. Only in 1989 did the protesters draw large segments of the urban population along with them in support. Farmers in the countryside, enjoying the fruits of household agriculture, took no part in these movements and appeared puzzled by their causes. And in virtually all cases the demands of politically active urbanites were aimed squarely at the national leadership and national policy—for political liberalization, a free press, and fairness in local elections.

Today's Protests

The protest wave that has affected China over the past 10 to 15 years has been very different. It is much less centered in the largest cities. Students, educated youths, and intellectuals have been far less active. Students have gone to the streets most often, but largely to express patriotic sentiment and anger at foreign powers. The wave of blue-collar protest that resulted from the downsizing of the state sector was not focused in China's major cities. Instead, it was scattered throughout the country, concentrated largely in the declining rust belt—around old Soviet plants from the 1950s, "third front" enterprises in the interior, or China's northeast.

Rural protest has been equally widespread, scattered across suburban villages as well as remote areas. These protests have been inspired by intensely local economic issues: the nonpayment of promised compensation or pensions to workers laid off during the restructuring or sale of a state-owned firm; excessive fees or taxes levied on farmers by village governments; and the unjust expropriation of land or homes from farmers or urban residents for commercial or industrial development projects.

These are all protests against local officials, and they invoke national law and charge local authorities with corruption or malfeasance. The protest leaders see higher levels of government as a solution to their problems, and their protests are largely aimed at ensuring the even-handed enforcement of national laws that they claim are grossly violated locally. In these struggles, appeals for help to higher authorities are common.

Inevitable Disputes

The upsurge of local protest—reportedly close to 80,000 events in 2005 according to official figures—is the result of profound changes in China's society and economy over the past 20 years. Under collective agriculture, village officials controlled the harvest, managed the land, and allocated incomes. With the shift to household farming, families controlled and farmed their own land, and rural officials had to extract fees and taxes from them in order to fund government activities. It was inevitable that this would breed conflict over extraction and land rights, especially in a country that was utterly without laws to govern extraction or institutions designed to adjudicate such disputes fairly.

Similarly, in the old socialist economy, job rights and associated pensions and benefits were guaranteed. When workers were stripped of rights in a wave of downsizing, restructuring, and privatization that was poorly regulated and that often benefited officials and managers in highly visible ways, conflict was inevitable. And China largely lacked the legal framework, or union and governmental institutions, that in mature market economies had evolved over generations to help regulate such conflict.

China's development model, meanwhile, has forced local officials throughout the country into a firm alliance with business interests, whether public or private, and this often makes them targets of collective protest, with charges of corruption and collusion leveled against them.

This is a very different sociopolitical landscape from that which existed in the 1980s. Farmers in that decade enjoyed rising incomes from household agriculture, and rural protest was rare. Urban workers were hit by inflation and feared future layoffs, but their job rights were still secure. The 1980s protests were concentrated in the key cities and directed at the central government. Today, the protests are dispersed across the landscape but are focused on local officials and enterprise managers.

Recent months have seen a resurgence of ethnic strife in Tibet and Xinjiang. Yet, as serious and deeply rooted as such problems may be, they exist in remote regions. And they represent little immediate threat, either to a regime that appears determined to suppress the strife, or to an urban Chinese public that shows little sympathy for the groups involved. These social conflicts create policy problems for the central government, but they are hardly the political challenge, or the political hazard, that was presented by the urban democracy movements concentrated in Beijing and other large cities in the 1980s—movements that constantly threatened to splinter China's leadership along factional lines.

In the Driver's Seat

Some observers view the overall volume of current protests as a harbinger of regime crisis, as if the sheer amount of protest activity determines the impact of protest on a national scale. One sometimes reads speculation that widespread dis- satisfaction in the countryside bodes ill for a regime that grew out of a rural guerrilla insurgency; some warn that the fate of the former Nationalist regime may as a result befall the Communists. This is a sobering reflection on China's recent history, but we need to recall that it took a revolutionary guerrilla insurgency and a massive foreign invasion and military occupation before peasants could be mobilized as a political force.

Other observers link the wave of protests to rising levels of inequality in China—certainly to levels not seen since the late 1940s—and it is now common to hear claims that China is one of the most unequal societies in the world. It is true that overall measures of inequality in China have risen since the late 1970s, when national inequality indices—as gauged by the Gini coef- ficient of income distribution—stood at around .32, roughly the same as in Taiwan at that time. The index for China rose rapidly to the mid-.40s by the late 1990s, and remains at this level today.

It is not true, however, that these levels are unusually high. Latin America has long had signif- icantly higher levels of income inequality (Brazil and Colombia are both at .58), and many African nations have much higher Gini measures than this. Recent data suggest that income inequality in China peaked in the late 1990s and has mod- erated slightly since then. In any case, inequal- ity per se is not directly connected to political

dissatisfaction—recent surveys in China indicate that citizens judge current levels of inequality far less harshly than do citizens in countries like Poland, which have a far more equal income dis- tribution. The reason is that most Chinese citi- zens have experienced economic improvement in recent years, and expect to enjoy further opportu- nity in the future.

These commonly cited portents of looming political instability are not what they are some- times claimed to be. They are symptoms of eco- nomic conflicts in a vastly transformed society, and in the context of a regime that is more sta- ble and that enjoys greater popular support than was the case during the first decade of economic reforms. Political change in China will remain a protracted affair, driven forward by forces that are fundamentally different from those that toppled so many economically stagnant and illegitimate communist regimes some two decades ago— and that briefly threatened the Chinese regime in 1989.

To be sure, the reforms of the past 30 years have bred severe economic conflicts. A prolonged fail- ure to address these conflicts with any measures other than repression could eventually culminate in renewed popular demands aimed squarely at the central leadership. For the time being, how- ever, popular protest is mostly creating pressure on China's government to create new institutions that fairly adjudicate the conflicts.

A RISING CHINA NEEDS A NEW NATIONAL STORY[*]

Orville Schell and John Delury

Every July, amid festivities and fireworks, the US and France mark their birth as nations. Accustomed as we are in the West to histories that begin with triumph—the signing of the Declaration of Independence, the storming of the Bastille—it may seem strange that China, the fast- rising dynamo of the East, marks the beginning of

its journey to modern nationhood in a very dif- ferent way: with the shock of unexpected defeat and the loss of national greatness.

Many Chinese date the start of their modern history to Aug. 11, 1842, when the Qing Dynasty, by signing the Treaty of Nanjing, capitulated to Great Britain in order to end the disastrous First Opium War (1839–42). It was from this and many other subsequent defeats that China's politi- cal elites—including the most progressive 20th- century reformers and revolutionaries—wove an

---

[*] This article was published in the *Wall Street Journal*, July 12, 2014.

entire national narrative of foreign exploitation and victimization. Even today, this fabric of ideas continues to hold powerful sway over China's relations with the rest of the world.

The artifacts of China's formative moment can be seen at the Temple of the Tranquil Seas, which sits on a narrow slice of land in the northwest part of Nanjing on the banks of the Yangzi River. It was here, in the oppressive heat of August 1842, that Chinese negotiators were forced to sit with their British counterparts and hammer out the crushing terms of the treaty. The negotiating chamber in the old temple has now been restored to something resembling its original state. A nearby exhibition covers the painful history of "China's unequal treaties," which imposed territorial concessions and onerous indemnities that remained in force until the 1940s.

The Temple of the Tranquil Seas serves as a curious porthole into this bitter past of foreign incursion and exploitation, from which both the Nationalist and Chinese Communist parties later constructed their ideologies. As the historical exhibit's first panel explains: "Those unequal treaties were like fettering ropes of humiliation that made China lose control of her political and military affairs ... It was one of the major causes that rendered China poor and weak in modern history ... and has become a symbol of the commencement of China's modern history."

For Chinese reformers, however, there was, in this record of impotence and inferiority, also a paradoxical promise of redemption. Being overwhelmed by materially stronger but culturally inferior foreign powers—Chinese leaders called them "barbarians"—may have been a profound humiliation, but it also served as motivation for China to regenerate itself as a great power. As Mao Zedong declared in founding the People's Republic in 1949, "The Chinese have always been a great courageous and industrious nation; it is only in modern times that they have fallen behind ... Ours will no longer be a nation subject to insult and humiliation."

This morality play continues to shape the Chinese imagination. As the last panel in the exhibit room of the Temple of Tranquil Seas explains: "It is hard to look back upon this humiliating history ...

But the abolishment of the unequal treaties has shown the Chinese people's unwavering spirit of struggle for independence and self-strengthening. To feel shame is to approach courage."

In this authorized version of modern Chinese history, 1842 is Year One. Every Chinese high-school student is expected to know the official narrative dividing Chinese history neatly into pre-Opium War and post-Opium War periods. It is China's counterpart to the familiar American exercise of learning the preamble of the Declaration of Independence.

To fully appreciate the trauma of these historical experiences, one must understand not just the shock of China's defeat in the First Opium War but also the cascade of further defeats that soon followed. Historically, the Chinese had very little experience in questioning the fundamental assumptions of their culture and ways of governance. When imperial officials finally began to understand that their country had become the hapless "sick man of Asia," in the words of Liang Qichao, a towering intellectual figure at the turn of the last century, they established an abiding view of China as having been preyed upon by its foreign rivals.

Today, the psychological and cultural habits developed during this dismal era of Chinese history continue to color and distort China's relations with the rest of the world, especially the US, which has taken the place of Great Britain as the world's superpower. In one of his first speeches as General Secretary of the Communist Party, President Xi Jinping recollected the "unusual hardship and sacrifice" suffered by his country in modern times. "But the Chinese people have never given in," Mr. Xi continued.

The historical memories on display at the Temple of the Tranquil Seas have had positive effects as well. One can hear their echo in China's determination to rejuvenate itself, regain wealth and power, and become a nation of consequence once again. It is this urge that Mr. Xi tries to encourage by speaking proudly of a "China Dream."

Still, it is time for China and the more vociferous propagandists in Beijing to move beyond declarations about China's "one hundred years of national humiliation." That period has come to an end. The world has changed, China and the West have changed, and a new narrative is necessary for China to achieve its declared aim of equality and a "new type of great power relationship."

Only when China is ready to define itself with a more constructive national story will it be able to take its place in full partnership with a nation born, in a moment of affirmation, on a distant Fourth of July.

CHINA AT THE TIPPING POINT?

Foreseeing the Unforeseeable[*]

Andrew J. Nathan

The consensus is stronger than at any time since the 1989 Tiananmen crisis that the resilience of the authoritarian regime in the People's Republic of China (PRC) is approaching its limits. To be sure, this feeling in part reflects the fevered atmosphere that surrounded the PRC's once-per-decade leadership succession at the Eighteenth Party Congress of November 2012. But, according to some of the best-informed observers, deep changes have been taking place that will eventually have major consequences.[1]

Regime transitions belong to that paradoxical class of events which are inevitable but not predictable. Other examples are bank runs, currency inflations, strikes, migrations, riots, and revolutions. In retrospect, such events are explainable, even overdetermined. In prospect, however, their timing and character are impossible to anticipate. Such events seem to come closer and closer but do not occur, even when all the conditions are ripe—until suddenly they do.

In analyzing what may sooner or later happen in China, it is helpful to review what we know about the dynamics of such events. Theories of "threshold models," "revolutionary bandwagons," and "informational cascades" share a logic that runs as follows.[2] Imagine that the forces arrayed against change are dominant—change fails to occur. Now imagine that the balance of forces shifts until the forces favoring and opposing change are closely balanced—a stalemate results.

Suppose again, however, that the balance shifts further, so that the forces in favor of change are stronger than those against it—and yet, nothing happens.

Why is this so? Because no actor knows for sure that the balance has actually tipped. People may speculate that it has, and some may gamble by taking action. But—and this is especially likely to be so under the kinds of conditions created by authoritarianism—the information that people need to make an informed choice about whether to come out in favor of change is hidden. Quoting Václav Havel's parable of the greengrocer who hangs a pro-regime slogan in his shop window "because everyone does it, and because ... if he were to refuse, there could be trouble"; Timur Kuran calls this phenomenon "preference falsification." A majority, even a vast one, may want change. But when each actor weighs the benefits of stepping forth against the danger of being punished for doing so, most stay silent.

Until, that is, a triggering event occurs. Theory does not tell us what this event has to be, or why it has the magic capability to unleash change when other, similar events do not. But whatever it is, the trigger moves a new group of citizens, still a minority, to reveal publicly their dissatisfaction with the status quo.

At this point, theorists ask us to imagine that the ratio between the desire for change and the fear of repression is unevenly distributed across the population. The dissidents and "troublemakers" who always act out regardless of consequences have ideals that are greater than their fears. But

[*] This article was published in the *Journal of Democracy* (January 2013).

they are a constant. What starts a cascade is the first group of ordinary citizens whose distaste for the status quo suddenly overwhelms their fear, or whose fear becomes less. Once that group has acted out, the group with the next largest desire-to-fear ratio perceives that support for change is more widely shared than they knew, and repression more costly and less likely. This shifts their desire-to-fear ratio enough for them to join the movement. This in turn affects the desire-to-fear ratio of those belonging to the next most fearful group, who also join.

In this way, an "informational cascade" occurs, as each shift in the publicly available information about the public mood alters the calculation of the next group. As Kuran puts it in his analysis of how the East European communist regimes collapsed in 1989, "seemingly unshakable regimes saw public sentiment turn against them with astonishing rapidity, as tiny oppositions mushroomed into crushing majorities."[3]

Something like this happened in China in 1989. The desire for change was strong and widespread, but people were afraid. Then a small group of students knelt before the Great Hall of the People on Beijing's Tiananmen Square to demand democratic reforms in the spirit of the recently deceased liberal leader Hu Yaobang. The regime failed to repress them promptly, sending a signal of indecision, and more students—the group with the next-strongest desire for change and a reduced fear of repression—came to the Square. When they in turn were not quickly punished, much of Beijing joined the demonstrations, followed by the citizens of more than three hundred other cities around the country.

No one knows why one "collective incident" and not another is capable of sparking a cascade. Perhaps the outbreaks that have been occurring ever more frequently in China have been too small and too local. Perhaps the regime has responded too deftly with a mix of punishments and concessions.

Moreover, the PRC is not East Germany. It is not the client of a hated foreign power, but a rising state proud of its prospects. Its economy is growing faster, not more slowly, than those of its neighbors.

Three other contrasts are important. First, citizens' access to information about what other people think is not as occluded in China today as it was in the East Germany of the 1980s. The rise of the Internet and social media—as well as a more sophisticated government propaganda strategy that floods citizens with harmless information and allows a limited level of grumbling for tension relief—has allowed citizens to know a fair amount about one another's desire for change. Everyone knows about the problems of corruption, land grabs, environmental pollution, and the polarization of wealth. Citizens are widely aware that the regime itself says the political system needs to be reformed.[4] Paradoxically, however, information overload may actually *weaken* the prospects of an informational cascade, because relatively routine outbreaks of protest send a less dramatic triggering signal than would be the case where protests are more rigorously suppressed. The kind of message the regime censors especially strictly is the type that proposes a concrete blueprint for change, such as the one found in Charter 08.[5] The difficulty that people have in envisioning an alternative to CCP rule is one of the greatest obstacles to voicing a demand for change.

Second, on the repressive side of the equation, the police in China are more numerous, better funded, more technologically advanced, and more skillful in the arts of repression than in other authoritarian regime.[6] They seem so far to have kept up—even if the race is a tight one—with the rise of the Internet and new social media, censoring messages that they view as threatening, posting messages that support the regime, and punishing messengers whom they consider particularly dangerous, such as Liu Xiaobo and Ai Weiwei. So while people may know more about one another's desire for change than they do in the classic cascade model, they also have a frightening picture of the regime's capacity and willingness to repress critics.

Third, the PRC regime as it stands today is more adaptive than other authoritarian regimes. The leadership proactively addresses the most neuralgic sources of popular dissatisfaction by making health and retirement insurance available, attacking corruption,[7] cracking down on the worst polluters, and increasing the appearance of transparency and accountability with devices such as e-government, opinion surveys, and limited-scope elections. The regime likes to *talk* about making itself more democratic, installing the rule of law, and promoting human rights. The apparent goal is to build a form of one-party rule that people will accept as responsive and legitimate. The PRC's rulers look to Singapore for an example of how that sort of thing can be done, even though conditions in that tiny and wealthy city-state are different from conditions in China.

Even if the East German scenario is unlikely to apply in its specifics, the general threshold model still might. Perhaps the key variable in the cascade model of political change is fear, and that seems to be diminishing. As it does so, the chances increase that the desire for change will find wide expression.

For change to happen, there will need to be a breakthrough moment. Do we feel that moment coming? We can imagine many possible triggers, including the bursting of the bubble economy, violent confrontations with local demonstrators, a protracted power struggle within the regime, or a natural disaster or public-health crisis that exposes scandalous incompetence or corruption. Even though the regime has recently survived several such scenarios (the Sichuan earthquake, the Western financial crisis, the tainted-milk scandal of 2008; the Wenzhou train collision of 2011; and the Bo Xilai incident of 2012), the occurrence of another could, unpredictably, lead to a different outcome. Perhaps the power-deflationary event to which this particular regime is most vulnerable is a foreign humiliation. That is one good reason why the PRC has been relatively cautious in its foreign relations—even, I would argue, as it ramps up its assertion of territorial claims in the South China and East China Seas.

No one, however, is able to say for sure whether, when, and how change will come. From where we sit, on the unpredictable side of what may turn out to be an inevitable event, fundamental change in fact continues to look unlikely. Small farmers are unhappy, but they live scattered across the countryside and far from the center of power. Worker unrest has increased, but it focuses on enterprises, not the government. Intellectuals are weak as a class, divided, and unable to spark resistance. Civil society is growing in scale and potential assertiveness, but remains under effective government surveillance and unable to form national linkages. Independent entrepreneurs have

ideas and means, and show increasing initiative, but their stake in stability makes them cautious.

The broad middle class sees through the regime, but is busy enjoying itself. National minorities such as the Uighurs, Tibetans, and Mongolians live on the periphery of a vast continental landmass and are culturally and socially cut off from the much larger Han Chinese majority. When it comes to defecting from the existing order, each group seems likely to look at the others and pipe up with a hearty "After you!"

So too with the forces and actors within the regime. The elite is evidently divided, to judge from the story of Bo Xilai, the high-flying, charismatic Chongqing Communist Party boss and political rising star who was undone by a scandal involving murder and corruption. Yet the damage from this embarrassing case has apparently been contained. The party's privileges remain intact. The military and security forces seem willing to keep doing their jobs. Local-level officials, who shoulder the impossible task of mediating between state and society, might have the most to gain from a change of system. Yet if they ever tried to link up with one another to form a bloc powerful enough to effect change, the risks that they would face would be staggering. This is not 1911, when power was dispersed, the center was weak, and the premodern state of the information and military technologies then prevalent in China kept central authorities from intervening strongly in the localities.

And yet, the expectation of dramatic change persists. The very anticipation of such change, even if it is unfounded, imparts a particular type of "meta-instability" to the Chinese system today. There is a sense of impermanence that we do not find in mature political systems—no matter how troubled in other ways—whose members operate on the assumption, wise or not, that their system is lasting.

Change—if and when it happens—will not necessarily come in a form that we envision or that Chinese actors prefer. Some Chinese form of democracy is one possible outcome, but since there is no well-developed opposition movement (as there was in Taiwan before its democratic transition in the late 1980s), the pro-democracy forces would have to come from inside the ruling Communist Party. A Chinese Vladimir Putin might emerge to reconsolidate authoritarian or semi-authoritarian institutions. A crisis might even galvanize a shift from social dissatisfaction to social support for the current regime. Or China might descend into disorder, a scenario that no pro-democracy activist, Chinese or foreign, wants. What one can say, however, as we wait for history to deliver its answer, is that more and more people believe some kind of change is coming.

NOTES

1. For another excellent analysis along such lines, see Yu Liu and Dingding Chen, "Why China Will Democratize," *Washington Quarterly* 35 (Winter 2012): 41–63.
2. Seminal statements are Mark Granovetter, "Threshold Models of Collective Behavior," *American Journal of Sociology* 83 (May 1978): 1420–43; Timur Kuran, "Now Out of Never: The Element of Surprise in the East European Revolution of 1989," *World Politics* 44 (October 1991): 7–48REFC; Susanne Lohmann, "The Dynamics of Informational Cascades: The Monday Demonstrations in Leipzig, East Germany, 1989–91," *World Politics* 47 (October 1994): 42–101.
3. Kuran, "Now Out of Never," 13.
4. On this point, among many sources, see Cheng Li, "The End of the CCP's Resilient Authoritarianism? A Tripartite Assessment of Shifting Power in China," *China Quarterly* 211 (September 2012): 599–602.
5. Jean-Philippe Béja, Fu Hualing, and Eva Pils, eds., *Liu Xiaobo, Charter 08, and the Challenges of Political Reform in China* (Hong Kong: Hong Kong University Press, 2012).
6. Xu Youyu and Hua Ze, eds., *Caoyu jingcha* [Close encounters with the Chinese PSB (Public Security Bureau)] (Hong Kong: Kaifang chubanshe, 2012).
7. Andrew Wedeman, *Double Paradox: Rapid Growth and Rising Corruption in China* (Ithaca: Cornell University Press, 2012).

About the Editor

David Shambaugh is a scholar, teacher, and writer about China and the international relations of Asia. He is Professor of Political Science and International Affairs and founding Director of the China Policy Program in the Elliott School of International Affairs at The George Washington University. The former editor of *The China Quarterly* and Reader in Chinese Politics at the School of Oriental and African Studies at the University of London, he is also now a nonresident Senior Fellow in the Foreign Policy Studies Program, Center for East Asian Policy Studies, and John L. Thornton China Center at the Brookings Institution. He is a member of the Council on Foreign Relations, the Board of Directors of the National Committee on US–China Relations, and other public policy and scholarly organizations.

ABOUT THE CONTRIBUTORS

Richard A. Bitzinger is a Senior Fellow with the S. Rajaratnam School of International Studies at Nanyang Technological University in Singapore.

Richard C. Bush is Senior Fellow in the Foreign Policy Studies Program and Director of the Center for East Asian Policy Studies at the Brookings Institution.

Jean-Pierre Cabestan is Professor and Head of the Department of Government and International Studies at Hong Kong Baptist University.

John Delury is Professor of History at Yonsei University in Seoul, Republic of Korea.

Bruce Dickson is Professor of Political Science & International Affairs and Director of the Sigur Center for Asian Studies at George Washington University.

Joshua Eisenman is Assistant Professor at the University of Texas at Austin's Lyndon Baines Johnson School of Public Affairs, and Senior Fellow for China Studies at the American Foreign Policy Council.

Peter Ferdinand is Reader in Politics and International Studies at the University of Warwick.

Joseph Fewsmith is Professor of International Relations and Political Science at Boston University.

Michael Fullilove is Executive Director of the Lowy Institute for International Policy in Sydney, Australia.

Merle Goldman is Professor Emeritus of History at Boston University, and Research Associate of the Fairbank Center for Chinese Studies at Harvard University.

Jamie Horsley is a Lecturer and Senior Research Scholar in Law, and Executive Director of the China Law Center at Yale University Law School.

Hu Jintao was President of the People's Republic of China and General Secretary of the Communist Party of China from 2002–2012, and Chairman of the Central Military Commission from 2004–2012.

Martin Jacques is an author and Visiting Fellow at the London School of Economics and Political Science Asia Research Center.

Andrew Kuchins is Director of the Russia and Eurasia Program at the Center for Strategic and International Studies (CSIS).

Joshua Kurlantzick is a Senior Fellow for Southeast Asia at the Council on Foreign Relations.

Li Lianjiang is Professor of Political Science at Chinese University of Hong Kong.

Kenneth Lieberthal is Professor Emeritus of Political Science and Business Administration at the University of Michigan, and Senior Fellow in the Foreign Policy Studies Program and Global Policy and Development Program at the Brookings Institution.

Justin Yifu Lin is Professor and Honorary Dean in the National School of Development at Peking University, and Member of the Standing Committee of the Chinese People's Political Consultative Congress.

Damien Ma is a Fellow at the Paulson Institute, University of Chicago.

Richard Madsen is Distinguished Professor of Sociology at the University of California, San Diego.

John J. Mearsheimer is R. Wendell Harrison Distinguished Service Professor of Political Science at the University of Chicago.

Rachel Murphy is Associate Professor of Sociology of China, St. Antony's College and Institute of Chinese Studies, University of Oxford.

Andrew J. Nathan is Class of 1919 Professor of Political Science at Columbia University.

Barry J. Naughton is Professor of Chinese Economy and Sokwanlok Chair of Chinese International Affairs in the School of International Relations & Pacific Studies at the University of California, San Diego.

Valérie Niquet is Research Fellow for Asia at the Fondation pour la Recherche Stratégique in Paris.

Joseph S. Nye is University Distinguished Service Professor, Kennedy School of Government, Harvard University.

Evan Osnos is a foreign affairs and politics staff writer at *The New Yorker* and nonresident Fellow at the John L. Thornton China Center at the Brookings Institution.

Minxin Pei is Pritzker Professor of Government and Director of the Keck Center for International and Strategic Studies at Claremont McKenna College.

Elizabeth J. Perry is Henry Rosovsky Professor of Government and Director of the Harvard-Yenching Institute, Harvard University.

Phillip C. Saunders is Distinguished Research Fellow and Director of the Center for the Study of Chinese Military Affairs in the Institute of National Strategic Studies at the US National Defense University.

Orville Schell is the Arthur Ross Director of the Center on US-China Relations at the Asia Society.

David Shambaugh is Professor of Political Science and International Affairs and Director of the China Policy Program at George Washington University, and nonresident Senior Fellow in the Foreign Policy Studies Program at the Brookings Institution.

Murray Scot Tanner is a Senior Research Scientist in CNA Corporation's China Studies Division.

Andrew G. Walder is Denise O'Leary and Kent Thiry Professor in the Department of Sociology and Senior Fellow in the Freeman Spogli Institute for International Studies at Stanford University.

Wang Feng is Professor of Sociology in the School of Social Sciences at the University of California-Irvine, and Nonresident Senior Fellow in the John L. Thornton China Studies Center at the Brookings Institution.

Wang Jisi is Professor and President of the Institute of International and Strategic Studies at Peking University.

Wang Yi is Foreign Minister of the People's Republic of China.

Odd Arne Westad is S.T. Lee Professor of US-Asia Relations in the Kennedy School of Government at Harvard University.

Martin King Whyte is John Zwaanstra Professor of International Studies and Sociology Emeritus at Harvard University.

Wu Xinbo is Professor, Executive Dean of the Institute of International Studies, and Director of the Center for American Studies at Fudan University.

Xi Jinping is President of the People's Republic of China, General Secretary of the Communist Party of China, and Chairman of the Central Military Commission.

Beina Xu was formerly an online editor/writer at the Council on Foreign Relations.

Xu Zhiyong is a lawyer and former Lecturer at Beijing University of Post and Telecommunications.

Yan Sun is Professor of Political Science at Queen's College, City University of New York.

Yun Sun is a Senior Associate in the East Asia Program at the Henry L. Stimson Center, and Nonresident Fellow in the Global Economy and Development Program's Africa Growth Initiative at the Brookings Institution.

Robert B. Zoellick is Chairman of Goldman Sachs' International Advisors and Nonresident Senior Fellow in the Belfer Center for Science and International Affairs, Kennedy School of Government, Harvard University.

Zhang Jiuhuan is the former Chinese ambassador to Thailand, and Associate of the China Institute of International Studies.

Zheng Bijian is a Member of the Standing Committee of the Chinese People's Political Consultative Congress.

Grateful acknowledgment is made to the following for permission to reprint previously published material:

The Brookings Institution

"The BRICS and China's Aspiration for the New International Order" by Yun Sun, published online, March 25, 2013.

"Fighting Corruption: A Difficult Challenge for Chinese Leaders" by Minxin Pei, from Cheng Li (ed.), *China's Changing Political Landscape: Prospects for Democracy* (Washington, DC: Brookings Institution Press, 2008).

China Perspectives

"The Many Facets of Chinese Nationalism" by Jeanne-Pierre Cabestan, *China Perspectives*, No. 59 (May–June 2005).

"Modernizing China's Military, 1997–2012" by Richard Bitzinger, *China Perspectives*, No. 4 (2011).

"China and Central Asia" by Valérie Niquet, *China Perspectives*, (September–October 2006).

Council on Foreign Relations

"China's 'Peaceful Rise' to Great-Power Status" by Zheng Bijian, *Foreign Affairs*, Vol. 84, No. 5 (2005).

"China's Governance Crisis" by Minxin Pei, *Foreign Affairs*, Vol. 81, No. 5 (Sept/Oct. 2002).

"China's Search for a Grand Strategy: A Rising Great Power Finds Its Way" by Wang Jisi, *Foreign Affairs* Vol. 90, No. 2 (March/April 2011).

"China's Search for a New Energy Strategy" by Damien Ma, *Foreign Affairs* (June 2013).

"China's Environmental Crisis" by Beina Xum, "Backgrounder," April 25, 2014.

"Fruitful Results and Broad Prospects: A Review of Twenty Years of China-ASEAN Relations" by Zhang Jiuhuan, *Foreign Affairs Journal*, (Spring 2011).

"Media Censorship in China" by Beina Xu, "Backgrounder," September 25, 2014.

"Work Together to Maintain World Peace and Security" by Xi Jinping, *Foreign Affairs Journal*, No. 105 (Autumn 2012).

Current History

"No 'Jasmine' for China" by Bruce J. Dickson, *Current History*, Vol. 110, No. 737 (September 2011);

"China's Beleaguered Intellectuals" by Merle Goldman, *Current History* (September 2009).

"Driven to Protest: China's Rural Unrest" by Lianjiang Li, *Current History* (September 2006).

"Citizen Contention and Campus Calm: The Paradox of Chinese Civil Society" by Elizabeth J. Perry, *Current History* (September 2014).

"China's Unpeaceful Rise" by John J. Mearsheimer, *Current History*, Vol. 105, No. 690 (April 2006).

"China's Population Destiny: The Looming Crisis" by Wang Feng, *Current History* (September 2010).

"China's Post-Socialist Inequality" by Martin King Whyte, *Current History* (September 2012).

"The Roots of China's Ethnic Conflicts" by Yan Sun, *Current History* (September 2014).

"The China-US Relationship Goes Global" by Kenneth Lieberthal, *Current History* (September 2009).

"Russia and China: The Ambivalent Embrace" by Andrew Kuchins, *Current History* (October 2007).

"China's Africa Strategy" by Joshua Eisenman and Joshua Kurlantzick, *Current History* (May 2006).

"Unruly Stability: Why China's Regime Has Staying Power" by Andrew G. Walder, *Current History* (September 2009).

The Economist

"Ideology in China: Confucius Makes a Comeback—You Can't Keep a Good Sage Down," *The Economist*, May 17, 2007.

"Building the (China) Dream, *The Economist*, April 19, 2014.

"Murder Mysteries," *The Economist* on April 6, 2013.

"Beneath the Glacier: Civil Society in China," *The Economist* on April 12, 2014.

"A Giant Cage: China's Internet," *The Economist*, April 6, 2013.

"China's Security State: The Truncheon Budget," *The Economist*, March 12, 2011.

"Political City: Democracy in Hong Kong," *The Economist* on September 6, 2014.

Journal of Democracy

"Is CCP Rule Fragile or Resilient" by Minxin Pei, Vol. 23, No. 1 (January 2012).

"The Upsurge of Religion in China" by Richard Madsen, Vol. 21, No. 4 (October 2010).

"China at the Tipping Point? Foreseeing the Unforeseeable" by Andrew J. Nathan, Vol. 24, No. 1 (January 2013).

The National Interest

"The Illusion of Chinese Power" by David Shambaugh, No. 132 (July–August 2014).

Penguin Books

"The Eight Differences That Define China" by Martin Jacques, from *When China Rules the World: The End of the Western World and the Birth of a New Global Order* (London: Penguin Books, revised second edition, 2012), 561–583.

Rowman & Littlefield Publishers

"Economic Growth: From High-Speed to High-Quality" by Barry Naughton; "Elite Politics: The Struggle for Normality" by Joseph Fewsmith; and "The Rule of Law: Pushing the Limits of Party Rule" by Jamie Horsley, from *China Today, China Tomorrow: Domestic Politics, Economy, and Society*, ed. Joseph Fewsmith, (Lanham, MD: 2010). "China's Role in Asia: Attractive or Assertive?" by Phillip C. Saunders, from *International Relations of Asia*, ed. David Shambaugh and Michael Yahuda, (Lanham, MD: 2014, second edition).

Routledge

"China and the Developing World" by Peter Ferdinand; "China's Roles in Global Security" by David Shambaugh; "Civil Society and Media in China" by Rachel Murphy, from David Shambaugh (ed.), *Charting China's Future: Domestic and International Challenges* (Abingdon, UK and New York: Routledge, 2011).

Wall Street Journal

"China's Soft Power Deficit" by Joseph S. Nye, May 8, 2012.

"A Rising China Needs a New National Story" by Orville Schell and John Delury, July 12, 2014.

The Washington Quarterly

"Agenda for a New Great Power Relationship" by Wu Xinbo (January 2014).

"China and the United Nations: The Stakeholder Spectrum" by Michael Fullilove (August 2011).

"China Rethinks Unrest" by Murray Scot Tanner (June 2004).

"Coping with a Conflicted China" by David Shambaugh (Winter 2011).

INDEX